New York

timeout.com/newyork

Published by Time Out Guides Ltd, a wholly owned subsidiary of Time Out Group Ltd.
Time Out and the Time Out logo are trademarks of Time Out Group Ltd.

© **Time Out Group Ltd 2007**
Previous editions 1990, 1992, 1994, 1996. 1997, 1998, 1999, 2000, 2001, 2002, 2003, 2004, 2005, 2006.

10 9 8 7 6 5 4 3 2 1

This edition first published in Great Britain in 2007 by Ebury Publishing
Ebury Publishing is a division of The Random House Group Ltd,
20 Vauxhall Bridge Road, London SW1V 2SA

Random House Australia Pty Limited 20 Alfred Street, Milsons Point, Sydney, New South Wales 2061, Australia
Random House New Zealand Limited 18 Poland Road, Glenfield, Auckland 10, New Zealand
Random House South Africa (Pty) Limited Isle of Houghton, Corner Boundary
Road & Carse O'Gowrie, Houghton 2198, South Africa

Random House UK Limited Reg. No. 954009

Distributed in USA by Publishers Group West
1700 Fourth Street, Berkeley, California 94710

Distributed in Canada by Publishers Group Canada
250A Carlton Street, Toronto, Ontario M5A 2L1

For further distribution details, see www.timeout.com

10 Digit ISBN: 1-84670-003-5
13 Digit ISBN : 9781846700033

A CIP catalogue record for this book is available from the British Library

Colour reprographics by Wyndeham Icon, 3 & 4 Maverton Road, London E3 2JE

Printed and bound in Germany by Appl

Papers used by Ebury Publishing are natural, recyclable products made from wood grown in sustainable forests.

Contents

Time Out Guides Limited
Universal House
251 Tottenham Court Road
London W1T 7AB
Tel + 44 (0)20 7813 3000
Fax + 44 (0)20 7813 6001
Email guides@timeout.com
www.timeout.com

Editorial

Editor Keith Mulvihill
Consultant Editor Elizabeth Barr for *Time Out New York*
Deputy Editor Anna Norman
Fact Checker/Researcher Chad Frade
Copy Editing Lesley McCave
Proofreader Tamsin Shelton
Indexer Jonathan Cox

Managing Director Peter Fiennes
Editorial Director Ruth Jarvis
Deputy Series Editor Lesley McCave
Financial Director Gareth Garner
Guides Co-ordinator Holly Pick
Accountant Kemi Olufuwa

Design

Art Director Scott Moore
Art Editor Pinelope Kourmouzoglou
Senior Designer Josephine Spencer
Graphic Designer Henry Elphick
Digital Imaging Simon Foster
Ad Make-up Jenni Prichard

Picture Desk

Picture Editor Jael Marschner
Deputy Picture Editor Tracey Kerrigan
Picture Researcher Helen McFarland

Advertising

Sales Director Mark Phillips
International Sales Manager Ross Canadé
International Sales Executive Simon Davies
Advertising Sales (New York) Siobhan Shea Rossi
Advertising Assistant Kate Staddon

Marketing

Group Marketing Director John Luck
Marketing Manager Yvonne Poon
Marketing & Publicity Manager, US Rosella Albanese

Production

Group Production Director Mark Lamond
Production Manager Brendan McKeown
Production Coordinator Caroline Bradford

Time Out Group

Chairman Tony Elliott
Financial Director Richard Waterlow
TO Magazine Ltd MD David Pepper
Group General Manager/Director Nichola Coulthard
Managing Director, Time Out International Cathy Runciman
TO Communications Ltd MD David Pepper
Group Art Director John Oakey
Group IT Director Simon Chappell

Contributors

History Kathleen Squires (*Sacred ground* Alan Mozes). **Architecture** Pablito Nash (*High times ahead* EJ Mundell). **Boom Town** Billie Cohen. **NYC Rivalries** Adapted from *Time Out New York* magazine. **New York Today** Howard Halle. **Where to Stay** Amy Plitt, Keith Mulvihill (*Something old, something new* Clare Lambe). **Tour New York** Keith Mulvihill. **Downtown** Billie Cohen. **Midtown**, **Uptown** Keith Mulvihill (*Green day* Eric Mendelsohn). **Brooklyn** Dan Avery. **Queens** John Roleke. **The Bronx**, **Staten Island** Kathleen Squires. **Museums** Clare Lambe. **Restaurants & Cafés**, **Bars** *Time Out New York* Eat Out staff. **Shops & Services** Kelly McMasters, Keith Mulvihill. **Festivals & Events** Keith Mulvihill. **Art Galleries** Emily Weiner. **Books & Poetry** Michael Miller. **Cabaret & Comedy** Adam Feldman (cabaret), Jane Borden (comedy). **Children** Keith Mulvihill. **Clubs** Bruce Tantum. **Film & TV** Joshua Rothkopf. **Gay & Lesbian** Beth Greenfield. **Music** Jay Ruttenberg (popular); Steve Smith (classical). **Sport & Fitness** Keith Mulvihill. **Theatre & Dance** David Cote (theatre), Amy Norton (dance). **Trips Out of Town** Adapted from *Time Out New York* magazine.

Maps john@jsgraphics.co.uk.

Photography Jonathan Perugia, except: page 14 Topfoto; 15, 16 North Wind Picture Archive; 19 Bridgeman Art Library; 21, 25 Bettmann/Corbis; 30 Patrick McMullan; 31 City of New York; 32, 36, 50, 59, 63, 65, 69, 73, 183, 190, 191, 192, 193, 196, 236, 238, 246, 249, 250, 253, 254, 260, 267, 272, 276, 285, 304, 338 Alys Tomlinson; 33 Michael Ficeto/Hearst Corporation; 34 Nathan Beck; 106 Christopher Dawson; 109, 355, 359 Corbis; 144 Sandra Roman; 198, 212, 245, 341 Sarina Finkelstein; 204 Talia Simhi; 257 Roxana Marroquin; 264 New York Road Runners; 266 Macy's East, Inc; 308 Liz Liguori; 320 Vito Fun; 323 Jane Hoffer; 329 Ken Howard/Metropolitan Opera; 334 Adam Coglianese/Nyra; 353 Paul Kolnik; 358 Andy Warhol, Shadows, 1978-79. Dia Art Foundation/photo: Bill Jacobson. The following images were provided by the featured establishment/artist: 70, 120, 357, 361, 362, 364.

The Editor would like to thank Elizabeth Barr, Carole Braden, Nestor Cervantes, Melisa Coburn, Billie Cohen, James Oliver Cury, Brian Farnham, Sarina Finkelstein, Anne Finn, Brian Fiske, Chad Frade, Gabriella Gershenson, Howard Halle, Stacy Hillegas, Killian Jordan, Eric Medelsohn, Amy Plitt, Leslie Price, Stephanie Rosenbaum, Mark Sinclair, Cyndi Stivers, Drew Toal, Alison Tocci, Reed Tucker and all contributors to previous editions of the *Time Out New York Guide*, whose work forms the basis for parts of this book.

Introduction

In *Here is New York,* published in 1949, American essayist EB White wrote: 'New York is nothing like Paris; it is nothing like London; and it is not Spokane multiplied by 60, or Detroit multiplied by four. It is by all odds the loftiest of cities. It even managed to reach the highest point in the sky at the lowest moment of the Depression.'

When a more recent black cloud settled over the city in the wake of the terrorist attacks of September 11, 2001, many feared its cherished skyline would never recover. Yet, it's partly through architecture – New York's favoured means of metaphorically expressing its greatness – that the city has pulled itself out from the dark days. There have been some, dare we say, lofty architectural developments of late that would make old EB proud. In September 2006 politicians and celebrities gathered together to inaugurate Sir Norman Foster's gleaming tribute to the city's renewed vigour: the 46-storey Hearst Tower, on the corner of Eighth Avenue and 57th Street – a glimpse of the city's transformed skyline of the future, which is likely to remain as emblematic as ever. In lower Manhattan, in particular, a wave of exciting new construction can be witnessed, with several more spectacular (and sometimes controversial) plans in the pipeline, including the High Line Park in western Manhattan and Frank Gehry's Atlantic Yards complex in Brooklyn. The path forward hasn't been free of setbacks, however, and plans for the World Trade Center Memorial remain uncertain even today.

This ambitious activity is nothing new, of course. New York has always been a city of superlatives, home at one time or another to the world's tallest buildings, longest bridges, busiest ports, crabbiest cabbies – as well as to many of the nation's richest and most media-, business- and fashion-savvy citizens. New Yorkers may not always live up to their irascible reputation – a 2006 *Reader's Digest* survey ranked New York number one in a list of the world's most courteous cities – but there's no denying that they're an opinionated bunch, who'll fight to defend their favourite bars, parks – even pizza. They may not always win, however, and the closing of the beloved punk rock bar CBGB is proof of that.

New York's cultural and scenic delights are renowned, and often immortalised on screen, yet it can take years of sifting through the ample offerings to determine the best in food, nightlife, shopping and entertainment. Take heart in the fact that this guide is written by die-hard locals eager to share their delight in scouring the city for all sorts of essential New York experiences, in the hope of making you her newest admirer. If it's classic New York you seek, might we suggest strolling over the Brooklyn Bridge at sunrise, rowing in Central Park or throwing back Martinis at the Carlyle Hotel. But keep in mind that every week some new club, bar or shop takes the place of something else; it pays to stray off the beaten path and keep your eyes peeled – you might stumble upon the next new thing that defines what it means to be a New Yorker for years to come.

ABOUT TIME OUT CITY GUIDES

The *Time Out New York Guide* is one of an expanding series of travel books produced by the people behind London's and New York's successful listings magazines. Our guides, now numbering about 50, are written and updated by resident experts who strive to provide you with the most up-to-date information you'll need to explore the city, whether you're a first-time visitor or a local. The staff of *Time Out New York* magazine worked on this, the 13th edition, of the *Time Out New York Guide*. TONY has been 'the obsessive guide to impulsive entertainment' for all city dwellers (and visitors just passing through) for over ten years. Many chapters have been written from scratch; all have been thoroughly revised and offer new feature boxes.

THE LOWDOWN ON THE LISTINGS

Above all, we've tried to make this book as useful as possible. Websites, phone numbers, transportation info, opening times, admission prices and credit-card details are included in our listings. And we've given details on facilities, services and events, all checked and correct at press time. However, owners and managers can change their policies with little notice. Before you go out of your way, we strongly advise you to call and check opening times,

dates of exhibitions and other particulars. While every effort has been made to ensure the accuracy of the information contained in this guide, the publishers cannot accept responsibility for any errors it may contain.

PRICES AND PAYMENT

We have noted whether venues accept credit cards and have listed the major ones: American Express (AmEx), Diners Club (DC), Discover (Disc), MasterCard (MC) and Visa (V). Many shops, restaurants and attractions will accept traveller's cheques issued by a major financial institution (such as American Express). The prices we've supplied should be treated as guidelines, not gospel. Fluctuating exchange rates and inflation can cause prices to change rapidly, especially in shops and restaurants. If costs vary wildly from those we've quoted, then ask whether there's a good reason – and please email us to let us know. We aim to give the best and most up-to-date advice, so we always want to know if you've been badly treated or overcharged.

THE LAY OF THE LAND

Many of our listings are divided up by the area demarcations described in our Sightseeing chapters, and are marked on maps on pages 402 to 412. The maps also pinpoint specific locations of hotels (❶), restaurants and cafés (❶) and bars (❶).

We've included cross streets with every address, so that you can easily find your way around. Fully indexed colour street maps, as well as subway and bus maps, are at the back of the guide, starting on page 402.

TELEPHONE NUMBERS

All telephone numbers printed in this guide are written as dialled within the United States. Note that you must always dial 1 and an area code, even if the number you're calling is in the same area code as the one you're calling from. Manhattan area codes are 212 and 646; those in Brooklyn, Queens, the Bronx and Staten Island are 718 and 347; generally (but not always), 917 is reserved for cell phones and pagers. Numbers preceded by 800, 877 and 888 can be called free of charge from within the US, and some of them can be dialled (though not necessarily for free) from the UK.

To dial numbers given in this book from abroad, use your country's exit code (00 in the UK), followed by 1, the area code and the phone number. When numbers are listed as letters for easy recall (as in 1-800-AIR-RIDE), dial the corresponding numbers on the telephone keypad. For more info on telephone usage, *see p381*.

ESSENTIAL INFORMATION

For practical information you might need for visiting the city – including visa and customs info, disabled access, emergency phone numbers, useful websites and the ins and outs of the local transportation network – see the Directory (*see pp366-386*) at the back of this guide.

LET US KNOW WHAT YOU THINK

We hope you enjoy the *Time Out New York Guide*, and we'd like to know what you think of it. We welcome tips for places that you believe we should include in future editions and appreciate your feedback on our choices. Please email us at guides@timeout.com.

Advertisers

There is an online version of this book, along with guides to over 100 international cities, at **www.timeout.com**.

Perfect place to plan All memorable Event

ToDai
Restaurant
NYC
sushi & seafood buffet

All Occasion
Catering

All Occasion
Party

All You Can Eat
Buffet

Todai is an upscale All-You-Can-Eat Japanese Seafood Buffet Restaurant. Todai offers quality food and services at an affordable price. New Todai NYC is designed to create a unique family atmosphere that seats up to 600 patrons. In addition, features a 160-foot seafood buffet counter with 40 different kinds of sushi, over 15 dishes are served at both the salad bar and hot entree island, and a dessert bar with over 20 different cakes and fruits.

Weekday Price: LUNCH $13.95 | DINNER $23.95
Weekend Price: LUNCH $15.95 | DINNER $25.95
(Prices are subject to change without notice)

LUNCH 11:30AM ~ 2:30PM (M - F) | 11:30AM ~ 3:00PM (Sat & Sun)
DINNER 6:00PM ~ 10:00PM (M - T) | 5:30PM ~ 10:00PM (Fri & Sat)
        5:00PM ~ 9:00PM (Sun)

6 E. 32nd St. New York, NY 10016
T. 212.725.1333   www.todai.com

In Context

The **Wall Street Crash** of 1929. *See p23.*

History

New York's rise to greatness (or something like it).

Our skyscraper-packed metropolis wasn't built by a bunch of mild-mannered do-gooders, bending over backwards to be nice to each other, got it? No sir, it took a combination of guts, nasty language and raised voices. Sure, there were some happy types who said 'thank you' and 'have a nice day' but, all told, there were generations of ambitious (some might even say back-stabbing) characters who made this city what it is. A brief look back at New York's history shows just how its residents earned their nerves-of-steel reputations, and explains why having a salty disposition has gotten them where they are today.

NATIVES AND NEWCOMERS

Members of the indigenous Lenape tribe were the original native New Yorkers. They lived among the meadows, forests and farms of the land they called Lenapehoking, pretty much undisturbed by outsiders for thousands of years – until 1524, when their idyll was interrupted by tourists from the later-named Old World. The first European sightseer to

cast his eyes upon this land was Giovanni da Verrazano, an Italian explorer commissioned by the French to find a shortcut to the Orient. Instead, he found Staten Island. Recognising that he was on the wrong track, Verrazano pulled up anchor nearly as quickly as he had dropped it, never setting foot on land. Eighty-five years later, Englishman Henry Hudson was more favourably disposed. Commissioned by the Dutch, and with the same goal of finding a shortcut to the Far East, Hudson sailed into Manhattan's natural deep-water harbour in September 1609, and was entranced by what lay before him. He lingered long enough to explore the entire length of the river that now bears his name, but it wasn't his fate to grow old in the place he admired and described in his logs as a 'rich and pleasant land': on a return trip in 1611, Hudson's crew mutinied and cast him adrift. Still, his tales of the lush, river-crossed countryside had captured the Dutch imagination, and in 1624 the Dutch West India Company sent 110 settlers to establish a trading post here. They planted themselves at the southern tip of the island called Mannahata and christened the colony New Amsterdam. In many bloody battles against the local Lenape, they did their best to drive the natives away from the little company town. But the Lenape were immovable.

In 1626 a man named Peter Minuit, New Amsterdam's first governor, thought he had solved the Lenape problem by pulling off the city's very first real-estate rip-off. The tribe had no concept of private land ownership, so Minuit made them an offer they couldn't refuse: he 'bought' the island of Manhattan – all 14,000 acres of it – from the Lenape for 60 guilders' worth of goods. Legend famously values the purchase price at $24, but modern historians set the amount closer to $500. (These days, that wouldn't cover a month's rent for a closet-size studio apartment.) It was a slick trick, and a precedent for countless ungracious business transactions that would occur here over the centuries.

The Dutch quickly made the port of New Amsterdam a centre for fur trading. The population didn't grow as fast as the business, however, and the Dutch West India Company had a hard time finding recruits to move to an unknown island an ocean away. The company instead gathered servants, orphans and slaves, and other, more unsavoury outcasts such as thieves, drunkards and prostitutes. The population grew to 400 within ten years, but given that one in every four structures was a tavern, drunkenness, crime and squalor prevailed. If the colony were to thrive, it needed a strong leader. Enter Dutch West India Company director Peter Stuyvesant.

THE FIRST IN-YOUR-FACE MAYOR

A one-legged, puritanical bully with a quick temper, Stuyvesant was less than popular: rudeness was a way of life for Peg-leg Pete, as he was known. But he was the colony's first effective governor. He made peace with the Lenape, formed the first policing force (consisting of nine men) and cracked down on debauchery by shutting taverns and outlawing drinking on Sunday. He established the first school, post office, hospital, prison and poorhouse. Within a decade, the population quadrupled, and the settlement became an important trading port.

Lined with canals and windmills, and dotted with gabled farmhouses, New Amsterdam began to resemble its namesake city. Newcomers arrived to work in the fur and slave trades, or to farm. Soon, a dozen and a half languages could be heard in the streets – a fact that made the bigoted Stuyvesant nervous. In 1654 he attempted to quash immigration by turning away Sephardic Jews who were fleeing the Spanish Inquisition. But, surprisingly for the time, the corporate honchos at the Dutch West India Company reprimanded him for his intolerance and overturned his decision, leading to the establishment of the earliest Jewish community in the New World. That was the first time the inflexible Stuyvesant was made to bend his ways. The second time would put an end to the 40-year Dutch rule for good.

YOU SAY YOU WANT A REVOLUTION?

In late August 1664 English warships sailed into the harbour, set on taking over the now prosperous colony. To avoid bloodshed and destruction, Stuyvesant quickly surrendered. Soon after, New Amsterdam was renamed New York (after the Duke of York, brother of King Charles II), and Stuyvesant quietly retired to his farm. Unlike Stuyvesant, the English battled with the Lenape; by 1695 those members of the tribe who weren't killed off were sent packing upstate, and New York's European population shot up to 3,000. Over the next 35 years, Dutch-style farmhouses and windmills gave way to stately townhouses and monuments to English royals. By 1740 the slave trade had made New York the third-busiest port in the British Empire. The city, now home to more than 11,000 residents,

The indigenous **Lenape** tribe. *See p14.*

The anti-British **Alexander Hamilton**.

continued to be prosperous for a quarter-century more. But resentment was beginning to build in the colony, fuelled by the ever-heavier burden of British taxation.

One very angry young man was Alexander Hamilton, the illegitimate son of a Scottish nobleman. Hamilton arrived in New York from the West Indies in 1772. A fierce intellectual, he enrolled in King's College (which is now Columbia University) and became politically active – writing anti-British pamphlets, organising an artillery company and serving as a lieutenant colonel in General George Washington's army. In these and other ways, Hamilton played a key role in a movement that would ultimately change the city – and the country – forever.

Fearing the brewing revolution, New York's citizenry fled the city in droves in 1775, causing the population to plummet from 25,000 to just 5,000. The following year, 100 British warships sailed into the harbour of this virtual ghost town, carrying an intimidating army of 32,000 men – nearly four times the size of Washington's militia. Despite the British presence, Washington organised a reading of the Declaration of Independence, and patriots tore the statue of King George III from its pedestal. Revolution was inevitable.

The battle for New York officially began on 26 August 1776, and Washington's army sustained heavy losses. Nearly a quarter of his men were slaughtered in a two-day period. As Washington retreated, a fire – thought to have been lit by patriots – destroyed 493 buildings, including Trinity Church, the tallest structure on the island. The British found a scorched city, and a populace living in tents.

The city continued to suffer for seven long years. Eventually, of course, Washington's luck turned. As the British left, he and his troops marched triumphantly down Broadway to reclaim the city as part of the newly established United States of America. A week and a half later, on 4 December 1783, the general bade farewell to his dispersing troops at Fraunces Tavern, which still stands on Pearl Street.

Alexander Hamilton, for his part, got busy in the rebuilding effort, laying the groundwork for New York City institutions that remain vital to this day. He started by establishing the city's first bank, the Bank of New York, in 1784. When Washington was inaugurated as the nation's first president in 1789, at Federal Hall on Wall Street, he brought Hamilton on board as the first secretary of the treasury. Thanks to Hamilton's business savvy, trade in stocks and bonds flourished, leading to the establishment in 1792 of what would eventually be known as the New York Stock Exchange. In 1801 Hamilton founded the *Evening Post* newspaper, still in circulation today as the *New York Post*. By 1804 he had helped make New York a world-leading financial centre. The same year that his dream was realised, however, Hamilton was killed by political rival Aaron Burr in a duel in Weehawken, New Jersey.

'A boom in maritime trades lured hundreds of European labourers, and the city – still crammed entirely below Houston Street – grew more and more congested.'

BOOMTOWN
New York continued to grow and prosper for the next three decades. Maritime commerce soared, and Robert Fulton's innovative steamboat made its maiden voyage on the Hudson River in 1807. Eleven years later, a group of merchants introduced regularly scheduled shipping (a novel concept at the time) between New York and Liverpool on the Black Ball Line. Reflecting the city's status as

America's shipping centre, the urban landscape was ringed with sprawling piers, towering masts and billowing sails. A boom in the maritime trades lured hundreds of European labourers, and the city – still entirely crammed below Houston Street – grew more and more congested. Where Dutch farms and English estates once stood, taller, more efficient structures took hold, and Manhattan real estate became the most expensive in the world.

The first man to conquer the city's congestion problem was Mayor DeWitt Clinton, a brilliant politician and a protégé of Alexander Hamilton. Clinton's dream was to organise the entire island of Manhattan in such a way that it could cope with the eventual population creep northwards. In 1807 he created a commission to map out the foreseeable sprawl. It presented its work four years later, and the destiny of this new city was made manifest: it would be a regular grid of crossing thoroughfares, 12 avenues wide and 155 streets long.

Then Clinton literally overstepped his boundaries. In 1811 he presented a plan to build a 363-mile canal linking the Hudson River with Lake Erie. Many thought it impossible: at the time, the longest canal in the world ran a mere 27 miles. But he pressed on and, with a silver tongue to rival a certain modern-day Clinton, raised a staggering $6 million for the project.

Work on the Erie Canal began in 1817 and was completed in 1825 – three years ahead of schedule. It shortened the journey between New York City and Buffalo from three weeks to one, and cut the shipping cost per ton1807 from about $100 to $4. Goods, people and money poured into New York, fostering a merchant elite that moved northwards to escape the urban crush. Estates multiplied above Houston Street even as 3,000 new buildings were erected below

If this tree could talk

Before there was a Greenwich Village, or even a George Washington, there was an English elm. Three hundred or so years later, it's still here, in the same spot, towering over the north-west corner of Washington Square Park. It's one of the oldest and, with a diameter of 61 inches, largest-known trees in the city. As a 17th-century sapling, it rested in what was then a forest north of the city. In the early 1800s the tree stood in a field used for duelling and for burying victims of the frequent cholera and yellow fever breakouts.

Because the field also hosted public hangings until 1819, the tree earned its name, the Hangman's Elm, and the persistent urban myth arose that criminals once hung from the tree itself. When the city bought the land in 1827, the elm survived landscaping and exhumation of the burial ground, and bore witness to a stately neighbourhood cropping up around the new park. Today, it's mostly the squirrels that pay attention to the elm, though it proudly bears a sign designating it as one of New York's Great Trees.

it – each grander and more imposing than its modest colonial forerunners. Once slavery was officially abolished in New York in 1827, free blacks became an essential part of the workforce. In 1831 the first public transportation system began operating, pulling passengers in horse-drawn omnibuses to the city's far reaches.

BUMMERTOWN

As the population grew (swelling to 170,000 by 1830), so did New York City's problems. Tensions bubbled between immigrant newcomers and those who could trace their American lineage back a generation or two. Crime rose and lurid tales filled the 'penny press', the city's proto-tabloids. While wealthy New Yorkers were moving as far 'uptown' as Greenwich Village, the infamous Five Points neighbourhood – the city's first slum – festered in the area now occupied by City Hall, the courthouses and Chinatown. Built on a fetid drained pond, Five Points became the ramshackle home of poor immigrants and blacks. Brutal gangs with colourful names like the Forty Thieves, Plug Uglies and Dead Rabbits often met in bloody clashes in the streets, but what finally sent a mass of 100,000 people scurrying from Downtown was an outbreak of cholera in 1832. In just six weeks, 3,513 New Yorkers died.

In 1837 a financial panic left hundreds of Wall Street businesses crumbling. Commerce stagnated at the docks, the real-estate market collapsed, and all but three city banks closed down. Some 50,000 New Yorkers lost their jobs, while 200,000 teetered on the edge of poverty. The panic also sparked an era of civil unrest and violence. In 1849 a xenophobic mob of 8,000 protesting the performance of an English actor at the Astor Place Opera House was met by a militia that opened fire, killing 22 people. But the Draft Riots of 1863, known as 'the bloodiest riots in American history', were much worse. After a law was passed exempting men from the draft for a $300 fee, the (mostly Irish) poor rose up, forming a 15,000-strong force that rampaged through the city. They trashed police stations, draft boards, newspaper offices, expensive shops and wealthy homes before the chaos took a racial turn. Fuelled by anger about the Civil War (for which they blamed blacks), and fearful that freed slaves would take away jobs, the rioters set fire to the Colored Orphan Asylum and vandalised black homes. Blacks were beaten in the streets, and some were lynched. A federal force of 6,000 men was sent to subdue the violence. After four days and at least 105 deaths, peace was finally restored.

PROGRESSIVE CITY

Amid the chaos of the mid 19th century, the pace of progress continued unabated. Compared with the major Southern cities, New York emerged nearly unscathed from the Civil War. The population ballooned to two million, and new technologies revolutionised daily life. The elevated railway, for example, helped extend the population into what is now the Upper East and Upper West Sides, while other trains connected the city with upstate New York, New England and the Midwest. By 1871 train traffic had grown so much that rail tycoon Cornelius Vanderbilt built the original Grand Central Depot, which could accommodate a then-considerable 15,000 passengers at a time. (It was replaced in 1913 by the current Grand Central Terminal.)

One ambitious project was inspired by the harsh winter of 1867. The East River froze over, halting water traffic between Brooklyn and Manhattan for weeks. Brooklyn, by then, had become the nation's third most populous city, and its politicians, businessmen and community leaders realised that the boroughs had to be linked. Thus, the New York Bridge Company was incorporated. Its goal was to build the world's longest bridge, spanning the East River between downtown Manhattan and south-western Brooklyn. Over 16 years (four times longer than projected), 14,000 miles of steel cable were stretched across the 1,595-foot span, while the towers rose a staggering 276 feet above the river. Disasters, worker deaths and corruption dogged the project, but the Brooklyn Bridge opened with triumphant fanfare on 24 May 1883. It remains one of the city's most beloved symbols.

'Financier JP Morgan was essential in bringing New York's, and America's, economy back to life.'

CORRUPT CITY

As New York recovered from the turmoil of the mid 1800s, one extremely indecorous man, William M 'Boss' Tweed, was pulling the strings. Using his ample charm, the six-foot-tall, 300-pound bookkeeper, chairmaker and volunteer firefighter became one of the city's most powerful politicians. He had been an alderman and district leader; he served in the US House of Representatives and as a state senator; and he was a chairman of the Democratic General Committee and leader of Tammany Hall, a political organisation that was formed by craftsmen to keep the wealthy class's political clout in check. But even though Tweed opened orphanages, poorhouses and hospitals, his good deeds were overshadowed by his and his cohorts' gross embezzlement of city funds.

By 1870 members of the 'Tweed Ring' had created a new city charter, granting themselves control of the City Treasury. Using fake leases and wildly inflated bills for city supplies and services, Tweed may ultimately have pocketed as much as $200 million, and caused the city's debt to triple. The work of cartoonist Thomas Nast, who lampooned Tweed in the pages of *Harper's Weekly*, helped to bring the Boss's transgressions to light. Tweed was eventually sued by the city for $6 million, and charged with forgery and larceny. In 1875, while being held in debtor's prison pending bail, he escaped. He was caught in Spain a year later and died in the can in 1878. But before his fall from power, Tweed's insatiable greed hurt many: as he was emptying the city's coffers, poverty spread. Then the bond market collapsed, the stock market took a nosedive, factories closed and railroads went bankrupt. By 1874 New York estimated its homeless population at 90,000. That winter, *Harper's Weekly* reported, 900 New Yorkers starved to death.

THE TWO HALVES

In September 1882 a new era dawned brightly when Thomas Alva Edison lit up half a square mile of lower Manhattan with 3,000 electric lamps. One of the newly illuminated offices belonged to a man known for brushing people aside when he strode down the sidewalks: financier JP Morgan, who was essential in bringing New York's, and America's, economy back to life. By bailing out a number of failing railroads, then merging and restructuring them, Morgan jump-started commerce in New York once again. Goods, jobs and businesses returned to the city, and soon aggressive businessmen with names like Rockefeller, Carnegie and Frick wanted a piece of the action (none of them, by the way, was noted for his courtesy, either). They made New York the HQ of Standard Oil and US Steel, corporations that would go on to shape America's economic future and New York's reputation as the country's centre of capitalism.

A shining symbol for less fortunate immigrants also made New York its home around that time: to commemorate America's freedom 100 years after the Declaration of Independence, and to celebrate an international friendship, the French gave the Statue of Liberty to the United States. Sculptor Frédéric-Auguste Bartholdi had created the 151-foot-tall Amazon using funds donated by French citizens, but their generosity could not cover the expense of building her base. Although the project was initially met with apathy by the US government, Hungarian immigrant and publisher Joseph Pulitzer used his *World* newspaper to

Robert Fulton's innovative steamboat made its maiden voyage in 1807. *See p16.*

encourage Americans to pay for a pedestal. When she was finally unveiled in 1886, Lady Liberty measured 305 feet high – taller than the towers of the Brooklyn Bridge.

Between 1892 and 1954 the statue welcomed more than 12 million immigrants into New York Harbor. Ellis Island opened as an immigration-processing centre in 1892, with expectations of accommodating 500,000 people annually; it processed twice that number in its first year. In the 34-building complex, crowds of would-be Americans were herded through examinations, inspections and interrogations. Fewer than two per cent were sent home, and others moved on, but four million stayed, turning New York into what British playwright Israel

Zangwill called 'the great melting pot where all the races of Europe are melting and reforming'.

Many of these new immigrants crowded into dark, squalid tenements on the Lower East Side, while millionaires like the Vanderbilts were building huge French-style mansions along Fifth Avenue. Jacob A Riis, a Danish immigrant and police reporter for the *New York Tribune*, made it his business to expose this dichotomy, however impolite it may have seemed to the wealthy. Employing the then relatively new technology of photography to accompany his written observations, Riis's 1890 book, *How the Other Half Lives,* revealed in graphic terms the bitter conditions of the slums. The intrepid reporter scoured filthy alleys and overcrowded,

Blast on the past

As former president of the New-York Historical Society and the editor of *The Encyclopedia of New York*, Columbia University professor Kenneth T Jackson has made a whole career out of local history. But when *Time Out* recently caught up with him, he sounded off on the once and future state of the city as a whole.

Time Out: You've said that many people are unaware of the city's rich historical legacy. Why do you think that's the case?
Kenneth T Jackson: If you want to give your children a history lesson, Americans tend to go to Colonial Williamsburg or Independence Hall. In New York, you're much more likely to go to Broadway. My argument would be that New York is the single most historic place in the United States. Not because of any one event, but just consistently over the generations more has happened in Manhattan than in any comparable city in the US and maybe even the world.

TO: It's been about ten years since you edited *The Encyclopedia of New York*. What's up with the new version?
KTJ: We have just begun working on a second edition, which we're hoping will be out by 2009. About 50 per cent of the existing entries will be revised, and we'll have about 1,000 new entries. So the book will be at least 50 per cent new.

TO: In what ways has the city evolved, and stayed the same, over the years?
KTJ: The physical structure of the city hasn't changed much – the streets, subways and

bridges are all in place – but what goes on inside has changed. New York was the biggest harbour and the most important manufacturing city in the world, but now that's no longer true. The kinds of economic dislocations that places like Detroit are going through now, New York went through years ago.

TO: What makes New York so resilient?
KTJ: Cities have a character almost like a person does. New York is a character. Everybody doesn't necessarily like it. It can be rough, it can be harsh, but it does have a personality and its own unique history. New York's ability to withstand challenges in the past [is due to] its historic openness to newcomers – not by being gracious or making it easy; what New York does do is give people a chance. I think that our tradition of diversity and tolerance is going to help New York withstand the pressures of globalisation and economic change.

TO: Speaking of change, what overall changes do you see in the city's future?
KTJ: I think that lower Manhattan could morph into something else and maybe something more interesting. Just think about it: 50 years ago, you did not want to be in lower Manhattan at 7pm, because nobody was there; now look at the explosion of residential opportunities and restaurants. Prices are up, crime is down, and the city seems to have recovered from much of the economic stress of the last six years. There's a good attitude among residents and visitors. Polls show people want to stay in New York.

unheated tenements, many of which lacked the barest minimum of light, ventilation and sanitation. Largely as a result of Riis's work, the state passed the Tenement House Act of 1901, which called for drastic housing reforms.

EXPANDING CITY

By the close of the 19th century, 40 fragmented governments had formed in and around Manhattan, creating political confusion on many different levels. On 1 January 1898 the boroughs of Manhattan, Brooklyn, Queens, Staten Island and the Bronx consolidated to form New York City, America's largest city. More and more companies started to move their headquarters to this new metropolis, increasing the demand for office space. With little land left to develop in lower Manhattan, New York embraced the steel revolution and grew skywards. Thus began an all-out race to build the tallest building in the world. By 1902 New York boasted 66 skyscrapers, including the 20-storey Fuller Building (which is now known as the Flatiron Building) at Fifth Avenue and 23rd Street, and the 25-storey New York Times Tower in Longacre (now Times) Square. Within four years, these two buildings would be completely dwarfed by the 47-storey Singer Building on lower Broadway, which enjoyed the status of tallest building in the world – but for only 18 months. The 700-foot Metropolitan Life Tower on Madison Square claimed the title from the Singer Building in 1909, but the 792-foot-tall Woolworth Building on Broadway and Park Place topped it in 1913 – and amazingly held the distinction for nearly two decades.

If that weren't enough to demonstrate New Yorkers' unending ambition, the city burrowed below the streets at the same time, starting work on its underground transit system in 1900. The $35-million project took nearly four and a half years to complete. Less than a decade after opening, it was the most heavily travelled subway system in the world, carrying almost a billion passengers on its trains every year.

CITY OF MOVEMENT

By 1909, 30,000 factories were operating in the city, churning out everything from heavy machinery to artificial flowers. Brutal conditions worsened the situation for workers, who toiled long hours for meagre pay. Young immigrant seamstresses worked 60-plus hours for just $5 a week. Mistrusted and abused, factory workers faced impossible quotas, had their pay docked for minor mistakes, and were often locked in the factories during working hours. In the end, it would take a tragedy for real changes to be made.

Italian immigrants in 1905. *See p20.*

On 25 March 1911 a fire broke out at the Triangle Shirtwaist Company. Though it was a Saturday, some 500 workers – most of them teenage girls – were toiling in the Greenwich Village factory. Flames spread rapidly through the fabric-filled building, but as the girls rushed to escape, they found many of the exits locked. Roughly 350 made it out on to the adjoining rooftops before the inferno closed off all exits, but 146 young women perished. Many jumped to their deaths from windows on the eighth, ninth and tenth floors. Even in the face of such tragedy, justice was not served: the two factory owners, tried for manslaughter, were acquitted. The disaster did spur labour and union organisations, which pushed for – and won – sweeping reforms for factory workers.

Another sort of rights movement was taking hold during this time. Between 1910 and 1913 New York City was the site of the largest women's suffrage rallies in the United States. Harriet Stanton Blatch (who was the daughter of famed suffragette Elizabeth Cady Stanton, and founder of the Equality League of Self Supporting Women) and Carrie Chapman Catt (the organiser of the New York City Women's Suffrage party) arranged attention-getting demonstrations intended to pressure the state into authorising a referendum on a woman's

Sacred ground

President George W Bush's 2006 National Monument designation aside, a passer-by might be forgiven for not immediately appreciating the enormous significance of this unassuming quarter-acre rectangle situated in the heart of lower Manhattan. But it's what lies beneath it that's of great importance: the 17th- and 18th-century remains of an estimated 20,000 African slaves and freed former slaves, who were stacked in layers, buried 16 to 25 feet under street level and spread across a five- to seven-acre stretch of what is now prime downtown real estate just north of City Hall. No colonial-era tombstones or markers speak of the lives and deaths of those interred. But the sheer scope of the burial ground offers a poignant testimony to a surprising fact: in its 18th-century infancy, New York City held the dubious distinction of being home to more enslaved Africans than any other English settlement save one (that being Charleston, South Carolina, which can claim sad bragging rights to top-dog status).

The slave trade first reached the Dutch colony named New Amsterdam in about 1625. After the British assumed control in 1664 the colony's African population was given permission to bury their dead in areas outside the town perimeters. Around 1795, by which point roughly a staggering 40 per cent of New York households owned at least one slave, the graveyard was closed down, surveyed, subdivided, and sold in lots. Construction landfill preserved the remains for nearly 200 years – it became a case of out of sight and mind – below a cityscape of 19th- and 20th-century office buildings and busy streets.

A 1991 excavation for the construction of a 34-storey office tower led to the rediscovery of the graveyard, the unearthing of 1.5 million burial artefacts and the disinterment of 419

right to vote. The measure's defeat in 1915 only steeled the suffragettes' resolve. Finally, with the support of Tammany Hall, the law was passed in 1919, challenging the male stranglehold on voting throughout the country. (With New York leading the nation, the 19th Amendment was ratified in 1920.)

In 1919, as New York welcomed troops home from World War I with a parade along Fifth Avenue, the city also celebrated its emergence on the global stage. It had supplanted London as the investment capital of the world, and it had become the centre of publishing, thanks to two men: Pulitzer and Hearst. The *New York Times* had become the country's most respected newspaper; Broadway was the focal point of American theatre; and Greenwich Village, once the home of an elite gentry, had become a middle-class bohemia, where flamboyant artists, writers and political revolutionaries gathered in galleries and coffeehouses. John Reed, reporter on the Russian revolution and author of *Ten Days*

That Shook the World, lived here, as did Edna St Vincent Millay, famous for her poetry and her public, unfettered love life.

The more personal side of the women's movement also found a home in New York City. A nurse and midwife who grew up in a family of 11 children, Margaret Sanger was a fierce advocate of birth control and family planning. She opened the first ever birth-control clinic in Brooklyn on 16 October 1916. Finding this unseemly, the police closed the clinic soon after and imprisoned Sanger for 30 days. She pressed on and, in 1921, formed the American Birth Control League – the forerunner of Planned Parenthood – which researched birth control and provided gynaecological services.

Forward-thinking women like Sanger set the tone for the Jazz Age, a time when women, now a voting political force, were moving beyond the moral conventions of the 19th century. The country ushered in the Jazz Age in 1919 by ratifying the 18th Amendment, which outlawed the distribution and sale of remains. A community uproar led to the nixing of building plans, the reinterment of remains and heated discussions regarding the building of a permanent memorial. Finally, in 2005, a government-led panel selected a stone memorial drafted by architect Rodney Leon, a 36-year-old African-American New Yorker. The two-storey-tall curved monument draws heavily on African architecture and contains a spiral path leading to an ancestral chamber. 'I wanted it to reflect the diversity of Africans who were buried there, and to address the sacredness of the place,' says Leon. 'It's a big responsibility, and you just hope you're doing the right thing.'

In February 2006 President Bush proclaimed the site a national monument.

'By creating this monument, we recognise that, as a nation, we were once blind and separated by the shame of slavery,' Secretary of the US Department of the Interior Gale Norton told ceremony attendees. 'Now we see, united by the hope that comes from repentance, remembrance and renewal.'

In addition to the memorial, which is slated to open early in 2007, there is an education and

interpretive centre located in the lobby of 290 Broadway, which contains commemorative artwork, a timeline and shows documentaries about the site and slavery in New York.

African Burial Ground National Monument

Duane Street, between Broadway & Centre Street, behind 290 Broadway (1-212 637 2019/www.africanburialground.com). Subway: N, Q, R, W to Canal Street; J, M, Z to Chambers Street; 4, 5, 6 to Brooklyn Bridge-City Hall. **Open** *9am-4pm Mon-Fri.* **Admission** *free.*

alcoholic beverages. Prohibition turned the city into the epicentre of bootlegging, speakeasies and organised crime. By the early 1920s, New York boasted 32,000 illegal watering holes – twice the number of legal bars before Prohibition.

In 1925 New Yorkers elected the magnetic James J Walker as the city's mayor. A charming ex-songwriter (as well as a speakeasy patron and skirt-chaser who would later leave his wife for a dancer), Walker was the perfect match for his city's flashy style, hunger for publicity and consequences be damned attitude. Fame flowed in the city's veins: home-run hero Babe Ruth drew a million fans each season to the New York Yankees' games, and sharp-tongued Walter Winchell filled his newspaper columns with celebrity titbits and scandals. Alexander Woollcott, Dorothy Parker, Robert Benchley and other writers met up daily to trade witticisms around a table at the Algonquin Hotel; the result, in February 1925, was *The New Yorker*.

The Harlem Renaissance blossomed at the same time. Writers such as Langston Hughes, Zora Neale Hurston and James Weldon Johnson transformed the African-American experience into lyrical literary works, and white society flocked to the Cotton Club to see genre-defining musicians like Bessie Smith, Cab Calloway, Louis Armstrong and Duke Ellington. (Blacks were not welcome here unless they were performing.) Downtown, Broadway houses were packed out, thanks to brilliant composers and lyricists like George and Ira Gershwin, Irving Berlin, Cole Porter, Lorenz Hart, Richard Rodgers and Oscar Hammerstein II. Towards the end of the '20s, New York-born Al Jolson wowed audiences in *The Jazz Singer*, the first ever talking picture.

THE FALL AND RISE
The dizzying excitement ended on Tuesday, 29 October 1929, when the stock market completely crashed and widespread hard times set in. Corruption eroded Mayor Walker's hold

Further reading

Herbert Asbury *The Gangs of New York: An Informal History of the Underworld*
A racy journalistic portrait of the city at the turn of the 19th century.

Robert A Caro *The Power Broker*
A biography of Robert Moses, New York's mid-20th-century master builder, and his chequered legacy.

Federal Writers' Project *The WPA Guide to New York City*
A wonderful snapshot of the 1930s by writers who were employed under FDR's New Deal.

Sanna Feirstein *Naming New York*
How Manhattan places got their names.

Mitchell Fink and Lois Mathias *Never Forget: An Oral History of September 11, 2001*
A collection of first-person accounts.

Alice Rose George (ed) *Here Is New York*
A collection of nearly 900 powerful amateur photos that document the aftermath of September 11, 2001.

Clifton Hood *722 Miles: The Building of the Subways and How They Transformed New York*
The title adequately describes the content.

Kenneth T Jackson (ed) *The Encyclopedia of New York City*
An ambitious and useful reference guide.

David Levering Lewis *When Harlem Was in Vogue*
A study of the Harlem Renaissance.

Shaun O'Connell *Remarkable, Unspeakable New York*
The history of New York as literary inspiration.

Mitchell Pacelle *Empire*
The story of the fight to build the Empire State Building.

Jacob A Riis *How the Other Half Lives*
A pioneering photojournalistic record of squalid tenement life.

Marie Salerno and Arthur Gelb *The New York Pop-up Book*
An interactive historical account of NYC.

Luc Sante *Low Life*
Opium dens and brothels in New York from the 1840s to the 1920s.

Mike Wallace and Edwin G Burrows *Gotham: A History of New York City to 1898*
The first volume in a planned mammoth history of NYC.

For other books on New York, see p385.

on the city: despite a tenure that saw the opening of the Holland Tunnel, the completion of the George Washington Bridge and the construction of the Chrysler and Empire State Buildings, Walker's lustre faded in the growing shadow of graft accusations. He resigned in 1932, as New York, caught in the depths of the Great Depression, had a staggering one million inhabitants who were out of work.

In 1934 an unstoppable force named Fiorello La Guardia took office as mayor, rolling up his sleeves to crack down on mobsters, gambling, smut and government corruption. La Guardia was the son of an Italian father and a Jewish mother. He was a tough-talking politician who was known for nearly coming to blows with other city officials, and he described himself as 'inconsiderate, arbitrary, authoritative, difficult, complicated, intolerant and somewhat theatrical'. La Guardia's act played well: he ushered New York into an era of unparalleled prosperity over the course of his three terms. During World War II, the city's ports and factories proved essential to the war effort. New Yorkers' sense of unity was never more visible than on 14 August 1945, when two million people spontaneously gathered in Times Square to celebrate the end of the war. The 'Little Flower', as La Guardia was known, streamlined city government, paid down the debt and updated the transportation, hospital, reservoir and sewer systems. Additional highways made the city more accessible, and North Beach (now La Guardia) Airport became the city's first commercial landing field.

Helping La Guardia to modernise the city was Robert Moses, a hard-nosed visionary who would do much to shape – and in some cases, destroy – New York's landscape. Moses spent 44 years stepping on toes to build expressways, parks, beaches, public housing, bridges and tunnels, creating such landmarks as Shea Stadium, the Lincoln Center, the United Nations complex and the Verrazano-Narrows Bridge.

THE MODERN CITY

Despite La Guardia's belt-tightening and Moses' renovations, New York began to fall apart financially. When World War II ended, 800,000 industrial jobs disappeared from the city. Factories in need of more space moved to the suburbs, along with nearly five million residents. But more crowding occurred as rural African-Americans and Puerto Ricans flocked to the metropolis in the '50s and '60s, only to meet with ruthless discrimination and a dearth of jobs. Robert Moses' Slum Clearance Committee reduced many neighbourhoods to rubble, forcing out residents in order to build huge, isolating housing projects that became

Home-run hero **Babe Ruth** during his glory years with the New York Yankees. *See p23.*

magnets for crime. In 1963 the city also lost Pennsylvania Station – McKim, Mead & White's architectural masterpiece. Over the protests of picketers, the Pennsylvania Railroad Company demolished the site to make way for a modern station and Madison Square Garden. It was a giant wake-up call to New Yorkers: architectural changes were hurtling out of control.

But Moses and his wrecking ball couldn't knock over one steadfast West Village woman. An architectural writer and urban-planning critic named Jane Jacobs organised local residents when the city unveiled its plan to clear a 14-block tract of her neighbourhood to make space for yet more public housing. Her obstinacy was applauded by many, including an influential councilman named Ed Koch (who would become mayor in 1978). The group fought the plan and won, causing Mayor Robert F Wagner to back down. As a result of Jacobs's efforts in the wake of Pennsylvania Station's demolition, the Landmarks Preservation Commission – the first such group in the US – was established in 1965.

At the dawning of the age of Aquarius, the city harboured its share of innovative creators. Allen Ginsberg, Jack Kerouac and their fellow Beats gathered in Village coffeehouses to create a new voice for poetry. A folk-music scene brewed in tiny clubs around Bleecker Street, showcasing musicians such as Bob Dylan. A former advertising illustrator from Pittsburgh named Andy Warhol began turning the images of mass consumerism into deadpan, ironic art statements. Gay men and women, long a hidden part of the city's history, came out into the streets in 1969's Stonewall riots, sparked when patrons at the Stonewall Inn on Christopher Street resisted a police raid – giving birth to the modern gay-rights movement.

'The angst of the time fuelled the angry punk culture that rose up around downtown clubs like CBGB.'

By the early 1970s deficits had forced heavy cutbacks in city services. The streets were dirty, subway cars and buildings were scrawled with graffiti, crime skyrocketed and the city's debt deepened to $6 billion. Despite the downturn, construction commenced on the World Trade Center; when completed, in 1973, its twin 110-storey towers were the world's tallest buildings. Even as the Trade Center rose, the city became so desperately overdrawn that Mayor Abraham Beame appealed to the federal government for financial assistance in 1975. Yet President Gerald Ford refused to bail out the city, and New Yorkers faced his decision, summed up by the immortal *Daily News* headline: 'Ford to city: drop dead'.

The President's callousness certainly didn't help matters during this time. Around the mid '70s, Times Square steadily degenerated into a sleazy morass of sex shops and porn palaces, drug use escalated and subway ridership hit an all-time low. To make situations worse, in 1977 serial killer Son of Sam terrorised the city, and a blackout one hot August night that same year led to widespread looting and arson. The angst of the time fuelled the angry punk culture that rose up around downtown clubs like CBGB, where the Ramones and other bands played fast and loud. At the same time, celebrities, designers and models converged on Midtown to disco their nights away at Studio 54.

The Wall Street boom of the '80s and some adept fiscal petitioning by then-mayor Ed Koch brought money flooding back into New York. Gentrification glamorised neighbourhoods like Soho, Tribeca and the East Village. But deeper ills persisted. In 1988 a demonstration against the city's efforts to impose a curfew and displace the homeless in Tompkins Square Park erupted into a violent clash with the police. Crack use was endemic in the ghettos, homelessness was rising and AIDS became a new scourge. By 1989 citizens were restless for change. They turned to David N Dinkins, electing him the city's first African-American mayor. A distinguished, soft-spoken man, Dinkins held office for only a single term – one marked by a record murder rate, flaring racial tensions in Washington Heights, Crown Heights and Flatbush, and the explosion of a terrorist bomb in the World Trade Center that killed six, injured 1,000 and foreshadowed the catastrophic attacks of 2001.

Deeming the polite Dinkins ineffective, New Yorkers voted in former federal prosecutor Rudolph Giuliani. Like his predecessors Peter Stuyvesant and Fiorello La Guardia, Giuliani was an abrasive leader who used bully tactics to get things done. His 'quality of life' campaign cracked down on everything from drug dealing and pornography to unsolicited windshield-washing. Even as multiple cases of severe police brutality grabbed the headlines, crime plummeted, tourism soared and New York became cleaner and safer than it had been in decades. Times Square was transformed into a family-friendly tourist destination, and the dot-com explosion brought a generation of young wannabe millionaires to the Flatiron District's Silicon Alley. Giuliani's second term as mayor would close, however, on a devastating tragedy.

On 11 September 2001 terrorists flew two hijacked passenger jets into the Twin Towers of the World Trade Center, collapsing the entire complex and killing nearly 2,800 people. But the attack triggered a citywide sense of unity, and New Yorkers did what they could to help their fellow citizens, from feeding emergency crews around the clock to cheering on workers en route to Ground Zero.

Two months later, billionaire Michael Bloomberg was elected mayor and took on the daunting task of repairing not only the city's skyline but also its battered economy and shattered psyche. He proved adept at steering the city back on the road to health as the stock market revived, downtown businesses re-emerged and plans for rebuilding the Trade Center were drawn. True to form, however, New Yorkers debated the future of the site for more than a year until architect Daniel Libeskind was awarded the redevelopment job in 2003. His plan, called 'Memory Foundations', aims to reconcile rebuilding and remembrance, with parks, plazas, a cultural centre, a performing arts centre, a memorial and a sleek new office tower. Nevertheless, conflict continues to plague every step of the project.

The summer of 2003 saw a blackout that shut down the city (and much of the eastern seaboard). New Yorkers were sweaty but calm, and again proved that they possessed surprisingly strong reserves of civility as the city's cafés set up candlelit tables and bodegas handed out free ice-cream.

And yet, despite Bloomberg's many efforts to make New York a more considerate and civil place – imposing a citywide smoking ban in bars and restaurants and a strict noise ordinance that would even silence the jingling of ice-cream vans – New Yorkers continue to uphold their hard-edged image. The 2004 Republican National Convention brought out hundreds of thousands of peace marchers who had no trouble expressing how they felt about the war in Iraq. Still, the oft-cranky citizenry swooned for Christo and Jeanne-Claude's The Gates – the 7,503 billowing orange fabric and metal gates that lined 23 miles of paths in Central Park for two weeks in February 2005. But just as quickly, it was back to business as usual: local belly-aching helped kill a plan to build a 75,000-seat stadium on Manhattan's West Side, squashing Bloomberg and Co's dream to bring the 2012 Olympic Games to the Big Apple.

But let's face it, if any of these rude, abrasive or inconsiderate people had their attitudes adjusted, New Yorkers wouldn't be where they are today: thriving in a city that is often looked upon as the capital of the world. And no doubt they would offer a big, disrespectful Bronx cheer to those who disagree.

Key NYC events

1524 Giovanni da Verrazano sails into New York Harbor.

1624 First Dutch settlers establish New Amsterdam at the foot of Manhattan Island.

1626 Peter Minuit purchases Manhattan for goods worth 60 guilders.

1639 The Broncks settle north of Manhattan.

1646 Village of Breuckelen founded.

1664 Dutch rule ends; New Amsterdam renamed New York.

1754 King's College (now Columbia University) founded.

1776 Battle for New York begins; fire ravages the city.

1783 George Washington's troops march triumphantly down Broadway.

1784 Alexander Hamilton founds the Bank of New York.

1785 New York becomes the nation's capital.

1789 President Washington inaugurated at Federal Hall on Wall Street.

1792 New York Stock Exchange founded.

1804 New York becomes the country's most populous city, with 80,000 inhabitants; New York Historical Society founded.

1811 Mayor DeWitt Clinton's grid plan for Manhattan introduced.

1825 New York Gas Light Company completes installation of first gas lamps on Broadway; Erie Canal completed.

1827 Slavery officially abolished in New York.

1833 The *New York Sun*'s lurid tales give birth to tabloid journalism.

1851 The *New York Daily Times* (now the *New York Times*) published.

1858 Work on Central Park begins; Macy's opens.

1870 Metropolitan Museum of Art founded.

1883 Brooklyn Bridge opens.

1886 Statue of Liberty unveiled.

1890 Jacob A Riis publishes *How the Other Half Lives*.

1891 Carnegie Hall opens with a concert conducted by Tchaikovsky.

1892 Ellis Island opens.

1895 Oscar Hammerstein's Olympia Theater opens, creating Broadway theatre.

1898 The city consolidates the five boroughs.

1902 The Fuller (Flatiron) Building becomes the world's first skyscraper.

1903 The New York Highlanders (later the New York Yankees) play their first game.

1904 New York's first subway line opens; Longacre Square becomes Times Square.

1908 First ball dropped to celebrate the new year in Times Square.

1911 The Triangle Shirtwaist Fire claims nearly 150 lives, spurring unionisation.

1923 Yankee Stadium opens.

1924 First Macy's Christmas Parade held – now the Thanksgiving Day Parade.

1929 The stock market crashes; Museum of Modern Art opens.

1931 George Washington Bridge completed; the Empire State Building opens; the Whitney Museum opens.

1934 Fiorello La Guardia takes office; Tavern on the Green opens.

1939 New York hosts a World's Fair.

1946 The New York Knickerbockers play their first game.

1950 United Nations complex completed.

1953 Robert Moses spearheads building of the Cross Bronx Expressway; 40,000 homes demolished in the process.

1957 The New York Giants baseball team moves to San Francisco; Brooklyn Dodgers move to Los Angeles.

1962 New York Mets debut at the Polo Grounds; Philharmonic Hall (later Avery Fisher Hall), the first building in Lincoln Center, opens; first Shakespeare in the Park performance.

1964 Verrazano-Narrows Bridge completed; World's Fair held in Flushing Meadows-Corona Park in Queens.

1970 First New York City Marathon held.

1973 World Trade Center completed.

1975 On the verge of bankruptcy, the city is snubbed by the federal government; *Saturday Night Live* debuts.

1977 Serial killer David 'Son of Sam' Berkowitz arrested; Studio 54 opens; 4,000 arrested during citywide blackout.

1989 David N Dinkins elected the city's first black mayor.

1993 A terrorist bomb explodes in the World Trade Center, killing six and injuring 1,000.

1997 Murder rate lowest in 30 years.

2001 Hijackers fly two jets into the Twin Towers, killing nearly 2,800 and demolishing the World Trade Center.

2004 The Statue of Liberty reopens for the first time since 9/11; the Republican National Convention brings out hundreds of thousands of protesters.

2005 Christo and Jeanne-Claude decorate Central Park with art installation *The Gates*; New York loses its bid for the 2012 Olympics.

Time Warner Center. *See p36.*

Architecture

Out of iron, steel and glass, a city rises.

Under New York's gleaming exoskeleton of steel and glass lies the heart of a 17th-century Dutch city. It began at the Battery and New York Harbor, one of the greatest naturally formed deep-water ports in the world. The former Alexander Hamilton Custom House, now the **National Museum of the American Indian** (*see p92*), was built by Cass Gilbert in 1907 and is a symbol of the harbour's significance in Manhattan's growth. Before 1913, the city's chief source of revenue was customs duties. Gilbert's domed marble edifice is suitably monumental – its carved figures of the Four Continents are by Daniel Chester French, the sculptor of the Lincoln Memorial in Washington, DC.

The Dutch influence is still traceable in the downtown web of narrow, winding lanes, reminiscent of the streets in medieval European cities. Because the Cartesian grid that rules the city was laid out by the Commissioners' Plan in 1811, only a few samples of actual Dutch

architecture remain, mostly off the beaten path. One of these is the 1785 **Dyckman Farmhouse Museum** (4881 Broadway, at 204th Street, www.dyckmanfarmhouse.org) in Inwood – Manhattan's northernmost neighbourhood. Its decorative brickwork and gambrel roof reflect the architectural fashion of the late 18th century. The oldest house still standing in the five boroughs is the **Pieter Claesen Wyckoff House Museum** (5816 Clarendon Road, at Ralph Avenue, Flatbush, Brooklyn, www.wyckoffassociation.org). Erected around 1652, it is a typical Dutch farmhouse with deep eaves and shingled walls. The **Lefferts Homestead** (Prospect Park, Flatbush Avenue, Prospect Heights, Brooklyn), built between 1777 and 1783, combines a gambrel roof with column-supported porches, a hybrid style popular during the Federal period.

In Manhattan, the only building extant from pre-Revolutionary times is the stately columned and quoined **St Paul's Chapel** (*see p97*),

In Context

completed in 1766 (a spire was added in 1796). George Washington, a parishioner here, was officially received in the chapel after his 1789 presidential inauguration. The Enlightenment ideals upon which this nation was founded influenced the church's democratic, non-hierarchical layout. **Trinity Church** (*see p97*) of 1846, one of the first and finest Gothic Revival churches in the country, was designed by Richard Upjohn. It's difficult to imagine now that Trinity's crocketed, finialed 281-foot-tall spire held sway for decades as the tallest structure in Manhattan.

> **'Iron and steel freed architects from the bulk, weight and cost of stone construction, allowing them to build taller structures.'**

Hold-outs remain from each epoch of the city's architectural history. An outstanding example of Greek Revival from the first half of the 19th century is the 1842 **Federal Hall National Memorial** (*see p97*), the mighty marble colonnade that was built to mark the site where George Washington took his oath of office. A larger-than-life statue of Washington by the sculptor John Quincy Adams Ward stands in front. The city's most celebrated blocks of Greek Revival townhouses, built in the 1830s, are known simply as the **Row** (1-13 Washington Square North, between Fifth Avenue & Washington Square West); they're exemplars of the more genteel metropolis of Henry James and Edith Wharton.

Greek Revival gave way to Renaissance-inspired Beaux Arts architecture, which reflected the imperial ambitions of a wealthy young nation during the Gilded Age of the late 19th century. Like Emperor Augustus, who boasted that he had found Rome a city of brick and left it a city of marble, the firm of McKim, Mead & White built noble civic monuments and palazzi for the rich. The best-known buildings of the classicist Charles Follen McKim include the main campus of **Columbia University** (*see p146*), which was begun in the 1890s, and the austere 1906 **Morgan Library** (*see p121*). His partner, socialite and bon vivant Stanford White (scandalously murdered by his mistress's husband in 1906) designed more festive spaces, such as the **Metropolitan Club** (1 E 60th Street, at Fifth Avenue) and the extraordinarily luxe Villard Houses of 1882, now incorporated into the **New York Palace Hotel** (*see p57*).

Another Beaux Arts treasure from the city's grand metropolitan era is Carrère & Hastings's sumptuous white-marble **New York Public Library** of 1911 (*see p126*), built on the site of a former Revolutionary War battleground; the site later hosted an Egyptian Revival water reservoir and, currently, the greensward of Bryant Park. The 1913 travertine-lined **Grand Central Terminal** (*see p131*) remains the elegant foyer of the city, thanks to preservationists (most prominently, Jacqueline Kennedy Onassis) who saved it from the wrecking ball.

UP, UP AND AWAY
Cast-iron architecture peaked in the latter half of the 19th century, coinciding roughly with the Civil War era. Iron and steel components freed architects from the bulk, weight and cost of stone construction and allowed them to build taller structures. Cast-iron columns – cheap to mass-produce – could support a tremendous amount of weight. The façades of many Soho buildings, with their intricate details of Italianate columns, were manufactured on assembly lines and could be ordered in pieces from catalogues.

This led to an aesthetic of uniform building façades, which had a direct impact on the steel skyscrapers of the following generation. To

The **Flatiron Building**. *See p31.*

High times ahead

is projected to open in spring 2008, according to Friends of the High Line, a non-profit group of community activists that is the heart and soul (and legwork) behind the project.

The last train to use the elevated High Line dropped off its final load in the early 1980s – a wagon of frozen turkeys. Not only was it the end of the line, it was the end of an era. Over the following two decades, the 22-block-long, three-storey-high ribbon of rail on Manhattan's far west side between Gansevoort Street in the Meatpacking District and 34th Street

After years of talk of turning an old defunct elevated train track on Manhattan's west side into a lush walkway, there's actual *action* taking place. In spring 2006 a bevy of politicians – including Mayor Bloomberg and Senator Hillary Clinton – were falling over each other in full-on self-congratulation mode at the ground-breaking ceremony (held on the elevated structure itself; *photo above*) to mark the start of construction of the High Line Park. We'll cut them some slack, though, since it's arguably the most fantastic idea to take hold of the local imagination in decades.

'It will be exciting to see this initiative move forward to create a great public amenity; a unique destination where New Yorkers will be able to find a peaceful oasis above the hustle and bustle of the city streets,' Senator Clinton told the crowd.

The first section of the park will run from Gansevoort Street to West 20th Street, and

in Midtown was abandoned – an urban afterthought made lush by nature.

In 2000 photos taken by renowned lensman Joel Sternfeld helped to awaken New Yorkers to the High Line's hidden beauty, which during the 1980s and '90s faced constant threat from the wrecking ball. Sternfeld's photos revealed something remarkable: a 1.5-mile-long artery of serene, verdant pasture coursing through the city's overstressed heart.

'What attracted me to saving the High Line was exactly that strangeness – this steel structure with wild flowers growing on top of it, in the middle of the city,' said Robert Hammond, 37, who in 1999 founded the Friends of the High Line with Joshua David, 43. The two Chelsea residents started pitching a simple idea to anyone who would listen: save the High Line and turn it into an elevated urban oasis.

enjoy one of the most telling vistas of skyscraper history, gaze northwards from the 1859 **Cooper Union** building in the East Village (*see p108*), the oldest existing steel-beam-framed building in America.

The most visible effect of the move towards cast-iron construction was the way it opened up solid-stone façades to expanses of glass. In fact, window-shopping came into vogue in the 1860s. Mrs Lincoln bought the White House china at the **Haughwout Store** (488-492 Broadway, at Broome Street). The 1857 building's Palladian-style façade recalls Renaissance Venice, but its regular, open fenestration was also a portent of

the future. (Look carefully: the cast-iron elevator sign is a relic of the world's first working safety passenger elevator, designed by Elisha Graves Otis in 1852.)

Once engineers perfected steel, which is stronger and lighter than iron, and created the interlocking steel-cage construction that distributed the weight of a building over its entire frame, the sky was the limit. New York is fortunate to have one building by the great skyscraper innovator Louis Sullivan, the 1898 **Bayard-Condict Building** (65-69 Bleecker Street, between Broadway & Lafayette Street). Though only 13 storeys tall, Sullivan's building,

Now, eight years later, the project has garnered the support of all major city politicians, and cultural heavyweights like Diane von Furstenberg and actor Edward Norton, all the while raising millions in public funding. In 2005 the line's owner, CSX Transportation, officially released it from the national rail grid, freeing it for development as a public trail. Note to visitors: for now, the High Line's mystery remains off-limits and trespassers will be prosecuted. But the winning design team – landscapers Field Operations plus architects Diller Scofidio + Renfro – has already drawn up breathtaking plans for a restored High Line (for details, go to www.thehighline.org). The proposed design 'opens the High Line to the public but still refers back to the magic we found it in, in its wild state,' David enthused. Instead of setting strict borders between walkways and vegetation, the planking tapers off raggedly, allowing wild flowers and grass to blur borders and soften the line's rusting rails. In one imaginative 'wetlands' segment, a glassed-in shoulder-high pond will flank those walking by. But David and Hammond say the design stresses the line's 1930s-era industrial identity too, celebrating the steel structure.

Once-neglected neighbourhoods touched by the High Line are undergoing rapid change; the park has already become a magnet for projects like the new DIA contemporary art museum (planned for the line's southern terminus), André Balazs's Standard Hotel at 13th Street, and a Frank Gehry-designed building between 18th and 19th Streets, already under construction (*see p35*). Even though the High Line's surface is still out of bounds, David and Hammond urge visitors to the city to walk under and alongside it, using the line as an 'overhead thread' linking the Meatpacking District, Chelsea and Hudson Yards.

They hope the High Line will inspire too. 'We were just a small community group against pretty big odds when we started this,' David said, looking back. 'We really hope that when visitors come and look at it they'll understand that they can do this in their cities too.'

covered with richly decorative terracotta, was one of the earliest to have a purely vertical design rather than a design that imitated the horizontal styles of the past. Sullivan wrote that a skyscraper 'must be tall, every inch of it tall.... From bottom to top, it is a unit without a single dissenting line'.

Chicago architect Daniel H Burnham's 1902 21-storey **Flatiron Building** (aka the Fuller Building; *see p119*) is another standout New York building; its height and modern design – breathtaking even today – combined with its traditional masonry decoration, was made possible only by its steel-cage construction.

The new century saw a frenzy of skyward manufacture, resulting in buildings of record-breaking height; the now modest-looking 30-storey, 391-foot-tall **Park Row Building** (15 Park Row, between Ann & Beekman Streets) was, when it was built in 1899, the tallest building in the world. That record was shattered by the 612-foot Singer Building in 1908 (demolished in the 1960s); the 700-foot **Metropolitan Life Tower** (1 Madison Avenue, at 24th Street) of 1909, modelled after the Campanile in Venice's Piazza San Marco; and Cass Gilbert's Gothic masterpiece, the 792-foot **Woolworth Building** (*see p100*).

The Woolworth reigned in solitary splendour until William van Alen's metal-spired homage to the Automobile Age, the 1930 **Chrysler Building** (see p132), soared to 1,046 feet.

In a highly publicised race, the Chrysler was outstripped 13 months later, in 1931, by Shreve, Lamb & Harmon's 1,250-foot-tall **Empire State Building** (see p125), which has since lost its title to other giants: the 1,450-foot Sears Tower in Chicago (1974); in Kuala Lumpur, Malaysia, the 1,483-foot Petronas Towers (1996); and the current record holder, the 1,671-foot Taipei 101 in Taiwan (2004). But the Empire State remains the quintessential skyscraper, one of the most recognisable buildings in the world, with its broad base, narrow shaft and distinctive needled crown. (The giant ape that scaled the side might have something to do with it too.)

The Empire State's setbacks, retroactively labelled art deco (such buildings were then simply called 'modern'), were actually a response to the zoning code of 1916, which required a building's upper storeys to be tapered in order not to block out sunlight and air circulation to the streets. The code engendered some of the city's most fanciful architectural designs, such as the ziggurat-crowned 1926 **Paramount Building** (1501 Broadway, between 43rd & 44th Streets) and the romantically slender spire of the former **Cities Service Building** (70 Pine Street, at Pearl Street), illuminated from within like a rare gem.

BOLD NEW WORLD

The post-World War II period saw the rise of the International Style, pioneered by such giants as Le Corbusier and Ludwig Mies van der Rohe. The style's most visible symbol was the all-glass façade, like that found on the sleek slab of the **United Nations Headquarters** (see p132). The International Style relied on a new set of aesthetics: minimal decoration, clear expression of construction, an honest use of materials and a near-Platonic harmony of proportions. **Lever House** (390 Park Avenue, between 53rd & 54th Streets), designed by Gordon Bunshaft of Skidmore, Owings & Merrill, was the city's first all-steel-and-glass structure when it was built in 1952 (it recently received an award-winning brush-up). It's almost impossible to imagine the radical vision this glass construction represented on the all-masonry corridor of Park Avenue, because nearly every building since has followed suit. Mies van der Rohe's celebrated bronze-skinned **Seagram Building** (375 Park Avenue, between 52nd & 53rd Streets), which reigns in imperious isolation in its own plaza, is the epitome of the architect's cryptic dicta 'Less is more' and 'God is in the details'. The Seagram's detailing is exquisite – the custom-made bolts securing the miniature bronze piers that run the length of the façade must be polished by hand annually to keep them from oxidising and turning green. It can truly be called the Rolls-Royce of skyscrapers.

'Too many postmodernist architects relied on fussy fenestration and passive commentary on other styles.'

High modernism began to show cracks in its façade during the mid 1960s. By then, New York had built too many such structures in Midtown and below, and besides, the public had never fully warmed to the undecorated style (though for those with a little insight, the best glass boxes are fully rewarding aesthetic experiences). And the International Style's sheer arrogance in trying to supplant the traditional city structure didn't endear the movement to anyone, either. The **MetLife**

The art deco **Chrysler Building**.

Building (200 Park Avenue, at 45th Street), originally the Pan Am Building of 1963, was the prime culprit, not so much because of its design by Walter Gropius of the Bauhaus, but because of its presumptuous location, straddling Park Avenue and looming over Grand Central. There was even a plan at the time to raze Grand Central and build a twin Pan Am in its place. The International Style had obviously reached its end when Philip Johnson, who was instrumental in defining the movement with his book *The International Style* (co-written with Henry-Russell Hitchcock), began disparaging the aesthetic as 'glass-boxitis'.

POSTMODERNISM AND BEYOND

Plainly, new blood was needed. A glimmer on the horizon was Boston architect Hugh Stubbins's silvery, triangle-topped **Citicorp Center** (Lexington Avenue, between 53rd & 54th Streets), which utilised daring contemporary engineering (the building cantilevers almost magically on high stilts above street level), while harking back to the decorative tops of yesteryear. The sly old master Philip Johnson turned the tables on everyone with the heretical Chippendale crown on his **Sony Building**, originally the AT&T Building (350 Madison Avenue, between 55th & 56th Streets), a bold throwback to decoration for its own sake.

Postmodernism provided a theoretical basis for a new wave of buildings that mixed past and present, often taking cues from the environs. Some notable examples include Helmut Jahn's 425 Lexington Avenue (between 43rd & 44th Streets) of 1988; David Childs's retro diamond-tipped **Worldwide Plaza** (825 Eighth Avenue, between 49th & 50th Streets) of 1989; and the honky-tonk agglomeration of Skidmore, Owings & Merrill's **Bertelsmann Building** (1540 Broadway, between 45th & 46th Streets) of 1990. But even postmodernism became old hat after a while. Too many architects relied on fussy fenestration and passive commentary on other styles, instead of creating vital new building façades.

The electronic spectacle of Times Square still provided, and continues to provide, one possible direction for architects. Upon seeing the myriad electric lights of Times Square in 1922, the British wit GK Chesterton remarked: 'What a glorious garden of wonder this would be, to anyone who was lucky enough to be unable to read.' This particular crossroads of the world continues to be at the cybernetic cutting edge: the 120-foot-tall, quarter-acre-in-area NASDAQ sign; the real-time stock tickers and jumbo TV screens; the news zipper on the original **New York Times Tower** (1 Times

Norman Foster's **Hearst Tower**. See p34.

Square, between Broadway & Seventh Avenue). The public's appetite for new images seems so insatiable that a building's fixed profile no longer suffices here – only an ever-shifting electronic skin will do. The iconoclastic critic Robert Venturi, who taught us how to learn from Las Vegas, calls this trend 'iconography and electronics upon a generic architecture'.

'The face of New York is being transformed by an influx of world-class architects.'

Yet, early 21st-century architecture is moving beyond applied symbolism to radical new forms facilitated by computer-based design methods. A stellar example is Kohn Pedersen Fox's stainless steel and glass 'vertical campus', the **Baruch College Academic Complex** (55 Lexington Avenue, between 24th & 25th Streets). The resulting phantasmic designs that curve and dart in sculptural space are so beyond the timid window-dressing of postmodernism that they deserve a new label.

Known for designs that owe as much to conceptual art as to architecture, the avant-garde firm Diller Scofidio + Renfro is working on an eye-popping addition to staid Chelsea, the **Eyebeam** art and technology centre, to be completed in 2007. The curvilinear walls of the planned museum are suggestive of film looping through a projector.

In the late 19th century New York City became the world's prime outdoor skyscraper museum. It may be founded on a very deliberate grid, but its growth has been organic. In the next decade Manhattan may come to look like a sculpture garden, as computer-aided designs bridge the gap between what is possible and what can be imagined.

NEW YORK CITY TODAY

Call it the invasion of the global architects. The face of New York is being transformed by an influx of world-class architects. Some projects have just been completed, some are under construction and others are still on the drawing boards, but New York ten years from now may well look radically different. British architect Norman Foster's faceted, 46-storey, 597-foot-high addition to the **Hearst Tower** (959 Eighth Avenue, between W 56th & W 57th Streets) is a glimpse of the cityscape to come. The tower's giant triangular windows play off the skyline in visually exciting ways.

Italian architect Renzo Piano is also making his mark on the city with his newly completed addition to the **JP Morgan Library & Museum** (*see p121*), a triumphant melding of airy, modernist glass forms with more traditional architectural styles. Piano's new 52-storey headquarters for the *New York Times* (Eighth Avenue, between W 40th & W 41st Streets), with its distinctive façade of shimmering ceramic glass rods, is due for completion in 2007.

Californian Frank Gehry, perhaps now the world's most recognised architect, with his own

Face facts: Santiago Calatrava

There are few architects working today who understand how natural forms – the human body, birds, flowers – allegorise function beyond the stereotypical modernist embrace of industrial form. Enter Santiago Calatrava, the Spanish architect who has given the world such icons as the Alamillo Bridge in Seville, Spain, which evokes the tension-filled vertical form of an archer reattaching a string to his bow. New Yorkers know him best as the man behind the breathtaking World Trade Center transit hub and its soaring glass rib cage (*photo above right*), currently under construction next to Ground Zero. Just as jaw-dropping are his plans for a futuristic-looking residential tower: an 835-foot-high stack of ten condos that will overlook the East River and South Street Seaport, with views to the north and west. Each glass-walled dwelling cube will have a rooftop garden and private elevator.

signature jewellery line from Tiffany's, is finally getting a chance to build in New York (previous plans for his Guggenheim addition in lower Manhattan fell through). Steel is already going into the ground for his unusual, ten-storey glass headquarters for Barry Diller's IAC/InterActiveCorp along the West Side Highway between W 18th and W 19th Streets. With diagonal glass walls, the bays of the riverfront property will resemble ships with billowing sails. Gehry is also working in collaboration with mega-developer Bruce Ratner on plans for the Atlantic Yards in Brooklyn. The development will include a basketball arena for the relocated Nets, a hotel, housing as well as commercial stores. He's also planning a 75-storey apartment building in Lower Manhattan.

Diller Scofidio + Renfro has its hand in the hotbed of architectural activity happening in Manhattan's Lower West Side, with its plans for a total reconception of the old High Line train tracks, which are being turned into a public park (*see p30* **High times ahead**). The architectural team envisions the 1.5-mile-long borderline between the urban and the natural as providing an experience in 'slowness, distraction and other-worldliness'.

Outside of Manhattan, another architect is making his debut on the New York scene. Steven Holl's Der Stijhl-like architectural addition connects two landmarked brick buildings of the Pratt Institute's architecture school in Brooklyn. And for Brooklyn's **Public Library for the Visual Performing Arts**, which will be built across the street from the Brooklyn Academy of Music, cutting-edge Mexican architect Enrique Norten, of TEN Arquitectos, has designed an aerodynamic, glass-walled building that will be shaped like a ship's prow. Construction is expected to be completed in 2008.

The Japanese firm of Sejima + Nishizawa/ SANAA have long been known within the profession as the architects' architect, but soon the New York public will become familiar with its work through the new home for the **New Museum of Contemporary Art** (*see p106*) at 235 Bowery on the Lower East Side. The museum's profile will be of stunningly proportioned and balanced crystalline rectangles.

Other ambitious plans still in the design stage include Spanish architect Santiago Calatrava's (*see p34* **Face facts**) much-anticipated World Trade Center PATH station, with its suspended, ribbed-steel, wing-shaped canopy (inspired by the image of a child releasing a dove) and gleaming white subterranean spaces that promise to rival Grand Central Terminal. (Light is planned

to shine down on to the station platforms 60 feet below street level.) If financing can be found, Calatrava will also build one of the world's most unusual residences – ten giant, four-storey glass cubes breathlessly suspended from narrow steel poles near the East River at 80 South Street. Calatrava has also proposed a barely-there spiderweb-like tram to Governors Island.

The World Trade Center-site project has been delayed several times by political infighting between developer Larry A Silverstein, Governor Pataki and other participants, but a list of architects for the new complex has now been announced, and includes two British lords – Norman Foster and Richard Rogers – who co-designed Paris's 'inside-out' Pompidou Centre in 1977, with Renzo Piano. So far, only David Childs's 52-storey, 750-foot-tall **7 World Trade Center** building has been completed, standing on a bomb-proof ten-storey pedestal. Daniel Libeskind will be redesigning a version of his 1,776-foot-tall Freedom Tower, and there will be a memorial in the footprints of the original towers to the 2,749 lives lost in the 2001 terrorist attack – although it has been greatly scaled back for budgetary reasons.

> **'Many contemporary architects working in New York are keenly aware of the importance of "green" design and sustainable development.'**

Also trimmed back were visionary plans for David Childs's revamp of the stoic Beaux Arts McKim, Mead & White **General Post Office** (421 Eighth Avenue, between 31st & 33rd Streets) – to be renamed **Moynihan Station** after former New York senator Daniel Patrick Moynihan. Moynihan was the propelling force behind the plan to transform the post office building into a multi-level train station. The idea is to recall the original McKim, Mead & White Penn Station, which previously lay across the street, but which was torn down in 1964, much to the despair of many New Yorkers. The 'potato chip' dome of the transit hall, in Childs's new plan, has been eliminated for cost reasons, but the bright new atrium will be illuminated by parabolic skylights.

Richard Rogers is also designing **Silvercup West**, a $1 billion, six-acre residential complex that will be built in Queens, just south of the Queensboro Bridge. The development will feature 1,000 apartments and eight new soundstages for Silvercup Studios – where HBO's television shows *Sex in the City* and *The Sopranos* were filmed.

This recent, sudden boom in high-profile projects by out-of-town architects was quietly preceded by a number of smaller-scale projects. French architect Christian de Portzamparc's eccentrically angled 23-storey **LVMH Tower** (19 E 57th Street, between Fifth & Madison Avenues), with its green and clear glass panels, stands like a postmodernist mini-glacier among the more traditional storefronts on Manhattan's premier shopping strip. Nearby, Austria native Raimund Abraham's **Austrian Cultural Forum** (11 E 52nd Street, between Fifth & Madison Avenues) glowers like a primitive mask, breaking free from the perpendicular street front. Midtown West looks decidedly more colourful with the addition of the Miami-based firm Arquitectonica's **Westin Hotel** (270 W 43rd Street, between Seventh & Eighth Avenues), a crisp-edged tower sheathed in purple, aqua and tangerine reflective glass.

Times Square has been revitalised as a tourist hub, although some of its character has been lost with the imposition of giant postmodernist skyscrapers like the **Conde Nast Building** (4 Times Square, at 42nd

Astor Place – condos for the rich.

Street) and the **Reuters Building** (3 Times Square, at 42nd Street), both by Fox & Fowle, alongside Kohn Pederson Fox's **5 Times Square** (Seventh Avenue, at 42nd Street) and David Childs's **Times Square Tower** (7 Times Square, between Broadway & Seventh Avenue). Fox & Fowle is adding yet another behemoth, the 35-storey **11 Times Square** (42nd Street, between Seventh & Eighth Avenues).

Not much further uptown, the recently opened set of twin towers, the **Time Warner Center** (10 Columbus Circle at Broadway), designed by David Childs, is a gleaming example of the fact that New York still dares to build them big. With its eye-catching mix of high-end stores, the Jazz at Lincoln Center performance space and an enormous Whole Foods gourmet food court, the upscale shopping mall has made a destination of what was once a near-dead neighbourhood.

Architects in New York are not only housing the arts in new museums, but also their well-heeled patrons. Gwathmey Siegel's curvaceous, all-glass 21-storey residential tower **Astor Place** (445 Lafayette Street, at the corner of Astor Place) features condos that sell for more than $12 million. Richard Meier has added a third minimalist glass tower (165 Charles Street, between West & Washington Streets) to his other postmodernist residences that overlook the Hudson on the lower west side.

Jean Nouvel is designing high price tag condominiums for hip hotelier Andre Balazs at 40 Mercer Street, while Balazs is also planning the International Style slab of the Standard Hotel on Washington Street in the Meatpacking District.

All of these projects provoke the question, however, can the city support and sustain all this new construction? Many contemporary architects working in New York City are keenly aware of the importance of so-called 'green' design and sustainable development, and a number of the city's newest skyscrapers, like **Bank of America Tower** at 1 Bryant Park, have been designed according to such precepts. The Bank of America Tower, like the New York Times Building and the planned Silvercup West (*see p35*) and Freedom Tower (*see p35*), uses elements like recycled water and specially treated glass that reduces solar heating, to limit the impact of new construction on the environment.

The best place to visit to keep tabs on upcoming architectural developments in the city – like Enrique Norten's exciting plans for a double slab skyscraper in Harlem and a condominium at 1 York Street in Tribeca – is the **AIA Center for Architecture** (*see p112*).

Boom Town

New York City's film industry is thriving once again, with movie sets blocking traffic all over town.

Once upon a time, New York played itself in the movies. A reliable and unique star, it seduced audiences in *On the Waterfront*, *West Side Story*, *Serpico* and almost everything by Woody Allen. In fact, the city was so popular that it became the first place in the world to establish an office for encouraging and dealing with all the movie-making interest: the Office of Film, Theatre & Broadcasting, inaugurated by Mayor John Lindsay in 1966.

But as time and the movie biz rolled on, the city's unique allure lost out to the desire to save a buck. Many films set in New York of the past 20 years weren't shot anywhere near the five boroughs. 'The great example is *Moonstruck*,' says Tim Williams, head of production at indie house GreeneStreet Films (*In the Bedroom*, *A Prairie Home Companion*). 'You look at *Moonstruck* and you're like, "That's not Brooklyn."' It was Toronto. Filmmakers have also ventured as far afield as South Africa, Australia, Bulgaria and the Czech Republic to make their New York movies for less money.

The city was seen as an overpriced, hassle-prone diva many filmmakers just didn't want to deal with. That unfortunate reputation stuck until 2004, when everything started to change.

THE TURNING POINT
'The slump was really based on the cost of filming in the United States, so there was all this runaway production to Canada,' says Ted Hope, co-founder of This Is That Productions and local indie pioneer Good Machine (which was acquired by Universal in 2002 and renamed Focus Features). Starting in 1997, productions shooting north of the border could get between a 20 and 40 per cent rebate on whatever they spent, and the American dollar was strong. Toronto and Montreal quickly became stand-ins for the Big Apple. It took a few years, but the US caught on and started to offer its own incentives: Louisiana was the first to jump in (landing *Ray* in 2002), followed by Pennsylvania, New Mexico, Florida and a host of others.

A major production
It takes a lot of planning (and cajoling) to shut down a landmark for a shoot.

The Empire State Building, the Statue of Liberty, Coney Island, Rockefeller Center: no city is more chock-a-block with cinematic icons than New York. But shooting a scene at one of these landmark locations isn't easy.

Ask Carla Raij, a savvy location manager who sweet-talked the city into giving her the Brooklyn Bridge – free of charge – for a two-week shoot during the 2004 production of Marc Forster's *Stay*. Every night from 10pm until 5am, Raij took over the Manhattan-bound lanes to stage a massive car accident. 'It was complicated,' she says. 'We had pyrotechnics, and required two weeks of electrical prerigging for our lights. Because the bridge has weight restrictions, trucks aren't allowed on; actors rode up to the location in golf carts.'

In another major endeavour, director Cameron Crowe filmed Tom Cruise in a deserted Times Square for *Vanilla Sky* early one morning in November 2000. Crowe managed to get 20 blocks sealed off for a few hours and bribed irritated pedestrians with coffee from a fleet of craft-service trucks.

Not every production has such free rein. When Adrian Lyne shot *Unfaithful* in 2001, the screenplay called for a scene featuring Diane Lane, as a commuting adulteress, at Grand Central Terminal. 'People can't miss their trains just because you're shooting a movie,' says location manager Rob Striem.

He arranged to film at off-peak times over two consecutive Saturdays. 'There was a wide shot of Diane walking through the station. We couldn't clear the floor, but we could surround her with extras. It's an imprecise science.'

If you want complete control of Grand Central, says Kyle McCarthy, special-events manager for Metro-North, you'll have to schedule a shoot between 2am and 4am – which is when Terry Gilliam filmed the 'ballroom' sequence for his 1991 flick *The Fisher King*. You'll also pay double time to any Metro-North employees that must be present.

Such shoots aren't as extensive, or necessary, as they once were. In 1981, when *Nighthawks* had Sylvester Stallone match wits with a hostage taker in the Roosevelt Island tram, the production bussed home unhappy islanders via Queens, according to Bradford Harlan of the Roosevelt Island Operating Corporation. Twenty years later, when Sam Raimi staged *Spider-Man*'s climactic battle, where the web-slinger rescues a tram full of children, he did only second-unit production at Roosevelt Island, building a miniature replica of the tram station on a soundstage.

Despite the challenges of shooting at a landmark, movie-makers hail the city for its openness. 'As long as you understand that there'll be restrictions and are willing to work within them,' Raij says, 'everything is doable.'

New York finally stepped back into the spotlight in 2004, pushed by Doug Steiner, a New Jersey real-estate developer who wanted to build a movie studio in the Brooklyn Navy Yard. Kaufman Astoria and Silvercup Studios had existed in the city for decades, but were mostly handling commercial and television production at that point. Steiner wanted to figure out a way to lure movie-makers back. In August of that year, with Mel Brooks on hand to announce *The Producers* as the first film to be shot at Steiner Studios, Governor Pataki signed a major tax incentive into law. Television and film productions that completed at least 75 per cent of their work within the state of New York would receive a ten per cent tax credit. Five months later, Mayor Bloomberg kicked in an additional five per cent for projects shot in the five boroughs.

The impact was immediate. The total number of 'shooting days' in the city hit 31,570 in 2005 (which works out as an average of 87 production companies shooting in the city every day), a 35 per cent increase over the figure from the previous year, and double the number of shooting days of 2002. In 2005 alone, New York State's film business generated 10,000 jobs and $1.5 billion in expenditures, with the lion's share of both going to New York City.

Suddenly, New York was teeming with film crews. 'We've been busy since we opened our doors,' Steiner says, citing an impressive roster that includes Nicole Kidman's *Fur*, Richard Gere's *Hoax*, Spike Lee's *Inside Man* and Uma Thurman's *My Super Ex-Girlfriend*. And many more high-profile projects are in the works or were recently completed in town: *The Devil Wears Prada*, starring Meryl Streep and Anne Hathaway; *Little Children*, featuring Kate Winslet and Jennifer Connelly; *Enchanted*, with Susan Sarandon and Patrick Dempsey; *The Good Shepherd*, starring Matt Damon, Robert De Niro and Angelina Jolie (and directed by De Niro); and *Fast Track*, with Zach Braff and Amanda Peet. Martin Scorsese's upcoming film *The Departed*, though set in Boston, was actually filmed here. (TV is also on an upswing, with more than a dozen pilots shot here in the past two years, increased from an average of one or two per year.)

'The turnaround in the mayor's office is what has changed everything in the film business in New York,' according to director Edward Burns, whose most recent New York production, comedy *The Groomsmen*, screened at the 2006 Tribeca Film Festival. 'I can tell you: I live in Tribeca, and again today my street is closed down for shooting – which is a good thing. I'd be the last guy to start complaining about that.'

GANGS OF NEW YORK

While the tax credit incentive programme is seen as a major catalyst, it wasn't the only reason the local film industry rebounded. 'The crew base is very solid, very large and very deep in New York,' says John Amman, business representative for the International Cinematographers Guild. 'I think that's been key to the recent surge in work. Tax incentives have been a spark plug, but you have an industry here that was willing to meet any challenge with the increase in production, which makes New York different from other communities. Louisiana, New Mexico – they had increased production, but it required bringing in crew and equipment from LA. That's not the case in New York.'

The person in charge of constantly reminding filmmakers of that fact is Katherine Oliver, commissioner of the Mayor's Office of Film, Theatre & Broadcasting. 'The message from the mayor when I took the job was that this agency is part of economic development for the city, that entertainment is a very viable industry in New York and that we needed to build this business,' she says. Oliver's first step was to drag her office into the 21st century. 'When I started here three and a half years ago, they were working on electric typewriters and processing permits by hand,' she recalls. Oliver quickly put permit applications online and reached out to filmmakers to let them know that shooting in New York was no longer the hassle it was perceived to be. Today, her office provides permits, parking tags, city-managed locations, police details and concierge services, such as assistance with budget planning and location scouting, all for free – as well as discounts at local vendors and some free advertising.

THE DAY AFTER TOMORROW

The question is whether the city can sustain this boom. The big piece of the puzzle is the tax incentive plan. The state budget will likely dish out $60 million annually in state funds through 2011, and the city budget could potentially toss another $30 million per year into the pot. So, it's likely that some sort of tax plan will remain in place, even if slightly curtailed, but if and when the credits do disappear, where will that leave New York?

'We've learned what the incentives do,' says Russ Hollander, eastern executive director of the Directors Guild of America. 'We saw what was happening to production when we didn't have them. So I would expect that if the incentives were to dry up, there'd be a substantial decline in production.'

Illustration by Henry Elphick

NYC Rivalries

Hatred! Loathing! Unkind words! New York is
a city of rivalries. Here we outline the top ten.

1. BROOKLYN VS MANHATTAN

Brooklyn Borough President Marty Markowitz
refers to the consolidation of NYC's boroughs
as the Great Mistake of 1898. He's joking, but
only a little. 'Many of us say we could have
done better if we'd stayed a separate city,' he
says. 'That said, the rivalry is a good rivalry.
Brooklyn doesn't want to be Manhattan, and
Manhattan doesn't want to be Brooklyn, I can
assure you.' The key difference, he says, is
that there are two types of life, 'and you have
to decide which life you want.'

'I wouldn't call it a rivalry, and I wouldn't
call it envy,' says Manhattan Borough
President Scott Stringer. 'But Brooklyn is
great because it's next to Manhattan.' He adds

magnanimously, 'I grant Manhattan citizenship
to everyone in Brooklyn who comes and works
in Manhattan. It's a dual citizenship. We're an
open-minded people.'

The competition between the BPs is amicable.
But it's not necessarily so friendly among the
laypersons. Every Manhattanite has suffered
the smug alternativism of a friend who has
'escaped' the noise, crowds and hectic pace of
the island, and who is now annoyingly proud
of having scored some only slightly less
ridiculously expensive apartment 20 blocks
away from the subway and 15 from the grocery
store. And every Brooklynite has endured the
Manhattitude of superiority and fabulousness
wielded to convince them that (a) anyone who

hightails it to Brooklyn simply cannot hack it in the big city and (b) it's cool to pay upwards of $14 for a cocktail.

While some playing fields are levelling (Brooklyn now has a viable dining scene, and rents have been shooting up in once dormant sections), each borough still offers things the other can't. Brooklyn has beaches, Prospect Park, its own brewery and *Welcome Back, Kotter*. Manhattan has the Met, Broadway, *Law & Order* and some of the most famous architecture, restaurants and residents in the world. And for crissakes, it's the City. No one means Brooklyn when they use that phrase. Not even Brooklynites.

2. THE POST VS DAILY NEWS

Post staffer Jared Paul Stern's alleged moonlighting as an extortionist was certainly a splashy scandal (even if nothing came of it), but for the *Daily News* it was so good that 'New York's Hometown Paper' gave it three continuous days of front-page coverage. The *Post*, meanwhile, seems equally committed to reporting every embarrassing blunder and gaffe of its tabloid rival, and was particularly elated when a printing error in last year's Scratch 'n' Match contest left hundreds of *News* readers thinking they had won $100,000. Unlike some media wars, this one doesn't seem to inspire better journalism, but it sure makes for entertaining reading.

3. YANKEE FANS VS MET FANS

If you're a native New Yorker, you probably didn't pick your baseball team – it picked you. Your so-called choice isn't simply a matter of Bronx vs Queens, nor anything so trivial as American League vs National League. You cheer for the Yankees and gleefully count the rings, regardless of that bloated payroll, because your father did, as his father did. You root for the scrappier Mets, whose fan base is at least perceived as being more working class – even though they were numbingly boring or hapless (or both) for years – because your mom would disown you if you didn't. 'The only thing better than a Mets win is a Yankees loss,' says Ralph Valente, 45, who has lived on the Upper East Side for 26 years and whose parents hail from Brooklyn. Die hard Bombers booster Amber Sexton, 37, was raised in the West Village and now calls Greenpoint home. Her argument: 'There's no good reason to cheer for the Mets. They have no history and they're not even remotely interesting.' You want interesting? Then check out the annual Subway Series when the two teams vie for bragging rights as to who is the better hometown team.

4. UPPER EAST SIDE VS UPPER WEST SIDE

Some shocking news for Upper East Siders came early in 2006: Pale Male and Lola, the famed red-tailed hawks who, since 1993, had nested on a slab of ornate moulding near the top of a chic apartment building at 927 Fifth Avenue, had flown off – to settle on Central Park West. No doubt the Gold Coast swells thought it gauche to desert such prime real estate for the uncouth, neo-Marxist neighbourhood across the park. Residents of the Upper West Side, however, had their own take on why the birds flew the coop: those blue bloods over on Fifth are so stuffy and boring, and the buildings on Central Park West are far superior architecturally. And thus the East vs West feud gained a notch in intensity.

'Even in high school I was always trying to prove that the Upper West Side had so much more culture to offer, was simply more hip,' says Caroline Bazbaz, 29, a record-label exec who's lived west of the park all her life. 'It's the home of *Seinfeld*. And what's more New York than *Seinfeld*? The Upper East Side has Grace's Marketplace [*see p138*] – yet compare that to Fairway [2127 Broadway]. Moms wear jeans on the Upper West Side, not slacks.'

But the UES has its share of supporters, of course – and its own celebrity residents. 'The Upper East Side is cleaner, and it's definitely less cold and windy in the winter,' says Alice Fixx, 63, who runs her own PR firm and lives on East 89th Street. 'You're just a very short ambulance ride away from most of the city's best hospitals. And where else can you count on seeing Woody Allen once a week or so?'

5. LOCAL PEDESTRIANS VS SLOW-WALKING TOURISTS

The relationship between out-of-towners and the rest of us trying to get to the office or the gym or anywhere in a hurry is usually a friendly one. Except in the summer months, that is, when the streets are sweltering, our shirt is soaked, and we're running late. We don't want to have to manoeuvre around you because your bum-bag posse has decided to occupy the entire sidewalk, or because you've unexpectedly veered left to peer into the Hard Rock Café window. Thank you for appreciating the wonders that fill our city. Now please move!

6. NYU VS THE VILLAGE

In the 1980s New York University (NYU) was able to house less than three-quarters of its freshmen. The institution decided that figure was too low – and so it began what *Newsday* called a campaign of 'relentless expansion' that has made it one of the city's biggest landlords.

Resentful locals think NYU is draining the Villages, both East and West, of character; the NYU-ification is continuing with the recent demolition of St Ann's Church on East 12th Street to make way for a planned 26-storey dorm, scheduled to open in 2009.

7. SHUBERTS VS NEDERLANDERS

While it's true that Gerald Schoenfeld, 82, and James Nederlander Jr, 84, haven't started any cane fights in Shubert Alley, that doesn't mean Broadway's biggest landlords aren't angling for supremacy. The Shubert dynasty, headed by Schoenfeld (its former lawyer), is the big dog, with 16 houses. The Nederlander Organization operates nine venues. And there are only 14 other Broadway houses. If any of these spaces were to come on to the market, there'd be a land scramble with a backstage drama to rival anything seen on the stages of Broadway.

8. TENANTS VS LANDLORDS

This battle flares up intensely every spring, when the Rent Guidelines Board decides how much landlords can increase leases. Landlords gripe that housing laws have long favoured the tenants; tenants counter that landlords constantly look for ways to increase rents in order to push them beyond the $2,000 mark (after which vacant apartments become destabilised). The difference of viewpoints (a tenant sees an apartment as home, a landlord as a business) will inevitably complicate what is possibly the most important relationship a New Yorker has.

9. CHINATOWN VS LITTLE ITALY

Despite its pasta-heavy diet, Little Italy has been shrinking for years as Chinatown expands, threatening to obliterate the Old World enclave. 'When I was a kid, everything north of Canal Street was Little Italy and south was Chinatown,' says Stefano Signorastri, longtime resident and manager of Il Cortile restaurant. 'Now, Little Italy is just Mulberry Street.' Time for the UN to redraw the boundaries.

10. THE *TODAY SHOW* VS *GOOD MORNING AMERICA*

Charles Gibson's departure from ABC's *Good Morning America* was the most recent twist in the show's 30-year rivalry with NBC's *Today*, which lost Katie Couric in 2006. Not only do the two television shows ferociously battle for on-air guests, but they're rumoured to poach audience members from the hordes lining up outside each other's studios.

Wack jobs

Competition, envy and just plain craziness fuel some of New York City's stranger rivalries.

Dog people vs non-dog people

The city's canine industry is booming, which is great news for puppy lovers and pooch-accoutrement peddlers. But what about people who aren't so amenable to the idea of dogs in sweaters – or dogs at all, for that matter? The whole thing can be a bit nauseating. 'I think they should all be put down,' says a particularly cantankerous Brooklyn writer. 'I'm talking about the owners!' she goes on. The pro-canine faction is a little more sanguine. 'Get a heart,' says an East Village marketing exec who attends a knitting class with her pug. 'Yes, it's kind of sickening,' she admits. 'But it's harmless, and Herbie looks so cute all dressed up!'

Lil' Kim vs Foxy Brown

'It's enough I got to put up with this doo-doo Brown chick,' Lil' Kim rhymed about former friend Foxy Brown on 'Came Back for You', from 2003's *La Bella Mafia*. After three years of verbal sparring for the title of original pint-size potty mouth, the rap divas' feud erupted in a gunfight between their respective posses outside Hot 97's studios in February of 2001. Later, the duo was allegedly offered a cool mill to record a duet. So now that Lil' Kim has finished her ten-month stint in prison (for lying to a federal grand jury about the events of the shoot-out) and Foxy Brown has recovered from hearing loss, maybe the two can finally settle their score and cash in.

Magnolia Bakery vs Buttercup Bake Shop

It was a sticky split. Jennifer Appel and Allysa Torey started Magnolia Bakery in the West Village in 1996, but parted ways – some say bitterly – three years later. In 1999 Appel launched Buttercup Bake Shop, while Torey still runs the show at the bustling Magnolia. 'Any relationship that Allysa and I had was a business one and a friendship, and that's no longer the case,' Appel says. Torey, for her part, plays down any competition. 'We have no rivalries going on with other bakeries making cupcakes,' Torey assures. 'We don't have negative feelings about any of these things.'

New York Today

The New York state of mind... remains positive.

The fifth anniversary of the September 11th terrorist attacks passed in 2006, and the way the occasion was marked says a lot about the city's contradictory mindset, which could be summed up as paying lip service to the past while also trying to forget it. There were the inevitable movies on television and in theatres, like Oliver Stone's *World Trade Center* that opened in August 2006, portraying the bravery of the police and fire departments in the aftermath of the attacks. Around the same time, the city's Emergency Management services released additional transcripts of 911 operators on that morning five years ago, responding to calls emanating from within the burning buildings – a gesture that had the strange effect of amalgamating in people's minds the real-world desperation of the victims with the trauma of Stone's fictional heroes.

During that same month, Rudy Giuliani visited South Carolina, where a key Republican Party primary election is set to take place in 2008; the former New York mayor was seemingly testing the waters to see whether his larger-than-life reputation, courtesy of his actions on and after September 11th 2001, might translate into the Presidency. And cashing-in on the tragedy wasn't confined to politics: on late-night television, a gold commemorative medallion was being advertised with an unusual feature: a tiny relief of the Twin Towers that pops up from the surface of the coin, leaving an empty indentation in the background.

In lower Manhattan, the hole that used to be Ground Zero remains largely empty, except for the men and machinery rumbling across its acreage in a strange sort of holding pattern. A long period of wrangling over what to do with the site (between the current mayor, Michael Bloomberg, the state's outgoing governor, George Pataki, and businessman Larry Silverstein, holder of the World Trade Center lease) appears to be have been settled with an agreement that the Port Authority of New York and New Jersey would take over supervision of the rebuilding effort's centrepiece, Freedom Tower. Yet it remains unclear as to whether all the insurance money earmarked for reconstruction will be coughed up under this new arrangement without a major court fight. The Port Authority has also assumed responsibility for erecting a September 11th memorial and museum; but cost overruns, drastic design revisions and the disgruntlement of the families who lost loved ones during the attacks also continue to delay that project. (Notwithstanding ground-breaking ceremonies for the memorial's foundation footings, which, like the cornerstone laying for the Freedom Tower three years ago, will probably remain a largely symbolic exercise for the foreseeable future.) Although the media in July 2006 made

much of the fact that the first of the giant steel columns for the Freedom Tower's foundation had rolled out of a foundry in Luxembourg, the truth is, the rebirth of Ground Zero seems further away now than it did in the months after September 11th, when New Yorkers pulled together and vowed to rebuild.

And yet, if some nagging sense of unfinished business is bothering the denizens of our fair metropolis, you'd be hard-pressed to find it: everywhere but Ground Zero, it seems, the city is exploding with vitality. For New Yorkers, then, the past year or so has so far proven to be the best of times, even if one might argue that they are shot through with a vague sense of anxiety. During the city's first major heatwave, for instance, in summer 2006, the usually surefooted Mayor Bloomberg seemed to slip up a bit when he didn't immediately resolve a blackout that plunged large sections of Queens into darkness for 14 days. But it didn't seem to hurt him politically, with most of the population intent on charging on with the business of being New Yorkers – grateful, perhaps, that these are not the worst of times, after all, as some feared, amid predictions that the attacks would ruin New York economically. Instead it remains what it's always been: a capital of culture, a churning maw of capitalism, a constant collision of humanity, high-born and low. In short, it remains the kind of place that ignores its inherent contradictions by transcending them.

> **'When it comes to building anything in New York, it's the market that decides when things happen.'**

RIP LMDC

In what may be considered a moment of true New York chutzpah, the Lower Manhattan Development Corporation (LMDC), the city-state authority tasked with overseeing the rebuilding of Downtown after September 11th, recently closed up shop, saying its mission had been accomplished. But there's more than the litany of messes cited above to suggest that the agency may have been kidding itself when it proclaimed as much. There was, for example, the debacle involving the so-called Freedom Center, a proposed museum for Ground Zero that the 9/11 families didn't much care for because its advisory programming committee included some known blame-America-first academics. Needless to say, the Freedom Center is history along with the LMDC itself. And yet, in all fairness, it must be said that the organisation was hamstrung from the very start by Governor

George Pataki, who often overruled its decisions for his own political ends. And not everything it did was a bust: the LMDC was instrumental, for instance, in keeping the residents of Downtown from fleeing the area after 9/11, thanks to a $300million rent subsidy programme. But the final lesson of the LMDC, perhaps, is that when it comes to building or rebuilding anything in New York, it's the market, not the government, that decides when things happen.

IT'S AN AD AD AD AD WORLD

One of the more interesting developments over the past year or so has been the spread of 'advertecture', the giant, building-size adverts and billboards that were once largely relegated to 42nd Street and the vicinity. The intersection of Seventh Avenue and 34th Street, for example, has become a veritable Times Square mini-me, replete with giant-screen video displays.

The corner of Houston Street and Broadway (the boundary between Noho and Soho) has likewise undergone a metamorphosis into an open-air honky-tonk of ginormous fashion models in underwear. The owners of the iconic Flatiron Building were forced to take down a 15,000-square-foot H&M advert, hung from scaffolding surrounding the place as it was undergoing renovation. Such signs are, in fact, outlawed by the city's Department of Buildings, although the rules have a loophole called a 'special district' regulation, which encourages such signage in areas like Times Square and Herald Square (site of Macy's). Outside these special districts, however, a colossal sign will cost a building owner $500 in fines. However, not only are such fines rarely given, they are

Unfinished business: the rebirth of **Ground Zero** is yet to be realised.

small potatoes compared to the tens of thousands of dollars advertisers typically pay a landlord to turn a building into a billboard. Recently, Manhattan's borough president, Scott Stringer, introduced legislation to toughen enforcement, raise fines and make it easier for New Yorkers to report violations. And if there's anything New Yorkers love, it's another opportunity to complain.

> **'New Yorkers feel that the quality of life overall has improved here.'**

HOW MAY I HELP YOU?

Or do they? Recently, the image of the irascible New Yorker suffered a blow, thanks to a *Reader's Digest* survey published in July 2006. The magazine sent 'undercover' reporters to 35 cities worldwide to measure courtesy. The Big Apple was ranked numero uno (and was the only American city to make the list), beating such presumably civilised metropolises as London and Toronto. Anecdotally, at least, this seems to be true: New Yorkers are likely to smile at strangers, and to offer directions when asked. Perhaps it's because, as another survey by Citizens for NYC points out, New Yorkers feel that the quality of life overall has improved here. Or maybe the answer is buried deeper in the same survey: when asked what the number one problem was with living in New York, the overwhelming majority answered 'street noise'. So maybe the new politeness is a cover for not hearing so well.

THE HIGH COST OF CULTURE

One thing New Yorkers should be complaining about is the high price of museum admission. The Museum of Modern Art started the wads of cash rolling when it began to charge a $20 admission fee for its newly enlarged facility. The venerable Metropolitan Museum of Art raised its suggested admission to the same price in 2006. (However, the savvy traveller should remember that admission to the Met is actually a donation, so you can pay whatever amount you want, as long as you pay something.) The skyrocketing costs could be attributed to fancy new architecture (as in MoMA's case), but certainly the astronomical cost of the artwork itself plays a role. In June 2006 cosmetics magnate Ronald Lauder paid $135 million for Gustav Klimt's 1906 portrait of Adele Bloch-Bauer, the largest sum ever paid for a single painting. The acquisition was for Lauder's Neue Galerie museum on Fifth Avenue; the crowds that flocked to see the works were huge, so the museum announced a special $50 fee for anyone caring to jump the line on nights set aside for members. The idea was quashed, though, when it caused an uproar.

The Met itself has been no slouch when it comes to shelling out big bucks for art, having paid $45 million for the 14th-century Duccio *Madonna and Child*, measuring 11 by eight inches. The painting was promptly denounced as a 19th-century forgery by Columbia University art historian James Beck, but the museum just as quickly pooh-poohed Beck's claim, saying its tests prove beyond doubt that the Duccio is legit. So for now, you will have to take its word that your suggested donation, in this case, is going towards the real deal.

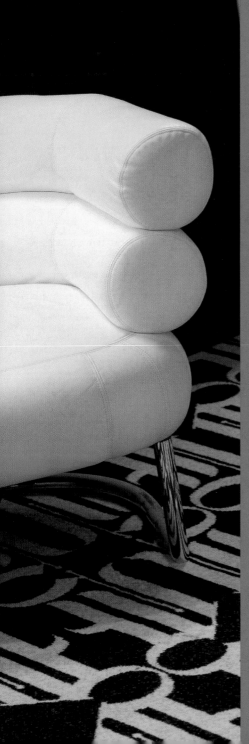

Where to Stay

Features

Night Hotel. *See p66.*

Where to Stay

I want to wake up… in the city… that never sleeps.

In many ways, New York is a city of numbers: from the massive grid of streets to the floors in a high-rise, right down to the square footage of tiny studio apartments. But, perhaps nowhere else is the numbers game more at play than with the city's hotel industry. In 2006 a record 43 million tourists passed through town, driving up hotel occupancy rates to roughly 85 per cent. What's more, Manhattan's skyrocketing real-estate market has caused the number of hotel rooms, which hovers around 63,000, to decrease. Many hotel owners have opted to cash in on their valuable property by converting it into luxury condominiums (see p70 **Something old, something new**). Of course, hotel guests are interested in numbers too – namely, how much money is going to have to be plunked down to rest weary bones after painting the town red. Brace yourself: the average nightly rate at a Manhattan hotel is teetering around $225 – with no sign of relenting. PKF Consulting, a New York City-based hotel industry advisory firm, advises that hotel room rates are expected to increase by ten per cent in 2007. Still, there has been a lot of chatter of late about the 5,000 new hotel rooms that are expected to up the inventory by 2007's end. But with so many conversions afoot, even this four-figure increase isn't expected to make much of an overall change in prices, although PKF does anticipate an increase in the number of mid-priced rooms available. So, what's a budget-minded traveller to do? A spate of budget hotels that opened in the past couple of years, like **Hotel QT** (see p71) and **Marrakech** (see p76), generated a huge amount of buzz with their minimalist-chic rooms for under $130 a night – but, now that these places are fully up and running, so are their prices. With some legwork you may be able to secure a clean, cramped room for under $150. Just be warned: the view will most probably be of a brick wall and there are likely to be zero amenities – not unlike residents' tiny studio apartments.

However, if you're lucky enough to be able to splurge on accommodation, you've come to the right town. There are so many stylish hotels

opening that it's hard to keep up. The most recent among them is **Night Hotel** (see p66), where the chic interiors are strictly black and white. Also, keep an ear out for word on Robert De Niro's Downtown Hotel, located in a purpose-built building in Tribeca, which is sure to generate plenty of buzz when it finally opens. (The project suffered a series of setbacks after designs initially failed to comply with zoning regulations for the historic district; the place is currently estimated to open in late 2006 or early 2007.)

The best way to begin your hotel search is to choose the price range and neighbourhood that interests you. Accommodation prices can vary quite wildly within a single property, and the rates quoted here, obtained from the hotels, reflect that disparity. We've classified hotels within each area heading (Downtown, Midtown, Uptown and Brooklyn) according to the price of a mid-season double room per night, beginning with the most expensive. The prices quoted are not guaranteed, but they should give a good indication of the hotel's average rack rates. And if you follow the tips below, you're likely to find

---

The best Hotels

… for views to die for
The **Hotel on Rivington** (see p53), the **Maritime Hotel** (see p65) and the **Bentley Hotel** (see p75).

… for celebrity spotting
The **Mercer** (see p49), the **Hotel Gansevoort** (see p49) and the **Four Seasons** (see p57).

… for style on the cheap
The **Chelsea Hotel** (see p69), the **Hudson** (see p71) and **Marrakech** (see p76).

… for cosy comfort
Blue Moon (see p51), the **Inn on 23rd Street** (see p62) and the **Harlem Flophouse** (see p76).

…for drama queens on a budget
The **Broadway Inn** (see p67), the **Americana Inn** (see p72) and the **Big Apple Hostel** (see p74).

---

❶ Green numbers in this chapter correspond to the location of each hotel as marked on the street maps. See pp402-412.

slashed room prices, package deals and special promotions on offer. Make sure to include New York's 13.625 per cent room tax and a $2 to $6 per-night occupancy tax when planning your travel budget.

Weekend travellers should be warned that many smaller hotels adhere to a strict three-night-minimum booking policy.

HOTEL-RESERVATION AGENCIES

Pre-booking blocks of rooms allows reservation companies to offer reduced rates. Discounts cover most price ranges, including economy; some agencies claim savings of up to 65 per cent, though 20 per cent is more likely. If you simply want the best deal, mention the rate you're willing to pay, and see what's available. The following agencies are free of charge, though a few require payment for rooms at the time the reservation is made.

Hotel Reservations Network

Suite 400, 10440 North Central Expressway, Dallas, TX 75231 (1-214 369 1264/1-800 246 8357/www.hotels.com).

Quikbook

3rd Floor, 381 Park Avenue South, New York, NY 10016 (1-212 779 7666/1-800 789 9887/ www.quikbook.com).

www.timeoutny.com

The *Time Out New York* website offers online reservations at more than 300 hotels. You can search for availability by arrival date or hotel name. (Full disclosure: *Time Out New York* receives a commission from sales made through our partner hotel reservation sites.)

APARTMENT RENTALS AND B&BS

Thousands of B&B rooms are available in New York, but in the absence of a central organisation, some are hard to find. Many B&Bs are unhosted, and breakfast is usually continental (if it's served at all), but the vibe is likely to be more personal in a B&B than a hotel. A sales tax of 8.625 per cent is added on hosted rooms, though not on unhosted apartments, if you stay for more than seven days. For a longer visit, it can be cheaper and more convenient to rent a place of your own; several of the agencies listed below specialise in short-term rentals of furnished apartments. One caveat: last-minute changes can be costly. For gay-friendly B&Bs (where straight guests are often welcome too), *see p304.*

CitySonnet

Village Station, PO Box 347, New York, NY 10014 (1-212 614 3034/www.citysonnet.com). **Rates** *B&B room* $90-$175; *unhosted artist's loft* $155-$600; *private apartment* $150-$275. **Credit** AmEx, Disc, MC, V.

This amiable artist-run agency specialises in downtown locations but has properties all over Manhattan on its books. B&B rooms and short-term apartment rentals are priced according to the size of the room, number of guests, and whether the bathroom is private or shared.

New York Habitat

Suite 306, 307 Seventh Avenue, between 27th & 28th Streets (1-212 255 8018/www.nyhabitat. com). **Rates** *unhosted studio* $115-$225; *unhosted 1-bedroom apartment* $155-$325; *unhosted 2-bedroom apartment* $250-$470. **Credit** AmEx, DC, Disc, MC, V. A variety of services is offered, from hosted B&Bs to short-term furnished-apartment rentals, which can be paid for by the day, week or month.

STANDARD HOTEL SERVICES

In the categories Luxury, Expensive and Moderate, every hotel has the following services (unless otherwise stated): alarm clock, business centre, cable TV, concierge, conference facility, currency exchange, dry-cleaning service, fax machine (in its business centre or in the rooms), hairdryer, in-room safe, laundry, minibar, modem line, parking, radio, one or more restaurants, one or more bars, room service and voicemail. Additional services are noted at the end of each listing. All hotels have air-conditioning unless otherwise noted.

Most hotels, in all categories, have access for the disabled, non-smoking rooms (and smoking rooms, at least on request) and an iron with ironing board in the room or on request. Call to confirm. 'Breakfast included' may mean either muesli and milk or a more generous continental spread. While many hotels claim 'multilingual' staff, that term may be used loosely.

Downtown

Luxury

Hotel Gansevoort

18 Ninth Avenue, at 13th Street (1-212 206 6700/ 1-877 726 7386/www.hotelgansevoort.com). **Subway:** *A, C, E to 14th Street; L to Eighth Avenue.* **Rates** $395-$475 single/double; $675-$725 suite; from $5,000 duplex penthouse. **Rooms** 187. **Credit** AmEx, DC, Disc, MC, V. **Map** p403 C28 ❶
For review, see p50 **Upscale Downtown.**
Hotel services *Pet-friendly. Spa.* **Room services** *CD player. Complimentary newspapers and magazines. Cordless phone. DVD player on request. High-speed wireless internet. LCD or plasma TV. Room service (24hrs).*

Mercer

147 Mercer Street, at Prince Street (1-212 966 6060/1-888 918 6060/www.mercerhotel.com). **Subway:** *N, R, W to Prince Street.* **Rates** $480-$680 single/double; $1,300-$2,500 suite. **Rooms** 75. **Credit** AmEx, DC, Disc, MC, V. **Map** p403 E29 ❷

Upscale Downtown

Enjoy the luxe life below 14th Street in one of these über-hip hotels.

Hotel Gansevoort

For listing, see p49.

It's hard to miss the Gansevoort (*photo above left*) – a soaring 14-floor contemporary structure that stands right out against the cobblestone streets and the warehouse storefronts of the Meatpacking District. Opened in early 2004, and designed by Stephen B Jacobs, this full-service luxury hotel gets strong marks for style. The hotel's entrance is framed by four 18ft light boxes, which change colour throughout the evening, and the world's tallest revolving door. Rooms are less colourful, but quarters are spacious and come with original photography from local artists and Molton Brown bath products. The private roof garden features a glassed-in heated pool with underwater music and 360-degree views of the city. Jeffrey Chodorow's glossy Japanese eaterie Ono has a covered terrace, private dining huts and a robatayaki bar. Guests also have their pick of the rooftop bar Plunge, or the subterranean spa that transforms into chic nightclub G-Spot nightly.

Mercer

For listing, see p49.

Although over seven years old, Soho's first luxury boutique hotel still has touches that keep it a notch above nearby competitors, which is perhaps why Marc Jacobs takes up residence here when he returns to New York. The lobby, with oversized white couches and chairs and shelves lined with colourful books, acts as a bar, library and lounge – open exclusively to hotel guests. Rooms are large by New York standards and feature furniture by Christian Liagre, oversize washrooms with tubs for two and Face Stockholm products. The restaurant, Mercer Kitchen (1-212 966 5454), serves Jean-Georges Vongerichten's stylish version of casual American cuisine.

60 Thompson

For listing, see p51.

Don't be surprised if you have to walk through a fashion shoot when you enter this slick hotel (*photo above right*) – it's a favoured location for fashionistas. A60, the exclusive guests-only rooftop bar, offers commanding city views and is very magazine-spread-worthy. Designed by Thomas O'Brien of Aero Studios, the hotel has been luring fashionable jet-setters since it opened five years ago. The modern rooms are dotted with pampering details like pure down duvets and pillows, and a 'shag bag' filled with fun items to get you in the mood. The acclaimed restaurant Kittichai serves creative Thai cuisine beside a pool filled with floating orchids.

Blue Moon.

For review, see p50 **Upscale Downtown**.
Hotel services *Book and magazine library.
CD/DVD library. Complimentary pass to nearby
gym. Mobile phone and laptop computer rental.
Pet-friendly. Ticket desk. Valet.* **Room services**
*Cassette and CD players. Complimentary newspaper.
DVD player and VCR on request. Fireplace in some
rooms. Plasma TV. PlayStation.*

60 Thompson

*60 Thompson Street, between Broome & Spring
Streets (1-212 431 0400/1-877 431 0400/www.
60thompson.com). Subway: C, E to Spring Street.*
Rates $229-$539 single/double; $650-$1,500 suite;
$3,500 penthouse suite. **Rooms** 98. **Credit** AmEx,
DC, Disc, MC, V. **Map** p403 E30 ❸
For review, see p50 **Upscale Downtown**.
Hotel services *CD/DVD library. Fitness centre.
Laptop computer on request. Mobile phone rental.
Valet.* **Room services** *CD/DVD player.
Complimentary newspaper. High-speed internet.
Microwave oven on request. Plasma TV.*

SoHo Grand Hotel

*310 West Broadway, between Canal & Grand
Streets (1-212 965 3000/1-800 965 3000/www.
sohogrand.com). Subway: A, C, E, 1 to Canal Street.*
Rates $309-$554 single/double; $1,699-$3,500 suite.
Rooms 366. **Credit** AmEx, DC, Disc, MC, V.
Map p403 E30 ❹
Right in the heart of Downtown, and regarded by
many as Soho's living room, the Grand makes
good use of industrial materials like poured
concrete, cast iron and bottle glass (used for the

staircase). Built in 1996, Soho's first high-end bou-
tique hotel features Bill Sofield-designed rooms,
which include two spacious penthouse lofts, use a
restrained palette of greys and beiges and sport
photos from local galleries. Sip cocktails in the
Grand Bar and Lounge, or dine on haute macaroni
and cheese in the Gallery.
Hotel services *Beauty salon. Fitness centre.
Mobile phone rental. Pet-friendly. Ticket desk.
Valet. Video library.* **Room services** *CD player.
High-speed internet. Plasma TV. VCR.*
Other locations: Tribeca Grand Hotel, 2 Sixth
Avenue, between Walker & White Streets,
Tribeca (1-877 519 6600).

Expensive

Blue Moon

*100 Orchard Street, between Delancey & Broome
Streets (1-212 533-9080). Subway: F to Delancey
Street.* **Rates** $275-$350 single/double. **Rooms** 22.
Credit AmEx, DC, Disc, MC, V. **Map** p403 F30 ❺
Next door to the Lower East Side Tenement
Museum (*see p107*), this eight-storey hotel (three
floors were added to the original five-storey build-
ing) aims to evoke Old World charm. There are
not a lot of amenities for the price but the location
is great. Orchard Street and the surrounding area
offer dozens of excellent restaurants, bars and
clubs. Some rooms come with views of the nearby
Williamsburg Bridge.
Room services *Whirlpool bath. Flat-panel TV.
Wireless internet.*

Hampton Inn Manhattan-Seaport.

Hampton Inn Manhattan-Seaport

320 Pearl Street, between Dover & Peck Slip Streets (1-212 571 4400). Subway: A, C, 2, 3, 4, 5 to Fulton Street-Broadway Nassau. **Rates** $180-$410 single/double. **Rooms** 65. **Credit** AmEx, Disc, MC, V. **Map** p402 F32 ❻

This new hotel caters to business travellers but weekenders might also enjoy the spot for its strolls to Tribeca and Chinatown. See if you can snag a room with a view of the Brooklyn Bridge.
Hotel services *Complimentary breakfast. Wireless internet in the lobby.* **Room services** *Cable TV. High-speed wireless internet.*

The Hotel on Rivington

107 Rivington Street, between Essex & Ludlow Streets (1-212 475 2600/www.hotelonrivington.com). Subway: F to Delancey Street; J, M, Z to Delancey-Essex Streets. **Rates** from $275 single/double; call or visit website for more information. **Rooms** 110. **Credit** AmEx, Disc, MC, V. **Map** p403 G29 ❼

Hotel on Rivington has a high cool factor, much like its trendy surroundings. Floor to ceiling windows are an extended theme throughout: the second-floor lobby overlooks the storefronts of Rivington Street, and every India Mahdavi-designed room has an unobstructed city view. Annie O (*see p233*), the hotel gift shop, features high-end trinkets; and the recently opened Thor Restaurant (*see p186*) and lounge is helmed by acclaimed chef Kurt Grutenbrunner. For the adventurous, wood-panelled drawers hide binoculars and an 'intimacy kit' stocked with surprises from nearby Toys in Babeland (*see p255*).

Hotel services *Complimentary breakfast. Fitness centre. Gift shop. Spa. Valet.* **Room services** *CD player. DVD library. Flat-panel TV. High-speed wireless internet. Room service (24hrs).*

Wall Street District Hotel

15 Gold Street, at Platt Street (1-212 232 7700/www.wallstreetdistricthotel.com). Subway: A, C to Broadway-Nassau Street; J, M, Z, 2, 3, 4, 5 to Fulton Street. **Rates** $199-$529 single/double; $299-$599 suite. **Rooms** 138. **Credit** AmEx, DC, Disc, MC, V. **Map** p402 F32 ❽

This small, tech-savvy hotel might be the best value for business travellers, nicely fusing comfort with amenities like automated check-in kiosks. For an additional $50, you can upgrade to a deluxe room with higher-tech amenities (PCs with free internet, white-noise machines); things to help prepare you for the big meeting (shoe shiner, trouser press, complimentary breakfast); and a few low-tech mood lifters (gummy bears!). The hotel's restaurant and bar, San Marino Ristorante, serves casual Italian cuisine.
Hotel services *Business centre. CD, periodical and video-game library. Fitness centre. Mobile phone rental. Pet-friendly.* **Room services** *CD player. Complimentary newspaper. Laptop-computer rental. Room service (24hrs). VCR on request. Web TV.*

Wall Street Inn

9 South William Street, at Broad Street (1-212 747 1500/www.thewallstreetinn.com). Subway: 2, 3 to Wall Street; 4, 5 to Bowling Green.

Rates $189-$399 single/double. Call for corporate and weekend rates. Rooms 46. **Credit** AmEx, DC, Disc, MC, V. **Map** p402 E33 🄉

The area surrounding this boutique hotel in the Financial District has seen a reincarnation in recent years, sprouting new pâtisseries, bars and restaurants along its cobblestone streets. The Wall Street Inn started a trend in 1998 by transforming the 1830s Lehman Brothers Bank building into tastefully appointed accommodation with marble baths. To lure travellers beyond financiers, the hotel offers hefty discounts on weekends. There's no restaurant or room service, but breakfast is included.

Hotel services *Complimentary breakfast. Fitness centre. Mobile phone rental. Video library.* **Room services** *Complimentary newspaper. High-speed wireless internet. Refrigerator. Two-line phone. VCR.*

Moderate

Abingdon Guest House

13 Eighth Avenue, between Jane & W 12th Streets (1-212 243 5384/www.abingdonguesthouse. com). Subway: A, C, E to 14th Street; L to Eighth Avenue. **Rates** $149-$199 single/double; $229-$239 suite. **Rooms** 9. **Credit** AmEx, DC, Disc, MC, V. **Map** p403 D28 🄉

This charm-saturated B&B (without the breakfast) is a good option if you want to be near the Meatpacking District but can't afford the Gansevoort. Named after nearby Abingdon Square, the nine-room townhouse offers European ambience for a reasonable price. Each room is painted a different colour and has plush fabrics, four-poster beds and private bath. The popular Brewbar Coffee doubles as a check-in desk and café, and you can sip your latte in the trellised garden (if you're lucky enough to get the garden room).

Hotel services *Coffeebar.* **Room services** *Complimentary local calls. Direct-dial phone numbers. High-speed wireless internet. VCR in some rooms.*

Cosmopolitan

95 West Broadway, at Chambers Street (1-212 566 1900/1-888 895 9400/www.cosmohotel.com). Subway: A, C, 1, 2, 3 to Chambers Street. **Rates** $149-$199 single/double. **Rooms** 120. **Credit** AmEx, DC, MC, V. **Map** p402 E31 🄉

Despite the name, you won't find any trendy pink cocktails at this well-maintained hotel (or even a bar to drink them in). That's because the Cosmopolitan is geared towards budget travellers with little need for luxury. Open continuously since the 1850s, it remains a tourist favourite for its Tribeca address and affordable rates. Mini-lofts – multilevel rooms with sleeping lofts – start at $119.

Hotel services *Discount parking.* **Room services** *Smoking permitted in all rooms.*

Off-Soho Suites Hotel

11 Rivington Street, between Bowery & Chrystie Street (1-212 979 9808/1-800 633 7646/ www.offsoho.com). Subway: B, D to Grand Street; F, V to Lower East Side-Second Avenue; J, M, Z to Bowery. **Rates** $129-$179 2-person suite with shared bath; $139-$209 4-person suite with private bath. **Rooms** 38. **Credit** AmEx, MC, V. **Map** p403 F30 🄉

These no-frills suites became a great deal more popular after the reclusive-hipster destination restaurant Freemans (*see p186*) opened at the end of the alley across the street. The suites are good value for the thriving Lower East Side (a couple of blocks from Soho). Rooms are bland but clean and spacious, and they have fully equipped kitchens.

Hotel services *Café. Fitness room. High-speed wireless internet. Pet-friendly.* **Room services** *Digital TV. Kitchen.*

Pioneer of SoHotel

341 Broome Street, between Elizabeth Street & Bowery (1-212 226 1482/www.sohotel-ny.com). Subway: J, M, Z to Bowery; 6 to Spring Street. **Rates** $149-$189 standard/double; $129-$139 suite. **Rooms** 105. **Credit** AmEx, DC, Disc, MC, V. **Map** p403 F30 🄉

At the time of writing, this European-style hotel was getting a complete renovation, but will remain open for business throughout the construction. The Pioneer lives up to its name – it's the only hotel in Nolita, a rapidly developing area known for its boutiques and cafés. Rooms are small and basic, but have decorative paintings and hardwood floors; most have private baths. Larger rooms have charming stucco walls and vaulted ceilings. Morning complimentary coffee is served in the lobby.

Hotel services *Complimentary coffee.*

St Mark's Hotel

2 St Mark's Place, at Third Avenue (1-212 674 0100/www.stmarkshotel.qpg.com). Subway: 6 to Astor Place. **Rates** $110-$140 single/double. **Rooms** 67. **No credit cards. Map** p403 F28 🄉

Positioned among all the tattoo parlours and piercing shops of St Mark's Place, this small hotel is unexpectedly bright, clean and understated (and the staff were surprisingly tattoo-less when we visited). The basic rooms have double beds with their own private baths. St Mark's biggest asset is its location – it's perfectly situated for immersing yourself in the East Village's historic punk-rock culture and newfound restaurant scene. Note that the hotel is in a pre-war walk-up building (no elevators).

Room services *Satellite TV.*

Washington Square Hotel

103 Waverly Place, between MacDougal Street & Sixth Avenue (1-212 777 9515/1-800 222 0418/ www.washingtonsquarehotel.com). Subway: A, B, C, D, E, F, V to W 4th Street. **Rates** $155-$185 single/double; $230-$250 quad. **Rooms** 165. **Credit** AmEx, MC, V. **Map** p403 E28 🄉

This quintessential Greenwich Village hotel has been a haven for writers and artists for decades, and also has something of a rock 'n' roll past: Bob Dylan and Joan Baez both lived here back when they sang for change in nearby Washington Square Park. Today, the century-old hotel remains popular with travellers aiming to soak up Village life. Recently, the deluxe rooms were expanded into

larger chambers decked out with art deco furnishings and leather headboards. Other recent renovations include a refurbished lobby and the addition of a cosy bar-lounge that serves afternoon tea and light fare. Rates include a complimentary continental breakfast – or you can splurge on the Sunday jazz brunch at North Square (1-212 254 1200), the hotel's restaurant.
Hotel services *Complimentary breakfast. Fitness centre. High-speed wireless internet. Massage service.* **Room services** *Complimentary newspaper. High-speed internet in some rooms.*

Budget

East Village Bed & Coffee

110 Avenue C, between 7th & 8th Streets (1-212 533 4175/www.bedandcoffee.com). Subway: F, V to Lower East Side-Second Avenue; L to First Avenue. **Rates** $80-$100 single; $90-$130 double/quad. **Rooms** 9. **Credit** AmEx, MC, V. **Map** p403 G28

Popular with European travellers, this unassuming East Village B&B (breakfast meaning coffee) is a great place in which to immerse yourself in downtown culture without splashing too much of the cash. The nine guest rooms come with eclectic furnishings and quirky themes, such as the Black and White Room and the 110 Downing Street room. Shared areas include three separate loft-like living rooms, bathrooms and fully equipped kitchens. In nice weather, sip your complimentary java in the private garden.

Hotel services *Digital cable. Fax. Free bicycle rental and local phone service. Garden. High-speed wireless internet. Kitchen. Stereo. VCR. Video library.* **Other locations**: Second Home on Second Avenue, 221 Second Avenue, between 13th & 14th Streets, East Village (1-212 677 3161/www.secondhome. citysearch.com).

Larchmont Hotel

27 W 11th Street, between Fifth & Sixth Avenues (1-212 989 9333/www.larchmonthotel.com). Subway: F, V to 14th Street; L to Sixth Avenue. **Rates** $80-$99 single; $109-$119 double; $129 queen. **Rooms** 60. **Credit** AmEx, DC, Disc, MC, V. **Map** p403 E28

Housed in a 1910 Beaux Arts building, the attractive, affordable Larchmont Hotel may be the best-value place in the heart of Greenwich Village. The decor (wicker furniture, floral bedspreads) recalls the set of *The Golden Girls*, but with prices this reasonable, you can accept low marks for style. All of the baths are shared, but your room comes equipped with a washbasin, a robe and a pair of slippers.
Hotel services *Complimentary breakfast. Kitchenette on some floors.* **Room services** *Digital TV.*

Union Square Inn

209 E 14th Street, between Second & Third Avenues (1-212 614 0500/www.nyinns.com). Subway: L to Third Avenue; N, Q, R, W, 4, 5, 6 to 14th Street-Union Square. **Rates** $89-$149 single/double. **Rooms** 45. **Credit** AmEx, MC, V. **Map** p403 F27

For review, *see p74* Murray Hill Inn.

The **Dream Hotel**, complete with Ayurvedic spa. *See p57.*

Hostels

Bowery's Whitehouse Hotel of New York

340 Bowery, between 2nd & 3rd Streets (1-212 477 5623/www.whitehousehotelofny.com). Subway: B, D, F, V to Broadway-Lafayette Street; 6 to Bleecker Street. **Rates** $34-$57 single/double; $71-$81 triple. **Rooms** 220. **Credit** AmEx, Disc, MC, V. **Map** p403 F29 ⑲

Even though the Bowery progressively looks more sleek than seedy, with pricey restaurants and flashy clubs popping up in recent years, the unapologetically second-rate Whitehouse Hotel remains steadfastly basic. Built in 1919 as housing for railroad workers, the renovated hotel offers semi-private cubicles (ceilings are an open latticework, so be warned that snorers or sleep talkers may interrupt your slumber) at unbelievably low rates. Towels and linens are provided. A microwave and large-screen TV are available in the lounge at all times.
Hostel services *Concierge. DVD library. DVD player, internet and TV in lobby. Fax. Luggage storage. Safe-deposit boxes. Self-service laundry. TV in some rooms.*

Midtown

Luxury

Dream Hotel

210 W 55th Street, between Broadway & Seventh Avenue (1-212 247 2000/1-866 437 3266/www.dreamny.com). Subway: N, Q, R, W to 57th Street. **Rates** $275-$575 single/double; $595-$3,000 suite. **Rooms** 216. **Credit** AmEx, Disc, MC, V. **Map** p405 D22 ⑳

In 2004 hotelier Vikram Chatwal, who brought us the Time Hotel, enlisted boldfaced names to turn the old Majestic Hotel into a luxury lodge with a trippy slumberland theme. David Rockwell dressed up the restaurant, an outpost of Serafina; Deepak Chopra conceived the Ayurvedic spa. The lobby sums up the resulting aesthetic – walls are cloaked in Paul Smith-style stripes, a crystal boat dangles from the ceiling and an enormous gold statue of Catherine the Great stands guard. The rooms are more streamlined, with white walls, satin headboards and an ethereal blue backlight that glows under the bed. Luxurious touches include feather-duvet-topped beds, plasma TV with movies on demand and an iPod – loaded with ambient music – with Bose speakers. Ava, the rooftop bar, has panoramic views of the city. **Photo** *p55.*
Hotel services *Fitness centre. Flat-panel TV. Pet-friendly. Spa.* **Room services** *CD/DVD player on request. High-speed internet. iPod. Movies on demand.*

Dylan

52 E 41st Street, between Madison & Park Avenues (1-212 338 0500/1-800 553 9526/www.dylan hotel.com). Subway: 42nd Street S, 4, 5, 6, 7 to
42nd Street-Grand Central. **Rates** $329-$549 single/double; $495-$1,200 suite. **Rooms** 107. **Credit** AmEx, DC, Disc, MC, V. **Map** p404 E24 ㉑

If you're a closet science geek, then you'll love this breathtaking boutique hotel, fashioned out of the once-crumbling 1903 landmark Chemist Club building. The lobby has a grand marble staircase, fluted columns and beautifully ornate mouldings. Most rooms are flooded with natural light and have 11ft-high ceilings. Bathrooms sport bowl sinks, and beakers stand in for water glasses. The stunning Gothic Alchemy Suite, modelled after a medieval alchemist's lab, has leaded floor-to-ceiling windows and a spacious outdoor terrace.
Hotel services *Fitness centre. Ticket desk. Valet.* **Room services** *CD player and VCR on request. Complimentary newspaper. High-speed wireless internet.*

Four Seasons Hotel

57 E 57th Street, between Madison & Park Avenues (1-212 758 5700/1-800 332 3442/www.fourseasons.com). Subway: N, R, W to Lexington Avenue-59th Street; 4, 5, 6 to 59th Street. **Rates** $455-$895 single/double; $1,550-$11,000 suite. **Rooms** 368. **Credit** AmEx, DC, Disc, MC, V. **Map** p405 E22 ㉒

For review, see pp58-9 **New York icons**.
Hotel services *Dry cleaning (24hrs). Fitness centre. Gift shop. Spa.* **Room services** *CD/DVD library. Flat-panel TV. High-speed internet. VCR in suites.*

Inn at Irving Place

56 Irving Place, between 17th & 18th Streets (1-212 533 4600/1-800 685 1447/www.innatirving. com). Subway: L, N, Q, R, W, 4, 5, 6 to 14th Street-Union Square. **Rates** $415-$565 standard/deluxe; $475-$495 junior suite. **Rooms** 12. **Credit** AmEx, DC, Disc, MC, V. **Map** p403 F27 ㉓

Inn at Irving Place may be one of Manhattan's smallest hotels, but it is also one of its most endearing. Housed in a pair of brownstones near Gramercy Park, it's dotted with fresh flowers and antique furnishings. While some rooms are petite, each is decorated with turn-of-the-19th century elegance. Leave the little ones at home (children under 12 are not permitted). At Lady Mendl's (1-212 533 4466, reservations required), the inn's pretty tearoom, damask love seats and a lavish tea and dessert menu create the perfect spot for brushing up on your manners. Edith Wharton would feel right at home.
Hotel services *Complimentary breakfast. Ticket desk.* **Room services** *CD player. Digital cable. High-speed internet. Room service (24hrs). VCR.*

New York Palace Hotel

455 Madison Avenue, between 50th & 51st Streets (1-212 888 7000/1-800 697 2522/www.new yorkpalace.com). Subway: E, V to Fifth Avenue-53rd Street. **Rates** $315-$745 single/double; $900-$12,000 suite. **Rooms** 896. **Credit** AmEx, DC, Disc, MC, V. **Map** p404 E23 ㉔

For review, see pp58-9 **New York icons**.

New York icons

In a New York state of mind? Check out these classic hotels.

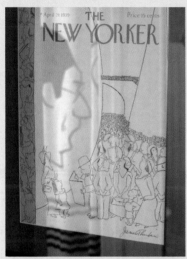

The Algonquin

For listing, see p61.

This landmark hotel (*photos above and left*) with a strong literary past (greats like Alexander Woollcott and Dorothy Parker gathered in the infamous Round Table Room to gossip) is beautifully furnished with upholstered chairs, old lamps and large paintings of figures from the Jazz Age. In 2004 the entire hotel was renovated; the small quarters were spiffed up with new bed-spreads and mahogany furniture, and many rooms now have flat-panel TVs. But a sense of old New York still exists: hallways are covered with *New Yorker*-cartoon wallpaper to commemorate Harold Ross, who secured funding for the magazine over long meetings at the Round Table, and the feel remains classic New York. Catch readings by local authors on some Mondays; cabaret performers take over in the Oak Room (*see p280*) Tuesday to Saturday.

Four Seasons Hotel

For listing, see p57.

New York's most quintessential hotel hasn't slipped a notch since its heyday. Everybody who's anybody – from music-industry executives to political figures – continue to drop in for a dose of New York luxury. Renowned architect IM Pei's sharp geometric design (in neutral cream and honey tones) is sleek and modern, and rooms are among the largest in the city (the three-bedroom Royal Suite measures 2,000sq ft). From the higher floors, the views of the city are superb. In 2004 the hotel spa was renovated and now features high-tech 'spa-ology', and in 2005 the Presidential suites were renovated and reopened. The hotel is known for catering to its guests' every need; your 4am hot-fudge sundae is only a room-service call away.

New York Palace Hotel
For listing, see p57.
Stepping inside the palace is like stepping inside a fairytale, complete with red carpet, twinkling lights and fancy tea parties. So it's hard to believe that the hotel was once owned by real-estate tycoon (and former jailbird) Leona Helmsley. Designed by McKim, Mead & White, the cluster of mansions now holds nearly 900 rooms ornamented in the art deco or neo-classical style. Triplex suites have a top-tier terrace, solarium and private rooftop garden. The restaurant Le Cirque 2000 is now closed, but you can still sip a Manhattan in the extravagant Louis XVI-style Villard Bar and Lounge. You can also sample New American fare and exotic cocktails at the elegant Istana Restaurant, which is also located in the hotel.

The Pierre
For listing, see p61.
A landmark of New York high society, the Pierre marked its 75th birthday in 2005. The hotel came under new management in the same year (it's now owned by the Taj Hotels group) and at the time of writing a $6million renovation was set to take place. In the meantime, the old-time glamour remains intact, with a black-and-white-chequered sidewalk that leads up to the gleaming gold lobby. Front rooms overlook Central Park, and wares from fancy neighbouring stores are on display in the lobby. There are three restaurants, including the opulent Café Pierre.

Waldorf-Astoria
For listing, see p67.
First built in 1893 on Fifth Avenue, the Waldorf-Astoria (*photo above right*) was the city's largest hotel (and the birthplace of the

Waldorf salad), but it was demolished to make way for the Empire State Building. The current art deco Waldorf on Park Avenue opened in 1931 and now has protected status as a historic hotel. In addition to history, it has spent $2million to make 24 rooms into 12 reconfigured Astor suites. It still caters to the high-and-mighty (famous guests have included Princess Grace, Sophia Loren as well as a long list of US Presidents). Double-check your attire before entering the hotel – you won't be allowed in if you're wearing a baseball cap, T-shirt or even trendy ripped jeans.

Warwick New York Hotel
For listing, see p67.
You'd never know it from its dated façade, but the grand Warwick was frequented by Elvis and the Beatles during their tours, and the top-floor suite with a wrap-around balcony was once the home of the actor Cary Grant. Built by William Randolph Hearst in 1927, the Warwick is listed by the National Trust for Historic Preservation. Rooms are exceptionally large by midtown standards, and have feminine touches like proper bedspreads and floral curtains. The in-house Murals on 54 restaurant has been refurbished to reveal a scenery of light-filled murals.

30 30

HOTEL THIRTY THIRTY

Hotel Thirty Thirty
30 East 30 th St.
New York NY 10016

Phone: (212) 689-1900
Reservations : (800) 497 6028
Email : info@thirtythirty-nyc.com
Web : www.thirtythirty-nyc.com

These top of the line trendy rooms are the ideal choice for the demanding traveler looking for luxury.

Accommodations to fit all types of travelers

Welcome to Hotel Thirty Thirty in New York City, a premier Midtown Manhattan hotel, perfectly located near most major business and leisure attractions. Our hotel offers the comfort and convenience of a European-style hotel at an affordable price. For your next business or leisure visit to New York City, the one hotel address worth talking about it Hotel Thirty Thirty.

Our room settings are arranged perfectly for business and leisure travelers, conference attendees, small or large families, or groups. Our hotel attracts business and leisure visitors from all over the world.

- Ideal Miidtown Manhattan hotel location, near Park Avenue
- 253 spacious, fully renovated and well-appointed Standard and Deluxe Executive Rooms
- Multilingual friendly staff
- Chic evening cocktail bar and intimate reception salo
- Fine dining at Zana's, where Chef Antonio serves unsurpassed Mediteranean cuisine
- High-speed Internet access in all rooms (small fee applie
- Valet laundry and dry-cleaning services, availble to a
- Daily parking nearby
- Pet-friendly accommodations (please see our pet friendly policy)
- Macres Florist in the hotel lobby, for deliveries throughto the hotel and Manhattan

Hotel services *Complimentary limousine service to Wall Street and shoe shine. Dry cleaning (24hrs). Fitness centre. Video library.* **Room services** *Complimentary breakfast, dessert and newspaper in suites. Dual-line phone. Room service (24hrs).*

The Pierre

2 E 61st Street, at Fifth Avenue (1-212 838 8000/ 1-800 743 7734/www.tajhotels.com). Subway: N, R, W to Fifth Avenue-59th Street. **Rates** $425-$950 single; $475-$995 double; $625-$3,800 suite. **Rooms** 201. **Credit** AmEx, DC, Disc, MC, V. **Map** p405 E22 **㉕**

For review, see pp58-9 **New York icons.**

Hotel services *Beauty salon. Mobile-phone rental. Dry cleaning (24hrs). Fitness centre. Free shuttle to Theater District. Ticket desk. Valet.* **Room services** *CD player. Exercise equipment. High-speed wireless internet. PlayStation and VCR on request.*

Expensive

The Algonquin

59 W 44th Street, between Fifth & Sixth Avenues (1-212 840 6800/www.thealgonquin.net). Subway: B, D, F, V to 42nd Street-Bryant Park; 7 to Fifth Avenue. **Rates** $200-$299 single/double; $299-$549 suite. **Rooms** 174. **Credit** AmEx, DC, Disc, MC, V. **Map** p404 E24 **㉘**

For review, see pp58-9 **New York icons.**

Hotel services *Fitness centre (24hrs). Ticket desk.* **Room services** *CD player and VCR in suites. Complimentary magazines and newspapers. High-speed wireless internet. Refrigerator in suites or on request.*

Bryant Park Hotel

40 W 40th Street, between Fifth & Sixth Avenues (1-212 642 2200/www.bryantparkhotel.com). Subway: B, D, F, V to 42nd Street-Bryant Park; 7 to Fifth Avenue. **Rates** $265-$395 single/double; $395-$615 suite. **Rooms** 128. **Credit** AmEx, DC, MC, V. **Map** p404 E24. **㉗**

This midtown hotel has seen a lot more action ever since Koi, the East Coast branch of the splashy Los Angeles restaurant, opened on site in spring 2005. Ian Schrager's partner Philip Pilevsky converted the 1924 American Radiator Building into his first New York property, and it seems as though the hotel has all the right accessories to lure a trendsetting crowd: there's a gorgeous 70-seat screening room with red velour chairs and built-in desks, and, thanks to the hotel's close proximity to Bryant Park, a well-heeled clientele, which checks in each year during Fashion Week. But, oddly, the rooms are stark, and – casting aside the LCD TVs – look as if they were furnished from the IKEA catalogue. You can always head downstairs for a cocktail in the vaulted Cellar Bar, however.

Hotel services *Beauty salon. Fitness centre. Screening room. Spa. Valet.* **Room services** *CD player. Digital movies on demand. High-speed internet. Room service (24hrs). VCR.*

Casablanca Hotel

147 W 43rd Street, between Sixth Avenue & Broadway (1-212 869 1212/1-800 922 7225/ www.casablancahotel.com). Subway: B, D, F, V to 42nd Street-Bryant Park; N, Q, R, W, 42nd Street S, 1, 2, 3, 7 to 42nd Street-Times Square. **Rates** $225-$365 single/double; $295-$395 suite. **Rooms** 48. **Credit** AmEx, DC, MC, V. **Map** p404 D24 **㉓**

Run by the same people who own the Library Hotel (*see p65*), this 48-room boutique hotel has a cheerful Moroccan theme. The lobby is an oasis in the middle of Times Square: walls are adorned with blue and gold Mediterranean tiles, and giant bamboo shoots stand in tall vases. The theme is diluted in the basic rooms, but wicker furniture, wooden shutters and new carpets and sofas warm up the space. Rick's Café serves free wine and cheese to guests Monday to Saturday. Breakfast is complimentary, as is your copy of *Casablanca*.

Hotel services *Complimentary breakfast and pass to nearby gym. Cybercafé. Mobile phone rental. Spa. Valet. Video library.* **Room services** *CD player. High-speed wireless internet. VCR.*

Flatotel

135 W 52nd Street, between Sixth & Seventh Avenues (1-212 887 9400/www.flatotel.com). Subway: N, R, W to 49th Street; 1 to 50th Street. **Rates** $229-$489 single/double; $600-$3,800 suite. **Rooms** 288. **Credit** AmEx, DC, MC, V. **Map** p404 D23 **㉙**

Upon entrance, the Flatotel seems ultra-hip: techno beats pump through the granite lobby, where dimly lit nooks and cowhide couches are filled with guests drinking cocktails. Rooms are less sleek, however, although still modern and very spacious, and some rooms have impressive views of the city. A slew of reality television shows, including *America's Next Top Model*, has been filmed in the penthouse suites. The in-house restaurant, Moda (1-212 887 9880), serves Italian-inspired fare; in temperate weather, catch a breeze with your cocktail in the restaurant's alfresco atrium. For private imbibing, call the Martini butler, who will mix the drink right in your room.

Hotel services *Fitness centre. Gift shop. Mobile phone rental. Spa. Valet.* **Room services** *CD player. High-speed internet. Microwave. Mini-fridge. Room service (24hrs). VCR.*

Hotel Chandler

12 E 31st Street, between Fifth & Madison Avenues (1-212 889 6363/www.hotelchandler. com). Subway: 6 to 33rd Street. **Rates** $290-$370 single/double; $525-$750 suite. **Rooms** 120. **Credit** AmEx, DC, Disc, MC, V. **Map** p404 E25 **㉚**

Rooms at this delightful hotel are style-conscious, with black-and-white photographs of New York streetscapes on the walls, chequered carpeting, and Frette robes and Aveda products in the bathroom. The in-house 12:31 bar offers cocktails and light nibbles. And turndown service means a chocolate on your pillow and a next-day weather forecast.

Hotel services *DVD library. Fitness centre. Valet.* **Room services** *CD/DVD player. High-speed internet. Nintendo/web TV (free).*

Hotel Elysée

60 E 54th Street, between Madison & Park Avenues (1-212 753 1066/www.elyseehotel.com). Subway: E, V to Lexington Avenue-53rd Street; 6 to 51st Street. **Rates** $285-$395 single/double; $675 suite. **Rooms** 101. **Credit** AmEx, DC, Disc, MC, V. **Map** p405 E22 ③①

The Hotel Elysée is a well-preserved piece of New York's Jazz Age: quarters are appointed with a touch of romance (period fabrics, antique furniture), and some rooms have coloured-glass conservatories and terraces. Elysée is popular with publishers and literary types, who convene over complimentary wine and cheese in the evening. Downstairs is the Steakhouse at Monkey Bar (1-212 838 2600), where a well-coiffed clientele dines on fine cuts. For sister hotels, see Casablanca Hotel (*see p61*), the Library Hotel (*see p65*) and the ultramodern Hotel Gansevoort (*see p49*).

Hotel services *Complimentary breakfast and pass to nearby gym. Valet. Video library.* **Room services** *CD player in suites. High-speed wireless internet. VCR.*

Hotel 41

206 W 41st Street, between Seventh & Eighth Avenues (1-212 703 8600/www.hotel41.com). Subway: N, Q, R, W to 42nd Street; S, 1, 2, 3, 7 to 42nd Street-Times Square. **Rates** $289-$309 single/double; $369-$589 suite. **Rooms** 47. **Credit** AmEx, Disc, MC, V. **Map** p404 D24 ③②

Although its look is cool, this tiny boutique hotel feels comfy-warm: reading lamps extend from dark-wood headboards, and triple-paned windows effectively filter out the cacophony from the streets below. The penthouse suite has a large private terrace with potted trees and views of Times Square. Bar 41 serves breakfast, lunch and dinner.

Hotel services *CD/DVD library. Complimentary breakfast. Espresso bar. Pet-friendly. Valet.* **Room services** *CD/DVD player. High-speed internet.*

Hotel Roger Williams

131 Madison Avenue, at 31st Street (1-212 448 7000/1-888 448 7788/www.rogerwilliamshotel.com). Subway: 6 to 33rd Street. **Rates** $255-$340 single/double; $325-$450 suite. **Rooms** 191. **Credit** AmEx, DC, Disc, MC, V. **Map** p404 E25 ③③

In 2004 an $8 million renovation brought in a vibrant colour palette of greens and tangerine to this small, stylish hotel. The soaring lobby has floor-to-ceiling windows, plenty of textured wood and a live jazz band (Wed-Fri). Room amenities, such as bottled water, Aveda bath products and a modern office area, make you feel at home – if you're lucky enough to live like this. Each room on the penthouse level has access to a shared wrap-around terrace. Lounge at the Roger, the hotel's new restaurant and bar, serves light fare and cocktails as well as room service, and the recently opened Veranda 411 is a fourth-floor garden open for private events.

Hotel services *Complimentary newspapers and magazines. Fitness centre. Mobile phone rental. Valet.* **Room services** *High-speed wireless internet. Plasma TV.*

Inn on 23rd Street

131 W 23rd Street, between Sixth & Seventh Avenues (1-212 463 0330/www.innon23rd.com). Subway: A, C, E to 14th Street; L to Eighth Avenue. **Rates** $209-$279 queen/king; $329-$359 suite. **Rooms** 14. **Credit** AmEx, MC, V. **Map** p404 D26 ③④

This real-deal B&B in the heart of Chelsea gives you a warm and fuzzy feeling from the moment that you enter – the sun-drenched library is brimming with comfy couches and chairs. Owners and innkeepers Annette and Barry Fisherman renovated a 19th-century townhouse into a homely inn with 14 themed rooms (all accessible by elevator and each with its own private bathroom). Rooms are exceptionally plush: pillow-topped mattresses, double-pane windows and white-noise machines will ensure a decent night's sleep. An expanded continental breakfast is served daily in the lobby or breakfast room.

Hotel services *Complimentary continental breakfast. High-speed wireless internet.* **Room services** *Complimentary high-speed internet. Complimentary local and national long distance phone calls.*

Iroquois

49 W 44th Street, between Fifth & Sixth Avenues (1-212 840 3080/1-800 332 7220/www.iroquois ny.com). Subway: B, D, F, V to 42nd Street-Bryant Park; 7 to Fifth Avenue. **Rates** $259-$459 single/double; $475-$685 suite. **Rooms** 114. **Credit** AmEx, DC, Disc, MC, V. **Map** p404 E24 ③⑤

The Iroquois is what you might find if you were to walk into a posh doorman apartment building on the Upper East Side. It boasts a polished-stone lobby, a mahogany-panelled library and spacious, elegant rooms – all the result of a massive renovation that morphed a modest inn into a full-service luxury hotel. Nine suites include additional treats like decorative fireplaces, jacuzzis and Frette bathrobes. The James Dean Suite (No.803), which is decorated with photographs of the rebel without a cause, commemorates the actor, who lived here in the 1950s. There's also a fitness centre, a sauna and a library with computer access. Haute French fare is served in the hotel's restaurant, Triomphe (1-212 453 4233).

Hotel services *Fitness centre. Mobile phone rental. Sauna. Ticket desk. Video library.* **Room services** *CD player. Flat-panel TVs. Room service (24hrs). VCR. Wireless internet.*

Kitano

66 Park Avenue, at 38th Street (1-212 885 7000/1-800 548 2666/www.kitano.com). Subway: 42nd Street S, 4, 5, 6, 7 to 42nd Street-Grand Central. **Rates** $250-$480 single/double; $400-$715 junior suite; $715-$2,100 suite. **Rooms** 149. **Credit** AmEx, DC, Disc, MC, V. **Map** p404 E24 ③⑥

Inn on 23rd Street. *See p62.*

DISCOVER MORE CITIES

Tell us what you think and you could win £100-worth of City Guides

Your opinions are important to us and we'd like to know what you like and what you don't like about the Time Out City Guides

For your chance to win, simply fill in our short survey at
timeout.com/guidesfeedback

Every month a reader will win £100 to spend on the Time Out City Guides of their choice – a great start to discovering new cities and you'll have extra cash to enjoy your trip!

The first and only Japanese-owned and operated hotel in New York City is also the only hotel to offer heated commodes. Rooms feature silk-covered walls, smooth stone floors, Shiseido bath products and complimentary green tea. A one-of-a-kind tatami suite boasts painted shoji screens and a separate tea-ceremony room. Dine with chopsticks at the hotel's two casual Japanese restaurants, Hakubai (1-212 885 7111) and Garden Café (1-212 885 7123).
Hotel services *Bar-lounge with jazz Wed-Sat. Complimentary pass to nearby gym. Gift shop. Laundry drop-off. Ticket desk. Valet.* **Room services** *CD player in some rooms. High-speed internet.*

Library Hotel

299 Madison Avenue, at 41st Street (1-212 983 4500/ www.libraryhotel.com). Subway: 42nd Street S, 4, 5, 6, 7 to 42nd Street-Grand Central; 7 to Fifth Avenue. **Rates** $335-$395 single/double; $435 suite. **Rooms** 60. **Credit** AmEx, DC, MC, V. **Map** p404 E24 ⑰
More than 6,000 books were handpicked from indie-fave bookstore the Strand to match the of the rooms they adorn at this literary-inspired boutique hotel. Even before you enter, you'll see quotes from famous authors inscribed in the sidewalk. Lodgings are organised according to the Dewey decimal system and furnished by subject (Botany, Fairy Tales). For instance, the Love Room is strewn with rose petals, and Casanova's autobiography sits on a bedside table in the Erotica Room. Rates include breakfast, evening wine and cheese gatherings in the second-floor Reading Room, and access to the mahogany-lined writer's den (which has a lovely tiny terrace and a glowing fireplace). The casual seafood destination, Branzini, is conveniently located in the lobby. Hotel Giraffe, which is a sister hotel, embodies modern European style 15 blocks south.
Hotel services *Complimentary breakfast, pass to nearby gym, and wine and cheese every evening. Mobile phone rental. Ticket desk. Valet. Video library.* **Room services** *CD player. High-speed internet. VCR.*
Other locations: Hotel Giraffe, 365 Park Avenue South, at 26th Street, Flatiron District (1-212 685 7700/1-877 296 0009/www.hotelgiraffe.com).

Maritime Hotel

363 W 16th Street, between Eighth & Ninth Avenues (1-212 242 4300/www.themaritimehotel. com). Subway: A, C, E to 14th Street; L to Eighth Avenue. **Rates** $295-$375 single/double; $650-$1,350 suite. **Credit** AmEx, DC, Disc, MC, V. **Map** p403 C27 ㉒
What are porthole windows doing on a hotel in Chelsea? Well, it's not *all* for show – the building is the former headquarters of the Maritime Union. In 2002 owners Eric Goode and Sean MacPherson took this nautical theme and spun it into the high-gloss Maritime Hotel, blending the look of a luxury yacht with a chic 1960s airport lounge. The lobby is a bit dank and dark, but the rooms are much more eye-catching. Modelled after ship cabins, each has one large porthole window and lots of glossy teak panelling. For more space, book one of the two penthouses, which have their own private terrace with an outdoor shower. The hotel offers

Maritime Hotel.

four food and drink spaces: Matsuri, a gorgeous Japanese restaurant; La Bottega (*see p202*), an Italian trattoria with a lantern-festooned patio; Cabana, an airy rooftop bar; and Hiro, a basement lounge that draws a buzzing crowd. **Photo p65.**
Hotel services *Complimentary pass to New York Sports Club. Discount parking and valet service. DVD library. Fitness centre. Pet-friendly.* **Room services** *CD player. Complimentary in-room movies. DVD player. Flat-panel TV. High-speed wireless internet. Room service (24hrs). Two-line telephone.*

Metropolitan Hotel

569 Lexington Avenue, at 51st Street (1-212 752 7000/1-800 836 6471/www.metropolitannyc.com). Subway: E, V to Lexington Avenue-53rd Street; 6 to 51st Street. **Rates** $189-$500 single/double; $379-$700 suite. **Rooms** 722. **Credit** AmEx, DC, Disc, MC, V. **Map** p404 F23 ❸❾
The Metropolitan has reinvented itself more times than Madonna: it was unveiled in 1961, and, known as the Summit, with an art deco look, later transformed into a more toned-down Loews Hotel in the '80s. In 2000 architect Morris Lapidus – designer of many 1950s-era hotels – returned the building to its original look. Its most recent reincarnation emerged in 2004, when hospitality-industry giant Doubletree acquired the place and a $35 million renovation added some badly needed style. Rooms are now freshly outfitted with fluffy down comforters, flat-panel TVs and original artwork. The Met Grill offers casual American cuisine, and a lobby lounge draws guests and local imbibers. In keeping with Doubletree tradition, everyone receives a warm chocolate-chip cookie at check-in.
Hotel services *Barbershop. Fitness centre (24hrs).* **Room services** *Cordless phone. High-speed internet. LCD TV.*

Night Hotel

132 W 45th Street, between Sixth & Seventh Avenues (1-212 835 9600). Subway N, Q, R, W to 42nd Street; S, 1, 2, 3, 7 to 42nd Street-Times Square. **Rates** $249-$429 single/double; $329-$529 suite; $2,500-$5,000 penthouse suite. **Rooms** 72. **Credit** AmEx, DC, Disc, MC, V. **Map** p404 D24 ❹⓿
At Midtown's Night Hotel, the new 72-room boutique property from Vikram Chatwal (of Dream Hotel and Time; *see p57* and *below*) out-of-town guests will see the city through the romantic lens of 21st-century Gothic Gotham. A nightcrawler's roost, the hotel's stylish black-and-white motif extends beyond the loungey lobby to the handsome (coffin-like) rooms. The Addams Family would love this place. **Photo** *p67.*
Hotel services *iPod Nano. Mobile phone on request. Personal shopper service. Valet.* **Room services** *Bose stereo. High-speed internet. Plasma TV.*

Park South Hotel

124 E 28th Street, between Park Avenue South & Lexington Avenue (1-212 448 0888/1-800 315 4642/www.parksouthhotel.com). Subway: 6 to 28th Street. **Rates** $209-$270 single/double; $330-$350 suite. **Rooms** 141. **Credit** AmEx, DC, Disc, MC, V. **Map** p404 E26 ❹❶

Everything about this quaint boutique hotel says 'I love New York'. The mezzanine library is crammed with books on historic Gotham, and the walls are covered with images from the New York Historical Society. Rooms are appointed in warm amber and brown tones, and some have dazzling views of the Chrysler Building. Bathrooms are stocked with essential oil products and thick terry-cloth bathrobes. The hotel's bar-restaurant, Black Duck (1-212 204 5240), provides live jazz with brunch.
Hotel services *Complimentary breakfast and newspaper. Fitness centre. Video library.* **Room services** *DVD player. High-speed internet.*

Roger Smith

501 Lexington Avenue, between 47th & 48th Streets (1-212 755 1400/1-800 445 0277/www.rogersmith. com). Subway: E, V to Lexington Avenue-53rd Street; 6 to 51st Street. **Rates** $265-$295 single/double; $330-$450 suite; $275-$400 junior suite. **Rooms** 130. **Credit** AmEx, DC, Disc, MC, V. **Map** p404 F23 ❹❷
The spacious chambers at this arty spot make it a good option for families. Each room is decorated with unique furnishings and colourful wallpaper. Lily's restaurant, situated in a bright space with playful murals, was only serving breakfast at the time of writing, but a full service is expected by the time this guide is published. The Roger Smith Gallery hosts rotating exhibitions, and a few interesting pieces by artist James Knowles (whose family owns the hotel) adorn the lobby.
Hotel services *Valet. Video library.* **Room services** *CD player. Coffeemaker. Complimentary local phone calls. High-speed wireless internet. Refrigerator. VCR.*

Time

224 W 49th Street, between Broadway & Eighth Avenue (1-212 320 2900/1-877 846 3692/ www.thetimeny.com). Subway: C, E, 1 to 50th Street; N, R, W to 49th Street. **Rates** $249-$429 single/double; $329-$529 suite; $2,500-$5,000 penthouse suite. **Rooms** 193. **Credit** AmEx, DC, Disc, MC, V. **Map** p404 D23 ❹❸
Have you ever wondered what it's like to feel, taste and smell colour? Adam Tihany designed this boutique hotel with the idea of stimulating the senses through a single primary colour (guest rooms are furnished entirely in either red, yellow or blue). Expect to find matching duvets, jelly beans and reading materials, as well as a chromatically inspired scent. At press time, Océo, the hotel's creative American restaurant, was closed but expected to reopen as a restaurant by another name.
Hotel services *Fitness centre. Mobile phone rental. Personal shopping. Ticket desk.* **Room services** *CD player and VCR on request. High-speed internet.*

W New York-Times Square

1567 Broadway, at 47th Street (1-212 930 7400/ 1-877 976 8357/www.whotels.com). Subway: N, R, W to 49th Street; 1 to 50th Street. **Rates** $279-$579 single/double; $699-$900 suite. **Rooms** 509. **Credit** AmEx, DC, Disc, MC, V. **Map** p404 D23 ❹❹

'Whatever, whenever' is the motto of this luxury boutique chain, and the hotel's concierge is always at the ready to fill your bathtub with champagne, chocolate or whatever else your heart desires. NYC's fifth and flashiest W location has a street-level vestibule with a waterfall (reception is on the seventh floor). To your right, the Living Room is a sprawl of white leather seating. Every private room features a floating-glass desk and a sleek bathroom stocked with Bliss spa products, but it's the bed-to-ceiling headboard mirror and sexy room service menu that get the mind racing. Steve Hanson's Blue Fin (1-212 918 1400) serves stellar sushi and cocktails.
Hotel services *Fitness centre. Gift shop. Mobile phone rental. Pet-friendly. Screening room. Spa. Valet.* **Room services** *CD/DVD player. High-speed wireless internet. VCR.*
Other locations: W New York, 541 Lexington Avenue, at 49th Street, Midtown (1-212 755 1200); W New York-The Court, 130 E 39th Street, between Park Avenue South & Lexington Avenue, Midtown (1-212 685 1100); W New York-The Tuscany, 120 E 39th Street, between Park Avenue South & Lexington Avenue, Midtown (1-212 686 1600); W New York-Union Square, 201 Park Avenue South, at 17th Street, Midtown (1-212 253 9119).

Waldorf-Astoria

301 Park Avenue, at 50th Street (1-212 355 3000/ 1-800 925 3673/www.waldorf.com). Subway: E, V to Lexington Avenue-53rd Street; 6 to 51st Street.
Rates $275-$450 single; $300-$450 double; $400-$900 suite. **Rooms** 1,425. **Credit** AmEx, DC, Disc, MC, V. **Map** p404 E23 ⓯
For review, see pp58-9 **New York icons**.
Hotel services *Beauty salon. Complimentary newspaper. Copier/printer. High-speed internet. Kitchenette in some suites. Mobile-phone rental. Refurnished fitness centre. Spa. 3 restaurants. Valet. Wi-Fi in lobby.*

Warwick New York Hotel

65 W 54th Street, at Sixth Avenue (1-212 247 2700/1-800 223 4099/www.warwickhotels.com). Subway: E, V to Fifth Avenue-53rd Street; F to 57th Street. **Rates** $189-$475 single/double; $405-$3,500 suite. **Rooms** 426. **Credit** AmEx, DC, MC, V. **Map** p405 E22 ⓰
For review, see pp58-9 **New York icons**.
Hotel services *Mobile-phone rental. New fitness centre. Refurnished business bentre. Valet (24hrs).* **Room services** *High-speed wireless internet. VCR on request.*

Moderate

Broadway Inn

264 W 46th Street, at Eighth Avenue (1-212 997 9200/ 1-800 826 6300/www.broadwayinn.com). Subway: A, C, E to 42nd Street-Port Authority. **Rates** $125-$299 single/double; $199-$399 suite. **Rooms** 41. **Credit** AmEx, DC, Disc, MC, V. **Map** p404 D23 ⓱

Noctural creatures flock to the gothic-inspired **Night Hotel**. *See p66.*

Time Out
Travel Guides

USA

**Available at all good bookshops
and at timeout.com/shop**

Time Out
Guides

Theatre junkies should take note: this endearing little hotel can arrange a 35-40% discount on theatre tickets; it also offers several Broadway dinner-and-show combinations. The warm lobby has exposed-brick walls, ceiling fans and shelves that are loaded with bedtime reading material. The fairly priced basic guest rooms and suites get lots of natural light. On the downside, there are no elevators, and the hotel is strict about its three night minimum policy on weekends and holidays.
Hotel services *Complimentary breakfast.*
Room services *High-speed wireless internet. Kitchenette in suites.*

Chelsea Hotel

222 W 23rd Street, between Seventh & Eighth Avenues (1-212 243 3700/www.hotelchelsea.com). Subway: C, E, 1 to 23rd Street. **Rates** *$125-$150 single/double with shared bath; $185-$275 single/double with private bath; $225 double studio; $325-$785 suite.* **Rooms** 400. **Credit** AmEx, DC, Disc, MC, V. **Map** p404 D26* ⓭
Built in 1884, the Chelsea has a long (and infamous) past: Nancy Spungen was murdered in Room 100 by her boyfriend, Sex Pistol Sid Vicious. This funky hotel has seen an endless parade of noteworthy guests: in 1912 Titanic survivors stayed here; other former residents include Mark Twain, Dee Dee Ramone, Thomas Wolfe and Madonna. Rooms are generally large with high ceilings, but certain amenities, like flat-panel TVs, washer-dryers and marble fireplaces, vary.

The lobby doubles as an art gallery, and the basement cocktail lounge, Serena (1-212 255 4646), draws a downtown crowd with nightly DJs.
Hotel services *Beauty salon. Fitness centre. Pet-friendly. Valet.* **Room services** *Fireplace. Flat-panel TV and kitchenette or refrigerator in some rooms. High-speed wireless internet. Washer-dryer in some rooms.*

414 Hotel

414 W 46th Street, between Ninth & Tenth Avenues (1-212 399 0006/www.414hotel.com). Subway: A, C, E to 42nd Street-Port Authority. **Rates** $99-$329 single/double. **Rooms** 22. **Credit** AmEx, MC, V. **Map** p404 C23 ⓭
This small hotel's shockingly affordable rates and reclusive location make it feel like a secret you've been lucky to stumble upon. Immaculate rooms are tastefully appointed with suede headboards, vases full of colourful roses and framed black-and-white photos of the city. There's a glowing fireplace and computer available to guests in the lobby and a leafy courtyard outside.
Hotel services *Complimentary breakfast. High-speed wireless internet.* **Room services** *Refrigerator in some rooms.*

Hotel Edison

228 W 47th Street, at Broadway (1-212 840 5000/ 1-800 637 7070/www.edisonhotelnyc.com). Subway: N, R, W to 49th Street; 1 to 50th Street. **Rates** $180

Chelsea Hotel.

Something old, something new

It may have a reputation as one of the world's most famous and best-loved grand hotels, but the five-star **Plaza Hotel** has been struggling of late, and is now converting most of its $300-plus per night rooms into luxury condominiums – which will likely cost between $2million and $32 million each. Slated for completion in autumn 2007, the $350million renovation project will see the French Renaissance-style icon converted into 182 luxury residences and 282 hotel rooms, as well as surrounding posh retail outlets and upscale restaurants.

'The Plaza is an elite landmark and we are building on that legacy,' Miki Naftali, president of Elad Properties – the hotel's new owner – has stated. 'We're making extraordinary apartments and the great public spaces will be thoughtfully restored.' In fact, eight of those public spaces, including the Oak Room, Palm Court and Grand Ballroom, are so great that they have now been designated as landmarks by the Landmarks Preservation Commission (LPC), which stepped in after there was a huge public outcry when the conversion was initially announced. Impressive features such as the Palm Court's intricate stained-glass ceiling are now being recreated in the

neo-classical style that architect Henry Hardenburgh intended (the original was painted over in the 1940s).

The upscale crash pad certainly has star qualities. Since opening in 1907, the Plaza has appeared in renowned books (including *The Great Gatsby,* and Kay Thompson's Eloise books); starred in movies (*North by Northwest, The Way We Were*); and hosted swank society events (such as Truman Capote's infamous Black and White Ball in 1966). And besides providing city pieds-à-terres for such diverse personalities as Alfred Hitchcock and Frank Lloyd Wright, over the years the hotel has hosted thousands of events for regular families looking to celebrate their weddings, engagements and bar mitzvahs in grand style. Perhaps that's why the recent auction of fixtures and furniture raked in $1.8 million (more than double the original valuation) as sentimental guests scrambled for souvenirs ranging from brass doorknobs to chandeliers and silverware. 'The Plaza resonates in so many people's lives and memories,' Robert Tierney, LPC's chairman, says. 'It's everyone's romantic dream of New York City.' *Plaza Hotel, Central Park South & 57th Street.*

Where to Stay

single; $195 double (each additional person $20, maximum 5 people); $265-$295 suite. **Rooms** 1,000. **Credit** AmEx, DC, Disc, MC, V. **Map** p404 D23 ⑤⓪ Theatre lovers flock to this newly renovated art deco hotel for its affordable rates and convenient location. Rooms are of a standard size but are decidedly spruced up. Café Edison (1-212 840 5000), a classic diner just off the lobby, is a long-time favourite of Broadway actors and their fans – Neil Simon was so smitten that he put it in one of his plays. **Hotel services** *Fitness centre. Gift shop. Ticket desk. Valet.* **Room services** *High-speed wireless internet.*

Hotel Metro

45 W 35th Street, between Fifth & Sixth Avenues (1-212 947 2500/1-800 356 3870/www.hotelmetro nyc.com). Subway: B, D, F, N, Q, R, V, W to 34th Street-Herald Square. **Rates** $195-$325 single/double; $275-$450 suite. **Rooms** 179. **Credit** AmEx, DC, MC, V. **Map** p404 E25 ⑤①
It's not posh, but the Metro has good service and a retro vibe. Black-and-white portraits of Hollywood legends adorn the lobby, and the tiny rooms are clean. Take in views of the Empire State Building from the rooftop bar of Metro Grill. **Hotel services** *Beauty salon. Complimentary breakfast. Fitness centre. Library. Ticket desk. Valet.* **Room services** *High-speed wireless internet. Refrigerator.*

Hotel Pennsylvania

401 Seventh Avenue, between 32nd & 33rd Streets (1-212 736 5000/1-800 223 8585/www.hotelpenn. com). Subway: A, C, E, 1, 2, 3 to 34th Street-Penn Station. **Rates** $139-$300 single/double; $350-$1,000 suite. **Rooms** 1,700. **Credit** AmEx, DC, Disc, MC, V. **Map** p404 D25 ⑤②
One of the city's largest hotels. Its reasonable rates and convenient location (directly opposite Madison Square Garden and Penn Station) make it popular with tourists. Rooms are basic but pleasant. The hotel's Café Rouge Ballroom once hosted such greats as Duke Ellington and the Glenn Miller Orchestra. **Hotel services** *Gift shop. Pet-friendly. Ticket desk. Valet.* **Room services** *Internet.*

Hotel QT

125 West 45th Street, between Sixth & Seventh Avenues (1-212 354 2323/www.hotelqt.com). Subway: N, Q, R, W, 42nd Street S, 1, 2, 3, 7, 9 to 42nd Street-Times Square. **Rates** $175-$285 single/double; $250-$375 suite. **Rooms** 140. **Credit** AmEx, Disc, MC, V. **Map** p404 D23 ⑤③
Celebrity hotelier André Balazs has mastered almost every type of property, from hip LA hotels (the Standard) to art deco resorts (the Raleigh) in Miami to luxury condominiums in Manhattan. In 2006 he took a stab at a youth hostel: albeit one with Egyptian cotton sheets, flat-panel TVs and a lobby pool with underwater music. Rooms start at a pretty low prices for a midtown hotel. This brand new stylish hotel for the budget-minded traveller is the last thing you'd expect to find in the middle of Times Square. That and the trippy corridors, which get smaller as you get to your room. Which is also likely to be narrow, but with fittings well adapted to the space. **Photo** *p73.*
Hotel services *Complimentary breakfast. Fitness centre. Magazine library. Pool.* **Room services** *Flat-panels TVs. Two-line speakerphones.*

Hotel Thirty Thirty

30 E 30th Street, between Madison Avenue & Park Avenue South (1-212 689 1900/1-800 497 6028/ www.thirtythirty-nyc.com). Subway: 6 to 28th Street. **Rates** $159-$269 single/double; $180-$375 suite. **Rooms** 250. **Credit** AmEx, DC, Disc, MC, V. **Map** p404 E25 ⑤④
Before it became a smart hotel, Thirty Thirty was a residence for single women, and 60 tenants still live here. Ambient music sets the tone in the spare, fashionable, block-long lobby. Rooms are small but sleek and complemented by clean lines and textured fabrics. Executive-floor rooms are slightly larger, with nifty workspaces and slate bathrooms. The hotel's restaurant, Zanna, serves Mediterranean fare. **Hotel services** *Complimentary pass to nearby gym. Florist. Ticket desk.* **Room services** *CD player. Internet.*

Hudson

356 W 58th Street, between Eighth & Ninth Avenues (1-212 554 6000/www.hudsonhotel.com). Subway: A, B, C, D, 1 to 59th Street-Columbus Circle. **Rates** $155-$295 single/double; $330-$5,000 suite. **Rooms** 803. **Credit** AmEx, DC, Disc, MC, V. **Map** p405 C22 ⑤⑤
Sure, the rooms get points for looks, but just try turning around, or even finding a place to put down your suitcase. Outside of its teeny bedrooms, though, the Hudson has lots to offer. A lush courtyard is shaded with enormous potted trees, a rooftop terrace overlooks the Hudson River, and a glass-ceilinged lobby with imported English ivy is crawling with beautiful people. The Hudson Cafeteria and the three on-site bars lure the fabulous. This is the third New York palace in Ian Schrager's hip-hotel kingdom, which includes Morgans and the Royalton. **Hotel services** *Fitness centre. Mobile phone rental. Rooftop terrace.* **Room services** *CD player. Internet.*
Other locations: Morgans, 237 Madison Avenue, between 37th & 38th Streets, Midtown (1-212 686 0300/1-800 334 3408); Royalton, 44 W 44th Street, between Fifth & Sixth Avenues, Midtown (1-212 869 4400/1-800 635 9013).

Marcel

201 E 24th Street, at Third Avenue (1-212 696 3800/www.nychotels.com). Subway: 6 to 23rd Street. **Rates** $197-$347 single/double. **Rooms** 97. **Credit** AmEx, DC, Disc, MC, V. **Map** p404 F26 ⑤⑥
Frequented by fashion-industry types because of its easy access to the Flatiron and Garment Districts, the Marcel features compact rooms with nice touches like modern wood furniture and multicoloured, padded headboards. An added bonus is the complimentary espresso bar in the lobby that's always

open. You'll find the same chic perks and low prices at four sister hotels: Ameritania Hotel, Amsterdam Court, the Moderne and the Bentley Hotel (see p75). **Hotel services** *Espresso bar. Ticket desk.* **Room services** *CD player. PlayStation. VCR on request.* **Other locations**: Ameritania Hotel, 230 W 54th Street, at Broadway, Midtown (1-888 664 6835); Amsterdam Court, 226 W 50th Street, between Broadway & Eighth Avenue, Midtown (1-888 664 6835); Moderne, 243 W 55th Street, between Broadway & Eighth Avenue, Midtown (1-888 664 6835).

Pickwick Arms

230 E 51st Street, between Second & Third Avenues (1-212 355 0300/1-800 742 5945/www.pickwick arms.com). Subway: E, V to Lexington Avenue-53rd Street; 6 to 51st Street. **Rates** $109-$229 single; $139-$145 double. **Rooms** 370. **Credit** AmEx, DC, MC, V. **Map** p404 F23 ⑤
Rooms at this no-frills hotel are clean and bright, and many have baths. (Some share an adjoining facility; otherwise, the lavatories down the hall.) There are two on-site restaurants and a rooftop garden. **Hotel services** *Internet in lobby.*

Roosevelt Hotel

45 E 45th Street, at Madison Avenue (1-212 661 9600/1-888 833 3969/www.theroosevelthotel.com). Subway: 42nd Street S, 4, 5, 6, 7 to 42nd Street-Grand Central. **Rates** $189-$499 single/double; $350-$750 suite. **Rooms** 1,013. **Credit** AmEx, DC, Disc, MC, V. **Map** p404 E23 ⑤

Several films have been shot here, including *Wall Street*, *The French Connection* and, more recently, *Maid in Manhattan*. Built in 1924, the enormous hotel was once a haven for celebs and socialites, and a certain nostalgic grandeur lives on in the lobby, which is decked with fluted columns and acres of marble. The Madison Club Lounge (1-212 885 6192) dispenses cocktails in a gentleman's club-like setting. **Hotel services** *Ballroom. Fitness centre. Gift shop. Ticket desk. Valet.* **Room services** *High-speed wireless internet. PlayStation. Room service (24hrs).*

Budget

Americana Inn

69 W 38th Street, at Sixth Avenue (1-212 840 6700/www.newyorkhotel.com). Subway: B, D, F, N, Q, R, V, W to 34th Street-Herald Square; B, D, F, V to 42nd Street. **Rates** $95-$105 standard/double. **Rooms** 53. **Credit** AmEx, MC, V. **Map** p404 E24 ⑤
This budget hotel near Times Square, has a speakeasy feel: the signage is discreet, and you'll have to ring the doorbell to enter. What the Americana might lack in ambience (with its linoleum floors and fluorescent lighting), it makes up for in location (a rhinestone's throw from the major Broadway shows) and reasonable prices (rooms start at just under $100). And although all bathrooms are shared, rooms come with a mini-sink and large walk-in closets. **Hotel services** *Ticket desk. Modem. Shared kitchenette.*

Booty call

Hotel amenities that push the envelope.

While every hotel tries to edge out the competition by offering unique amenities to lure guests, a few manage to stand out from the crowd. Sometimes, it's the little things that can make a big difference, like the (often needed but rarely found in hotel bathrooms) toothbrush and toothpaste you'll find at the Lower East Side's recent arrival, **Blue Moon** (see p51). Of course, in a tough town like New York, it's going to take a lot more to really wow guests than complimentary brushing. Since most of us just want to be pampered with yummy bath products, our hats are off to **W New York-Times Square** (see p66) for its truly scrumptious Bliss body soaps and lotions. Nothing beats lemon and sage shower gel and body butter after a long day of pounding the pavements. Aiming for a lift of a different sort, the recently opened **Night Hotel** (see p66) supplies patrons with a fully loaded iPod, complete with three playlists (Day, Night and Late-night) compiled by local

DJs. Speaking of getting your groove on, over at **The Hotel on Rivington** (see p53), visitors who are in the mood for a little lovin' can indulge in the 'intimacy kit'. Put together by those wild, uninhibited gals at nearby Toys in Babeland (see p255), the goodie-bag contains condoms, lube and a bullet-shaped mini-vibrator. If it's spiritual cleansing you seek, on the other hand, look no further than the **Dream Hotel** (see p57). Upon check-in, you can fill out an Ayurveda-themed questionnaire to help pinpoint which of your doshas (vata, pitta or kapha) need balancing. Herbal products – to start the healing process – are delivered to your room.

Last but not least, we have to wax lyrical about the quality of service offered at the **Four Seasons** (see p57), where 'I need it now' hotel guests simply call the front desk to have their craving satisfied.

Intrepid travellers, get out there and get the goods!

aggressively charming that reservations fill up quickly. (Psst! There's no sign outside, so be sure to write down the address.)
Room services *High-speed wireless internet. Kitchenette and VCR in suites.*

Chelsea Star Hotel

300 W 30th Street, at Eighth Avenue (1-212 244 7827/1-877 827 6969/www.starhotelny.com). Subway: A, C, E to 34th Street-Penn Station. **Rates** $30 per person dorms; $69-$105 single/double/triple/quad with shared bath; $129-$149 double with private bath; $159-$179 suite. **Rooms** 30. **Credit** AmEx, MC, V. **Map** p403 D25 ⑫
Tired of sleeping in a boring beige box? Check in to this whimsical place, where your quarters might be decked out with Japanese paper screens (the Madame Butterfly). The 16 themed rooms are on the small side though less pricey, and lavatories are shared. A recent renovation more than doubled the hotel's size; there are now 18 superior rooms and deluxe suites with custom mahogany furnishings, flat-panel TVs and private baths. Ultra-cheap, shared hostel-style dorm rooms are also available. **Hotel services** *Bicycle and in-line-skate rental. Internet kiosk. Laundry. Safe-deposit boxes.* **Room services** *DVD and flat-panel TV in some rooms.*

Gershwin Hotel

7 E 27th Street, between Fifth & Madison Avenues (1-212 545 8000/www.gershwinhotel.com). Subway: N, R, W, 6 to 28th Street. **Rates** $30-$60 per person in 4- to 8-bed dorm; $109-$329 for 1-3 people in private room; $209-$369 suite. **Rooms** 58 beds in dorms; 133 private. **Credit** AmEx, MC, V. **Map** p404 E26 ⑬
Works by Lichtenstein line the hallways, and an original Warhol soup-can painting hangs in the lobby of this funky Pop Art-themed budget hotel. Rates are extremely reasonable for a location just off Fifth Avenue. All rooms received a facelift in 2005, which brought in new chairs and upholstery. If you can afford a suite, book the Lindfors (named after the building's designer), which has screen-printed walls and a sitting room. Just off the lobby, but unaffiliated, is Gallery at the Gershwin, a bar and lounge with glowing counter-tops and mod Lucite orbs.
Hotel services *Internet kiosk. Transportation desk.*

Hotel 17

225 E 17th Street, between Second & Third Avenues (1-212 475 2845/www.hotel17ny.com). Subway: L to Third Avenue; N, Q, R, W, 4, 5, 6 to 14th Street-Union Square. **Rates** $99-$120 single/double; $75-$150 triple. **Rooms** 120. **Credit** MC, V. **Map** p403 F27 ⑭
Equivalent to a good dive bar, Hotel 17's grungy cachet is the draw here. Except for a recent sprucing up of the lobby, the place remains a little rough and funky. The hotel has been used for numerous films (Woody Allen shot scenes from *Manhattan Murder Mystery* here), as well as magazine shoots. Labyrinthine corridors lead to tiny high-ceilinged rooms filled with discarded

Style for a steal, at **Hotel QT**. *See p71.*

Carlton Arms Hotel

160 E 25th Street, at Third Avenue (1-212 679 0680/www.carltonarms.com). Subway: 6 to 23rd Street. **Rates** $70-$87 single; $88-$101 double; $112-$122 triple. **Rooms** 54. **Credit** MC, V. **Map** p404 F26 ⑳
The Carlton Arms Art Project started in the late 1970s, when a small group of creative types brought new paint and fresh ideas to a run-down shelter. Today, the site – in the heart of Chelsea – is home to a bohemian, tastefully decorated and very clean hotel with themed spaces (check out the English-cottage room). Discounts are offered for students, overseas guests and patrons on weekly stays. Most guests share baths; tack on an extra $15 for a private lavatory. Rooms are usually booked early, so reserve well in advance.
Hotel services *Safe. Telephone in lobby.*

Chelsea Lodge

318 W 20th Street, between Eighth & Ninth Avenues (1-212 243 4499/www.chelsealodge. com). Subway: C, E to 23rd Street. **Rates** $99-$114 single/double with shared bath; $135-$150 deluxe with private bath; $195-$225 suite with private bath (each additional person $15; maximum 4 people). **Rooms** 26. **Credit** AmEx, DC, Disc, MC, V. **Map** p403 D27 ㉛
If Martha Stewart decorated a log cabin, it would end up looking something like this 22-room inn, which is housed in a landmark brownstone. All of the rooms (including the four suites down the block at 334 West 20th Street) have new beds, televisions, showers and air-conditioning. Although most are fairly small in size, the rooms are so

102Brownstone. *See p76.*

dressers and mismatched 1950s wallpaper. Expect to share the hallway bathroom with other guests. The affiliated Hotel 31 (*see below*) has less ambience, but it suffices as a Gramercy budget hotel.
Room services *VCR in some rooms.*

Hotel 31

120 E 31st Street, between Park Avenue South & Lexington Avenue (1-212 685 3060/www. hotel31.com). Subway: 6 to 33rd Street. **Rates** $85-$120 single/double; $125-$140 triple. **Rooms** 60. **Credit** MC, V. **Map** p404 E25 ⑤
For review, *see p73* Hotel 17.

Murray Hill Inn

143 E 30th Street, between Lexington & Third Avenues (1-212 683 6900/1-888 996 6376/ www.nyinns.com). Subway: 6 to 28th Street. **Rates** $89-$99 double with shared bath; $129 single/double with private bath. **Rooms** 50. **Credit** AmEx, MC, V. **Map** p404 F25 ⑥
A recent renovation to Murray Hill Inn added hardwood floors and new bathrooms – most of which are private – to this affordable inn. Discounted weekly and monthly rates are available. Book well in advance, or try the sister locations: Amsterdam Inn (*see p76*), Central Park Hostel (*see p76*) and Union Square Inn (*see p55*).

Hotel services *Complimentary breakfast. High-speed wireless internet. Flat-panel TVs.*

Hostels

Big Apple Hostel

119 W 45th Street, between Sixth & Seventh Avenues (1-212 302 2603/www.bigapplehostel.com). Subway: B, D, F, V to 42nd Street; N, Q, R, S, W, 1, 2, 3, 7 to Times Square-42nd Street. **Rates** $35-$60 dorm; $92 private room. **Rooms** 112 dorm beds; 11 private. **Credit** AmEx, DC, Disc, MC, V. **Map** p404 D23 ⑦
Increasingly popular with backpackers, this basic hostel is lacking in frills, but rooms are spotless and as cheap as they come. The Big Apple puts you just steps from the Theater District and Times Square. Beware if you're travelling in August: dorm rooms aren't air-conditioned. Take refuge in the breezy back patio, equipped with a grill for summer barbecues. Linens are provided, but remember to pack a towel.
Hostel services *Air-conditioning in private rooms.*

Chelsea Center

313 W 29th Street, between Eighth & Ninth Avenues (1-212 643 0214/www.chelseacenterhostel.com). Subway: A, C, E to 34th Street-Penn Station; 1 to 28th Street. **Rates** $35 per person in dorm. **Beds** 20.

Relive your student days in a small, women-only hostel with shared rooms and a communal kitchen and living area. Bathrooms are clean, and a patio garden is out back. Rooms are non-smoking and lack air-con, but the rate includes breakfast.
Hostel services *Garden. Internet. Kitchen. TV.*

Uptown

Expensive

Lucerne
201 W 79th Street, at Amsterdam Avenue (1-212 875 1000/1-800 492 8122/www.thelucerne hotel.com). Subway: 1 to 79th Street. **Rates** $210-$310 single/double; $220-$400 suite. **Rooms** 187. **Credit** AmEx, DC, Disc, MC, V. **Map** p405 C19 ⑥⑨
The elaborate pre-war façade and ornate columns of this historic hotel may fool you into thinking that the rooms are equally stunning. They are, however, far from fabulous. Instead, seek style in the hotel's breezy ground-floor French bistro, Nice Matin (1-212 873 6423), or on the rooftop patio, which offers lovely views of Central Park and the Hudson River.
Hotel services *Fitness centre.* **Room services** *High-speed internet. Plasma TV.*

Moderate

Bentley Hotel
500 E 62nd Street, at York Avenue (1-212 644 6000/1-888 664 6835/www.nychotels.com). Subway: F to Lexington-63rd Street; 4, 5, 6 to 59th Street. **Rates** $180-$300 single/double; $200-$275 suite. **Rooms** 200. **Credit** AmEx, DC, Disc, MC, V. **Map** p405 G22 ⑦⓪
It's hard to notice anything in the Bentley's sleek rooms other than the sweeping vistas from the floor-to-ceiling windows. Converted from an office building in 1998, this slender 21-storey hotel is an ideal getaway for weary execs, thanks to solid sound-proofing and blackout shades. Sip cappuccinos in the mahogany-panelled library or take in even more views from the glittering rooftop restaurant.
Hotel services *Complimentary pass to nearby gym.* **Room services** *CD player. Complimentary newspaper. High-speed wireless internet.*
Other locations: Ameritania Hotel, 230 W 54th Street, at Broadway, Midtown (1-888 664 6835); Amsterdam Court, 226 W 50th Street, between Broadway & Eighth Avenue, Midtown (1-888 664 6835); Marcel (*see p71*); Moderne, 243 W 55th Street, between Broadway & Eighth Avenue, Midtown (1-888 664 6835).

Country Inn the City
270 W 77th Street, between Broadway & West End Avenue (1-212 580 4183/1-800 572 4969/www.countryinnthecity.com). Subway: 1 to 79th Street. **Rates** $150-$210 single/double. **Rooms** 4. **No credit cards.** **Map** p405 C19 ⑦①
The name of this charming B&B on the West Side is pretty accurate: here, you can escape to the country without leaving the city. Four-poster beds, flagons of brandy and moose heads in the hallways make this intimate inn a special retreat.
Room services *Complimentary local phone calls. Kitchenette.*

Hotel Beacon
2130 Broadway, between 74th & 75th Streets (1-212 787 1100/1-800 572 4969/www.beaconhotel.com). Subway: 1, 2, 3 to 72nd Street. **Rates** $195-$265 single/double; $280-$600 suite. **Rooms** 245. **Credit** AmEx, DC, Disc, MC, V. **Map** p405 C20 ⑦②
The Hotel Beacon offers very good value in a desirable residential neighbourhood that's only a short walk from Central and Riverside Parks. Rooms are clean and spacious and include marble baths. For only $5, guests can purchase a pass to the nearby Synergy gym. But make sure you quell your post-workout hunger at the classic diner Viand Café.
Hotel services *Babysitting. Internet.* **Room services** *Kitchenette.*

Hotel Belleclaire
250 W 77th Street, at Broadway (1-212 362 7700/www.hotelbelleclaire.com). Subway: 1 to 79th Street. **Rates** $100-$119 single with shared bath; $189-$219 single/double with private bath; $229-$289 suite. **Rooms** 200. **Credit** AmEx, DC, Disc, MC, V. **Map** p405 C19 ⑦③

Housed in a landmark building near Lincoln Center and Central Park, the sleek Belleclaire is a steal for savvy budget travellers. Rooms feature goose-down comforters, sleek padded headboards and mod lighting fixtures. Every room comes with a refrigerator – perfect for chilling your protein shake while you're hitting the state-of-the-art fitness centre. **Hotel services** *Fitness centre. Gift shop. Massage service. Mobile phone rental.* **Room services** *CD player. Direct-dial phone numbers. Internet. Nintendo.*

Marrakech

2688 Broadway at 103rd Street (1-212 222 2954). Subway: 1 to 103rd Street. **Rates** $160-$220 single/double. **Rooms** 125. **Credit** AmEx, DC, Disc, MC, V. **Map** p406 C16 ⑦
Nightclub and restaurant designer Lionel Ohayon (Crobar, Koi) was enlisted to make over this newly renovated Upper West Side hotel, formerly the Hotel Malibu. As the name implies, rooms are warm-toned with simple Moroccan embellishments. The clean no-frills hotel is likely to appeal to twentysomethings who are not that interested in amenities (which are few), or bothered by the fact that there is no elevator. **Hotel services** *High-speed internet in lobby.* **Room services** *Plasma TV.*

On the Ave Hotel

222 W 77th Street, between Broadway & Amsterdam (1-212 362 1100/1-800 509 7598/www.ontheave-nyc.com). Subway: 1 to 79th Street. **Rates** $129-$229 single/double; $350-$450 suite; $459 penthouse. **Rooms** 266. **Credit** AmEx, DC, Disc, MC, V. **Map** p405 C19 ⑦
Stylish additions to On the Ave include industrial-style bathroom sinks and penthouse suites with fantastic balcony views of Central Park. (All guests have access to a balcony on the 16th floor of the hotel.) On the Ave's Citylife Hotel Group sibling is Hotel Thirty Thirty (*see p71*). **Hotel services** *Video library.* **Room services** *CD player. Complimentary newspaper. High-speed internet. Plasma TV. VCR.*

102Brownstone

102 W 118th Street, between Malcolm X Boulevard (Lenox Avenue) & Adam Clayton Powell Jr Boulevard (Seventh Avenue) (1-212 662 4223/www.102brownstone.com). Subway: 2, 3 to 116th Street. **Rates** $250 studio apartment; $200 suite. **Rooms** 6. **Credit** AmEx, MC, V. **Map** p407 D14 ⑦
Located near Marcus Garvey Park on a landmark, tree-lined street, 102 features five substantial suites, all renovated and individually themed by lively proprietor Lizette Lanoue, who owns and lives in the 1892 Greek Revival row house with her husband. She says 102 is 'not your typical B&B. We aren't up in your face. We want to give you the experience of what it would be like to live here in Harlem, in your own apartment'. **Photos** *p74 and p75.* **B&B services** *DVD player. High-speed internet. Jacuzzi. Kitchenette in some rooms.*

Budget

Amsterdam Inn

340 Amsterdam Avenue, at 76th Street (1-212 579 7500/www.amsterdaminn.com). Subway: 1 to 79th Street. **Rates** $89-$109 single/double with shared bath; $109-$169 with private bath. **Rooms** 30. **Credit** AmEx, MC, V. **Map** p405 C19 ⑦
For review, *see p74* Murray Hill Inn.

Efuru Guest House

106 W 120th Street, at Malcolm X Boulevard (Lenox Avenue) (1-212 961 9855/www.efuru-nyc.com). Subway: 2, 3 to 116th Street. **Rates** $95-$135 double with shared or private bath. **Rooms** 3. **Credit** MC, V. **Map** p407 D14 ⑦
Efuru, a Nigerian word meaning 'daughter of heaven', is the brainchild of Lydia Smith, who bought the once-abandoned property through a lottery system in the late 1990s, and then endured a five-year renovation process. The result is a homey inn where guests can enjoy total privacy (each garden-level room has an entrance and patio) or mingle in a communal living room decorated with antique couches and a working fireplace. The three suites, painted in serene hues of green and blue, are basic but clean and comfy. All have queen beds and refrigerators, most have private baths and some have a kitchenette. **B&B services** *Garden. High-speed internet. Kitchenette in some rooms. TV in rooms.*

Harlem Flophouse

242 W 123rd Street, between Adam Clayton Powell Jr Boulevard (Seventh Avenue) & Frederick Douglass Boulevard (1-212 662 0678/www.harlemflophouse.com). Subway: A, C, B, D to 125th Street. **Rates** $100-$150 single/double with shared bath. **Rooms** 4. **Credit** MC, V. **Map** p407 D14 ⑦
The dark-wood interior, moody lighting and lilting jazz make the Flophouse feel more like a 1930s speakeasy than a 21st-century B&B. The airy suites have restored tin ceilings, glamorous chandeliers and working sinks in antique cabinets. For $15 per person ($25 per couple), you can eat a home-cooked breakfast in the communal dining room or garden. Want to stay in your PJs? A staff member will bring your meal to your room. **Hotel services** *Garden. High-speed wireless internet. Laundry service.* **Room services** *Private sink and dressing areas.*

Hostels

Central Park Hostel

19 W 103rd Street, at Central Park West (1-212 678 0491/www.centralparkhostel.com). Subway: B, C to 103rd Street. **Rates** $29-$45 for a bed in shared room; $109-$149 private room with shared bath. **Beds** 250. **Credit** MC, V. **Map** p406 D16 ⑦
Housed in a recently renovated brownstone, this tidy hostel offers dorm-style rooms that sleep four, six or eight people; private chambers with two beds are also available. All baths are shared. **Hostel services** *Lockers. Travel desk.*

Hostelling International New York

891 Amsterdam Avenue, at 103rd Street (1-212 932 2300/www.hinewyork.org). Subway: 1 to 103rd Street. **Rates** *$29-$40 dorm rooms; $120 family rooms; $135 private room with bath.* **Beds** *624.* **Credit** *AmEx, DC, MC, V.* **Map** *p406 C16* ㉛
This budget lodging is actually the city's only 'real' hostel (being a non-profit accommodation that belongs to the International Youth Hostel Federation), but it's also one of the most architecturally stunning. The gabled, Gothic-inspired brick-and-stone building spans the length of an entire city block. The immaculate rooms are spare but air conditioned and there is a shared kitchen and a large backyard.
Hostel services *Café. Conference facility. Courtyard. Fax. Games room. Gift shop. Internet kiosk. Library. Lockers. Self-service laundry. Shuttles. Travel desk. TV lounge.* **Room services** *Air-conditioning.*

International House

500 Riverside Drive, at Tiemann Place (1-212 316 8436/www.ihouse-nyc.org). Subway: 1 to 125th Street. **Rates** *$120-$130 single; $135-$145 double/suite.* **Rooms** *11.* **Credit** *MC, V.* **Map** *p407 B13* ㉜
Primarily a dormitory for foreign graduate students, this housing facility is a good reliable bet for short-term summer travellers (when all the students have checked out). Located on a peaceful block overlooking Grant's Tomb and the small but well-tended Sakura Park, this hostel has simple rooms with private bathrooms and refrigerators.
Hostel services *Bar. Cafeteria. Self-service laundry.* **Room services** *Air-conditioning. Cable TV.*

Jazz on the Park Hostel

36 W 106th Street, between Central Park West & Manhattan Avenue (1-212 932 1600/www.jazzon thepark.com). Subway: B, C to 103rd Street. **Rates** *$27-$32, 4- to 12-bed dorm; $50-$90 2-bed dorm (maximum 2 people); $90-$130 private room with bath.* **Beds** *310.* **Credit** *MC, V.* **Map** *p406 D16* ㉝
Jazz on the Park might be the trendiest hostel in the city – the lounge is kitted out like a space-age techno club and sports a piano and pool table. But some visitors have been known to complain about the customer service, so make sure to double-check your room type and check-in date before you arrive. In summer, the back patio hosts a weekly barbecue. Linens and a continental breakfast are complimentary, while lockers come with a surcharge.
Hostel services *Air-conditioning. Café. Complimentary breakfast. Fax. Internet. Private lockers. Self-service laundry. TV room.* **Other locations**: Jazz on the Town Hostel, 307 E 14th Street, between First & Second Avenues, East Village/Gramercy Park (1-212 228 2780); Jazz on Harlem, 104 W 128th Street, between Adam Clayton Powell Jr Boulevard (Seventh Avenue) & Malcolm X Boulevard (Lenox Avenue), Harlem (1-212 222 5779).

Brooklyn

Expensive

Bed & Breakfast on the Park

113 Prospect Park West, between 6th & 7th Streets, Park Slope (1-718 499 6115/www.bbnyc. com). Subway: F to Seventh Avenue. **Rates** *$155-$300 single/double; $250-$325 suite.* **Rooms** *7.* **Credit** *AmEx, MC, V (cheques preferred).* **Map** *p410 T12* ㉞
Staying at this 1895 parkside brownstone is like taking up residence on the set of *The Age of Innocence.* The parlour floor is crammed with antique furniture, and guest rooms are furnished with love seats and canopy beds swathed in French linens.

Moderate

Akwaaba Mansion

347 MacDonough Street, between Lewis & Stuyvesant Avenues, Bedford-Stuyvesant (1-718 455 5958/www.akwaaba.com). Subway: A, C to Utica Avenue. **Rates** *$150 single/double weekdays; $165 single/double weekends (each additional person $30, maximum 4 people).* **Rooms** *4.* **Credit** *MC, V.* **Map** *p410 W10* ㉟
Akwaaba means 'welcome' in Ghanaian, a fitting name for this gorgeous restored 1860s mansion with a wide screened-in porch and flower gardens. The individually themed rooms are decorated with African artefacts and textiles. A hearty Southern-style breakfast and complimentary afternoon tea are served in the dining room or on the porch.

Awesome Bed & Breakfast

136 Lawrence Street, between Fulton & Willoughby Streets, Fort Greene (1-718 858 4859/ www.awesome-bed-and-breakfast.com). Subway: A, C, F to Jay Street-Borough Hall; M, R to Lawrence Street; 2, 3 to Hoyt Street. **Rates** *$99-$130 single/double; $140-$150 triple/quad.* **Rooms** *7.* **Credit** *AmEx, MC, V.* **Map** *p410 T10* ㊱
'Awesome' isn't normally a word used to describe a B&B, but this bi-level guesthouse is an exception. The themed rooms could be a setting for MTV's *The Real World*, with details like giant daisies and purple drapes. The equally snazzy bathrooms are communal, and a complimentary breakfast is delivered to your door promptly at 8am. Plans to double the capacity are in the works.

Union Street Bed & Breakfast

405 Union Street, between Hoyt & Smith Streets, Carroll Gardens (1-718 852 8406). Subway: F, G to Carroll Street. **Rates** *$100 single; $165 double.* **Rooms** *7.* **Credit** *AmEx, MC, V.* **Map** *p410 S10* ㊲
This quasi-Victorian-style inn is housed in an 1898 brownstone with a pleasant back garden. Room prices decrease with each additional night's stay. Great restaurants are just steps away on Smith Street, Brooklyn's restaurant row.

5 FAMOUS ATTRACTIONS
ONE AMAZING PRICE
AVOID MOST TICKET LINES

Empire State Building Observatory

2 hour Circle Line Harbor Cruise

American Museum of Natural History

Museum of Modern Art

Guggenheim Museum

VALID 9 DAYS

ON SALE AT THESE ATTRACTIONS.
Buy it at the first one you visit! For more info visit **www.citypass.com** or call **(707) 256-0490**.
Pricing and programs are subject to change.

Only **$59.00**
A $112.00 Value
(Youth 6-17 $49.0

Atlanta · Boston · Chicago · Hollywood · Philadelphia · San Francisco · Seattle · So. California · Toron

Sightseeing

Introduction

Getting the most out of the action-packed metropolis.

Most newcomers arriving in New York City have a pretty good idea what they're in for – non-stop sightseeing, shopping, eating and drinking. Then there's dancing, art gazing and people-watching. No, visiting New York is not for the easily winded. You'll fare better if you devise even the most rudimentary plan of attack. Start by jotting down a few of your must-see and -do destinations. Remember, whole days can be spent wandering such enormous institutions as the Metropolitan Museum of Art or the American Museum of Natural History. If that's exactly how you want to spend your time, hey, we certainly won't judge you. But if you are looking to see as much as possible then plan on spending just a few hours at your destination of choice. Walk across the Brooklyn Bridge (*see p162* **Step to it**), take in the jaw-dropping view at the top of the Rockefeller (*see p128* **Top this!**) or stroll through Central Park (*see p134* **Step to it**). Then, catch your breath: hang out at a café or raise a glass at a neighbourhood bar. And, for God's sake, don't be shy – maybe that conversation you strike up could lead you to one of the city's many hidden gems just waiting to be discovered.

THE LIE OF THE LAND

New York City is made up of five boroughs: Brooklyn, the Bronx, Manhattan, Queens and Staten Island. What the island of Manhattan lacks in land mass (it's the smallest of the bunch), it more than makes up for in cultural and commercial power. Manhattan is bordered by New Jersey, just over the Hudson River, to the west; Brooklyn and Queens are due east, on the other side of the East River; the Bronx is just to the north, above the Harlem River; and Staten Island is south, at the mouth of New York Harbor. Within each borough, areas of varying size are broken down into neighbourhoods like Midtown, Chinatown and the Upper East Side (*see p82* **New York at a glance**), all marked on the maps at the back of this book.

New York at a glance

Broadway & Times Square (p123)
Night-time under the world's most famous array of twinkling lights is positively thrilling.

Chelsea (p114)
The city's gayest neighbourhood is also home to hundreds of art galleries west of Tenth Avenue, between 19th and 26th Streets.

Chinatown (p102)
You'll feel like you are in another country walking among the Asian restaurants and groceries here. Canal Street offers myriad designer knock-offs.

East Village (p107)
Tompkins Square Park (just off Avenue A) is the heart of this young, edgy 'hood. No specific tourist destinations to mention (aside from now-defunct CBGB), but fun to wander nonetheless.

Fifth Avenue (p125)
The well-heeled still shop here (Tiffany's, Cartier, Bergdorf Goodman), but mall stores are beginning to nudge in on the action. Landmarks aplenty, among them the Empire State Building, Rockefeller Center, St Patrick's Cathedral.

Greenwich Village (p110)
Leafy streets and bohemian Washington Square Park, where folks embrace a slower pace. Literary associations abound.

Harlem (p148)
Broad, sunny boulevards with stunning examples of late 19th- and early 20th-century architecture. And soul food galore.

Lower East Side (p105)
See how waves of immigrants lived at the Lower East Side Tenement Museum. Today, young hipsters have recently opened up all kinds of indie boutiques and hot new bars, but the delis and pickle shops remain.

Midtown East (p131)
Lots of office buildings and bustling streets, but it's the United Nations and Grand Central Terminal that beckon.

Soho (p101)
The city's former art district is now a must-see stop for trendy shoppers. Tons of cafés and restaurants to cool your heels.

Tribeca (p101)
Actor Robert De Niro put this area on the map when he debuted the Tribeca Film Festival here in 2002. Chic bars and restaurants nestle among warehouses (now loft apartments).

Upper East Side (p137)
Super-rich and important, full of embassies and billionaires. Museums such as the Met and the Guggenheim up the culture quotient.

Upper West Side (p143)
Lovely turn-of-the-century architecture and lush green havens on either side (Central Park to the east, Riverside Park to the west).

Wall Street (p97)
The oldest area of the city and the epicentre of capitalism. Offers a glimpse of traders (between trades) and a chance to stroll narrow streets darkened by skyscrapers. Home of the New York Stock Exchange and Trinity Church.

West Village & Meatpacking District (p112)
Quiet, cobblestone streets offer plenty of opportunity to peer into picturesque 19th-century brownstones. The trendy restaurants and bars on Ninth Avenue buzz at night.

Beyond Manhattan
Particularly worth the trip over to Brooklyn are **Williamsburg** (see *p164*), with dozens of über-hip cafés, bars and shops; **Brooklyn Heights** (*p154*) and its breathtaking views; and Coney Island's **Astroland Amusement Park** (*p165*).

STREET SMARTS
Setting out into our teeming streets, we guarantee that you're going to feel overwhelmed, if not downright lost. Take heart: although much of Manhattan is laid out on a grid system, even New Yorkers get turned around and frequently can't remember which way is which. The older streets of Lower Manhattan, in particular, can cause confusion. Your best bet is to take a few moments to study our maps on pages 402-412 before hitting the streets, and to read the **Getting Around** section (*see p368*) at the back of this book.

VISITING MUSEUMS
Visiting several venues in a single day can be exhausting. Similarly, it's self-defeating to attempt to hit all the major collections during one visit to an institution as large as

the Met or the American Museum of Natural History. So plan, pace yourself, and don't forget to eat: a host of excellent museum cafés and restaurants afford convenient breaks. Delicious spots for refuelling include Sarabeth's at the **Whitney Museum of American Art** (*see p138*); the elegant Café Sabarsky at the **Neue Galerie** (*see p138*); the **Jewish Museum**'s Café Weissman (*see p139*); and a more formal option, the Modern, at the **Museum of Modern Art** (MoMA; *see p127*). It may be tempting to save museums for a rainy day, but remember that most sites offer cool, air-conditioned relief on sticky summer days and cosy warmth come winter.

If the weather is too gorgeous to stay indoors, bear in mind that gardens are the hidden gems of several New York museums. The Brooklyn Museum abuts the **Brooklyn Botanic Garden** (*see p161*) where enticements include a Japanese garden complete with pavilion, wooden bridges and a Shinto shrine. The **Cloisters** (*see p153*), in northern Manhattan's Fort Tryon Park, was John D Rockefeller's gift to New York. The reconstructed monastery houses the Met's stellar collection of medieval art. In summer, bring a picnic and relax on lush grounds that provide spectacular views of the Hudson River and the rocky cliffs of New Jersey's Palisades.

Sightseeing

Hands up to the **Statue of Liberty**.
See p91.

Sightseeing

Brace yourself for local admission prices; they can be steep (tickets to the recently renovated MoMA cost $20 per adult). This is because most of the city's museums are privately funded and receive little or no government support. Even so, a majority of them, including MoMA, the Whitney and the Guggenheim, either waive admission fees or make them voluntary at least one evening a week. Most museums also offer discounts to students and senior citizens with valid IDs. And although the Met suggests a $12 donation for adults, you can pay what you wish whenever you visit.

Nothing is more exciting than discovering the secrets of a new museum on your own, but many institutions offer tours that are both entertaining and educational. For example, the audio tour at the **Ellis Island Immigration Museum** (*see p95*) and the (mandatory) guided tours at the **Lower East Side Tenement Museum** (*see p105*) and the **Museum of Jewish Heritage** (*see p96*) offer fascinating insights into NYC's immigrant roots.

Most New York museums are closed on major US holidays (*see p383* **Holidays**). Nevertheless, some institutions are open on certain Monday holidays, such as Columbus Day and Presidents' Day. A few places, like **Dia:Beacon** (*see p357*) and the **Queens Museum of Art** (*see p169*), change their hours seasonally; it's wise to call before setting out.

Security has been tightened at most museums. Guards at all public institutions will ask you to open your bag or backpack for inspection; umbrellas and large bags must be checked (free of charge) at a cloakroom.

Most museums are accessible to people with disabilities, and furnish free wheelchairs.

PACKAGE DEALS

If you're planning to take in multiple museums – and you're likely to add a Circle Line tour or a visit to a major attraction – consider buying a nine-day **CityPass** for $63 ($46 6-17s, free under-6s), which also allows you to bypass the first queue at the Empire State Building. Similarly, the **New York Pass** covers entry to over 40 of the city's top attractions and cultural institutions, and gives discounts on shopping, eating and other activities. The card is $54 for the day ($39 2-12s) and $144 for the week ($104 2-12s). You can compare benefits and buy at www.citypass.com and www.newyorkpass.com.

What price vice?

Don't do the crime if you can't pay the fine.

New York's anything-goes era is long gone, but some of us still insist on behaving naughtily in plain view. To better weigh up the risks of sparking up that spliff on your hotel steps, consider these penalties for the most popular public transgressions. Note to foreigners: in addition to the fine, you just might find yourself deported, never to return again. Judge wisely!

Open container of alcohol on the street: $25

It's a mere $25 ticket, payable by mail. And the cops are unlikely to be fooled by the old paper-bag trick.

Smoking a cigarette inside a bar: $100

The law allows for up to a $100 fine, although this ticket is almost never issued.

Playing your music too loudly: $250

Disturbing the peace is one of the most common charges in the city, and can mean 15 days in the can or $250 out of your pocket.

Sex on the beach: $500

The law calls it 'public lewdness'. It's $500 plus three months behind bars, where sex ain't so nice.

Smoking a joint: $500

A class-B misdemeanour that can cost you up to three months in the pokey, and your savings up in smoke.

Jumping the subway turnstile: $1,000

That's called stealing city services, a class-A misdemeanour, punishable by up to a year in jail and a $1,000 fine – way more than a MetroCard.

Urinating in public: $2,000

Fines range from $50 all the way to a pissed-away $2,000, depending on what violation the cop decides to hit you with.

Letting off fireworks: $10,000

The NYPD declared zero tolerance for fireworks in 2006, and getting caught could cost you $1,000-$10,000 or up to 30 days in jail.

84 Time Out New York

Sightseeing

Flatiron Building. *See p119.*

New York City.
Now in convenient
wallet size.

MetroCard can take you to all the famous places in the entire city. And, with an Unlimited Ride Card, you can hop on and off New York City Transit subways and local buses as many times as you like, all day long. It's the fastest, least expensive way to see it all.

You can choose from several Unlimited Ride MetroCards, including our 1-Day Fun Pass and our 7-Day Unlimited Ride MetroCard.

You can buy MetroCard at many hotels, the New York Convention & Visitors Bureau (810 7th Avenue at 53rd Street), the New York Transit Museum in Brooklyn Heights, and at the Museum's Gallery & Store at Grand Central Terminal. You can also buy it at subway station vending machines with your debit or credit card, or cash.

Visit **www.mta.info** and click on the MetroCard icon to get MetroCard information, including promotions, and tips for travel and sightseeing. Or call 800-METROCARD (800-638-7622); in NYC, 212-METROCARD. And remember to keep MetroCard in your wallet at all times. Welcome to New York!

New York City Transit *Going your way*

www.mta.info

Tour New York

See the city's best places and faces in style.

There are just too many must-see attractions to cram into a single visit to New York; but, thankfully, there's also a myriad of options to help you take in the sites. You can sit back and enjoy the ride on a double-decker bus, rickshaw or ferry. If you need a bit more personal control, you can rent a bike or pound the pavement, or take a walking tour. For additional inspiration, refer to the Around Town section of *Time Out New York* magazine, where you'll find a weekly listing of urban outings.

By bicycle

For more city biking, *see pp336-337*.

Bike the Big Apple

1-877 865 0078/www.bikethebigapple.com. **Tours** Call or visit website for schedule. **Tickets** $49-$69 (includes bicycle & helmet rental). **Credit** AmEx, DC, Disc, MC, V.

Licensed guides take cyclists through both historic and newly hip neighbourhoods. Half- and full-day rides are family-friendly and gently paced, and they can be customised to your interests and riding level. Check the website for seasonal events and deals.

Central Park Bike Tours

Bite of the Apple Tours (1-212 541 8759/www. centralparkbiketour.com). **Tours** *Apr-Oct* 9am, 10am, 11am, 1pm, 4pm daily. *Nov-Mar* by reservation only. **Tickets** $35; $20 under-15s (includes bicycle rental). **Credit** AmEx, Disc, MC, V.

Bite of the Apple focuses on Central Park. The main tour visits the John Lennon memorial at Strawberry Fields, Belvedere Castle and the Shakespeare Garden. Film buffs will enjoy the Central Park Movie Scenes Bike Tour (10am, 1pm, 4pm Sat, Sun), passing locations for *When Harry Met Sally…* and *Wall Street*. Most tours run a leisurely two hours; hard-core cyclists might consider the three-hour Manhattan Island Bicycle Tour ($45, by appointment only).

By boat

Adirondack

Chelsea Piers, Pier 62, 22nd Street, at the Hudson River (1-646 336 5270/www.sail-nyc.com). Subway: C, E to 23rd Street. **Tours** *1 May-15 Oct* 1pm, 3.30pm, 6pm, 8.30pm daily. **Tickets** $35 for day sails; $50 for evening & Sunday-brunch sails. **Credit** AmEx, MC, V.

Built in 1994, the *Adirondack* is a beautiful three-masted replica of a classic 19th-century schooner. Sip your complimentary glass of wine (or beer) as

the ship sails from Chelsea Piers to Battery Park, past Ellis Island, to the Statue of Liberty and around to Governors Island and the Brooklyn Bridge.

Circle Line Cruises

Pier 83, 42nd Street, at the Hudson River (1-212 563 3200/www.circleline.com). Subway: A, C, E to 42nd Street-Port Authority. **Tours** Call or visit website for schedule. **Tickets** $29 for 3hrs; $24 seniors; $16 children. **Credit** AmEx, DC, Disc, MC, V.

Circle Line's famed three-hour guided circumnavigation of Manhattan is a fantastic way to see the city's sights. The themed tours include a New Year's Eve cruise, a DJ dance party or an autumn foliage ride to Bear Mountain in the Hudson Valley. From April to October, there's a fun 30-minute speedboat ride on *The Beast*.
Other locations: South Street Seaport, Pier 16, by Burling Slip & Fulton Street, Downtown (1-212 630 8888).

Less legwork, more sights. *See p88.*

NY Waterway

*Pier 78, 38th Street, at the Hudson River (1-800
533 3779/www.nywaterway.com). Subway: A, C,
E to 42nd Street-Port Authority.* **Tours** Call or
visit website for schedule. **Tickets** 2hr Manhattan
cruise $24; $20 seniors; $13 children. **Credit**
AmEx, Disc, MC, V.

The scenic two-hour ride makes a complete circuit
around Manhattan's landmarks. A 60-minute tour
focuses on the skyline of lower Manhattan.
Other locations: World Financial Center Pier,
Pier 11, Wall Street, Downtown.

Pioneer

*South Street Seaport Museum, 207 Front Street,
between Beekman & Fulton Streets (1-212 748 8786/
www.southstreetseaportmuseum.org). Subway: A, C
to Broadway-Nassau Street; J, M, Z, 2, 3, 4, 5 to
Fulton Street.* **Tours** Call for schedule. **Tickets**
$30; $15 under-12s. **Credit** AmEx, MC, V.

Built in 1885, the 102ft *Pioneer* is the only iron-hulled
merchant sailing ship still in existence. Sails billow
as you cruise the East River and New York Harbor.
Educational children's programmes are also offered.

Shearwater Sailing

*North Cove, Hudson River, between Liberty
& Vesey Streets (1-212 619 0885/1-800 544 1224/
www.shearwatersailing.com). Subway: R, W to City
Hall; A, C, 2, 3, 4, 5 to Fulton Street/Broadway-
Nassau Street.* **Tours** 15 Apr-15 Oct 5 times daily.
Call for schedule. **Tickets** $45; $25 children.
Credit AmEx, DC, Disc, MC, V.

Set sail on the *Shearwater*, an 82ft luxury yacht built
in 1929. The champagne brunch or full-moon sail
options are lovely ways to take in the skyline.

Staten Island Ferry

*Battery Park, South Street, at Whitehall Street
(1-718 727 2508/www.siferry.com). Subway: 1 to
South Ferry; 4, 5 to Bowling Green.* **Open** 24hrs
daily. **Tickets** free.

During this commuter barge's 25-minute crossing,
you get superb panoramas of lower Manhattan and
the Statue of Liberty. Boats leave South Ferry at
Battery Park. Call or see the website for schedules.

By bus

Gray Line

*777 Eighth Avenue, between 47th & 48th Streets
(1-212 445 0848/1-800 669 0051 ext 3/www.gray
linenewyork.com). Subway: A, C, E to 42nd Street-Port
Authority.* **Tours** Call or visit website for schedule.
Tickets $37-$81. **Credit** AmEx, Disc, MC, V.

This is your grandma's classic red double-decker
(the line runs other buses too), but with something
to interest everyone. Gray Line offers more than 20
bus tours, from a basic two-hour ride (with more
than 40 hop-on, hop-off stops) to the guided
Manhattan Comprehensive, which lasts eight and a
half hours and includes lunch, admission to the
United Nations tour and a boat ride to Ellis Island
and the Statue of Liberty.

By helicopter, carriage or rickshaw

Liberty Helicopter Tours

*Downtown Manhattan Heliport, Pier 6, East
River, between Broad Street & Old Slip (1-212 967
6464/1-800 542 9933/www.libertyhelicopters.com).
Subway: R, W to Whitehall Street; 1 to South Ferry.*
Tours 9am-7pm daily. **Tickets** $69-$186.
Credit AmEx, MC, V.

There'll be no daredevil swooping and diving
(Liberty's helicopters provide a fairly smooth flight)
but the views are excitement enough. Even a five-
minute ride (durations vary) is long enough to get a
thrilling look at the Empire State Building.
Other locations: VIP Heliport, Twelfth Avenue, at
30th Street, Midtown.

Manhattan Carriage Company

*200 Central Park South, at Seventh Avenue
(1-212 664 1149/www.ajnfineart.com/mcc.html).
Subway: N, Q, R, W to 57th Street.* **Tours** 10am-
2am Mon-Fri; 8am-2am Sat, Sun. **Tickets** $40/
20min ride (extended rides by reservation
only). Hours and prices vary during holidays.
Credit AmEx, MC, V (reserved tours only).

The beauty of Central Park seems even more romantic from the seat of a horse-drawn carriage. Choose
your coach from those lined up on the streets along
the southern end of the park, or book in advance.

Manhattan Rickshaw Company

1-212 604 4729/www.manhattanrickshaw.com.
Tours noon-midnight Tue-Sun and by appointment.
Tickets $10-$50, depending on duration and number
of passengers. **No credit cards.**

Manhattan Rickshaw Company's pedicabs operate
in Greenwich Village, Soho, Times Square and the
Theater District. If you see one that's available, hail
the driver. (Determine your fare before you jump
in.) For a pre-arranged pick-up, make reservations
24 hours in advance.

On foot

Adventure on a Shoestring

1-212 265 2663. **Tours** Mon-Sun. Call for schedule
and reservations. **Tickets** $5. **No credit cards.**

The motto of this organisation, now in its 44th year,
is 'Exploring the world within our reach... within
our means', and founder Howard Goldberg is dedicated to revealing the 'real' New York. Walks take
you from one charming neighbourhood to another,
and topics can include Millionaire's Row and
Haunted Greenwich Village. Special celebrity theme
tours, including tributes to Jackie O, Katharine
Hepburn and Marilyn Monroe, are also available.

Big Onion Walking Tours

1-212 439 1090/www.bigonion.com. **Tours** Sept-
May 11am, 1pm and major holidays. June-Aug 1pm,
5pm Mon, Wed-Sun. **Tickets** $15; $12 seniors; $10
students. **No credit cards.**

Cab fabulous

2007 marks the 100th anniversary of the gas-powered taxi in New York City. Today, more than 13,000 cabs blaze through the city's streets, with many racking up as many as 70,000 miles a year on their odometers. While the vast majority (11,637, at last count) are the Ford Crown Victoria model, the fleet also boasts just over 1,000 mini-vans and a few dozen Ford Explorer sports utility vehicles. Recently, they have even bumped up the number of alternative fuel cabs to 254, and 54 cabs are now wheelchair accessible.

In coming years, the taxicab as we know it may get a makeover. In 2006 city officials, taxi commission honchos and designers launched a campaign to redesign the city's taxicabs – and we're not talking about just adding more legroom. Ideas that have surfaced include sunroofs, front passenger seats that face the backseat, and the possibility of hailing a cab with a mobile phone. But that flashy shade of yellow is staying put.

You can see some of the new designs on display in April 2007 at the New York International Auto Show (*see p261*).

New York was known as the Big Onion before it became the Big Apple. The tour guides will explain why, and they should know – all guides hold advanced degrees in history (or a related field), resulting in astoundingly informative tours of the city's historic districts and ethnic neighbourhoods. Check the website for meeting locations. Private tours are also available.

Bronx Tours

1-646 685 7725/www.bronxtours.net. **Tours** Call for schedule and to make reservations. **Tickets** $40. **Credit** AmEx, Disc, MC, V.
On these van tours, Bronx native Maurice Valentine shows that there's more to his borough than Yankee Stadium and the Bronx Zoo. Hip hop music provides a funky aural backdrop as passengers are guided through unsung neighbourhoods like Fordham, Hunts Point and Mott Haven.

Greenwich Village Literary Pub Crawl

1-212 613 5796/www.geocities.com/newensemble. *Tour meets at the White Horse Tavern, 567 Hudson Street, at 11th Street. Subway: 1 to Christopher Street-Sheridan Square.* **Tours** 2pm Sat (reservations requested). **Tickets** $15; $12 seniors, students (drinks not included). **No credit cards**.
Local actors from the New Ensemble Theatre Company take you to the past haunts of famous writers. Watering stops include Chumley's (a former speakeasy) and Cedar Tavern, where Jack Kerouac and a generation of abstract expressionist painters, including Jackson Pollock, drank with their peers.

Harlem Heritage Tours

1-212 280 7888/www.harlemheritage.com. **Tours** Call or visit website for schedule and meeting locations. **Tickets** $20-$100 (reservations required). **Credit** AmEx, MC, V.

Sightseeing

Now operating more than 15 bus and walking tours, Harlem Heritage aims to show visitors the soul of the borough. The Harlem Song, Harlem Nights tour takes tourists to landmarks like the Apollo Theater. The Renaissance tour walks you to Prohibition-era speakeasies, clubs and one-time residences of artists, writers and musicians.

Municipal Art Society Tours

1-212 935 3960/recorded information 1-212 439 1049/www.mas.org. **Tours** Call or visit website for schedule and meeting locations. **Tickets** $12-$15 weekends; $10-$12 weekdays (reservations may be required for some tours). **No credit cards**.
The Municipal Art Society (MAS) organises bus and walking tours in New York and even New Jersey. Many – like Art Deco Midtown – reflect the society's focus on contemporary architecture, urban planning and historic preservation. There's also a free guided walk through Grand Central Terminal on Wednesdays at 12.30pm (suggested donation $10). Private tours are available by appointment.

Rock 'n' Roll Walking Tour

Rock Junket NYC (1-212 696 6578/www.rock junket.com). **Tours** Mon-Fri by appointment; 1pm Sat. **Tickets** $20. **No credit cards**.
Rocker guides and liggers supreme Bobby Pinn and Ginger Ail lead this East Village walk to legendary rock, punk and glam sites (from famous album-cover locations, to where the Ramones called home) from the 1960s to the present day.

Soundwalk

1-212 674 7407/www.soundwalk.com. **Tours** CDs and MP3s are available for purchase from website and in various stores. **Tickets** vary.
These inventive self-guided audio tours ('for people who don't normally take audio tours') provide insight into life in Chinatown, Times Square, Little Italy, Dumbo and other neighbourhoods. The cinematic soundtracks layer the voices of narrators, selected for their connection to the 'hood, with sound clips and street noises. Writer Paul Auster recently narrated the Ground Zero Sonic Memorial Soundwalk.

Downtown

The seeds of the Big Apple.

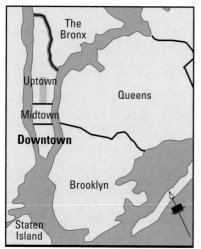

Manhattan's downtown neighbourhoods are a microcosm of nearly everything that's going on in the rest of the city. The swankification of the shops in the West Village, the condo-isation of the Lower East Side and the East Village, the rejuvenation of Chinatown and even the rebirth of the area around Ground Zero – these developments mirror similar debates and changes taking place in all five boroughs. But here, like nowhere else in the city, the small, amorphously shaped neighbourhoods bump against each other, and in some cases overlap like jigsaw pieces, the product of the city's early, unplanned and somewhat disorganised growth and the ungridded street layout that went with that. These neighbourhoods are alive with the city's history, as well as its future. Downtowners would argue that everything you need is here below 14th Street (and many of them joke that they never venture north of that dividing line). So tie on comfortable shoes, grab your wallet and your appetite and see for yourself.

Battery Park

Manhattan doesn't generally feel like an island – until you reach the southern tip. Down here, Atlantic Ocean breezes remind you how millions of people once travelled to New York:

on overcrowded, creaking sailing ships. Trace their journey past the golden torch of the **Statue of Liberty**, through the immigration and quarantine centres of **Ellis Island** (for both, *see p95*) and, finally, to the statue-dotted **Battery Park promenade**. If it's summertime, this strip – the closest thing this largely green area has to a main drag – will pull you back to the present as you behold a harbour filled with sailboats and jet-skiers, and sidewalks crowded with hurried urbanites who have just been ferried to work from their Staten Island homes.

The promenade is a bench-lined location for quiet contemplation, but also a stage for applause- (and money-) hungry performers, who entertain crowds waiting to hop on to the boats to the Statue of Liberty and Ellis Island. The park itself plays host to a variety of events, including the **River to River Festival** (www.rivertorivernyc.com), a celebration of downtown culture featuring free outdoor goings-on from music and movies to comedy and kids' programmes on summer evenings. **Castle Clinton**, in the park, is an intimate, open-air setting for concerts. Built in 1812 to defend against attacks by the British, the castle, really a former fort, has been a theatre and an aquarium; it now also serves as a visitors' centre and ticket booth for Statue of Liberty and Ellis Island tours.

As you join the throngs making their way to Lady Liberty, you'll head south-east along the shore from which several ferry terminals jut into the harbour. The **Whitehall Ferry Terminal** is the boarding place for the famous **Staten Island Ferry** (*see p88; photo p96*). First onstructed in 1907, it has been completely rebuilt in recent years, after being damaged by fire in 1991. The new terminal opened in 2005; it's the place to catch one of the city's three new ferry boats: the *Guy V Molinari*, named after the former Staten Island borough president; the *Sen John J Marchi*, honouring the veteran Republican legislator; and the *Spirit of America*, which commemorates the teamwork of Staten Islanders on 9/11. The 25-minute ride to the Staten Island shore is one of the few things in New York City that is free; quite a bargain, considering it offers an unparalleled view of the downtown Manhattan skyline and, of course, a closer look at the iconic statue. In the years before the

Face facts: Amanda Sutphin

Amanda Sutphin is not accustomed to being in the limelight. As Director of Archeology for the city's Landmark Preservation Commission (LPC), her days typically involve lots of research, meetings, looking at maps and examining excavation plans. But for the Department of Archaeology, these are not typical days. In 2006 Sutphin was among the city and Metropolitan Transportation Authority (MTA) officials who announced the discovery of a wall that dated to at least the 18th century, unearthed by workers building the new South Ferry subway station in Battery Park.

'It's huge,' Sutphin says, describing the wall – although the description applies to the find as well. 'Eight feet wide and about 40feet long,' she continues. 'I mean, we don't have anything like it.' No one is sure yet exactly what the wall was, although prevailing theories locate it as part of a 17th-century fort or an 18th-century battery. Experts do agree, though, that it's a pre-Revolutionary War structure.

After the find, no one was sure what to do with the thing. The wall was directly in the way of where the subway tunnel is supposed to go – a fact the MTA was none too happy about; work halted around the wall for months after the discovery. The MTA hired a conservation firm to assess the structure and figure out how best to excavate it; the big question was whether it should be removed and replaced elsewhere or whether it should remain where it is (the less likely option). Sutphin's main hope was that the public would have access to the wall, and in the summer of 2006, her dream was temporarily realised: a section of the wall was put on display at Castle Clinton in Battery Park. 'We have heard talk that eventually the wall will be displayed in the new South Ferry subway station,' says Sutphin.

Sutphin's department has jurisdiction only when a project is done on public land or financed with public money, as with the Battery Park wall. If someone's remodelling their kitchen in Park Slope and happens across some historical artefacts, it's up to him or her what to do with them, no matter what wonderful thing might be on the site.

In many ways, what's good about being an archaeologist in New York City is also what's bad about it. 'New York is a city that's always been focused on development,' she says. 'People are constantly tearing down and rebuilding, and tearing down and rebuilding again.' That dynamic means that archaeologists have many opportunities to get a look at what's underneath, but it also means that a lot of history gets destroyed.

It's vexing, she admits, but Sutphin remains focused on matters that she can affect – like the wall.

Brooklyn Bridge was built, the Battery Maritime Building (11 South Street, between Broad & Whitehall Streets) served as a terminal for ferry services between Manhattan and Brooklyn. Get a better view of the harbour, cocktail in hand, from the terrace of the Rise Bar, located on the 14th floor of the luxe Ritz-Carlton New York Battery Park hotel (2 West Street, 1-917 790 2626).

Once you're refreshed, head north of Battery Park to the triangle of **Bowling Green**, the city's oldest park and the recipient of an expensive makeover completed in 2004. This grass triangle is also the front lawn of the 1907 Beaux Arts Alexander Hamilton Custom House,

now home to the **National Museum of the American Indian** (see p93). On its north side, sculptor Arturo DiModica's muscular bronze bull represents the potent capitalism of the Financial District, while to the east sits the **Skyscraper Museum** (see p96), where you can learn about the high-rise buildings that have made the city's skyline iconic, and explore the World Trade Center Dossier, an exhibit about the fallen towers and what will replace them.

Other see-worthy historical sites are close by: the rectory of the **Shrine of St Elizabeth Ann Seton** (see p95), a 1790 Federal building dedicated to the first American-born saint; and

New York Unearthed, a tiny offshoot of the South Street Seaport Museum (*see p99*), whose collection documents 6,000 years of New York's archaeological past. The **Fraunces Tavern Museum** (*see below*) is a restoration of the alehouse where George Washington celebrated his victory over the British. After a bite, you can examine the Revolution-era relics displayed in the tavern's period rooms. The **New York Vietnam Veterans Memorial** (55 Water Street, between Coenties Slip & Hanover Square, www.nyvietnamveteransmemorial. org) stands one block to the east. Erected in 1985, and refreshed with a newly designed plaza a few years ago, it features the Walk of Honor – a pathway inscribed with the names of the 1,741 New Yorkers who lost their lives fighting in that South-east Asian conflict – and a touching memorial etched with excerpts from letters, diary entries and poems written during the war.

Nearby, the **Stone Street Historic District** is built around one of Manhattan's oldest roads. The once-derelict bit of Stone Street between Coenties Alley and Hanover Square is charming; office workers and visitors now frequent its restaurants and bars, including popular watering hole Ulysses (95 Pearl Street, at Stone Street, 1-212 482 0400) and Financier Patisserie (62 Stone Street, between Hanover Square & Mill Lane, 1-212 344 5600).

Fraunces Tavern Museum

54 Pearl Street, at Broad Street (1-212 425 1778/ www.frauncestavernmuseum.org). Subway: J, M, Z to Broad Street; 4, 5 to Bowling Green. **Open** noon-5pm Tue-Fri; 10am-5pm Sat. **Admission** $4; $3 seniors, 6-18s; free under-6s. **No credit cards.** **Map** p402 E33.

This 18th-century tavern was George Washington's watering hole and the site of his famous farewell to the troops at the Revolution's close. During the mid to late 1780s, the building housed the fledgling nation's departments of war, foreign affairs and treasury. In 1904 Fraunces became a repository for artefacts collected by the Sons of the Revolution in the State of New York. Ongoing exhibits include 'George Washington: Down the Stream of Life', which examines America's first President. The tavern and restaurant (1-212 968 1776) serve hearty fare at lunch and dinner, Monday to Saturday.

National Museum of the American Indian

George Gustav Heye Center, Alexander Hamilton Custom House, 1 Bowling Green, between State & Whitehall Streets (1-212 514 3700/www.nmai. si.edu). Subway: R, W to Whitehall Street; 1 to South Ferry; 4, 5 to Bowling Green. **Open** 10am-5pm Mon-Wed, Fri-Sun; 10am-8pm Thur. **Admission** free. **Map** p402 E33.

This branch of the Smithsonian Institution displays its collection around the grand rotunda of the 1907 Custom House, at the bottom of Broadway (which, many moons ago, began as an Indian trail). The life

Burn up some energy, and then recharge, at **Battery Park**. *See p91.*

and culture of Native Americans is presented in rotating exhibitions – from intricately woven fibre Pomo baskets to beaded buckskin shirts – along with contemporary artwork. On show throughout summer 2007 is 'Beauty Surrounds Us', a collection of musical instruments, games and ceremonial clothing that celebrates the importance of decorative art in native cultures.

Shrine of St Elizabeth Ann Seton

7 State Street, between Pearl & Whitehall Streets (1-212 269 6865/www.setonshrine.org). Subway: R, W to Whitehall Street. **Open** 6.30am-5pm Mon-Fri; by appointment only Sat; before and after 11am Mass Sun. **Admission** free. **Map** p402 E34.

Statue of Liberty & Ellis Island Immigration Museum

Statue of Liberty (1-212 363 3200/www.nps.gov/stli). Travel: R, W to Whitehall Street; 1 to South Ferry; 4, 5 to Bowling Green; then take the Statue of Liberty ferry (1-866 782 8834), departing every 25 mins from gangway 4 or 5 in southernmost Battery Park. **Open** Ferry runs 8.30am-4.30pm daily. Purchase tickets at Castle Clinton in Battery Park. **Admission** $11.50; $9.50 seniors; $4.50 3-12s; free under-3s. **Credit** AmEx, MC, V.

Trust us, even if your blood doesn't run red, whit and blue you will not be underwhelmed by either of these two landmarks. But, contrary to some mistaken notions, the mother of all American statues is not on Ellis Island, though that historic place and its resident Ellis Island Immigration Museum can be reached by the same ferry.

Frédéric-Auguste Bartholdi's *Liberty Enlightening the World*, a gift from the people of France, was unveiled in 1886. Although security concerns placed the statue off-limits after 9/11, Lady Liberty's insides were reopened for guided tours (reservations required; call 1-866-782-8834) in 2004. However, you still can't climb up to the crown, and backpacks and luggage are not permitted on the island. Still, you can take in the carving on the pedestal, which features the 1883 Emma Lazarus poem that includes the renowned lines 'Give me your tired, your poor/your huddled masses yearning to breathe free'. On the way back to Manhattan, the ferry will stop at the popular Immigration Museum, on Ellis Island, through which more than 12 million people entered the country between 1892 and 1954. The exhibitions are a moving tribute to the immigrants from so many different countries who made the journey to America, dreaming of a better life. The $6 audio tour, narrated by Tom Brokaw, is informative and inspiring.

Battery Park City & Ground Zero

The streets around **Ground Zero**, the former site of the **World Trade Center**, have been drawing crowds since the terrorist attacks of 2001. Not that there's been much to see. The site

of the worst attack on US soil, on 11 September 2001, took nearly 2,800 lives and left a hole where one of the most recognisable American icons, the Twin Towers, had been. It's taken nearly five years of bureaucratic red tape, but construction on the site is finally under way, with completion of the entire project, including the much-debated Freedom Tower (a 1,776-foot spire planned as the world's tallest building but stalled by security issues in 2005) and a funding-challenged memorial, due sometime around 2012. Unfortunately, the optimism that the site's new, soaring architecture was supposed to inspire has been dampened by infighting among state and city governments, the real-estate developer who leases the land, the insurance companies that have been trying to get out of covering the damage, the architects whose designs have been neutered, and the families of the victims and survivors. The good news: one building, 7 World Trade Center, has been completed and is now open for tenants. Designed by the same architect who's now designing the Freedom Tower, 7 WTC is one of the first commercial buildings in New York City to be certified 'green', thanks to its low-energy heating and cooling systems and refined use of electricity.

Immediately to the west of Ground Zero, the city-within-a-city **World Financial Center** (*see p97*) is fully recovered from its 9/11 injuries, and is a pretty place for a walk-through. Completed in 1988, architect Cesar Pelli's four glass-and-granite, postmodern office towers – each crowned with a different geometric form – surround an upscale retail area and a series of eatery-lined plazas ringing a marina where private yachts and water taxis to New Jersey are docked. The glass-roofed **Winter Garden** is a popular venue for concerts. To the east of Ground Zero, shopaholics can amuse themselves at the enormous discount-designer-duds vault Century 21 (*see p236*).

Just west of the World Financial Center lies **Battery Park City**, devised by Nelson A Rockefeller (the governor of New York from 1959 to 1973) as a site of apartment housing and schools in an area that is otherwise all business. Home to roughly 9,000 people, the self-contained neighbourhood includes restaurants, cafés, shops and a marina amid 92 glorious riverside acres. Sweeping views of the Hudson River and close proximity to the downtown financial scene have also made this an ideal spot for office space. Still, the most impressive aspects of BPC are its esplanade, a paradise for bikers, skaters and joggers, and the strolling park (officially called Nelson A Rockefeller Park), both of which run along the Hudson River north of the Financial Center and connect to Battery Park at the south. Close by the marina is the 1997 **Police**

Sightseeing

The **Staten Island Ferry**. See p91.

Memorial (Liberty Street, at South End Avenue), a granite pool and fountain that symbolically trace the lifespan of a police officer through the use of moving water, with names of the fallen etched into the wall. The **Irish Hunger Memorial** (Vesey Street, at North End Avenue) is here too, paying tribute to those who suffered during the Irish Famine.

One of the larger chunks of green along this stretch is Rockefeller Park's sprawling **North Lawn**. This spot, located adjacent to the well-respected Stuyvesant High School, becomes a veritable beach in summer, when sunbathers, kite fliers and soccer players vie for turf. Basketball and handball courts, concrete tables inlaid with chess and backgammon boards, and playgrounds with swings are some of the built-in recreation options. Continue north and you'll find a jogging and bike trail and, on Piers 25 and 26, all kinds of activities, from kayaking and fishing to a trapeze-swinging school.

Situated between Battery Park City and Battery Park are the inventively designed South Cove, the new **Teardrop Park** – a two-acre space designed to evoke the Hudson River Valley – and Robert F Wagner Jr Park, where an observation deck offers fabulous views of the harbour and the Verrazano-Narrows Bridge. New York City's Holocaust-remembrance archive, the **Museum of Jewish Heritage** (*see below*), is tucked in amid the green spots, and the entire park area is dotted with sculptures, including Tom Otterness's whimsical *The Real World*, which, by the way, has nothing to do with

MTV's long-running reality show of the same name, although both debuted the same year: 1992. Just across the street, anyone with a fascination for tall buildings will want to duck into the **Skyscraper Museum** (*see below*).

Battery Park City Authority

1-212 417 2000/www.batteryparkcity.org.
The neighbourhood's official website lists events taking place and has a very useful map of the area.

Museum of Jewish Heritage

Robert F Wagner Jr Park, 36 Battery Place, at First Place (1-646 437 4200/www.mjhnyc.org). Subway: 1, 9 to South Ferry; 4, 5 to Bowling Green. **Open** 10am-5.45pm Mon-Tue, Thur, Sun; 10am-8pm Wed; 10am-3pm Fri, eve of Jewish holidays (until 5pm in the summer). **Admission** $10; $7 seniors; $5 students; free under-12s. Free 4-8pm Wed. **Credit** AmEx, MC, V. **Map** p402 E34.
Opened in 1997 and expanded in 2003, this museum offers one of the most moving cultural experiences in the city. Detailing the horrific attacks on (and inherent joys of) Jewish life during the past century, the collection consists of 24 documentary films, 2,000 photographs and 800 cultural artefacts, many donated by Holocaust survivors and their families. The Memorial Garden features English artist Andy Goldsworthy's permanent installation *Garden of Stones*: 18 fire-hollowed boulders, each planted with a dwarf oak sapling.

Skyscraper Museum

39 Battery Place, between Little West Street & 1st Place (1-212-968-1961/www.skyscraper.org). Subway: 4, 5 to Bowling Green. **Open** noon-6pm Wed-Sun. **Admission** $5; $2.50 seniors, students. **Map** p402 E34.

In just 5,000sq ft – very modest by institutional standards – this space manages to evoke the scale and aspirations of the Skyscraper Museum's subject matter.

World Financial Center & Winter Garden

From Albany to Vesey Streets, between the Hudson River & West Street (1-212 945 2600/www.world financialcenter.com). Subway: A, C to Broadway-Nassau Street; E to World Trade Center; J, M, Z, 2, 3, 4, 5 to Fulton Street. **Map** p402 D32.
Go online to download a calendar of free events ranging from folk concerts to silent-film festivals.

Wall Street

Since the city's earliest days as a fur-trading post, wheeling and dealing has been New York's main activity, and commerce has been the backbone of its prosperity. The southern tip of Manhattan is generally known as the Financial District because, in the days before telecommunications, banks established their headquarters here to be near the city's active port. While this nabe is bisected vertically by the ever-bustling Broadway, it's that east-west thoroughfare Wall Street (or 'the Street' in trader lingo) that is synonymous with the world's greatest den of capitalism.

Wall Street, which took its name from a defensive wooden wall built by the Dutch in 1653 to mark what was then the northern limit

Statue of Liberty. *See p91.*

of New Amsterdam, is big on legend but is less than a mile long – it's truncated by Broadway on its western end, and therefore only spans about half the width of the island. Here at Broadway rises the Gothic Revival spire of **Trinity Church** – proof, perhaps, that God and capitalism are not mutually exclusive. This Episcopalian house of worship was the island's tallest structure when it was completed in 1846 (the original burned down in 1776; a second was demolished in 1839). A set of gates north of the church on Broadway allows access to the adjacent cemetery, where cracked and faded tombstones mark the final resting places of dozens of past city dwellers, including signatories of the Declaration of Independence and the Constitution. The church is also home to the **Trinity Church Museum** (*see p98*), which displays an assortment of historic diaries, photographs, sermons and burial records.

St Paul's Chapel (*see p98*), a satellite of Trinity Church, is an oasis of peace in the midst of frantic business activity. The chapel is the city's only extant pre-Revolutionary building (it dates from 1766) and one of the finest Georgian structures in the country. Miraculously, both landmark churches survived the World Trade Center attack; although mortar fell from their façades, the steeples remained intact.

A block east of Trinity Church, the **Federal Hall National Memorial** is an august Greek Revival building in its own right, and – in a previous incarnation – the site of George Washington's inauguration in 1789.

It was along this stretch that corporate America made its first audacious architectural statements, and a continued walk eastwards offers much evidence of what money can buy. Notable structures include **40 Wall Street** (between Nassau & William Streets), which went head-to-head with the Chrysler Building in 1929 battling for the title of 'world's tallest building' (the Empire State Building trounced them both a year later), and the former **Merchants' Exchange** at 55 Wall Street (between Hanover & William Streets), with its stacked rows of Ionic and Corinthian columns, giant doors and a remarkable 12,000-square-foot ballroom inside. Back around the corner is another example: the **Equitable Building** (120 Broadway, between Cedar & Pine Streets), whose greedy use of vertical space helped to instigate the zoning laws now governing skyscrapers (stand across the street from the building to get the optimal view).

The nerve centre of the US economy is the **New York Stock Exchange** (11 Wall Street, between Broad & New Streets). For security reasons, the Exchange is no longer open to the public, but the street outside offers an endless pageant of brokers, traders and their minions. For a lesson on Wall Street's influence over the years, visit the **Museum of American Financial History** (*see p98*), on the ground floor of what was once JD Rockefeller's Standard Oil Building.

Federal Reserve Bank

33 Liberty Street, between Nassau & William Streets (1-212 720 6130/www.newyorkfed.org). Subway: 2, 3, 4, 5 to Wall Street. **Open** 9am-5pm Mon-Fri. **Tours** every hour on the half-hour, last tour 2.30pm. Tours must be arranged at least 1 week in advance; tickets are sent by mail. Call for reservations. **Admission** free. **Map** p402 E33.

Here's your chance to descend 80ft below street level and commune with the planet's most precious metal. Roughly a quarter of the world's gold (more than $100 billion dollars) is stored here in a gigantic vault that rests on the bedrock of Manhattan Island.

Museum of American Financial History

28 Broadway, between Beaver Street & Exchange Place (1-212 908 4110/www.financialhistory.org). Subway: 1 to Rector Street. **Open** 10am-4pm Tue-Sat. **Admission** $2. **Credit** AmEx, MC, V. **Map** p402 E33.

The permanent collection, which traces the development of Wall Street and America's financial markets, features ticker tape from the morning of the big crash of 29 October 1929, an 1867 stock ticker and the earliest known photograph of Wall Street.

New York City Police Museum

100 Old Slip, between South & Water Streets (1-212 480 3100/www.nycpolicemuseum.org). Subway: 2, 3 to Wall Street; 4, 5 to Bowling Green. **Open** 10am-5pm Mon-Sat. **Admission** suggested donation $5; $3 seniors; $2 6-18s; free under-6s. **No credit cards. Map** p402 F32.

The NYPD's self-tribute features exhibits on its history and the tools and transportation of the trade. You can also buy officially licensed NYPD paraphernalia.

St Paul's Chapel

209 Broadway, between Fulton & Vesey Streets (1-212 233 4164/www.saintpaulschapel.org). Subway: A, C to Broadway-Nassau Street; J, M, Z, 2, 3, 4, 5 to Fulton Street. **Open** 10am-6pm Mon-Sat; 9am-4pm Sun. **Map** p402 E32.

Trinity Church Museum

89 Broadway, at Wall Street (1-212 602 0872/www.trinitywallstreet.org). Subway: R, W to Rector Street; 2, 3, 4, 5 to Wall Street. **Open** 9-11.45am, 1-3.45pm Mon-Fri; 10am-3.45pm Sat; 1-3.45pm Sun. Closed during concerts. **Admission** free. **Map** p402 E33.

South Street Seaport

New York's importance as a port has diminished, but its initial fortune rolled in on the swells that crash around its deep-water harbour. The city was perfectly situated for trade with Europe; after 1825, goods from the Western Territories arrived via the Erie Canal and the Hudson River. By 1892 New York had become the point of entry for many millions of immigrants, and thus its character was, of course, shaped by more than commodities – it grew from the waves of humanity that arrived at its docks. The South Street Seaport is the best place to appreciate this seafaring heritage.

If you enter the Seaport area from Water Street, the first thing you'll notice is the whitewashed *Titanic* **Memorial Lighthouse**, originally erected on top of the Seaman's Church Institute (Coenties Slip & South Street) in 1913 – the year after the great ship sank. The monument was moved to its current location in 1976. Check out the fine views of the **Brooklyn Bridge** that this corner of the neighbourhood offers.

The **South Street Seaport**, which was redeveloped in the mid 1980s, is lined with reclaimed and renovated buildings that have been converted to shops, restaurants, bars and a museum. It's not an area that New Yorkers often visit, despite its rich history. The Seaport's public spaces, including blocks of both Fulton and Front Streets, where cars are barred, are a favourite of street performers. At 11 Fulton Street, the Fulton Market (open daily), with its gourmet food stalls and seafood restaurants, is a great place for people-watching and oyster-slurping. Familiar national-chain stores such as J Crew and Abercrombie & Fitch line the surrounding thoroughfares. The shopping area of Pier 17, though little more than a picturesque mall by day and an after-work watering hole by night, is worth a quick walkthrough. (Outdoor concerts in summertime actually do attract locals, and may justify a sitdown, even for determined sightseers.) Antique vessels are docked at neighbouring piers. The street right in front of Pier 17 used to support the famous Fulton Fish Market, a bustling, early-morning trading centre that dated back to the mid 1800s, where much of the city's food industry purchased fresh seafood for their daily menus. In early 2006 the market was relocated to a larger, more modern and more sanitary facility in the Bronx, making it the second-largest fish market in the world (second to Tokyo), and is no longer open for tours. Plans for the former site are up in the air, although cynical New Yorkers suspect the historic site, one of the last vestiges of the city's working waterfront, will probably be turned into condos, instead of, say, being annexed by the **South Street Seaport Museum** (*see p99*), which details New York's maritime history. The museum is located inside the restored 19th-century buildings of Schermerhorn Row (2-18 Fulton Street, 91-92 South Street and 189-195 Front Street).

South Street Seaport Museum

Visitors' Center, 12 Fulton Street, at South Street (1-212 748 8600/www.southstseaport.org). Subway: A, C to Broadway-Nassau Street; J, M, Z, 2, 3, 4, 5 to Fulton Street. **Open** *Apr-Oct* 10am-6pm Tue-Sun. *Nov-Mar* 10am-6pm Fri-Sun. **Admission** $8; $6 seniors, students; $4 5-12s; free under-5s. **Credit** AmEx, MC, V. **Map** p402 F32.

Occupying 11 blocks along the East River, the museum is an amalgam of galleries, historic ships, 19th-century buildings and a visitors' centre. Wander around the rebuilt streets and pop in to see an exhibition on marine life and history before climbing aboard the four-masted 1911 *Peking*. The seaport is generally thick with tourists, but it's still a lively place to spend an afternoon, especially for families with children, who are likely to enjoy the atmosphere and intriguing seafaring memorabilia. In spring 2007 the museum launches World Port New York, an ambitious exhibition highlighting the economic and social importance of New York's bustling seaport to the city, country and world beyond.

Civic Center & City Hall

The business of running New York takes place in the many grand buildings of the **Civic Center**, an area that formed the budding city's northern boundary in the 1700s. **City Hall Park** was treated to an extensive renovation just before the millennium arrived, and the pretty landscaping and abundant benches make it a popular weekday lunching spot for local office workers. At the south end you'll find a granite 'time wheel' tracking the park's history. Like the steps of City Hall, the park has been the site of press conferences and political protests for years. (Under former mayor Rudy Giuliani, the steps were closed to such activities unless they were approved by Hizzoner's office. A federal district judge declared the ban unconstitutional in April 2000, after a celebration of the Yankees' World Series victory took place, but an event commemorating World AIDS Day was snuffed.) **City Hall**, at the northern end of the park, houses the mayor's office and the legislative chambers of the City Council, and is therefore usually buzzing with preparations for VIP comings and goings. When City Hall was completed in 1812, its architects were so confident the city would grow no further north that they didn't bother to put any marble on its northern side. The building, a beautiful blend of Federalist form and French Renaissance detail, is closed to the public (except for scheduled group tours). Facing City Hall, the much larger, golden-statue-topped **Municipal Building** contains other civic offices, including the marriage bureau; note the nervous, blushing brides- and grooms-to-be awaiting their ceremonies, particularly in the early morning.

Park Row, east of City Hall Park, is now lined with cafés, electronics shops and the campus of **Pace University**. It once held the

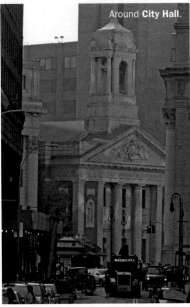

Around **City Hall**.

Soho.

offices of 19 daily papers and was known as Newspaper Row (these days, scoop-driven crime reporters from the major newspapers share one cramped office, affectionately known as 'the Shack', which is located nearby at 1 Police Plaza). This strip was also the site of Phineas T Barnum's sensationalist American Museum, which burned down in 1865.

Facing the park from the west is Cass Gilbert's famous **Woolworth Building** (233 Broadway, between Barclay Street & Park Place), a vertically elongated Gothic cathedral-style office building considered by many to be the Mozart of skyscrapers (and, alternatively, nicknamed the Cathedral of Commerce). Be sure to look skywards, both as you face the striking façade and as you stand in the stunning lobby.

The houses of crime and punishment are also located in the Civic Center, near Foley Square, which was once a pond and later the site of the city's most notorious 19th-century slum, Five Points. These days, you'll find the State Supreme Court in the **New York County Courthouse** (60 Centre Street, at Pearl Street), a hexagonal Roman Revival building; the beautiful rotunda is decorated with the mural *Law Through the Ages*. The **United States Courthouse** (40 Centre Street, between Duane & Pearl Streets) is a Corinthian temple crowned with a golden pyramid. Next to City Hall, on Chambers Street, is the 1872 Old New York County Courthouse, more popularly known as the **Tweed Courthouse**, a symbol of the runaway corruption of mid 19th-century municipal government. William 'Boss' Tweed, leader of the political machine Tammany Hall, famously pocketed some $10 million of the building's huge $14 million construction budget. What he didn't steal bought a beautiful edifice; the Italianate detailing is exquisite. These days, the Tweed houses the city's Department of Education, a considerably less lucrative machine.

The **Criminal Courts Building & Bernard Kerik Detention Complex** (100 Centre Street, between Leonard & White Streets), still known as 'the Tombs' despite its official renaming in 2001, is the district's most intimidating pile. The hall's architecture – great granite slabs and looming towers guarding the entrance – is downright Kafkaesque. (Kerik is a former commissioner of the New York Police Department, who in summer 2006 pleaded guilty to accepting thousands of dollars in gifts from people associated with the mob. No word yet on whether his name will be taken off the Tombs.)

All of these courts are open to the public on weekdays from 9am to 5pm. Your best bets for legal drama: the Criminal Courts. If you can't slip into a trial, you can at least observe legal eagles and their clients. Or, for a grim twist on dinner theatre, observe the pleas here at the Arraignment Court (the action lasts till 1am).

A major archaeological discovery, the **African Burial Ground** (Duane Street, between Broadway & Centre Street) is a small remnant of a five-and-a-half-acre cemetery where between 10,000 and 20,000 African men, women and children were buried more than 200 years ago. The cemetery, which closed in 1794, was unearthed during construction of a federal office building in 1991 and designated a National Historic Landmark (*see p22* **Sacred ground**). In 2006 President Bush upgraded it to a National Monument.

City Hall

City Hall Park, from Vesey to Chambers Streets, between Broadway & Park Row (1-212 788 3000/ www.nyc.gov). Subway: J, M, Z to Chambers Street; 2, 3 to Park Place; 4, 5, 6 to Brooklyn Bridge-City Hall. **Map** p402 E32.
For group tours only; call two weeks in advance.

Tribeca & Soho

Tribeca (the Triangle Below Canal Street) is a textbook example of the gentrification process in lower Manhattan. Much of the neighbourhood throbs with energy, but a few pockets appear abandoned – the cobblestones crumbling and dirty, the cast-iron buildings chipped and unpainted. Don't let your eyes fool you; derelict areas like these are transformed with deluxe makeovers, seemingly overnight.

The rich and famous weren't really here first, but visible gentrification has led some to think of them as pioneers: many big-name celebs (Robert De Niro, Christy Turlington) and established, successful artists (Richard Serra) live in the area. There's a host of haute eateries here, including Chanterelle (2 Harrison, at Hudson Street, 1-212 966 6960) and Nobu (105 Hudson, at Franklin Street, 1-212 334 4445); the long-running Odeon (145 West Broadway, at Duane Street, 1-212 233 0507), immortalised by Jay McInerney in his 1984 novel *Bright Lights, Big City*, is still a beautiful-people hotspot.

Many of the buildings in Tribeca are large, hulking former warehouses; those near the river, in particular, are rapidly being converted into modern condos, but fine small-scale cast-iron architecture still stands along White Street and the parallel thoroughfares. You'll find galleries, salons, furniture stores, spas and other businesses here that cater to the neighbourhood's stylish residents. Architecture star Frank Gehry designed the multimillion-dollar interior for the Tribeca Issey Miyake boutique (119 Hudson Street, at North Moore Street, 1-212 226 0100).

Tribeca is also the unofficial headquarters of New York's film industry. De Niro's **Tribeca Film Center** (375 Greenwich Street, at Franklin Street) houses screening rooms and production offices in the old Martinson Coffee Building; his restaurant, Tribeca Grill, is on the ground floor. A few blocks away, his recently acquired **Tribeca Cinemas** (54 Varick Street, at Laight Street, 1-212 966 8163) hosts film premières and parties when it is not acting as a venue for the **Tribeca Film Festival** (*see p261*), which grows each year. In 2006 there were so many screenings (more than 800 in two weeks) that the festival had to expand beyond Tribeca, showing movies in Midtown and the Upper West Side.

Soho, New York's glamorous downtown shopping destination, was once an industrial zone known as Hell's Hundred Acres. In the 1960s the neighbourhood was earmarked for destruction, but its signature cast-iron warehouses were saved by the many artists who inhabited them. (Urban-planning theorist Chester A Rapkin coined the name Soho, for South of Houston Street, in a 1962 study of the neighbourhood.) The **King** and **Queen of Greene Street** (respectively, 72-76 Greene Street, between Broome & Spring Streets, and 28-30 Greene Street, between Canal & Grand Streets) are prime examples of the area's beloved architectural landmarks. Not surprisingly, as loft living became fashionable and buildings were renovated for residential use, landlords sniffed the potential for profits, and Soho morphed into a playground for the young, the beautiful and the rich. While it can still be a pleasure to stroll around the cobblestone streets on weekdays, large chain stores have moved in among the boutiques and bistros, bringing with them a shopping mall at Christmas-time crush every Saturday and Sunday. The commercialism and crowds have caused a number of hip shops to head to other neighbourhoods, and most of the galleries that made Soho an art mecca in the 1970s and '80s have decamped to cheaper (and now trendier) neighbourhoods like West Chelsea and Brooklyn's Dumbo. Surprisingly, some garment-factory sweatshops remain in Soho, especially near Canal Street, though the same elegant buildings may also house design studios, magazine publishers and record labels.

Upscale hotels like the Mercer, 60 Thompson (for both, *see p50* **Upscale Downtown**) and SoHo Grand (*see p51*) keep the fashionable coming to the area; high-end clothing stores include Prada and Agnès b, and swanky home furnishings rule at Euro-cool design stores such as Moss and Cappelletti. And the goods aren't all that's worldly in these parts. West Broadway, Soho's main thoroughfare, is a magnet for out-

Sightseeing

of-towners. At weekends, you're as likely to hear French, German and Italian as you are to catch a blast of Brooklynese. The **New Museum of Contemporary Art** (*see p106* **Ultra modern**) has left the neighbourhood (it's inhabiting a temporary space in Chelsea until its new home on the Bowery is ready in 2007). A remaining museum in Soho that is worth a tour is the **New York City Fire Museum** (*see below*), a former fire station housing a collection of antique engines dating from the 1700s.

Just west of West Broadway, tenement- and townhouse-lined streets contain remnants of the Italian community that once dominated the area. Elderly men and women walk along Sullivan Street to the St Anthony of Padua Roman Catholic Church (No.155, at W Houston Street), which was dedicated in 1888. You'll find old-school neighbourhood flavour in businesses such as Joe's Dairy (No.156, between Houston & Prince Streets, 1-212 677 8780), Pino's Prime Meat Market (No.149, between Houston & Prince Streets, 1-212 475 8134) and, on Prince Street, the Vesuvio Bakery (160 Prince Street, between Thompson Street & West Broadway, 1-212 925 8248), whose old-fashioned façade has appeared in dozens of commercials.

New York City Fire Museum

278 Spring Street, between Hudson & Varick Streets (1-212 691 1303/www.nycfiremuseum. org). Subway: C, E to Spring Street; 1 to Houston Street. **Open** 10am-5pm Tue-Sat; 10am-4pm Sun. **Admission** suggested donation $5; $2 seniors, students; $1 under-12s. **Credit** AmEx, DC, Disc, MC, V. **Map** p403 D30.

An active firehouse from 1904 to 1959, this museum is filled with gadgetry and pageantry, from late 18th-century hand-pumped fire engines to present-day equipment. The museum also houses a permanent exhibit commemorating firefighters' heroism after the attack on the World Trade Center.

Little Italy & Nolita

Little Italy, which once ran from Canal to Houston Streets, between Lafayette Street and the Bowery, hardly resembles the insular community famously portrayed in Martin Scorsese's *Mean Streets*. Italian families have fled Mott Street and gone to the suburbs, Chinatown has crept north, and rising rents have forced mom-and-pop businesses to surrender to the stylish boutiques of Nolita: North of Little Italy (a misnomer, since it technically lies within Little Italy). Another telling change in the 'hood: St **Patrick's Old Cathedral** (260-264 Mulberry Street, between Houston & Prince Streets) now holds services in English and Spanish, not Italian. Completed in 1809 and restored after a fire in 1868, this was

New York's premier Catholic church until it was demoted, upon consecration of the Fifth Avenue cathedral of the same name. But ethnic pride remains. Italian-Americans flood in from the outer boroughs to show their love for the old neighbourhood during the **Feast of San Gennaro** (*see p265*) every September. Tourist-oriented Italian cafés and restaurants line Mulberry Street between Canal and Houston Streets, but nearby pockets of the past still linger. Elderly locals (and in-the-know young ones) buy olive oil and fresh pasta from venerable shops such as DiPalo's Fine Foods (200 Grand Street, at Mott Street, 1-212 226 1033) and sandwiches packed with salami and cheeses at the Italian Food Center (186 Grand Street, at Mulberry Street, 1-212 925 2954).

Of course, Little Italy is the site of several notorious Mafia landmarks. The brick-fronted store occupied by accessories boutique Amy Chan (247 Mulberry Street, between Prince & Spring Streets) was once the Ravenite Social Club – Mafia kingpin John Gotti's HQ from the mid 1980s until his arrest (and imprisonment) in 1990. Mobster Joey Gallo was shot to death in 1972 while celebrating a birthday at Umberto's Clam House, which has since moved around the corner to 178 Mulberry Street, at Broome Street (1-212 431 7545). The restaurants in the area are mostly undistinguished grill-and-pasta houses, but two reliable choices are Il Cortile (125 Mulberry Street, between Canal & Hester Streets, 1-212 226 6060) and La Mela (167 Mulberry Street, between Broome & Grand Streets, 1-212 431 9493). Drop in for dessert at Caffè Roma (385 Broome Street, at Mulberry Street, 1-212 226 8413), which opened in 1891.

Chi-chi restaurants and boutiques have taken over **Nolita**. Elizabeth, Mott and Mulberry Streets, between Houston and Spring Streets in particular, are now the source of everything from perfectly cut jeans to hand-blown glass. The young, the insouciant and the vaguely European still congregate outside hip eateries like Bread (20 Spring Street, between Elizabeth & Mott Streets, 1-212 334 1015) and Café Habana (*see p184*). Even before the Nolita boom, the grand Police Headquarters Building (240 Centre Street, between Broome & Grand Streets) had been converted into pricey apartments.

Chinatown

Take a walk in the area south of Broome Street and west of Broadway, and you'll feel as though you've entered a completely different continent. You won't hear much English spoken along the crowded streets of **Chinatown**, lined by fish-, fruit- and vegetable-stocked stands. Manhattan's Chinatown is one the largest

Chinese communities outside Asia. Even though some residents eventually decamp to one of the four other Chinatowns in the city (two each in Queens and Brooklyn), a steady flow of new arrivals keeps this hub full-to-bursting, with thousands of legal and illegal residents packed into the area surrounding East Canal Street. Many work and live here and rarely leave the neighbourhood. Chinatown's busy streets get even wilder during the **Chinese New Year** festivities, in February (see p266).

Food is everywhere. The markets on Canal Street sell some of the best and most affordable seafood and fresh produce in the city – you'll see buckets of live eels and crabs, stacks of greens and piles of hairy rambutans (cousins of the lychee). Street vendors sell satisfying snacks such as pork buns and sweet egg pancakes by the bagful. Mott Street, between Kenmare and Worth Streets, is lined with restaurants representing the cuisine of virtually every province of mainland China and Hong Kong; the Bowery, East Broadway and Division Street are just as diverse. Adding to the mix are myriad Indonesian, Malaysian, Thai and Vietnamese eateries and stores.

Canal Street, a bargain hunter's paradise, is infamous as a source of (illegal) knock-off designer handbags, perfumes and other goods. The area's many gift shops are stocked with fun, inexpensive Chinese products.

One site of historical interest is Wing Fat Shopping, a strange little subterranean mall with its entrance at Chatham Square (No.8, to the right of the OTB parlour), rumoured to have been a stop on the Underground Railroad 25 years before the Chinese began populating this area in the 1880s.

A statue of the philosopher marks **Confucius Plaza**, at the corner of the Bowery and Division Street. In Columbus Park, at Bayard and Mulberry Streets, elderly men and women gather around card tables to play mah-jong and dominoes (you can hear the clacking tiles from across the street), while younger folks practise martial arts. The **Museum of Chinese in the Americas** hosts exhibitions and events that explore the Chinese immigrant experience in the western hemisphere. In the **Eastern States Buddhist Temple of America**, you'll be dazzled by the glitter of hundreds of Buddhas and the aroma of wafting incense. Donate $1 and you'll receive a fortune slip. For both, see p104.

For a different perspective on the area's culture, visit the noisy, dingy Chinatown Fair (at the southern end of Mott Street), an amusement arcade where some of the East Coast's best Street Fighter players congregate. Older kids hit Chinatown to eat and drink: Joe's Shanghai (9 Pell Street, between Bowery & Mott Street, 1-212 233 8888) is known for its soup dumplings, boiled pillows of dough filled with pork and broth;

Chinatown.

and Happy Ending (302 Broome Street, between Eldridge & Forsyth Streets, 1-212 334 9676), a popular nightspot for denizens of every ethnicity, occupies a former massage parlour (the name of the bar is a nod to its sexually charged roots).

Eastern States Buddhist Temple of America

64 Mott Street, between Bayard & Canal Streets (1-212 966 6229). Subway: J, M, N, Q, R, W, Z, 6 to Canal Street. **Open** *9am-6pm daily.* **Map** p403 F29.

Museum of Chinese in the Americas

2nd Floor, 70 Mulberry Street, at Bayard Street (1-212 619 4785/www.moca-nyc.org). Subway: J, M, N, Q, R, W, Z, 6 to Canal Street. **Open** noon-5pm Tue-Sat. **Admission** suggested donation $3; $1 seniors, students; free under-12s. Free Fri. **No credit cards.** **Map** p402 F31.

In the heart of downtown Manhattan's Chinatown, a century-old former schoolhouse holds a two-room museum focused on Chinese-American history

South of the border

The latest downtown acronym: BelDel.

There's something happening in a part of the Lower East Side south of Delancey Street. A three-by-four-block neighbourhood roughly bounded by Delancey to the north, Canal to the south, Essex to the east and Allen to the west, that used to be an eating and drinking no-man's land, was the scene of a flurry of construction over the course of 2005 and 2006. This led to the opening of a dozen or so new bars and restaurants by canny entrepreneurs, and a buzz to the air, with many of the new eateries contributing to the new upbeat yet laid-back vibe (think Latin American street food joints). The

neighbourhood has attracted enough attention to earn itself its own acronym: 'BelDel', short for 'Below Delancey'.

Development in this part of town was inevitable. The proliferation of restaurants and bars on Ludlow, Rivington and Orchard Streets north of Delancey – and the backlash against the noise and crowds that they attract – has made it hard to open new spots there: bar owners now have to fight for liquor licences, and rents are soaring. So while Delancey once served as the highway that divided booze-infused revellers from the rest of the Lower East Side, it was only a matter of time before restaurateurs discovered the vacant storefronts and failing lingerie stores that litter BelDel. 'For better or for worse, the old Orchard Street businesses are getting priced out,' says Dylan Dodd, co-owner of the two-and-a-half-year-old Mexican eaterie Barrio Chino.

BelDel, then, is a new world to explore, and one that poses two seemingly opposing questions: will enough foot traffic find its way across the divide? And, more worrisome, will the neighbourhood become just an extension of the already cluttered über-trendy 'hoods of the Lower East Side? Danny Milan, who opened the tiny bar-café King Size in December 2005, believes BelDel is still off most people's radar. 'It feels as if most people stumble into this neighbourhood by accident,' he says. 'Even people who grew up in Manhattan haven't been down here.' And yet, he's also aware that the unveiling of these destinations could signal the end of one of Downtown's last undeveloped enclaves. 'We wouldn't want this neighbourhood to be like it is above Delancey. That's really out of control.' The lingering question that remains is, can you have it both ways?

and the Chinese immigrant experience. The huge archive holds thousands of rare and important papers and artefacts. Call for details about walking tours of the neighbourhood.

Lower East Side

The **Lower East Side** was shaped by New York's immigrants, millions upon millions of whom poured into the city from the late 19th century onwards. The resulting patchwork of dense communities is great for dining and exploration – though today, the Lower East Side is less and less dominated by Asian, Jewish and Latino families, and more and more ruled by chic boutiques, restaurants and the stylish types who frequent them. Early inhabitants of this area were mostly Eastern European Jews, and mass tenement housing was built to accommodate the 19th-century influx of immigrants, which included many German, Hungarian, Irish and Polish families. The unsanitary, airless and overcrowded living conditions suffered by these people were documented near the end of that century by photographer and writer Jacob A Riis in *How the Other Half Lives*; the book's publication fuelled reformers, who prompted the introduction of building codes. To better understand how these immigrants lived, tour the **Lower East Side Tenement Museum** (*see p107*).

Between 1870 and 1920, hundreds of synagogues and religious schools were established. Yiddish newspapers and associations for social reform and cultural studies flourished, as did vaudeville and classic Yiddish theatre. (The Marx Brothers, Jimmy Durante, Eddie Cantor, and George and Ira Gershwin were just a few of the entertainers who once lived in the district.) Currently, only about ten per cent of the LES population is Jewish; the **Eldridge Street Synagogue** often has a hard time rounding up the ten adult males required to conduct a service. Still, the synagogue has not missed a Sabbath or holiday service in more than 115 years. **First Shearith Israel Graveyard** (on the southern edge of Chinatown) is the burial ground of the country's first Jewish community. It has gravestones that date from 1683, including those of Spanish and Portuguese Jews who fled the Inquisition.

Puerto Ricans and Dominicans began to move to the Lower East Side after World War II. Colourful awnings still mark the area's bodegas, and many restaurants serve Caribbean standards.

In the 1980s a new breed of immigrant began moving in: young artists and musicians attracted by the low rents. Bars, boutiques and

Soak up the culture in the **Lower East Side**.

music venues sprang up on and around Ludlow Street, creating an annex to the East Village. This scene is still thriving, though rents have risen like mercury in August. One casualty of the heat was the Luna Lounge, a Ludlow Street stalwart that offered free concerts and cheap comedy shows, both of which were breeding grounds for big names. It was torn down in 2005 to make way for, you guessed it, an apartment building. For live music, you can still check who's playing at Arlene's Grocery (*see p311*), the Bowery Ballroom (*see p314*) and Tonic (*see p319*). The sign at Pianos (*see p318*), a popular bi-level bar, is a remnant from the piano store that occupied its address for decades. A local art scene has also taken root here; Rivington Arms and Participant Inc (for both, *see p268*) are storefront galleries showcasing young artists.

The Lower East Side's reputation as a haven for political radicals lives on at ABC No Rio (*see p278* SOS: Sunday Open Series), which was established in 1980 after squatters took over an abandoned ground-floor space; it now houses a gallery and performance space. Meanwhile, luxe apartment complexes have moved in. The flash Hotel on Rivington (*see p53*), a 21-storey glass tower, is one of the new crop of high-rise buildings in this low-rise 'hood, and is therefore difficult to miss.

Sightseeing

Despite the trendy shops that have cropped up along the block, Orchard Street below Stanton Street remains the heart of the **Orchard Street Bargain District**, a row of stores selling utilitarian goods. This is the place for cheap hats, luggage, sportswear and T-shirts. In the 1930s Mayor Fiorello La Guardia forced pushcart vendors off the streets and into large indoor marketplaces. Although many of these bazaars are now a thing of the past, **Essex Street Markets** (120 Essex Street, between Delancey & Rivington Streets) is still going strong and is packed with purveyors of all sorts of things Latino, Jewish and Chinese, from plantains to kosher wine and soy dumplings.

Another vestige of the neighbourhood's Jewish roots remains: Katz's Delicatessen (205 E Houston Street, at Ludlow Street, 1-212 254 2246) sells some of the best pastrami in New York (FYI, Meg Ryan's famous 'orgasm' scene in *When Harry Met Sally…* was filmed here).

The Lower East Side is a carb-craver's paradise. Pay tribute to the neighbourhood's Eastern European origins with a freshly baked bialy from Kossar's Bialystoker Kuchen Bakery (367 Grand Street, between Essex & Norfolk Streets, 1-212 473 4810). If you're in need of a sweeter hunk of dough, head a few doors over to the Doughnut Plant (379 Grand Street, between Essex & Norfolk Streets, 1-212 505 3700), for high-quality organic doughnuts.

Eldridge Street Synagogue

12 Eldridge Street, between Canal & Division Streets (1-212 219 0888/www.eldridgestreet.org). Subway: F to East Broadway. **Tours** 11am-4pm Tue, Wed, Thur, Sun and by appointment. Guided tours on the hour 11am-3pm. **Admission** $5; $3 seniors and students. **Map** p402 F31.

Ultra modern
The New Museum really is new.

The **New Museum of Contemporary Art**'s relocation to a permanent site at 235 Bowery, on the Lower East Side, embodies its mission statement: 'New Art, New Ideas'. The museum's latest address also confirms its other primary calling, to cut 'clear, smart and bold' moves within the field of contemporary art.

The 65,000-square-foot museum, which is scheduled to open in autumn 2007, will remain dedicated, first and foremost, to contemporary art with emphases on emerging media and surveys of important but 'under-recognised' artists (recent exhibitions, at the museum's temporary location, have showcased the work of Ana Mendieta, Tom Friedman and Andrea Zittel). For a museum with this much cultural capital, relocating to the (former) skids of the Bowery is a pioneering step, but chief curator Richard Flood sees the new space dovetailing with the museum's legacy as the city's most innovative 'laboratory for change' as far as contemporary art goes. The new building reflects the New Museum's spirit, housed on a former parking lot wedged between Stanton and Rivington Streets, in a neighbourhood that's known more for its restaurant supply wholesalers and flophouses than for high-end conceptual art.

Encased in rippling silver metal, the seven-storey museum was designed by the Tokyo-based firm Sejima + Nishizawa/SANAA. The interior challenges the clean white cube of the conventional art gallery, featuring unusual light sources, a sun-flooded lobby and other site-specific quirkiness. Keep an attentive eye out for interesting corners and hidden pockets where art will be tucked. Other features in the building include a black box auditorium accommodating 180 people, and offering downtown art lovers a much-needed venue for an array of public programmes.
For further info, visit www.newmuseum.org.

First Shearith Israel Graveyard
55-57 St James Place, between James & Oliver Streets. Subway: J, M, Z to Bowery. **Map** p402 F31.

Lower East Side
Tenement Museum
108 Orchard Street, at Broome Street (1-212 431 0233/www.tenement.org). Subway: F to Delancey Street; J, M, Z to Delancey-Essex Streets. **Open** *Visitors' center* 11am-5.30pm Mon; 11am-6pm Tue-Fri; 10.45am-6pm Sat, Sun. **Admission** $15; $11 seniors, students. **Credit** AmEx, MC, V. **Map** p403 G30.

Housed in an 1863 tenement building along with a gallery, shop and video room, this fascinating museum is accessible only by guided tour. The tours, which regularly sell out (definitely book ahead), explain the daily life of typical tenement-dwelling immigrant families. (See the website for 360-degree views of the museum's interior.) From April to December, the museum also leads walking tours of the Lower East Side.

East Village

Scruffier than its genteel western counterpart, the **East Village** has a long history as a countercultural hotbed. Originally considered part of the Lower East Side, the neighbourhood boomed in the 1960s, when writers, artists and musicians moved in, transforming it into the hub for the period's social revolution.

Clubs and coffeehouses thrived, including the Fillmore East, on Second Avenue, between 6th and 7th Streets (the theatre has been demolished), and the Dom (23 St Marks Place, between Second & Third Avenues), where the Velvet Underground often headlined (the building is now a condo). In the '70s the neighbourhood took a dive as drugs and crime prevailed – but that didn't stop the influx of artists and punk rockers. In the early '80s East Village galleries were among the first to display the work of groundbreaking artists Jean-Michel Basquiat and Keith Haring. The nabe's past as an alt-scene nexus of arts and politics gets a nod with **Howl!** (*see p264*), a late-summer festival organised by the Federation of East Village Artists. Poetry, music and film events celebrate the community's vibrant heritage.

The area east of Broadway between Houston and 14th Streets is less edgy today (the arrival of high-priced faux-hippie grocery stores Whole Foods and Trader Joes signal an imminent influx of wealthy residents), but remnants of its spirited past endure. A generally amiable population of ravers, punks, yuppies, hippies, homeboys, vagrants and trustafarians (those wannabe bohos funded by family money) has crowded into the neighbourhood's tenements, alongside a few elderly holdouts from previous

waves of immigration. Check out the indie record shops, bargain restaurants, grungy bars, punky clubs and funky, cheap clothing stores.

Looking for a portal into the 19th century? Make a social call at No.29 E 4th Street – the **Merchant's House Museum** (*see p110*). Built in 1832, the home is the best example of domestic life of the period.

For a historical and cultural tour of the neighbourhood, start on the corner of 10th Street and Second Avenue. Here, on the eastern end of historic Stuyvesant Street (one of only a few streets in this area that break the grid), sits the East Village's unofficial cultural centre: **St Mark's Church in-the-Bowery**. St Mark's was built in 1799 on the site of Peter Stuyvesant's farm, and the old guy himself, one of New York's first governors, is buried in the adjacent cemetery. The Episcopal church holds regular services, and also hosts arts groups, such as the experimental theatre troupe Ontological at St Mark's (1-212 533 4650).

St Marks Place (8th Street, between Lafayette Street & Avenue A) is the East Village's main drag. In 1917 the Bolshevik Leon Trotsky ran a printing press at No.77 (between First & Second Avenues), and poet WH Auden lived at the address from 1953 to 1972. Lined with stores, bars and street vendors, St Marks stays packed until the wee hours with crowds browsing for bargain T-shirts, records and books. Since tattooing became legal again in New York City in 1997 (it had been banned in 1961), a number of parlours have opened up, including the famous Fun City (94 St Marks Place, between First Avenue & Avenue A, 1-212 353 8282), whose awning advertises cappuccino and tattoos.

Astor Place, with its 1970s balanced-cube sculpture – which made news in 2005, when it disappeared overnight (turns out the Parks Department took it away for cleaning) – is always swarming with young skateboarders and other modern-day street urchins. It is also the site of Peter Cooper's **Cooper Union** – home to schools of art, architecture and engineering, it bears the distinction of being the only full-scholarship (as in free) private college in the United States. During the 19th century, Astor Place marked the boundary between the slums to the east and some of the city's most fashionable homes. **Colonnade Row** (428-434 Lafayette Street, between Astor Place & E 4th Street) faces the distinguished Astor Public Library building, which theatre legend Joseph Papp rescued from demolition in the 1960s. Today, the old library is the **Public Theater** (*see p348*), a haven for first-run American plays, the headquarters of the Shakespeare in Central Park festival (*see p262*) and the trendy Joe's Pub (*see p316*).

Washington Square Park. *See p110.*

Below Astor Place, Third Avenue (one block east of Lafayette Street) becomes the **Bowery**. The street, for ages the city's famous flophouse strip and the home of missionary organisations catering to the down-and-out, has in recent years been sanitised and invaded by swanky restaurants and clubs. Hallowed CBGB, the birthplace of American punk, is even about to get the boot – its pedigree couldn't protect it from rising rents. The club had been embroiled in a legal battle with its landlord for months, and, at the time of writing, was facing eviction in October 2006. On the upside, owner

and East Village character Hilly Kristal has announced that he's searching for a new location for the historic venue, and might even open a sister club in Las Vegas. Apparently, you really can't stop the rock.

Whatever happens to CBGB, many other bars and clubs in the East Village still successfully apply the cheap-beer-and-loud-music formula, including Continental (*see p315*) and the Mercury Lounge (*see p317*).

East 7th Street is a Ukrainian stronghold; the focal point is the Byzantine **St George's Ukrainian Catholic Church** at No.30.

Across the street, there's often a long line of beefy fraternity types waiting to enter McSorley's Old Ale House (*see p219*), which touts itself as the city's oldest pub in a single location (1854); it still serves just one kind of beer – its own brew, available in light and dark formulas. For those who would rather shop than sip, the eclectic boutiques of young designers and vintage-clothing dealers dot 7th, 8th and 9th Streets.

Curry Row, on 6th Street, between First & Second Avenues, is one of several Little Indias in New York. Roughly two dozen Indian restaurants sit side by side (contrary to an oft-told joke, they do not share a single kitchen), and they remain popular with diners on an extremely tight budget. The line of shiny Harleys on 3rd Street, between First & Second Avenues, tells you that the New York chapter of the **Hell's Angels** is based here.

Alphabet City, so-called because it occupies Avenues A, B, C and D, stretches towards the East River. The once largely working-class Latino (and in particular, Puerto Rican) population has now been overtaken by professionals willing to pay higher rents. Avenue C is known as Loisaida Avenue, an approximation of 'Lower East Side' when pronounced with a Spanish accent. An important cultural melting pot in the 1970s and '80s, the area has lost some of its cultural energy in recent years with the change in demographics; the positive aspect of gentrification is cleaner streets and lower crime rates – the neighbourhood's long romance with the drug trade is now mostly a thing of the past.

For those who appreciate funky charm, Alphabet City has its attractions. Two churches on 4th Street are built in the Spanish colonial style: San Isidro y San Leandro (345 E 4th Street, between Avenues C & D) and Iglesia Pentecostal Camino Damasco (289 E 4th Street, between Avenues B & C). The Nuyorican Poets Café (*see p278*), a more than 30-year-old clubhouse for espresso-drinking beatniks, is famous for its poetry slams, in which performers do lyric battle before a score-keeping audience. **Tompkins Square Park** (from 7th to 10th Streets, between Avenues A & B; **photo** *p110*), which honours Daniel D Tompkins, governor of New York from 1807 to 1817 and vice-president during the Monroe administration, has a past as a site for demonstrations and rioting. The last major uprising was about 15 years ago, when the city evicted squatters from the park and renovated it to suit the area's increasingly affluent residents; in the summer of 2004 a permit request for a 20,000-person protest camp during the Republican National Convention was denied. The square also plays host to the city's on-again, off-again drag celebration, Wigstock. This is the community park of the East Village, and a place where Latino bongo beaters, longhairs with acoustic guitars, punky squatters, mangy dogs, yuppie stroller-pushers and the homeless all mingle.

North of Tompkins Square, around First Avenue and 11th Street, are remnants of earlier communities: discount fabric dealers, Italian cheese shops, Polish butchers and two great Italian coffee-and-cannoli houses: De Robertis

Local legend

Sightseeing

In 1917 **Edna St Vincent Millay**, already a gifted poet, moved to Greenwich Village, where she immediately took to the bohemian lifestyle; here women were allowed to smoke in public, dress casually and go out at night unaccompanied. Embracing unconventionality, Millay freely took both male and female lovers. In 1921 she wrote *Recuerdo*, a romantic poem about being up all night and riding the Staten Island Ferry: 'We were very tired, we were very merry/We had gone back and forth all night on the ferry.' In 1923 she was the first woman to be awarded the Pulitzer Prize for poetry. That same year she moved into 75½ Bedford Street, one of the narrowest homes in the city, measuring a mere nine and a half feet wide. A talented actress, St Vincent Millay also helped found the Cherry Lane Theater around the corner on Commerce Street, an experimental theatre landmark.

Tompkins Square Park. *See p109.*

(176 First Avenue, between 10th & 11th Streets, 1-212 674 7137) and Veniero's Pasticceria and Caffè (342 E 11th Street, at First Avenue, 1-212 674 7264).

Merchant's House Museum

29 E 4th Street, between Lafayette Street & Bowery (1-212 777 1089/www.merchantshouse.com). Subway: B, D, F, V to Broadway-Lafayette Street; 6 to Bleecker Street. **Open** noon-5pm Thur-Sun. **Admission** $8; $5 seniors, students. **Credit** AmEx, MC, V. **Map** p403 F29.

New York City's only preserved 19th-century family home is an elegant, late Federal-Greek Revival house stocked with the same furnishings and decorations that filled its rooms when it was inhabited from 1835 to 1933 by hardware tycoon Seabury Treadwell and his descendants.

Greenwich Village

Stretching from Houston Street to 14th Street, between Broadway and Sixth Avenue, **Greenwich Village**'s leafy streets have inspired bohemians for almost a century. It's a place for idle wandering, candlelit dining in out-of-the-way restaurants, and for hopping between bars and cabaret venues. The Village often gets mobbed in mild weather and has lost some of its quaintness, but much of what has always attracted painters and poets to New York still exists. Sip a fresh roast in honour of the Beats – Jack Kerouac, Allen Ginsberg and their buddies – as you sit in their former haunts. Kerouac's favourite was Le Figaro Café

(184 Bleecker Street, at MacDougal Street, 1-212 677 1100). The Cedar Tavern (82 University Place, between 11th & 12th Streets, 1-212 929 9089), which was originally at the corner of 8th Street, is where the leading figures of abstract expressionism's boys' club discussed how best to apply paint: Franz Kline, Jackson Pollock, Larry Rivers and Willem de Kooning drank under this banner in the 1950s.

The hippies who tuned out in **Washington Square Park** (**photo** *p108*), once a potter's field, are still there in spirit, and often in person: the park hums with musicians and street artists (though the once-ubiquitous pot dealers have disappeared thanks to hidden surveillance cameras). In warmer months, this is one of the best people-watching spots in the city. Chess hustlers and students from New York University join in, along with today's new generation of idlers: hip-hop kids, who drive down to West 4th Street in their booming Jeeps, and Generation-Y skateboarders, who clatter around the fountain and near the base of the Washington Arch. A modest-size replica of Paris's Arc de Triomphe, the arch was built in 1895 to honour George Washington, and was recently unveiled after a seemingly endless refurbishment. A $16million redesign of the park will begin sometime in late 2006 or early 2007.

The Village has been fashionable since the 1830s, when the wealthy built handsome townhouses around Washington Square. A few of these properties are still privately owned and occupied; many others have become part of the ever-expanding **New York University** campus. NYU also owns the Washington Mews, a row of charming 19th-century buildings that were once stables; they line a tiny cobblestone alley just north of the park between Fifth Avenue and University Place. Several literary figures, including Henry James, Herman Melville and Mark Twain, lived on or near the square. In 1871 the local creative community founded the **Salmagundi Club** (*see p112*), America's oldest artists' club, which is now situated north of Washington Square on Fifth Avenue. The landmark building hosts exhibitions, lectures and art auctions.

Greenwich Village continues to change with the times, for better and for worse. Eighth Street is currently a long procession of piercing parlours, punky boutiques and shoe stores; in the 1960s it was the closest New York got to San Francisco's Haight Street. (Jimi Hendrix's Electric Lady Studios is still at 52 W 8th Street, between Fifth & Sixth Avenues.)

Once the dingy but colourful stomping ground of Beat poets and folk and jazz musicians, the well-trafficked strip of Bleecker Street between La Guardia Place and Sixth Avenue is now simply an overcrowded stretch of poster shops, cheap restaurants and music venues for

Feeling bookish?

Roll-up for a magical (weekend) literary tour.

Friday Writing about Times Square, GK Chesterton proclaimed, 'What a glorious garden of wonders this would be, to any who was lucky enough to be unable to read,' Literate New Yorkers should head elsewhere, however – to the shade-dappled outdoor Bryant Park Reading Room (42nd Street side of park, between Fifth & Sixth Avenues, www.bryantpark.org; closes at 5pm), a great place for a spot of afternoon relaxation. Then follow Library Walk, 96 bronze sidewalk plaques with quotes (41st Street, between Fifth & Park Avenues), to the deluxe Library Hotel (299 Madison Avenue at 41st Street, 1-212 204 5498, www.libraryhotel.com), which has book-themed rooms organised according to the Dewey decimal system. Truman Capote might have approved of the cocktail named after him (gin, Cointreau, lime juice and orange bitters; $12); sip one in the rooftop Bookmarks Lounge.

Saturday Take the 2 or 3 train to the NYPL's Schomburg Center for Research in Black Culture (515 Malcolm X Blvd, at Lenox Avenue, enter at 103 W 135th Street, 1-212 491 2200, www.nypl.org), which has more than ten million books, manuscripts and photos. Then drop by the hotspot Hue-Man Bookstore and Café (2319 Frederick Douglass Blvd, at Eighth Avenue, between 124th & 125th Streets, 1-212 665 7400, www.huemanbookstore.com). You may know

about the Algonquin's 'Round Table' legacy, but have you made it to the Lenox Lounge (288 Malcolm X Blvd, at Lenox Avenue, between 124th & 125th Streets, 1-212 427 0253, www.lenoxlounge.com)? End your day with crab-cakes and jazz at the former hangout of James Baldwin and Langston Hughes.

Sunday Get jump-started with a latte and a granola bar at Housing Works Used Books Café (*see p252*), which hosts great events, and benefits homeless New Yorkers living with HIV. Some of the city's best reading series can be found at Happy Ending, KGB Bar and the Bowery Poetry Club (*see p278*).

Finally, imbibe like a literary legend at Chumley's (86 Bedford Street, between Barrow & Grove Streets, 1-212 675 4449). Striking book jackets and photos of the likes of Ring Lardner Jr and JD Salinger line the walls at this hidden Prohibition-era speakeasy.

The rose fades
and is renewed again
by its seed, naturally
but where

save in the poem
shall it go
to suffer no diminution
of its splendor

the college crowd. Bob Dylan lived at and owned 94 MacDougal Street (on a row of historic brownstones near Bleecker Street) through much of the 1960s, performing in Washington Square Park and at clubs such as Cafe Wha? on MacDougal Street, between Bleecker and West 3rd Streets. The famed Village Gate jazz club once stood at the corner of Bleecker and Thompson Streets; it's been carved up into a CVS pharmacy and a small theatre, though the Gate's sign is still in evidence. The new **AIA Center for Architecture** (*see below*), a comprehensive resource for building and planning in New York, is just up the street, on La Guardia Place.

In the triangle formed by Sixth Avenue, Greenwich Avenue and 10th Street, you'll see the Gothic-style Jefferson Market Library (a branch of the New York Public Library); the lovely flower-filled garden facing Greenwich Avenue once held the art deco Women's House of Detention (Mae West did a little time there in 1926, on obscenity charges stemming from her Broadway show *Sex*), which was torn down in 1974. On Sixth Avenue at West 4th Street, stop by 'the Cage' – outdoor basketball courts where outstanding schoolyard players showcase their high-flying moves. Across the street lies the new state-of-the-art IFC movie theatre, an arthouse spot that took the place of the formerly grungy and subsequently long-abandoned Waverly Cinema.

AIA Center for Architecture

536 La Guardia Place, between Bleecker & W 3rd Streets (1-212 683 0023/www.aiany.org). Subway: A, B, C, D, E, F, V to W 4th Street. **Open** 9am-8pm Mon-Fri; 11am-5pm Sat. **Admission** free. **Map** p403 E29.

After five years of planning, the Center for Architecture opened to acclaim in autumn 2003. Founded in 1867, the organisation languished for years on the sixth floor of a Lexington Avenue edifice, far out of sight (and mind) of all but the most devoted architecture aficionados. In 1997, recognising its isolation and perceived insularity, the American Institute of Architects (AIA) began searching Soho and the Village for new digs, finally opting for a vacant storefront in an early 20th-century industrial building. After a design competition, Andrew Berman Architect was chosen to transform the space into a fitting home for architectural debate.

The sweeping, light-filled design is a physical manifestation of AIA's goal of promoting transparency in its access and programming. Berman cut away large slabs of flooring at the street and basement levels, converting underground spaces into bright, museum-quality galleries. He also installed a glass-enclosed library and conference room – open to the public – on the first floor, and a children's gallery and workshop on the mezza-

nine level. The building is New York's first public space to use an energy-efficient geothermal system. Water from two 1,260ft wells is piped through the building to help heat and cool it.

Salmagundi Club

47 Fifth Avenue, at 12th Street (1-212 255 7740/ www.salmagundi.org). Subway: L, N, Q, R, W, 4, 5, 6 to 14th Street-Union Square. **Open** 1-5pm daily for exhibitions only; phone for details. **Admission** free. **Map** p402 E28.

West Village & Meatpacking District

While the **West Village** now harbours a wide range of celebrities (Sarah Jessica Parker and hubby Matthew Broderick live here, as does former NYC mayor Ed Koch, and the trio of Richard Meier towers at the end of Perry and Charles Streets houses A-listers galore), a low-key, everyone-knows-one-another feel remains.

The area west of Sixth Avenue to the Hudson River, from 14th Street to Houston Street, still possesses the features that moulded the Village's character. Only in this neighbourhood could West 10th Street cross West 4th Street, and Waverly Place cross...Waverly Place. (The West Village's layout follows not the regular grid pattern but the original horse paths that settlers used to navigate it.) Locals and tourists fill bistros along Seventh Avenue and Hudson Street (aka Eighth Avenue), the neighbourhood's main drags, and patronise the increasingly high-rent shops,

The **Meatpacking District**.

including three Marc Jacobs boutiques, three Ralph Lauren outposts and a new James Perse shop, at this newly hot end of Bleecker Street.

The north-west corner of this area is known as the **Meatpacking District**. Beginning in the 1930s, it was primarily a wholesale meat market; until the 1990s, it was also a choice haunt for prostitutes, many of them transsexual. In recent years, however, the atmospheric cobblestone streets of this landmark district have seen the arrival of a new type of tenant: the once-lonely Florent (69 Gansevoort Street, between Greenwich & Washington Streets, 1-212 989 5779), a 24-hour French diner that opened in 1985, is now part of a chic scene that includes some swinging watering holes and the restaurants Pastis (9 Ninth Avenue, at Little W 12th Street, 1-212 929 4844), 5 Ninth (5 Ninth Avenue, at Little W 12th Street, 1-212 929 9460) and Spice Market (403 W 13th at Ninth Avenue, 1-212 675-2322), among many others. When the boutique Hotel Gansevoort (*see p50* **Upscale Downtown**) opened in 2004, it made this area an official tourist destination. It's now trendsetting again with the new G Spa and Lounge, a kooky blend of bar and spa, in which the treatment rooms become VIP coves at night. The district also lures the fashion faithful with hot spots such as Jeffrey New York, Alexander McQueen, Stella McCartney and rockin' Le Dernier Cri. As rents rose, many of the meatpacking plants were forced out to make space for the trendy (on hot summer days, however, you can still smell the meat dealers that remain).

The neighbourhood's bohemians may have dwindled – they surely could not afford the current astronomic rents in this area – but several historic nightlife spots soldier on to the south in the West Village: the White Horse Tavern (567 Hudson Street, at 11th Street, 1-212 989 3956) is supposedly where poet Dylan Thomas went on his last drinking binge before his death, in 1953. Earlier in the century, John Steinbeck and John Dos Passos passed time at Chumley's (*see p220*), a still-unmarked Prohibition-era speakeasy at 86 Bedford Street. Writer Edna St Vincent Millay lived at 75½ Bedford Street (*see p109* **Local legend**), built in 1873; subsequent inhabitants include Cary Grant and John Barrymore. Only nine and a half feet wide, it's one of the narrowest residential buildings in the entire city. On and just off Seventh Avenue South are jazz and cabaret clubs, including Village Vanguard (*see p325*).

The West Village is also renowned as a gay neighbourhood, though the scene is more happening in Chelsea these days (*see p114*). The Stonewall (*see p305*), on Christopher Street, is next to the original Stonewall Inn, the site of the 1969 rebellion that marked the birth of the modern gay-liberation movement. Same-sex couples stroll along Christopher Street (from Sheridan Square to the Hudson River), and plenty of shops, bars and restaurants are out and proud. The Hudson riverfront features grass-covered piers, food vendors, picnic tables and volleyball courts – ideal for warm-weather dawdling by folks of any sexual persuasion.

Midtown

Get swept away, New York-style.

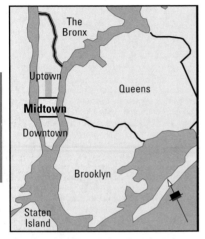

If you're new to New York and you haven't spent much time in a big city, then brace yourself. The strip of land roughly between 14th Street and 59th Street teems with tens of thousands of people every day. No time to stop and smell the roses here, especially above 34th Street. Marvel at the flowing river of people walking shoulder to shoulder along the avenues. Just keep apace as you ponder where all those navy blue suits come from, and be sure to watch your step to avoid getting run over by a speeding yellow cab or bike messenger. This is the beating heart of the city: high-powered bankers, lawyers and advertising executives pack glass-fronted skyscrapers doing untold important works, helped by a veritable army of Starbucks baristas who keep everyone's caffeine levels surging (there are about 100 branches of Starbucks in this part of town alone). Of course, New York City's most famous landmarks – the **Empire State Building**, the **Chrysler Building**, **Times Square**, **Rockefeller Center**, and **Grand Central Terminal** – are located here. But there's more to Midtown than glistening towers and high-octane commerce. Cultural heavyweights such as the **Museum of Modern Art**, **Broadway** and the **Theater District**, **New York Public Library** and **Carnegie Hall** draw their own

crowds. Midtown is also where you'll find the **Union Square Greenmarket**, an agrarian oasis, and the quaint tree-lined streets of **Chelsea**, **Tudor City** and **Gramercy Park**. Everywhere you look, you'll see an opportunity to part with your hard-earned cash, from street peddlers pushing designer knock-offs to charming boutiques and world-class department stores. If city life is for you, you've come to the right place – smack-bang in the middle of the maddening crowd.

Chelsea

Up until the 1980s, Chelsea was a mostly working-class and industrial neighbourhood. Now it's the epicentre of the city's gay life, but residents of all types inhabit the blocks between 14th and 29th Streets west of Fifth Avenue. There's a generous assortment of bars and restaurants, most of which are clustered along Eighth Avenue, the main hub of activity. Pioneers such as **Dia:Chelsea** (*see p117*) led the art crowd northwards from Soho, and the whole western edge of Chelsea is now the city's hottest gallery zone (*see p270* **Art attack**). This far-west warehouse district is now a nesting ground for fashionable lounges and nightclubs, and has become much more residential in recent years. The most exciting thing to happen to Chelsea of late are the plans to turn a defunct elevated train, known as the High Line, into a 1.5-mile-long promenade (*see pp30-31* **High times ahead**).

Don't miss the weekend flea markets tucked between buildings in parking lots on 25th Street, between Sixth Avenue and Broadway, or the rummage-worthy **Garage** (*see p249*). Ornate wrought-iron balconies distinguish the **Chelsea Hotel** (*see p67*), which has been a magnet for international bohemians since the 1950s. In the '60s and '70s Andy Warhol's superstars (the Chelsea Girls) made the place infamous; punk rock conferred its notoriety in the '80s, when Nancy Spungen was stabbed to death by boyfriend Sid Vicious in Room 100. Stop by for a peek at the lobby artwork and the grunge-glamorous guests, and linger over a drink in the luxe basement lounge, Serena. Occupying the long stretch of 23rd Street, between Ninth and Tenth Avenues, London Terrace is a distinctive 1920s Tudor-

Chelsea.

style apartment complex that's home to some famous names, including Debbie Harry, Chelsea Clinton and Teri Hatcher (of *Desperate Housewives*).

Chelsea has its fair share of cultural offerings. The **Joyce Theater** (*see p351*) is a brilliantly renovated art deco cinema that presents better-known contemporary dance troupes. The **Dance Theater Workshop** (*see p352*) performs at the Bessie Schönberg Theater (219 W 19th Street, between Seventh & Eighth Avenues, 1-212 691 6500), and towards the river on 19th Street sits the **Kitchen** (*see p352*), a pioneering experimental-arts centre. Looking to kick-start your libido? Head to Fifth Avenue and check out the **Museum of Sex** (*see below*).

One of the most talked-about additions to the neighbourhood is the billowing nine-storey glass-sheathed Frank Gehry building on the West Side Highway, between 18th and 19th Streets. The building will be the East Coast headquarters for media and e-commerce mogul Barry Diller.

Cushman Row (406-418 W 20th Street, between Ninth & Tenth Avenues), in the Chelsea Historic District, is an example of how the area looked when it was developed in the mid 1800s (although its grandeur was later affected by the intrusion of noisy elevated railways). Just north is the block-long **General Theological Seminary of the Episcopal Church** (*see below*), whose gardens offer a pleasant respite for reflection. The seminary's land was part of the estate known as Chelsea, owned by the poet Clement Clarke Moore (best known for 'Twas the night before Christmas').

The former Nabisco plant on Ninth Avenue, where the first Oreo cookie was made, in 1912, has been renovated and is now home to the **Chelsea Market** (75 Ninth Avenue, between 15th & 16th Streets, www.chelseamarket.com). The former factory site is a conglomeration of 18 structures built between the 1890s and the 1930s. The ground-floor food arcade offers artisanal bread, lobster, wine, hand-decorated cookies and imported Italian foods, among other treats. Upper floors house several media companies, including the Oxygen Network and the Food Network studios, where shows such as *Emeril Live* and *Molto Mario* are taped.

Chelsea's art galleries, occupying former warehouses on streets W 20th to W 29th, west of Tenth Avenue, draw an international audience, especially at weekends. Many of the major galleries that were priced out of Soho (replaced by retail shops) found new homes here; bars and restaurants on the prowl for cheaper space followed suit. Evolving much like Soho did, the area has become just as pricey.

In 2006 the **New Museum of Contemporary Art** (*see p118*) will call the neighbourhood home and new digs are being built all the time.

On Seventh Avenue, at 27th Street, is the **Fashion Institute of Technology** (www.fitnyc.edu), a state college for those who aspire to vie with renowned alumni, including Calvin Klein, in making their mark on fashion. Fashionistas won't want to miss the school's museum (*see below*) a block away, which mounts stellar free exhibitions.

You can watch the sunset from one of the spectacular Hudson River piers, which were once terminals for the world's grand ocean liners. Many other city piers remain in a state of ruin, but the four between 17th and 23rd Streets have been transformed into the mega sports centre and TV- and film-studio complex **Chelsea Piers**. When you're down by the river, the **Starrett-Lehigh Building** (601 W 26th Street, at Eleventh Avenue) comes into view. The stunning 1929 structure was left to fall into disrepair until the dot-com boom of the late '90s, when media companies, photographers and fashion designers snatched up the loft-like spaces.

Dia:Chelsea

548 W 22nd Street, between Tenth & Eleventh Avenues (1-212 989 5566/www.diachelsea.org). **Closed** until early 2008. **Map** p404 C26.
The Chelsea branch of this New York stalwart, usually given to single-artist projects, is seeking a new home in the trendy Meatpacking District, and hopes to reopen sometime in early 2008. For information on visiting Dia:Beacon, *see p357*.

General Theological Seminary of the Episcopal Church

175 Ninth Avenue, between 20th & 21st Streets (1-212 243 5150/www.gts.edu). Subway: C, E to 23rd Street. **Open** *Gardens* noon-3pm Mon-Thur; 11am-3pm Fri, weather permitting. **Admission** free. **Map** p403 C27.

Museum at FIT

Seventh Avenue, at 27th Street (1-212 217 5800/ www.fitnyc.edu). Subway: 1 to 28th Street. **Open** noon-8pm Tue-Fri; 10am-5pm Sat. **Admission** free. **Map** p404 D26.
The Fashion Institute of Technology houses one of the world's most important collections of clothing and textiles, curated by the influential fashion historian Valerie Steele. Incorporating everything from extravagant costumes to sturdy denim work clothes, the exhibitions touch on the role fashion has played in society since the beginning of the 20th century.

Museum of Sex

233 Fifth Avenue, at 27th Street (1-212 689 6337/ www.museumofsex.org). Subway: N, R, W, 6 to 28th Street. **Open** 11am-6.30pm Mon-Fri, Sun; 11am-8pm Sat. **Admission** $14.50; $13.50 students. Under-18s not admitted. **Credit** AmEx, MC, V. **Map** p404 E26.

The cutting-edge **Flatiron Building**. See p119.

Ever-lively **Union Square**. See p119.

Despite the subject matter, don't expect too much titillation at this museum, which opened in 2002 to mixed reviews. Instead, you'll find presentations of historical documents and items – many of which were too risqué to be made public in their own time – that explore prostitution, burlesque, birth control, obscenity and fetishism. In 2002 the museum acquired an extensive collection of pornography from a retired Library of Congress curator (apparently, he applied his professional knowledge to recreational pursuits as well). Thus, the Ralph Whittington Collection features thousands of items, including 8mm films, videos, blow-up dolls and other erotic paraphernalia.

New Museum of Contemporary Art

Temporary location *556 W 22nd Street, at Eleventh Avenue (1-212 219 1222/www.newmuseum.org). Subway: C, E to 23rd Street.* **Open** noon-6pm Tue, Wed, Fri, Sat; noon-8pm Thur. **Admission** $6; $3 seniors, students; free under-18s. Half-price 6-8pm Thur. **Credit** AmEx, Disc, MC, V. **Map** p404 C26. While its new digs on the Bowery are under construction (the opening is slated for late autumn 2007), the New Museum will occupy 7,000sq ft of ground-floor space in the Chelsea Art Museum. Its retrospectives of mid-career artists – South Africa's William Kentridge, Los Angeles's Paul McCarthy, New York's Carroll Dunham – attract serious crowds, though not every group show is strong.

Flatiron District & Union Square

The Flatiron District, which extends from 14th to 29th Streets, between Fifth and Park Avenues, gives Downtown a run for its money in terms of cachet – and cool. This chic enclave is full of retail stores that are quite often less expensive but just as stylish as those below 14th Street. The area is compact enough that tourists can hit all the sights on foot and then relax with a cocktail at a local watering hole.

Two public commons lie within the district: Madison and Union Squares. **Madison Square** (from 23rd to 26th Streets, between Fifth & Madison Avenues) was the site of PT Barnum's Hippodrome and the original Madison Square Garden – the scene of the scandalous murder of its architect, Stanford White (recounted in EL Doctorow's novel *Ragtime*, also adapted as a film). After years of neglect, the statue-filled Madison Square Park finally got a facelift in 2001. For ages, the vicinity bordering the park's east side was notable only for the presence of the monolithic New York Life Insurance Company Building (51 Madison Avenue, between 25th & 26th Streets) and the Appellate Division Courthouse

(35 E 25th Street, at Madison Avenue). Now, numerous swank dining options have injected some café-society liveliness, including Tom Colicchio's glorious side-by-side-by-side trio of eateries, 'wichcraft, Craft and Craftbar (*see p205*).

During warmer months, stop by Danny Meyer's Shake Shack (south side of Madison Square Park, near 23rd Street, at Madison Avenue, 1-212 889 6600), a hot-dog, hamburger and ice-cream stand where you can dine alfresco, surrounded by lush foliage.

Just south of Madison Square is a famously triangular Renaissance palazzo, the **Flatiron Building** (175 Fifth Avenue, between 22nd & 23rd Streets; **photo *p118***). The 22-storey edifice is clad in white terracotta: its light colour was revealed again by cleaning and restoration in the early 1990s. The surrounding neighbourhood was christened in honour of the structure, which was the world's first steel-frame skyscraper.

In the 19th century the neighbourhood went by the moniker of Ladies' Mile, thanks to the ritzy department stores that lined Broadway and Sixth Avenue to the west. These huge retail palaces attracted the carriage trade, wealthy women who bought the latest imported fashions and household goods. By 1914 most of the department stores had moved north, leaving their proud cast-iron buildings behind. Today, the area is peppered with bookshops and photo studios and labs (it was known as New York's photo district well into the 1990s), and supermodels. The area has also reclaimed its fashionable history and is once again a prime shopping destination. Broadway between 14th and 23rd Streets is a tasteful home-furnishings strip; be sure to take a spin through the eclectic, expensive six-storey home-design store **ABC Carpet & Home** (*see p250*). Fifth Avenue below 23rd Street is a clothing mecca: many upscale shops, including the exclusive Paul Smith, showcase the latest designs. In the mid 1990s big internet companies began colonising the lofts on Fifth Avenue and Broadway, and the district was dubbed Silicon Alley, a name that stuck even after the boom flattened out.

Union Square (from 14th to 17th Streets, between Union Square East & Union Square West; **photo *p118*.**) is named after neither the Union of the Civil War nor the lively labour rallies that once took place here, but simply for the union of Broadway and Bowery Lane (now Fourth Avenue). From the 1920s until the early 1960s, Union Square had a reputation as the favourite location for rabble-rousing political oratory, from AFL-CIO rallies to anti-Vietnam War protests. Following September 11, 2001, the park became a focal point for the city's outpouring of grief. Today, it's probably best known as the home of the **Union Square Greenmarket** (*see p121*), an excellent farmers' market fast becoming a New York institution. The buildings flanking the square are used for a variety of commercial purposes. They include the W New York-Union Square hotel, the giant Zeckendorf Towers residential complex (1 Irving Place, between 14th & 15th Streets), a Virgin Megastore and a Barnes & Noble bookstore. Facing south, look up (and slightly east) and marvel at what three million

Keeping it regional at the **Union Square Greenmarket**.

Returning champion

The Morgan Library's new look.

In 2003 the Morgan Library (established by Pierpont Morgan (father of JP) to house his growing collection of rare books, manuscripts and artworks) locked its doors and embarked on its largest growth spurt since 1928. Those New Yorkers who are obsessed with certain NYC institutions missed this particular one with a nerdiness that bordered on the insane.

Finally, in April 2006, the museum, designed by Pritzker Prize-winning architect Renzo Piano, reopened, with double the amount of exhibition space and new amenities added to the old complex's three buildings. But has this new Super Morgan shed the slightly esoteric vibe that previously made it so endearing?

Let's be frank here: the Morgan was never the Met or MoMA. When tourists come to visit the city, the first thing on their to-do lists is not an exhibition of 16th-century Flemish drawings. But the homely atmosphere of the Morgan, with its small, digestible galleries, unusual artworks and historical display of Pierpont's actual home library made it a rare treat. The buildings were just so pretty, so warm and so rarely crowded that they felt like an oasis for those in the know. 'People have long felt it is a very special place in New York where objects of great quality can be viewed in an intimate setting,' the director of communications, Patrick Milliman, explained. 'We haven't changed that with the expansion. Our galleries are still relatively small and intimate but we have more of them.'

Milliman isn't wrong. The new Morgan keeps the focus on the complex's original trio of historical structures, slyly connecting them through Piano's glass and steel additions, and unobstructively adding 75,000 square feet, mostly underground. A giant translucent cube enclosing the central court between the buildings now transforms the once loosely connected edifices into a seamless campus, complete with an airy Italian-style piazza.

The Morgan seems to be making a bid to be taken seriously as a major cultural attraction. Exhibit A is, quite simply, the architecture. In an era when a building's design is often judged to be as important as what's inside, Piano's melding of historic and modern is a laudable feat that's beautiful in itself.

Exhibit B is the new 280-seat performance hall. Blanketed in cherrywood, the acoustically outfitted concert space will not only host musical events, but also readings, lectures and an inaugural series featuring playwright Edward Albee, author Pete Hamill, poet Seamus Heaney and baritone Thomas Hampson.

Exhibit C: the exhibitions. The museum will now be able to display more of its 350,000 objects than ever, and the opening shows mine those treasures. You'll see drawings by Michelangelo, Rembrandt and Picasso; a first edition of Malory's King Arthur tales from 1485; a copy of *Frankenstein* annotated by Mary Shelley; manuscripts by Dickens, Poe, Twain, Steinbeck and Wilde; and sheet-music drafts by the likes of Beethoven and Mozart.

And the there's the most convincing evidence of the Morgan's transformation: an exhibition on Bob Dylan in autumn 2006. With this show of handwritten lyrics, instruments and personal objects from Dylan's early career, the Morgan made an unexpected move, spicing up its brainy character with a bit of pop-culture relevance.

bucks can buy: the ugly sculpture-wall before you, called *Metronome,* was installed in 1999 (and remains one of the largest private commissions of public art in the city's history). What the hell is it? We thought you'd never ask: 'The entire work symbolises the intangibility of time,' according to its makers (artists Kristin Jones and Andrew Ginzel). Reading from left to right, the digital read-out on the installation's main panel displays the current time.

If you worked up an appetite contemplating the hour of the day, several decent restaurants are in close proximity, most notably the elegant (and famously expensive) Union Square Café (21 E 16th Street, between Fifth Avenue & Union Square West, 1-212 243 4020). In summer, the outdoor Luna Park bar (Union Square Park, 17th Street, between Broadway & Park Avenue South, 1-212 475 8464) beckons the cocktail crowd, while skateboarders commandeer the Greenmarket space during the evenings. Just off the square to the east is the **Vineyard Theatre** (*see p349*), an Off-Broadway venue featuring the works of such well-respected playwrights as Craig Lucas and Paula Vogel. Tony-award-winning musical *Avenue Q* got its start here.

Union Square Greenmarket

From 16th to 17th Streets, between Union Square East & Union Square West (1-212 788 7476). Subway: L, N, Q, R, W, 4, 5, 6 to 14th Street-Union Square. **Open** 8am-6pm Mon, Wed, Fri, Sat. **Map** p403 E27.
Shop elbow-to-elbow with top chefs for all manner of regionally grown culinary pleasures. **Photo** *p119.*

Gramercy Park & Murray Hill

You need a key to enter **Gramercy Park**, a tranquil, gated green square at the bottom of Lexington Avenue (between 20th & 21st Streets). Who gets a key? Only the lucky people who live in the beautiful townhouses and apartment buildings that ring the park. Anyone, however, can enjoy the charms of the surrounding district. Gramercy Park was developed in the 1830s to resemble a London square. The Players (16 Gramercy Park South, between Park Avenue South & Irving Place), a private club and residence, is housed in an 1845 brownstone formerly owned by actor Edwin Booth; the 19th-century superstar was the brother of Abraham Lincoln's assassin, John Wilkes Booth. Edwin had the interior revamped as a club for theatre professionals. Next door (No.15) is the Gothic Revival Samuel Tilden House, which now houses the **National Arts Club**, whose members often donate their work in lieu of annual dues. The busts of famous writers (Shakespeare, Dante) that grace the

façade were chosen to reflect Tilden's library, which, along with his vast fortune, helped create the New York Public Library.

Irving Place, a strip leading south from the park to 14th Street, is named after author Washington Irving. Near the corner of 15th Street, **Irving Plaza** (*see p316*), a medium-size live-music venue that has been around since the early 1990s (when the Dave Matthews Band played here as an opening act), hosts everyone from old-timers like Van Morrison to newer acts like Ted Leo + Pharmacists. At the corner of Park Avenue South and 17th Street stands the final headquarters of the once-omnipotent Tammany Hall political machine. Built in 1929, the building now houses the New York Film Academy and a theatre.

A few blocks away, the **Theodore Roosevelt Birthplace**, a national historic site, holds a small museum. The President's actual birthplace was demolished in 1916, but it has since been fully reconstructed, complete with period furniture and a trophy room. The low, fortress-like 69th Regiment Armory (68 Lexington Avenue, between 25th & 26th Streets), now used by the New York National Guard, hosted the sensational 1913 Armory Show, which introduced Americans to Cubism, Fauvism and Dadaism. The tradition continues at the annual **Armory Show** (*see p260*).

The largely residential area bordered by 23rd and 30th Streets, Park Avenue and the East River is known as **Kips Bay**, named after Jacobus Henderson Kip, whose farm covered the area in the 17th century. Third Avenue is the neighbourhood's main thoroughfare, and a locus of ethnic eateries representing a variety of eastern cuisines, including Afghan, Tibetan and Turkish, along with nightspots such as the **Rodeo Bar & Grill** (*see p325*), a Texas-style roadhouse that offers food and live roots music. Lexington Avenue, between 27th and 30th Streets, has been dubbed Curry Hill because of its many Indian restaurants and grocery stores.

Murray Hill spans 30th to 40th Streets, between Third and Fifth Avenues. Townhouses of the rich and powerful were once clustered around Madison and Park Avenues. While it's still a fashionable neighbourhood, only a few streets retain the elegance that made Murray Hill so distinctive. Sniffen Court (150-158 E 36th Street, between Lexington & Third Avenues) is an unspoilt row of 1864 carriage houses located within earshot of the Queens Midtown Tunnel's ceaseless traffic. One of the area's most impressive attractions, the **Morgan Library** (*see p122*), also located on 36th Street, reopened in 2006 after an extensive renovation (*see p120* **Returning champion**).

The charming exhibition space occupies two buildings (one of which was J Pierpont Morgan's personal library) and holds books, manuscripts, prints, and silver and copper collections accumulated by the famously acquisitive banker. If contemporary European culture interests you more, visit nearby **Scandinavia House: the Nordic Center in America** (*see below*).

Morgan Library

225 Madison Avenue, at 36th Street (1-212 685 0008/www.morganlibrary.org). Subway: 6 to 33rd Street. **Open** 10.30am-5pm Tue-Thur; 10.30am-9pm Fri; 10am-6pm Sat; 11am-6pm Sun. **Admission** $12; $8 12-16s, seniors, students; free under 12s. **Credit** AmEx, MC, V. **Map** p404 E25. *See p120* **Returning champion**.

National Arts Club

15 Gramercy Park South, between Park Avenue South & Irving Place (1-212 475 3424/ www.nationalartsclub.org). Subway: 6 to 23rd Street. **Open** for exhibitions only. Call or visit website for current exhibition information. **Map** p404 E27.

Scandinavia House: The Nordic Center in America

58 Park Avenue, between 37th & 38th Streets (1-212 879 9779/www.scandinaviahouse.org). Subway: 42nd Street S, 4, 5, 6, 7 to 42nd Street-Grand Central. **Open** noon-6pm Tue-Sat. **Admission** suggested donation $3; $2 seniors, students. **Credit** AmEx, MC, V. **Map** p404 E24. You'll find all things Nordic, from IKEA designs to the latest Finnish film, at this modern centre, the leading cultural link between the US and the five Nordic countries (Denmark, Finland, Iceland, Norway and Sweden). As well as exhibitions, it stages films, concerts, lectures, symposia and readings, plus kid-friendly programming. The AQ Café is a bustling lunch spot with a menu by NYC's most famous Swedish chef, Marcus Samuelsson.

Theodore Roosevelt Birthplace

28 E 20th Street, between Broadway & Park Avenue South (1-212 260 1616/www.nps.gov/thrb). Subway: 6 to 23rd Street. **Open** 9am-5pm Tue-Sat. **Tours** 10am-4pm Tue-Sat; tours depart on the hour. **Admission** $3; free under-18s. **No credit cards.** **Map** p403 E27.

Herald Square & Garment District

The heart of America's multibillion-dollar clothing industry is New York's **Garment District** (roughly from 34th to 40th Streets, between Broadway & Eighth Avenue), where platoons of designers – and thousands of workers – create the clothes we'll be wearing next season. The main drag, Seventh Avenue, has a fitting (although rarely used) moniker, Fashion Avenue. Although most garment manufacturing has left Manhattan, the area is still gridlocked by delivery trucks and workers pushing racks of clothes up and down the streets. Trimming, button and fabric shops line the sidewalks, especially on 38th and 39th Streets. At the north-east corner of 39th Street and Seventh Avenue, you'll spy a gigantic needle and button sculpture, signalling that you are in the fashion centre. The **Fashion Center Information Kiosk** alongside the sculpture provides spools of information to

Face facts: Irving Chais

'There isn't a doll that we can't repair... we fix them even if they were made before the birth of Christ,' claims Irving Chais, owner of New York Doll Hospital (787 Lexington Avenue, at 61st Street, 1-212 838 7527). Chais's family started the business in 1900, and today the second-floor shop is cluttered with mounds of doll limbs and lone heads. Chais explains that many customers come to him because he can often repair a beloved Barbie or teddy the same day (unlike many other repair shops, which sometimes require a wait of several weeks for similar work). But some 'operations' can't be rushed: he once pieced together a porcelain head that had shattered into 40 tiny shards. 'It took me six months,' Chais says, 'but it looked like new again.'

Everything is illuminated – quite literally, in **Times Square**.

professional and budding designers, buyers and manufacturers. A once-thriving fur market is in retreat, now occupying only 28th to 30th Streets, between Seventh and Eighth Avenues.

Beginning on 34th Street, at Broadway, and stretching all the way to Seventh Avenue, **Macy's** (*see p230*) is still the biggest – and busiest – department store in the world. Across the street, at the junction of Broadway and Sixth Avenue, is **Herald Square**, named after a long-gone newspaper, surrounded by a retail wonderland. The area's lower section is known as **Greeley Square**, after Horace Greeley, owner of the *Herald*'s rival, the *Tribune* (which employed Karl Marx as a columnist); the previously grungy square now offers bistro chairs and rest areas for weary pedestrians. To the east, the many restaurants and shops of Koreatown line 32nd Street, between Broadway and Madison Avenue.

The giant circular building on Seventh Avenue, between 31st and 33rd Streets, is the sports and entertainment arena **Madison Square Garden** (*see p311*). It occupies the site of the old Pennsylvania Station, a McKim, Mead & White architectural masterpiece that was razed in the 1960s – an act so soulless, it spurred the creation of the Landmarks Preservation Commission. The railroad terminal, now known as **Penn Station**, lies beneath the Garden and serves approximately 600,000 people daily, more than any other station in the country. Fortunately, the aesthetic tide has turned. The city has

approved a $788 million restoration-and-development project to move Penn Station across the street, into the General Post Office (formally known as the James A Farley Post Office Building; 421 Eighth Avenue, between 31st & 33rd Streets, 1-800 275 8777), another McKim, Mead & White design. The project will connect the post office's two buildings with a soaring glass-and-nickel-trussed ticketing hall and concourse. When the new Penn Station is finally realised (no earlier than 2007), Amtrak services will roll in (along with rail links to Newark, La Guardia and JFK airports); the current Penn Station will remain a hub for New Jersey Transit and the Long Island Rail Road.

Broadway & Times Square

Around 42nd Street and Broadway, an area sometimes called 'the crossroads of the world', the night is illuminated not by the moon but by acres of glaring neon and sweeping arc lamps. Even native New Yorkers are electrified by this larger-than-life light show of corporate logos. No area better represents the city's glitter than **Times Square**, where zoning laws actually require businesses to include a certain level of illuminated signage on their façades.

Originally called Longacre Square, Times Square was renamed after the *New York Times* moved to the site in the early 1900s; it announced its arrival with a spectacular New Year's Eve fireworks display. At the present

1 Times Square building (formerly the Times Tower), the *Times* erected the world's first ticker sign, and the circling messages – the stockmarket crash of 1929, JFK's assassination, the 2001 World Trade Center attack – have been known to stop the midtown masses in their tracks. The Gray Lady is now located on 43rd Street, between Seventh and Eighth Avenues, but will soon move to a new $84 million tower on Eighth Avenue, between 40th and 41st Streets. However, the sign remains at the original locale and marks the spot where New Year's Eve is traditionally celebrated.

Times Square is really just the elongated intersection of Broadway and Seventh Avenue, but it's also the heart of the **Theater District**.

More than 40 stages showcasing extravagant dramatic productions are situated on the streets that cross Broadway. Times Square's once-famous sex trade is now relegated to short stretches of Seventh and Eighth Avenues (just North and South of 42nd Street).

The Theater District's transformation began in 1984, when the city condemned many properties along 42nd Street ('the Deuce'), between Seventh and Eighth Avenues. A few years later, the city changed its zoning laws, making it harder for adult-entertainment establishments to operate. The results include places like Show World (669 Eighth Avenue, between 42nd & 43rd Streets), formerly a noted sleaze palace that now gets by with X-rated video sessions instead of live 'dance' shows.

The streets west of Eighth Avenue are filled with eateries catering to theatre-goers, especially along **Restaurant Row** (46th Street, between Eighth & Ninth Avenues). This stretch is also popular after the theatres let out, when the street's bars host stand-up comedy and campy drag cabaret.

The area's office buildings are filled with entertainment companies: recording studios, record labels, theatrical agencies and screening rooms. The Brill Building (1619 Broadway, at 49th Street) has long been the headquarters of music publishers and producers, and such luminaries as Jerry Lieber, Mike Stoller, Phil Spector and Carole King wrote and auditioned their hits here. Visiting rock royalty and aspiring musicians drool over the selection of new and vintage guitars (and other instruments) for sale along **Music Row** (48th Street, between Sixth & Seventh Avenues). Eager teenagers congregate under the windows at MTV's home base (1515 Broadway, at 45th Street), hoping for a wave from a guest celebrity like Beyoncé from the second-floor studio above. The glittering glass case that serves as headquarters to the magazine-publishing giant Condé Nast (Broadway, at 43rd Street) gleams at 4 Times Square – which is home to *Vogue, GQ* and *The New Yorker*, among many other titles. The NASDAQ electronic stock market is housed in the same building, and its MarketSite Tower, a cylindrical eight-storey video screen, dominates Times Square.

Glitzy attractions strive to outdo one another in ensnaring the endless throngs of tourists. **Madame Tussaud's New York**, a Gothamised version of the London-based wax-museum chain, showcases local legends such as Woody Allen and Jennifer Lopez. On Broadway, the noisy **ESPN Zone** (1472 Broadway, at 42nd Street, 1-212 921 3776) offers hundreds of video games and enormous TVs showing all manner of sporting events, and the 110,000-square-foot **Toys 'R' Us** flagship boasts a 60-foot-tall indoor Ferris wheel.

Make a brief detour uptown on Seventh Avenue for a glimpse of the great classical music landmark **Carnegie Hall** (*see p328*), on 57th Street, two blocks south of Central Park. Nearby is the famous Carnegie Deli (854 Seventh Avenue, at 55th Street, 1-212 757 2245), master of the Reuben sandwich. **ABC Television Studios**, at 7 Times Square, draw dozens of early-morning risers hoping to catch a glimpse of the *Good Morning America* crew.

West of Times Square, in the vicinity of the Port Authority Bus Terminal (on Eighth Avenue) and the Lincoln Tunnel's traffic-knotted entrance, is an area historically known as **Hell's Kitchen**, where a gang- and crime-ridden Irish community scraped by during the 19th century. Italians, Greeks, Puerto Ricans, Dominicans and other ethnic groups followed. The neighbourhood maintained its tough reputation into the 1970s, when, in an effort to invite gentrification, local activists renamed it Clinton, after one-time mayor (and governor) DeWitt Clinton. Crime has indeed abated, and in-the-know theatre-goers fill the ethnic eateries along Ninth Avenue, which cost less and serve more interesting food than the traditional pre-theatre spots.

The extreme West Side remains somewhat desolate, but in the past year a burgeoning theatre scene has taken root. Since plans for a new stadium in the neighbourhood were quashed last year, hopes for expanding the unlovely Jacob K Javits Convention Center (Eleventh Avenue, between 34th & 39th Streets) have been stalled. Still, the massive black glass structure draws huge crowds to its various

trade shows. Maritime enthusiasts will appreciate the area along the Hudson River between 46th and 52nd Streets. The **Intrepid** (*see below*), a retired naval aircraft carrier, houses a sea, air and space museum (and a Concorde jet), and big crowds flock to the river whenever cruise ships, especially the world's largest ocean liner, the *Queen Mary 2*, dock at the terminal near 50th Street. During Fleet Week (the last week in May), the West Side fills with white-uniformed sailors on shore leave. The Circle Line Terminal is on 42nd Street, at Pier 83.

Intrepid Sea-Air-Space Museum

USS Intrepid, Pier 86, 46th Street, at the Hudson River (1-212 245 0072/www.intrepidmuseum.org). Travel: A, C, E to 42nd Street-Port Authority, then M42 bus to Twelfth Avenue. **Closed** until 2009. **Map** p404 B23.
The retired aircraft carrier is closed for renovations and repairs; it will reopen at some point in 2009.

Madame Tussaud's New York

234 W 42nd Street, between Seventh & Eighth Avenues (1-800 246 8872/www.nycwax.com). Subway: A, C, E to 42nd Street-Port Authority; N, Q, R, W to 42nd Street; S, 1, 2, 3, 7 to 42nd Street-Times Square. **Open** 10am-8pm daily. **Admission** $29; $26 seniors; $23 4-12s; free under-4s. **Credit** AmEx, MC, V. **Map** p404 D24.
A must if you are a fan of frozen life-sized celebs; every few months the place rolls out a new posse of freshly waxed victims.

Times Square Visitors' Center

1560 Broadway, between 46th & 47th Streets, entrance on Seventh Avenue (1-212 869 1890/ www.timessquarebid.org). Subway: N, R, W to 49th Street; 1 to 50th Street. **Open** 8am-8pm daily. **Map** p404 D23.

Fifth Avenue

Synonymous with the chic and the moneyed, Fifth Avenue caters to the elite; it's also the main route for the city's many ethnic (and inclusive) parades: National Puerto Rican Day (*see p262*), St Patrick's Day (*see p260*), Gay & Lesbian Pride (*see p262*), and many more. Even without a parade, the street hums with activity as the sidewalks fill with all types, from gawking tourists to smartly dressed society matrons.

The **Empire State Building** (*see p127*), located smack-bang in the centre of Midtown, is visible from most parts of the city and beyond (at night, it's lit in showy colours to celebrate a holiday or special event in progress; *see p126* **High-rise & shine**). Craning your neck at the corner of 34th Street to see storey after storey extend into the sky gives a breathtaking perspective of the gargantuan structure. The building's 86th-floor observation deck offers brilliant views in every direction; go at sunset to glimpse the longest urban shadow you'll ever see, cast from Manhattan all the way across the river to Queens. For a weekday break from sightseeing, catch a few winks in a cosy MetroNaps pod (1-212 239 3344), located in the famous skyscraper. This new company welcomes midtown executives and others looking to recharge with a quick powernap.

High-rise & shine

Originally illuminated with one large searchlight in 1932 to herald Franklin D Roosevelt's presidential election, the Empire State Building now requires nearly 1,400 lights for its iconic nightly display. White light remains the basic ESB staple, though coloured lights were introduced in 1976, during the bicentennial, to bathe the tower in patriotic red, white and blue. The pizza-sized coloured gels take a full four hours to fit and are used in dozens of colour combinations to celebrate holidays (red and green at Christmas) and charity causes (pink for breast-cancer awareness). Lights come on at sundown and turn off, Cinderella-like, at the stroke of midnight each night except New Year's Eve, New Year's Day, St Patrick's Day, Christmas Eve and Christmas Day. On these nights the edifice becomes the world's largest night-light, shining on until 3am.

Impassive stone lions, dubbed Patience and Fortitude by Mayor Fiorello La Guardia, guard the steps of the humanities and science collection of the **New York Public Library** (*see p130*), a beautiful Beaux Arts building at 41st Street. (A lovely library gift shop is just across Fifth Avenue.) The Rose Main Reading Room, on the library's top floor, is a hushed sanctuary of 23-foot-long tables and matching oak chairs, where bibliophiles can read, write and do research. Situated behind the library is **Bryant Park**, a well-cultivated green space that hosts a dizzying schedule of free entertainment during the summer (*see p261*), when it also attracts outdoor internet users with its free wireless access. The luxury **Bryant Park Hotel** (*see p61*) occupies the former American Radiator Building on 40th Street. Designed by architect Raymond Hood in the mid 1920s, and recently renovated, the structure is faced with near-black brick and trimmed in gold leaf. Alexander Woollcott, Dorothy Parker and friends held court and traded barbs at the **Algonquin** (*see p61*); the lobby is still a great place to meet for a drink.

Veer off Fifth Avenue into the 19 buildings of **Rockefeller Center** (*see p131*) and you'll see why this interlacing of public and private space is so lavishly praised. After plans for an expansion of the Metropolitan Opera on the site fell through in 1929, John D Rockefeller Jr, who had leased the land on behalf of the Met, set about creating a complex to house radio and television corporations. Designed by Raymond Hood and many other prominent architects, the 'city within a city' grew over the course of more than 40 years, with each new building conforming to the original master plan and art deco design. In autumn 2005 the legendary observation deck atop 30 Rockefeller Plaza reopened after 20 years (*see p128* **Top this!**).

As you stroll through the Channel Gardens from Fifth Avenue, the stately **General Electric Building** gradually appears above you. The sunken plaza in the complex is the winter home of an oft-packed ice-skating rink (*see p338*); a giant Christmas tree looms above it each holiday season. The plaza is the most visible entrance to the restaurants and shops in the underground passages that link the buildings. It is also home to the famous art auction house **Christie's** (*see p127*).

The centre is filled with murals, sculptures, mosaics and other artwork. Perhaps the most famous pieces are the rink-side *Prometheus* sculpture, by Paul Manship, and José María Sert's murals in the GE Building. But wander around, and you'll be treated to many more masterworks. On weekday mornings, a (mainly tourist-filled) crowd gathers at the **NBC** television network's glass-walled, ground-level studio (where the *Today* show is shot), at the south-west corner of Rockefeller Plaza and 49th Street (*see p130*). When the show's free concert series in the plaza hosts big-name guests like Norah Jones, Sting and Queen Latifah, the throng swells mightily.

Radio City Music Hall, on Sixth Avenue, at 50th Street, was the world's largest cinema when it was built, in 1932. This art deco jewel (the backstage tour is one of the best in town) was treated to a $70 million restoration in 1999; it's now used for music concerts and for traditional Christmas and Easter shows featuring the renowned Rockettes.

Facing Rockefeller Center is the beautiful **St Patrick's Cathedral** (*see p131*), the largest Catholic cathedral in the United States. A few blocks north, a cluster of museums – the **American Folk Art Museum** (*see below*), the **Museum of Arts & Design** (*see p128*) and the **Museum of Television & Radio** (*see p129*) – is anchored by the recently renovated **Museum of Modern Art** (*see p129*). Swing Street, or 52nd Street, between Fifth and Sixth Avenues, is a row of 1920s speakeasies; the only venue still open from that period is the '21' Club (21 W 52nd Street, between Fifth & Madison Avenues, 1-212 582 7200). The bar buzzes at night; upstairs, the restaurant is a popular power-lunch spot.

The blocks off Fifth Avenue, between Rockefeller Center and Central Park South, showcase expensive retail palaces bearing names that were famous long before the concept of branding was developed. Along the stretch between Saks Fifth Avenue (49th to 50th Streets; *see p230*) and Bergdorf Goodman (at 58th Street; *see p229*), the rents are the highest in the world; tenants include Cartier, Versace, Tiffany & Co and Gucci. Fifth Avenue is crowned by Grand Army Plaza at 59th Street. A gilded statue of General William Tecumseh Sherman presides over this public space; to the west stands the elegant Plaza Hotel building (which is closed until October 2007 while being transformed into condos; *see p70* **Something old, something new**); to the north lies the luxe Pierre hotel. From here, you can access Central Park (*see p133*), where the city din gives way to relative serenity.

American Folk Art Museum

45 W 53rd Street, between Fifth & Sixth Avenues (1-212 265 1040/www.folkart museum.org). Subway: E, V to Fifth Avenue-53rd Street. **Open** 10.30am-5.30pm Tue-Thur, Sat, Sun; 10.30am-7.30pm Fri. **Admission** $9; $7 seniors, students; free under-12s. Free to all 5.30-7.30pm Fri. **Credit** AmEx, Disc, MC, V. **Map** p404 E22.

Celebrating traditional craft-based work is the American Folk Art Museum (formerly the Museum of American Folk Art). Designed by architects Billie Tsien and Tod Williams, the architecturally stunning eight-floor building is four times larger than the original Lincoln Center location (now a branch of the museum) and includes a café. The range of decorative, practical and ceremonial folk art encompasses pottery, trade signs, delicately stitched log-cabin quilts and wind-up toys.
Other locations: 2 Lincoln Square, Columbus Avenue, between 65th & 66th Streets, Upper West Side (1-212 595 9533).

Christie's

20 Rockefeller Plaza, 49th Street, between Fifth & Sixth Avenues (1-212 636 2000/www.christies.com). Subway: B, D, F, V to 47-50th Streets-Rockefeller Center. **Open** 9.30am-5.30pm Mon-Fri. **Admission** free. **Map** p404 E23.

Dating from 1766, Christie's joins Sotheby's as one of New York's premier auction houses. The building is worth a visit purely for the architecture – in particular to see the cavernous three-floor lobby featuring a specially commissioned mural by artist Sol LeWitt. Most auctions are open to the public, with viewing hours scheduled in the days leading up to the sale. Hours vary with each exhibition; call or visit the website.

Empire State Building

350 Fifth Avenue, between 33rd & 34th Streets (1-212 736 3100/www.esbnyc.com). Subway: B, D, F, N, Q, R, V, W to 34th Street-Herald Square. **Open**

Mid Sept-late June 8am-midnight daily (last elevator at 11.15pm). *Late June-mid Sept* 8am-midnight Sun-Wed (last elevator at 11.15pm); 8am-2am Thur-Sat (last elevator at 1.15am). Closed during extreme weather. **Admission** *86th-floor observatory* $16; $14 seniors, 12-17s; $10 6-11s; free under-6s. *102nd-floor observatory* an additional $14. **Credit** AmEx, DC, Disc, MC, V with valid ID. **Map** p404 E25.

In late 2005 the 102nd-floor observatory was reopened to the public and reigns as the city's highest lookout. The view from the 86th floor isn't too shabby either, where, on a clear day, you can see all five boroughs and five states. (Psst! In summer, the roof deck now remains open until 2am.) The relocation of the ticket office and queuing area to the second floor (from the basement) makes for a much more pleasurable experience. Just be warned: waits can last as long as two hours on busy days. We recommend buying your tickets online to save time. If you have money to burn, you can take advantage of the $40 express ticket option, which gets you to the top in about 20 minutes. The

informative (but hokey) audio tour is worth the extra six bucks if you want to get more than just an eyeful.

The Empire State Building was financed as a speculative venture by General Motors executive John J Raskob; builders broke the ground in 1930. It sprang up in 14 months with amazing speed, completed more than a month ahead of schedule and $5 million under budget. The 1,250ft tower snatched the title of world's tallest building from under the nose of the months-old, 1,046ft Chrysler Building (*see p132*), conveniently showing up Raskob's Detroit rival Walter P Chrysler.

Museum of Arts & Design

40 W 53rd Street, between Fifth & Sixth Avenues (1-212 956 3535/www.madmuseum.org). Subway: E, V to Fifth Avenue-53rd Street. **Open** 10am-6pm Mon-Wed, Fri-Sun; 10am-8pm Thur. **Admission** $9; $7 seniors, students; free under-12s. Voluntary donation 6-8pm Thur. **Credit** AmEx, Disc, MC, V. **Map** p404 E23.

Formerly the American Crafts Museum, this is the

Top this!

The Empire State Building no longer has a lock on the killer-view market. A new viewing spot has arisen that has something that the Empire State will never have: a view of, well, the Empire State Building. First, some back story. In 1933 John D Rockefeller Jr saw the completion of the monumental 30 Rockefeller Center, aka the RCA Building (now referred to as the General Electric Building) – the crown jewel in one of the country's most significant (and copied) urban design projects. Back in the day, the top floor, 70 storeys up, was done up like the upper decks of a 1930s ocean liner, replete with deck chairs and air vents resembling smoke stacks.

One of the most impressive elements of the art deco tower was its stunning observation decks, with unparalleled 360-degree views of Manhattan. This was declared off-limits in 1986, when another RCA landmark, the glamorous Rainbow Room on the 65th floor, underwent a renovation and expansion, cutting off access to the roof. Twenty years later, the observatory, which occupies the 67th to 70th floors, opened with great fanfare in the autumn of 2005. 'Every inch of the place that we could restore to its original glamour, we did,' says Peter Dillon of Rockefeller Center. (Those details include the cast-aluminium fleur-de-lis panels and tiled mosaics).

While the view alone is worth the price of admission, the folks at 30 Rock have also designed an exciting dreamy lobby housing a modern gallery space that explores the storied history of Rockefeller Center. Even the elevator gets in on the act, with a video projection on its glass-panelled ceiling of bygone decades as it rockets up, up and away.

Top of the Rock

30 Rockefeller Plaza, just off W 50th Street, between Fifth & Sixth Avenues (1-212 698 2000/tickets 1-877 692 7625/www.topoftherocknyc.com). Subway: B, D, F, V to 47-50th Streets-Rockefeller Center. **Open** 8.30am-midnight daily. **Admission** $17.50; $16 seniors; $11.25 6-11s. **Credit** AmEx, MC, V. **Map** p404 E23.

The **Museum of Modern Art (MoMA)** – for 20th-century art at its finest. *See p127.*

country's leading museum for contemporary crafts in clay, cloth, glass, metal and wood. It changed its name to emphasise the harmonious relationships between art, design and craft. The museum plans to move to a new home in the former Huntington Hartford building at 2 Columbus Circle in 2008, but for now, visitors can peruse the jewellery, ceramics and other objects displayed on four floors here. The exhibition 'Radical Lace & Subversive Knitting' looks at the resurgence in the intricate crafts, and displays works made from silk, wool, paper clips and rubber hosing (25 Jan-6 May). 'Intelligent Design' showcases the work of a dozen artists who meld art and science (17 May-2 Sept).

Museum of Modern Art (MoMA)

11 W 53rd Street, between Fifth & Sixth Avenues (1-212 708 9400/www.moma.org). Subway: E, V to Fifth Avenue-53rd Street. **Open** 10.30am-5.30pm Mon, Wed, Thur, Sat, Sun; 10.30am-8pm Fri. **Admission** (includes admission to film programmes) $20; $16 over-65s; $12 full-time students; free under-16s (must be accompanied by an adult). Free to all 4-8pm Fri. **Credit** AmEx, MC, V. **Map** p404 E23.

While *Starry Night* may be the attraction that keeps the tourists coming to the Museum of Modern Art, even the most jaded New Yorkers swoon when they enter the spacious galleries and the soaring atrium. MoMA contains the world's finest and most comprehensive holdings of 20th-century art, and, thanks to a sweeping redesign by architect Yoshio Taniguchi, completed in 2004, it is now able to show off much more of its immense permanent collection in serene, high-ceilinged galleries that almost outshine the art on display. Inside the soaring five-storey atrium is the central artery from which six curatorial departments – Architecture and Design, Drawings, Painting and Sculpture, Photography, Prints and Illustrated Books, and Film and Media – display works that include the best of Matisse, Picasso, Van Gogh, Giacometti, Lawrence, Pollock, Rothko and Warhol, among many others. Outside, Philip Johnson's sculpture garden has been restored to its original, larger plan from 1953, and its powerful minimalist sculptures and sheer matte-black-granite-and-glass wall are overlooked by the sleek high-end restaurant and bar the Modern, which is run by Midas-touch restaurateur Danny Meyer. The museum's eclectic exhibition of design objects is a must-see, with examples of art nouveau, the Bauhaus and the Vienna Secession lining up alongside a vintage 1946 Ferrari and architectural drawings and models from the likes of Rem Koolhaas and Mies van der Rohe.

Planned 2007 exhibitions: the spring survey of Canadian artist Jeff Wall's career brings 40 of his instantly recognisable large-scale lightbox photographs to the sixth-floor gallery (25 Feb-14 May). In 'Comic Abstraction: Image Breaking, Image Making', artists like Arturo Herrera and Ellen Gallagher mutate traditional cartoons and animation into striking new forms of social and political commentary – MoMA surveys the critical and playful nature of the works (4 Mar-11 June). Such is the scale of Richard Serra's enormous site-specific sculptures, that MoMA has strengthened the floors to accommodate summer 2007's retrospective of the artist's 40-year body of work (3 June-10 Sept).

Museum of Television & Radio

25 W 52nd Street, between Fifth & Sixth Avenues (1-212 621 6600/www.mtr.org). Subway: B, D, F, V to 47-50th Streets-Rockefeller Center; E, V to Fifth Avenue-53rd Street. **Open** noon-6pm Tue-Sun; noon-8pm Thur. **Admission** $10; $8 seniors, students; $5 under-14s. **No credit cards. Map** p404 E23.

This nirvana for boob-tube addicts and pop-culture

junkies contains an archive of more than 100,000 radio and TV programmes. Head to the fourth-floor library to search the computerised system for your favourite *Star Trek* or *I Love Lucy* episodes, then walk down one flight to take a seat at your assigned console. (The radio listening room operates the same way.) Screenings of modern cartoons, public seminars and special presentations are offered. Recent programmes were devoted to television superheroes, American political ads and the history of gay and lesbian characters on TV.

NBC

30 Rockefeller Plaza, 49th Street, between Fifth & Sixth Avenues (1-212 664 3700/www.nbc.com). Subway: B, D, F, V to 47-50th Streets-Rockefeller Center. **Admission** $17.95; $15.50 seniors, groups of 15 or more, 6-16s. Under-6s not admitted. **Tours** 8.30am-5.30pm Mon-Sat; 9.30am-4.30pm

Sun. Tours depart every 15-mins. **Credit** AmEx, MC, V. **Map** p404 E23.

Peer through the *Today* show's studio window with a horde of fellow onlookers, or pay admission (at the NBC Experience Store, www.shopnbc.com) for a guided tour of the studios. The tours are led by pages, many of whom – Ted Koppel, Kate Jackson, Michael Eisner, Marcy Carsey, and others – have gone on to bigger and better things in showbiz. (For information on NBC tapings, *see p299*.)

New York Public Library

455 Fifth Avenue, at 42nd Street (1-212 930 0830/ www.nypl.org). Subway: B, D, F, V to 42nd Street-Bryant Park; 7 to Fifth Avenue. **Open** 11am-7.30pm Tue, Wed; 10am-6pm Thur-Sat. **Admission** free. **Map** p404 E24.

When people mention the New York Public Library,

Sex it up

Oh, *don't* behave, on this naughty tour of all things sexy.

Friday Snatch your honey and make time to take in all the dirty, pretty things this city has to offer. Start with some aphrodisiac action at the **Grand Central Oyster Bar & Restaurant** (42nd Street, at Park Avenue, 1-212 490 6650); stand at the Whispering Gallery outside and murmur filthy intentions to your blushing lover, who will hear you clearly from 20 feet away. Then it's on to **Pink Elephant** (527 W 27th Street, between Tenth & Eleventh Avenues, 1-212 463 0000), a Chelsea hotspot that blows pheromone-laced scents on to writhing dancers while they suck down pricey beverages. Bring your evening to a climax at tryst-friendly **La Semana Hotel** (25 W 24th Street, between Fifth & Sixth Avenues,

1-212 255 5944). Spend three glorious hours in a room with a dodgy duvet cover, a hot tub and mirror-lined walls, for just $82.

Saturday After a quickie tour of the **Museum of Sex** (*see p117*), while away the afternoon browsing for gifts. **Kiki de Montparnasse** (79 Greene Street, between Broome & Spring Streets, 1-212 965 8150) is perfect for stocking up on essentials like a Swarovski crystal-encrusted, gold-plated travel vibrator or a diamond-studded cock ring. Hardcore shoppers can scour **Purple Passion DV8** (211 W 20th Street, between Seventh & Eighth Avenues, 1-212 807 0486): the walls are lined with bondage gear, corsets, butt plugs and ball gags. Come dinner-time, red-blooded Romeos can eat their hearts out at **Robert's Steakhouse**, inside classy gentlemen's refuge the Penthouse Executive Club (603 W 45th Street, at Eleventh Avenue, 1-212 245 0002). Then head to **CasBar** in Greenwood Heights, Brooklyn (BYOB), where scantily clad straight couples and bi women mingle in a converted warehouse (www.srcasbar.com), or, if it's the third Saturday of the month, hot young LGBTs (no heteros!) will want to hit Park Slope, strip to their undies and go at it at **SPAM** (www.submitparty.com/spam).

Sunday A bracing morning stroll through the Ramble in Central Park could reward voyeurs with glimpses of skin in the bushes. After that, it's back to your pad to sleep off the weekend's excesses.

most are referring to this imposing Beaux Arts building. (In fact, it houses only NYPL's humanities and social sciences collection; for other locations, *see p375*.) Two massive stone lions, dubbed Patience and Fortitude by former mayor Fiorello La Guardia, flank the main portal. Free guided tours (at 11am and 2pm) stop at the beautifully renovated Rose Main Reading Room and the Bill Blass Public Catalog Room, which offers free internet access. Lectures, author readings and special exhibitions are definitely worth checking out.

Radio City Music Hall

For listing, see p319. **Tours** 11am-3pm daily. **Admission** $17; $14 seniors; $10 under-12s. **Credit** AmEx, MC, V. **Map** p404 E23.

Rockefeller Center

From 48th to 51st Streets, between Fifth & Sixth Avenues (1-212 332 6868/tickets 1-212 664 7174/ www.rockefellercenter.com). Subway: B, D, F, V to 47-50th Streets-Rockefeller Center. **Admission** $12; $10 seniors, 6-16s. Under-6s not admitted, groups of 10 or more. **Tours** 10am-5pm Mon-Sat; 10am-4pm Sun. Tours depart on the hour. **Credit** AmEx, MC, V. **Map** p404 E23.

Exploring the centre is free. For guided tours in and around the historic buildings, however, advance tickets are necessary and available by phone, online or at the NBC Experience Store. For information about newly opened Top of the Rock, the observation deck at 30 Rockefeller Center, *see p128* **Top this!**

St Patrick's Cathedral

Fifth Avenue, between 50th & 51st Streets (1-212 753 2261). Subway: B, D, F to 47-50th Streets-Rockefeller Center; E, V to Fifth Avenue-53rd Street. **Open** 6.30am-8.45pm daily. **Admission** free. **Tours** Call for tour dates and times. **Map** p404 E23.
St Patrick's adds Gothic grace to Fifth Avenue. The diocese of New York bought the land for an orphanage in 1810, but then, in 1858, it switched gears and began construction on what would become the country's largest Catholic church. Today, the white marble spires are dwarfed by Rockefeller Center, but, inside, visitors are treated to a still-stunning array of vaulted ceilings, stained-glass windows from Charres and altars by Tiffany & Co.

Midtown East

The area east of Fifth Avenue may seem less appealing to visitors than Times Square or Rockefeller Center. Although the neighbourhood is home to some of the city's most recognisable landmarks – the United Nations, Grand Central Terminal and the Chrysler Building – the grid of busy streets is lined with large, imposing buildings, and the bustling sidewalks are all business. The area is a little thin on plazas and street-level attractions, but it compensates with a dizzying array of world-class architecture.

Grand Central Terminal, a 1913 Beaux Arts train station, is the city's most spectacular point of arrival, even though it isn't a national gateway (unlike Penn Station, Grand Central is used only for commuter trains). The station stands at the junction of 42nd Street and Park Avenue, the latter rising on a viaduct that curves around the terminal. The station played an important role in the nation's historic preservation movement, after a series of legal battles that culminated in the 1978 Supreme Court decision affirming NYC's landmark laws. Since its 1998 renovation, the terminal has become a destination in itself, with classy restaurants and bars, such as the Campbell Apartment cocktail lounge (off the West Balcony, 1-212 953 0409), the expert and attitudinous Grand Central Oyster Bar & Restaurant (Lower Concourse, 1-212 490 6650) and star chef Charlie Palmer's Métrazur (East Balcony, 1-212 687 4600). The Lower Concourse food court spans the globe with its fairly priced lunch options. One notable oddity: the constellations on the Main Concourse ceiling are drawn in reverse, as if seen from heaven.

Rising like a phoenix behind Grand Central, the **MetLife Building**, formerly the Pan Am Building, was once the world's largest office tower. Now its most celebrated tenants are the peregrine falcons that nest on the roof and feed on pigeons snatched mid-air. On Park Avenue is the famed **Waldorf-Astoria** (*see p67*), formerly located on Fifth Avenue but rebuilt here in 1931 after the original was demolished to make way for the Empire State Building. Other must-see buildings in the area include **Lever House** (390 Park Avenue, between 53rd & 54th Streets), the **Seagram Building** (375 Park Avenue, between 52nd & 53rd Streets), **Citicorp Center** (from 53rd Street to 54th Street, between Lexington & Third Avenues) and the stunning art deco skyscraper that anchors the corner of Lexington Avenue and 51st Street, formerly the **General Electric Building** (and before that, the RCA Victor Building). A Chippendale crown tops Philip Johnson's postmodern icon, the **Sony Building** (550 Madison Avenue, between 55th & 56th Streets), formerly the AT&T Building. Inside, the Sony Wonder Technology Lab (*see p286*) delivers a hands-on thrill zone of science in action.

Along the river to the east lies **Tudor City**, a pioneering 1925 residential development and a high-rise version of England's Hampton Court. The neighbourhood is dominated by the **United Nations Headquarters** (*see p132*) and its famous glass-walled Secretariat building. Although you don't need a passport, you will be leaving US soil when you enter the UN complex – it's an international zone, and the vast buffet at the Delegates Dining Room (fourth floor, 1-212 963 7626) puts cultural diversity on the table. The grounds and the Peace Garden along the East River are off-limits for security reasons. Unless you pay for a guided tour, the only accessible attractions are the exhibitions in the lobby and the bookstore and gift shop on the lower level. But right across First Avenue is **Dag Hammarskjöld Plaza** (47th Street, between First & Second Avenues), named for the former UN secretary general. Here, you can stroll through a lovely garden honouring Katharine Hepburn (who used to live nearby in Turtle Bay Gardens, a stretch of townhouses on 48th and 49th Streets, between Second and Third Avenues). Nearby is the **Japan Society** (*see below*).

East 42nd Street holds still more architectural distinction, including the Romanesque Revival hall of the former **Bowery Savings Bank** (No.110) and the art deco details of the **Chanin Building** (No.122). Completed in 1930, the gleaming **Chrysler Building** (at Lexington Avenue) pays homage to the automobile. Architect William Van Alen outfitted the main tower with colossal radiator-cap eagle 'cargoyles' and a brickwork relief sculpture of racing cars complete with chrome hubcaps. A needle-sharp stainless-steel spire was added to the blueprint so the finished product would be taller than 40 Wall Street, which was under construction at the same time. The Daily News Building (No.220), another art deco gem designed by Raymond Hood, was immortalised in the *Superman* films; although the namesake tabloid no longer has its offices here, the lobby still houses the paper's giant globe.

Grand Central Terminal

From 42nd to 44th Streets, between Vanderbilt & Lexington Avenues. Subway: 42nd Street S, 4, 5, 6, 7 to 42nd Street-Grand Central. **Tours** Call 1-212 697 1245 for information. **Map** p404 E24.

Japan Society

333 E 47th Street, at First Avenue (1-212 832 1155/www.japansociety.org). Subway: E, V to Lexington Avenue-53rd Street; 6 to 51st Street. **Open** 11am-6pm Tue-Thur; 11am-9pm Fri; 11am-5pm Sat, Sun. **Admission** $12; $10 seniors, students; free under-16s. **Credit** AmEx, Disc, MC, V. **Map** p404 F23.

In a serene space complete with waterfall and bamboo garden, the Japan Society presents performing arts, lectures, exchange programmes and special events, and a language centre and library are open to members and students. In 2007 the society celebrates its 100th anniversary, and a year of special events, performances and exhibitions is planned. The newly refurbished gallery space will showcase 'Awakenings: Zen Figure Painting in Medieval Japan' – an exhibition exploring the ideology behind the little-understood Zen Buddhist figure paintings from the 13th to the 17th centuries (22 Mar-17 June). An interactive symposium on robotics and Japan's cutting-edge technology industry is planned for the autumn.

United Nations Headquarters

UN Plaza, First Avenue, between 42nd & 48th Streets (1-212 963 7710/tours 1-212 963 8687/www.un.org). Subway: 42nd Street S, 4, 5, 6, 7 to 42nd Street-Grand Central. **Admission** $12; $8.50 seniors; $8 students; $7 5-14s. Under-5s not admitted. **Tours** *Mar-Dec* 9.30am-4.30pm Mon-Fri; 10am-4.30pm Sat, Sun. *Jan, Feb* 9.30am-4.45pm Mon-Fri. **Credit** AmEx, MC, V. **Map** p404 G24.

Queuing for tickets – a **Broadway** tradition. *See p123.*

Uptown

Museums, greenery and all that jazz.

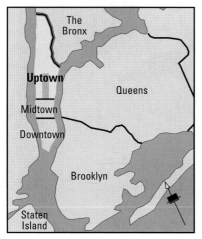

If we've heard it once, we've heard it a thousand times: Uptown is where the rich people live. While it's true that, above 57th Street, the Upper East Side and Upper West Side (the neighbourhoods bordering Central Park) boast a nice clutch of millionaires (and a few billionaires) there's definitely more to this part of Manhattan than well-heeled socialites. For starters, the area is positively brimming with culture: **Lincoln Center**, the **Metropolitan Museum of Art**, the **Guggenheim** and the **Studio Museum in Harlem** all call Uptown home.

Once a bucolic getaway for 18th-century New Yorkers living at the southern tip of the island, much of this area can still feel blissfully serene. Strolling past the flower gardens in **River Side Park**, meandering the curvy paths of **Central Park** (*see p134* **Step to it**), or taking in the breathtaking views of the Hudson River from the grounds surrounding the **Cloisters** can be just what the doctor ordered when the frenetic pace of Downtown overwhelms. But, if you came to New York to *escape* the trees, you're still in luck in these parts: the increasingly diverse **Harlem** offers a myriad of urban pleasures, and window-shopping along **Madison Avenue** cannot fail to give you the cosmopolitan lift you seek.

Central Park

An emerald, 843-acre rectangle, this patch of the great outdoors was the first man-made public park in the US. In 1853 the newly formed Central Park Commission chose landscape designer Frederick Law Olmsted and architect Calvert Vaux to turn a vast tract of rocky swampland into a rambling oasis of greenery. The commission, inspired by the great parks of London and Paris, imagined a place that would provide city dwellers with respite from the crowded streets. A noble thought, but one that required the eviction of 1,600 mostly poor or immigrant inhabitants, including residents of Seneca Village, the city's oldest African-American settlement. But clear the area they did, and the rest is history.

The park celebrated its 150th anniversary in 2003, and it has never looked better, thanks to the Central Park Conservancy, a private, non-profit civic group formed in 1980 that has been instrumental in the park's restoration and maintenance. A horse-drawn carriage is still the sightseeing vehicle of choice for many tourists (and even a few romantic locals, though they'd never admit to it); plan on paying $34 for a 20-minute tour. (You can usually hail a carriage on Central Park South, where they line up between Fifth Avenue and Columbus Circle.) If walking is more your speed, *see p134* **Step to it**.

The park is dotted with landmarks. **Strawberry Fields**, near the West 72nd Street entrance, memorialises John Lennon, who lived in the nearby Dakota Building. Also called the International Garden of Peace, this sanctuary features a mosaic of the word 'imagine', donated by the Italian city of Naples. More than 160 species of flowers and plants bloom here (including strawberries, of course). The statue of Balto, a heroic Siberian husky (East Drive, at 67th Street), is a favourite sight for tots. Slightly older children appreciate the statue of Alice in Wonderland, just north of the **Conservatory Water** at the East 74th Street park entrance (*see also p288* **Go ask Alice**).

In winter, ice skaters lace up at **Wollman Rink** (midpark, at 62nd Street; *see also p338*), where the skating comes with a picture-postcard view of the fancy hotels surrounding the park. A short stroll to about 64th Street

Step to it Green day

Start: Columbus Circle
Finish: Roof Garden, Metropolitan Museum of Art
Distance: About 1.5 miles
Time: About 3 hours

Winners of the modestly named 'Central Park Design Competition' in 1857, Calvert Vaux and Frederick Law Olmsted set about creating a park where 'every tree and bush, every arch, roadway and walk, has been fixed where it is with a sense of purpose'. Welcome to New York City's own 843-acre backyard, where history, scenery and boundless opportunities for 'leisurely contemplation' await.

Your day begins at Columbus Circle, located at the south-west corner of the park. This 1892 monument got a makeover in 2005 but the real reason to celebrate is the (newish) neighbour to the west – the **Time Warner Center** (*see p143*) – a hub of shops including a Whole Foods market in the basement (*see p246*) and Bouchon Bakery on the third floor: perfect for coffee and croissants before setting off into the woods.

Enter the park through its south-west gate (called the Merchants Entrance), diagonally across the street from the statue of Mr Columbus (look for the welcoming arms of a gilt-covered woman atop the imposing entry monument.) Walking straight ahead (east) you'll hit the roadway that snakes through much of the park. Follow this to the right until you come to **Heckscher Playground**, the city's largest and oldest playground. Head past the restrooms and go north (a left turn) and you'll soon hit another kid-friendly attraction, the **Central Park Carousel** (aka the Friedsam Memorial Carousel; *see p137*), operated on the same site in one form or another since 1871. A masterpiece of 1900s folk art, it sports 58 of the largest hand-carved horses ever constructed. The original calliope still cranks out organ music, and there's a psychotic frieze of Cupid shooting rabbits.

Leave the spinning horses behind, make a sharp left, and head north up a small hill where you will soon discover the park's undisputed spot for great city views – **Sheep Meadow** (*see p137*). The sheep were evicted in the 1930s, replaced by city sunbathers who pack in, sardine-like, on warm days. Follow the meadow around to the west and you'll find the Mineral Springs Café, a snack bar. Passing by the café, stay to your right and soon enough you'll come to a roadway. Cross over, and look for the statue of Daniel Webster on your right. Don't waste a minute on this American politician and orator, as he is now just a guidepost to the celebrated **Strawberry Fields** (*see p133*), memorial to one of the world's most adored cultural icons, John Lennon. Just up the hill you'll find the marble mosaic (a gift from Naples, Italy) inscribed with one word: 'imagine'.

A short walk west takes you out of the park and straight up to the **Dakota** apartment

134 Time Out New York

building (*see p145*). Built in 1884, it's the last home (and murder site) of John Lennon. The German Renaissance-styled structure has not only been home to Lauren Bacall and Yoko Ono but it's also the exterior for Roman Polanski's film *Rosemary's Baby* and a crucial setting in Jack Finney's beloved novel *Time and Again*.

A jaunt up smart Central Park West will take you past the **New-York Historical Society** (*see p145*) where exhibitions celebrate New York's fascinating past. But if you like your history to come with more bite, keep looking for the medieval turret of the **American Museum of Natural History** (*see p145*), with its celebrated collection of dinosaur skeletons.

Dip back into the park at 77th Street and follow the entry path down to the roadway, then cross it and head south (a right turn). You'll be treated to a view of water opening up on your left-hand side and you can follow this around for quite some time until you arrive at Cherry Hill Fountain. Head down to the water's edge to witness the park's most expansive panorama: the lake.

In the distance you will see the graceful cast-iron **Bow Bridge**. Stroll past it down to the undisputed heart of the park and meet the queen who reigns there at **Bethesda Fountain** (*see p137; photo left*), with its winged *Angel of the Waters* statue. The only statuary commissioned for the original park's design, it is also featured in the film *Angels in America*.

Following the path closest to the water's edge, head up and over a small hill leading to the **Loeb Boathouse** (*see p137*). Boat rentals and a famed restaurant (plus a cheaper snackbar) can be found; it's also the spot where Carrie Bradshaw of *Sex and the City* made a big splash attempting to kiss Mr Big. (Psst! Naturalists alert! A bench in the snackbar area is the designated location for the Central Park Bird Log – an obsessive, fascinating communal diary with sightings of everything from warblers and green herons to red-tailed hawks.)

Stuffed and sated, exit the Boathouse heading straight down to the roadway. Cross over and follow the small footpath to another icon of the park's seemingly endless supply, the **Conservatory Water** (*see p133*), better known as the Boat Pond. Used by generations of Manhattan's children to sail toy ships, it is flanked on two sides by well-loved statues.

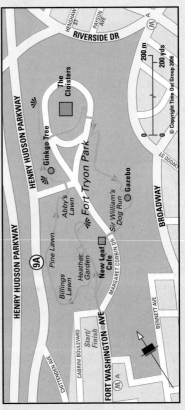

One is Hans Christian Andersen, but it's the other – featuring a certain Mad Hatter, a White Rabbit and an infamous blonde – that gets worldwide attention.

When you've finished up here, it's time for one last look at the park. Make a beeline north and follow the path to the **Metropolitan Museum of Art** (*see p138*). Turn right and exit out on to Fifth Avenue – the museum is just north. Once inside, head to the Roof Garden (ask the nearest guard for directions; open May to late autumn, weather permitting). Once there, have some wine and get drunk on the brilliant sunset. The view is every Woody Allen movie rolled into one impossibly long Manhattan panorama of trees, buildings and endless sky.

Sightseeing

Central Park. See p133.

brings you to the **Friedsam Memorial Carousel**, still a bargain at $1.50 a ride. (For more park activities for children, see p286.)

Come summer, kites, Frisbees and soccer balls fly every which way across **Sheep Meadow**, the designated quiet zone that begins at 66th Street. The sheep are gone (they grazed here until 1934), replaced by sunbathers improving their tans and scoping out the throngs. The hungry (and affluent) can repair to the glitzy **Tavern on the Green** (Central Park West, at 67th Street, 1-212 873 3200), which sets up a grand outdoor café in the summer, complete with a 40-foot bar made with trees from city parks. However, picnicking alfresco (or snacking on a hot dog from one of the park's food vendors) is the most popular option. East of Sheep Meadow, between 66th and 72nd Streets, is the **Mall**, where you'll find volleyball courts and plenty of in-line skaters. East of the Mall's **Naumburg Bandshell** is **Rumsey Playfield** – site of the annual Central Park SummerStage series (see p262), an eclectic roster of free and benefit concerts held from Memorial Day weekend to Labor Day weekend. One of the most popular meeting places in the park is the grand **Bethesda Fountain & Terrace**, near the midpoint of the 72nd Street Transverse Road. *Angel of the Waters*, the sculpture in the centre of the fountain, was created by Emma Stebbins, the first woman to be granted a major public-art commission in New York. North of it is the **Loeb Boathouse** (midpark, at 75th Street), where you can rent a rowing boat or gondola to take out on the lake, which is crossed by the elegant Bow Bridge. The bucolic park views enjoyed by diners at the nearby **Central Park Boathouse Restaurant** (midpark, at 75th Street, 1-212 517 2233) make it a lovely place for brunch or drinks, with an outdoor terrace and bar that's idyllic in summer. The thickly forested **Ramble**, between 73rd and 79th Streets, is a favourite spot for birdwatching, offering glimpses of more than 70 species.

Further north is the popular **Belvedere Castle**, a restored Victorian building that sits atop the park's second-highest peak. It offers excellent views and also houses the **Henry Luce Nature Observatory** (see below). The open-air **Delacorte Theater** hosts Shakespeare in the Park (see p348), a summer tradition of free performances of plays by the Bard and others. The **Great Lawn** (midpark, between 79th & 85th Streets) is a sprawling stretch of grass that doubles as a rally point for political protests and a concert spot for just about any act that can rally a six-figure audience, as well as free shows by the Metropolitan Opera and the New York Philharmonic during the summer. (At other times, it's the favoured spot of seriously

competitive soccer teams and much less cutthroat teams of Hacky Sackers and their dogs.) Several years ago, the Reservoir (midpark, between 85th & 96th Streets) was renamed in honour of the late Jacqueline Kennedy Onassis, who used to jog around it.

Central Park Zoo

830 Fifth Avenue, between 63rd & 66th Streets (1-212 439 6500/www.centralparkzoo.org). Subway: N, R, W to Fifth Avenue-59th Street. **Open** *Apr-Oct* 10am-5pm Mon-Fri; 10am-5.30pm Sat, Sun. *Nov-Mar* 10am-4.30pm daily. **Admission** $8; $4 seniors; $3 3-12s; free under-3s. **No credit cards. Map** p405 E21.
This is the only place in New York City where you can see a polar bear swimming underwater. The Tisch Children's Zoo was recently spiffed up, and the roving characters on the George Delacorte Musical Clock delight kids every half-hour.

Charles A Dana Discovery Center

Park entrance on Malcolm X Boulevard (Lenox Avenue), at 110th Street (1-212 860 1370/ www.centralparknyc.org). Subway: 2, 3 to 110th Street-Central Park North. **Open** 10am-5pm Tue-Sun. **Admission** free. **Map** p406 E15.
Stop by for weekend family workshops, cultural exhibits and outdoor performances on the plaza next to the Harlem Meer. From April to October, the centre lends out fishing rods and bait, and on selected Thursday mornings park rangers lead bird-watching walks. Call ahead for the schedule.

Dairy

Park entrance on Fifth Avenue, at 65th Street (1-212 794 6564/www.centralparknyc.org). Subway: N, R, W to Fifth Avenue-59th Street. **Open** 10am-5pm daily. **Admission** free. **Map** p405 D21.
Built in 1872 to show city kids where milk comes from (cows, in this case), the Dairy is now the Central Park Conservancy's information centre, complete with interactive exhibits, videos explaining the park's history and a gift shop.

Henry Luce Nature Observatory

Belvedere Castle, midpark, off the 79th Street Transverse Road (1-212 860 0210). Subway: B, C to 81st Street-Museum of Natural History. **Open** 10am-5pm Tue-Sun. **Admission** free. **Map** p405 D19.
During the spring and autumn hawk migrations, park rangers discuss the various birds of prey found in the park and help visitors spot raptors from the castle roof. You can also borrow binoculars, maps and bird-identification guides.

Upper East Side

Gorgeous pre-war apartments owned by blue-blooded socialites, soigné restaurants filled with the Botoxed ladies-who-lunch set… this is the picture most New Yorkers have of the Upper East Side, and you'll certainly see plenty of supporting evidence on Fifth, Madison and Park

Avenues. There's a history to this reputation: encouraged by the opening of Central Park in the late 19th century, the city's more affluent residents began building mansions along Fifth Avenue. By the beginning of the 20th century, even the superwealthy had warmed to the idea of giving up their large homes for smaller quarters – provided they were near the park. As a result, flats and hotels began springing up. (A few years later, working-class folks settled around Second and Third Avenues, following construction of an elevated East Side train line.) Architecturally, the overall look of the neighbourhood, especially from Fifth to Park Avenues, is remarkably homogeneous. Along the expanse known as the Gold Coast – Fifth, Madison and Park Avenues from 61st to 81st Streets – you'll see the great old mansions, many of which are now foreign consulates. The structure at 820 Fifth Avenue (at 64th Street) was one of the earliest luxury apartment buildings on the avenue. New York's ultimate gingerbread house is 45 East 66th Street (between Madison and Park Avenues). Stanford White designed 998 Fifth Avenue (at 81st Street) in the image of an Italian Renaissance palazzo. Some wonderful old carriage houses adorn 63rd and 64th Streets.

Philanthropic gestures made by the moneyed class over the past 130 years have helped to create a cluster of art collections, museums and cultural institutions. In fact, Fifth Avenue from 82nd to 104th Streets is known as Museum Mile because it is flanked by the **Metropolitan Museum of Art** (see p139); the Frank Lloyd Wright-designed **Solomon R Guggenheim Museum** (see p140); the **Cooper-Hewitt** (see p139), which houses the National Design Museum in Andrew Carnegie's former mansion; the **Jewish Museum** (see p139); the **Museum of the City of New York** (see p140) and **El Museo del Barrio** (see p139).

Madison Avenue from 57th to 86th Streets is New York's world-class ultra-luxe shopping strip. The snazzy department store **Barneys New York** (see p228) offers chic designer fashions and witty, sometimes audacious, window displays. For a post-spree pick-me-up, order a cup of divinely rich hot chocolate and a Paris-perfect pastry at **La Maison du Chocolat** (see p244). While bars and restaurants dominate most of the north-south avenues, hungry sightseers can pick up a snack (or picnic supplies) at the well-stocked **Grace's Market Place** (1237 Third Avenue, between 71st & 72nd Streets, 1-212 737 0600) or at the Italian gourmet food shop **Agata & Valentina** (1505 First Avenue, at 79th Street, 1-212 452 0690). Savour your meal on a park bench along the East River promenade leading

Reel history

New York, New York, it's a hell of a town with a hell of a story. Since 1624 people on this little island have been fighting to live the American dream on a daily basis. Now, witness the evolution of the metropolis for yourselves: *Timescapes*, a 25-minute multimedia film showing daily at the Museum of the City of New York (*see below*), uses specially made digital maps with historic images and film footage to piece together the rise of New York City over four centuries – bringing to life buildings and street corners you might otherwise breeze by.

to **Carl Schurz Park** (see p143). The ritzy neighbourhood is also home to the **Asia Society & Museum** (see below), the **China Institute** (see below), the **Frick Collection** (see p139), the **Goethe-Institut New York/German Cultural Center** (see p139), the **Neue Galerie** (see p140) and the **Whitney Museum of American Art** (see p142).

Asia Society & Museum

725 Park Avenue, at 70th Street (1-212 288 6400/www.asiasociety.org). Subway: 6 to 68th Street-Hunter College. **Open** 11am-6pm Tue-Thur, Sat, Sun; 11am-9pm Fri. **Admission** $10; $7 seniors; $5 students; free under-16s. Free 6-9pm Fri. **No credit cards. Map** p405 E20.

The Asia Society sponsors study missions and conferences while promoting public programmes in the US and abroad. The headquarters' striking galleries host major exhibitions of art culled from dozens of countries and time periods – from ancient India and medieval Persia to contemporary Japan – and assembled from public and private collections, including the permanent Mr and Mrs John D Rockefeller III collection of Asian art. A spacious, atrium-like café, with a pan-Asian menu, and a beautifully stocked gift shop, make the society a one-stop destination for anyone who has an interest in Asian art and culture.

China Institute

125 E 65th Street, between Park & Lexington Avenues (1-212 744 8181/www.chinainstitute.org). Subway: F to Lexington Avenue-63rd Street; 6 to 68th Street-Hunter College. **Open** 10am-5pm Mon, Wed, Fri, Sat; 10am-8pm Tue, Thur. **Admission** $5; $3 seniors, students; free under-12s. Free Tue, Thur. **Credit** AmEx, MC, V. **Map** p405 E21.

Consisting of just two small galleries, the China Institute is somewhat overshadowed by the nearby Asia Society. But its rotating exhibitions, including works by female Chinese artists and selections from the Beijing Palace Museum, are compelling. The institute offers lectures and courses on myriad subjects such as calligraphy, Confucius and cooking.

Cooper-Hewitt, National Design Museum

2 E 91st Street, at Fifth Avenue (1-212 849 8400/ www.cooperhewitt.org). Subway: 4, 5, 6 to 86th Street. **Open** 10am-5pm Tue-Thur; 10am-9pm Fri; 10am-6pm Sat; noon-6pm Sun. **Admission** $12; $7 seniors, students; free under-12s. **Credit** AmEx, Disc, MC, V. **Map** p406 E18.

The Smithsonian's National Design Museum was once the home of industrialist Andrew Carnegie (there is still a lovely lawn behind the building – his former garden). Now it's the only museum in the US dedicated to domestic and industrial design, boasting a fascinating roster of temporary exhibitions. From late 2006 to June 2007, there's a celebration of Eugene Thaw's collection of staircase models, most of which come from 19th-century France; and from August 2007 to March 2008, the museum will examine the historical and contemporary use of sampling formats (sample books featuring a physical example of a technique – as tools for marketing or recording designs and techniques in a wide variety of media).

El Museo del Barrio

1230 Fifth Avenue, between 104th & 105th Streets (1-212 831 7272/www.elmuseo.org). Subway: 6 to 103rd Street. **Open** 11am-5pm Wed-Sun. **Admission** $6; $4 seniors, students; free under-12s when accompanied by an adult. Seniors free Thur. **Credit** AmEx, MC, V. **Map** p406 E16.

Located in Spanish Harlem (aka El Barrio), El Museo del Barrio is dedicated to the work of Latino artists who reside in the US as well as Latin American masters. The 8,000-piece collection ranges from pre-Columbian artefacts to contemporary installations. 2007's programmes include 'The Disappeared', a powerful collection of works commemorating the tens of thousands of people kidnapped, tortured and murdered by right-wing military in South America during the 1970s and '80s (22 Feb-17 June). From July until December, El Barrio stages its fifth biennial, 'The (S) Files/The Selected Files', a major survey of innovative works by more than 40 Latino and Latin-American artists living in NYC.

Frick Collection

1 E 70th Street, between Fifth & Madison Avenues (1-212 288 0700/www.frick.org). Subway: 6 to 68th Street-Hunter College. **Open** 10am-6pm Tue-Sat; 11am-5pm Sun. **Admission** $15; $10 seniors; $5 students, 10-18s (under-16s must be accompanied by an adult; under-10s not admitted). Voluntary donation 11am-1pm Sun. **Credit** AmEx, Disc, MC, V. **Map** p405 E20.

The opulent residence that houses this private collection of great masters (from the 14th to the 19th centuries) was originally built for industrialist Henry Clay Frick. The firm of Carrère & Hastings (which designed the New York Public Library) created the 1914 structure in an 18th-century European style, with a beautiful interior court and reflecting

pool. The permanent collection boasts world-class paintings, sculpture and furniture by the likes of Rembrandt, Vermeer, Renoir and French cabinet-maker Jean-Henri Riesener. In autumn 2006 two works from a series by Italian Renaissance master Cimabue were reunited and displayed together for the first time in America.

Goethe-Institut New York/ German Cultural Center

1014 Fifth Avenue, at 82nd Street (1-212 439 8700/ www.goethe.de/ins/us/ney). Subway: 4, 5, 6 to 86th Street. **Open** *Gallery* 10am-5pm Mon, Wed, Fri, Sat; 10am-7pm Tue, Thur. *Library* noon-7pm Tue, Thur; noon-5pm Wed, Fri, Sat. **Admission** free. **Map** p405 E19.

The Goethe-Institut New York is a branch of the international German cultural organisation founded in 1951. Housed in a landmark Fifth Avenue mansion across from the Metropolitan Museum of Art, the institute mounts shows featuring German-born contemporary artists, and presents concerts, lectures and film screenings. German-language books, videos and periodicals are available in the library.

Jewish Museum

1109 Fifth Avenue, at 92nd Street (1-212 423 3200/ www.thejewishmuseum.org). Subway: 4, 5 to 86th Street; 6 to 96th Street. **Open** 11am-5.45pm Mon-Wed, Sun; 11am-9pm Thur; 11am-3pm Fri. Closed on Jewish holidays. **Admission** $10; $7.50 seniors, students; free under-12s when accompanied by an adult. Voluntary donation 5-8pm Thur. **Credit** AmEx, MC, V. **Map** p405 E18.

The Jewish Museum, in the 1908 Warburg Mansion, contains a fascinating collection of over 28,000 works of art, artefacts and media installations. A two-floor permanent exhibit, 'Culture and Continuity: The Jewish Journey', examines Judaism's survival and the essence of Jewish identity. Temporary exhibitions in 2007 include 'Alex Katz paints Ada'; the American artist is famous for his still-lifes and landscapes, but here the museum displays 39 tender, intimate portraits of his beloved wife, Ada (to 18 Mar). Also showing is 'Louise Nevelson: A Story in Sculpture'; originally from Kiev, Russia, Nevelson (1899-1988) migrated to America and became one of the country's most influential sculptors (4 May-16 Sept). The museum's Café Weissman serves contemporary kosher fare.

Metropolitan Museum of Art

1000 Fifth Avenue, at 82nd Street (1-212 535 7710/ www.metmuseum.org). Subway: 4, 5, 6 to 86th Street. **Open** 9.30am-5.30pm Tue-Thur, Sun; 9.30am-9pm Fri, Sat. No strollers Sun. **Admission** suggested donation (incl same-day admission to the Cloisters) $20; $10 seniors, students; free under-12s. **Credit** AmEx, DC, Disc, MC, V. **Map** p405 E19.

Many locals shuddered in anger in summer 2006 when the Met announced that its suggested fee would be jumping up to $20. We say, chill out. It's only a suggested amount, after all. And thank God for that, since it would take many, many visits to cover the Met's 2 million sq ft of gallery space. Besides the enthralling temporary exhibitions, there are excellent collections of African, Oceanic and Islamic art, along with more than 3,000 European paintings from the Middle Ages up to the fin-de-siècle period, including major works by Titian, Brueghel, Rembrandt, Vermeer, Goya and Degas, as well as the controversial *Madonna and Child* – stop by and decide whether you think the $45 million piece is the handiwork of medieval master Duccio, or some latter-day forger, as one art historian recently claimed. Egyptology fans should head straight for the glass-walled atrium housing the Temple of Dendur. The Greek and Roman halls have received a graceful makeover, and the incomparable medieval armour collection – a huge favourite with adults and children – was recently enriched by gifts of European, North American, Japanese and Islamic armaments.

The Met has also made significant additions to its modern-art galleries, including major works by American artist Eric Fischl and Chilean surrealist Roberto Matta. Contemporary sculptures are displayed each year in the Iris and B Gerald Cantor Roof Garden (May to late autumn, weather permitting). If you're in town for a long holiday weekend, don't despair. The Met opens its doors on Monday holidays, including Martin Luther King Day, Presidents' Day, Memorial Day and the Monday between Christmas and New Year's Day.

A large, round desk in the Great Hall (staffed by volunteers who speak multiple languages) is the hub of the museum's excellent visitors' resources. (Foreign-language tours are available; call 1-212 570 3711 for information.) Once you've found the type of art that interests you most – from Greek kouroi to colourful Kandinskys – we recommend seeking out a spot of relative privacy and calm. The Met is dotted with plenty of choices – you just have to know where to look. The Engelhard Court, which borders Central Park, has benches, a trickling fountain, trees, ivy and stunning examples of Tiffany stained-glass to encourage restful contemplation. (And if you'd like to grab a drink or a snack in less-than-hectic surroundings, try the recently opened American Wing Café.) Astor Court, on the second floor, is a garden modelled on a Ming-dynasty scholar's courtyard. Wooden paths border a naturally lit, gravel-paved atrium. The nearby Asian galleries, full of superb bronzes, ceramics and rare wooden Buddhist images, seldom get heavy foot-traffic. At the western end of the museum, rest on a bench in the Robert Lehman Wing, then commune with Botticelli's *Annunciation*.

Planned 2007 exhibitions include 'Coaxing the Spirits to Dance: Art of the Papuan Gulf', with sacred objects, sculptures and photographs from Papua New Guinea that explore the place of supernatural beings in the region's folklore (to 2 Sept); 'Louis Comfort Tiffany – An Artist's Country Estate', bringing together the surviving works from Tiffany's country home, which was created as a showcase for his lavish paintings, ceramics and stained-glass windows (to 20 May); and 'Venice and the Islamic World 828-1797', showing how Venetian artworks were influenced by the Islamic world during this 1,000-year period (27 Mar-8 July).

Museum of the City of New York

1220 Fifth Avenue, between 103rd & 104th Streets (1-212 534 1672/www.mcny.org). Subway: 6 to 103rd Street. **Open** 10am-5pm Tue-Sun. **Admission** suggested donation $9; $5 seniors, students, children; $20 families. **Credit** AmEx, MC, V. **Map** p405 E16.
Located at the northern end of Museum Mile, this institution contains a wealth of city history and includes paintings, sculptures, photographs, military and naval uniforms, theatre memorabilia, manuscripts, ship models and rare books. The extensive toy collection, full of New Yorkers' playthings dating from the colonial era to the present, is especially well loved. Toy trains, lead soldiers and battered teddy bears share shelf space with exquisite bisque dolls (decked out in extravagant Paris fashions) and lavishly appointed dolls' houses. Don't miss the amazing Stettheimer Dollhouse, created during the 1920s by Carrie Stettheimer, whose artist friends re-created their masterpieces in miniature to hang on the walls. Look closely and you'll even spy a tiny version of Marcel Duchamp's famous *Nude Descending a Staircase*. Don't miss the museum's *Timescapes*, a 25-minute multimedia film that tells NYC's glorious story from 1624 to the present. The film is free with admission and plays throughout the day.

Neue Galerie

1048 Fifth Avenue, at 86th Street (1-212 628 6200/ www.neuegalerie.org). Subway: 4, 5, 6 to 86th Street. **Open** 11am-6pm Mon, Sat, Sun; 11am-9pm Fri. **Admission** $15; $10 seniors, students, 12-16s (must be accompanied by an adult); under-12s not admitted. **Credit** AmEx, MC, V. **Map** p405 E18.
This elegant museum is devoted entirely to late 19th- and early 20th-century German and Austrian fine and decorative arts. The creation of the late art dealer Serge Sabarsky and cosmetics mogul Ronald S Lauder, it has the largest concentration of works by Gustav Klimt and Egon Schiele outside Vienna. There's also a bookstore, a chic design shop and Café Sabarsky, serving updated Austrian cuisine and ravishing Viennese pastries.

Solomon R Guggenheim Museum

1071 Fifth Avenue, at 89th Street (1-212 423 3500/ www.guggenheim.org). Subway: 4, 5, 6 to 86th Street. **Open** 10am-5.45pm Mon-Wed, Sat, Sun; 10am-8pm Fri. **Admission** $18; $15 seniors, students with a valid ID; free under-12s (must be accompanied by an adult). Half-price 5.45-8pm Fri. **Credit** AmEx, MC, V. **Map** p406 E18.
Even if your hectic museum-hopping schedule doesn't allow time to view the collections, you must get a glimpse (if only from the outside) of this dramatic spiral building, designed by Frank Lloyd Wright. In addition to works by Manet, Kandinsky, Picasso, Chagall and Bourgeois, the museum owns Peggy Guggenheim's trove of cubist, surrealist and abstract expressionist works, along with the Panza di Biumo

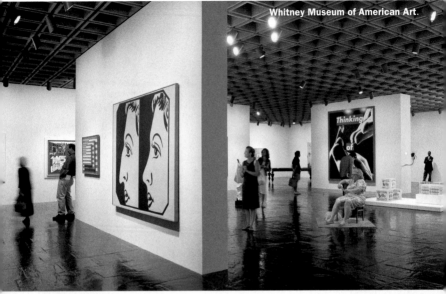

Collection of American minimalist and conceptual art from the 1960s and '70s. In 1992 the addition of a ten-storey tower provided space for a sculpture gallery (with views of the park), an auditorium and a café.

Planned 2007 exhibitions: the Guggenheim will no doubt draw huge crowds with 'El Greco to Picasso: Time, Truth and History', a survey of the most important Spanish artists of the last 500 years (ends spring 2007). A major retrospective of American artist Richard Prince follows later in the spring. Famous for his joke paintings, repurposed adverts and car bonnet sculptures, Prince has become something of an art world pop idol.

Whitney Museum of American Art

945 Madison Avenue, at 75th Street (1-212 570 3676/1-800 944 8639/www.whitney.org). Subway: 6 to 77th Street. **Open** 11am-6pm Wed, Thur, Sat, Sun; 1-9pm Fri. **Admission** $15; $10 seniors, students; free under-12s. Voluntary donation 6-9pm Fri. **Credit** AmEx, MC, V. **Map** p405 E20.
Like the Guggenheim, the Whitney is set apart by its unique architecture: it's a Marcel Breuer-designed grey granite cube with an all-seeing upper-storey 'eye' window. When Gertrude Vanderbilt Whitney, a sculptor and art patron, opened the museum in 1931, she dedicated it to living American artists. Today, the Whitney holds about 15,000 pieces by nearly 2,000 artists, including Alexander Calder, Willem de Kooning, Edward Hopper (the museum holds his entire estate), Jasper Johns, Louise Nevelson, Georgia O'Keeffe and Claes Oldenburg. Still, the museum's reputation rests mainly on its temporary shows, particularly the exhibition every-

one loves to hate, the Whitney Biennial. Held in even-numbered years, the Biennial remains the most prestigious (and controversial) assessment of contemporary art in America. The Whitney's small midtown Altria branch, located in a corporate atrium space across the street from Grand Central Terminal, mounts solo commissioned projects. At the main building, there are free guided tours daily and live performances on select Friday nights. Sarabeth's, the museum's café, is open daily till 4.30pm, offering sandwiches and the like.

Planned 2007 exhibitions: Asian punk boy Terence Koh's sensuous monochromatic lobby installation uses burned objects and shards of mirrored glass to stunning effect in a piece he created specially for the Whitney (Jan-May), and a retrospective of the short, shining career of American conceptual artist Gordon Matta-Clark (1943-78) includes films, drawings and photographs of buildings with cut-out walls to expose their inner core (opens Feb).
Other locations: Whitney Museum of American Art at Altria, 120 Park Avenue, at 42nd Street, Midtown (1-917 663 2453).

Yorkville

Not much remains of the old German and Hungarian immigrant communities that filled Yorkville with delicatessens, beer halls and restaurants. Two flashbacks are the 71-year-old **Elk Candy Company** (1628 Second Avenue, between 84th & 85th Streets, 1-212 585 2303), famous for its chocolates and marzipan, and the nearly 50-year-old **Heidelberg** (1648 Second Avenue, at 85th Street, 1-212 650 1385), where dirndl-wearing waitresses serve steins of Spaten and platters of sausages from the wurst-meisters at nearby butcher shop Schaller & Weber.

Gracie Mansion (*see below*), at the eastern end of 88th Street, is the only Federal-style mansion in Manhattan, and it's been New York's official mayoral residence since 1942 – the current mayor, billionaire Michael Bloomberg, famously eschewed this traditional address in favour of his own Beaux Arts mansion at 17 East 79th Street (between Fifth & Madison Avenues). The green-shuttered yellow edifice, built in 1799 by Scottish merchant Archibald Gracie, was originally constructed as a country house for the wealthy businessman. Today, the stately house is the focal point of tranquil **Carl Schurz Park**, named in honour of the German immigrant who became a newspaper editor and US senator. In 2002 Gracie Mansion's living quarters were opened to public tours for the first time in 60 years. Reservations are a must.

The **Henderson Place Historic District** (at East End Avenue, between 86th & 87th Streets), one block from Gracie Mansion, consists of two dozen handsome Queen Anne row houses, which were commissioned by furrier and real-estate developer John C Henderson. Twenty-four of the original 32 houses remain, with the original turrets, double stoops and slate roofs. Nearby, you can also check out what's for sale at **Sotheby's** (*see below*).

Although the city is home to approximately 400,000 Muslims, the dramatic **Islamic Cultural Center** (1711 Third Avenue, at 96th Street, 1-212 722 5234), built in 1990, is New York's first major mosque.

Gracie Mansion Conservancy

Carl Schurz Park, 88th Street, at East End Avenue (1-212 570 4751). Subway: 4, 5, 6 to 86th Street. **Tours** *Mar-mid Nov* 10am, 11am, 1pm, 2pm Wed. **Admission** $7; $4 seniors, students; free under-12s. Reservations required. Tours last 45mins; same-day reservations not permitted. **No credit cards**. Map p406 G18.

Sotheby's

1334 York Avenue, at 72nd Street (1-212 606 7000/ www.sothebys.com). Subway: 6 to 68th Street-Hunter College. **Open** 10am-5pm Mon-Sat (hours change seasonally, call ahead). **Admission** free.
Sotheby's, with offices from London to Singapore, is the world's most famous auction house. The New York branch regularly holds public sales of antique furniture and jewellery in one lot, and pop-culture memorabilia in another. Spring and autumn see the big sales of modern and contemporary art. Public viewings are held prior to each auction; call or visit Sotheby's website for details of dates and times.

Upper West Side

Housing a population that's older than Downtown's, but more bohemian than the Upper East Side's, this four-mile-long stretch west of Central Park is culturally rich and cosmopolitan. As on the UES, New Yorkers were drawn here during the late 19th century, after the completion of Central Park, the opening of local subway lines and Columbia University's relocation to Morningside Heights. In the 20th century many central Europeans found refuge here; in the 1960s Puerto Ricans settled along Amsterdam and Columbus Avenues. These days, new real-estate development is reducing eye-level evidence of old immigrant life, and the neighbourhood's long-standing intellectual, politically liberal spirit has waned (a bit) as apartment prices have risen. Still, sections of Riverside Drive, West End Avenue and Central Park West continue to rival the grandeur of the East Side's Fifth and Park Avenues.

The gateway to the UWS is **Columbus Circle**, where Broadway meets 59th Street, Eighth Avenue, Central Park South and Central Park West – a rare rotary in a city of right angles. The architecture around it could make anyone's head spin. A 700-ton statue of Christopher Columbus, positioned at the entrance to Central Park, goes almost unnoticed in the shadow of the **Time Warner Center** across the street, which houses the offices of the media conglomerate, along with luxury apartments, hotel accommodation and **Jazz at Lincoln Center**'s stunning Frederick P Rose Hall (*see p322*). The first seven levels of the enormous glass complex are filled with high-end retailers and gourmet restaurants, including **Per Se** (*see p211*), the four-star venture of celebrated chef Thomas Keller. On the south side of the circle is a windowless white-granite structure, built as a modern-art gallery by Huntington Hartford in 1964. The **Museum of Arts & Design** (*see p127*) has bought the building and, after renovation, will move into its new home in 2007. The circle also bears Donald Trump's signature: he stuck his name on the former Gulf & Western Building when he converted it into the predictably glitzy Trump International Hotel & Tower.

The Upper West Side's seat of highbrow culture is **Lincoln Center** (*see p328*), a complex of concert halls and auditoriums built in the 1960s. It is home to the New York Philharmonic, the New York City Ballet and the Metropolitan Opera, along with a host of other arts organisations. The big circular fountain in the central plaza is a popular gathering spot, especially in summer, when amateur dancers

Payton place

Philip A Payton Jr isn't a household name, but for blacks at the turn of the 20th century, he was 'the man' to see about scoring a crib in Harlem. Payton opened the Afro-American Realty Company in 1904, becoming the biggest realtor in Harlem, thanks initially to an argument between two white landlords: one of them, itching to get even with the other, turned a building over to Payton to fill with African-American tenants. He was so successful that soon he was managing houses for other white owners. Payton wasn't just buying and selling the Harlem dream – he lived it, residing in a Victorian Gothic row house at 13 West 131st Street until his death in 1917. Through his efforts, Harlem became the capital of black America – and Payton became known as the father of Harlem.

converge on it to dance alfresco at Midsummer Night Swing (*see p262*). Lincoln Center has begun a billion-dollar overhaul that includes a redesign of public spaces, refurbishment of the various ageing halls and construction of new buildings. Nearby you can also check out the **New York Public Library for the Performing Arts** (*see p146*).

The other, less formal, cultural venues on the Upper West Side include the **Makor/Steinhardt Center** (35 W 67th Street, between Central Park West & Columbus Avenue, 1-212 601 1000, www.makor.org), where the public can attend lectures, films, readings and live music performances, often with a folky or Jewish flavour; **Symphony Space** (*see p331*), where the World Music Institute programmes music and dance performances and rated actors read short stories aloud as part of the Selected Shorts programme; and **El Taller Latino**

Americano (2710 Broadway, at 104th Street, 1-212 665 9460, www.tallerlatino.org), which offers a full range of cultural events.

Around Sherman and Verdi Squares (from 70th to 73rd Streets, where Broadway and Amsterdam Avenue intersect) classic early 20th-century buildings stand cheek-by-jowl with newer, often mundane high-rises. The jewel is the 1904 **Ansonia Hotel** (2109 Broadway, between 73rd & 74th Streets). Over the years, Enrico Caruso, Babe Ruth and Igor Stravinsky have lived in this Beaux Arts masterpiece, which was also the site of the Continental Baths (the gay bathhouse and cabaret where Bette Midler got her start) and Plato's Retreat (a swinging '70s sex club). On Broadway, the crowded 72nd Street subway station, which opened in 1904, is notable for its Beaux Arts entrance. The **Beacon Theatre** (*see p314*), formerly Manhattan's only rococo

1920s movie palace, is now one of the city's premier mid-size concert venues, presenting an eclectic menu of music, African-American regional theatre and headliner comedy events.

Once Central Park was completed, magnificently tall residential buildings rose up along Central Park West to take advantage of the views. The first of these great buildings was the **Dakota** (at 72nd Street). The fortress-like 1884 luxury apartment building is known as the setting for *Rosemary's Baby* and the site of John Lennon's murder in 1980 (Yoko Ono still lives here). You might recognise 55 Central Park West (at 66th Street) from the movie *Ghostbusters*. Built in 1930, it was the first art deco building on the block. Heading north on Central Park West, you'll spy the massive twin-towered San Remo Apartments (at 74th Street), which also date from 1930. A few blocks north, the **New-York Historical Society** (*see p146*) is the city's oldest museum, built in 1804. Across the street, the glorious **American Museum of Natural History** (*see below*) has been given an impressive facelift, making even the fossils look fresh again. Dinosaur skeletons, a permanent rainforest exhibit and an IMAX theatre (which shows Oscar-winning nature documentaries) lure adults and school groups. Perhaps most popular is the museum's newest wing, the amazing, glass-enclosed Rose Center for Earth & Space, which includes the retooled Hayden Planetarium.

The cluster of classic groceries and restaurants lining the avenues of the neighbourhood's northern end is where the Upper West Side shops, drinks and eats. To see West Siders in their natural habitat, get in line at the perpetually jammed smoked-fish counter at gourmet market **Zabar's** (*see p246*). **Café Lalo** (201 W 83rd Street, between Amsterdam Avenue & Broadway, 1-212 496 6031) is famous for its lavish desserts; **H&H Bagels** (*see p186* **Daily bread**) is the city's largest bagel purveyor; and the legendary (though scruffy) restaurant and deli **Barney Greengrass** ('the Sturgeon King', 541 Amsterdam Avenue, at 86th Street, 1-212 724 4707) has specialised in smoked fish, and what may be the city's best chopped liver, since 1908.

Designed by Central Park's Frederick Law Olmsted, **Riverside Park** is a sinuous stretch of riverbank that starts at 72nd Street and ends at 158th Street, between Riverside Drive and the Hudson River. The stretch of park below 72nd Street, called Riverside Park South, includes a pier and beautiful patches of grass with park benches, and is a particularly peaceful city retreat. You'll probably see yachts, along with several houseboats, berthed at the 79th Street Boat Basin; in the summertime, there's an

open-air café in the adjacent park, where New Yorkers unwind with a beer and watch the sun set over the Hudson River. Several sites provide havens for reflection. The Soldiers' and Sailors' Monument (89th Street, at Riverside Drive), built in 1902 by French sculptor Paul EM DuBoy, honours Union soldiers who died in the Civil War, and a 1908 memorial (100th Street, at Riverside Drive) pays tribute to fallen firemen. **General Grant National Memorial** (aka Grant's Tomb), the mausoleum of former president Ulysses S Grant, is also located in the park. Across the street stands the towering Gothic-style Riverside Church (Riverside Drive, at 120th Street, 1-212 870 6700, www.theriversidechurchny.org), built in 1930. The tower contains the world's largest carillon: 74 bells, played every Sunday at 10.30am.

American Museum of Natural History/Rose Center for Earth & Space

Central Park West, at 79th Street (1-212 769 5100/www.amnh.org). Subway: B, C to 81st Street-Museum of Natural History. **Open** 10am-5.45pm daily. **Admission** suggested donation $14; $10.50 seniors, students; $8 2-12s; free under-2s. **Credit** AmEx, MC, V. **Map** p405 C/D19.

Home to the largest and arguably most fabulous collection of dinosaur fossils in the world, AMNH's fourth-floor dino halls have been blowing people's minds for decades. Roughly 80% of the bones on

Madison Avenue. See p133.

display were actually dug out of the ground by Indiana Jones types. The thrills begin when you cross the threshold of the Theodore Roosevelt Rotunda, where you're confronted with a towering barosaurus that's rearing high on its hind legs to protect its young from an attacking allosaurus – an impressive welcome to the world's largest museum of its kind. During the museum's mid 1990s renovation, several specimens were remodelled to incorporate discoveries made during that time. The Tyrannosaurus rex, for instance, was once believed to have walked upright, Godzilla-style; it now stalks prey with its head lowered and tail raised parallel to the ground.

The rest of the museum is equally dramatic. The Hall of Biodiversity examines world ecosystems and environmental preservation, and a life-size model of a blue whale hangs from the cavernous ceiling of the Hall of Ocean Life. The impressive Hall of Meteorites was brushed up and reorganised in 2003. The space's focal point is Ahnighito, the largest iron meteor on display anywhere in the world, weighing in at 34 tons (more than 30,000kg). The spectacular $210 million Rose Center for Earth & Space – dazzling to come upon at night – is a giant silvery globe where you can discover the universe via 3-D shows in the Hayden Planetarium and light shows in the Big Bang Theater. An IMAX theatre screens larger-than-life nature programmes, and you can always learn something new from the innovative temporary exhibitions, an easily accessible research library (with vast photo and print archives), several cool gift shops and friendly, helpful staff.

From October 2006 to May 2007, visitors can mingle with 500 live specimens of tropical butterflies in the specially constructed conservatory in the Hall of Oceanic Birds. Until August 2007 the museum stages 'Gold', an exhibition that looks at mankind's obsession with the precious metal and that features gleaming icons such as Olympic medals and the Academy Award's Oscar. From May 2007 to the end of the year there'll be a major show exploring mythical creatures such as dragons, unicorns and mermaids through an astonishing collection of tapestries, sculpture, ceremonial masks and fossils – even live crocodiles.

General Grant National Memorial

Riverside Drive, at 122nd Street (1-212 666 1640). Subway: 1, 9 to 125th Street. **Open** 9am-5pm daily. **Admission** free. **Map** p407 B14.
Who's buried in Grant's Tomb? No one, it appears – the crypts of Civil War hero and 18th president Ulysses S Grant and his wife, Julia, are in full aboveground view, however. Note: the memorial is closed on Thanksgiving, Christmas and New Year's Day.

New-York Historical Society

170 Central Park West, between 76th & 77th Streets (1-212 873 3400/www.nyhistory.org). Subway: B, C to 81st Street-Museum of Natural History. **Open** 10am-6pm Tue-Sun. **Admission** $10; $5 seniors, students; free under-12s when accompanied by an adult. **No credit cards. Map** p405 D20.

New York's oldest museum, founded in 1804, was one of America's first cultural and educational institutions. Highlights in the vast Henry Luce III Center for the Study of American Culture include George Washington's Valley Forge camp cot, a complete series of the extant watercolours from Audubon's *The Birds of America* and the world's largest collection of Tiffany lamps. A fascinating ongoing multimedia exhibition on slavery and its social, economic and political impact on New York is in the Luce Center; and, until 3 September 2007, 'New York Divided: Slavery and the Civil War' examines the city's relationship to slavery and the abolitionist movement in and around the Civil War years.

New York Public Library for the Performing Arts

40 Lincoln Center Plaza, at 65th Street (1-212 870 1630). Subway: 1 to 66th Street-Lincoln Center. **Open** noon-6pm Tue, Wed, Fri, Sat; noon-8pm Thur. **Admission** free. **Map** p405 C21.
One of the world's great performing-arts research centres, the New York Library for the Performing Arts houses a seemingly endless collection of films, letters, manuscripts, video – and half a million sound recordings. Visitors can browse through books, scores and recordings, or attend a concert or lecture.

Morningside Heights

Morningside Heights runs from 110th Street (also known west of Central Park as Cathedral Parkway) to 125th Street, between Morningside Park and the Hudson River. The Cathedral Church of St John the Divine and the campus of Columbia University exert considerable influence over the surrounding neighbourhood.

One of the oldest universities in the US, **Columbia** (*photo p148*) was chartered in 1754 as King's College (the name changed after the Revolutionary War). It moved to its present location in 1897. Thanks to the large student population of Columbia and its sister school, Barnard College, the area has an academic feel, with bookshops, inexpensive restaurants and coffeehouses lining Broadway between 110th and 116th Streets. **Mondel Chocolates** (2913 Broadway, at 114th Street, 1-212 864 2111) was the chocolatier of choice for the late Katharine Hepburn, and **Tom's Restaurant** (2880 Broadway, at 112th Street, 1-212 864 6137) did duty for the exterior shots for the countless diner scenes on TV's *Seinfeld*.

If you wander into Columbia's campus entrance at 116th Street, you won't fail to miss the impressive Low Memorial Building: it's the only one modelled on Rome's Pantheon. The former library, completed in 1897, is now an admin building. The real attraction, however, is the student body sprawled out on its steps (or lawns out front), catching rays between classes.

Hanging on and around **Malcolm X Boulevard** (Lenox Avenue).

The **Cathedral Church of St John the Divine** (*see below*) is the seat of the Episcopal Diocese of New York. Known affectionately by locals as St John the Unfinished, the enormous cathedral (already larger than Notre Dame in Paris) will undergo hammering and chiselling well into this century. Just behind is the green expanse of **Morningside Park** (from 110th to 123rd Streets, between Morningside Avenue & Morningside Drive) and across the street is the **Hungarian Pastry Shop** (1030 Amsterdam Avenue, between 110th & 111th Streets, 1-212 866 4230), a great place for coffee, dessert and mingling with cute Columbia co-eds.

Cathedral Church of St John the Divine

1047 Amsterdam Avenue, at 112th Street (1-212 316 7540/www.stjohndivine.org). Subway: B, C, 1 to 110th Street-Cathedral Parkway. **Open** 8am-6pm daily. **Admission** suggested donation $5; $4 seniors, students. **Credit** MC, V. **Map** p406 C15.
Construction on 'St John the Unfinished' began in 1892 in Romanesque style, was put on hold for a Gothic Revival redesign in 1911, then ground to a halt in 1941, when the US entered World War II. It resumed in earnest in 1979, but a fire in 2001 destroyed the church's gift shop and damaged two 17th-century Italian tapestries, which has delayed completion further. In addition to Sunday services,

the cathedral hosts concerts and tours. It bills itself as a place for all people – and it means it. Annual events include both winter and summer solstice celebrations; the Blessing of the Animals during the Feast of St Francis, which draws pets and their people from all over the city; and, would you believe it, the Blessing of the Bikes, which kicks off the bicycle season each spring.

Harlem

Despite the big-name chain stores lining 125th Street – and the roll of gentrification steadily making its way ever northward – Harlem, thankfully, remains Harlem. Here, ancestral beats bounce between hip hop, zouk and reggae. Sundays spill sweet gospel sounds and enticing biscuit aromas on to house front steps that have seen poets, prophets, preachers and even Presidents come and go. Harlem has long been the cultural capital of black America and home to such luminaries as Duke Ellington, Thurgood Marshall and Jacob Lawrence. The neighbourhood – which runs from the East River to the Hudson and from 110th Street to the 160s – saw its once-glorious reputation overshadowed by images of poverty and crime during the second half of the 20th century. Today, Harlem can no longer be described as the neglected 'raisin in the sun', as it was in

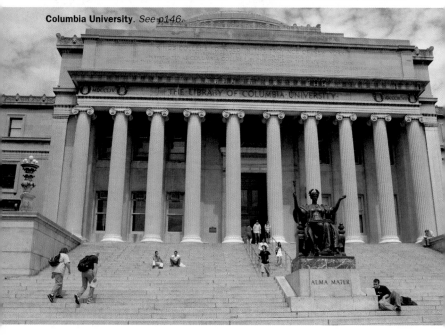

Columbia University. See p146.

Langston Hughes's famous poem 'Harlem: A Dream Deferred' (1959). (The poet's line inspired Lorraine Hansberry's eponymous groundbreaking play, the first black work on Broadway, which is still running today.) And it's not the powder keg of the 1960s that his words presaged, either. The Harlem Renaissance of the 1920s and '30s – the cultural explosion that gave us the likes of Hughes, Zora Neale Hurston and Duke Ellington – continues to live on in memory and has helped spur a new Harlem renaissance, jump-started largely by private real-estate investment and government support for local entrepreneurs and business development.

Harlem began as a suburb for well-to-do whites in the 19th century, after the West Side railroad was built. Around 1900, plans to extend the subway along Lenox Avenue to 145th Street triggered a housing boom that went bust just a few years later. White landlords, previously unwilling to lease to blacks, were now desperate for tenants, and, slowly but surely, changed their leasing habits. Blacks reportedly paid up to $5 more per month than whites at this time, to rent similar flats; yet it was a watershed for the city's resident African-American community: for the first time in NYC's history, they had an opportunity to live in well-built homes in a stable community. By 1914 the black population of Harlem rose above 50,000.

The area is blessed with stately brownstones in varying stages of renovation, often right next to blocks of towering public housing. Thanks to a thriving black middle-class community, Harlem's cultural and religious institutions are seeing renewed interest and funding, and new commercial enterprise abounds. Yet, the neighbourhood's history remains visible. Some of the fabled locations from the original Harlem Renaissance have been restored, and while many stages in the celebrated jazz clubs, theatres and ballrooms have been replaced by pulpits, the buildings still stand.

West Harlem

West Harlem, between Fifth and St Nicholas Avenues, is the Harlem of popular imagination, and 125th Street ('the one-two-five') is its lifeline. Start at the crossroads: the 274,000-square-foot **Harlem USA Mall** (300 W 125th Street, between Adam Clayton Powell Jr Boulevard [Seventh Avenue] & Frederick Douglass Boulevard [Eighth Avenue], www.harlem-usa.com). The mall features a Magic Johnson multiplex movie theatre (1-212 665 6923) and the well-stocked Hue-Man Bookstore (1-212 665 7400), specialising in African-American titles, plus the usual retail megastores. Across the street is the **Apollo Theater**, which still

hosts live concerts, a syndicated television programme and the classic Amateur Night held every Wednesday. A few blocks west, other touches of old Harlem linger: **Showman's Bar** (375 W 125th Street, between St Nicholas & Morningside Avenues, 1-212 864 8941), a mecca for jazz lovers, and the reconstituted **Cotton Club** (656 W 125th Street, at Riverside Drive, 1-212 663 7980), which hosts gospel brunches and evening jazz and blues sessions.

To the east of the mall is the **Lenox Lounge** (*see p322*), still cooking with old-school jazz. A well-regarded fine arts centre, the **Studio Museum in Harlem** (*see p150*) exhibits work by many local artists. Just a block away is the vibrant new **Harlem Lanes** (*see p151* **Face facts**); there are 24 gleaming lanes here and you aren't likely to find cheaper bowling anywhere in Manhattan. The first-floor family area caters mostly to birthday parties. If you don't have kids in tow, head upstairs to the grown-ups' lounge: it's hip and cosy, featuring a bar, plush jewel-toned banquettes and exposed brick.

The offices of former president Bill Clinton are at 55 W 125th Street (between Fifth Avenue & Malcolm X Boulevard [Lenox Avenue]). Harlem's rich history is preserved in the archives of the **Schomburg Center for Research in Black Culture** (*see p150*). This branch of the New York Public Library contains more than five million documents, artefacts, films and prints relating to the cultures of peoples of African descent, with an emphasis on the African-American experience. The **Abyssinian Baptist Church** (*see p150*), where Harlem's controversial 1960s congressman Adam Clayton Powell Jr once preached, is celebrated for its history, political activism and rousing gospel choir. It harbours a small museum dedicated to Powell, the first black member of New York's City Council.

Harlem has become a destination for stylish plus-size fashions. Check out the **Soul Brothers Boutique** (115 W 128th Street, between Malcolm X Boulevard [Lenox Avenue] & Adam Clayton Powell Jr Boulevard [Seventh Avenue], 1-212 749 9005), where you can find T-shirts that celebrate the neighbourhood, black political figures and '70s blaxploitation films. (You may also want to visit Freedom Hall, an active radical-politics lecture facility and bookstore next door.)

That generously sized clothing will come in handy if you sample the smothered pork chops and collard greens with fatback at **Sylvia's** (328 Malcolm X Boulevard [Lenox Avenue], between 126th & 127th Streets, 1-212 996 0660), Harlem's tourist-packed soul-food specialist. **Bayou** (308 Malcolm X Boulevard [Lenox Avenue], between 125th & 126th Streets, 1-212

Sightseeing

426 3800), the handsome Cajun eaterie down the street, is a more attractive alternative.

Walk off some of your meal with a stroll around **Marcus Garvey Park** (aka Mount Morris Park, 120th to 124th Streets, between Madison Avenue & Mount Morris Park West), where the brownstone revival is in full swing.

Abyssinian Baptist Church

132 W 138th Street, between Malcolm X Boulevard (Lenox Avenue) & Adam Clayton Powell Jr Boulevard (Seventh Avenue) (1-212 862 7474/www.abyssinian. org). Subway: 2, 3 to 135th Street. **Open** 9am-5pm Mon-Fri. **Admission** free. **Map** p407 E11.

Harlem Lanes

3rd Floor, 2116 Adam Clayton Powell Jr Boulevard (Seventh Avenue), at 126th Street (1-212 678 2695/ www.harlemlanes.com). Subway 2, 3, A, B, C, D to 125th Street. **Open** 11am-11pm Mon-Thur; 11am-2am Fri, Sat; 11am-9pm Sun. **Cost** from $5.50 per game. **Credit** AmEx, MC, V. **Map** p407 D13.

Schomburg Center for Research in Black Culture

515 Malcolm X Boulevard (Lenox Avenue), at 135th Street (1-212 491 2200). Subway: 2, 3 to 135th Street. **Open** noon-8pm Tue, Wed; noon-6pm Thur, Fri; 10am-6pm Sat. **Admission** free. **Map** p407 D12. An extraordinary trove of vintage literature and historical memorabilia relating to black culture and the African diaspora is housed in an institution founded in 1926 by its first curator, bibliophile Arturo Alfonso Schomburg. The centre also hosts jazz concerts, films, lectures and tours.

Studio Museum in Harlem

144 W 125th Street, between Malcolm X Boulevard (Lenox Avenue) & Adam Clayton Powell Jr Boulevard (Seventh Avenue) (1-212 864 4500/www.studio museum.org). Subway: 2, 3 to 125th Street. **Open** noon-6pm Wed-Fri, Sun; 10am-6pm Sat. Guided tours by appointment. **Admission** suggested donation $7; $3 seniors, students; free under-12s. Free 1st Sat of mth. **No credit cards**. **Map** p407 D13.
When the Studio Museum opened in 1968, it was the first black fine-arts museum in the country, and it remains the place to go for historical insight into African-American art and that of the African diaspora. Under the leadership of director Lowery Stokes Sims (formerly of the Met) and chief curator Thelma Golden (formerly of the Whitney), this favourite has evolved into the city's most exciting showcase for contemporary African-American artists.

Mount Morris & Strivers' Row

Harlem's historic districts continue to gentrify. The **Mount Morris Historic District** (from 119th to 124th Streets, between Malcolm X Boulevard [Lenox Avenue] & Mount Morris Park West) contains charming brownstones and a collection of religious buildings in a variety of architectural styles. These days, new boutiques, restaurants and pavement cafés dot the walk down the double-wide **Malcolm X Boulevard** (Lenox Avenue). **Harlemade** (No.174, between 118th & 119th Streets, 1-212 987 2500, www.harlemade.com) sells T-shirts with Afro- and Harlem-centric messages and images, along with postcards, books and other neighbourhood memorabilia.

Another area with a historic past is **Strivers' Row**, also known as the St Nicholas Historic District. Running from 138th to 139th Streets, between Adam Clayton Powell Jr Boulevard (Seventh Avenue) and Frederick Douglass Boulevard (Eighth Avenue), these blocks of majestic houses were developed in 1891 by David H King Jr and designed by three different architects, including Stanford White. In the 1920s prominent members of the black community, the legendary Eubie Blake and WC Handy among them, lived in this area. Now, more upwardly mobile strivers are moving in, and so are stylish boutiques such as **Grandview** (2531 Frederick Douglass Boulevard [Eighth Avenue], between 135th & 136th Streets, 1-212 694 7324), which sells eclectic contemporary clothing and accessories, mostly by African-American designers. Along the way, there's plenty of good eating: **Londel's Supper Club** (2620 Frederick Douglass Boulevard [Eighth Avenue], between 139th & 140th Streets, 1-212 234 0601), owned by former police officer Londel Davis, serves some of the best blackened catfish in town, and **Home Sweet Harlem Café** (270 W 135th Street, at Frederick Douglass Boulevard [Eighth Avenue], 1-212 926 9616) is the place for smoothies, soy burgers and hearty soups.

The 'hood comes alive after dark, especially at the not-to-be-missed **St Nick's Pub** (773 St Nicholas Avenue, at 149th Street, 1-212 283 9728), where you can hear live jazz every night (except Tuesday) for a small cover charge.

Heading east on West 116th Street, you'll pass through a dizzying smörgåsbord of cultures. There's a West African flavour between Malcolm X and Adam Clayton Powell Jr Boulevards (Lenox and Seventh Avenues), especially at the Senegalese restaurant **Le Baobab** (No.120, 1-212 864 4700). On the north side of the street is one of the Reverend Al Sharpton's favourite restaurants, **Amy Ruth's** (No.113, 1-212 280 8779). While tour buses may favour nearby Sylvia's, locals who know better head to this cosy restaurant instead. Each dish is named after a prominent African-American New Yorker; try the Terry Rivers, honey-dipped fried chicken. Continue east, past the silver-domed **Masjid Malcolm Shabazz** (No.102, 1-212 662 2200), the mosque of Malcolm X's ministry, to the **Malcolm Shabazz Harlem**

Face facts:
Sharon Joseph & Gail Richards

Time Out: You and your business partner, Gail Richards, have opened the first bowling alley Harlem's had in decades. What was it that made you want to bring this sport to the neighbourhood?
Sharon Joseph: What we really enjoy about bowling is that it's a sport that everyone can participate in, whether it's a child or a senior. We want Harlem Lanes to be an epicentre for the community, a place where people can come together and enjoy themselves. We're overwhelmed by the response of the community so far. An 86-year-old woman stopped by the other day and wanted to know why we didn't open it ten years ago.

TO: Are you and Gail Harlemites?
SJ: Yes. I grew up in Harlem. Gail has already owned businesses in the neighbourhood. She opened one of the first $10 shops here, and she also owned a number of real-estate properties. Before Harlem was popular, Gail talked about where the community was going. It's really nice to see some of the ideas coming to fruition.

TO: Has Harlem's gentrification been a positive thing so far?
SJ: Yes, it's great to see the ethnic and economic diversity. There's concern about Harlem becoming pricey, but it's actually no different to the rest of Manhattan in needing more affordable housing. You used the word 'gentrification', but I really think we're seeing another renaissance – for Harlem and for bowling, too.

For further info on Harlem Lanes, see p149.

Market (No.52, 1-212 987 8131), an outdoor bazaar that buzzes with vendors, most from West Africa, selling clothes, jewellery, sculpture and other traditional goods from covered stalls.

East Harlem

East of Fifth Avenue is East Harlem, sometimes called Spanish Harlem but better known to its primarily Puerto Rican residents as El Barrio.

North of 96th Street and east of Madison Avenue, El Barrio moves to a different beat. Its main east–west cross-street, East 116th Street, shows signs of a recent influx of Mexican immigrants, but between Fifth and Park Avenues, the thoroughfare's main attraction is actually the unusually high concentration of botanicas, or shops that supply candles, charms, oils, potions, orisha-priestess readings and other elements of the Catholic-tinged

Harlem. See p148.

Santeria religion. **Rendon Otto Chicas** (60 E 116th Street, at Madison Avenue, 1-212 289 0378) is particularly kid- and tourist-friendly. From 96th to 106th Streets, a little touch of East Village-style bohemia can be detected in such places as **Carlito's Café y Galería** (1701 Lexington Avenue, between 106th & 107th Streets, 1-212 348 7044), which presents music, art and poetry performances. Nearby is the **Graffiti Hall of Fame** (106th Street, between Madison & Park Avenues), a schoolyard that celebrates great old- and new-school 'writers'. Be sure to check out **El Museo del Barrio** (*see p138*), Spanish Harlem's community museum.

Hamilton Heights

Hamilton Heights (named after Alexander Hamilton, who owned a farm and estate here in 1802) extends from 125th Street to the Trinity Cemetery at 155th Street, between Riverside Drive and St Nicholas Avenue. The former factory neighbourhood developed after the West Side elevated train was built in the early 20th century. Today, it's notable for the elegant turn-of-the-20th-century row houses in the Hamilton Heights Historic District, which extends from 140th to 145th Streets, between Amsterdam and Edgecomb Avenues – just beyond the Gothic Revival-style campus of the City College of New York (Convent Avenue, at 138th Street).

Washington Heights & Inwood

The area from West 155th Street to Dyckman (200th) Street is called Washington Heights; venture north of that and you're in Inwood, Manhattan's northernmost neighbourhood, where the Harlem and Hudson Rivers converge. A growing number of artists and young families are relocating to these parts, attracted by the art deco buildings, big parks, hilly streets and (comparatively) low rents.

The area's biggest claim to fame is the **Morris-Jumel Mansion** (*see p153*), a stunning Palladian-style mansion that served as a swanky headquarters for George Washington during the autumn of 1776.

Since the 1920s waves of immigrants have settled in Washington Heights. In the post-World War II era, many German-Jewish refugees (including Henry Kissinger, Dr Ruth Westheimer and Max Frankel, a former executive editor of the *New York Times*) moved to the western edge of the neighbourhood. Broadway once housed a sizeable Greek population – opera singer Maria Callas lived here in her youth. But in the last few decades, the southern and eastern parts of the area have become predominantly Spanish-speaking due to a large population of Dominican settlers. The **Hispanic Society of America** (*see below*) has its headquarters here.

A trek along Fort Washington Avenue from about 173rd Street to Fort Tryon Park puts you in the heart of what is now being called **Hudson Heights** – the posh area of Washington Heights. Start at the George Washington Bridge, the city's only bridge across the Hudson River. A pedestrian walkway (also a popular route for cyclists) allows for dazzling Manhattan views. Under the bridge on the New York side is a diminutive lighthouse – those who know the children's book *The Little Red Lighthouse and the Great Gray Bridge*, by Hildegarde Swift, will recognise it immediately. When the 85-year-old landmark wasn't needed any more (after the bridge was completed) fans of the book rallied against plans to put it up for auction. To see it up close, look for the footpath on the west side of the interchange on the Henry Hudson Parkway at about 170th Street. If you need to refuel, stop at Bleu Evolution (808 W 187th Street, between Fort Washington & Pinehurst Avenues, 1-212 928 6006) for a downtown-style vibe, or hold out for the lovely New Leaf Café (1 Margaret Corbin Drive, near Park Drive, 1-212 568 5323) within the Frederick Law Olmsted-designed **Fort Tryon Park**.

At the northern edge of the park are the **Cloisters** (*see below*), a museum built in 1938 using segments of five medieval cloisters shipped from Europe by the Rockefeller clan. It houses the Metropolitan Museum of Art's permanent medieval art collection, including the exquisite Unicorn Tapestries (c1500).

Inwood stretches from Dyckman Street up to 218th Street, the last residential block in Manhattan. Dyckman buzzes with streetlife and nightclubs from river to river, but, north of that, the island narrows considerably and the parks along the western shoreline culminate in the wilderness of **Inwood Hill Park**, another Frederick Law Olmsted legacy. Some believe that this is the location of the legendary 1626 transaction between Peter Minuit and the Native American Lenapes for the purchase of a strip of land called Manahatta – a plaque at the south-west corner of the ballpark near 214th Street marks the purported spot. The 196-acre refuge contains the island's last swathes of virgin forest and salt marsh. Today, with a bit of imagination, you can hike over the

hilly terrain, scattered with massive glacier-deposited boulders (called erratics), and picture Manhattan as it was before development. In recent years, the city's Parks Department has used the densely wooded area as a fledging spot for newly hatched bald eagles.

Cloisters
Fort Tryon Park, Fort Washington Avenue, at Margaret Corbin Plaza (1-212 923 3700/www.metmuseum.org). Subway: A to 190th Street, then take the M4 bus or follow Margaret Corbin Drive north, for about the length of 5 city blocks, to the museum. **Open** *Mar-Oct* 9.30am- 5.15pm Tue-Sun. *Nov-Feb* 9.30am-4.45pm Tue-Sun. **Admission** suggested donation (includes admission to the Metropolitan Museum of Art on the same day) $20; $10 seniors, students; free under-12s (must be accompanied by an adult). **Credit** AmEx, DC, Disc, MC, V. **Map** p409 B3.
Set in a lovely park overlooking the Hudson River, the Cloisters houses the Met's medieval art and architecture collections. A path winds through the peaceful grounds to a castle that seems to have survived from the Middle Ages. (It was built a mere 70 years ago, using pieces of five medieval French cloisters.) Be sure to check out the famous Unicorn Tapestries, the 12th-century Fuentidueña Chapel and the *Annunciation Triptych* by Robert Campin.

Hispanic Society of America
Audubon Terrace, Broadway, between 155th & 156th Streets (1-212 926 2234/www.hispanicsociety.org). Subway: 1 to 157th Street. **Open** 10am-4.30pm Tue-Sat; 1-4pm Sun. **Admission** free. **Map** p408 B9.
The Hispanic Society has the largest assemblage of Spanish art and manuscripts outside Spain. Look for two portraits by Goya and the lobby's bas-relief of Don Quixote. The collection is dominated by religious artefacts, including 16th-century tombs from the monastery of San Francisco in Cuéllar, Spain. Also on display are decorative art objects and thousands of black-and-white photographs that document life in Spain and Latin America from the mid 19th century to the present. Note that the library is closed on Sundays.

Morris-Jumel Mansion
65 Jumel Terrace, between 160th & 162nd Streets (1-212 923 8008/www.morrisjumel.org). Subway: C to 163rd Street-Amsterdam Avenue. **Open** 10am-4pm Wed-Sun. **Admission** $3; $2 seniors, students; free under-12s. **No credit cards.** **Map** p408 C8.
Built in 1765, Manhattan's only surviving pre-Revolutionary manse was originally the heart of a 130-acre estate that stretched from river to river (on the grounds, a stone marker points south with the legend 'new york, 11 miles'). George Washington planned the Battle of Harlem Heights here in 1776, after the British colonel Roger Morris moved out. The handsome 18th-century Palladian-style villa offers fantastic views. Its former driveway is now Sylvan Terrace, which boasts the largest continuous stretch (one block) of old wooden houses in Manhattan.

Brooklyn

If Manhattan is the pulse-pounding heart of New York,
then Brooklyn is its nourishing soul.

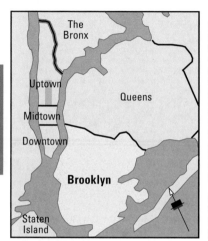

While Manhattanites may view Brooklyn as
something of a country cousin, the borough
(which would be America's fourth largest
city if it were still independent) has a unique
character, historical charm and enough cultural,
recreational and entertainment options to
make it a premier destination in its own right.

With 2.6 million inhabitants – almost 30 per
cent of New York City's entire population –
Brooklyn (or Kings County, as it's also known)
is the city's most populous municipality. Thanks
to an improved housing market and a lowering
of the crime rate in recent years, it has become
a borough in flux. Large-scale developments
are either under way or being proposed for
numerous sectors, including Red Hook, Fort
Greene and the Downtown/Fulton Street area.
One of the largest projects under consideration
is Atlantic Yards, a massive real-estate venture
designed by Frank Gehry for developer Bruce
Ratner. If approved, the development would be
situated between Prospect Heights and Fort
Greene, and would feature 16 new skyscrapers
and an 18,000-seat stadium for the New York
Nets. While many view projects like Atlantic
Yards as a natural development of the area's
economic, social and cultural growth, others
fear the borough's character and more relaxed
pace will be sacrificed in the name of progress.

Progress, though, has been in Brooklyn's
blood since Europeans first settled here in the
early 1600s. Brooklyn (originally the Dutch
settlement of Breuckelen) was an independent
city from 1834 until 1898, when it became
an official borough. Today, the region's
diversity is still reflected in its long-established
neighbourhoods. From Russian enclaves in
Brighton Beach and the Polish residents of
Greenpoint to the Italians in Bensonhurst,
Chinese expats in Sunset Park and Arab
immigrants in Cobble Hill, almost 40 per cent
of the people who call Brooklyn home were
born outside the United States. As a distinctive
traffic marker proudly proclaims, the borough
is 'Home to Everyone from Everywhere!'.

If that makes Brooklyn sound like a quaint
old-world attraction, think again. Among
the contemporary playgrounds for adults
(not to mention kids) are the hipster enclaves
of Williamsburg, the world-class Brooklyn
Museum and a wealth of outdoor beauty in
Prospect Park and the Brooklyn Botanic Garden.

For more details on what the borough has
to offer, contact **Brooklyn Information &
Culture** (1-718 855 7882, www.brooklynx.
org) or **Heart of Brooklyn: A Cultural
Partnership** (1-718 638 7700, www.heartof
brooklyn.org). We've also put together a walk,
past a few of the borough's most stunning sites;
see p162 **Step to it**.

Brooklyn Heights & Dumbo

Brooklyn's toniest address, **Brooklyn Heights**,
is an area steeped in American history. After
British troops landed on Long Island in 1776,
General George Washington withdrew his
troops here after heavy losses and was able
to plot a skillful retreat across the East River
to Manhattan. The area's life as a residential
neighbourhood, though, began in 1814, when
inventor Robert Fulton's first steam-powered
ferry linked Manhattan to the quiet fishing
village on the western edge of Long Island.

The streets of Brooklyn Heights –
particularly Cranberry, Hicks, Pierrepont and
Willow – are lined with well-preserved Greek
Revival and Italianate row houses dating from
the 1820s, a legacy of the area being designated
Brooklyn's first historic district in 1965. Today,

both Henry and Montague Streets are crammed with shops, restaurants and bars. At the end of Montague, the **Brooklyn Heights Promenade** offers spectacular waterfront vistas of Manhattan, especially on the Fourth of July when the Macy's firework display lights up the harbour sky. Just a short jaunt away is the venerable **Brooklyn Bridge** (*see p156*), a marvel of 19th-century engineering that connected two cities and became an important symbol of progress. The first to use steel suspension cables, the bridge was the vision of German-born civil engineer John Augustus Roebling, who died before it was completed. The 5,989-foot-long transverse, connecting downtown Brooklyn with Manhattan, offers striking views of the Statue of Liberty and New York Harbor. If time permits, it's well worth a stroll across the pedestrian walkway. If you prefer your history beneath street-level, a stop at the **New York Transit Museum** (*see p157*) – housed in a former subway station – is a must. Visitors can learn about the complex engineering and construction feats that helped establish the city's century-old subway system.

More remnants of bygone Breuckelen abound at the **Brooklyn Historical Society** (*see p156*) building, which, when completed in 1881, was the first in New York to use locally produced terracotta on its façade. The seat of local government, the grand **Borough Hall** (209 Joralemon Street, at Court Street, www.brooklyn-usa.org), stands as a monument to Brooklyn's

past as an independent municipality. Completed in 1851, the Greek Revival edifice – later crowned with a Victorian cupola – was renovated in the late 1980s. The building is linked to the **New York State Supreme Court** (360 Adams Street, between Joralemon Street & Tech Place) by **Cadman Plaza** (from Prospect Street to Tech Place, between Cadman Plaza East & Cadman Plaza West). Nearby, at the junction of Court and Remsen Streets, farmers peddle produce on Tuesdays, Thursdays and Saturdays throughout most of the year.

In sharp contrast to the historic Heights is the still-evolving waterside neighbourhood of **Dumbo** (Down Under the Manhattan Bridge Overpass), an artists' community providing equally impressive sightlines to Manhattan. First-rate views are to be had below the Brooklyn Bridge at the **Fulton Ferry Landing**, which juts out over the East River at Old Fulton and Water Streets, and is close to two newly refurbished parks – **Empire-Fulton Ferry State Park** and **Brooklyn Bridge Park** (riverside, between the Manhattan and Brooklyn Bridges). Also at the water's edge is a dock for the **New York Water Taxi** (1-212 742 1969, www.nywater taxi.com), an affordable and picturesque way to travel from Manhattan to Williamsburg, Red Hook and points in-between. Along the same pier is the posh and pricey River Café (1 Water Street, at Old Fulton Street, 1-718 522 5200); breathtaking views of the Manhattan skyline

Whatever the time of day, **Brooklyn Bridge** never fails to impress.

Walking tall (and small) on **Brooklyn Heights Promenade**. *See p155.*

have made the adjacent pier a favourite photo site for Asian wedding parties. Cap an afternoon of sightseeing with a scoop from the **Brooklyn Ice Cream Factory** (Fulton Ferry Landing, between Old Fulton & Water Streets, 1-718 246 3963). This area is also home to the **Fulton Ferry Historic District**. When a steam-powered ferry service between Brooklyn and Manhattan kicked off in 1814, the area made way for the construction of several Greek Revival, Italianate and cast-iron buildings.

Drawn by the cobblestone streets and loft spaces in red-brick warehouses, artists flocked to **Dumbo** in the 1970s and '80s, and then kept on coming. The arrival of several chic boutiques and home stores has some people saying that the area has lost its rough-hewn charm. Don't believe it. You can still get lost among the quiet side streets, and the **dumbo arts center** (30 Washington Street, between Plymouth & Water Streets, 1-718 694 0831, www.dumboartscenter. org) continues to promote community artists through its gallery and sponsorship of the annual **d.u.m.b.o. art under the bridge** festival (*see p265*), held in mid October. **St Ann's Warehouse** (38 Water Street, between Dock & Main Streets, 1-718 254 8779) hosts offbeat concerts, readings and theatre productions that often feature high-profile artists.

Dumbo dining also boasts its share of attractions, like **Grimaldi's** (19 Old Fulton Street, between Front & Water Streets, 1-718 858 4300), where pizza lovers can share a coal-fired pie. For more substantial fare, **Five Front** (5 Front Street, 1-718 625 5559), tucked under the Brooklyn Bridge, dishes out creative takes on comfort food like jumbo lump crab-cake and goat's cheese gnocchi. **Superfine** (126 Front Street, 1-718 243 9005) is both a first-rate restaurant and chic bar, but if you prefer sweets to sweet vermouth, head down to the packed **Jacques Torres Chocolate Heaven** shop (*see p244*) for one of its fabulous hot chocolates.

Brooklyn Bridge
Subway: A, C to High Street; J, M, Z to Chambers Street; 4, 5, 6 to Brooklyn Bridge-City Hall.
Map p411 S8, S9.
The stunning views and awe-inspiring web of steel cables will take your breath away. As you walk, bike or rollerblade along its wide wood-planked promenade, look for plaques detailing the history of the bridge's construction. **Photo** *p155.*

Brooklyn Historical Society
128 Pierrepont Street, at Clinton Street, Brooklyn Heights (1-718 222 4111/www.brooklynhistory.org). Subway: A, C, F to Jay Street-Borough Hall; M, R to Court Street; 2, 3, 4, 5 to Borough Hall. **Open** noon-5pm Wed-Sun. **Admission** $6; $4 seniors, students, 12-18s; free under-12s. **Credit** AmEx, MC, V.
Map p411 S9.
Founded in 1863, the society is located in a landmark four-storey Queen Anne-style building and houses numerous permanent and ongoing exhibits, including 'It Happened in Brooklyn', highlighting local links to crucial moments in American history. A major photo and research library – featuring historic

maps and newspapers, notable family histories, and archives from the area's prominent abolitionist movement – are accessible by appointment. Boat tours of the waterfront in summer are fun and fascinating.

New York Transit Museum
Corner of Boerum Place & Schermerhorn Street, Brooklyn Heights (1-718 694 1600/www.mta. info/mta/museum). Subway: A, C, G to Hoyt-Schermerhorn. **Open** 10am-4pm Tue-Fri; noon-5pm Sat, Sun. **Admission** $5; $3 seniors, 3-17s; free under-3s. **No credit cards. Map** p410 S10.
Located in an authentic 1930s subway station, the Transit Museum allows visitors to climb aboard an exceptional collection of vintage subway and El cars, explore a working signal tower and check out ongoing exhibitions such as 'The Triborough Bridge: Robert Moses and the Automobile Age'. The museum also has a great gallery and gift shop in Grand Central Terminal.
Other locations: New York Transit Museum Gallery Annex & Store, Grand Central Terminal, adjacent to stationmaster's office, Main Concourse, 42nd Street, at Park Avenue, Midtown (1-212 878 0106).

Boerum Hill, Carroll Gardens, Cobble Hill & Red Hook

One of the most striking examples of Brooklyn's rapid gentrification can be found on **Smith Street**, stretching from **Boerum Hill** to **Carroll Gardens** and known as the borough's **Restaurant Row**. This strip was targeted for urban renewal in the 1990s, receiving a facelift that included wrought-iron streetlamps and new sidewalks. It boasts charming, walkable historic districts lined with mid 19th-century Greek Revival and Italianate homes and storefronts. Today, affordable restaurants and cafés pack in the diners. Hot eateries along trendy Smith Street include classic bistro Bar Tabac (No.128, at Dean Street, Boerum Hill, 1-718 923 0918); the Grocery (No. 288, between Sackett & Union Streets, Carroll Gardens, 1-718 596 3335) and New American favourite, Chestnut (No.271, between DeGraw & Sackett Streets, Carroll Gardens, 1-718 243 0049). Many of the area's shops are run by artists and designers selling wares that rival anything in Soho or the East Village. Playful, pretty women's clothing is for sale at Frida's Closet (No.296, between Sackett & Union Streets, Carroll Gardens, 1-718 855 0311) and Flirt (No.252, between DeGraw & Douglass Streets, 1-718 858 7931), where many of the pieces are made by local designers.

Along nearby **Atlantic Avenue** are haute home furnisher City Foundry (No.365, between Bond & Hoyt Streets, Boerum Hill, 1-718 923 1786); Rico (No.384, between Bond & Hoyt Streets, 1-718 797 2077), which sells art, lighting

and furnishings; and stylish women's clothier Butter (No.389, between Bond & Hoyt Streets, 1-718 260 9033). On the western fringes of Cobble Hill and Brooklyn Heights, Magnetic Field (No. 97, between Henry & Hicks Streets, 1-718 834 0069) draws area hipsters with its campy Western theme and edgy live acts.

The mile-long stretch of Atlantic Avenue between Henry and Nevins Streets, affectionately nicknamed the **Fertile Crescent**, was once crowded with Middle Eastern restaurants and markets, though gentrification and geo-political tensions threaten the community's cohesion. The granddaddy of them all still exists, though; Sahadi Importing Company (No.187, between Clinton & Court Streets, Cobble Hill, 1-718 624 4550) is a 59-year-old neighbourhood institution that sells olives, spices, cheeses, nuts and other gourmet treats. Atlantic Avenue is also considered the northern border of **Cobble Hill**, a quaint neighbourhood with a small-town feel. Less restaurant-heavy than nearby Smith Street, shady **Court Street** is dotted with boutiques, shops and cafés such as Book Court (No.163, between Pacific & Dean Streets, 1-718 875 3677), which carries Brooklyn guidebooks and histories, and the charming Sweet Melissa (No.276, between Butler & Douglass Streets, 1-718 855 3410), which serves brunch, lunch and afternoon tea in a pretty back garden. Further south, you'll cross into the still predominantly Italian-American **Carroll Gardens**. Pick up a prosciutto loaf from the Caputo Bakery (No.329, between Sackett & Union Streets, Carroll Gardens, 1-718 875 6871) or an aged soppressata salami from Esposito and Sons (No.357, between President & Union Streets, 1-718 875 6863); then relax in Carroll Park (from President to Carroll Streets, between Court & Smith Streets) and watch the old-timers play bocce (lawn bowling). Take a walk over the Brooklyn-Queens Expressway to the industrial waterfront of Cobble Hill and the corner building housing hip Mexican bistro Alma (*see p215*). The open-air rooftop dining area has a great view of the East River and lower Manhattan.

To the south-west of Cobble Hill and Carroll Gardens, the rough-and-tumble industrial neighbourhood of **Red Hook** (*see p158* **Get hooked**) has long avoided urban renewal, but the arrival of luxury condos and gourmet grocer Fairway (1-718 694 6868, www.fairwaymarket. com) on Van Brunt Street has put it on the fast track to gentrification. The area offers singular views of New York Harbor from Valentino Pier, as well as an eclectic variety of artist studios, bars and eateries, including Hope & Anchor (347 Van Brunt Street, at Wolcott Street, 1-718 237 0276), a retro bar and grill that attracts scenesters and old-timers alike. Getting to the

Get hooked

Ten reasons to check out Red Hook.

Louis J Valentino Jr Park & Pier

Still the best spots on dry land from which to view Lady Liberty. The pier is frequented by anglers looking for an out-of-the-way place, and by the Gowanus Dredgers Canoe Club, who launch their boats and kayaks here in the warmer months.
Coffey Street, at Ferris Street/www.nycgov parks.org.

Foodie opportunities galore

Foodies can thank Hope & Anchor for Van Brunt Street's reputation as an emerging restaurant row. When this stylish diner opened in 2002, the neighbourhood was a culinary wasteland. These days, seats are constantly filled with people chowing down on the famed juicy burgers and chicken potpies or all-day breakfast fare.
347 Van Brunt Street, at Wolcott Street (1-718 237 0276).

Old-school baking

After co-founding West Village sweet spot the Chocolate Bar, Matt Lewis decided to bring his sugar skills to Brooklyn. He opened the retro bakery Baked, where cool kids and young moms hang out in bright orange chairs and indulge in old-school confections like the Diner Double Dark layer cake, mixed-berry bars and jumbo marshmallows.
359 Van Brunt Street, at Wolcott Street (1-718 222 0345).

Authentic Key Lime Pies

For more than 25 years, Steve Tarpin has been making his infamous Key Lime Pies the same way – with only freshly squeezed juice. Find his unassuming storefront and snag that frozen chocolate-dipped key lime pie novelty on a stick, the Swingle, or your own miniature pie.
204 Van Dyke Street, at Pier 41 (1-718 858 5333/www.stevesauthentic.com).

Latin American flavours

Every weekend from spring to early autumn in Red Hook Park, Central and South American locals set up griddles and grills to serve pan-Latin street food. At the makeshift food bazaar women fashion tortillas for toothsome quesadillas and fry up El Salvadoran *pupusas* (hot patties oozing with cheese). Few items cost more than $5.
Red Hook Park, 155 Bay Street, between Clinton & Henry Streets.

Quirky bars

Opened by four friends who simply wanted a bar in their neighbourhood that they could count on to be open every night, Bait & Tackle sits in the former home of – what else – a bait and tackle shop. The spot is quirkily decorated with taxidermy, and, in addition to an array of beers, displays an impressive collection of whiskeys and bourbons.
Bait & Tackle, 320 Van Brunt Street, at Pioneer Street (1-718 797 4892).

The Hook music venue

The Hook could never exist in Manhattan; the location is what makes the venue work. A genuine community has flourished here: bands from the city and outlying areas love the warm, muscular sound and expansive stage; no one in the audience is there by accident. For big shows, the Hook even runs a free shuttle bus from the Carroll Street F and G stop.
18 Commerce Street, between Columbia & Richards Streets (1-718 797 3007/ www.thehookmusic.com).

Real ale, locally brewed

The Sixpoint Craft Ale Brewery affords adjacent Liberty Heights Tap Room the distinct ability to offer a rotating selection of 13 house brews. Open Thursday to Sunday, the Tap Room also has a full menu with burgers and brick-oven pizzas, a pool table, a roof deck and an open-mic night on Thursdays (8.30pm). Stop by Sixpoint on Saturdays at 1pm for a free tour.
34 Van Dyke Street, at Dwight Street (1-718 246 8050).

The Brooklyn Collective

The gallery-like Brooklyn Collective is a co-operative boutique that brings together the work of area artists and artisans. A rotating cast of photographers, painters, jewellery and fashion designers shares the space.
198 Columbia Street, between DeGraw & Sackett Streets (1-718 596 6231).

Vintage furniture & antiques

Equal parts furniture rehabber and antique shop, Atlantis offers restoration and repair services, and also carries ready-to-buy goods from yesteryear, including reupholstered slipper chairs and mid-century lamps.
351 Van Brunt Street, between Dikeman & Wolcott Streets (1-718 858 8816).

Getting there

(See map p410 S11 and vicinity)
Easy: Take the F or G train to the Smith-9th Streets station and catch bus B77 right outside. It carries you past the housing projects to Red Hook's (relatively) glitzy Van Brunt strip. Other alternatives are the A, C or F train to Jay Street-Borough Hall, and the 2, 3, 4 or 5 train to Borough Hall; then get on the B61, which stops at the corner of Jay and Willoughby Streets and trundles down Columbia Street on to Van Brunt Street.
Breezy: On weekends, New York Water Taxi operates an hourly service between Pier 11 (South Street, at Wall Street) and the Beard Street Pier terminus at Van Brunt Street. A one-way trip costs between $5 and $10 (www.nywatertaxi.com).
Lazy: For a rather reasonable $20 (from downtown Manhattan) or $22 (from Midtown) one way, Eastern Car Service (1-718 499 6227) will collect you and drop you anywhere in Red Hook – or take you back at closing time.

Brooklyn Museum. *See p161.*

'hood is a challenge – from the F and G subway station at Smith-9th Street, it's either a long walk or a transfer to the B77 bus. The **New York Water Taxi** (1-212 742 1969, www.nywater taxi.com) has improved the situation somewhat by adding stops to the Beard Street Pier. Though progress gallops apace (an outpost of Swedish furniture superstore IKEA is set to open in 2007), you can still catch a glimpse of the rough-and-ready life of old New York. Decaying piers are an appropriately moody backdrop for massive cranes, empty warehouses and trucks clattering over cobblestone streets. To check out the work of local artists, look for the word 'Gallery' hand-scrawled in block letters on the doors of the Kentler International Drawing Space (353 Van Brunt Street, between Sullivan & Wolcott Streets, 1-718 875 2098). The Brooklyn Working Artists Coalition (BWAC) hosts large group shows in the spring and autumn. Visit the website (www.bwac.org) or call 1-718 596 2507 for a calendar. At the **Red Hook Recreation Area** (155 Bay Street, between Clinton & Henry Streets) you can play softball, basketball or soccer, watch from the sidelines, or dine on Latin delicacies from the makeshift food bazaar. For more on events and developments in Red Hook, visit B61 Productions (www.b61productions.com).

Park Slope & Prospect Heights

Though home to young families, sleepy Victorian brownstones and stoop sales galore, **Park Slope** is no mere bedroom community. The neighbourhood has some of the best dining and shopping options in the borough. Fifth Avenue is the prime locale for restaurants,

including the beloved Venetian mainstay al di là (248 Fifth Avenue, at Carroll Street, 1-718 783 4565); the eclectic favourite Blue Ribbon Brooklyn (*see p189*); and kid-friendly Peruvian sensation Coco Roco (No. 392, between 6th & 7th Streets, 1-718 965 3376). Park Slope's gay and lesbian community is one of the Big Apple's strongest: explore Sapphic lore at the **Lesbian Herstory Archives** (*see p302*), then do field research at Cattyshack (49 4th Avenue, 1-718 230 5740) or Ginger's Bar (*see p307*). Both welcome the boys, but Park Slope's gay gents usually habituate Excelsior (390 5th Avenue, 1-718 832 1599), a low-key watering hole with a vibrant jukebox and lush backyard garden. Seventh Avenue is the main commercial district (between President Street & 11th Street) – ideal for a post-shopping oolong tea and blueberry scone. Innovative boutiques have cropped up along Fifth Avenue as well, including eco-friendly home furnisher 3r Living (No. 276, between Garfield Place & 1st Place, 1-718 832 0951); urban gear depot Brooklyn Industries (No. 206, at Union Street, 1-718 789 2764) and Beacon's Closet (No. 220, at Union Street, 1-718 230 1630), a must for vintage clothing aficionados. Along the western edge of Prospect Park, extending for a full 19 blocks, is a section of the **Park Slope Historic District**. Brownstones and several fine examples of Romanesque Revival and Queen Anne residences grace these streets. Particularly charming are the brick edifices that line Carroll and Montgomery Streets.

Central Park may be bigger and more famous, but **Prospect Park** (main entrance on Flatbush Avenue, at Grand Army Plaza, Prospect Heights, 1-718 965 8999, www. prospectpark.org) has a more rustic quality.

It's entirely possible to take a short stroll into its lush green expanse and forget you're in the midst of a bustling metropolis. This masterpiece, which designers Frederick Law Olmsted and Calvert Vaux said was more in line with their vision than Central Park (their previous project), is a great spot for bird-watching, especially with a little guidance from the **Prospect Park Audubon Center at the Boathouse** (park entrance on Ocean Avenue, at Lincoln Road, Prospect Heights, 1-718 287 3400). Or pretend you've left the city altogether by boating or hiking amid the waterfalls, pools and wildlife habitats of the recently restored Ravine Park (park entrances on Prospect Park West, at 3rd, 9th & 15th Streets, Park Slope). The rolling green park was created with equestrians in mind; you can saddle a horse at the nearby Kensington Stables (*see p337*) or hop on a bike and pedal alongside rollerbladers and runners. Children enjoy riding the hand-carved horses at the park's antique Carousel (Flatbush Avenue, at Empire Boulevard) and playing with animals in the **Prospect Park Zoo** (park entrance on Flatbush Avenue, near Ocean Avenue, Prospect Heights, 1-718 399 7339).

A 15-minute walk from Prospect Park is the verdant necropolis of **Green-Wood Cemetery** (*see below*). A century ago, this site vied with Niagara Falls as New York State's greatest tourist attraction. Filled with Victorian mausoleums, cherubs and gargoyles, Green-Wood is the final resting place of some half-million New Yorkers, including Jean-Michel Basquiat, Leonard Bernstein and Mae West. The spectacular, soaring arches of the main gate are carved from New Jersey brownstone. Intricate details of death and resurrection, carved in Nova Scotia sandstone, are the handiwork of John Moffit. **Battle Hill**, the highest point in Brooklyn, is on cemetery grounds.

Near the main entrance to Prospect Park sits the massive Civil War memorial arch at **Grand Army Plaza** (intersection of Flatbush Avenue, Eastern Parkway & Prospect Park West) and the central branch of the **Brooklyn Public Library** (Grand Army Plaza, Prospect Heights, 1-718 230 2100). The library's Brooklyn Collection includes thousands of artefacts and photos tracing the borough's history. Just around the corner are the tranquil **Brooklyn Botanic Garden** and the **Brooklyn Museum** (for both, *see below*), which has a renowned Egyptology collection and engaging temporary exhibits that explore the current culture.

Brooklyn Botanic Garden

900 Washington Avenue, at Eastern Parkway, Prospect Heights (1-718 623 7200/www.bbg.org). Subway: B, Q, Franklin Avenue S to Prospect Park; 2, 3 to Eastern Parkway-Brooklyn Museum.

Open *Apr-Sept* 8am-6pm Tue-Fri; 10am-6pm Sat, Sun. *Oct-Mar* 8am-4.30pm Tue-Fri; 10am-4.30pm Sat, Sun. **Admission** $5; $3 seniors, students; free under-16s. Free Tue; 10am-noon Sat; Sat, Sun mid Nov-Feb. **Credit** MC, V. **Map** p410 U11.
This 52-acre haven of luscious greenery was founded in 1910. April is when Sakura Matsuri, the annual Cherry Blossom Festival, takes place, where prize buds and Japanese culture are in full bloom. The recently renovated Eastern Parkway entrance and the Osborne Garden – an Italian-style formal garden – are also well worth a peek.

Brooklyn Museum

200 Eastern Parkway, at Washington Avenue, Prospect Heights (1-718 638 5000/www.brooklyn museum.org). Subway $5; 2, 3 to Eastern Parkway-Brooklyn Museum. **Open** 10am-5pm Wed-Fri; 11am-6pm Sat, Sun; 11am-11pm 1st Sat of mth (except Sept). **Admission** $8; $4 seniors, students; free under-12s (must be accompanied by an adult). Free 5-11pm 1st Sat of mth (except Sept). **Credit** AmEx, MC, V. **Map** p410 U11.
Brooklyn's premier institution is a tranquil alternative to Manhattan's big-name spaces; it's rarely crowded. Among the museum's many assets is a rich, 4,000-piece Egyptian collection, which includes a gilded-ebony statue of Amenhotep III and, on a ceiling, a large-scale rendering of an ancient map of the cosmos. You can even view a mummy preserved in its original coffin.

Masterworks by Cézanne, Monet and Degas, part of an impressive European painting and sculpture collection, are displayed in the museum's skylighted Beaux-Arts Court. On the fifth floor, American paintings and sculptures include native son Thomas Cole's *The Pic-Nic* and Louis Rémy Mignot's *Niagara*. Don't miss the renowned Pacific Island and African galleries (this was the first American museum to display African objects as art).

In March 2007 the museum begins a major survey of feminist art with Judy Chicago's installation *The Dinner Table* as centrepiece, plus the exhibition 'Pharaohs, Queens & Goddesses', which features artefacts from the Egyptian collection. Also opening in March 2007 is 'James Tissot: The Life of Christ', which will show more than 150 of the French artist's works depicting the New Testament. **Photo** *p160*.

Green-Wood Cemetery

Fifth Avenue, at 25th Street, Sunset Park (1-718 768 7300/www.green-wood.com). Subway: M, R to 25th Street. **Open** 8am-5pm daily. **Admission** free. **Map** p410 S13.

Fort Greene & Williamsburg

With its stately Victorian brownstones and other grand buildings, **Fort Greene** has undergone a major revival over the past decade. It has long been a centre of African-American life and business – Spike Lee, Branford Marsalis and Chris Rock have

Step to it A bridge not far

Sightseeing

Start: Brooklyn Bridge (Manhattan side)
Finish: Fulton Ferry Water Taxi Landing, Dumbo
Distance: About 2 miles
Time: 2-3 hours

Standing in City Hall Park, just outside the Brooklyn Bridge-City Hall subway entrance, face east (in the direction of the **Brooklyn Bridge**; *photo left*). As you cross over Centre Street, to the bridge's pedestrian walkway, say goodbye to Manhattan. The 3,460-foot-long suspension bridge you are walking on was the first to use steel for its stunning web of cable wires and was the longest suspension bridge in the world on the day it opened – 24 May 1883. On that day, more than 150,000 people paid one cent to stroll across the bridge and marvel at the Gothic towers that rise out of the East River. As you walk, be sure to take a few minutes to read the panels that inform about the bridge's storied construction. As you near the Brooklyn side of the bridge the path splits; stay to the left and go down the stairs to the street. You'll come out on Cadman Plaza East. Turn left and cross over Prospect Street (Cadman Plaza becomes Washington Street at this point). Walk down the hill for two blocks on Washington Street and turn right on to Front Street.

Welcome to **Dumbo** (*see p155*), short for Down Under the Manhattan Bridge Overpass. This hip little enclave became a fashionable residential area as artists took over warehouses that were once part of the booming Fulton Ferry commercial waterfront (which thrived after the steam-powered ferry came on the scene in 1814). Nowadays, locals load up on caffeine and art supplies at Dumbo General Store (111 Front Street). Continue along Front Street until you get to Pearl Street. Look up; this is the **Manhattan Bridge**, which opened in 1909. Turn left on Pearl Street and follow it to the East River. At John Street, turn left and head into **Brooklyn Bridge Park**. Follow the gravel path along the water (past the mini beach) at the flagpole and cross over the pavement and enter Empire-Fulton Ferry State Park – the surrounding Fulton Ferry Landing dates back to 1642. Curve your way around and exit between the two tobacco warehouses through the Dock Street gate. (Note: there's a public toilet in the State Park office to the left.) Turn right on Water Street. As the road bends consider having a bite to eat. For something upscale, try the **River Café** (1 Water Street, 1-718 522 5200); many people consider it the best restaurant in Brooklyn – and maybe the most expensive. The romantic waterside

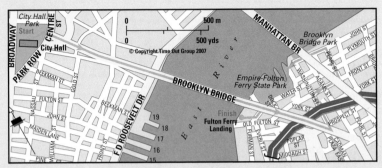

eaterie, which could easily skate by on its views of downtown Manhattan, has spawned a long roster of great chefs. If you're in the mood for something cheaper, you have two choices: just past River Café is the **Brooklyn Ice Cream Factory** (Old Fulton Street, at Water Street, 1-718 246 3963; *photo below*); the parlour's recipe is as old-fashioned as its 1920s fireboat-house building – all cream and no eggs. If you take a left and walk a block north on the north side of Old Fulton Street, you'll come to **Grimaldi's Pizza** (No.19, 1-718 858 4300). A pie from the brick-walled coal oven at this old-fashioned place is a favourite snack among locals.

After you've had your fill, hop on a water taxi for a breezy ride back to Manhattan at the **Fulton Ferry Landing** (in front of the Brooklyn Ice Cream Factory). If the ferry's not running (or you only have two dollars left in your pocket), take the subway – just a short walk away. To get there, cross over to the south side of Old Fulton Street and head east (passing in front of the Eagle Warehouse & Storage Co building). As the road bends right, just past Henry Street, it turns into Cadman Plaza West. The High Street-Brooklyn Bridge station is barely one block further. There, you can board an A or C train to Manhattan.

all lived here. **Fort Greene Park** (from Myrtle to DeKalb Avenues, between St Edwards Street & Washington Park) was conceived in 1846 at the behest of poet Walt Whitman (then editor of the *Brooklyn Daily Eagle*); its masterplan was fully realised by the omnipresent Olmsted and Vaux in 1867. At the centre of the park stands the Prison Ship Martyrs Monument, erected in 1909 in memory of 11,000 American prisoners who died on British ships that were anchored nearby during the Revolutionary War.

Despite its name, the 34-storey **Williamsburg Savings Bank** located at the corner of Atlantic and Flatbush Avenues is in Fort Greene, not Williamsburg. The 512-foot-tall structure is the tallest in the borough and, with its unique four-sided clocktower, doubtlessly the most recognisable feature of the Brooklyn skyline. Though mostly serving as office space in recent years, the building is set to be converted into luxury condominiums. Planners vow, though, that the famous clocktower will remain untouched.

Though originally founded in Brooklyn Heights, the **Brooklyn Academy of Music** (*see p328*) moved to its current site on Fort Greene's southern border in 1901. BAM is America's oldest operating performing arts centre. It once hosted the likes of Edwin Booth and Sarah Bernhardt and was the home of the Metropolitan Opera until 1921; now it's known for ambitious cultural performances of all varieties. More recently, it has added several venues that show cutting-edge dance, theatre, music and film programmes and draw audiences from throughout the metropolitan area. From October to December, BAM hosts the Next Wave Festival (*see p265*). Also world-famous – though perhaps to a different audience – is the cheesecake at Junior's Restaurant (386 Flatbush Avenue, at DeKalb Avenue, 1-718 852 5257), just three blocks away. A slew of popular hangouts can be found on or near **DeKalb Avenue**, including the funky South African i-Shebeen Madiba (No.195, at Carlton Avenue, 1-718 855 9190); lively bistro Chez Oskar (No.211, at Adelphi Street, 1-718 852 6250); and the Francophilic iCi (No. 246, at Vanderbilt Avenue, 1-718 789 2778).

Williamsburg is further along in hipness than Fort Greene, especially if you're 22, have a blog and are sufficiently pierced. Just one subway stop from the East Village (on the L line), **Bedford Avenue** is the neighbourhood's main thoroughfare. You'll also find plenty of restaurants and nightspots along North 6th Street and Grand Avenue. During the day, Verb Café (218 Bedford Avenue, between North 4th & 5th Streets, 1-718 599 0977) is the nabe's prime slacker hangout; at night, the scene

moves to eateries like the Thai palace SEA (*see p215*), funky Japanese Bozu (296 Grand Street, between Havemeyer & Roebling Streets, 1-718 384 7770) and upscale diner Relish (225 Wythe Ave, at North 3rd Street, 1-718 963 4546), housed in a formerly abandoned railcar. Locals with mortgages prefer neighbourhood fixture Peter Luger (*see p215*), which grills what many people consider to be the best steak in the entire city.

The area also has dozens of art galleries, such as the local fave Pierogi (*see p274*). But the core of the art scene is the **Williamsburg Art & Historical Center** (135 Broadway, at Bedford Avenue, 1-718 486 7372, www. wahcenter.org), in a landmark 1929 bank building. The music scene thrives, too; worth-a-trip spaces include Galapagos (*see p315*), Northsix (*see p318*), Pete's Candy Store (709 Lorimer Street, 1-718 302 3770) and Warsaw (261 Driggs Avenue, at Eckford Street, 1-718 387 0505), which doubles as the Polish National Home. Formerly a community swimming hole, **McCarren Park Pool** at Lorimer Street and Driggs Avevue (www.thepoolparties.com) is now a distinctive outdoor concert venue hosting local and national acts alike.

But long before the hipster invaded, Billyburg's waterfront location made it ideal for industry; after the Erie Canal linked the Atlantic Ocean to the Great Lakes in 1825,

Williamsburg.

the area became an even more bustling port. Companies such as Pfizer and Domino Sugar started here, but by the late 20th century businesses began to abandon the area's enormous industrial spaces. A sign of the area's rapid gentrification, the Domino refinery finally closed in 2004, though its signature sign is still a local landmark. The beloved **Brooklyn Brewery** (79 North 11th Street, between Berry Street & Wythe Avenue, 1-718 486 7422, www.brooklynbrewery.com) took up residence in a former ironworks. Visit during happy 'hour' (Friday evenings from 6pm to 11pm) for $3 drafts or take a tour on Saturdays from noon to 5pm.

Williamsburg is one of New York's many curious multi-ethnic amalgams. To the south, Broadway divides a Latino neighbourhood from a lively community of Hasidic Jews, while the northern half extending into Greenpoint contains Polish and Italian settlements (with old-time delis and restaurants to match).

Brighton Beach & Coney Island

In the cultural hodgepodge that is New York City, **Brighton Beach** stands out for being unapologetically Russian. But this seaside borscht belt welcomes anyone in the mood for unfamiliar flavours, bargain shopping and seriously over-the-top entertainment. In the 1970s an ageing population – mainly of Jews of Eastern European descent – moved or died out, leaving the neighbourhood marred by vacant storefronts. It was during those years that refugees from the Soviet Union began transforming the 'hood into what soon became known as Little Odessa. It may not have major museums or galleries but it does have the ocean and lots of places to eat, drink and buy inexpensive electronics. Brighton Beach Avenue, the main artery here, is packed with Russian-speaking shopkeepers hawking glassware, caviar and DVDs from nearly every former Soviet Republic. Wander the aisles of M&I International Foods (No.249, between Brighton 2nd & 3rd Streets, 1-718 615 1011), a huge Russian deli and grocery, where locals stock up on kielbasa, kefir (a popular sour cultured-milk drink) and legendary butter from the Russian city of Vologda. At Primorski Restaurant (No.282, between Brighton 2nd & Brighton 3rd Streets, 1-718 891 3111), immigrants from the Georgian region dine on indigenous delicacies, including walnut-stuffed aubergine, meaty xhingali dumplings and solyanka, a thick and spicy soup made from sturgeon. Want something showier?

Make a reservation at the National (No.273, at Brighton 2nd Street, 1-718 646 1225), an infamous Moscow-style nightclub where the dress is flashy, the food and vodka are plentiful and the over-the-top burlesque shows are downright trippy.

Coney Island, on the peninsula just west of Brighton Beach, is mainly a summertime destination. After decades of decay, the weirdly wonderful community – known for its amusement park, beach and boardwalk – has made a comeback. The biggest improvement is seaside KeySpan Park, home to the **Brooklyn Cyclones** (see p333), a minor league baseball affiliate of the New York Mets. If you're a thrill-seeker, take a spin on the Cyclone at **Astroland Amusement Park** (see p283): a ride on the 79-year-old wooden rollercoaster lasts less than two minutes, but the first drop is nearly vertical, and the cars clatter along the 2,640 feet of track at speeds of up to 60 miles per hour. Consider saving the funnel cake and cotton candy for after your ride.

Further down the boardwalk, the **New York Aquarium** (see p289) is the nation's oldest marine preserve and home to more than 350 aquatic species, including the California sea-lions who perform daily at the outdoor, 1,600-seat Aquatheater. Don't forget to look up: a recent wave of local artists has focused its creative energy on adding some colour to the local signage.

The oddball Sideshows by the Seashore is put on by **Coney Island USA** (see below), an organisation that keeps the torch burning for early 20th-century Coney life. You won't want to miss a minute of the show, which includes legendary freaks like human pincushion Scott Baker (aka the Twisted Shockmeister), pain-proof Eak the Geek and the heavily tattooed Insectavora, who dines on flames and climbs the dangerous Ladder of Swords.

The **Mermaid Parade** (see p262) and Nathan's Famous Fourth of July Hot Dog Eating Contest are two quirky summertime rituals at Coney Island. In 2006 six-time winner Takeru Kobayashi scoffed down 53¾ dogs – complete with buns – in a mere 12 minutes, joining the likes of Lance Armstrong and Michael Jordan in the pantheon of enduring world champions. On Friday evenings throughout the summer, a fireworks display (9.30pm) is the perfect nightcap to a day of sandy adventures.

Coney Island USA

1208 Surf Avenue, at W 12th Street, Coney Island (1-718 372 5159/www.coneyislandusa.com). Subway: D, F, N, Q to Coney Island-Stillwell Avenue. **Open** Call or visit website for schedule. **Admission** $5; $3 under-12s. **No credit cards**.

Queens

NYC's biggest borough defines the term 'melting pot'.

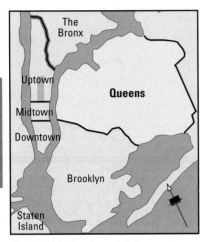

Almost 200,000 people come to Queens every day via JFK and La Guardia airports. Yet most visitors are in such a a rush to get to Manhattan that they don't realise they're missing parts of the city that some would describe as the 'real New York'. Middle-class but not yuppified, and definitely rough around the edges, Queens is a great day trip if you want to experience the full flavour of New York City's melting pot.

Queens is the city's huge eastern borough. It's the largest borough in terms of size, and demographers predict it will also surpass Brooklyn as the most populous in a matter of years. Its tremendous recent growth is thanks largely to a tidal wave of immigration – notable even by New York standards. The borough is the most diverse urban area the country has ever seen, with close to half the 2.2 million residents hailing from another land.

Except for the **US Open** and possibly a Mets game, haughty Manhattanites don't dare waggle a foot east of the East River, to the homeland of dysfunctional TV characters like *Seinfeld*'s George Costanza. But what do they know? Just minutes from Midtown, the borough offers cutting-edge art at **P.S.1**, jazz history at the **Louis Armstrong House** and cheap, delicious and honest ethnic eats.

As in the rest of New York, it's all about the neighbourhoods here. Take a globe-trotting tour on the elevated 7 subway, nicknamed the

International Express for the microcosm of nations you find represented beneath its tracks. That's no joke – like the Appalachian Trail, the 7 train is a designated National Millennium Trail. Get a MetroCard and head out to Queens for lunch to enjoy whatever cuisine gets your mouth watering. There are French bistros in Long Island City, Irish pub grub and Turkish kebabs in Sunnyside, knock-your-socks-off Thai curry in Woodside, more curry in Jackson Heights' Little India, Indonesian satay in Elmhurst, hearty steaks and tacos in pan-Latino Corona and Chinese dumplings and Korean barbecue in Flushing, the train's last stop.

The word is out about Queens – overlooked no longer – and a steady flow of New Yorkers priced out of Manhattan and Brooklyn have moved into immigrant neighbourhoods, pushing up prices. A few years ago the trailblazers were artists looking for cheap spaces in Long Island City's factories, followed by MoMA's temporary visit in 2003, while its midtown home was being expanded. Since then the row houses and pre-war apartment buildings of western Queens have been staked out by young college grads and professionals ready to start families. They've brought new tastes, which means you'll find fries served with garlic aïoli in Long Island City, iPods on parade in Astoria and Bugaboo strollers in Jackson Heights.

Long Island City

Long Island City is undergoing the most radical transformation of all the borough's nabes, on its way from being a land of industry to an extension of Midtown Manhattan, with multiple residential apartment towers rising on the East River waterfront, where a Queens tour normally starts. Get off the 7 subway at its first stop, Vernon Boulevard-Jackson Avenue, to see old and new Queens at literally the same address. Nothing says *new* Queens like the **Watertaxi Beach** (2-03 Borden Avenue, at 2nd Street, Long Island City, www.watertaxibeach.com), a man-made beach on the East River. The up-close views of Midtown Manhattan look even better when you're chomping on a burger and downing cold draft beer with your toes in the sand. Next door (but with the same address) you'll find Long Island City history in the boxing-themed **Waterfront Crabhouse** (2-03 Borden

Avenue, at 2nd Street, 1-718 729 4862), an old-time saloon and oyster bar. If you'd prefer a more sedate setting for Manhattan gazing, try **Gantry Plaza State Park** (48th Avenue, at Center Boulevard), named after the hulking 19th-century railroad gantries that transferred cargo from ships to trains. Both these watery outposts are directly across the East River from the United Nations, with postcard-worthy views of the skyline, making them superb perches for the Fourth of July fireworks show.

A few blocks east on Jackson Avenue is **P.S.1 Contemporary Art Center** (*see p170*), a progressive cultural outpost affiliated with MoMA that highlights the work of up and coming art stars and throws the DJed Warm Up (*see p264*) summer art parties on its courtyard. Cross the street for a close-up on the graffiti-covered building that is **5 Pointz** (Crane Street & Jackson Avenue). Art studios now inhabit this former warehouse, but it's the outdoor canvas you'll want to inspect. Close by, a well-preserved block of 19th-century row houses in an array of styles constitutes the **Hunters Point Historic District** (45th Avenue, between 21st & 23rd Streets).

Hop back aboard the 7 subway and you'll get treated to a view of the Manhattan skyline through the elegant spans of the 59th Street Bridge (aka **Queensboro Bridge**). Completed in 1909, it signifies glamorous New York in everything from F Scott Fitzgerald's novel *The Great Gatsby* to Woody Allen's film *Manhattan* to Simon & Garfunkel's hit 'The 59th Street Bridge Song (Feelin' Groovy)'.

Back when Los Angeles was a sleepy orange grove, western Queens was America's film capital, and these days it buzzes with cinematic goings-on once more. The mounted 'Silvercup' sign visible from the Queensboro Plaza subway platform announces Silvercup Studios, once a bakery and today a TV and film production stage, where *Sex and the City* and *The Sopranos* were made. WC Fields and the Marx Brothers clowned at Famous Players/Lasky Studios, now called Kaufman Astoria Studios, which houses the **Museum of the Moving Image** (*see p170*). Dub your voice into the *Wizard of Oz*, learn what creative minds are fashioning out of video games and check out classic, foreign and experimental films. To get there, you'll need to transfer to the N or W trains at Queensboro Plaza.

Astoria

The N or W train also chugs north to Astoria, a lively neighbourhood – of Greeks, but also Brazilians, Egyptians and everyone else – that's favoured by post-grads sharing row-house digs. You can alight at Broadway for a hike to the

Numbers game
What's up with Queens addresses?

According to the Topographical Bureau of the Borough President's office, Queens has had a hyphenated address system since at least the 1930s. The first number in the address refers to the cross-street, and the number after the hyphen is the actual house number, which, as with most addresses around the US, corresponds to the distance the house is from the street corner. Every 20 feet, that second number increases by two, with odd numbers organising the north and west sides, and even numbers the south and east. For example, if you're heading east on Hillside Avenue at 146th Street in Jamaica, the first address you'll find is 146-02 Hillside Avenue. The entire borough uses this system, except for the Rockaways and Ridgewood.

indoor-outdoor **Noguchi Museum** (*see p170*), which shows works by the visionary Japanese sculptor and others. Nearby is **Socrates Sculpture Park** (Broadway, at Vernon Boulevard, Long Island City, www.socrates sculpturepark.org), a riverfront art space given to concerts and summer film screenings on Wednesday nights. At the end of the subway line (Astoria-Ditmars Boulevard), walk west to Astoria Park (from Astoria Park South to Ditmars Boulevard, between Shore Boulevard & 19th Street), for its dramatic views of two bridges: the **Triborough Bridge**, Robert Moses's automotive labyrinth connecting Queens, the Bronx and Manhattan; and the 1916 **Hell Gate Bridge**, a single-arch steel tour de force that was the template for the Sydney Harbour Bridge in Australia.

As New York's Greek-American stronghold, Astoria is known for Hellenic eateries specialising in impeccably grilled seafood. Taverna Kyclades (33-07 Ditmars Boulevard, between 33rd & 35th Streets, 1-718 545 8666) offers a breezy Aegean atmosphere and a smoker-friendly patio. Lovely Agnanti (19-06 Ditmars Boulevard, between 19th & 21st Streets, 1-718 545 4554) is adjacent to Astoria Park and serves meze and grilled catch of the day. One of the city's last central European beer gardens, Bohemian Hall (29-19 24th Avenue, at 29th Street, 1-718 274 4925), hosts Czech-style dining and drinking on weeknights and weekends. Better arrive early on weekends to

Sightseeing

get a table in the linden tree-shaded courtyard. South of Astoria Boulevard, enjoy *shisha* – a (legal) hookah pipe – with thick Turkish coffee in the Egyptian cafés along Steinway Street. Over at **Steinway & Sons** you can glimpse masterful piano artisans at work on a tour of the still-thriving red-brick 1871 factory (*see p170* **Don't miss**).

Jackson Heights

Find your way back to an E, F, G, R or 7 train and ride to the 74th Street-Broadway stop. This is the crossroads of Jackson Heights, a dizzyingly multicultural neighbourhood even by Queens standards, and a cheap-eats paradise. Step off the subway into Little India. Dosa Diner (35-66 73rd Street, between 35th & 37th Avenues, 1-718 205 2218) is packed on weekends with families feasting on the south Indian dosa crêpe specialities. Ashoka's fresh all-you-can-eat buffet is unfurled at lunch and dinner (74-14 37th Avenue, between 74th & 75th Streets, 1-718 898 5088). Shops selling saris, spices, Bollywood DVDs and intricate gold jewellery line 74th Street, between Roosevelt and 37th Avenues.

Jackson Heights claims a roughly 30-square-block landmark district of notable mock Tudor and neo-Gothic-style co-op apartment buildings, with attached houses characterised by tree-dotted lawns and park-like courtyards. Outstanding examples of these 1920s beauties are found on 70th Street, between 34th Avenue and Northern Boulevard, and on 34th Avenue, between 76th and 77th Streets, and 80th and 81st Streets.

Jackson Heights and its adjoining 'hoods have welcomed successive waves of Latin American immigrants and their cuisines. Colombians and Argentinians are old school in these parts: get a taste of Buenos Aires at La Fusta, a convivial steakhouse (80-32 Baxter Avenue, between Broadway & Layton Street, Elmhurst, 1-718 429 8222). Thatch-covered Gran Rancho Jubilee (23-04 94th Street, at 23rd Avenue, East Elmhurst, 1-718 335 1700) lies just a block from the airport, but offers a full ride into Dominican life, with home-cooking and live merengue shows.

Flushing

At the end of the 7 train lies historic Flushing. Egalitarian Dutchmen staked their claim to 'Vlissingen' in the 1600s and were shortly joined by pacifist Friends, or Quakers, seeking religious freedom in the New World. These liberal settlers promulgated the Flushing Remonstrance, a groundbreaking 1657 edict extending 'the law of love, peace and liberty'

to Jews and Muslims. It is now regarded as a forerunner of the United States Constitution's First Amendment.

The plain wooden Friends Meeting House (137-16 Northern Boulevard, between Main & Union Streets, Flushing, 1-718 358 9636), built in 1694, creates a startling juxtaposition to prosperous Chinatown – New York's second largest – that now surrounds its weathered wooden walls. Religious freedom is still a draw in the neighbourhood, which boasts hundreds of active temples and churches thick with immigrants from Korea, China and South Asia. **St George's Church** (Main Street, between 38th & 39th Streets, 1-718 359 1171), an Episcopalian steeple chartered by King George III, was once a dominant site on Main Street, but now competes for attention with a parade of local shops and restaurants, including a major shopping development opening across the street in 2007. The interior of St George is worth a brief visit to see two examples of Queens-made Tiffany stained-glass – and to hear church services in Caribbean-accented English, Chinese and Spanish. Ambitious explorers will want to make the jaunt south to the **Hindu Temple Society** (*see p169*), a Ganesh temple whose ornate stone exterior was hand-carved in India.

The restaurants and dumpling stalls of Flushing's Chinatown are another way to commune with the divine, with lamb specialities from northern China and Malaysian's savoury roti canai just a couple of examples of the hundreds of heavenly options. Teenagers love the bubble tea – sweet, milky tea loaded with tapioca balls – that you can find in cafés like donut-serving Sago (39-02 Main Street, 1-718 353 2899) or tea-specialists Ten Ren (135-18 Roosevelt Avenue, 1-718 461 9305). For brunch at the weekend, sit side by side with local families for dim sum at banquet-sized, chandelier-lit Gum Fung (136-28 39th Avenue, 1-718 762 8821).

Flushing Town Hall (*see p169*), built during the Civil War in the fanciful Romanesque Revival style, showcases local arts groups and hosts jazz concerts, chamber music and multimedia exhibits. It's hard to believe the gorgeous exterior survived utter abandonment in the early 1980s when the building was overrun by derelicts. Here you can catch the **Queens Jazz Trail** (*see p169*), a monthly trolley tour of the homes of jazz legends who have resided in the borough, including Louis Armstrong, Count Basie, Ella Fitzgerald, Dizzy Gillespie, Billie Holiday and John Coltrane. The tour's centrepiece is the **Louis Armstrong House** in Corona (*see p169*), a modest brick home in a working-class community that 'Satchmo' never abandoned, despite his global fame.

The site in Queens that gets the most visitors every year is rambling **Flushing Meadows-Corona Park** (*see below*), where the 1939 and 1964 World's Fairs were held. Larger than Central Park, Flushing Meadows is home to the **Queens Zoo**, where natural environments include a lush parrot habitat; **Queens Theatre in the Park**, an indoor amphitheatre designed by the late Philip Johnson; the **New York Hall of Science** (*see p170*), an acclaimed interactive museum; the **Queens Botanical Garden**, a 39-acre cavalcade of greenery; and the **Queens Museum of Art** (*see p170*), which exhibits increasingly avant-garde shows that nicely tie art to local immigrant experience – fittingly enough for the building that was the first home of the United Nations. The museum's mesmerising pièce de résistance is the *Panorama of the City of New York*, a 9,335-square-foot, 895,000-building scale model (1 inch equals 100 feet) of all five boroughs. Flushing Meadows also encompasses **Shea Stadium**, home base of the Mets baseball team (*see p333*); the USTA (United States Tennis Association) National Tennis Center, where the US Open (*see p336*) raises a racket at summer's end (the general public can play here during the other 11 months of the year); and the 140-foot-high Unisphere, a mammoth steel globe that became famous as the symbol of the 1964 World's Fair – and the final battle scene between humans and aliens in the first *Men in Black* movie.

For an 'I can't believe this is New York' experience, take the E or F express subways out to 71st Avenue and stroll through **Forest Hills Gardens**, the remarkably preserved (and ritzy) 'garden city' developed in 1910 and inspired by the English Arts and Crafts movement. The planned community is a genius stroke in the history of suburban development. At the end of boutique-heavy Austin Street is another neighbourhood genius – Nick's Pizza (108-26 Ascan Avenue, at Austin Street, 1-718 263-1126), a great place to sample a New York pizza pie.

Rap fans should continue on the E or F trains out to Jamaica and Hollis, the hometowns of Run-DMC, LL Cool J and 50 Cent. The teenagers who throng Jamaica Avenue are hip hop taste-makers, and you'll find the latest fashions from Baby Phat and more near 164th Street. It's about as far as you can get from Manhattan by subway, but you'll find tons of New York attitude.

The website Queens.About.com is a great source of cultural and entertainment information, and DiscoverQueens.info is the official tourism website for Queens.

Flushing Meadows-Corona Park

From 111th Street to Van Wyck Expressway, between Flushing Bay & Grand Central Parkway (1-718 760 6565/Queens Zoo 1-718 220 510/www.queenszoo. com). Subway: 7 to Willets Point-Shea Stadium.

Most people come out to these parts to catch a game at Shea Stadium, home of the New York Mets, but don't overlook the 1964 World's Fair sculptures.

Flushing Town Hall/Flushing Council on Culture & the Arts/Queens Jazz Trail

137-135 Northern Boulevard, at Linden Place, Flushing (1-718 463 7700/www.flushingtownhall. org). Subway: 7 to Main Street. **Open** 9am-5pm Mon-Fri; noon-5pm Sat, Sun. **Admission** *Exhibits* free. *Jazz Trail* $30; first Sat of the mth at 10am; reservations recommended. **Credit** AmEx, MC, V.
Jazz diehards will love the three-hour Queens Jazz Trail trolley tour that stops by Addisleigh Park and showcases haunts of jazz greats like Louis Armstrong, Ella Fitzgerald, Billie Holiday and Dizzy Gillespie. The 30 bucks also gets you a cool illustrated guide.

Hindu Temple Society

4557 Bowne Street, between Holly & 45th Avenues, Flushing (1-718 460 8484/www.nyganeshtemple. org). Subway: 7 to Main Street. **Open** 8am-9pm Mon-Fri; 7.30am-9pm Sat, Sun.
Dutch colonists who stood up for religious freedom in the New World might be shocked to see this ornate stone façade dedicated to the Hindu deity Ganesh. The first Hindu temple in the US welcomes visitors. Afterwards, try the dosas at next door's tiny Dosa Hutt.

Louis Armstrong House

34-56 107th Street, between 34th & 37th Avenues, Corona (1-718 478 8274/www.satchmo.net). Subway: 7 to 103rd Street-Corona Plaza. **Open** 10am-5pm Tue-Fri; noon-5pm Sat, Sun. *Tours* 10am-4pm Tue-Fri, on the hour; noon-4pm Sat, Sun, on the hour. **Admission** $8; $6 seniors, students; free under-4s. **Credit** MC, V ($15 minimum).

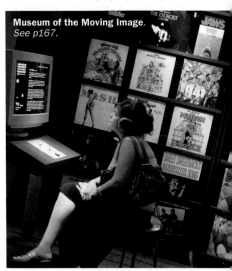

Museum of the Moving Image.
See p167.

Sightseeing

Don't miss Steinway & Sons

1 Steinway Place, between 19th Avenue & 38th Street, Astoria (1-718 721 2600/ www.steinway.com/factory/tour). Travel: N, W, 7 to Queensboro Plaza or E, F, G, R to Queens Plaza, then take the Q101 bus to 20th Avenue. **Tours** *are conducted in spring & autumn. Call for information. Reservations required. No children allowed.* **Admission** *free.* This (roughly) 2.5-hour tour of how a Steinway grand piano is painstakingly pieced together (all 12,000 parts) is quite simply amazing. And what's more, it's free!

Jazz lovers will have to make the pilgrimage, but though this is Louis's house, it was his wife Lucille who dealt with its upkeep – so be warned, her decor can overshadow the legendary life of Armstrong.

Museum of the Moving Image

35th Avenue, at 36th Street, Astoria (1-718 784 0077/www.movingimage.us). Subway: G, R, V to Steinway Street. **Open** *11am-5pm Wed, Thur; 11am-8pm Fri; 11am-6.30pm Sat, Sun.* **Admission** *$10; $7.50 seniors, students; $5 5-18s; free under-5s. Free 4-8pm Fri. No strollers.* **Credit** *AmEx, MC, V.*
Only 15 minutes by subway from Midtown, MMI is one of the city's most dynamic institutions. Located in the restored complex that once housed the original Kaufman Astoria Studios, it offers daily film, video and video game programming. The museum also displays famous movie props, including the chariot driven by Charlton Heston in *Ben-Hur* and the Yoda puppet used in *The Empire Strikes Back*.

New York Hall of Science

47-01 111th Street, at 47th Avenue, Flushing Meadows-Corona Park (1-718 699 0005/www.ny science.org). Subway: 7 to 111th Street. **Open** *July, Aug 9.30am-5pm Mon-Fri; 10am-6pm Sat, Sun. Sept-June 9.30am-2pm Mon-Thur; 9.30am-5pm Fri; 10am-6pm Sat, Sun.* **Admission** *$11; $8 seniors, students, children. Free 2-5pm Fri Sept-June. Science playground extra $3 (open summer only).* **Credit** *AmEx, DC, Disc, MC, V.*
The fun-for-all-ages New York Hall of Science, built for the 1964 World's Fair, and recently expanded, demystifies its subject through colourful hands-on exhibits, with topics such as Marvelous Molecules and The Realm of the Atom. Children can burn off their excess energy – and perhaps learn a thing or two – in the 30,000 sq ft outdoor science playground (summer only, $3 in addition to museum entry).

Noguchi Museum

9-01 33rd Road, between Vernon Boulevard & 10th Street, Long Island City (1-718 204 7088/www. noguchi.org). Travel: N, W to Broadway, then bus Q104 to 11th Street; or 7 to Vernon Boulevard-Jackson Avenue, then Q103 bus to 10th Street. **Open** *10am-5pm Wed-Fri; 11am-6pm Sat, Sun.* **Admission** *$10; $5 seniors, students. No strollers.* **No credit cards.**
In addition to his famous lamps, artist Isamu Noguchi (1904-88) created large-scale sculptures of supreme simplicity and beauty. The museum is located in a 1920s-era factory; galleries surround a serene sculpture garden designed by Noguchi himself. The second-floor galleries are devoted to Noguchi's interior design, a new café and a shop. A shuttle service from Manhattan is available on weekends (call or see website for more information).

P.S.1 Contemporary Art Center

22-25 Jackson Avenue, at 46th Avenue, Long Island City (1-718 784 2084/www.ps1.org). Subway: E, V to 23rd Street-Ely Avenue; G to 21st Street-Jackson Avenue; 7 to 45th Road-Court House Square. **Open** *noon-6pm, Thur-Sun.* **Admission** *suggested donation $5; $2 seniors, students.* **Credit** *AmEx, MC, V.*
Cutting-edge shows and an international studio programme make each visit to this contemporary art space a treasure hunt, with artwork turning up in every corner. In a Romanesque Revival building (a former public school), the MoMA affiliate mounts shows that appeal to art fans and open-minded neophytes.

Queens Museum of Art

New York City Building, park entrance on 49th Avenue, at 111th Street, Flushing Meadows-Corona Park (1-718 592 9700/www.queensmuseum.org). Subway: 7 to 111th Street. Walk south on 111th Street, then turn left on to 49th Avenue. Continue into the park and over Grand Central Parkway Bridge. **Open** *26 June-5 Sept 1-8pm Wed-Sun. 6 Sept-25 June 10am-5pm Wed-Fri; noon-5pm Sat, Sun.* **Admission** *$5; $2.50 seniors, students; free under-5s.* **No credit cards.**
Located in the grounds of the 1939 and 1964 World's Fairs, the QMA holds one of the area's most amazing sights: a 9,335sq ft scale model of New York City, accurate down to the square inch – at least up to 1994, the date of its last major renovation. Contemporary and outsider exhibits have grown more bold and inventive here, garnering increasing acclaim.

The Bronx

Gentrification: the final frontier.

The Bronx

Uptown
Queens
Midtown
Downtown
Brooklyn
Staten
Island

Change doesn't come easy in the **Bronx**. This probably has to do with the sad truth that it contains one of the poorest Congressional districts in the country. But many are hoping that the renaissance it has been promised for years will finally be realised, following an influx of cash and community support and as an army of folks seeking more affordable housing flees Manhattan and Brooklyn. In fact, so much activity is afoot that the Bronx should be called the 'hard-hat' borough, as cranes and scaffolding dominate the skyline. In 2006 Mayor Bloomberg announced the creation of the South Bronx Initiative, which aims to develop and sustain revitalisation of the area, and organisations like Sustainable South Bronx (www.ssbx.org) are pledging to make way for more parks. The area was even hailed as one of the five hot markets in the country by local real-estate guru Barbara Corcoran, causing her peers to nickname the area 'SoBro'. New condos are sprouting up, old warehouses are being redeveloped, once-crumbling tenements are being refurbished and chain stores are moving in. Young families are snapping up the stately townhouses on Alexander Avenue, furnishing them from the thoroughfare's rejuvenated antique stores, while industrial lofts on Bruckner Boulevard are becoming homes to artists. An especially thriving corner of the area is **Hunts Point**,

which may still look like an industrial wasteland, but has become increasingly popular as a live–work destination for artists. In 1994 a group of artists and community leaders converted a 12,000-square-foot industrial building into the **Point Community Development Corporation** (940 Garrison Avenue, at Manida Street, 1-718 542 4139, www.thepoint.org), a performance space, gallery and business incubator. The Point also leads lively walking tours (call for reservations) like Mambo to HipHop, which covers the history of locally born music genres. Creative types stage performances at the nearby **Bronx Academy of Arts & Dance (BAAD)** (*see p175*), and more than a dozen painters and sculptors work in the academy's studios. Those wanting a closer look at the up-and-coming arts scene should hop on the **Bronx Culture Trolley** (*see p175*), a free shuttle that visits the area's most happening galleries, performance spaces and museums. After much delay, in November 2005 Hunts Point also became the new home for the city's **Fulton Fish Market** (1-718 378 2356, www.newfultonfishmarket.com) in a modern, temperature-controlled $86 million indoor facility. Visitors can explore the new digs for $5.

Settled in the 1630s by the family of Jonas Bronck, a Swedish farmer who had a 500-acre homestead in what is now the south-eastern Morrisania section, the area became known as 'the Broncks' farm. Over the centuries, the name stuck, though its spelling was altered. The area was originally part of Westchester county, but like the other boroughs, it was incorporated into New York City in 1898.

Throughout the early 1900s, the Bronx, like Queens and Brooklyn, drew much of its population from the ever-expanding pool of Irish, German, Italian and Eastern European Jewish immigrants who flocked to the area for its cheap rents and open spaces. After World War II, as the borough grew more urbanised, the descendants of the European immigrants moved further out to the suburbs of Long Island and Westchester, and fresh waves of newcomers, hailing from Central America, Puerto Rico, Albania and Russia, as well as Hispaniola and other points in the West Indies, took their places.

Along with the population shifts, from the late 1940s until the early '70s the Bronx probably witnessed more upheaval than the rest of the city combined, baring the brunt of city planner Robert Moses's drastic remaking of the city. Thousands of residents saw their apartment buildings razed to make room for the Whitestone and Throgs Neck Bridges, the east-to-west Cross Bronx Expressway and the north-to-south Bruckner Boulevard extension of the New England Thruway. Many neighbourhoods fell into neglect, a condition exacerbated by the economic and social downturns that plagued the entire city in the '60s and '70s. The community felt (rightly so) cut off, forgotten and left to rot.

But the Bronx always drew sightseers for its long-standing gems like **Yankee Stadium** (*see p333*), located at 161st Street and River Avenue. Baseball's most famous legends made history on its diamond, from Babe Ruth and Joe DiMaggio to Derek Jeter. When there isn't a day game, the Yankees organisation gives tours of the clubhouse, the dugout and the famous centre-field Monument Park. Enjoy 'the house that Ruth built' while you can: in 2009 the Yankees will move to their new home – a brand new $800 million stadium across the street. When George Steinbrenner unveiled the plan in 2005, he put an end to years of threats of abandoning the borough for Manhattan or New Jersey, finally ensuring that the Bombers will remain in the Bronx. The new stadium met with some opposition, however, by groups concerned about it encroaching on parkland. Ground-breaking began, however, in summer 2006. The original will be torn down and replaced by a park.

Just under the Major Deegan Expressway, south of Yankee Stadium, lies the site of another controversial development – the former **Bronx Terminal Market**, once the largest wholesaler of ethnic and tropical produce on the East Coast. It closed in 2006 after 80 years of business; plans for replacing the cluster of buildings with a one-million-square-foot shopping mall are under way: The $400 million project is one of the largest private investments in the borough's history.

A few blocks east lies the six-and-a-half-mile **Grand Concourse**, which is also undergoing a facelift as its centennial approaches (2009). Around $18 million has been set aside to rebuild the area near Yankee Stadium. Plans include adding a terraced park, planting new trees and flowers, installing new streetlights, paving a bike lane and laying down cobblestones. Once the most prestigious drag in the Bronx, it's still a must for lovers of architecture. Engineer Louis Risse designed the boulevard, which stretches from 138th Street to Mosholu Parkway, in 1892, patterning it after Paris's Champs-Elysées. Starting at 161st Street and heading south, look for the permanent street plaques that make up the **Bronx Walk of**

Fame, honouring famous Bronxites from Regis Philbin to Colin Powell to Afrika Bambaataa. The buildings heading north date mostly from the 1920s to the early '40s and display the country's largest array of art deco housing. Erected in 1937 at the corner of 161st Street, 888 Grand Concourse has a concave entrance of gilded mosaic and is topped by a curvy metallic marquee. Inside, the mirrored lobby's central fountain and sunburst-patterned floor could rival those of any hotel on Miami's Ocean Drive. But the grandest building on the Concourse is the landmark **Andrew Freedman Home**, a 1924 French-inspired limestone palazzo between McClennan and 166th Streets. Freedman, a millionaire subway contractor, set aside the bulk of his $7 million estate to build a poorhouse for the rich – those who lost their fortunes, that is. It now houses the Family Preservation Center (FPC), a community-based social service agency. Across the street, the **Bronx Museum of the Arts** (*see p175*), established in 1971, and housed in a former synagogue, exhibits high-quality contemporary and historical works by Bronx-based artists, including many of African-American, Asian and Latino heritage. Near the intersection of Fordham Road, keep an eye out for the freshly refurbished **Loew's Paradise Theater**, with its recently landmarked interior. The Italian rococo exterior of the building was landmarked in 1997.

Due north to Kingsbridge Road, lovers of literature will enjoy the **Edgar Allan Poe Cottage** (*see p175*), a small wooden farmhouse where the writer lived from 1846 to 1849. Moved to the Grand Concourse from its original spot on Fordham Road in 1913, the museum has period furniture and details about Poe and his work. Nearby, a neighbourhood enjoying a notable resurgence is Bronx's **Little Italy**, centred around Arthur Avenue (*see p173* **On the avenue**), lined with Italian delis, restaurants, markets and cafés. Browse and nibble at the Arthur Avenue Retail Market (Crescent Avenue, at 186th Street), an indoor bazaar built in the 1940s when former mayor Fiorello La Guardia campaigned to get pushcarts off the street. (The market is closed on Sundays.) Inside is Mike's Deli (2344 Arthur Avenue, between Crescent Avenue & E 186th Street, 1-718 295 5033), where you can try the trademark schiacciata sandwich of grilled vegetables, or Big Mike's Combo, a roll loaded with provolone cheese and cold cuts. If you're in the mood for a full meal, try old-style red-sauce joints Mario's (2342 Arthur Avenue, between Crescent Avenue & E 186th Street, 1-718 584 1188) or Roberto's (603 Crescent Avenue, between Hughes & Arthur Avenue, 1-718 733 9503).

On the avenue

Experience a little Italy on Bronx's legendary Arthur Avenue.

The Arthur Avenue district in the heart of working-class Belmont is small and utilitarian-looking – just six blocks, densely packed with a colourful collection of third- and fourth-generation restaurants, butchers, bakers, fishmongers and grocers. These days, one notices more and more Albanian and Spanish signage, as the local demographic shifts. But the neighborhood remains the city's best source for everything Italian, from St Francis medals for pets (Catholic Goods Center, 630 E 187th Street) to Sicilian salt-packed capers and Francesconi canned tomatoes, sold by the case (Teitel Brothers, 2372 Arthur Avenue). By day, the offerings spilling out on to the sidewalks include homemade lemon, chocolate and cremolata ices, and curbside raw bars manned by waiters in crisp white aprons. Meat vendors display skinned rabbits and baby lambs, dangling on hooks over bins piled high with tripe and trotters.

Pop into Mike's Deli (2344 Arthur Avenue, between 183rd & 186th Streets, 1-718 295 5033), an overstocked butcher and café

located in the city's most beloved food- and kitchen-supplies market. The glossy menu may paralyse you with indecision – it lists more than 50 different sandwiches.

While Albanians increasingly populate these streets (just as in Rome, Naples and other Italian cities), the flavour of the old country – garlic and basil aromas wafting out of eateries and Mediterranean-tinged gardens – is more intact here than it is in Manhattan's stage-set Little Italy or in Brooklyn's rapidly gentrifying Carroll Gardens. In fact, Belmont's ambience has been preserved for more than 80 years by those who came to find refuge, not only from the poverty of Europe, but from the suffocating tenements of Mulberry Street. Before leaving, take a detour for a cannoli in classic Italian-American pastry shop Edigio's (622 E 187th Street, 1-718 295 6077).

T-shirts on sale in neighbourhood stores here boldly proclaim Belmont to be 'New York's real Little Italy'. They may have a point. *For more info, visit www.arthuravenue bronx.com.*

The serene 250 acres of the **New York Botanical Garden** (*see p175*) are a magical respite from cars and concrete, comprising 50 gardens and plant collections, the Rockefeller Rose Garden, the Everett Children's Adventure Garden and the last 50 original acres of a forest that once covered all of New York City. In springtime, the gardens are frothy with pastel blossoms, as clusters of lilac, cherry, magnolia and crab apple trees burst into bloom, followed in autumn by vivid foliage in the oak and maple groves. On a rainy day, you can stay warm and sheltered inside the Enid A Haupt Conservatory, a striking glass-walled greenhouse – the nation's largest – built in 1902. It offers seasonal exhibits as well as the World of Plants, a series of environmental galleries that will send you on an ecotour through tropical rainforests, deserts and a palm-tree oasis. Just next door is the borough's most famous attraction, the **Bronx Zoo** (*see p175*), opened in 1899 by Theodore Roosevelt in an attempt to preserve game. At 265 acres, it's the largest urban zoo in the US. The zoo shuns cages in favour of indoor and outdoor environments that mimic the natural habitats of more than 4,000 mammals, birds and reptiles. Nearly 100 species,

including monkeys, leopards and tapirs, live inside the lush, steamy Jungle World, a re-creation of an Asian rain forest inside a 37,000-square-foot building. The super-popular Congo Gorilla Forest has turned six and a half acres into a dramatic Central African rainforest habitat. A glass-enclosed tunnel winds through the forest, allowing visitors to get close to the dozens of primate families in residence, including 26 majestic western lowland gorillas. For those who prefer cats, Tiger Mountain has six adult Siberian tigers, who look particularly regal on snowy days. The zoo's newest additions include African wild dogs; an aquatic aviary; a butterfly garden, featuring 1,000 colourful flutterers; and the adjacent Bug Carousel.

Pelham Bay Park (take the 6 train to Pelham Bay), in the borough's north-eastern corner, is NYC's biggest park, once home to the Siwonay Indians. Take a car or a bike if you want to explore the 2,765 acres. Get a map at the Ranger Nature Center, near the entrance on Bruckner Boulevard at Wilkinson Avenue. The **Bartow-Pell Mansion Museum** (*see p174*), in the park's south-eastern quarter, overlooks Long Island Sound. Finished in 1842, the elegantly furnished Greek Revival building

Bronx Zoo. *See p175.*

faces a reflecting pool ringed by gardens. The park's 13 miles of coastline skirt the Hutchinson River to the west and the Long Island Sound and Eastchester Bay to the east. In summer, locals hit Orchard Beach; set up in the 1930s, it's a rare Robert Moses project loved by all.

Riverdale, along the north-west coast of the Bronx, reflects the borough's suburban past. Huge homes perch on narrow, winding streets overlooking the Hudson River. Theodore Roosevelt, Mark Twain and Arturo Toscanini have all lived in **Wave Hill House** (*see p175*), an 1843 stone mansion set on a former private estate that is now a cultural and environmental centre. The 28 acres of cultivated gardens and woodlands provide fine views of the river – especially during sunset. The art gallery shows nature-themed exhibits, and the organisation presents year-round concerts and performances, t'ai chi classes and events like the 'barefoot dancing' series. If you need a day outdoors on foot or on bike, try the quiet pathways of the Hudson River-hugging **Riverdale Park**. Enter this swath of forest preserve along Palisade Avenue, between 232nd and 254th Streets.

The nearby 1,146-acre **Van Cortlandt Park** (entrance on Broadway, at 244th Street) often hosts cricket teams made up mostly of West Indians. You can hike through a 100-year-old forest, play golf on the nation's first municipal course or rent horses at stables in the park. **Van Cortlandt House Museum** (*see p175*), a fine example of pre-Revolutionary Georgian architecture, was built by Frederick van Cortlandt in 1748; it served as a headquarters for George Washington in the Revolutionary War. Donated to the city by the van Cortlandt family, it's the oldest building in the borough. Abutting the park is **Woodlawn Cemetery**, which houses over 300,000 bodies, including Elizabeth Cady Stanton, Duke Ellington, Miles Davis, FW Woolworth and Damon Runyon. Maps are available at the visitors' entrance at Webster Avenue and E 233rd Street. About five blocks

south on Bainbridge Avenue, history buffs will also enjoy stopping in at the Bronx Historical Society's **Museum of Bronx History** (*see p175*), set in a lovely 1758 stone farmhouse.

Despite all the recent redevelopment, there is an organised effort to retain the unique New England-like charm of **City Island**. Located just east of Pelham Bay Park and ringed by the waters of Eastchester Bay and the Long Island Sound, City Island was settled in 1685 and was once a prosperous shipbuilding centre with a busy fishing industry, a history reflected in the streets lined with Victorian captains' houses. Nautical activity still abounds, especially in the summer, but recreational boating is the main industry now. The island's main drag, City Island Avenue, brims with art galleries and antique shops, while seafood restaurants, marine-themed bars, yacht clubs and sail-makers crowd the docks. Join the warm-weather hordes at **Johnny's Famous Reef Restaurant** (No.2, at Belden Street, 1-718 885 2086) for steamed clams, cold beer and great views. Few commercial fishermen remain, but you'd hardly know it at **Rosenberg's Boat Livery** (No.663, 1-718 885 1843), a bait-and-tackle shop that rents motorboats by the day. The Livery also doubles as a bustling bar. Timeless treasures like these prove that the lure of the Bronx never really went away – they just need to be dusted off and discovered by a new generation.

Bartow-Pell Mansion Museum

895 Shore Road North, at Pelham Bay Park (1-718 885 1461/www.bartowpellmansionmuseum.org). Travel: 6 to Pelham Bay Park, then take the Bee-Line bus 45 (ask driver to stop at the Bartow-Pell Mansion; bus does not run on Sunday), or take a cab from the subway station. **Open** noon-4pm Wed, Sat, Sun. **Admission** $5; $3 seniors, students; free under-6s. Free Wed. **No credit cards.**
Operating as a museum since 1946, this stunning estate dates from 1654, when Thomas Pell bought the land from the Siwonay Indians. It was Robert Bartow who added the Grecian-style stone mansion.

Bronx Academy of Arts & Dance (BAAD)

2nd Floor, 841 Barretto Street, between Garrison & Lafayette Avenues (1-718 842 5223/www.bronx academyofartsanddance.org). Subway: 6 to Hunts Point Avenue. **Open** Check website for performances and prices.

A myriad dance, theatre and visual arts events including OUT LIKE THAT! – the borough's only fest celebrating works by lesbian, gay, bisexual and transgender artists; and BAAD! ASS WOMEN, a cultural celebration of works by women.

Bronx Culture Trolley

The Bronx Council on the Arts, 1738 Hone Avenue (1-718 931 9500 ext 33/www.bronxarts.org). Subway: 2, 4, 5 to 149th Street-Grand Concourse. **Open** Feb-Aug, Oct-Dec 1st Wed of mth. 5.30pm, 6.30pm & 7.30pm from the Longwood Art Gallery at the Hostos Center for the Arts & Culture (450 Grand Concourse).* Admission free.

The trolley is a replica of an early 20th-century trolley that shuttles you (for nothing!) to a whole host of galleries and performing arts venues. It also takes riders to the Artisans Marketplace – a giant craft fair with all sorts of attractive handmade stuff. Visit the website for a schedule of seasonal events.

Bronx Museum of the Arts

1040 Grand Concourse, at 165th Street (1-718 681 6000/www.bxma.org). Subway: B, D to 167th Street Grand Concourse; 4 to 161st Street-Yankee Stadium. **Open** noon-9pm Wed; noon-6pm Thur-Sun. **Admission** $5; $3 seniors, students; free under-12s. Free Wednesday. **No credit cards**.

Founded in 1971 and featuring more than 800 works, this multicultural art museum shines a spotlight on 20th- and 21st-century artists of African, Asian and Latin American ancestry.

Bronx Zoo/Wildlife Conservation Society

Bronx River Parkway, at Fordham Road (1-718 367 1010/www.bronxzoo.org). Travel: 2 to Pelham Parkway, then walk two blocks, turn left at Boston Road and follow as it bears right to the zoo's Bronxdale entrance; or Metro-North's Harlem Line to Fordham, then take the Bx9 bus south to the zoo entrance, or the Bx12 bus east to Southern Boulevard, and walk east to the zoo entrance. **Open** Apr-Oct 10am-5pm Mon-Fri; 10am-5.30pm Sat, Sun, holidays. Nov-Mar 10am-4.30pm daily. **Admission** Apr-Oct $12; $9 seniors, children; free under-2s. Nov-Mar $8; $6 seniors, children; free under-2s. Voluntary donation Wed. (Some rides and exhibitions are extra.) **Credit** AmEx, DC, Disc, MC, V.

Home to more than 4,500 creatures, including African wild dogs (the latest additions). For visitors who want a bird's-eye view, the Skyfari, an aerial tram ride over the zoo, is wonderful. Highlights include an underwater viewing area; the Congo Gorilla forest; Tiger Mountain, which educates visitors about tigers and conservation; and an indoor Asian rainforest. **Photo** *p174*.

Edgar Allan Poe Cottage

2640 Grand Concourse, at Kingsbridge Road (1-718 881 8900/www.bronxhistoricalsociety.org). Subway: D, 4 to Kingsbridge Road. **Open** 10am-4pm Sat; 1-5pm Sun. **Admission** $3; $2 seniors, students. **No credit cards**.

Pay homage to Poe in the very house where he wrote literary gems including *Annabel Lee* and *The Bells*. A presentation film and guided tour are available.

Museum of Bronx History

Valentine-Varian House, 3266 Bainbridge Avenue, between Van Cortlandt Avenue & E 208th Street (1-718 881 8900/www.bronxhistoricalsociety.org). Subway: D to Norwood-205th Street. **Open** 10am-4pm Sat; 1-5pm Sun. **Admission** $3; $2 seniors, students & children. **No credit cards**.

Operated by the Bronx County Historical Society, the Museum of Bronx History is located in the Valentine-Varian House, a Federal-style fieldstone residence built in 1758. The society offers tours that explore the neighbourhoods and historic periods.

New York Botanical Garden

Bronx River Parkway, at Fordham Road (1-718 817 8700/www.nybg.org). Travel: B, D to Bedford Park Boulevard, then take the Bx26 bus to Garden gate; or Metro-North (Harlem Line local) from Grand Central Terminal to Botanical Garden. **Open** Apr-Oct 10am-6pm Tue-Sun, Mon federal holidays. Nov-Mar 10am-5pm Tue-Sun. **Admission** $20; $18 seniors, students; $5 2-12s; free under-2s. Grounds only $6; free 10am-5pm Wed; noon-5pm Sat. **Credit** AmEx, DC, MC, V.

The $20 ticket buys entry to current exhibitions, the Adventure Garden, the Haupt Conservatory and tram tours. If you're coming from Manhattan, look into specials from Metro-North's Harlem line train from Grand Central Terminal, which may include a round-trip ticket with admission.

Van Cortlandt House Museum

Van Cortlandt Park, entrance on Broadway, at 246th Street (1-718 543 3344/www.vancortlandthouse.org). Subway: 1 to 242nd Street-Van Cortlandt Park. **Open** 10am-3pm Tue-Fri; 11am-4pm Sat, Sun. **Admission** $5; $3 seniors, students; free under-12s. Free Wed. **No credit cards**.

A one-time wheat plantation that has been turned into a colonial museum.

Wave Hill House

W 249th Street, at Independence Avenue (1-718 549 3200/www.wavehill.org). Travel: Metro-North (Hudson Line local) from Grand Central Terminal to Riverdale. **Open** mid Apr-May, Aug-mid Oct 9am-5.30pm Tue-Sun. June, July 9am-5.30pm Tue, Thur-Sun; 9am-9pm Wed. Mid Oct-mid Apr 9am-4.30pm Tue-Sun. **Admission** $4; $2 seniors, students; free under-6s. Free all day Tue, 9am-noon Sat. **No credit cards**.

Laze on 28 lush acres overlooking the Hudson River at Wave Hill, a former estate that has housed Mark Twain, Teddy Roosevelt and conductor Arturo Toscanini. It's now a spectacular nature preserve and conservation centre, where you can see art exhibits and dance and music performances.

Sightseeing

Staten Island

It's not easy being the city's greenest borough.

In May 2006 New York was rocked by a shocking crime on Staten Island. A woman ambushed a man at the doorstep of his home, shooting him four times. What surprised New Yorkers wasn't the actual crime, though, but the nature of the man's dwelling – a 90-person commune known as 'Ganas'. A free-loving, toothpaste-sharing, tree-hugging counterculture… in Staten Island? Looking past the working-class neighbourhoods and the ordinary strip malls, however, maybe it shouldn't be such a shock – at one time or another the entire island has struggled to establish a Utopia among the urban sprawl.

The first visitor looking to drop out and tune in to a bucolic new world was Giovanni da Verrazano, who set down his anchor on the island in 1524. But the spot wasn't named until 1609, when Henry Hudson sailed in and christened it *Staaten Eylandt* (Dutch for 'State's Island'). Early settlements were repeatedly decimated by Native Americans – the island's first true preservationists. But the Dutch finally took hold in 1661, establishing shipping and manufacturing communities on the northern shore, and farms and small hamlets in the south. Despite being incorporated as one of the five boroughs in 1898, the predominantly rural area remained a somewhat isolated Eden until 1964, when the Verrazano-Narrows Bridge joined the island to Brooklyn's Bay Ridge neighbourhood.

The **Staten Island Ferry** (*see p88*), however, is the borough's best-known connection to the rest of the city, linking lower Manhattan to the island's St George terminal, which was revamped in 2005 in honour of its 100th birthday. Once a dreary through-station, the terminal is now marked by floor-to-ceiling glass, providing commuters with panoramic views of the harbour and lower Manhattan's skyline. A new outdoor promenade surrounding the area is in the works to provide easier access to the neighbourhood's many attractions, including *Postcards*, a sculpture by Japanese architect Masayuki Sono – a memorial to the 253 Staten Islanders lost on 9/11. Another addition to the area will be the **National Lighthouse Center & Museum** (1-718 556 1681, www.lighthousemuseum.org) scheduled to open in 2007. The complex will include a restored lighthouse, a lightship, piers and exhibits just east of the ferry terminal. Along Richmond Terrace lies the **Richmond County Savings Bank Ballpark**, home of the three-time minor league champions the Staten Island Yankees (www.siyanks.com), a great place to catch a game and a harbourside view. Across the street, look for the **Borough Hall's** (10 Richmond Terrace) distinctive clocktower and step inside for a peek at the *Works Progress Administration* murals depicting local history. Also worth popping into is the Spanish baroque-styled lobby of the newly restored **St George Theater** (35 Hyatt Street, 1-718 442 2900, www.stgeorgetheater.com), just two blocks inland. You can expect exhibits on anything from baseball cards to beetles at the **Staten Island Museum** (75 Stuyvesant Place, 1-718 727 1135, www.statenislandmuseum.org), the city's only general interest museum, just another two blocks north. Continuing north and then west along Richmond Terrace to Westervelt Avenue, then uphill two blocks to St Marks Place, you'll come upon the **St George-New Brighton Historic District**, a landmark neighbourhood full of Queen Anne and Colonial Revival buildings dating from the early 1830s. Moving south to Bay Street near Victory Boulevard, vintage fashion fans will enjoy the various thrift shops dotting the strip.

Dozens of pastoral attractions lie further inland. You can spend an entire day looking around the 83-acre **Snug Harbor Cultural Center** (*see p178*), a short bus ride west along Richmond

The **Staten Island Ferry**. *See p176.*

Terrace. Stately Greek Revival structures form the nucleus of the former maritime hospital and sailors' home dating from 1833. The centre was converted in the 1970s into a visual and performing arts complex that includes the **Art Lab** and **Newhouse** art galleries, the **Staten Island Children's Museum** and the verdant **Staten Island Botanical Garden** (for all, *see p178*), as well as the **Noble Maritime Collection**, with artworks by artist John A Noble (1-718 447 6490, www.noblemaritime.org). Slightly further inland, the **Staten Island Zoo** (*see p178*), adjacent to the Clove Lakes Park, boasts an aquarium, a rainforest and one of the East Coast's largest reptile collections.

Buses and the single-line Staten Island Railroad depart from St George for destinations along the eastern half of the island. Along Hylan Boulevard, one of Staten Island's major arteries, lies photographer **Alice Austen**'s house (*see p178*), a 15-minute bus ride east of the ferry. The 18th-century cottage has breathtaking harbour views and 3,000 of Austen's glass negative photos. At the east end of Bay Street, historic **Fort Wadsworth** (*see p178*) is one of the oldest military sites in the nation. There, visitors can explore the Civil War-era gun batteries or take in the vista of the Verrazano bridge and downtown Manhattan from one of NYC's highest points. Further along the eastern coast, residents and tourists stroll along the two-mile **FDR Boardwalk** of South Beach, the fourth longest in the world. It's also a great area for picnicking, cycling and fishing.

In the centre of the island, on Lighthouse Avenue, many seek refuge at the **Jacques Marchais Museum of Tibetan Art** (*see p178*), a reproduction of a Himalayan mountain temple with tranquil meditation gardens and a small collection of Tibetan and Buddhist objects of interest. The museum also hosts meditation workshops. Nearby, guides in period garb offer tours of the 27 restored buildings of **Historic Richmond Town** (*see p178*), the island's one-time county seat.

Among the group are Voorlezer's House (the nation's oldest former schoolhouse circa 1695). Just a stone's throw away, **High Rock Park** (*see p178*) is the entry point for more than 30 miles of hiking trails. It's part of the 2,800-acre **Greenbelt** (www.sigreenbelt.org) and includes golf, archery, baseball, birdwatching, a carousel and a nature centre.

The island's south-eastern coast (a 40-minute ride on the S78 bus) is especially pleasant in the summer, when you can swim, picnic and fish at **Wolfe's Pond Park** (Cornelia Avenue, at Hylan Boulevard, 1-718 984 8266). A little further south, the historic **Conference House** (*see p178*) was the site for a failed attempt at peace between American and British forces in 1776 and is now a museum of colonial life. A short walk away, you'll find yourself at the very tip of the island on Tottenville Beach. Here, you can relax and admire the passing sailboats.

Staten Island's rural respites are growing with the addition of the **Fresh Kills Park**, a 2,200-acre parcel of land that was once the city's garbage dump and which is now slated to become the city's largest park, at almost three times the size of Central Park. While the project's completion is 30 years away, parts of the park are scheduled to open in 2007, and the Parks Department currently offers guided tours of the site twice a month (visit www.nycparks.org for more info). The grand plan includes cycling trails, tennis courts, a sports stadium, gardens, stables, and a memorial to the World Trade Center on the spot where its wreckage rested after 9/11. Another new development for the island is drawing fierce opposition from environmentalists – NYC's very own NASCAR track, proposed for 450 acres near the Goethals Bridge. Conservationists have banded together to stall the project, as part of efforts to reduce overdevelopment in general, proving that a 'green' sentiment is spreading throughout the borough. After all, you don't have to be part of a tree-hugging commune to cherish, and preserve, some of the city's most idyllic charms.

Alice Austen House

*2 Hylan Boulevard, between Bay & Edgewater
Streets (1-718 816 4506/www.aliceausten.org).
Travel: from the Staten Island Ferry, take the S51
bus to Hylan Boulevard.* **Open** *Mar-Dec* noon-5pm
Thur-Sun. Closed major holidays. **Admission**
suggested donation $2. **No credit cards**.
History buffs will marvel at Austen's beautiful turn-
of-the-19th-century photographs. The restored house
and lovely grounds often host concerts and events.

Conference House (Billopp House)

*7455 Hylan Boulevard, at Craig Avenue (1-718 984
2086/www.theconferencehouse.org). Travel: from the
Staten Island Ferry, take the S78 bus to Craig Avenue.*
Open *1 Apr-15 Dec* 1-4pm Fri-Sun. **Admission** $3;
$2 seniors, children. **No credit cards**.
Britain's Lord Howe parleyed with John Adams and
Benjamin Franklin in this 17th-century manor house
in 1776, in an attempt to stop the American Revolution.

Fort Wadsworth

*East end of Bay Street (1-718 354 4500). Travel:
from the Staten Island Ferry, take the S51 bus to
Fort Wadsworth on weekdays, Von Briesen Park
on weekends.* **Open** dawn-dusk daily. *Visitors'
Center* 10am-5pm Wed-Sun. **Tours** Call for
schedule. **Admission** free.
Explore the fortifications that guarded NYC for
almost 200 years, or take one of the creatively themed
tours, like the popular evening lantern-light tours.

High Rock Park

*200 Nevada Avenue, at Rockland Avenue (1-718 667
2165/www.sigreenbelt.org). Travel: from the Staten
Island Ferry, take the S62 bus to Manor Road, then
the S54 bus to Nevada Avenue.* **Open** dawn-dusk daily.
*Greenbelt Nature Center Visitors' Center (1-718 351
3450)* 10am-5pm Tue-Sun. **Admission** free.
Covering 90 acres of land, where visitors may hike
the mile-long Swamp Trail, climb Todt Hill or explore
trails through forests, meadows and wetlands.

Historic Richmond Town

*441 Clarke Avenue, between Richmond Road &
St Patrick's Place (1-718 351 1611/www.historic
richmondtown.org). Travel: from the Staten Island
Ferry, take the S74 bus to St Patrick's Place.* **Open**
8 Jan-30 June 1-5pm Wed-Sun. *July-Aug* 10am-5pm
Wed-Fri; 1-5pm Sat, Sun. *Sept-Dec* 1-5pm Wed-Sun.
Closed major holidays and 1-7 Jan. **Admission** $5;
$4 seniors; $3.50 5-17s; free under-5s. **No credit cards**.
A colonial era 'living museum'.

Jacques Marchais
Museum of Tibetan Art

*338 Lighthouse Avenue, off Richmond Road, Staten
Island (1-718 987 3500/www.tibetanmuseum.org).
Travel: from the Staten Island Ferry, take the S74
bus to Lighthouse Avenue.* **Open** 1-5pm Wed-Sun.
Admission $5; $3 seniors, students; $2 under-12s.
Credit AmEx, MC, V.
This tiny museum contains a formidable Buddhist
altar, lovely gardens and a large collection of Tibetan
art. A Tibetan festival takes place each October.

Staten Island Zoo

*614 Broadway, between Glenwood Place & West
Raleigh Avenue (1-718 442 3100/www.statenisland
zoo.org). Travel: from the Staten Island Ferry, take
the S48 bus to Broadway.* **Open** 10am-4.45pm daily.
Closed major holidays. **Admission** $7; $5 seniors;
$4 3-14s; free under-3s. Free 2-4.45pm Wed
(suggested donation $2). **No credit cards**.
The home of 'Staten Island Chuck', NYC's furry
Groundhog Day forecaster, holds one of the largest
reptile and amphibian collections on the East Coast.

Snug Harbor Cultural Center

Art Lab

*Snug Harbor Cultural Center, Building H
(1-718 447 8667/www.artlab.info).* **Open** 9am-
8pm Mon-Thur; 9am-5pm Fri-Sun. **Admission** free.
This non-profit space runs classes in fine arts,
crafts and photography for children and adults.
The Art Lab Gallery exhibits the work of a different local artist every month.

Newhouse Center for
Contemporary Art

*Snug Harbor Cultural Center, Building C
(1-718 448 2500/www.snug-harbor.org/newhouse).*
Open 10am-5pm Tue-Sun. **Admission** $3 adults;
$2 seniors, under-12s. **Credit** AmEx, MC, V
Staten Island's premier space for contemporary art.

Snug Harbor Cultural Center

*1000 Richmond Terrace, between Snug Harbor
Road & Tysen Street (1-718 448 2500/tickets
1-718 815 7684/www.snug-harbor.org). Travel:
from the Staten Island Ferry, take the S40 bus to
the north gate (tell the bus driver).* **Open** *Galleries*
10am-5pm Tue-Sun. **Admission** $3; $2 seniors,
under-12s. **Credit** AmEx, MC, V.
In addition to the venues that are listed here, Snug
Harbor also houses a 400-seat auditorium and the
city's oldest concert venue.

Staten Island Botanical Garden

*Snug Harbor Cultural Center, Building H (1-718
273 8200/www.sibg.org).* **Open** dawn-dusk daily.
Admission *Chinese Scholar's Garden* $5; $4 seniors,
students, children. *Grounds & other gardens* free.
Credit AmEx, MC, V.
Stroll through more than 20 themed gardens, from
the White Garden (based on Vita Sackville-West's
creation at Sissinghurst Castle) and the tranquil,
pavilion-lined Chinese Scholar's Garden to the
delightful Secret Garden, complete with child-size
castle, maze and a secluded walled garden.

Staten Island Children's Museum

*Snug Harbor Cultural Center (1-718 273 2060/
www.statenislandkids.org).* **Open** *School year*
noon-5pm Tue-Fri; 10am-5pm Sat-Sun. *Summer*
10am-5pm Tue; 10am-8pm Wed; 10am-5pm
Thur-Sun. **Admission** $5. **Credit** AmEx, MC, V.
This museum's hands-on exhibits, workshops and
after-school programmes entertain kids of all ages.

Eat, Drink, Shop

Craftsteak. *See p203.*

Restaurants & Cafés

A feast for the eyes as well as the appetite.

Eating out in New York remains a huge business that knows no boundaries, with cavernous, luxurious new spaces opening weekly (see p195 **Massive attack**). The bulk of these fancy newcomers over the last few years have been Japanese restaurants, such as **Megu Midtown** (see p210), **Buddha Bar** (see p198) and **EN Japanese Brasserie** (see p198), which pair rare sake lists with exotic delicacies beyond the usual kobe beef and blowfish. During 2006, however, the Asian focus started to shift towards China; noteworthy additions to the Chinese restaurant landscape include Philadelphia entrepreneur Stephen Starr's **Buddakan** (see p201), located in the Meatpacking District; **Chinatown Brasserie** (see p197) – the $6 million initiative of John McDonald and Joshua Pickard (of Lever House and Lure) at the space formerly occupied by Time Café; and organic Chinese eaterie **Ginger** (see p214) uptown, which won the 2006 *Time Out New York's* Readers' Choice Eat Out award for best new Upper East Sider (see p182 **The winner is...**). Chinese food is no longer just for take-out.

Meat eaters have been offered many more steakhouse options of late – a few of which are run by former employees of **Peter Luger** (the famed Brooklyn steakhouse; see p215). To keep up with these younger and hipper steakhouses, Michael Stillman – son of Smith & Wollensky founder Alan Stillman – closed Manhattan Ocean Club, a 22-year-old seafood palace in Midtown, replacing it with **Quality Meats** (see p208). It is literally the choice of a new generation – they've converted a once-dull space into a highly stylised industrial theme park. Speaking of theme parks, Tom Colicchio's enormous steakhouse **Craftsteak** (see p203) is about as open and bright as a beef emporium can be: 16-foot ceilings and giant windows lend it a luxurious airiness. The meat line-up reads like a wine list – diners can select by cattle breed, type of feed, cut and time spent ageing. The word is still out on whether the new kids on the block can compete with the master originals, but to learn about how

all those fine cuts of meat are selected by the steakhouse pioneers, see p200 **Meat market**.

It's no surprise that offshoots do well in this city. New Yorkers know exactly what they like and aggressively follow talented chefs to their new digs. The latest batch? Josh DeChellis (of Sumile fame) opened the Italian **Jovia** (see p212) in 2005 (although departed in late 2006), Marc Meyer (Five Points) unveiled the organic **Cookshop** (see p199), Laurent Tourondel has followed up his elegant BLT Steak (see p211) with slick **BLT Fish** (21 W 17th Street, between Fifth & Sixth Avenues, 1-212 691 8888) and Geoffrey Zacharian (Town) has given us the very high-end **Country** (see p204). Read *Time Out's* interview with Zacharian, where he gives his take on the latest chapter of **Le Cirque** (see p209), which recently debuted its third incarnation (see p204 **Face facts**).

The best Restaurants

... for weekend brunch
Clinton Street Baking Company (see p185), Freemans (see p186), Balthazar (see p190).

... for cheap eats
Peanut Butter & Co (see p194), Mama Empanada (p207), Gray's Papaya (p211).

... for the hippest scene
Café Habana (see p184), Thor (see p186), Ditch Plains (see p199).

... for burgers and fries
Fanelli's Café (see p190), Corner Bistro (see p197), Bar Americain (see p206).

... for vegetarians
Caravan of Dreams (see p194), Blossom (see p204), Pure Food & Wine (see p205).

... for late-night grub
Blue Ribbon (see p189), Empire Diner (see p200), Pre:Post (see p200).

... for dining alfresco
La Bottega (see p202), Central Park Boathouse Restaurant (see p213), DuMont (see p214).

---

❶ Purple numbers given in this chapter correspond to the location of each restaurant and café as marked on the street maps. See pp402-412.

GETTING IN

The hardest part about eating out in New York City is the simple fact that there are hundreds, no, make that thousands, of choices. It's downright crazy even for locals to try to keep up with all the new places while still trying to visit old favourites. Naturally, with all the madness, snagging reservations can be difficult, so always be sure to call ahead. Super trendy spots can be fully booked weeks in advance. Luckily, the vast majority require only a few days' notice, or less. Most restaurants fill up between 7pm and 9pm and it's harder to bag reservations on weekends than weekdays. If you don't mind eating early (5pm) or late (after 10pm), your chances of getting in somewhere popular will improve greatly. Alternatively, you can try to nab a reservation by calling at 5pm on the day you want to dine and hoping for a last-minute cancellation. Dress codes are rarely enforced any more, but some ultra-fancy eateries do require men to don a jacket and tie. If in doubt, call ahead and ask. But take heart: you can never really overdress in this town.

The winner is…

Every year *Time Out* recognises the best offerings from the city's thousands of restaurants. The judgements of our culinary experts and the votes of *Time Out New York* readers are combined to form a list of outstanding eateries. Below are some of the winners from the 2006 awards:

Best new Mexican restaurant
La Esquina (*see p185*).

Best hot dog
Gray's Papaya (*see p211*).

Best new tapas restaurant that actually serves Spanish food
Las Ramblas (*see p199*).

Best new hotel restaurant
Thor (*see p186*).

Best new restaurant design
Stanton Social (*see p189*).

Best reason to skip dinner
Room 4 Dessert.(*see p184*).

Best alternative to mega-restaurant mayhem
Naka Naka (*see p202*).

SMOKE BREAK

A strict citywide smoking ban in 2003 has changed the carousing habits of many smokers: some go to bars and restaurants that allow smoking, but these are few and far between. The only legal indoor places to smoke are either venues that largely cater to cigar smokers (and actually sell cigars and cigarettes) or spaces that have created areas specifically for smokers, and that somehow pass legal muster. For a few of our favourite spots, *see p227* **Smoke signal**.

Downtown

Tribeca & south

American

Bouley Bakery & Market
130 West Broadway, at Duane Street (1-212 608 5829). Subway: A, C, 1, 2, 3 to Chambers Street. **Open** *Bakery* 7.30am-7.30pm daily. *Restaurant* 6-11pm Tue-Sat. **Main courses** $19. **Sandwich** $9. **Credit** AmEx, DC, Disc, MC, V. **Map** p402 E31 ❶
Chef David Bouley's new bakery has pastries, breads, sandwiches, salads and pizza on the ground floor; a cellar full of fresh seafood, produce, meats and cheeses; and on the first floor, a dining room with a sushi bar and cocktails by renowned bar chef Albert Trummer. Sidewalk seats appear in warm weather.

French

Landmarc
179 West Broadway, between Leonard & Worth Streets (1-212 343 3883). Subway: 1 to Franklin Street. **Open** noon-2am Mon-Fri; 11am-2am Sat, Sun. **Main courses** $23. **Credit** AmEx, DC, Disc, MC, V. **Map** p402 E31 ❷
Chef Marc Murphy has a great kids' menu, which helps to ensure that the grown-ups have time to savour the really good stuff: tender braised lamb shanks, steaks grilled in an open hearth, mussels steamed with chorizo and onions. An enticing wine list features a good range of bottles that are also provided as half-bottles. The $3 tasting portions of desserts such as blueberry crumble and crème brûlée will please calorie-counters.

Italian

Adrienne's Pizza Bar
54 Stone Street, between Mill Street & Coenties Alley (1-212 248 3838). Subway: A, C, E to Canal Street. **Open** 11am-11pm Mon-Thur; 11am-midnight Fri; 10.30am-midnight Sat, Sun. **Main courses** $20. **Credit** AmEx, DC, MC, V. **Map** p402 F33 ❸
A bright, modern pizzeria on a quaint, cobbled pedestrian street. You can get pizza by the slice or thin-crust pie, and wolf it down at the infamous standing-room

Stanton Social. *See p189.*

bar, or savour it in the sit-down dining area. Dinner guests will find an extended menu of small plates and entrées, and plenty of outdoor seating.

Other locations: Bread, 20 Spring Street, between Elizabeth & Mott Streets, Little Italy (1-212 334 1015).

Chinatown, Little Italy & Nolita

American

Barmarché
14 Spring Street, at Elizabeth Street (1-212 219 2399). Subway: N, R, W to Prince Street; 6 to Spring Street. **Open** 11am-2am Mon-Fri; 9am-2am Sat, Sun. **Main courses** $15. **Credit** AmEx, MC, V. **Map** p403 F30 ➍
Peer inside this bright, white-on-white brasserie, and you'll be tempted to go in and join the party: the dining room is often filled with beautiful people and lively groups, and the kitchen keeps them happy and well fed with generous portions of reliable bistro hits. The menu is American in the melting-pot sense, covering all the greatest hits and no-nonsense dishes from around the world: homemade fettuccine with pesto, thick gazpacho with a dollop of guacamole, tuna tartare with grated Asian pear and citrus ponzu, and a made-in-the-USA juicy burger.

Porcupine
20 Prince Street, between Elizabeth & Mott Streets (1-212 966 8886). Subway: N, R, W to Prince Street; 6 to Spring Street. **Open** 11am-11pm Mon-Fri; 11am-11.30pm Sat, Sun. **Main courses** $20. **Credit** AmEx. **Map** p403 F29 ➎
Jacques Ouari is mixing things up once again: in early 2005 he closed his short-lived French brasserie, Mix It, and reopened it as a café-tavern called Porcupine, preparing audacious seasonal dishes from local artisanal ingredients. For lunch, you can try hearty sandwiches like the croque-madame with fried egg and vinegar radishes, and grilled leg of lamb with prune-hyssop butter and arugula (rocket). Dinners are meaty, too: suckling pig with apple and celeriac, or mustard-braised veal with lemon pickles. Non-meat dishes could include Taylor Bay scallop and blackfish stew with almond milk and acorn squash.

Room 4 Dessert
17 Cleveland Place, between Kenmare & Spring Streets (1-212 941 5405). Subway: 6 to Spring Street; F, V to Broadway-Lafayette. **Open** 6pm-midnight Mon-Thur; 6pm-1am Fri, Sat. **Average dessert** $11. **Credit** AmEx, MC, V. **Map** p403 F30 ➏
Yes, you could plan to stop by this dessert-only restaurant *after* you've had a meal somewhere else, but you'd be full, and your taste buds wouldn't be optimally receptive to Will Goldfarb's spectrum of flavours. Instead, why not have dessert for dinner once in your life?

Chinese

Golden Bridge
50 Bowery, between Bayard & Canal Streets (1-212 227 8831). Subway: B, D to Grand Street; J, M, N, Q, R, W, Z, 6 to Canal Street. **Open** 9am-11pm daily. **Dim sum** $2. **Credit** AmEx, DC, Disc, MC, V. **Map** p403 F31 ➐
Dim sum devotees often pick places in Flushing, Queens, over Manhattan options, but they should reconsider this serious Cantonese venue. An armada of carts offers flavourful standards like clams in black-bean sauce, plus unusual items like egg tarts with a soft taro crust. Look for the elusive cart filled with an irresistible, lightly sweetened tofu.

Cuban

Café Habana
17 Prince Street, at Elizabeth Street (1-212 625 2001). Subway: N, R, W to Prince Street; 6 to Spring Street. **Open** 9am-midnight daily. **Main courses** $10. **Credit** AmEx, MC, V. **Map** p403 F29 ➑
Hipsters storm this café day and night for its addictive grilled corn doused in butter and rolled in grated cheese and chilli powder. Other staples include crisp beer-battered catfish *tortas*, and juicy marinated skirt steak with rice and black beans.
Other locations: 757 Fulton Street, at South Portland Avenue, Fort Greene, Brooklyn (1-718 858 9500); Café Habana to Go, 229 Elizabeth Street, between Houston & Prince Streets, Soho (1-212 625 2002).

Eclectic

Public
210 Elizabeth Street, between Prince & Spring Streets (1-212 343 7011). Subway: N, R, W to Prince Street; 6 to Spring Street. **Open** 6-11.30pm Mon-Fri; 6-12.30pm Sat; 6-10.30pm Sun. **Main courses** $20. **Credit** AmEx, MC, V. **Map** p403 F29 ➒

Tax and tipping

Most New York restaurants don't add a service charge to the bill unless there are six or more people in your party. So it's customary to give 15 to 20 per cent of the total bill as a tip. The easiest way to figure out the amount is to double the 8.625 per cent sales tax. Complain – preferably to a manager – if you feel the service is under par, but only in the most extreme cases should you completely withhold a tip. Remember that servers are paid far below minimum wage and rely on tips to pay the rent. Bartenders get tipped, too; $1 a drink should ensure friendly pours until last call.

This gorgeous industrial space, designed by AvroKo, is high on concept: machine-age glass lamps, pre-war office doors and a library card catalogue make sly references to public spaces. Chef Brad Farmerie, who worked at London's acclaimed Providores, has created the menu in tandem with Providores colleagues New Zealanders Anna Hansen and Peter Gordon. Look for a Kiwi influence in dishes like grilled kangaroo on coriander falafel and New Zealand venison with pomegranates and truffles. Desserts are equally eclectic.

Mexican

La Esquina

106 Kenmare Street, at Cleveland Place (1-646 613 7100). Subway: 6 to Spring Street. **Open** 6pm-midnight daily. **Main courses** $18. **Credit** AmEx, MC, V. **Map** p403 F30 ❿

Many first-time diners here stand on the corner of Lafayette and Kenmare Streets staring at the deli sign, wondering if they wrote down the wrong address. After watching dozens of people who in no way look like employees walk through a door marked 'employees only', it becomes clear that the restaurant does lurk within. Dishes like spicy sirloin with poblano chillies, Mayan shrimp coated in a chipotle glaze and grilled fish with avocado salsa somehow taste better when served amid exposed brick, wrought iron and wax-dripping candelabras.

Pan-Asian

Kitchen Club

30 Prince Street, at Mott Street (1-212 274 0025). Subway: N, R, W to Prince Street; 6 to Spring Street. **Open** 12.30-4pm, 5.30-11.30pm Mon-Sat; 12.30-4pm, 5.30-10.30pm Sun. **Main courses** $21. **Credit** AmEx, MC, V. **Map** p403 F29 ⓫

The quasi host of this inviting pan-Asian spot is diminutive Chibi – a French bulldog who defers only to chef-owner Marja Samsom. Eclectic dishes with a Japanese tinge are carefully made and prettily presented. The dumplings are a justifiable source of pride, with tasty, inventive fillings including salmon tartare and tofu with chrysanthemum. And meat eaters will find sweet bliss in venison glazed with a spicy raspberry sauce and sprinkled with huckleberries.

Lovely Day

196 Elizabeth Street, between Prince & Spring Streets (1-212 925 3310). Subway: J, M, Z to Bowery; 6 to Spring Street. **Open** noon-11pm Mon-Thur; noon-midnight Fri; 11am-midnight Sat; 11am-11pm Sun. **Main courses** $10. **Credit** AmEx. **Map** p403 F30 ⓬

Cash-strapped twentysomethings (and their admirers) pack this inexpensive Nolita eaterie to gossip and dine on an assortment of Thai-themed curries and noodle dishes. If you're looking for a little heat, try the ginger-fried chicken served with spicy aïoli and lime sauce. The laid-back decor of simple red booths is

matched at times by the slow service. Relax and hold out for the crispy banana rolls served with vanilla ice-cream, honey and sesame – you'll be glad you did.

Pizza

Lombardi's

32 Spring Street, between Mott & Mulberry Streets (1-212 941 7994). Subway: 6 to Spring Street. **Open** 11.30am-11pm Mon-Thur; 11.30am-midnight Fri, Sat; 11.30am-10pm Sun. **Large pizza** $15. **No credit cards**. **Map** p403 F30 ⓭

Lombardi's is the city's oldest pizzeria, established in 1905, and offering pies at their best – made in a coal-fired oven and with a chewy, thin crust. The pepperoni is fantastic, as are the killer meatballs in tomato sauce. The setting is classic pizza-parlour, with wooden booths and red-and-white checked tablecloths.

Vietnamese

Doyers Vietnamese Restaurant

11 Doyers Street, between Bowery & Pell Street (1-212 513 1521). Subway: J, M, N, Q, R, W, Z, 6 to Canal Street. **Open** 11am-10pm Mon-Thur, Sun; 11am-11pm Fri, Sat. **Main courses** $8. **Credit** AmEx. **Map** p402 F31 ⓮

The search to find this restaurant is part of the fun: it's tucked away in a basement on a zigzagging Chinatown alley. The 33 appetisers include balls of grilled minced shrimp wrapped around sugarcane sticks and a delicious Vietnamese crêpe filled with shrimp and pork. Hot-pot soups, served on a table-top stove, are made with an exceptional fish-broth base and brim with vegetables. For maximum enjoyment, come with a six-pack of Singha in tow (the restaurant is BYOB).

Lower East Side

American creative

Clinton Street Baking Company

4 Clinton Street, between Houston & Stanton Streets (1-646 602 6263). Subway: F to Delancey Street; J, M, Z to Delancey-Essex Streets. **Open** 8am-11pm Mon-Fri; 10am-4pm, 6-11pm Sat; 10am-4pm Sun. **Main courses** $13. **Credit** AmEx, DC, MC, V. **Map** p403 G29 ⓯

The warm buttermilk biscuits here are reason enough to face the brunchtime crowds; if you want to avoid the onslaught, however, the homey Lower East Side spot is just as reliable at lunch and dinner, when locals drop in for fish tacos, grilled pizzas and a daily $10 beer-and-burger special: 8oz of Black Angus topped with Swiss cheese and caramelised onions, served with a Brooklyn lager. To better your odds for getting a table at brunch (the best in town), show up between 9am and 10am, when coffee and pastries are served before the rest of the kitchen opens.

Eat, Drink, Shop

Freemans

2 Freeman Alley, off Rivington Street, between
Bowery & Chrystie Street (1-212 420 0012).
Subway: F, V to Lower East Side-Second Avenue;
J, M, Z to Bowery. **Open** 5pm-midnight Mon-
Fri; 11am-4pm, 6pm-midnight Sat, Sun. **Main**
courses $22. **Credit** AmEx, DC, Disc, MC, V.
Map p403 F29 ⓰

Once you eventually find this secret restaurant
(hidden at the end of Freeman Alley) you will feel
as though you have stepped into a ski lodge on a
mountaintop in Aspen, Colorado. Those in the
know feast on affordable dishes like juicy trout,
warm artichoke dip, rich wild-boar terrine and
perfect batches of mac and cheese, plus a few retro
oddities like 'devils on horseback' (prunes stuffed
with blue cheese and wrapped in bacon), all
served under the gaze of mounted animal heads.
Brunch, when raised waffles with banana-maple
syrup are served and the sun streams through the
front windows, is a rather more tranquil affair.
This is also a popular spot for cocktails.

Austrian

Thor

107 Rivington Street, between Essex & Ludlow
Streets (1-212 796-8040). Subway: F to Delancey.
Open 7am-midnight Mon-Wed; 7am-1am Thur,
Fri; 11am-1am Sat; 11am-midnight Sun. **Main**
courses $22. **Credit** AmEx, Disc, DC, MC, V.
Map p403 G29 ⓱

A nice lobby and a solid ribeye don't cut it any
more at the city's top hotels. Restaurateurs are hir-
ing celebrity chefs and cutting-edge designers and
expecting the food to taste as good as the place
looks. At Thor, the marriage was an instant success: crowds packed the Lower East Side hotspot
(its name is an acronym for The Hotel On
Rivington) to savour one of Downtown's most fashionable scenes and delicious meals. The à la carte
menu is organised by temperature; cold dishes are
listed first, followed by warm ones, leading up to
the fully hot. Each (vaguely Austrian) dish is artfully positioned on a large white plate.

Daily bread

Like many New Yorkers, bagels travelled
from afar to make this metropolis their home.
When Jewish Eastern European immigrants
began arriving in New York City in the late
19th century, they brought with them a
taste for dense, chewy breads, including
a ring-shaped roll known by the Yiddish
word *beygl*, derived from the German
word *beugel*, meaning 'bracelet' or 'ring'.

Peddlers walked the crowded, tenement-
lined streets of the Lower East Side (a
common destination for Jewish newcomers),
brandishing long sticks stacked with fresh
bagels. Competition was fierce, and in 1907
a very exclusive bagel bakers' union formed
in New York City. (One of its rules stipulated
that only the sons of members could become
apprentices.) The union knew the real secret

Cafés

Brown

*61 Hester Street, between Essex & Ludlow Streets
(1-212 477 2427). Subway: F to East Broadway.*
Open 9am-11pm Tue-Sat; 9am-6pm Sun. **Main
courses** $12. **Credit** AmEx. **Map** p403 G30 ⑱
Owner Alejandro Alcocer opened this small café to
compensate for the lack of a decent cup of joe in the
'hood. Not only can you get a mean latte here, but
now you can also choose from more than 20 entrées
made from organic ingredients. Daily specials,
scribbled on the front-door glass, usually include a
soup, a frittata and a cheese-and-fruit plate, and
sandwiches are also available. Alcocer recently
started serving beer and wine and introduced a dinner menu. Sculpted wooden-plank tables, benches
and stump-like stools give the place the feel of an
afternoon picnic straight from the glossy pages of
Surface. A great spot in which to linger with a
newspaper, or from which to watch the outside
street action from the bay window seats.

Chinese

Congee Village

*100 Allen Street, between Broome & Delancey Streets
(1-212 941 1818). Subway: F to Delancey Street; J,
M, Z to Delancey-Essex Streets.* **Open** 10.30am-2am
daily. **Main courses** $12. **Credit** AmEx, MC, V.
Map p403 F30 ⑲
If you've never indulged in the starchy comfort of
congee, this mainly Cantonese restaurant is a good
place to be initiated. The rice porridge, cooked to
bubbling in a clay pot over a slow fire, is at its best
early in the day; pick a chunky version from the 30
or so options on offer, such as the treasure-laden
seafood or sliced fish. Crab is impeccably fresh, as
is the well seasoned whole fish served over glistening Chinese broccoli. Rice and noodle dishes are also
available, with rice dishes served in bamboo pots,
and there's a good range of dim sum. It may seem
incongruous, but the Congee does a great Pina
Colada – and it will only cost you $3 during the
weekday happy hour (4-7pm).

of making a fine bagel: give it
a quick bath in boiling water
before baking. This brief dunk
is responsible for the bagel's
signature shiny crust and
chewy interior.

As Jews in New York began
moving out of the Lower East
Side, they took their culinary
traditions with them. Bagels,
which became a standard offering
in delicatessens throughout the
city, were typically flavoured with
onions or poppy seeds and topped
with a thick schmear of cream
cheese and a piece of the salty smoked
salmon known as lox. As Jewish humour
and traditions became part of the city's
cultural fabric, so did bagels. For Jews
and gentiles alike, weekend brunch in the
city just isn't complete without bagels,
coffee and the plump Sunday edition
of the *New York Times*.

Although bagels can be found everywhere
these days, from Starbucks to McDonald's,
tracking down the traditional boiled and baked
version can be tough. Most bakeries use
mechanised ovens that steam-mist the dough
instead of boiling it, which results in soft,
puffy rolls without the classic chewy crust.

For a taste of the real old-fashioned thing,
visit the legendary H&H Bagels (*photos left*

and above), either the Upper West Side shop
(2239 Broadway, at 80th Street, 1-212 595
8003) or the big factory in Hell's Kitchen
(639 W 46th Street, between Eleventh &
Twelfth Avenues, 1-212 595 8000), across
from the Intrepid Sea-Air-Space Museum.
Both are open 24/7.

While H&H's creations are the perfect
snack, just one roll from Ess-a-Bagel (359
First Avenue, at 21st Street, 1-212 980 1010;
831 Third Avenue, at 51st Street, 1-212 980
4315) could easily be a meal for two or three.
Since 1976 this family-run operation has
been making monstrously big bagels with
exceptional texture and flavour. Just be sure
to come early on weekends, or you risk
waiting in a line that snakes out the door.

Eat, Drink, Shop

Eclectic

Schiller's Liquor Bar
131 Rivington Street, at Norfolk Street (1-212 260 4555). Subway: F to Delancey Street; J, M, Z to Delancey-Essex Streets. **Open** 11am-4am Mon-Fri; 10am-4am Sat, Sun. **Main courses** $12. **Credit** AmEx, MC, V. **Map** p403 G29 ⑳
Decorated with old mirrors and antique subway tiles, Keith McNally's latest is a playful all-day bohemian hangout that attracts a variety show of a clientele, from suits to drag queens and artfully tousled locals. No dish, except steak, costs more than $16. The menu is a mix of French bistro classics (steak-frites), British pub faves (Welsh rarebit) and Louisiana lunch choices (oyster po'boys). Traversing the wine list is a cinch: it's a mere six bottles long, designated 'cheap', 'decent' or 'good'. Desserts are mandatory.

Stanton Social
99 Stanton Street, between Ludlow & Orchard Streets (1-212 995 0099). Subway: F, V to Lower East Side-Second Avenue. **Open** 11am-4am Mon-Fri; 10am-4am Sat, Sun. **Main courses** $14. **Credit** AmEx, DC, Disc, MC, V. **Map** p403 G29 ㉑
Plenty of trendy spots have opened on the LES, but none with as much eye candy as this. Chandeliers, lizard-skin banquettes and retro booths only hint at the 1940s-inspired elegance of the three-level restaurant. Chris Santos has created 40 shareable, international plates (light dishes followed by heavier ones) that all receive special treatment. French onion soup comes in dumpling form; red-snapper tacos are covered with a fiery mango and avocado salsa. The only discernible miss is the Peking duck quesadilla, a needlessly sweet fusion of Asian and Spanish flavours. **Photo** *p183.*

Italian

Falai
68 Clinton Street, between Rivington & Stanton Streets (1-212 253 1960). Subway: F, J, M, Z to Delancey-Essex Streets **Open** 6-11pm Tue-Thur; 6pm-midnight Fri-Sun. **Main courses** $20. **Credit** AmEx, MC, V. **Map** p403 G29 ㉒
Former Bread Tribeca chef Iacopo Falai has opened his own eatery, and it's much smaller and more precious than his last spot: just 40 seats, in an all-white room. You'll see hints of his past, though, like a boisterous, fashionable crowd, a modern Italian menu and a sexy location (on the LES's restaurant row). Portions are quite small but prices are reasonable and dishes inspired and well executed. **Photos** *p190 and 191.*

Japanese

Cube 63
63 Clinton Street, between Rivington & Stanton Streets (1-212 228 6751). Subway: F to Delancey Street; J, M, Z to Delancey-Essex Streets. **Open** 5pm-midnight Mon-Thur, Sun; 5pm-1am Fri, Sat. **Sushi meal** $19. **Credit** MC, V. **Map** p403 G29 ㉓

This glowing lime-green dining room is tiny, but the inventive flavours created by sushi chefs Ben and Ken Lau (brothers who worked at Bond Street) are bigger than you'll find just about anywhere else. Jumbo speciality rolls are the main draw: shrimp tempura hooks up with eel, avocado, cream cheese and caviar in the Tahiti roll; the Volcano is crab and shrimp topped with spicy lobster salad then set aflame with a blowtorch in an eruption of melding flavours.

Spanish

Oliva
161 E Houston Street, at Allen Street (1-212 228 4143). Subway: F, V to Lower East Side-Second Avenue. **Open** 5.30pm-midnight Mon-Thur; 5.30pm-1am Fri; 11.30am-3.30pm, 5.30pm-1am Sat, Sun. **Main courses** $17. **Tapas** $5. **Credit** AmEx. **Map** p403 F29 ㉔
A bright red *toro* (bull) is stencilled on each table at Oliva. Young downtowners read the daily selections from an inscribed mirror over the bar; pintxos change daily. Serrano ham croquettes or tortilla are a tasty prelude to heartier dishes, such as seafood-heavy paella. On Wednesday and Sunday sangria flows freely while a Latin band keeps the place jumping.

Suba
109 Ludlow Street, between Delancey & Rivington Streets (1-212 982 5714). Subway: F to Delancey Street; J, M, Z to Delancey-Essex Streets. **Open** 6pm-2am Mon-Thur; 6pm-4am Fri, Sat; 6pm-midnight Sun. **Main courses** $24. **Credit** AmEx, MC, V. **Map** p403 G30 ㉕
Down the suspended steel staircase from the loud tapas bar is another scene entirely. Suba fuses traditional Spanish dishes with modern techniques. Duck breast with white-peach coulis and cinnamon sauce is undeniably sexy, especially when followed by the sultry dark-chocolate almond cake or a lime-pie cocktail.

Soho

American

Blue Ribbon
97 Sullivan Street, between Prince & Spring Streets (1-212 274 0404). Subway: C, E to Spring Street. **Open** 4pm-4am Tue-Sun. **Main courses** $22. **Credit** AmEx, DC, MC, V. **Map** p403 E30 ㉖
Where else, at 3am, can you slurp down just-shucked oysters and smear bone marrow on toast? The city's off-duty chefs long ago elected this Soho sleeper to be their post-work playhouse, and it's still an industry favourite. Every night past midnight, the Bromberg brothers' flagship restaurant begins filling up with a *Who's Who* of the restaurant biz. You might need patience landing even a perch at the bar. Ask for a menu while you wait and decide if you're going upscale (sevruga caviar) or down (matzo-ball soup). **Other locations**: Blue Ribbon Brooklyn, 280 Fifth Avenue, between Garfield Place & 1st Street, Park Slope, Brooklyn (1-718 840 0404).

Fanelli's Café

94 Prince Street, at Mercer Street (1-212 226 9412). Subway: N, R, W to Prince Street. **Open** 10am-2.30am Mon-Thur; 10am-3am Fri, Sat; 11am-12.30am Sun. **Main courses** $10. **Credit** AmEx, MC, V. **Map** p403 E29 ㉗

Deemed the second-oldest restaurant in New York, Fanelli's has stood at this cobblestoned intersection since 1847, and local artists and worldly tourists pour into the lively landmark for perfectly charred beef patties on toasted onion rolls. The long bar, prints of boxing legends and checked tablecloths add to the charm. Specials, such as pumpkin ravioli or grilled mahimahi with lime and coriander, are surprisingly good offerings in a sea of pub grub.

French

Balthazar

80 Spring Street, between Broadway & Crosby Street (1-212 965 1414). Subway: N, R, W to Prince Street; 6 to Spring Street. **Open** 7.30-11.30am, noon-5pm, 6pm-1am Mon-Wed; 7.30-11.30am, noon-5pm, 6pm-1.30am Thur; 7.30-11.30am, noon-5pm, 6pm-2am Fri; 10am-4pm, 6pm-2am Sat; 10am-4pm, 5.30pm-midnight Sun. **Main courses** $21. **Credit** AmEx, MC, V. **Map** p403 E30 ㉘

Not only is Balthazar still trendy, but the kitchen rarely puts a foot wrong. At dinner, the place is perennially packed with rail-thin lookers in head to toe Prada. But the bread is great, the food is good and the service is surprisingly friendly. The three-tiered seafood platter casts the most impressive shadow of any appetiser in town. The frisée aux lardons is exemplary. Roasted chicken on mashed potatoes for two, délicieux. Don't hate the patrons because they're beautiful – just join them. Brunch is a must here.

Félix

340 West Broadway, at Grand Street (1-212 431 0021). Subway: A, C, E, 1 to Canal Street. **Open** noon-midnight daily. **Main courses** $19. **Credit** AmEx. **Map** p403 E30 ㉙

Antique ads, large glass doors that open on to the sidewalk and a pressed-tin ceiling provide a timeless backdrop for a modish scene (you may recognise it from films like *Igby Goes Down*). The food has actually improved over Félix's 13-year tenure. You come here to eat steak-frites – choose among peppercorn, béarnaise or roquefort sauces to accompany a very tender piece of meat and golden frites. Félix is most frenzied at weekend brunch, when patrons spill out of the front door with Caipirinhas in hand.

Italian

Ama

48 MacDougal Street, between Houston & Prince Streets (1-212 358 1785). Subway: C, E to Spring Street. **Open** 11am-3pm, 5-11pm daily. **Main courses** $19. **Credit** AmEx, Disc, MC, V. **Map** p403 E29 ㉚

Falai. See p189.

Although Donatella Arpaia gave her name to the uptown restaurant she runs with chef David Burke (davidburke & donatella) her heart seems to be here, at this much smaller, much homier new Soho spot. She named the place after the Italian word for love; it is indeed a lovely little restaurant. The food is a tribute to the cuisine of her mom's native Puglia. Chef Turibio Girardi serves rustic fare with upscale twists, such as rabbit stuffed with chestnuts, and cod with cream of fava beans and wild chicory. If you don't have time for dinner, stop by the bar for an espresso and a plate of homemade almond cookies.

Turkish

Antique Garage

41 Mercer Street, between Broome & Grand Streets (1-212 219 1019). Subway: J, M, N, Q, R, W, Z, 6 to Canal Street. **Open** noon-midnight daily. **Main courses** $11. **Credit** AmEx, MC, V. **Map** p403 E30 ③
Formerly an auto-repair shop, the Antique Garage has good acoustics and ample Turkish carpeting to control the volume of its garrulous crowd, which comes for the live music as well as the food. Other assets: faded paintings and peeling mirrors on the walls, heirloom plates and antique chandeliers – all of which are for sale. The kitchen manages to live up to the decor with decent portions of borek (feta-stuffed filo), creamy houmous with fried toast points, and seared tuna doused in red pepper purée.

East Village

Cuban

Cafecito

185 Avenue C, at 12th Street (1-212 253 9966). Subway: L to First Avenue. **Open** 6-10pm Tue, Thur, Sun; 6pm-2am Fri, Sat. **Main courses** $12. **No credit cards. Map** p403 G28 ③
The relaxed outdoor bar is just one of the authentic touches at Cafecito ('tiny coffee'). You can sip a Mojito and nibble on green plantain chips as you contemplate menu choices: the aborcito de Cuba gives you a taste of each of the small hot appetisers – the best of which are the bollos, corn and black-bean fritters. In addition to blackboard specials like char-grilled skirt steak with chimichurri sauce, the place does a perfectly pressed Cuban sandwich, which is always spot on.

Eclectic

Ludo

42 E 1st Street, between First & Second Avenues (1-212 777 5617). Subway: F, V to Lower East Side-Second Avenue. **Open** 6-11pm daily. **Main courses** $22. **Credit** AmEx, MC, V. **Map** p403 F29 ③
The space formerly known as Chez es Saada has now reopened as Ludo, an equally sensuous restaurant and lounge with blue lighting that ripples off

Aroma.

stone walls, mimicking the movement of water. The name means 'I play' in Latin, and chef Einat Adimony has created a menu of global meze plates to reflect that idea. Cantaloupe gelato is encrusted with almonds and wrapped in prosciutto while the pork-belly spring rolls come with a tangy tamarind dipping sauce. Descending the steps from the ground-level bar to the grotto-like dining area below is still a thrill.

French

Jules Bistro

65 St Marks Place, between First & Second Avenues (1-212 477 5560). Subway: L to First Avenue. **Open** 11am-4pm, 5pm-1am Mon-Fri; 10am-4pm, 5pm-1am Sat, Sun. **Main courses** $14. **Credit** AmEx. **Map** p403 F28 ㉞

Habitués at this chic enclave may have scored high-paying jobs Uptown, but they still prefer to play Downtown. Candles flicker, tables are separated by groovy beaded partitions and the live jazz has a swinging, loungey feel (lively groups like to be near the bar; quieter diners head for the narrow back room). The kitchen turns out exceedingly good traditional Parisian bistro fare: beef stew simmered in red wine or spiced lamb shanks with figs; veal scaloppine comes with gnocchi bathed in gorgonzola and truffle oil. The $9.50 brunch features organic eggs that can be cooked in a variety of ways.

Indian

Spice Cove

326 E 6th Street, between First & Second Avenues (1-212 674 8884). Subway: F, V to Lower East Side-Second Avenue. **Open** 11.30am-midnight Mon-Fri; 11.30am-12.30am Sat, Sun. **Main courses** $12. **Credit** AmEx, DC, Disc, MC, V. **Map** p403 F28 ㉟

Curry Row is looking less rough around the edges, as new restaurants like this one, with snazzy decor and a refined menu, replace the old garish curry houses. Bright orange walls, stone archways and candles provide a seductive setting; St Germain stands in for sitar music; and in place of an all you can-eat buffet are chef Muhammed Ahmed Ali's specialities. Expect properly spiced dishes such as chickpeas stir-fried with coriander, cumin and cinnamon and fenugreek-scented Atlantic salmon crowned with tomato masala.

Italian

Aroma

36 E 4th Street, between Bowery & Lafayette Street (1-212 375 0100). Subway: 6 to Astor Place. **Open** 5pm-midnight Tue-Thur; 6pm-1am Fri; 12.30am-3.30pm, 6pm-2am Sat; 5pm-1am Sun. **Main courses** $18. **Credit** AmEx, DC, MC, V. **Map** p403 F29 ㊱

This enchanting, slender wine bar has been carved out of a former streetwear boutique; raindrop crystal chandeliers hang from the ceiling, olives are laid out single file in porcelain vessels, and a long brick wall

5pm-1am Fri; 11.30am-4pm, 5pm-1am Sat;
11.30am-4pm, 5-11pm Sun. **Main courses** $11.
Credit AmEx, MC, V. **Map** p403 G28 ⑱
This Mexican newcomer features wood, tiles and
stucco from Mexico, a thatched roof inside the dining room and an elaborate hacienda-style courtyard
outside. In the kitchen, chef Patricio Sandoval creates dishes inspired by the cuisine of southern
Mexico, like smoked mahimahi ceviche, ribeye
steak with cactus salad and tomatillo-avocado
chimichurri, plus six kinds of tacos sold by weight.
At brunch, breakfast tacos and Mexican sausage
are a welcome break from bacon and eggs.

Seafood

Jack's Luxury Oyster Bar
*246 E 5th Street, between Second & Third Avenues
(1-212 673 0338). Subway: F, V to Lower East Side-
Second Avenue; 6 to Astor Place.* **Open** 6-11pm Mon-
Sat. **Prix fixe** $75 (4 courses). **Credit** AmEx, DC,
Disc, MC, V. **Map** p403 F29 ⑲
Jack and Grace Lamb, who revealed themselves as
obsessively detail-oriented with Jewel Bako, have
transformed the first two floors of their romantic
5th Street townhouse into a doll's house of a restaurant. The real magic unfolds in the tiny upstairs dining room, where a mere dozen or so guests settle in
near a fireplace for each night's dinner party, a phenomenal five-course feast by chef Maxime Bilet. On
the menu, you might find decadent lobster Newburg
or pan-seared halibut in a vermouth-camomile
sauce with chive blossoms.

Mermaid Inn
*96 Second Avenue, between 5th & 6th Streets (1-212
674 5870). Subway: F, V to Lower East Side-Second
Avenue.* **Open** 5.30-11pm Mon-Thur; 11.30pm-
midnight Fri, Sat; 5-10pm Sun. **Main courses** $20.
Credit AmEx, DC, Disc, MC, V. **Map** p403 F28 ⑳
The menu changes seasonally, but there's always the
award-winning overstuffed lobster roll and spaghetti
with spicy shrimp, scallops and calamari, topped with
arugula (rocket). Everything tastes even better in
summer, when you can sit in the back garden. The
only non-maritime menu item is the complimentary
dessert, which is whatever the chef feels like making. This Mermaid's lure is irresistible, so make reservations or suffer in the queue.

Thai

Pukk
*71 First Avenue, between 4th & 5th Streets (1-212
253 2740). Subway: F, V to Lower East Side-Second
Avenue.* **Open** 11am-11pm daily. **Main courses** $7.
Credit MC, V. **Map** p403 F29 ㉑
Strip this groovy little hole in the wall of its East
Village clientele and you might mistake it for an
empty pool: some of the stools and tables are crafted
from concrete and small circular tiles (they grow out
of the walls like pool steps), and the space basks in

displays the Italian wines (including Gragnano, a rare
sparkling red). Chef Christopher Daly's dishes are
carefully conceived: a duck salad is loaded with lardons, wild chicory and a soft-poached egg. The excellent 'lamb three ways' consists of a tower of braised
shoulder, a patty of neck meat, pine nuts, raisins and
capers, and a juicy, rosemary-rubbed chop.

Poetessa
*92 Second Avenue, between 5th & 6th Streets
(1-212 387 0065). Subway: F, V to Lower East
Side-Second Avenue; 6 to Astor Place.* **Open** 5-11pm
Mon-Thur; noon-4.30pm, 5pm-2am Fri, Sat; 5-10pm
Sun. **Main courses** $18. **Credit** AmEx, Disc, MC,
V. **Map** p403 F28 ⑰
Chef Pippa Calland has been working in the food biz
since she was 14, and now she's taken over this space
(which previously housed East Post) to share what
she's learned. The dining room is comfortably familiar – exposed brick walls, wooden furniture, ceiling
fans. And Calland follows through with flavourful
Italian dishes: parmesan-battered soft-shell crab with
courgettes and fresh peas; sizzling own-made pork
meatballs; and plenty of hearty pasta dishes.

Mexican

Mercadito
*179 Avenue B, between 11th & 12th Streets
(1-212 529 6493). Subway: 6 to Astor Place.*
Open 5pm-midnight Mon-Thur; noon-4pm,

a mysterious yellow-green glow. The folks behind Highline and Peep have opened this third spot with a twist: they're cooking only vegetarian Thai dishes. So instead of pork and duck, you'll get your thrills from sweet breaded-and-fried tofu, seriously spicy tom yum soup, linguine in yellow curry and more.

Vegetarian/organic

Caravan of Dreams

405 E 6th Street, between First Avenue & Avenue A (1-212 254 1613). Subway: F, V to Lower East Side-Second Avenue; 6 to Astor Place. **Open** 11am-11pm Mon-Fri, Sun; 11am-midnight Sat. **Main courses** $15. **Credit** AmEx, MC, V. **Map** p403 F28 ㊷

Vegetarians, vegans and raw-foodists unite! A long-time East Village hangout now offers both regular meat-free dishes – grilled-seitan nachos, black-bean chilli, stir-fries – and 'live foods' made from uncooked fruits, vegetables, nuts and seeds. Live 'houmous' (whipped up from cold-processed tahini and raw almonds instead of the usual chickpeas) can be scooped up with pressed flaxseed 'chips'; the live Love Boat pairs almond-Brazil nut 'meatballs' with mango chutney and cool marinara sauce on a napa cabbage leaf. Naturally, there are loads of salads and some macrobiotically balanced rice-and-seaweed combos. The kitchen is kosher-certified.

Venezuelan

Caracas Arepa Bar

91 E 7th Street, at First Avenue (1-212 228 5062). Subway: F, V to Lower East Side-Second Avenue; 6 to Astor Place. **Open** noon-11pm Tue-Sat; noon-10pm Sun. **Arepa** $4. **Credit** AmEx, DC, Disc, MC, V. **Map** p403 F28 ㊸

This endearing little Venezuelan spot, with flower-patterned, vinyl-covered tables, zaps you straight to South America. The secret is in the house-made arepas: each golden patty is made from scratch, daily. The golden pitta-like pockets are stuffed with a choice of 18 fillings, such as chicken and avocado or mushrooms with tofu. The simplest ones, like plain butter or nata (Venezuelan sour cream), are the best. Top off your snack with a cocada, a thick and creamy milkshake made with freshly grated coconut and cinnamon.

Greenwich Village/Noho

American

Jane

100 W Houston Street, between La Guardia Place & Thompson Street (1-212 254 7000). Subway: C, E to Spring Street; 1 to Houston Street. **Open** 11.30am-midnight Mon-Sat; 11am-11pm Sun. **Main courses** $19. **Credit** AmEx, MC, V. **Map** p403 E29 ㊹

One visit, and you too will suffer a Jane's addiction. This popular neighbourhood spot has warm lighting, plush banquette seating and sunny sidewalk tables;

they all match well with the good vibe and pleasant menu. A flavourful bouquet of baby arugula (rocket), blue cheese and pear is sprinkled with dried cranberries and toasted pumpkin seeds; fluffy pillows of ricotta gnocchi sit in a rich pool of white truffle and parmesan sauce. And at brunch, hollandaise-glossed poached eggs top delicious crab and crawfish cakes.

American creative

Blue Hill

75 Washington Place, between Washington Square West & Sixth Avenue (1-212 539 1776). Subway: A, B, C, D, E, F, V to W 4th Street. **Open** 5.30-11pm Mon-Sat; 5.30-10pm Sun. **Main courses** $25. **Credit** AmEx, DC, MC, V. **Map** p403 E28 ㊺

This beloved gourmand destination has a knack for scoring the best local produce all year round. Chefs Dan Barber and Michael Anthony succeed so consistently with their dishes because of their solid foundation in classical French cooking. When in season, Blue Hill's strawberries have more berry flavour, and its heirloom tomatoes are juicier than anyone else's. The poached foie gras, duck breast in beurre blanc, tender roasted chicken and mango sorbet are sublime.

Cafés

Peanut Butter & Co

240 Sullivan Street, between Bleecker & W 3rd Streets (1-212 677 3995). Subway: A, B, C, D, E, F, V to W 4th Street. **Open** 11am-9pm Sun-Thur; 11am-10pm Fri, Sat. **Sandwich** $6. **Credit** AmEx, DC, Disc, MC, V. **Map** p403 E29 ㊻

To Americans, nothing brings on an attack of 'happy childhood' nostalgia like a peanut butter sandwich. Every day, the staff at Peanut Butter & Co grind out a fresh batch of peanut butter, which is used to create gooey mood-pacifiers like the popular Elvis – the King's infamous grilled favourite of peanut butter, banana and honey. Owner Lee Zalben confesses to a weakness for the warm sandwich of cinnamon-raisin peanut butter, vanilla cream cheese and tart apple slices. Goober-free menu items, like tuna melts and bologna sandwiches, continue the brown-bag theme.

Italian

Il Buco

47 Bond Street, between Lafayette Street & Bowery (1-212 533 1932). Subway: B, D, F, V to Broadway-Lafayette Street; 6 to Bleecker Street. **Open** 6pm-midnight Mon; noon-4pm, 6pm-midnight Tue-Thur; noon-4pm, 6pm-1am Fri, Sat; 5pm-midnight Sun.* **Main courses** $28. **Credit** AmEx, MC, V. **Map** p403 F29 ㊼

The old-world charm of well-worn communal tables and flickering lamps may help explain why a 12-year-old restaurant is still tough to get into on a Saturday night. Seasonal produce shapes the menu of chef Ed Witt (Daniel, River Café). Dunk the warm

Massive attack

The conversion of the Meatpacking District from meat market to meet market did more than ignite New York's club scene. The massive scale of the restaurants that moved into the vast former warehouses evoke Sin City more than the Big Apple. In fact, Tom Colicchio's sleek and sophisticated **Craftsteak** (*see p203*) is an offshoot of a concept that debuted at Las Vegas's MGM Grand. Stephen Starr, a celebrity restaurateur in Philadelphia, didn't start small when he broke into New York. For **Buddakan** (*see p201*), he hired designer Christian Liaigre to convert 16,000 square feet of raw space into a Chinese palace with French influences including carved woodwork created and shipped in from France. Liaigre rose to the challenge of creating warmth and personality in a huge area by creating a series of distinct spaces, each one with its own style. Around the corner, Starr's 12,000-square-foot **Morimoto** (*see p202*) combines sushi bar seating, communal tables, private dining nooks with a downstairs lounge and striking design details like a wall of more than 17,000 Ty Nant Spring Water bottles. Hell, even the loo gets in on the act with fully automated toilets outfitted with built-in seat warmers. Architect Glen Coben faced the challenge of creating a space that would live up to the expectations of Mario Batali, Lidia Bastianach and Joe Bastianach for **Del Posto** (*see p202*). To satisfy their demands for a restaurant that would capture the essence of a Venetian palazzo or European grand hotel – and to increase the number of seats – Coben designed a second level of seating that evokes an opera balcony, while also creating an intimate experience in the 22,000-square-foot space, with an elevator and stairs that connect from the basement all the way up to the mezzanine floor. Now, if only the prices weren't being scaled up to match the enormous spaces.

country bread in Umbrian olive oils produced exclusively for Il Buco. *Primi* include a thin-crust pizza with fresh porcini, shallots and aged Asturian goat's cheese; entrées include an excellent suckling pig snuggled into warm polenta. Book a table in the candlelit wine cellar for a rustic, charming vibe.

La Lanterna di Vittorio

129 MacDougal Street, between 3rd & 4th Streets (1-212 529 5945). **Open** 10am-3am Mon-Thur, Sun; 10am-4am Fri, Sat. **Main courses** $28. **Average pizza** $9. **Credit** AmEx, DC, Disc, MC, V. **Map** p403 E29 ⑬

Woo your darling by the fire or under the stars at a romantic Village spot that has been helping to smooth the course of true love for 28 years. The 200-year-old garden was once owned by Aaron Burr; its history is heard in the wind rustling through the dense green canopy of apple and cherry trees and the worn walls are strung with ivy. (In wintertime, four fireplaces spark your courting.) Choose a bottle from the extensive wine list to go with light café eats like panini, crostini, smoked duck breast with salad, or thin-crust pizza.

Lupa

170 Thompson Street, between Bleecker & Houston Streets (1-212 982 5089). Subway: A, B, C, D, E, F, V to W 4th Street. **Open** noon-3pm, 5-11.30pm Mon-Fri; 11.30am-2.30pm, 5-11.30pm Sat, Sun. **Main courses** $14. **Credit** AmEx, MC, V. **Map** p403 E29 ⑭

Fans of this 'poor man's Babbo' (celeb-chef Mario Batali's pricier restaurant around the corner) keep reclaiming their seats. Here's the ritual they recommend: first, a cutting-board of fatty-delicious cured meats like tender prosciutto and spirited coppi. Move on to sublime pasta, like the ricotta gnocchi with sausage and fennel. Then choose a meaty main, like oxtail alla vaccinara or a classic saltimbocca. By the time the panna cotta with apricot arrives, you'll be ready to become a regular too.

Employees Only.

Eat, Drink, Shop

Pan-Asian

Chinatown Brasserie
*380 Lafayette Street, at Great Jones Street
(1-212 533 7000). Subway: B, D, F, V to Broadway-
Lafayette Street; 6 to Bleecker Street.* **Open** 11.30am-
3.30pm, 5-11.30pm Mon-Thur; 11.30am-3.30pm,
5pm-12.30am Fri; 5pm-12.30am Sat; 5-11.30pm Sun
Main courses $19. **Credit** AmEx, Disc, MC, V.
Map p403 F29 ⑤⓪
Many of the menu options here could appear at
some spot with Wok or Empire in its name, except
that the prices run about 50% higher. While the
menu lists fried-egg rolls, wok-fried noodles and
fried rice, this brasserie specialises in dim sum. The
decor is stunning: dark brocade curtains, wooden
room dividers and red-and-yellow silk lanterns
greet you upstairs, while a downstairs lounge
shoots for tiki cool with the help of a koi pond and
low to the ground lounge chairs.

Steakhouse

Strip House
*13 E 12th Street, between Fifth Avenue & University
Place (1-212 328 0000). Subway: L, N, Q, R, W, 4,
5, 6 to 14th Street-Union Square.* **Open** 5-11.30pm
Mon-Thur; 5pm-midnight Fri, Sat; 5-11pm Sun.
Main courses $32. **Credit** AmEx, DC, Disc, MC,
V. **Map** p403 E28 ⑤①
Strip House cultivates a retro-sexy vibe with its
suggestive name, red furnishings and vintage pin-
ups. But it's still a modern meat shrine flaunting
French influences. Executive chef David Walzog
makes sure that his New York strips arrive at
your table still sizzling and seasoned with sea salt
and peppercorns – they are a sublime combination of a perfectly charred outside with a luscious
rare-red inside. Don't miss the black-truffle
creamed spinach, one of several gourmet takes
on classic steak sides.

Thai

Prem-On Thai
*138 W Houston Street, between Sullivan &
MacDougal Streets (1-212 353 2338). Subway:
C, E to Spring Street.* **Open** noon-11.30pm Mon-
Fri; noon-midnight Sat, Sun. **Main courses** $17.
Credit AmEx, DC, MC, V. **Map** p403 E29 ⑤②
In one of several stylish rooms (Prem-on Thai is
refreshingly bamboo-free), you'll watch in awe as
dramatically plated Thai dishes and cocktails are
carried through the dining room. Prem-On Thai
doesn't hold back, either visually or with the seasoning: a whole fried sea bass fillet is served
upright and loaded with basil and roasted chilli
paste sauce. Red snapper is smothered with an
extra-sweet pineapple and lychee sauce, and pork
hand rolls are an impressive trio of towers with a
punchy sesame-chilli rice-vinegar sauce.

West Village & Meatpacking District

American

Corner Bistro
*331 W 4th Street, at Jane Street (1-212 242 9502).
Subway: A, C, E to 14th Street; L to Eighth Avenue.*
Open 11.30am-4am daily. **Burgers** $5. **No credit
cards. Map** p403 D28 ⑤③
There's only one reason to come to this legendary pub:
the place serves up the city's best burgers – and beer
is just $2 a mug (well, that makes two reasons). The
patties here are cheap, delish and no-frills, served on a
flimsy paper plate. To get your hands on one, you may
have to queue for a good hour, especially on weekend
nights. Fortunately, the game is on the tube, and a jukebox covers everything from Calexico to Coltrane.

Eclectic

Employees Only
*510 Hudson Street, between Christopher & W 10th
Streets (1-212 242 3021). Subway: 1 to Christopher
Street-Sheridan Square.* **Open** 6pm-4am daily.
Main courses $22. **Credit** AmEx, Disc, MC, V.
Map p403 C28 ⑤④
The psychic palm-reader in the window is part of
the high-concept decor, inspired by the speakeasies
of yore. Peek behind the purple curtain in the foyer
and you'll see mahogany walls, a working fireplace,
a shiny tin ceiling and a collection of vintage cocktail books and bottles – inspiration for co-owner
Jason Kosmas's interesting drinks. The 'rustic
European' menu features butternut-squash riga-
toni and house-cured gravlax. Swing by late at
night, and you can nosh on oysters, baked brie and
veal goulash until 4am. **Photo** *p196.*

5 Ninth
*5 Ninth Avenue, between Gansevoort & Little W 12th
Streets (1-212 929 9460). Subway: A, C, E, L to 14th
Street.* **Open** 5.30pm-midnight Mon-Thur; 5.30pm-
1am Fri, Sat; 11am-midnight Sun. **Main courses**
$15. **Credit** AmEx, MC, V. **Map** p403 C28 ⑤⑤
This spare, brick-walled duplex of dining rooms
has a hotter-than-hot location smack bang in the
middle of the Meatpacking District. Chef Zak
Pelaccio's Asian-inflected instincts are as sharp as
ever: thick chips of bacon teeter atop four tiny oysters, each on a spoonful of vivid-green sweet-pea
purée. Poached lobster in a ginger beurre blanc and
the kobe ribeye in chunky coconut chutney are too
good to share. In the summer, sip a cocktail on the
peaceful back deck.

Spotted Pig
*314 W 11th Street, at Greenwich Street (1-212
620 0393). Subway: A, C, E to 14th Street; L to
Eighth Avenue.* **Open** noon-2am Mon-Fri; 11am-
2am Sat, Sun. **Main courses** $15. **Credit** AmEx,
MC, V. **Map** p403 D28 ⑤⑥

Eat, Drink, Shop

Buddha Bar

Brick archways, a pressed-tin ceiling and retro farm-animal pictures make this perpetually jammed two-room pub feel like a piece of England. Most of the beer is brewed in Brooklyn, and the menu… well, it's actually quite Italian, thanks to consultant Mario Batali and chef April Bloomfield, a British import from London's highly regarded, Italian-inspired River Café. The small menu changes daily but always includes Bloomfield's melt-in-your-mouth ricotta gnudi and rich smoked haddock chowder, as well as a handful of heartier dishes like pork sausages with polenta – a sly spin on bangers and mash.

Italian

Barbuto

775 Washington Street, between Jane & W 12th Streets (1-212 924 9700). Subway: A, C, E to 14th Street; L to Eighth Avenue. **Open** noon-11pm Mon-Fri; noon-midnight Sat; noon-10pm Sun. **Main courses** $18. **Credit** AmEx, Disc, MC, V. **Map** p403 D28 ⑰
For such an industrial-chic space (housed in a former garage), this bright corner restaurant serves surprisingly rustic food. Owner Fabrizio Ferri (who runs the Industria Superstudio complex upstairs) teamed with chef Jonathan Waxman to create a seasonal kitchen anchored by both a brick and a wood oven. Marvellously light calamari comes in lemon-garlic sauce; chitarra all'aia mixes pasta with

crushed walnuts, garlic, olive oil and parmesan; Vermont veal is perfectly fried. In the summer, the garage doors go up and a breeze sweeps through the airy dining room.

Japanese

EN Japanese Brasserie

435 Hudson Street, at Leroy Street (1-212 647 9196). Subway: 1 to Houston Street. **Open** 5pm-2am Mon-Sat; 5pm-midnight Sun. **Main courses** $15. **Credit** AmEx, DC, Disc, MC, V. **Map** p403 D29 ㊳
On the main floor of the multi-level space, Bunkei and Reika Yo have built tatami-style rooms; on the mezzanine level, they've recreated the living room, dining room and library of a Japanese home from the Meiji era (1868-1912). Chef Koji Nakano runs with the theme by offering handmade miso paste, tofu and yuba (soya-milk skin) in dishes like Berkshire pork belly braised in sansho miso; foie gras and poached daikon steak with white miso vinegar.

Pan-Asian

Buddha Bar

25 Little W 12th Street, between Ninth Avenue & Washington Street (1-212 647 7314). Subway: A, C, E to 14th Street; L to Eighth Avenue. **Open** 6pm-4am daily. **Main courses** $35. **Credit** AmEx, MC, V. **Map** p403 C28 ㊴

Eat, Drink, Shop

The irony is obvious: Buddhism emphasises moderation, and Buddha Bar is a temple of excess. Statues line the entrance tunnel. A glass-encased smoking room spares puffers from having to walk outside. As a nightclub party spot, Buddha Bar succeeds on many levels. It's visually stimulating, very Vegas, and the lounge scene bustles. Feasting on the Pan-Asian menu, however, requires patience. The entrées come out whenever they are ready. **Photo** *p198*.

Seafood

Ditch Plains

29 Bedford Street, at Downing Street (1-212 633 0202). Subway: A, B, C, D, E, F, V to W 4th Street; 1 to Houston Street. **Open** *7am-2am daily.* **Main courses** $12. **Credit** AmEx, MC, V. **Map** p403 D29 ⑥
Ditch Plains, named after a favourite surfing spot off Long Island, is a casual oyster bar and fish shack fitted with yellow pine tabletops, sheet-metal walls and flat-screen TVs showing aquatic-themed films. Breakfast plates, like eggs Benedict with chorizo or blood sausage, are available all day long. Think of it as a surfer special.

Spanish

Las Ramblas

170 W 4th Street, between Cornelia & Jones Streets (1-646 415 7924). Subway: A, B, C, D, E, F, V to W 4th Street-Washington Square. **Open** *4pm-2am daily.* **Small plate** $8. **No credit cards. Map** p403 D28 ⑥①

The authenticity of Las Ramblas (the chef's from Pamplona) is apparent in every centimetro of the place; three flavours of sangria are mixed to order; and the intimate space fosters interaction. Food portions (aged serrano ham, grilled chorizo, patatas bravas, Spanish cheeses) are just the right size, and price, for sharing.

Vegetarian/organic

'sNice

45 Eighth Avenue, at W 4th Street (1-212 645 0310). Subway: A, C, E to 14th Street: L to Eighth Avenue. **Open** *7.30am-10pm Mon-Fri; 8am-10pm Sat, Sun.* **No credit cards. Map** p403 D28 ⑥②
Someone who hasn't eaten meat for 20 years is bound to know a thing or two about what vegetarians like to eat. Mike Walter opened this sandwich shop as a haven for the herbivore – a simple spot to spend a few hours reading, snacking or working on a laptop.

Midtown

Chelsea

American

Cookshop

156 Tenth Avenue, at 20th Street (1-212 924 4440). Subway: C, E to 23rd Street. **Open** *noon-midnight daily.* **Main courses** $22. **Credit** AmEx, MC, V. **Map** p403 C27 ⑥③

'sNice.

Vicki Freeman and chef-husband co-owner Marc Meyer, want Cookshop to be a platform for sustainable ingredients from independent farmers. True to its mission, Cookshop's ingredients are consistently top-notch – and the menu changes daily.

Empire Diner

210 Tenth Avenue, at 22nd Street (1-212 243 2736). Subway: C, E to 23rd Street. **Open** 24hrs daily. **Main courses** $13. **Credit** Disc, MC, V. **Map** p404 C26 ⓺⓸

It's three in the morning and you're hungry – do you know where your middle-of-the-night grub is? This Fodero-style diner provides the answer for those who find themselves in Chelsea and in need of sustenance. It looks like a classic diner – gleaming stainless-steel walls and rotating stools – but few other hash houses have candlelight, sidewalk café tables and a pianist playing dinner music. Fewer still attempt such dishes as sesame noodles with chicken, and linguine with smoked salmon, watercress and garlic.

Pre:Post

547 W 27th Street, between Tenth & Eleventh Avenues (1-212 695 7270). Subway: C, E to 23rd Street. **Open** 5pm-5am Tue-Thur; 5pm-7am Fri, Sat. **Main courses** $19. **Credit** AmEx, MC, V. **Map** p404 B26 ⓺⓹

There's a seating option for every kind of customer here: cabanas for table-service types, regular tables for quiet wallflowers and private birchwood log booths for couples that don't mind sitting far apart from one another. The menu wisely sticks to classic comfort food: burgers, sandwiches, meat loaf and chicken. Generally, the greasier the dish, the better the taste.

American creative

Bette

461 W 23rd Street, at Tenth Avenue (1-212 366 0404). Subway: C, E to 23rd Street. **Open** 6-11.30pm Mon-Sat. **Main courses** $25. **Credit** AmEx, MC, V. **Map** p404 C21 ⓺⓺

Meat market
Whose beef tastes best?

There's no shortage of steakhouses in this city: in 2006, just weeks after the openings of Harry's Steak, Wolfgang's Tribeca and Craftsteak came the news that two high-profile steakhouses will launch in the Time Warner Center: Marc Murphy's Landmarc and Michael Lomonaco's Porter House. Every chef claims to have the tastiest cut of meat, but USDA (United States Department of Agriculture) Prime is no longer the gold standard in New York City. Pioneering types are seeking out new sources of beef, experimenting with breeds and feed, and challenging preconceived notions of what tastes best. They are rebelling against a system that has become largely irrelevant: the USDA's classification system dates back to 1927.

'Back then, there were five breeds of cattle, everything was fed corn, and facilities did 40 to 50 head an hour,' says Peter Alpert of Ridgefield Farms, a South Dakota breeder whose corn-fed premium Hereford cattle are used at Tom Colicchio's Craftsteak (*see p203*). 'Today there are 89 breeds, which create 5,000 cross-combinations, and the average plant runs 300 to 400 head an hour,' he adds. In 2005 the USDA graded more than 20 billion pounds of beef. Prime was three per cent of that total – the most tender, juicy, flavourful cut, thanks to excellent 'marbling' (the streaks of fat in lean

meat). Lesser grades are, in descending order, Choice, Select, Standard, Commercial, Utility, Cutter and Canner.

Peter Luger Steakhouse (*see p215*), long known as the city's (if not the country's) best steakhouse, uses USDA Prime beef, and many have suggested that the eaterie's superior product results from the fact that it gets first crack at the good stuff. 'We all have our hands actively on the meat,' says Jody Storch, whose family has operated the restaurant since 1950. She, along with her aunt and mother, personally selects every piece of meat. She claims that Prime isn't only scarce, but subjective. 'Prime is not necessarily Prime,' Storch explains. 'Many times we reject half of what we see, despite the fact that it has a Prime grade on it.'

At **Quality Meats** (*see p208*), executive chef Craig Koketsu doesn't care so much about what kind of cow he's using or whether it's got the Prime stamp of approval – he's more keen to find unusual cuts of meat that taste great. Order the 64-ounce, 28-day dry-aged, double rib steak for two and you get a slab of beef with a bone six inches longer than anything you've seen before, which gives the cut more intense flavour. Diners order it in droves, but it's not USDA Prime; it's merely a Choice form of Black Angus.

Amy Sacco, the beauty and brains behind Bungalow 8 and Lot 61, has opened a serious restaurant in Chelsea. The space is relatively small, but tastefully decorated with designer touches: art by Richard Phillips and stemware from Lalique. Executive chef Tom Dimarzo serves lofty fare like lobster gazpacho and seared tuna with basil, capers and tapenade.

Cafés

Wild Lily Tea Room

511 W 22nd Street, between Tenth & Eleventh Avenues (1-212 691 2258). Subway: C, E to 23rd Street. **Open** noon-9pm Tue-Sun. **Main courses** $11. **Credit** AmEx, MC, V. **Map** p404 C26 ⓺⓻
Goldfish swim among floating candles in a round stone pool at the front of Wild Lily Tea Room's peaceful tri-level space. The food is precious pan-Asian and often creatively incorporates tea: black sticky-rice risotto with mascarpone shares space with steamed turbot and shiitake mushrooms in a slightly sweet jasmine tea broth; a shrimp salad is delicately flavoured with a lavender-mint dressing. The $25 tasting of five carefully chosen, well-described sakés is a bargain.

Chinese

Buddakan

75 Ninth Avenue, between 15th & 16th Streets (1-212 989 6699). Subway: A, C, E to 14th Street; L to Eighth Avenue. **Open** 5pm-midnight Mon-Wed, Sun; 5pm-1am Thur-Sat. **Main courses** $20. **Credit** AmEx, MC, V. **Map** 403 C27 ⓺⓼
Buddakan relies almost entirely on the shock and awe of 16,000 stunning square feet of space. Open the giant gate of a door and you are greeted by a hotel-style line-up of hosts. Continue inside and you pass a bustling front bar, dominated by giant square tables, a birdcage filled with taxidermy, Buddha pictures and European tapestries, all leading to a grand staircase that descends into a soaring, golden-hued main room with a 35ft ceiling and a long communal table. The food – yes, there is food

At **Craftsteak** (*see p203*), chef-owner Tom Colicchio never buys Prime. Instead, he sources beef from ranchers who provide a product they believe is better than anything the US government grades. 'Wanting Prime and not being able to get Prime creates an inventory and menu nightmare,' says Summerfield Farms' Jamie Nicoll. 'So Tom chose to go with the premium Hereford.' Originally cultivated for British aristocracy, the Hereford is generally labelled USDA Choice.

Lineage and breeding alone do not determine a steak's flavour; feed can affect it too. Colicchio and Albrecht use grass-fed cattle born and bred in Hawaii by Kulana Foods. The cuts, which offer a robust, onion-like flavour, are hand-selected for Colicchio by Kulana's owner. The beef is aged for 21 days in Hawaii and an additional 21 days at the restaurant to increase tenderness and flavour.

While Prime will continue to be the official apex of the USDA grading system, there are clearly outside alternatives. Japan's marbling scale runs from 0 to 12, 12 being practically unobtainable. According to Albrecht, 'USDA Prime falls at about a four on that scale.' In May 2006 Craftsteak debuted its first batch of Australian Blackmore Ranch 56-day dry-aged platinum-graded pure Wagyu. Is it better than grass-fed Hawaiian or Prime? That's up to you to decide.

Eat, Drink, Shop

here, too – sounds more fancy, by the descriptions on the menu, than it really is. Noodle and rice dishes offer great bang for the buck.

Italian

Del Posto

85 Tenth Avenue, between 15th & 16th Streets (1-212 497 8090). Subway: A, C, E to 14th Street; L to Eighth Avenue. **Open** 5.30-11.30pm Tue-Sat. **Main courses** $28. **Credit** AmEx, MC, V. **Map** p403 C27 ⑳
Del Posto is a huge deal in every sense of the word. The 24,000sq-ft space is backed by heavyweights Mario Batali, Mark Ladner, and Lidia Bastianich and her son, Joseph. It has a basement for private banquets, a main floor with a 60-seat dining room and a 40-seat lounge, a mezzanine with opera house-like balcony tables and a 50,000-bottle wine cellar. The menu features high-end modern Italian cuisine such as house-made salami, pasta and bread. Big meaty dishes of lamb, venison and halibut are carved tableside.

La Bottega

Maritime Hotel, 88 Ninth Avenue, at 17th Street (1-212 243 8400). Subway: A, C, E to 14th Street; L to Eighth Avenue. **Open** 7-11.30am, 5pm-1am Mon, Tue; 7-11.30am, 5pm-2am Wed, Thur; 7-11.30am, 5pm-3am Fri; 11am-4pm, 5pm-3am Sat; 11am-4pm, 5pm-1am Sun. **Main courses** $18. **Credit** AmEx, DC, Disc, MC, V. **Map** p403 C27 ⑳

Given how popular this space is – especially during the summer, when the vast lantern-lit terrace is jam packed with a fashionable Euro crowd – the reasonably priced chow is much better than it needs to be. La Bottega has the classic trattoria mix: pasta, meat, fish and pizzas, and is open for breakfast and lunch, as well as dinner.

Japanese

Morimoto

88 Tenth Avenue, between 15th & 16th Streets (1-212 989 8883). Subway: A, C, E to 14th Street; L to Eighth Avenue. **Open** 5pm-midnight Mon-Thur, Sun; 5pm-1am Fri, Sat. **Main courses** $36. **Credit** AmEx, MC, V. **Map** p403 C27 ⑳
See p195 **Massive attack**.

Naka Naka

458 W 17th Street, between Ninth & Tenth Avenues (1-212 929 8544). Subway: A, C, E to 14th Street; L to Eighth Avenue. **Open** 6pm-midnight Tue-Sat. **Average sushi roll** $8. **Credit** AmEx, MC, V. **Map** p403 C27 ⑳
Naka Naka's kitchen produces tasty traditional dishes, starting with spicy lotus root, delicate mixed-vegetable tempura and deliciously dense shrimp dumplings. The sushi is neither phenomenal nor disappointing, but considering how difficult it is to find peace and quiet over dinner in this part of town, we can't complain.

Blossom. *See p204.*

Pan-Asian

Rickshaw Dumpling Bar

61 W 23rd Street, between Fifth & Sixth Avenues (1-212 924 9220). Subway: F, N, R, V, W to 23rd Street. **Open** 11.30am-9.30pm Mon-Sat; 11.30am-8.30pm Sun. **Dumplings** $5 (6). **Credit** AmEx, MC, V. **Map** p404 E26

Annisa chef Anita Lo has designed a simple menu consisting of six different dumplings, each inspired by an Asian cuisine and matched with its own dipping sauce: classic Chinese pork and chive with a soy vinegar, for instance, or Thai chicken with peanut satay. If you're hungry enough for a full meal, you can pair your dumplings with a big bowl of noodle soup, then top it all off with a green-tea milkshake or a dessert dumpling of molten chocolate in a mochi wrapper.

Sapa

43 W 24th Street, between Broadway & Sixth Avenue (1-212 929 1800). Subway: F, N, R, V, W to 23rd Street. **Open** 5.30-11pm Mon-Thur; 5.30-11.30pm Fri, Sat; 5.30-10.30pm Sun. **Main courses** $24. **Credit** AmEx, Disc, MC, V. **Map** p404 E26 ⑦

This savvy AvroKo-designed dining room is a perfect setting for inventive cocktails like a yellow-tomato version of a Bloody Mary, and has a French-Vietnamese menu by chef Patricia Yeo. Sapa's roll bar serves variations on spring and summer rolls, including ones with raw wild salmon and cucumber, or foie gras and duck. Among the adventurous main dishes are cider-braised monkfish, and scallops marinated in cane sugar.

Spanish

Tia Pol

205 Tenth Avenue, between 22nd & 23rd Streets (1-212 675 8805). Subway: C, E to 23rd Street. **Open** noon-3pm, 5pm-midnight Mon-Thur; noon-3pm, 5pm-1am Fri, Sat; 11am-3pm, 6pm-midnight Sun. **Small plate** $7. **Credit** AmEx, MC, V. **Map** p404 C26 ⑦

This tiny tapas restaurant keeps things simple with traditional tapas like sautéed cockles and razor clams. Other dishes showcase unlikely combinations: tomato-covered bread with lima bean purée, and chorizo and chocolate on bread rounds. The all-Spanish wine list is well priced, with selections that pair well with the spicy food.

Steakhouse

Craftsteak

85 Tenth Avenue, between 15th & 16th Streets (1-212 400 6699). Subway: A, C, E to 14th Street; L to Eighth Avenue. **Open** 5.30-10pm Mon-Thur, Sun; 5.30-11pm Fri, Sat. **Main courses** $35. **Credit** AmEx, MC, V. **Map** p403 C27 ⑦
See p200 **Meat market.**

Face facts: Geoffrey Zakarian

Chef-owner of both **Town** (in the Chambers Hotel) and **Country** (*see p204*) restaurants, author of a new cookbook and former chef at the original **Le Cirque** (*see p209*).

TO: How did you feel about Le Cirque reopening at One Beacon Court, its third space since its 1974 debut?
GZ: I didn't think they could do it again – it's hard to keep remaking a place – but Sirio Maccioni is unstoppable. It's very open and modern and light, and it hasn't been that before, ever. The original Le Cirque was a great room for that time, and the second Le Cirque at the Palace Hotel would have been if it hadn't been overdone. Le Cirque never

had this type of loftiness before. I think it's great that Sirio has included a casual café. It's like the old-world Le Cirque in a modern setting.

TO: Does any one restaurant these days command the majesty or respect of the Le Cirque that you worked at?
GZ: Most of those places are gone. There aren't too many people doing [the fancy French thing], except maybe La Grenouille. They've all sort of gone. [La Caravelle, Lutèce and La Cote Basque all closed], and now we're redefining what old is. At Country, we're keeping a lot of the old stuff [like the Tiffany dome and original glass-mosaic floors] and updating it.

TO: In your latest book, *Town/Country: 150 Recipes for Life Around the Table*, you present two recipes each for 65 ingredients – one in a refined 'Town' style and one in a more casual 'Country' mode. You suggest that a similar duality was found at Le Cirque when servers adapted spaghetti primavera with tableside 'flourishes'. What did they do exactly?
GZ: They took the tomatoes and the garlic and the broccoli and the vegetables and the pine nuts and the cream and the pasta, and each waiter made it differently, depending on where he was from. The Italian waiters made it with more tomato, and the French waiters would make it with more cream. [In the book] I try to treat the ingredients in the 'Town' versions as slightly more urbane, more complicated, something you wouldn't attempt on a school night. The 'Country' dishes aren't any less sophisticated, but they're more classical, more able to be served family-style.

Eat, Drink, Shop

Vegetarian/organic

Blossom
187 Ninth Avenue, between 21st & 22nd Streets (1-212 627 1144). Subway: C, E to 23rd Street. **Open** 11.45am-3.30pm, 5-10.30pm Mon-Sat; noon-3.30pm, 5-10pm Sun. **Main courses** $16. **Credit** AmEx, DC, Disc, MC, V. **Map** 404 C26 ⑰
Blossom offers a big surprise: all the egg-less pastas and mock meats actually taste pretty good. For vegans, it's a candlelit godsend. Try the pan-seared seitan medallions, unusually satisfying mock veal with capers, served with broccoli rabe and buttery-tasting polenta (without butter, of course). Or consider the fake-

chicken mole, seitan steak or a tofu BLT. The South Asian lumpia – a chickpea pancake filled with curried potato – is a spicy starter that would be right at home in a good Indian restaurant. **Photos** *pp202-3*.

Gramercy & Flatiron

American creative

Country
Carlton Hotel, 90 Madison Avenue, at 29th Street (1-212 889 7100). Subway: 6 to 28th Street. **Open** 5.30-11pm Mon-Sat. **Prix fixe** $85. **Credit** AmEx, MC, V. **Map** p404 F25 ⑱

Geoffrey Zakarian's Carlton Hotel restaurant is an enthrallingly sophisticated addition to the Flatiron dining scene. The prix-fixe menu (which changes frequently) draws heavily on French influences, but adds American and Italian elements. The dress code here is formal; jackets are required for men. A more casual café serves less expensive fare in the subterranean basement. **Photos** *p206 and p207*.

Craftbar

900 Broadway, at 20th Street (1-212 461 4300).
Subway: N, R, W, 6 to 23rd Street. **Open** noon-11pm Mon-Thur, Sun; noon-midnight Fri, Sat.
Main courses $25. **Credit** AmEx, DC, Disc, MC, V. **Map** p404 E27 ⓲

Tom Colicchio's flashy spin-off of his upscale restaurant Craft recently moved to a bigger and brighter space around the corner from the original Craftbar. The dining room is still positively raucous, and the busy bar is jammed with chatty, wine-swigging groups. Appetisers rate highest, especially a lavish platter of Italian, Spanish and house-cured meats and the addictive pork-stuffed sage leaves. Desserts like chocolate pot de crème and steamed lemon pudding are sheer heaven.
Other locations: Craft, 43 E 19th Street, between Broadway & Park Avenue South, Flatiron District (1-212 780 0880); 'wichcraft, 49 E 19th Street, between Broadway & Park Avenue South, Flatiron District (1-212 780 0577).

French

Le Express

249 Park Avenue South, at 20th Street (1-212 254 5858). Subway: 6 to 23rd Street. **Open** 24hrs daily. **Main courses** $13. **Credit** AmEx, MC, V. **Map** p404 E27 ⓱

It's 3am, and, if you want to dodge that hangover, you'd better eat something. So why not consider this bustling bistro, which stays open 24 hours a day, seven days a week? You're likely to find it as crowded in the wee hours as it is at 8pm. Bistro standards like steak au poivre, seared tuna steak, along with monkfish and chorizo brochettes, are satisfying at any hour.

Indian

Dévi

8 E 18th Street, at Fifth Avenue (1-212 691 1300).
Subway: N, R, W, 6 to 23rd Street. **Open** noon-2.30pm, 5.30-10.30pm Mon-Thur; noon-2.30pm, 5.30-11pm Fri, Sat; 5.30-10.30pm Sun. **Main courses** $21. **Credit** AmEx, Disc, MC, V. **Map** p404 E27 ⓱

Dangling from the ceiling like clusters of shiny hard candies, ornate multicoloured lanterns cast a warm glow over diners, who are surrounded by gauzy saffron draperies in the split-level dining room. Start your evening with a citrusy Dévi Fizz cocktail, nibble some crisp samosas, then pamper yourself with inspired Indian dishes like velvety

yam dumplings in a spiced tomato gravy; stuffed baby aubergine bathed in spicy peanut sauce; or moist chunks of chicken with pistachios, cilantro (coriander) and green chillies.

Spanish

Casa Mono/Bar Jamón

Casa Mono, 52 Irving Place, at 17th Street; Bar Jamón, 125 E 17th Street, at Irving Place (1-212 253 2773). Subway: L to Third Avenue; N, Q, R, W, 4, 5, 6 to 14th Street-Union Square. **Open** *Casa Mono* noon-midnight daily. *Bar Jamón* 5pm-2am Mon-Fri; noon-2am Sat, Sun. **Small plate** $9. **Credit** AmEx, MC, V. **Map** p404 F27 ⓲

Part of Mario Batali's ever-expanding restaurant spread, this busy and tiny tapas restaurant (Bar Jamón is the equally teeny wine bar around the corner) specialises in making 'difficult' meats irresistible. Fried sweetbreads in a nutty batter, oxtail-stuffed piquillo peppers, baby squid with plump white beans, tripe with sausage – it's all good, especially with a glass of wine or sherry from the extensive Iberian-heavy list.

Vegetarian/organic

Pure Food & Wine

54 Irving Place, between 17th & 18th Streets (1-212 477 1010). Subway: L, N, Q, R, W, 4, 5, 6 to 14th Street-Union Square. **Open** 5.30-11pm Mon-Sat; 5.30-10pm Sun. **Main courses** $23. **Credit** AmEx, DC, MC, V. **Map** p403 E27 ⓳

The dishes delivered to your table – whether out in the leafy patio or inside the ambient dining room – are minor miracles, not only because they look gorgeous and taste terrific, but also due to the fact that they come from a kitchen that lacks a stove. Everything here is raw and vegan – from the pad thai appetiser to the lasagne, a rich stack of zucchini, pesto and creamy 'cheese' made from cashews. Wines, mostly organic, are top-notch, as are the desserts, especially the confoundingly fudgy chocolate layer cake.

Midtown West

American

Dave & Busters

3rd Floor, 234 W 42nd Street, between Seventh & Eighth Avenues (1-646 495 2015). Subway: N, Q, R, S, W, 1, 2, 3 to 42nd Street-Times Square. **Open** 11am-12am Mon-Thur, Sun; 11am-2am Fri, Sat. **Main courses** $15. **Credit** AmEx, MC, V. **Map** p405 D24 ⓴

The latest addition to Times Square's restaurant collection of giant theme-park eateries is this behemoth food-entertainment venue, which offers virtual reality simulators, video games galore and Skee-Ball – plus Philly cheese steaks, salads and burgers. **Photo** *p212*.

Eat, Drink, Shop

Market Café

*496 Ninth Avenue, between 37th & 38th Streets
(1-212 967 3892). Subway: C, E to 34th Street.*
Open 11am-11pm daily. **Main courses** $12.
No credit cards. Map p404 C24 ⑮
Park yourself at one of the gleaming formica tables
and prepare to eat downright delicious seasonal
food, and plenty of it. House-made gnocchi are
bathed in chunky tomato sauce with peas, ham and
fresh ricotta; plump seared scallops sit on a bed of
whipped potatoes drizzled with brown butter; and
some of the best houmous in town comes with tri-
angles of char-grilled flatbread.

American creative

Bar Room at the Modern

*9 W 53rd Street, between Fifth & Sixth Avenues
(1-212 333 1220). Subway: E, V to Fifth Avenue-
53rd Street.* **Open** noon-2.15pm, 6-9.30pm Mon-
Thur; noon-2.15pm, 5.30-10.30pm Fri; 5.30-10.30pm
Sat. **Small plate** $12. **Credit** AmEx, DC, Disc,
MC, V. **Map** p404 E23 ㊱
The main culinary attraction at the new MoMA
opened a little after the museum, but to fans of chef
Gabriel Kreuther, the Modern was worth the wait.
Those who can't afford to drop a pay cheque at the

formal dining room should drop into the equally
stunning and less pricey bar room (which shares
the same kitchen). From the 30 savoury dishes on the
menu (which features several small and medium size
plates), standouts include Arctic char tartare and
sweetbread ravioli in a balsamic-sage sauce. Desserts
come courtesy of pastry chef Marc Aumont, and the
wine list is extensive.

American regional

Bar Americain

*152 W 52nd Street, between Sixth & Seventh
Avenues (1-212 265 9700). Subway: 1 to 50th
Street; N, R, W to 49th Street.* **Open** noon-11pm
daily. **Main courses** $28. **Credit** AmEx, DC, Disc,
MC, V. **Map** p404 D23 ㊲
Bobby Flay, the high-spirited, red-headed grill guy
from the Food Network, opened this flashy eaterie
in April 2005, 15 years after he opened his last NYC
restaurant, Mesa Grill. The menu is a good ol' boy's
take on a traditional European brasserie: rack of
pork comes with apple-ginger chutney, creamed
corn and sour mash; barbecued lamb gets hominy
flecked with yellow peppers. While you're waiting
for a table, you can take a seat at the bar and sip one
of 50 classic cocktails.

Country. See p204.

Argentine

Mama Empanada

763 Ninth Avenue, at 51st Street (1-212 698 9008). Subway: C, E to 50th Street. **Open** 9am-midnight daily. **Empanada** $2. **Credit** MC, V. **Map** p404 C23 ⑱

This vibrant South American spot serves 40 varieties of empanadas. Fillings range from traditional (mozzarella in a corn-flour empanada) to more creative versions like Cuban and cheese steak. The Elvis comes with peanut butter and bananas, and the Viagra with prawns, crab and scallops.

French

Marseille

630 Ninth Avenue, at 44th Street (1-212 333 3410). Subway: A, C, E to 42nd Street-Port Authority. **Open** noon-3pm, 5.15-11.30pm Mon-Fri; 11am-3pm, 5.15-11.30pm Sat; 11am-3pm, 5.15-10pm Sun. **Main courses** $23. **Credit** AmEx, MC, V. **Map** p404 C24 ⑲

This bustling corner restaurant with floor-to-ceiling windows, proscenium arches, a weathered bar and damask wallpaper will instantly transport you to the notorious port city in France. While Marseille's version of bouillabaisse is not textbook, it is undeniably tasty: haddock, skate, cod and mussels are cooked separately, then added to a light broth with a generous dose of garlic. As well as main course dishes, the extensive menu also features a huge selection of salads, sandwiches, starters and brunch fodder. Sipping and snacking are encouraged in the bustling bar: you can order every meze on the menu for only $24.

Seppi's

123 W 56th Street, between Sixth & Seventh Avenues (1-212 708 7444). Subway: F, N, Q, R, W to 57th Street. **Open** noon-2am Mon-Sat; 10.30am-2am Sun. **Main courses** $21. **Credit** AmEx, DC, Disc, MC, V. **Map** p405 D22 ⑳

We can't decide what we like best about this classic French bistro: the decor is spot on (black-and-white booths, pressed-tin ceilings); the hours are rare for Midtown (order until 2am nightly); the steak au poivre is properly peppery; and then there's Bob Baxter, an 85-year-old suspenders-sportin' magician who stops by your table late at night. Chocoholics come on Sundays to indulge in the divine $24 prix-fixe chocolate brunch, which starts with a chocolate mimosa and follows with a buffet of chocolate delicacies.

Italian

Abboccato

138 W 55th Street, between Sixth & Seventh Avenues (1-212 265 4000). Subway: F, N, Q, R, W to 57th Street. **Open** 6.30-10.30am, noon-3pm, 5.30-10pm Mon; 6.30-10.30am, noon-3pm, 5.30-11pm Tue-Thur; 6.30-10.30am, noon-3pm, 5.30pm-midnight Fri, Sat; 6.30-10.30am, noon-10pm Sun. **Main courses** $28. **Credit** AmEx, DC, Disc, MC, V. **Map** p405 D22 ㉛

Each dish at Jim Botsacos's new Sinatra-esque restaurant (low ceilings, circular leather banquettes) is associated with a region of Italy: there's Umbrian-style quail, and octopus with Sicilian oregano. Carbonara subs in flavourful duck eggs for a richer sauce. His vaniglia e cioccolato, meanwhile, combines two classic dishes into one: vanilla-scented veal cheeks and wild boar stewed in red wine, spices and chocolate. It's dinner and dessert rolled into one.

Japanese

Koi

Bryant Park Hotel, 40 W 40th Street, between Fifth & Sixth Avenues (1-212 642 2100). Subway: B, D, F, V to 42nd Street-Bryant Park; 7 to Fifth Avenue. **Open** noon-2.30pm, 6-10pm Mon, Sun; noon-2.30pm, 5.30-11pm Tue-Sat. **Main courses** $23. **Credit** AmEx, Disc, MC, V. **Map** p404 E24 ㉜

The newly opened Koi is a spin-off of the sceney LA Japanese restaurant. The decor embodies the four elements of feng shui: earth (bamboo stalks), wind (a ceiling installation modelled after a fluttering fishnet), fire (chandeliers of amber glass) and water (a fountain at the entrance). Chef Sal Sprufero, who worked at Ilo, put his own spin on Koi's menu, adding a white asparagus salad with crab, osetra and watercress pesto, rock shrimp tempura and duck breast with green-tea soba.

Nobu 57

40 W 57th Street, between Fifth & Sixth Avenues (1-212 757 3000). Subway: F to 57th Street; N, R, W to Fifth Avenue-59th Street. **Open** 11.45am-2.15pm, 5.45-10.15pm Mon-Fri; 5.45-10.15pm Sat, Sun. **Main courses** $23. **Sushi roll** $6. **Credit** AmEx, DC, Disc, MC, V. **Map** p405 E22 ㉝

Tables at this soaring new midtown location are almost as hard to come by as at the venerable Tribeca mothership – and that's any night of the week. Chef Nobu Matsuhisa continues his sushi revolution with paper-thin slices of seared fish with a hint of yuzu. The salmon-skin roll is as stellar as its reputation: slices of cucumber enfold salty salmon skin and bits of fish along with avocado, pickled burdock, shiso and rice so fresh it has a translucent sheen. A heaping bowl of rock-shrimp tempura with ponzu or Nobu's special creamy, spicy dipping sauce proves irresistible. If you can't get a table here, you can always try your luck at the downtown Next Door Nobu, the no-reservations sibling (105 Hudson Street, at Franklin Street, 1-212 334 4445).

Mexican

El Centro

824 Ninth Avenue, at 54th Street (1-646 763 6585). Subway: C, E to 50th Street. **Open** 5-11pm Mon, Tue, Sun; 5pm-midnight Wed-Sat. **Main courses** $12. **Credit** AmEx, DC, MC, V. **Map** p405 C22 ㉞

To start the party right, indulge in one of the frozen Margaritas, available with guava or raspberry. The menu's tried-and-true offerings – tacos, burritos, enchiladas, fajitas and so on – are all solid; especially good is the quesadilla with fat chunks of shrimp and melted monterey jack cheese, and a tostada appetiser with black beans, lettuce, tomato, sour cream and thick, juicy slices of grilled skirt steak.

Steakhouse

Quality Meats

57 W 58th Street, between Fifth & Sixth Avenues, (1-212 371 7777). Subway: F to 57th Street; N, R, W to Fifth Avenue-59th Street. **Open** 5-11.30pm daily. **Main courses** $35. **Credit** AmEx, MC, V. **Map** p405 E22 ㉟

See p200 **Meat market**.

Thai

Breeze

661 Ninth Avenue, between 45th & 46th Streets (1-212 262 7770). Subway: A, C, E to 42nd Street-Port Authority. **Open** 11.30am-11.30pm Mon-Wed; 11.30am-12.30am Thur, Fri; 10.30am-12.30am Sat; 10.30am-11.30pm Sun. **Main courses** $17. **Credit** AmEx, DC, MC, V. **Map** p404 C23 ㊱

Breeze sails past the other Thai contenders, with tangerine walls, triangular mirrors, a long backlit bar and a menu (printed on old 45s and CD cases) that doesn't stick to tradition. Chef Jeff Hardinger melds haute French techniques with Thai ingredients, and the outcome is spellbinding: fried dumplings cradle wild mushrooms and caramelised onions in a soy-black truffle foam, while succulent braised short ribs appear in a cinnamon-anise broth with celery hearts and fresh rice noodles.

Midtown East

American

PS 450

450 Park Avenue South, between 30th & 31st Streets (1-212 532 7474). Subway: 6 to 33rd Street. **Open** 11.30am-4am daily. **Main courses** $15. **Credit** AmEx, MC, V. **Map** p404 E25 ㊲

This is what happens when a distinctly unsexy, quiet neighbourhood gets a big new playground: the place is packed. An admirable selection of finger food pairs nicely with cocktails, including tasty duck-confit taquitos with tomatillo and pear salsa, tender pulled-pork sliders, and satisfying

Face facts: Aaron Isaacson

at Windows on the World. I've been in the spice business for 12 years now.

TO: How many different spices do you sell?
MR: I have 200 products from 20 to 25 different countries. I'm always adding new ones, going to new places and finding new things. [Among my new pepper finds:] Tellicherry double-hulled extra-extra-bold black pepper, Malaysian creamy white pepper (which smells like feet) and Aleppo red pepper from Syria and Turkey.

You might think that the city's top chefs get their spices from gourmet shops or from secret contacts in far-off lands. Some do. Many, however, go to Aaron Isaacson, aka Mr Recipe. *Time Out* sat down with Mr Recipe to find out what makes his products so special.

Time Out: How did you get involved in the spice market?
Mr Recipe: In 1983 I graduated from the Culinary Institute of America and went to work at some of the best restaurants in New York City – La Côte Basque, the Russian Tea Room – and later consulted

TO: Can you name a few places that use your spices?
MR: Gilt, Craft, Babbo. They are using my salt on the table at Del Posto. They have these beautiful Italian-made grinders where you can see the salt crystals.

TO: How do you get your moustache to stay like that?
MR: Viagra! No, I use a wax from Germany called Brother's Love. You can't get it here; you have to get it out of the country and smuggle it in.

entrées such as a wood-grilled hangar steak sliced over chorizo hash with lobster butter. Chef Dominic Giuliano's food is better than you'd find at most lounges and clubs – just don't plan on enjoying a quiet meal.

Cafés

Penelope
159 Lexington Avenue, at 30th Street (1-212 481 3800). Subway: 6 to 28th Street. Open 8am-11pm daily. **Main courses** $9. **No credit cards.** Map p404 F25 ⓾
This pretty little café and wine bar is the last thing you'd expect to find in Curry Hill, with its generic hot-table curry houses. The kitchen here cranks out dishes with care: creamy houmous with toast, chicken potpies and a terrific grilled cheese are just a few of the homespun dishes. The soup of the day is listed on a chalkboard and is served with chunks of good, earthy bread; the skins are left on the handcut french fries. Penelope is also a popular brunch spot; you may have to wait for a table.

French

Brasserie
100 E 53rd Street, between Park & Lexington Avenues (1-212 751 4840). Subway: 6 to 33rd Street. Open 7am-midnight Mon-Thur; 7am-1am Fri; 11am-1am Sat; 11am-10pm Sun. **Main courses** $23. **Credit** AmEx, DC, Disc, MC, V. Map p405 E23 ⓿
The trouble with cutting-edge design is that it soon becomes passé. Such is the case with Brasserie's high-concept interior. So it's a good thing that the food holds its own. Old-school French classics (steak-frites, escargots) never go out of style, and mix well with more inventive dishes, like an appetiser of tuna tartare with mango-chilli marmalade. The days when Brasserie stayed open all night are long gone, but at least it still serves food after most of the neighbourhood has shut down.

Le Cirque
One Beacon Court, 151 E 58th Street, between Lexington & Third Avenues (1-212 644 0202). Subway: N, R, W to Fifth Avenue-59th Street; 4,

Eat, Drink, Shop

Japanese cuisine for the modern age, at **Megu Midtown**.

5, 6 to 59th Street. **Open** 11.45am-10.45pm
Mon-Sat; 11.45am-9.45pm Sun. **Main courses**
$40. **Credit** AmEx, MC, V. **Map** p405 F27
After an 18-month hiatus, Sirio Maccioni, 74, has
stepped back into the limelight with the third incarnation of the legendary Le Cirque. The centrepiece
of the 16,000sq-ft restaurant: a 27ft-high illuminated circus tent; the imaginatively designed glass
bar is another impressive architectural element.
Main courses here include the likes of warm Maine
lobster salad, chicken comsommé with mushroom
ravioli, and sautéed red mullet with tomato com-
pote and rocket chutney.

Indian

Mint
*150 E 50th Street, between Lexington & Third
Avenues (1-212 644 8888). Subway: E, V to
Lexington Avenue-53rd Street; 6 to 51st Street.*
Open 11.30am-3pm, 5-11pm daily. **Main courses**
$19. **Credit** AmEx, MC, V. **Map** p404 F23 ⓴
At this Indian eatery, chefs pull all sorts of traditional baked goods from the fiery clay oven – fluffy
nan, roti and kulcha – but the best is the aloo paratha:
warm, chewy, slightly charred rounds with a layer
of soft, spicy potato in the middle. The secret's in the
seasoning and the precisely heated oven.

Japanese

Megu Midtown
*845 UN Plaza, Trump World Tower, First Avenue,
at 47th Street (1-212 964 7777). Subway: E, V
to Lexington Avenue-53rd Street; 6 to 51st Street.*
Open 5.30-10.30pm Mon-Wed; 5.30-11.30pm Thur-
Sat. **Main courses** $32. **Prix fixe** $70 (4 courses).
Map 404 F24 ⓵⓶
The 115-seat dining room has 24ft ceilings, 16ft-long
lampshades, black wood panelling, a monumental
mural of white tigers and a Buddha ice sculpture. From
the open kitchen, an army of chefs produces pristine
sushi and meat dishes (kobe beef, foie gras) the likes
of which you won't find elsewhere. If the $70 prix-fixe
menu isn't enough to impress, ask about the 'wagon
service', featuring rare ingredients, jetted in daily.

Pan-Asian

Tao
*42 E 58th Street, between Madison & Park Avenues
(1-212 888 2288). Subway: N, R, W to Fifth Avenue-
59th Street.* **Open** 11.30am-midnight Mon, Tue;
11.30am-1am Wed-Fri; 5pm-1am Sat; 5pm-midnight
Sun. **Main courses** $22. **Credit** AmEx, DC, MC, V.
Map p405 E22 ⓵⓷

A magnificent, scenic palace, Tao is packed with glowing Chinese lanterns, wealthy businesspeople, trendy Manhattanites and intrepid tourists. The bar (see p224) is always packed, and the stunning dining room has an over-the-top Far Eastern vibe, thanks to curly bamboo, Asian art and a 16ft stone Buddha. The menu offers generic small plates (dumplings, satay) and decent entrées.

Steakhouse

BLT Steak

106 E 57th Street, between Park & Lexington Avenues (1-212 752 7470). Subway: N, R, W to Lexington Avenue-59th Street; 4, 5, 6 to 59th Street. **Open** 11.45am-2.30pm, 5.30-11pm Mon-Thur; 11.45am-2.30pm, 5.30-11.30pm Fri; 5.30-11.30pm Sat. **Main courses** $32. **Credit** AmEx, DC, Disc, MC, V. **Map** p405 E22 🄽

BLT (Bistro Laurent Tourondel) Steak is an interpretation of an American steakhouse, in an elegant room with ebony tables and walnut floors. There's Caesar salad or shrimp cocktail to start, or trust Tourondel's whims and try beef carpaccio with lemon and arugula (rocket), or tuna tartare with soy-lime dressing. The meats are marvellous, if modest – only the 40oz porterhouse for two is really humungous – but no one can complain about the selection of sides: eight takes on potato and ten additional vegetables and starches (don't miss the heavenly onion rings).

Uptown

Upper West Side

American

Bouchon Bakery

3rd Floor, Time Warner Center, 10 Columbus Circle, at Broadway (1-212 823 9366). Subway: A, C, B, D, 1 to 59th Street-Columbus Circle. **Open** 11.30am-5.30pm Mon, Tue; 11.30am-9pm Wed-Sat. **Main courses** $12. **Credit** AmEx, MC, V. **Map** p405 D22 🄽

It has taken chef Thomas Keller, of Per Se, three years to open the New York outpost of his famous French bistro and boulangerie, Bouchon Bakery. The sleek 60-seat café is on the third floor of the mall; a chic take away shop sits around the corner. The menu – served throughout the space whether you sit at the espresso/wine bar, the communal table or a marble-topped table – includes savoury tartines, hearty soups, rustic pâtés, chocolate tarts and other affordable treats.

Gray's Papaya

2090 Broadway, at 71st Street (1-212 799 0243). Subway: 1, 2, 3 to 72nd Street. **Open** 24hrs. **Hot dog** 95 cents. **No credit cards. Map** p405 C20 🄽

A great number of New Yorker's think Gray's Papaya exemplifies the classic New York dog. The meat itself (all beef) boasts the ever-alluring combination of salty and sweet. It is cooked on a flat grill that renders the exterior (or casing) slightly crunchy. You'll find mustard, sauerkraut, sautéed onions and ketchup on the counter. At 95 cents apiece, the price is certainly right.

Telepan

72 W 69th Street, at Columbus Avenue (1-212 580 4300). Subway: B, C to 72nd Street; 1 to 66th Street. **Open** 5-11pm Tue; 11.30am-2.30pm, 5-11pm Wed, Thur; 11.30am-2.30pm, 5pm-midnight Fri; 11am-2.30pm, 5pm-midnight Sat; 11am-2.30pm, 5-10.30pm Sun. **Main courses** $28. **Prix fixe** $55. **Credit** AmEx, Disc, MC, V. **Map** p405 C21 🄽

This place isn't fancy, but it gets things right. Diners can customise their $55 prix-fixe dinners by selecting three dishes from any three columns; they can ask for assistance and get smart feedback; and they can count on a fresh, Greenmarket-inspired menu featuring stuff like hen-of-the-woods mushrooms, brook trout and organic lamb.

Cafés

Alice's Tea Cup

102 W 73rd Street, at Columbus Avenue (1-212 799 3006). Subway: B, C, 1, 2, 3 to 72nd Street. **Open** 8am-8pm Mon-Thur; 8am-10pm Fri; 10am-10pm Sat; 10am-8pm Sun. **Sandwich** $8. **Credit** AmEx, Disc, MC, V. **Map** p405 C20 🄽

Wander into this basement and you'll be transported to the end of a rabbit hole. This quirky *Alice in Wonderland*-themed boutique-cum-bakeshop is the perfect refuge for afternoon tea. Choose from scrumptious scones and muffins, overstuffed sandwiches like curried chicken salad and croque-monsieur, and sprightly salads like warm lentil with ginger dressing. Or you can have the full teatime treatment (dubbed the Mad Hatter) for $27 ($7 extra to share). *See also p289* **Go ask Alice**.

Eclectic

Per Se

4th Floor, Time Warner Center, 10 Columbus Circle, at Broadway (1-212 823 9335). Subway: A, B, C, D, 1 to 59th Street-Columbus Circle. **Open** 5.30-10pm Mon-Thur; 11.30am-1.30pm, 5.30-10.30pm Fri, Sat; 11.30am-1.30pm, 5.30-10pm Sun. **Prix fixe** $125-$150. **Credit** AmEx, MC, V. **Map** p405 D22 🄽

Rules are meant to be broken – unless you're Thomas Keller, and then they're not. Keller insists on perfection at Per Se. All he asks in return is that diners rise to the occasion and dress for it. Truth be told, a few guests are let off the hook. Mick Jagger got to wear jeans, and an occasional VIP is allowed to dine in a button-down without being forced to don the house jacket. Otherwise, those who are lucky or patient enough to get a reservation willingly suit up for the

Dave & Busters. *See p205.*

meal. For doing so, they're treated to nearly flawless, epic tasting menus, from the crunch of the classic opening bite – Keller's salmon-topped tuile cone – to the last little macaroon on the petits fours tray.

French

Nice Matin

201 W 79th Street, at Amsterdam Avenue (1-212 873 6423). Subway: 1 to 79th Street. **Open** 8am-3.30pm, 5.30pm-midnight daily. **Main courses** $18. **Credit** AmEx, DC, MC, V. **Map** p405 C19 **⑩**
Nice Matin draws mature locals seeking a relaxed night out. Chef Andy D'Amico's southern French fare isn't particularly inventive, but it's tasty and well executed. The optical-illusion wallpaper and carousel-top columns make for date-friendly surroundings. If only the waitstaff's attention didn't wander so.

Mexican

Rosa Mexicano

61 Columbus Avenue, at 62nd Street (1-212 977 7700). Subway: 1 to 66th Street-Lincoln Center. **Open** noon-3pm, 5-10pm Mon-Fri; 5-10pm Sat; noon-3pm, 4-10pm Sun. **Main courses** $23. **Credit** AmEx, DC, Disc, MC, V. **Map** p405 C21 **⑪**
The jazzy technicolour journey up vivid terrazzo steps to the cavernous dining room is alone worth the trip uptown. But the famous guacamole is still a main draw, smashed to order at your table. As the waiter unwraps a parchment package of braised

lamb shank, the rich aroma of chilli, cumin and clove envelopes the table. Veracruz-style red snapper is stuffed with crab and brightened with a punchy sauce of tomatoes, olives and capers.

Vietnamese

Monsoon

435 Amsterdam Avenue, at 81st Street (1-212 580 8686). Subway: B, C to 81st Street-Museum of Natural History; 1 to 79th Street. **Open** 11.30am-11.30pm Mon-Thur, Sun; 11.30am-midnight Fri, Sat. **Main courses** $15. **Credit** AmEx, MC, V. **Map** p405 C19 **⑫**
Ceiling fans, bamboo shades and a lush garden mural create a pleasant space for locals to satisfy their cravings for lemongrass, ginger, gingko and aromatic fresh herbs. The ample selections start with a long list of dim sum and unusual summer rolls. Chicken-mango rolls with wasabi-jalapeño sauce are delicious, as is the beef bun with bean sprouts, scallions and nuoc cham. Ginger sneaks in everywhere, but is best at dessert, where big, pungent chunks are buried in the ice-cream.

Upper East Side

American

Jovia

135 E 62nd Street, between Park & Lexington Avenues (1-212 752 6000). Subway F to Lexington Avenue-63rd Street. **Open**

5.30-10.30pm Mon-Thur, Sun; 5.30-11.30pm Fri, Sat. **Main courses** $28. **Credit** AmEx, MC, V. **Map** p405 E21 **113**
At Jovia, deer meat has been turned into one of the tastiest entrées in town, by massaging New Zealand venison loin with Barolo, roasting each serving over a nest of juniper branches in a pot sealed with a pastry lid, and serving the meat with roasted chestnuts, matsutake mushrooms and a sprinkle of juniper salt. You can taste the wild earth in every tender bite.

Lexington Candy Shop
1226 Lexington Avenue, at 83rd Street (1-212 288 0057). Subway: 4, 5, 6 to 86th Street. **Open** 7am-7pm Mon-Sat; 9am-6pm Sun. **Main courses** $9. **Credit** AmEx, Disc, MC, V. **Map** p405 E19 **114**
You won't find much candy for sale at Lexington Candy Shop. Instead, you'll find a preserved retro diner, lined with chatty locals digging into gigantic chocolate malts or peanut butter and bacon sandwiches. The shop was founded in 1925 and has appeared in numerous films, including the Robert Redford classic *Three Days of the Condor*.

Austrian

Café Sabarsky
Neue Galerie, 1048 Fifth Avenue, at 86th Street (1-212 288 0665). Subway: 4, 5, 6 to 86th Street. **Open** 9am-6pm Mon, Wed; 9am-9pm Thur-Sun. **Main courses** $14. **Credit** AmEx, MC, V. **Map** p406 E18 **115**
Nearby museum-goers come to this elegant Viennese café on Fifth Avenue for lunch plates such as smoked trout and goulash with spaetzle. But the savoury stuff is little more than a prelude to the real works of art that come after – apple strudel in crackling golden pastry, feather-light quark cheesecake, luscious Sachertorte and magnificent cream-topped (mit schlag) coffee. Breakfast is a particularly serene moment for appreciating the beautifully carved dark-wood walls and the leafy park views.

French

Le Bilboquet
25 E 63rd Street, between Madison & Park Avenues (1-212 751 3036). Subway: F to Lexington Avenue-63rd Street. **Open** noon-11pm daily. **Main courses** $22. **Credit** AmEx, MC, V. **Map** p405 E21 **116**
It's hard to believe that the skinny, skin-baring beauties who flock here on a Friday night can put away the portions this tiny bistro dishes out. With its loud, flirty rock 'n' roll ambience, Le Bilboquet knows how to get sexy and raw. Thick chunks of fresh tuna teeter between layers of lightly fried wonton skins; rich, piquant steak tartare comes with a tower of crisp frites. The unmarked entrance makes this feel like an upscale speakeasy.

Italian

Spigolo
1561 Second Avenue, at 81st Street (1-212 744 1100). Subway: 4, 5, 6 to 86th Street. **Open** 5pm-2am Mon-Sat. **Main courses** $19. **Credit** AmEx, DC, Disc, MC, V. **Map** p405 F19 **117**
Scott and Heather Fratangelo met in the kitchen at Union Square Café. The two talented chefs decided to move uptown in 2005. In passing, you might mistake the brick-walled place for just another pasta-slinging joint. It's not. Fat slices of grilled cotechino sausage marinated in red wine and bursting with flavour, and a brick-roasted baby chicken compete for top menu billing with a wild mushroom sauce and side of soft polenta. Heather handles desserts; her caramel affogato and bombolini are sublime.

Uva
1486 Second Avenue, at 77th Street (1-212 472 4552). Subway: 6 to 77th Street. **Open** noon-1am Mon-Thur, Sun; noon-2am Fri, Sat. **Main courses** $15. **Credit** AmEx, MC, V ($30 minimum). **Map** p405 F19 **118**
Although the Upper East Side has plenty of rustic Italian restaurants, the neighbourhood could still do with a few more wine bars. Luigi Lusardi and his brother Mauro opened Uva to fill the void. A 200-year-old wooden floor and antique couches give the place a warm, worn-in feel, and as per the wine bar formula, you can take your pick of cured meats and cheeses to pair with most Italian wines (30 are available by the glass).

Seafood

Central Park Boathouse Restaurant
Central Park Lake, park entrance on Fifth Avenue, at 72nd Street (1-212 517 2233). Subway: 6 to 68th Street-Hunter College. **Open** *Apr-Nov* noon-4pm, 5.30-11pm Mon-Fri; 9.30am-4pm, 6-11pm Sat, Sun. *Dec-Mar* noon-4pm Mon-Fri; 9.30am-4pm Sat, Sun. **Main courses** $26. **Credit** AmEx, MC, V. **Map** p405 D20 **119**
Paying for location is par for the course in New York; here, it's well worth it. The Boathouse salad is a gorgeous sculpture of tomatoes, cucumbers, red onion, olives and large, rectangular chunks of feta cheese. Crab-cakes, more crab than cake, are worth every penny. Fish and fowl are fresh and beautifully presented, if a bit bland.

116th Street & above

American

Kitchenette Uptown
1272 Amsterdam Avenue, between 122nd & 123rd Streets (1-212 531 7600). Subway: 1 to 125th Street. **Open** 8am-11pm daily. **Main courses** $16. **Credit** AmEx, DC, MC, V. **Map** p407 C14 **120**

Eat, Drink, Shop

Riding the wave of South Harlem gentrification, Kitchenette Uptown brings Tribeca-style country dining to a sunlit space in Morningside Heights. At brunch, order the BLT on challah bread – it does cartwheels around the egg dishes. Cheese grits with own-made turkey sausage also make a great meal, followed by a homely slice of cherry pie. All-day breakfast and weekend brunch attract a lively group of university types, as does the BYOB dinner with chicken potpie and four-cheese macaroni.

American regional

Miss Maude's Spoonbread Too

547 Malcolm X Boulevard (Lenox Avenue), between 137th & 138th Streets (1-212 690 3100). Subway: B, C to 135th Street. **Open** 11.30am-9.30pm Mon-Sat; 11am-8pm Sun. **Main courses** $12. **Credit** AmEx, MC, V. **Map** p407 D11 ⓬①

Norma Jean Darden knows that sometimes nothing will do but real home cookin'. The three-year-old off-shoot of Darden's original Morningside Heights spot makes everything from scratch. Get a load of fall-off-the-bone short ribs, flaky cornmeal-crusted catfish, or thick-cut pork chops smothered in creamy gravy, and dig into sides like smoky collard greens. Weekend brunch includes nap-inducing favourites like pecan waffles, fried fish and biscuits.

Chinese

Ginger

1400 Fifth Avenue, at 116th Street (1-212 423 1111). Subway: 2, 3 to 116th Street-Lenox Avenue; 6 to 116th Street-Lexington Avenue. **Open** 5.30-10.30pm Mon-Thur; 5.30-11.30pm Fri; 11.30am-3pm, 5.30-11.30pm Sat; 5.30-10pm Sun. **Credit** AmEx, DC, Disc, MC, V. **Main courses** $15. **Map** p407 E14 ⓬②

Big-name developers aren't the only people breaking new ground in East Harlem. What's novel about this organic Chinese restaurant – aside from the fact that it's on East 116th Street – is what executive chef James Marshall (Vong, China Grill) won't do to the food: there will be no deep frying and no excessive use of oil or salt. Instead, fresh vegetables and lean meats are doused in citrusy sauces; the menu lists a pineapple-and-mango-glazed pork chop as well as an apricot-glazed chicken. The decor mixes traditional with modern. Is it authentic Chinese cooking? Not really, but you don't care when the food is this good – and healthy.

Pizza

Patsy's

2287 First Avenue, between 117th & 118th Streets (1-212 534 9783). Subway: 6 to 116th Street. **Open** 11am-11pm Mon-Sat; 1-10pm Sun. **Average pizza** $12. **No credit cards. Map** p407 F14 ⓬③

This is East Harlem's favourite parlour, and with good reason. Sit down for a pie or stand up for a slice at the 71-year-old uptown joint.

Brooklyn

American

Applewood

501 11th Street, at Seventh Avenue, Park Slope (1-718 768 2044). Subway: F to Seventh Avenue. **Open** 5-11pm Tue-Sat; 10am-3pm Sun. **Main courses** $20. **Credit** AmEx, Disc, MC, V. **Map** p410 T12 ⓬④

David and Laura Shea met at the Culinary Institute of America and then returned to New York to open this charming eatery with country style and organic produce. Tables are adorned with bundles of fresh herbs, there's a working fireplace, and many ingredients come from a friend's upstate farm. On the opening menu: ricotta dumplings with braised pork shoulder, roasted chicken with chanterelle-sage gravy, and wild striped bass with roasted corn and curried mussel chowder.

Brooklyn Fish Camp

162 Fifth Avenue, between DeGraw & Douglass Streets, Park Slope (1-718 783 3264). Subway: 2, 3 to Bergen Street. **Open** noon-3pm, 6-11pm Mon-Sat. **Main courses** $19. **Credit** AmEx, MC, V. **Map** p410 T11 ⓬⑤

Brooklyn Fish Camp is no flop: the cultish lobster roll, rosemary-stuffed whole fish and succulent lobster knuckles are fresh and delicious. Spicy calamari tossed with grape tomatoes and chickpeas are equally satisfying. You'll eat well here, and while the weather's nice you can eat outside on the lovely deck out back.

Schnäck

122 Union Street, at Columbia Street, Carroll Gardens (1-718 855 2879). Subway: F, G to Carroll Street. **Open** 11am-1am daily. **Burgers** $5. **No credit cards. Map** p410 S10 ⓬⑥

A greasy spoon with a sense of humour, Schnäck has a knack for burgers: you can order up to five small patties stacked on a single bun, with a full array of toppings (the likes of 'schnäck sauce', spicy onions, chilli and kraut). The $2 quickie – a mini-burger with a 'children's portion' of beer – is one of the best deals in Brooklyn. Buttermilk-soaked onion rings fry up flaky-crisp and are sprinkled with salt and parsley seasoning. The award-winning beer milkshake tastes just like a regular milkshake, but has a buzz.

American creative

DuMont

432 Union Avenue, between Devoe Street & Metropolitan Avenue, Williamsburg (1-718 486 7717). Subway: G to Metropolitan Avenue; L to Lorimer Street. **Open** 11am-3pm, 6-11pm daily. **Main courses** $12. **Credit** MC, V. **Map** p411 V8 ⓬⑦

DuMont is the kind of place where Byron, Shelley and Keats might have gathered for a drink – a gently worn joint with pressed-tin ceilings, a wooden bar, retro brown leather booths and plenty of candles. A private den in the back doubles as a bar and holding pen for those who are waiting to dig into excellent seasonal American dishes like frothy lobster bisque with a dollop of curry butter, or braised duck leg risotto. Lucky for all of us, the lardon-laced macaroni and cheese never disappears.

Italian

DOC Wine Bar

83 North 7th Street, at Wythe Avenue, Williamsburg (1-718 963 1925). Subway: L to Bedford Avenue. **Open** 6pm-midnight Mon-Thur; 6pm-1am Fri-Sun. **Small plate** $7. **No credit cards. Map** p411 U7 **128**
Tucked on a quiet side street, this unpretentious spot charms with brown-paper-covered tables and menus held together with wooden spoons. Peruse the list of 70 Italian wines, and a menu of small plates: vegetarian carpaccio serves up as a mound of thin, perfectly rolled slices of carrot and courgette topped with parmesan shavings. Pistokku – traditional flatbread from Sardinia – is served pizza-style, warm and crisp with toppings such as bresaola (air-cured beef), goat's cheese and arugula (rocket).

Mexican

Alma

187 Columbia Street, at DeGraw Street, Cobble Hill (1-718 643 5400). Subway: F, G to Carroll Street. **Open** 5.30-10pm Mon-Fri; 6-11pm Sat, Sun. **Main courses** $15. **Credit** MC, V. **Map** p410 S10 **129**
From the subway, it's a long walk west (when you get to the far side of the BQE overpass, you're almost there), but if you want to chill with local Margarita-lovin' arty types, head over to this sexy Mexi spot. Have a drink at the ground-floor bar, B61, then head upstairs to Alma's colourful dining room. In good weather, snag a table on the rooftop deck, which has industrial-chic views of the Brooklyn waterfront and the downtown Manhattan skyline. Citrusy ceviche of shrimp, scallop and bass has a hint of jalapeño; a side of black beans with sticky, luscious sautéed plantains is pure south-of-the-border comfort.

Steakhouse

Peter Luger

178 Broadway, at Driggs Avenue, Williamsburg (1-718 387 7400). Subway: J, M, Z to Marcy Avenue. **Open** 11.30am-10pm Mon-Thur, Sun; 11.30am-11pm Fri, Sat. **Steak for two** $65. **No credit cards. Map** p411 U7 **130**
Does this Williamsburg landmark deserve its rep as one of the best steakhouses in America? A four-star experience this isn't, but the quality of the beef may make you forgive any shortcomings. Established as a German beer hall in 1887, the restaurant serves only one cut: a porterhouse that's char-broiled black on the outside, tender and pink on the inside. Service is slow, provided by waiters

who would rather give out wisecracks than water. Remember to stuff your wallet before you stuff your face; Luger's doesn't take credit cards (although it will accept US debit cards).

Thai

SEA Thai Restaurant & Bar

114 North 6th Street, at Berry Street, Williamsburg (1-718 384 8850). Subway: L to Bedford Avenue. **Open** 11.30am-12.30am Mon-Thur, Sun; 11.30am-1.30am Fri, Sat. **Main courses** $9. **Credit** AmEx, MC, V. **Map** p411 U7 **131**
SEA could be mistaken for a nightclub, given the reverberating dance music and a mod lounge complete with bubble-chair swing. Get a table by the reflecting pool and flip through the campy postcard menu. For a place so stylish, prices are cheap and the food good. Stuffed with shrimp and real crab, jade seafood dumplings come with a nutty Massaman sauce, while Queen of Siam beef with basil and red chilli is best when you ask the kitchen to fire it up.

Queens

French

718

35-01 Ditmars Boulevard, at 35th Street, Astoria (1-718 204 5553). Subway: N, W to Astoria-Ditmars Boulevard. **Open** 5.30-10.30pm Mon-Thur; 5.30pm-1am Fri; noon-5pm, 5.30pm-1am Sat; noon-4pm, 5.30-10.30pm Sun. **Main courses** $15. **Credit** AmEx, DC, Disc, MC, V. **Map** p412 X3 **132**
Queens achieved a certain critical mass two and a half years ago when French chef Alain Allaire co-opened 718 on a promising corner of Ditmars Boulevard's restaurant row. The joint has since become a consistent crowd-pleaser. It is at once a bar, a warm-weather café, a brunch hang, a late-night tapas haunt, a weekly belly-dancing-and-salsa club and (crucially) a dependable kitchen.

Greek

Cavo

42-18 31st Avenue, between 42nd & 43rd Streets, Astoria (1-718 721 1001). Subway: G, R, V to Steinway Street. **Open** 5pm-2am Mon-Sat; noon-4am Sun. **Main courses** $18. **Credit** AmEx, MC, V. **Map** p412 X4 **133**
Space-starved New Yorkers love to luxuriate in the immense outdoor garden of this upscale Astoria restaurant, bar and lounge. The menu features Greek classics such as whole-roasted fish, along with modern inspirations like the giant filo-wrapped shrimp drizzled with Cretan honey. Don't miss the keftedakia – crispy beef and pork meatballs oozing with kefalograviera, a goat and cow's milk cheese, and dressed with ladolemono, an olive oil and lemon emulsion.

Bars

The lush life is waiting for you, in a town where great bars are always on tap.

Welcome to boozers' paradise. Here you can drink up, down and all around town. We've got nearly 5,000 bars, pubs and clubs to keep your favourite libation flowing from 8am until 4am – which leaves you with a few hours to catch some shut-eye before starting up all over again.

Our 'average drink' price covers a standard 'well drink' (a spirit from a bar) plus a mixer, or the equivalent.

Downtown

Tribeca & South

Another Room

249 West Broadway, between Beach & North Moore Streets (1-212 226 1418). Subway: A, C, E to Canal Street. **Open** 5pm-4am daily. **Average drink** $7. **No credit cards. Map** p402 E31 ❶
Like its siblings, this sleek and civilised bar doubles as an art gallery. You won't find any hard liquor, but the selection of fine beer and wine is varied and vast and the crowd (gay, straight, fashionistas, 9-to-5 execs) interesting. If the weather is decent, sit at the picnic table out front.
Other locations: The Other Room, 143 Perry Street, between Greenwich & Washington Streets, Tribeca (1-212 645 9758); The Room, 144 Sullivan Street, between Houston & Prince Streets, Soho (1-212 477 2102).

Brandy Library

25 North Moore Street, at Varick Street (1-212 226 5545). Subway: 1 to Franklin Street. **Open** 4pm-4am daily. **Average drink** $12. **Credit** AmEx, MC, V. **Map** p402 E31 ❷
Cocktail connoisseurs and spirit snobs will find themselves at home inside this handsome cognac-coloured liquor lounge. Wood panelling, low couches, a long bar and blue-note jazz create an atmosphere that begs for a smoking jacket (you can smoke cigars on the heated terrace out front).

Bubble Lounge

228 West Broadway, between Franklin & White Streets (1-212 431 3433). Subway: 1 to Franklin Street. **Open** 5pm-2am Mon, Tue; 5pm-3am Wed; 5pm-4am Thur; 4.30pm-4am Fri; 6pm-4am Sat. **Average drink** $22. **Credit** AmEx, DC, Disc, MC, V. **Map** p402 E31 ❸

---

❶ Pink numbers given in this chapter correspond to the location of each bar as marked on the street maps. *See pp402-412.*

This warm L-shaped and couch-filled champagne and sparkling wine bar doesn't get jammed until late. In a festive mood? Ask to have your bottle opened in the traditional celebratory way: with a sabre.

Dekk

134 Reade Street, between Greenwich & Hudson Streets (1-212 941 9401). Subway: 1, 2, 3 to Chambers Street. **Open** 11am-4am Mon-Fri; 10am-4am Sat, Sun. **Average drink** $8. **Credit** AmEx, MC, V. **Map** p402 E31 ❹
Decorated with antique Parisian subway seats and French doors, Dekk has a screening room in the back that shows depraved films like *Cecil B Demented* and *Tromeo and Juliet*. A long list of wines by the glass complements a menu of thin-crust pizzas and northern Italian pastas.

Megu Kimono Bar

62 Thomas Street, between Church Street & West Broadway (1-212 964 7777). Subway: A, C, 1, 2, 3 to Chambers Street. **Open** 11.30am-2.30pm, 5.30-11.30pm Mon-Fri; 5.30-11.30pm Sat, Sun. **Average drink** $16. **Credit** AmEx, DC, Disc, MC, V. **Map** p402 E31 ❺
The lounge of this high-end, high-profile Japanese restaurant is show-stopping: white columns are fashioned from porcelain rice bowls, and saké bottles and kimono fabrics abound. Kimono's cocktails are similarly fancy: Autumn Rain is a refreshing blend of citrus vodka, elderflower syrup, Asian-pear purée and ginger.

Ulysses Folk House

58 Stone Street, at Hanover Square (1-212 482 0400). Subway: 4, 5 to Bowling Green. **Open** 11am-4am Mon-Sat; noon-4am Sun. **Average drink** $6. **Credit** AmEx, DC, Disc, MC, V. **Map** p402 E33 ❻
Photos of the late, great author adorn the exposed-brick walls; he looks on knowingly as the harried help pours pints of Guinness and 16 other draught brews.

Chinatown, Little Italy & Nolita

Odea

389 Broome Street, at Mulberry Street (1-212 941 9222). Subway: J, M, Z to Bowery; 6 to Spring Street. **Open** 6pm-2am Tue-Wed; 6pm-4am Thur-Sat. **Average drink** $10. **Credit** AmEx, DC, Disc, MC, V. **Map** p403 F30 ❼
This sleek AvroKO-designed lounge nails the industrial-chic look – high ceilings, wood beams and brick walls painted black – but also includes some old-fashioned touches that soften the room. Stay long enough, and you'll find yourself nibbling on tasty tapas such as figs wrapped in prosciutto.

Centovini. See p219.

Palais Royale

*173½ Mott Street, between Broome & Grand Streets
(1-212 941 6112). Subway: J, M, Z to Bowery; 6 to
Spring Street.* **Open** 1pm-2am Mon-Wed; 1pm-4am
Thur-Sun. **Average drink** $6. **Credit** AmEx, MC,
V. **Map** p403 F30 ❽
Palais Royale might be the city's first haute dive bar.
The owners, who also run Double Happiness and
Orchard Bar, are serious about booze – they're
serving 30 types of bourbon – but they're having
fun with the menu: Hungry-Man and Lean Cuisine
microwaveable meals. A pool table and televisions
above the bar add to the 'dive' quotient.

Xicala Wine & Tapas Bar

*151B Elizabeth Street, between Broome & Kenmare
Streets (1-212 219 0599). Subway: J, M, Z to
Bowery.* **Open** 5pm-2am daily. **Average drink**
$8. **Credit** AmEx, MC, V. **Map** p403 F30 ❾
Everything about this Spanish spot, located on an
ungentrified block, is incongruous. A bright neon
sign leads to a dark, tiny space. Classic tapas –
chorizo, codfish, olives – co-exist with chocolate fon-
due, and powerhouse wines are properly chilled and
generously poured. Full capacity is 20 people, so in
warm weather patrons spill out on to the pavement.

Lower East Side

Barrio Chino

*253 Broome Street, between Ludlow & Orchard
Streets (1-212 228 6710). Subway: F to Delancey
Street; J, M, Z to Delancey-Essex Streets.* **Open** 6pm-
2am Mon-Thur, Sun; 6pm-4am Fri, Sat. **Average
drink** $8. **Credit** MC, V. **Map** p403 G30 ❿
Neighbourhood cool kids have taken up positions
at Barrio Chino's rough-hewn wooden bar. Owners
Patrick Durocher and Dylan Dodd aim to 'give
tequila credibility as a sipping liquor, like Scotch'.
Fifty tequilas are available, at $6 to $25 per shot.
Each comes with a slice of mango and a glass of
Sangrita, a tomato-citrus palate-cleanser. There's
also a list of unusual but delicious Margaritas.

The Delancey

*168 Delancey Street, at Clinton Street (1-212
254 9920). Subway: F to Delancey Street; J, M,
Z to Delancey-Essex Streets.* **Open** 4pm-4am
daily. **Average drink** $6. **Credit** MC, V.
Map p403 G30 ⓫
The tropical-themed rooftop is what keeps luring the
cool crowd – a wooden deck lined with potted palms,
equipped with a fishpond, a bar and a Margarita
machine. When the alfresco party ends, at midnight,
you can head down to the main floor for DJ music,
or into the basement to catch a live show.

East Side Company Bar

*49 Essex Street, at Grand Street (1-212 614 7408).
Subway: F to Delancey Street; J, M, Z to Delancey-
Essex Streets.* **Open** 8pm-4am daily. **Average
drink** $8. **Credit** AmEx, MC, V. **Map** p403 G30 ⓬
If you still can't get into Milk & Honey (the exclusive reservation-only bar owned by Sasha Petraske),
you'll fare much better at his new Lower East Side
spot: the phone number is listed, and you can also
walk in off the street. The snug new space also has
a 1940s-era vibe (leather booths, classic cocktails),
as well as a few additions, such as a raw bar.

'inoteca

*98 Rivington Street, at Ludlow Street (1-212 614
0473). Subway: F to Delancey Street; J, M, Z to
Delancey-Essex Streets.* **Open** noon-3am Mon-Fri;
10am-3am Sat, Sun. **Average drink** $8.
Credit AmEx, MC, V. **Map** p403 G29 ⓭
Where chefs drink, their partisans follow. So Jason
Denton and his partners at the microscopic wine bar
'ino opened a bigger space across town. Same warm
atmosphere, same foodie crowd, but there's also a
menu of great pan-Italian share-plates and enough
space to give your glass a proper swirl. The downstairs wine cellar is more conversation-friendly.

Punch & Judy

*26 Clinton Street, between Houston & Stanton
Streets (1-212 982 1116). Subway: F to Delancey
Street; J, M, Z to Delancey-Essex Streets.* **Open**
6pm-2am Mon-Wed, Sun; 6pm-4am Thur-Sat.
Average drink $10. **Credit** AmEx, MC, V.
Map p403 G29 ⓮

Eat, Drink, Shop

This stylish, modern wine bar and lounge, furnished with 1930s theatre seats and red couches, offers 150 wines that pair beautifully with nibbles like a lobster club sandwich, cheese plates or a Caprese salad, where the ingredients are rolled up sushi-style.

Schiller's Liquor Bar
For listing, see p189. **Map** p403 G29 ⑮
Keith McNally's downtown bar attracts the hep cats with decidedly unsnobbish wine-list categories ('cheap', 'decent' and 'good').

Soho

Fanelli's Café
94 Prince Street, at Mercer Street (1-212 226 9412). Subway: N, R, W to Prince Street. **Open** 10am-1.30am Mon-Thur, Sun; 10am-3.30am Fri, Sat. **Average drink** $5. **Credit** AmEx, MC, V. **Map** p403 E29 ⑯
On a lovely cobblestoned corner, this 1847 joint claims to be the second-oldest continuously operating bar and restaurant in the city. Prints of boxing legends and one of the city's best burgers add to the easy feel. The banter of locals and the merry clinking of pint glasses sound just like the old days.

Brew's crews

Long confined to Coney Island, Skee-Ball (a ball-rolling arcade game) has now rolled into the East Village thanks to Brewskee-Ball, the world's first beer-fuelled Skee-Ball league. Thirty-two teams, boasting such colourful monikers and appropriately themed costumes as Skee3PO and Skee's Company – battle it out on Wednesdays and Sundays at Ace Bar (*see right*), for the honour of quaffing from the Brewskee-Ball Mug at the championship. Says Will Guidara of reigning champs Skee Patrol, 'We play for companionship and victory, that's it. Oh, and beer.'
For details, visit www.brewskeeball.com.

Fiamma Osteria
206 Spring Street, between Sixth Avenue & Sullivan Street (1-212 653 0100). Subway: C, E to Spring Street. **Open** noon-2.30pm, 5.30-11pm Mon-Thur, Sun; noon-2.30pm, 5.30pm-midnight Fri; 5.30pm-midnight Sat.* **Average drink** $13. **Credit** AmEx, Disc, MC, V. **Map** p403 E30 ⑰
After a short glass-elevator ride up to the second floor, you find a hidden lounge that looks like an upscale building-material showroom: stone walls, hardwood floors, leather banquettes and a brigade of tealights. Regulars get giddy over the smooth Cappuccino Martini, but wine aficionados come for a sampling of one of the city's best wine lists.

Grand Bar & Lounge
SoHo Grand Hotel, 310 West Broadway, between Canal & Grand Streets (1-212 965 3000). Subway: A, C, E, 1 to Canal Street. **Open** noon-1.30am Mon-Wed, Sun; noon-2.30am Thur-Sat. **Average drink** $12. **Credit** AmEx, DC, Disc, MC, V. **Map** p403 E30 ⑱
They've been around for a while, but the second-floor bar and lounge still draw a media-industry crowd. The two spaces – a wood-panelled bar and a plush lounge drenched in chocolate hues – are linked by a long corridor. Sip a pricey cocktail or glass of wine while you take in evening sessions of newly released lounge imports. Hungry drinkers can order grilled salmon BLTs or truffled turkey burgers.

MercBar
151 Mercer Street, between Houston & Prince Streets (1-212 966 2727). Subway: B, D, F, V to Broadway-Lafayette Street; N, R, W to Prince Street; 6 to Bleecker Street. **Open** 5pm-2am Mon, Tue, Sun; 5pm-2.30am Wed; 5pm-3am Thur; 5pm-4am Fri, Sat. **Average drink** $9. **Credit** AmEx, MC, V. **Map** p403 E29 ⑲
Need a sharp-looking place to try with a blind date? Head to the MercBar, where the well-coiffed after-work crowd comes to engage in polite conversation and to avoid mingling. The interior (soft lighting, log-cabin-like walls, landscape paintings and a canoe hanging above the sleek wooden bar) feels like your rich friend's parents' mountain lodge, but the drinks are city-slick – the Concorde blends apple schnapps, Bacardi Limón and grape juice.

East Village

Ace Bar
531 E 5th Street, between Avenues A & B (1-212 979 8476). Subway: F, V to Lower East Side-Second Avenue. **Open** 2pm-4am daily. **Average drink** $5. **Credit** AmEx, MC, V. **Map** p403 G28 ⑳
Recreational opportunities abound at roomy bar Ace – Big Buck Hunter, two pool tables (the bar even has a league going), and the daily 4-to-7pm happy hour is perfect for the serious afternoon drinker (14 beers on tap let you keep the pints rotating). For the Wednesday and Sunday Skee-Ball contest, *see left* **Brew's crews**.

Baraza

133 Avenue C, between 8th & 9th Streets (1-212 539 0811). Subway: L to First Avenue; 6 to Astor Place. **Open** 7.30pm-4am daily. **Average drink** $5. **No credit cards. Map** p403 G28 ㉑
One of the pioneers on Avenue C, this lively Latin spot is famous for its good $5 Caipirinhas and Mojitos, which draw a sleek boho crowd (the place is always packed). In the candlelit lounge past the bar, patrons puzzle over the Barbie aquarium, in which the plastic diva and Ken enjoy a lovely beach scene.

DBA

41 First Avenue, between 2nd & 3rd Streets (1-212 475 5097). Subway: F, V to Lower East Side-Second Avenue. **Open** 1pm-4am daily. **Average drink** $6. **Credit** AmEx, DC, Disc, MC, V. **Map** p403 F29 ㉒
DBA is a true beer hall for the true beer connoisseur – 130 brews (20 or so on tap), from the expensive (Belgian wheat drafts) to the unpronounceable (Schlenkerla Rauchbier). If you're not already paralysed by indecision, add more than 130 single malts and 50 tequilas to muddy your thinking.

In Vino

215 E 4th Street, between Avenues A & B (1-212 539 1011). Subway: F, V to Lower East Side-Second Avenue. **Open** 5.30pm-midnight Mon-Thur, Sun; 5.30pm-1am Fri, Sat. **Average drink** $8. **Credit** MC, V. **Map** p403 G29 ㉓
Come here to savour southern Italian vinos: the small cave-like space offers hundreds of regional wines that can accommodate such tasty, rustic appetisers as tomato-and-truffle crostini.

Le Souk

47 Avenue B, between 3rd & 4th Streets (1-212 777 5454). Subway: F, V to Lower East Side-Second Avenue. **Open** 6pm-4am daily. **Average drink** $9. **Credit** MC, V. **Map** p403 G29 ㉔
In the early evening, the muted lighting and *shishas* (hookas) give this two-room lounge the feel of a North African teahouse; a few hours on, it's a bump-and-grind bar; later still, when the tables and chairs are cleared away, it seems like a private after-hours party. Le Souk is an absolute hit every night, whether for weeknight belly dancing, the weekend's Arabic-infused house beats or Sunday night's legendary progressive house party.

McSorley's Old Ale House

15 E 7th Street, between Second & Third Avenues (1-212 473 9148). Subway: N, R, W to 8th Street-NYU; 6 to Astor Place. **Open** 11am-midnight Mon-Sat. **Average drink** $2. **No credit cards. Map** p403 F28 ㉕
It would take days to read the newspaper clips on the walls of this 1854 drinking landmark. Order a house beer – Dark Ale (sweet and smooth) or Light Ale (smooth with a bite) – and the veteran Irish waiters will bring you double mugs of suds. The sawdusted floor and never-dusted chandelier add to the old-time feel. Look up bartender-poet Geoffrey Bartholomew's *The McSorley Poems* before stopping by.

Sutra Lounge

16 First Avenue, between 1st & 2nd Streets (1-212 677 9477). Subway: F, V to Second Avenue-Lower East Side. **Open** 9pm-4am Mon-Sat. **Average drink** $8. **Credit** AmEx, MC, V. **Map** p403 F29 ㉖
Sutra wants to put you in the mood: you're seduced with incense and warm amber lighting the moment you enter. A downstairs cave is preserved as an old Turkish gentleman's club, and an upstairs bar and billiards room is lined with red velvet banquettes and bordello-style lamps. You can nibble on delicacies such as chocolate-covered strawberries and sip concoctions like the Sutra Martini, with vodka, vermouth and crème de cassis.

Greenwich Village & Noho

Bar Next Door

129 MacDougal Street, between 3rd & 4th Streets (1-212 529 5945). Subway: A, B, C, D, E, F, V to W 4th Street. **Open** 6pm-2am Mon-Thur, Sun; 6pm-3am Fri, Sat. **Average drink** $7. **Cover** $5 (Tue-Thur, Sun). **Credit** AmEx, DC, Disc, MC, V. **Map** p403 E29 ㉗
Hidden in the basement of a beautifully restored townhouse, Bar Next Door feels like a special secret you're lucky to know about. The romantic nook evokes old New York, as well as owner Vittorio Antonini's home town on the Italian Riviera. Low ceilings, exposed brick and stone walls provide superb acoustics for the regularly scheduled live jazz performances (Tuesday to Sunday). If you'd like something to nibble on, a full menu is offered until 2am (3am on weekends) from the adjacent trattoria, La Lanterna di Vittorio (*see p195*).

Centovini

25 W Houston Street, at Greene Street (1-212 219 2113). Subway: B, D, F, V to Broadway-Lafayette Street; 6 to Bleecker Street. **Open** 8am-midnight Mon; 8am-2am Tue-Fri; 9am-2am Sat; 9am-midnight Sun. **Average drink** $15. **Credit** AmEx, MC, V. **Map** p403 E29 ㉘
The design snobs at Soho's Moss have partnered with the wine geeks at I Trulli and Vino to open a wine bar with 100 Italian wines available by the glass, bottle and case. Much of the decor can be purchased around the corner at Moss. **Photo** *p217.*

Marion's Continental Restaurant & Lounge

354 Bowery, between Great Jones & E 4th Streets (1-212 475 7621). Subway: B, D, F, V to Broadway-Lafayette Street; 6 to Bleecker Street. **Open** 5.30pm-2am daily. **Average drink** $7. **Credit** AmEx, DC, Disc, MC, V. **Map** p403 F29 ㉙
Marion's hasn't been serving old-fashioned cocktails forever, but it sure feels that way. Decorated with thrift-shop paintings and bric-a-brac, this retro shrine to 1950s New York nightlife assumes the air of a festive but down-to-earth supper club, with fabulous music that varies from lounge and Latin to soul.

Eat, Drink, Shop

Views and booze mix to perfect effect at **230 Fifth**. *See p222.*

Pegu Club

77 W Houston Street, between West Broadway & Wooster Street (1-212 473 7348). Subway: 6 to Bleeker Street; B, D, F, V to Broadway-Lafayette Street. **Open** 5pm-2am Mon, Wed-Sun; 5pm-4am Thur-Sat. **Average drink** $12. **Credit** AmEx, Disc, DC, MC, V. **Map** p403 E29 ③⓪

Located on an unassuming Soho block, this bar is both hidden and welcoming. Upstairs, an elegant space with a long maple bar greets cocktail connoisseurs. Owner-mixologist Audrey Saunders stubbornly discourages trendy vodkas – gin is the basis for most of the menu. Asian-inspired snacks complement the drinks perfectly.

Von Bar

3 Bleecker Street, between Bowery & Elizabeth Street (1-212 473 3039). Subway: B, D, F, V to Broadway-Lafayette Street; 6 to Bleecker Street. **Open** 5pm-2am Mon-Wed, Sun; 5pm-4am Thur-Sat. **Average drink** $7. **Credit** AmEx, MC, V. **Map** p403 F29 ③①

This low-key two-room lair, all candlelit dark wood and exposed brick, is a perfect first-date spot. A large blackboard trumpets an extensive selection of (mostly French) wines by the glass, but the bar also has a full liquor licence. Pick a full-bodied red, like the Vacqueyras, take your friend by the hand, and head for one of the benches in the back room.

West Village & Meatpacking District

APT

For listing, see p295. **Map** p403 C27 ③②

By shifting its focus from door attitude to DJs, APT lives up to India Mahdavi's sleek, polished design.

Arthur's Tavern

57 Grove Street, between Bleecker Street & Seventh Avenue South (1-212 675 6879). Subway: 1 to Christopher Street-Sheridan Square. **Open** 7pm-4am daily. **Average drink** $8 (2-drink minimum). **No credit cards. Map** p403 D28 ③③

For about 60 years, this no-nonsense dive with year-round Christmas decorations and cheap suds has attracted tourists, old Village bohemians, fans of Dixieland jazz and the odd drag queen. Free live jazz and blues often make the two-drink minimum worthwhile. Best bet: the early-evening piano slot with Eri Yamamoto, Thursday to Saturday.

Chumley's

86 Bedford Street, between Barrow & Grove Streets (1-212 675 4449). Subway: 1 to Christopher Street-Sheridan Square. **Open** 4pm-midnight Mon-Thur; 4pm-2am Fri; noon-2am Sat, Sun. **Average drink** $6. **No credit cards. Map** p403 D29 ③④

The two unmarked entrances to Chumley's reflect its speakeasy roots. Since its opening in 1922, the place has poured pints for a fair share of famous authors; notice the countless book covers displayed on the walls. A working fireplace, free-roaming labradors and sawdusted floors maintain the scruffy yet genteel vibe.

5 Ninth

For listing, see p197. **Map** p403 C28 ③⑤

The bar inside the rustic restaurant, in a charming three-storey 1848 house, vibrates with speakeasy charm; old-school Scotches, cognacs and whiskeys are the main ingredients of the heady cocktails (like the fizzy Floridora) named after Broadway shows. Fireplaces, exposed brick and one of the city's loveliest gardens contribute to the intimacy, which encourages chatting up strangers.

Little Branch

20-22 Seventh Avenue South, at Leroy Street (1-212 929 4360). Subway: 1 to Houston Street. **Open** 7pm-3am Mon-Fri; 9pm-3am Sat. **Average drink** $9. **No credit cards. Map** p403 D29 ㊱

Milk & Honey owner Sasha Petraske is letting commoners into his candlelit, subterranean spot to sample his legendary cocktails. No reservations needed.

Spice Market

403 W 13th Street, at Ninth Avenue (1-212 675 2322). Subway: A, C, E to 14th Street; L to Eighth Avenue. **Open** 6pm-2am daily. **Average drink** $12. **Credit** AmEx, DC, MC, V. **Map** p403 C27 ㊲

Glide down the dramatic staircase and enter a glamorous world where votives flicker over a fashionable crowd that comes for the scene, the fruity cocktails and the street-market-inspired dishes.

Turks & Frogs

323 W 11th Street, between Greenwich & Washington Streets (1-212 691 8875). Subway: A, C, E to14th Street; L to Eighth Avenue. **Open** 5pm-4am daily. **Average drink** $7. **Credit** AmEx, MC, V. **Map** p403 C28 ㊳

In addition to the Turkish and French pottery doing decoration duty, visitors will find 50 wines (including some from Cakir's native Turkey) and a small menu of prepared foods (there's no oven on the premises) made with aubergine, cheese, grape leaves and other Mediterranean ingredients. Cakir has managed to pack an antique couch, a small bar and a few tables into the 800sq ft place. It makes for a nice getaway from the Meatpacking crowd.

Midtown

Chelsea & Flatiron

Bar Veloce

176 Seventh Avenue, between 20th & 21st Streets (1-212 629 5300). Subway: 1 to 18th Street. **Open** 5pm-3am daily. **Average drink** $8. **Credit** AmEx, MC, V. **Map** p403 D27 ㊴

This new outpost of the popular East Village Italian wine bar has a similar layout: a long wood bar and wine bottles stacked horizontally on artfully designed racks. The all-Italian wines pair well with an assortment of snacks including panini, bruschette and meat and cheese plates.

Double Seven

418 W 14th Street, between Ninth & Tenth Avenues (1-212 981 9099). Subway: A, C, E to 14th Street; L to Eighth Avenue. **Open** 6pm-4am Mon-Fri; 8pm-4am Sat. **Average drink** $16. **Credit** AmEx, MC, V. **Map** p403 C27 ㊵

Eventually, clubbers have to grow up, and Lotus owner David Rabin has just the place for them when they do – his new cocktail lounge across the street from his sceney Meatpacking District den. It's small – just 75 seats – and built for conversation rather than craziness. Drinks (by consultant Sasha

Petraske of Milk & Honey) are a whopping $16, but each one is served with Debauve & Galais chocolates. There's no need to queue: the place takes reservations for parties of four or more.

Flatiron Lounge

37 W 19th Street, between Fifth & Sixth Avenues (1-212 727 7741). Subway: F, N, R, V, W to 23rd Street; 1 to 18th Street. **Open** 5pm-2am Mon-Wed, Sun; 5pm-4am Thur-Sat. **Average drink** $10. **Credit** AmEx, MC, V. **Map** p403 E27 ㊶

To get to the 30ft mahogany bar (built in 1927), follow an arched hallway warmed by the soft glow of candles. You'll find an art deco space with red leather booths, round glass tables, flying-saucer-shaped lamps and an imaginative cocktail menu you'll want to dive straight into. Co-owner Julie Reiner is the mistress of mixology: the Persephone, for instance, is a subtle pomegranate Martini named for the queen of Hades.

Hiro

Maritime Hotel, 371 W 16th Street, at Ninth Avenue (1-212 727 0212). Subway: A, C, E to 14th Street; L to Eighth Avenue. **Open** 10pm-4am daily. **Average drink** $12. **Credit** AmEx, MC, V. **Map** p403 C27 ㊷

Past the guard at the speakeasy window is a vast, vaulted room lined with backlit paper screens. The place is often filled with girls in tube tops and the banker types who love them, as well as an occasional Rolling Stones heiress (Elizabeth Jagger, Theodora Richards). Signature cocktails, such as the Sakenade (saké, fresh ginger and lemon juice), are the kinds of delicious drinks that taste benign but quickly kick your ass – as they should, for $12.

Opus 22 Turntable Lounge

559 W 22nd Street, at Eleventh Avenue (1-212 243 1851). Subway: C, E to 23rd Street. **Open** 5pm-2am daily. **Average drink** $7. **Credit** AmEx, MC, V. **Map** p404 C26 ㊸

Sunsets over the Hudson remain the draw at this sleek space off the West Side Highway. But new owner Eddie Lee brought in a menu of upscale eats, like macaroni au gratin with ham and parmesan, and cream of melon soup with pepper and mint. Lee has revamped the open-air room, covering the space in Brazilian cherry wood and charcoal-grey upholstery. A custom-designed sound system and DJ booth lure aspiring artists during open-turntable sessions.

Park Bar

15 E 15th Street, between Fifth Avenue & Union Square West (1-212 367 9085). Subway: L, N, Q, R, W, 4, 5, 6 to 14th Street-Union Square. **Open** 3pm-5am daily. **Average drink** $7. **Credit** AmEx, MC, V. **Map** p403 E27 ㊹

What's small, dark and packed all over? Park Bar's dusky den of a room might be teensier than the average studio apartment, but for all that it has charm to spare. You'll need to arrive early to have any hope of a seat at the bar. Hungry drinkers often order pizza from nearby Giorgio's.

Eat, Drink, Shop

Bamboo 52.

Passerby

436 W 15th Street, between Ninth & Tenth Avenues (1-212 206 7321). Subway: A, C, E to 14th Street; L to Eighth Avenue. **Open** 6pm-2am Mon-Sat. **Average drink** $8. **Credit** AmEx, MC, V. **Map** p403 C27 ⓘ

The unmarked Passerby is a sort of clubhouse for arty types. Flashing coloured floor panels, created by artist Piotr Uklansky, pulse with the DJ's beats and lend an ambient glow. Early evening, this is a civilised place for a drink; later, things can get deliciously raucous.

230 Fifth

230 Fifth Avenue, between 26th & 27th Streets (1-212 725 4300). Subway: N, R, W to 28th Street. **Open** 4pm-4am daily. **Average drink** $11. **Credit** AmEx, MC, V. **Map** p404 E26 ⓘ

The rooftop bar dazzles with truly spectacular views of the Manhattan skyline, but the indoor lounge – with its wraparound sofas and bold lighting – should not be overlooked. Drinks are expensive and unremarkable, but the crowd is too busy bopping to the fantastic '80s music to mind much. **Photo** *p220.*

Midtown West

Ava Lounge

Majestic Hotel, 210 W 55th Street, between Seventh Avenue & Broadway (1-212 956 7020). Subway: N, Q, R, W to 57th Street. **Open** 5pm-3am Mon, Tue; 5pm-4am Wed-Fri; 6pm-4am Sat; 6pm-3am Sun. **Average drink** $9. **Credit** AmEx, Disc, MC, V. **Map** p405 D22 ⓘ

The top of the Majestic Hotel has been transformed into a penthouse lounge and rooftop deck with views of both the twinkling cityscape and the blondes in black who serve Key Lime Martinis and Flirtinis.

Modern, chic and slick but not overdesigned, the space is often used for private parties, and the outdoor patio is a lure for smokers.

Bamboo 52

344 W 52nd Street, between Eighth & Ninth Avenues (1-212 315 2777). Subway: C, E to 50th Street. **Open** 4pm-4am daily. **Average drink** $8. **Credit** AmEx, MC, V. **Map** p404 C23 ⓘ

This Hell's Kitchen eaterie has a front porch, a bamboo garden, a sushi bar and a drinks menu listing saké champagne, Asian microbrews and Japanese single-malt whiskey.

Hudson Bar

The Hudson, 356 W 58th Street, between Eighth & Ninth Avenues (1-212 554 6500). Subway: A, B, C, D, 1 to 59th Street-Columbus Circle. **Open** 4pm-2am Mon-Sat; 4pm-1am Sun. *Library bar* noon-2am Mon-Sat; noon-1am Sun. **Average drink** $10. **Credit** AmEx, DC, Disc, MC, V. **Map** p405 C22 ⓘ

Like a lime-green stairway to heaven, an escalator leads to the lobby of Ian Schrager's Hudson hotel, where you'll find three separate bars. Most dazzling is the postmodern Hudson Bar, with a backlit glass floor. The Library bar marries class (leather sofas) and kitsch (photos of cows in pillbox hats). If that's too cute, then get some air in the seasonal Private Park (open April to November), the leafy, cigarette-friendly outdoor bar lit by candle chandeliers.

Kemia Bar

630 Ninth Avenue, at 44th Street (1-212 582 3200). Subway: A, C, E to 42nd Street-Port Authority. **Open** 6pm-1am Tue-Fri; 8pm-2am Sat. **Average drink** $8. **Credit** AmEx, MC, V. **Map** p404 C24 ⓘ

Descending into this lush Middle Eastern oasis is like penetrating the fourth wall of a brilliant stage set. Gossamer fabric billows from the ceiling,

ottomans are clustered around low tables, and dark-wood floors are strewn with rose petals. A soulful DJ helps, as do the luscious libations.

Marseille

630 Ninth Avenue, at 44th Street (1-212 333 3410). Subway: A, C, E to 42nd Street-Port Authority. **Open** noon-1am daily. **Average drink** $9. **Credit** AmEx, MC, V. **Map** p404 C24 ⑤

Oenophiles line up at this slice of Paris, eager to taste selections from the 300 varieties kept in a cellar that once served as a bank vault. Wine director Sterling Roig has received accolades for putting together an eclectic list with overlooked vintages from France's Languedoc-Roussillon and Loire regions, as well as Sardinia and Sicily, in Italy. More than a dozen wines are sold by the glass.

Single Room Occupancy

360 W 53rd Street, between Eighth & Ninth Avenues (1-212 765 6299). Subway: B, D to Seventh Avenue; C, E to 50th Street. **Open** 7.30pm-2am Mon, Tue; 7.30pm-4am Wed-Sat. **Average drink** $8. **Credit** AmEx. **Map** p405 C23 ⑤

It's hard to overstate the importance of feeling like a New York insider. At this wine and beer speakeasy, where you must ring the doorbell to enter, you'll be deliciously in the know. SRO comfortably fits 20 or so, but more have been known to squeeze into the cave-like medieval-modern space. Locals think of owner Markos as the host of their favourite nightly party, and on one random evening a month, he rewards them with go-go dancers.

Sortie

329 W 51st Street, between Eighth & Ninth Avenues (1-212-265-0650). Subway: C, E to 50th Street. **Open** 5pm-4am daily. **Average drink** $9. **Credit** AmEx, MC, V. **Map** p404 C23 ⑤

The owners of this sultry bordello-like bar made sure their subterranean space would never be boring. They painted the walls a deep red and added velvet banquettes and studded black-leather café tables. They also hired flamenco dancers and serious guest DJs, and came up with a menu that specialises in tapas, cocktails and 30 artisanal beers.

Town

Chambers Hotel, 15 W 56th Street, between Fifth & Sixth Avenues (1-212 582 4445). Subway: F to 57th Street; N, R, W to Fifth Avenue-59th Street. **Open** noon-1am daily. **Average drink** $12. **Credit** AmEx, DC, Disc, MC, V. **Map** p405 E22 ⑤

Moneyed drinkers in their middle years pick from four designated drinking areas: the narrow bar at the head of the passageway leading to the restaurant; the spacious back balcony bar; the hotel's lofty lobby bar; and the mezzanine bar. There's a pricey wine list, but you might prefer a sassy house cocktail like the Town Plum, made with plum nectar.

Midtown East

Artisanal

2 Park Avenue, at 32nd Street (1-212 725 8585). Subway: E, V to Lexington Avenue-53rd Street; 6 to 51st Street. **Open** noon-11pm Mon-Thur; noon-midnight Fri, Sat; 11am-10pm Sun. **Average drink** $11. **Credit** AmEx, DC, Disc, MC, V. **Map** p404 E25 ⑤

Wine and cheese move into the realm of art at this restaurant's boisterous bar. There are 150-plus wines by the glass, and 250 or so cheeses – enough permutations for you to forever swear off chardonnay and brie. (Pairing flights of wine can help the uninitiated.) The bar area is packed for dinner, when fondue-craving hordes await their tables.

Brasserie

For listing, see p209. **Map** p404 E23 ⑤⑥

Take an architectural tour: this striking spot, in the basement of Mies van der Rohe's much-lauded Seagram Building, was outfitted by Diller + Scofidio. It features backlit bottles stored horizontally behind opaque glass, a long granite bar and curved walls made of pear-tree wood. You can spy on new arrivals via stop-motion images on screens mounted above the bar.

PJ Clarke's

915 Third Avenue, at 55th Street (1-212 317 1616). Subway: E, V to Lexington Avenue-53rd Street; 6 to 51st Street. **Open** 11.30am-4am daily. **Average drink** $7. **Credit** AmEx, DC, Disc, MC, V. **Map** p405 F22 ⑤⑦

PJ Clarke's has been a beloved saloon since 1884, but the storied, hard-drinking hacks, pols, molls and palookas of yore have been supplanted by briefcase-toting execs, cashmere-clad couples and baseball-capped buddies. Recently restored to vintage perfection, Clarke's also draws the likes of Johnny Depp and Bill Murray. Bartenders are polite and the pours generous. Must-peeks: the Tiffany stained-glass in the men's room and the cosy dining alcove where Renée Zellweger and Salma Hayek order steak to amp up their real-girl cred.

Sakagura

211 E 43rd Street, between Second & Third Avenues (1-212 953 7253). Subway: 42nd Street S, 4, 5, 6, 7 to 42nd Street-Grand Central. **Open** noon-2.30pm, 6pm-midnight Mon-Thur; noon-2.30pm, 6pm-1am Fri; 6pm-1am Sat; 6-11pm Sun. **Average drink** $7. **Credit** AmEx, DC, Disc, MC, V. **Map** p404 F24 ⑤⑧

The winner is…

Every year *Time Out New York* recognises the best offerings from among the city's thousands of bars. The selection of the most outstanding bars is the result of our expert drinkers' opinions combined with the votes of *Time Out* readers. Listed below are some of the winners from the 2006 awards:

Best new cocktail bar
Pegu Club. *See p220.*

Best new wine bar
Uva. *See p225.*

Best dive bar
Subway Inn. *See p225.*

Most innovative use of exotic spices
Loft. *See right.*

At Sakagura, you'll have to do a little work: walk through the unmarked lobby of an office building, down a few stairs and along a basement corridor. Finally, enter a quiet room of bamboo and blond wood and prepare to learn about saké. The 200 kinds available here, categorised by region, are served in delicate handblown glass vessels. If you can't decide, try a Sakagura Tasting Set, which teams an appetiser, entrée and dessert with three corresponding sakés. Check out the candlelit restrooms, cleverly fashioned from giant saké casks.

Tao

For listing, see p210. **Map** p405 E22 ⑤⑨

This sceney palace is forever packed with suits and skirts; a 16ft stone Buddha towers over the dining room. Drinks include many, many sakés and a list of appealing Asian-inflected cocktails.

Uptown

Upper West Side

Bin 71

237 Columbus Avenue, at 71st Street (1-212 362 5446). Subway: B, C to 72nd Street. **Open** 5pm-midnight Mon, Tue; 11am-1am Wed-Sun. **Average drink** $8. **Credit** AmEx, Disc, MC, V. **Map** p405 C20 ⑥⓪

This classy new wine bar from father and son Anselmo and Lawrence Bondulich helps fill the neighbourhood's 'inoteca void. Anselmo is coming out of retirement to create dishes like pink-snapper sashimi with garlic oil, and meatballs braised in white wine, lemon and bay leaves. Snackers can share antipasto platters or cheese plates, paired with wines from California, Italy, France and Spain. Of course, there's plenty of fine beer too.

Café del Bar

945 Columbus Avenue, between 106th & 107th Streets (1-917 741 0270). Subway: B, C to 103rd Street. **Open** 6pm-4am Tue-Sat; 8pm-2am Sun. **Average drink** $4. **Credit** AmEx, MC, V. **Map** p406 C16 ⑥①

If you can't get to Jamaica, Red Stripes here are $4 and the soundtrack is pure reggae. Located next door to the tiny French-Caribbean bistro A, the bar specialises in island drinks like a potent Dark & Stormy, made with ginger beer and spiced rum, or a Sorrel-a-Go-Go, made with rum, Cointreau and sorrel.

Loft

505 Columbus Avenue, between 84th & 85th Streets (1-212 362 6440). Subway: B, C to 86th Street. **Open** 6pm-midnight Mon-Thur, Sun; 6pm-4am Fri, Sat. **Average drink** $10. **Credit** AmEx, DC, Disc, MC, V. **Map** p406 C18 ⑥②

Ginger Martinis recently became the equivalent of the bindi on Gwen Stefani's forehead: the exotic co-opted as mere fashion. But at this sexy Moroccan-accented lounge and restaurant, the addition of pungent spices makes for some profoundly unusual drinking. The

Eat, Drink, Shop

Galapagos. *See p227.*

Sirocco, a blast of bourbon and lime juice, gets its sweet and vicious snap from lavender-flower honey. And for its Basil Mojito, Loft boils down sugarcane. This concoction is also available by the carafe; it's as intoxicating as absinthe and similarly addictive.

Upper East Side

Central Park Boathouse

Central Park Lake, Park Drive North, at 72nd Street (1-212 517 2233). Subway: 6 to 68th Street-Hunter College. **Open** noon-4pm, 5.30-9.30pm Mon-Fri; 9.30am-4pm, 6-9.30pm Sat, Sun. **Average drink** $7. **Credit** AmEx, DC, MC, V. **Map** p405 D20 ⑥③

The view from the tree-shaded deck bordering the boat-freckled lake looks like a shot framed by Woody Allen. Step into the film at the outdoor bar after Sunday brunch (the Bloody Marys are mighty powerful). Plush leather armchairs near the fireplace beckon in winter. A Boathouse Martini (Bacardi Limón, triple sec and a splash each of lime and cranberry juices) will make you smile all year long.

Lexington Bar & Books

1020 Lexington Avenue, at 73rd Street (1-212 717 3902). Subway: 6 to 77th Street. **Open** 5pm-3am Mon-Wed, Sun; 5pm-4am Thur-Sat. **Average drink** $10. **Credit** AmEx, DC, MC, V. **Map** p405 E20 ⑥④

Order a drink here, and the barman offers you an ashtray. Yes, it's a legal cigar bar – and one with class: walls are lined with books and fine brandies,

beer and Martini glasses are frosted, and the selection of single-malt Scotches and cognacs is topflight. If James Bond was an East Sider, you would find him here.

Subway Inn

143 E 60th Street, between Lexington & Third Avenues (1-212 223 8929). Subway: N, R, W to Lexington Avenue-59th Street; 4, 5, 6 to 59th Street. **Open** 8am-4am daily. **Average drink** $3. **No credit cards. Map** p405 F22 ⑥⑤

The bar near the Lexington Avenue and 60th Street subway exit is a 74-year-old watering hole that really is a hole. The clientele varies based on the time of day, but you're likely to see a mix of what appears to be Bowery-bum-like boozers, regular guys and confused tourists, seated either in decrepit booths or at the bar. Drinks prices are lost in a time warp too – beer starts at $3.50.

Uva

1486 Second Avenue, at 77th Street (1-212 472 4552). Subway: 6 to 77th Street. **Open** noon-2am Mon-Thur, Sun; noon-3am Fri, Sat. **Average drink** $9. **Credit** AmEx, MC, V ($30 minimum). **Map** p405 F19 ⑥⑥

The Upper East Side has plenty of rustic Italian restaurants but it could use a few more wine bars. A 200-year-old wooden floor and antique couches give this one a warm, worn-in feel. You can take your pick of cured meats and cheeses to pair with many Italian wines (30 are available by the glass).

Above 116th Street

Den

2150 Fifth Avenue, between 131st & 132nd Streets (1-212 234 3045). Subway: 2, 3 to 135th Street. **Open** 6pm-1am Mon-Thur; 6pm-4am Fri, Sun. **Average drink** $9. **Credit** AmEx, Disc, MC, V. **Map** p407 E12 ⑥⑦

Under the glow of a classic old streetlamp, a dapper doorman tips his derby and welcomes visitors to a subterranean lounge set in a Harlem brownstone. Designer Carlos Jimenez, whose resumé includes industry (food) and Flow, has cast a lush red haze over the 1920s-era room lined with exposed brick and accented by a copper-topped bar.

Lenox Lounge

288 Malcolm X Boulevard (Lenox Avenue), between 124th & 125th Streets (1-212 427 0253). Subway: 2, 3 to 125th Street. **Open** noon-4am daily. **Average drink** $5 (cover varies). **Credit** AmEx, DC, MC, V. **Map** p407 D13 ⑥⑧

This is where a street hustler named Malcolm worked before he found religion and added an X to his name. Now the famous Harlem bar, lounge and jazz club welcomes a mix of old-school cats and unobtrusive booze hounds. Settle into the refurbished art deco area at the front or take a table in the zebra-papered back room, then tune in to the haunting presence of Billie Holiday and Miles Davis.

Eat, Drink, Shop

Bembe. *See p227.*

Brooklyn

Bembe
81 South 6th Street, at Berry Street, Williamsburg (1-718 387 5389). Subway: J, M, Z to Marcy Avenue; L to Bedford Avenue. **Open** 7.30pm-4am Mon-Thur; 7pm-4am Fri-Sun. **Average drink** $5. **No credit cards. Map** p411 U8 ⑥
At an unmarked hideaway under the Williamsburg Bridge, the swinging clientele dances by candlelight to Latin beats laid down by sexy DJs. Take a breather from the salsa and refuel with tequila shots at the sleek wooden bar. Regulars swear by the post-shot practice of sucking the lime after dipping one side in fresh coffee and the other in sugar. **Photos** *p226.*

Boogaloo
168 Marcy Avenue, between Broadway & South 5th Street, Williamsburg (1-718 599 8900). Subway: J, M, Z to Marcy Avenue. **Open** 7pm-4am Tue-Thur; 8pm-4am Fri-Sun. **Average drink** $6. **Credit** AmEx, Disc, MC, V. **Map** p411 U8 ⑦
This sleek white hideaway oozes *Barbarella* cool. A long, narrow front room leads to a small dancefloor and DJ station (Latin, house, hip hop and funk); the rooftop space is open in warm weather. Rum is a speciality, but bartenders can fix any combo. None is especially cheap, but that seems to suit Boogaloo's patrons just fine.

Brooklyn Social
335 Smith Street, between Carroll & President Streets, Carroll Gardens (1-718 858 7758). Subway: F, G to Carroll Street. **Open** 6pm-2am Mon-Thur; 6pm-4am Fri, Sat; 5pm-2am Sun. **Average drink** $6. **No credit cards. Map** p410 S10 ⑦

Smoke signal

Despite the strict citywide smoking ban of 2003, there are still a few places where you can legally light up:
Circa Tabac 32 Watts Street, between Sixth Avenue & Thompson Street (1-212 941 1781).
Club Macanudo 26 E 63rd Street, between Madison & Park Avenues (1-212 752 8200).
Karma 51 First Avenue, between 3rd & 4th Streets (1-212 677 3160).
Velvet Cigar Lounge 80 E 7th Street, at First Avenue (1-212 533 5582).
At the time of writing, smoking was still permitted at many outdoor patios and roof decks. If the weather is nice, head for:
Ava Lounge (*see p222*).
Central Park Boathouse (*see p225*).
Glass 287 Tenth Avenue, between 26th & 27th Streets (1-212 904 1580).

When Matt Dawson heard that Società Riposto was closing, he thought the old Sicilian social club would make an ideal hipster watering hole. So he gutted the bland card-playing room and installed designer touches, right? Fuhgeddaboudit. He kept every detail he could and even hung photographs of the original members on the walls. The bar has been kept simple, but there's one major add-on: a backyard with a patio.

Galapagos
For listing, see p315. **Map** p411 U7 ⑦
This perennial Williamsburg fave doubles as a performance space for all kinds of art. **Photo** *p225.*

Moto
394 Broadway, at Hooper Street, Williamsburg (1-718 599 6895). Subway: J, M to Hewes Street. **Open** 6pm-2am Mon-Thur, Sun; 6pm-3am Fri, Sat. **Average drink** $6. **No credit cards. Map** p411 V8 ⑦
Owners Billy Phelps and John McCormick have somehow created a café-bar evocative of 1930s Paris in a former cheque-cashing store beneath the J-M elevated tracks. (The documentary *Eat This New York* captured Moto's rocky transformation on celluloid.) However, the menu is Italian, the wines are handpicked and the beers include Belgian Corsendonk. The pan-Euro attitude, easy subway access and good food and drink in an intimate triangular room make Moto a Williamsburg must-go.

Superfine
126 Front Street, at Pearl Street, Dumbo (1-718 243 9005). Subway: A, C to High Street; F to York Street. **Open** 11.30am-3pm, 6pm-1am Tue-Thur; 11.30am-3pm, 6pm-4am Fri; 2pm-4am Sat; 11am-3pm, 6pm-1am Sun. **Average drink** $6. **Credit** AmEx, MC, V. **Map** p411 T9 ⑦
Praised for its weekend Southwestern Chili Brunch, this eaterie is also a fine place for drinks any evening of the week (there's also a tiny art gallery and scruffy types in smart-guy glasses). The worn-in mix-and-match furniture is usually occupied by young, suited professionals downing Cosmos, or arty locals who hang at the pool table. You might even see regulars from the Federation of Black Cowboys, who hitch their horses at the door before sitting at the bar.

Queens

Bohemian Hall & Beer Garden
29-19 24th Avenue, between 29th & 31st Streets, Astoria (1-718 274 0043). Subway: N, W to Astoria Boulevard. **Open** 5pm-2am Mon-Fri; noon-3am Sat, Sun. **Average drink** $4. **Credit** MC, V ($10 minimum). **Map** p412 X3 ⑦
Echt Mitteleuropa in the Greek precinct of Astoria? Czech! This authentic (c1910) beer hall is a throwback to the time when hundreds of such places dotted the town; the vibe manages to combine the ambience of that era with the youthful spirit of a junior year in Prague. Go for the platters of Czech sausage, $4 Stolis, Spaten Oktoberfests and the rockin' juke. In summer, the huge, tree-canopied beer garden beckons.

Eat, Drink, Shop

Shops & Services

These streets were made for walking… and shopping.

If there's one thing New York has plenty of, it's beautiful things to buy. So arm yourself with fistfuls of cash and credit cards and don't look back, because we're taking you on a shopping spree. Whether your tastes lean towards Soho chic, Fifth Avenue posh or vintage treasures (see p240 **Good as old**), a mountain of glorious goods is ready and waiting to be snapped up. Listed on the following pages are a dizzying array of shops to help you part with your hard-earned money. But before you get started, here's a tactical spending tip: it's best to arrange your shopping excursions by neighbourhood. And, while all the top designers have shops here, be sure to pay a visit to the independent local stores for something nobody at home will be wearing.

DO AS NEW YORKERS DO

There are a few key shopping events in this town that can reap major finds: Barneys' ever-popular twice-yearly warehouse sales, and designers' frequent sample sales are excellent sources for reduced-price clothing by fashion's biggest names. To find out where the sales are during any given week, consult the Check Out section of *Time Out New York*. Top Button (www.topbutton.com) and the SSS Sample Sales hotline (1-212 947 8748, www.clothingline. com) are also great discount resources. Sales are usually held in the designers' shops or in rented loft spaces. Typically, loft sales are not equipped with changing rooms, so bring a courageous spirit with you (and plenty of cash) and remember to wear appropriate undergarments. Speaking of showing some skin, if you're looking to do it up with a new tattoo be sure to read **Ink well** (see p257) for the city's best tattoo artists.

RETAIL RECONNAISSANCE

Harlem, the Meatpacking District and Brooklyn's Williamsburg are the city's latest fashion stops – that they're relatively far-flung areas distinguishes the willing-to-travel fashion fiends from the less obsessive. However, serious shoppers agree that the most cutting-edge labels are to be found in Nolita, along Mott and Mulberry Streets, although Uptown's Fifth Avenue (between 42nd & 59th Streets) is difficult to beat. Over on the west side of the island, the West Village's Bleecker Street has become hot property seemingly overnight, touting the likes of Intermix, Lulu Guinness, Cynthia Rowley,

Ralph Lauren (which has three stores here – one for men, one for women and a co-ed shop), along with three Marc Jacobs stores. Now you can window-shop like you're Uptown with a cupcake from Magnolia Bakery. To find out the latest stores and hotspots making waves on New York's design scene, visit www.timeout newyork.com, click on Check Out. And, if you're the type that needs a little extra guidance, check out our day-long shopping itineraries (see p232 and p233 **Clothes lines**).

If the weather is disagreeable and you need a shopping fix, head to one of New York's shopping malls. You won't get the best deal or the uniqueness of a boutique, but the Manhattan Mall (Sixth Avenue, at 33rd Street), the Shops at Columbus Circle (Time Warner Center, 10 Columbus Circle, at 59th Street), and the myriad stores in Trump Tower (Fifth Avenue, at 56th Street), Grand Central Terminal (42nd Street, at Park Avenue) and South Street Seaport's cobblestoned Pier 17 (Fulton Street, at the East River) are convenient options.

Thursday is the unofficial shop-after-work night; most stores remain open until at least 7pm. Stores downtown generally stay open an hour or so later than those uptown. Some of the shops listed here have more than one location; we have given up to two branches. For bigger chains, check the website or the business pages in the phone book for further addresses.

One-stop

Department stores

Barneys New York

660 Madison Avenue, at 61st Street (1-212 826 8900/www.barneys.com). Subway: N, R, W to Fifth Avenue-59th Street; 4, 5, 6 to 59th Street. **Open** 10am-8pm Mon-Fri; 10am-7pm Sat; 11am-6pm Sun. **Credit** AmEx, MC, V.

The top designers are represented at this bastion of New York style. At Christmas time, Barneys has the most provocative windows in town (see p252 **Season's greetings**). Its co-op branches carry young designers, as well as secondary lines from heavies like Marc Jacobs and Theory. Every February and August, the Chelsea co-op hosts the Barneys Warehouse Sale, when prices are slashed by 50% to 80%. **Photo** p229.
Other locations: throughout the city.

Barneys New York. See p228.

Bergdorf Goodman

754 Fifth Avenue, at 57th Street (1-212 753 7300/ www.bergdorfgoodman.com). Subway: E, V to Fifth Avenue-53rd Street; N, R, W to Fifth Avenue-59th Street. **Open** 10am-8pm Mon-Fri; 10am-7pm Sat; noon-6pm Sun. **Credit** AmEx, DC, MC, V.

If Barneys aims for a young, trendy crowd, then Bergdorf's is dedicated to an elegant, understated clientele that has plenty of disposable income. Luxury clothes, accessories and even stationery are found here, along with an over-the-top beauty floor. Handily, the famed men's store is just across the street (745 Fifth Avenue).

Bloomingdale's

1000 Third Avenue, at 59th Street (1-212 705 2000/ www.bloomingdales.com). Subway: N, R, W to Lexington Avenue-59th Street; 4, 5, 6 to 59th Street. **Open** 10am-8.30pm Mon-Fri; 10am-7pm Sat; 11am-7pm Sun. **Credit** AmEx, MC, V.

Bloomies is a gigantic, glitzy department store offering everything from handbags and cosmetics to furniture and designer duds. Brace yourself for the crowds – this store ranks among the city's most popular tourist attractions, right up there with the Empire State Building. Check out the cool new (little) sister branch in Soho.

Other locations: 504 Broadway, between Broome & Spring Streets, Soho (1-212 279 5900).

Henri Bendel

712 Fifth Avenue, at 56th Street (1-212 247 1100/ www.henribendel.com). Subway: E, V to Fifth Avenue-53rd Street; N, R, W to Fifth Avenue-59th Street. **Open** 10am-8pm Mon-Sat; noon-7pm Sun. **Credit** AmEx, DC, Disc, MC, V.

Bendel's lavish quarters resemble an opulent townhouse. Naturally, there are elevators – no one expects you to walk, this is Fifth Avenue – but it's nicer to saunter up the elegant, winding staircase. Prices are comparable to those of other upscale stores, but the merchandise somehow seems more desirable here – we guess it must be those darling brown-striped shopping bags.

Jeffrey New York

449 W 14th Street, between Ninth & Tenth Avenues (1-212 206 1272/www.jeffreynewyork.com). Subway: A, C, E to 14th Street; L to Eighth Avenue. **Open** 10am-8pm Mon-Wed, Fri; 10am-9pm Thur; 10am-7pm Sat; 12.30-6pm Sun. **Credit** AmEx, MC, V.

Jeffrey Kalinsky, a former Barneys shoe buyer, was a Meatpacking District pioneer with his namesake shop. Designer clothing abounds here – Helmut Lang, Versace and Yves Saint Laurent among other brands. But the centrepiece is without doubt the shoe salon, which features Manolo Blahnik, Prada and Robert Clergerie.

Lord & Taylor

424 Fifth Avenue, between 38th & 39th Streets (1-212 391 3344/www.lordandtaylor.com). Subway: B, D, F, V to 42nd Street-Bryant Park; 7 to Fifth Avenue. **Open** 10am-8.30pm Mon-Fri; 10am-7.30pm Sat; 11am-7pm Sun. **Credit** AmEx, Disc, MC, V.

Classic is the word at Lord & Taylor, for both the clothing stocked and the presentation; this is where the tradition of dramatic Christmas window displays began. Check out two recent dining additions: An American Place and the Signature Café, run by celebrity chef Larry Forgione.

Eat, Drink, Shop

Macy's

151 W 34th Street, between Broadway & Seventh Avenue (1-212 695 4400/www.macys.com). Subway: B, D, F, N, Q, R, V, W to 34th Street-Herald Square; 1, 2, 3 to 34th Street-Penn Station. **Open** 10am-9pm Mon-Sat; 11am-8pm Sun. **Credit** AmEx, MC, V.

Behold the real miracle on 34th Street. Macy's has everything a shopper could ever want: designer labels and lower-priced knockoffs, a pet-supply shop, a restaurant in the Cellar (the housewares section), a Metropolitan Museum of Art gift shop and – gulp – a McDonald's on the kids' floor. The store also offers Macy's by Appointment, a free service that allows you to order goods or clothing over the phone and have them shipped anywhere in the world (1-800 343 0121).

Saks Fifth Avenue

611 Fifth Avenue, at 50th Street (1-212 753 4000/www.saksfifthavenue.com). Subway: E, V to Fifth Avenue-53rd Street. **Open** 10am-7pm Mon-Wed, Fri, Sat; 10am-8pm Thur; noon-6pm Sun. **Credit** AmEx, DC, Disc, MC, V.

Although Saks maintains a presence in 24 states, the Fifth Avenue location is the original, established in 1924 by New York retailers Horace Saks and Bernard Gimbel. The store features all the big names in women's fashion, from Armani to Yves Saint Laurent, plus an excellent menswear department and a children's section. There are also fine household linens, La Prairie skincare and attentive customer service. New management is exploring the possibility of a major overhaul this year; at the time of writing, Frank Gehry's name had made the rumour mill as the architect.

Takashimaya

693 Fifth Avenue, between 54th & 55th Streets (1-212 350 0100/www.ny-takashimaya.com). Subway: E, V to Fifth Avenue-53rd Street. **Open** 10am-7pm Mon-Sat; noon-5pm Sun. **Credit** AmEx, DC, MC, V.

Step out of the Fifth Avenue hustle-bustle and into Takashimaya to experience the Zen garden of the retail world. Explore floor by floor, indulging your senses as you pass beauty essentials, furniture and the men's and women's signature clothing collections. A cup of tea in the basement Tea Box makes the perfect end to a trip to consumer nirvana.

National chains

Many New Yorkers regard chain stores as unimaginative places to shop, but that doesn't mean you won't have to stand behind a long line of locals while waiting at the register. Stores such as American Apparel, Anthropologie, Banana Republic, Express, H&M, Old Navy, Target and Urban Outfitters abound in New York. To find the nearest location of your favourite chain, refer to the phone book.

Fashion

Flagships

These big-name designers have clothes horses chomping at the bit for their latest designs.

Alexander McQueen

417 W 14th Street, between Ninth & Tenth Avenues (1-212 645 1797/www.alexandermcqueen.com). Subway: A, C, E to 14th Street; L to Eighth Avenue. **Open** 11am-7pm Mon-Sat; 12.30-6pm Sun. **Credit** AmEx, DC, Disc, MC, V.

A barrel-vaulted ceiling and serene lighting make the rebellious Brit's Meatpacking District store feel like a religious retreat. But the top-stitched denim skirts and leather jeans are far from monastic.

Ben Sherman

96 Spring Street, at Mercer Street (1-212 680 0160/www.benshermanusa.com). Subway: C, E to Spring Street; N, R, W to Prince Street. **Open** 10am-9pm Mon-Sat; 11am-7pm Sun. **Credit** AmEx, MC, V.

Bringing a touch of London's Carnaby Street to Soho, Ben Sherman, the eponymous streetwear brand born of the original swinging '60s mod god, has dropped its first US flagship. As a salute to its English roots, the co-ed emporium is peppered with mannequins and an antique settee covered in a Union Jack pattern.

Bottega Veneta

699 Fifth Avenue, between 54th & 55th Streets (1-212 371 5511/www.bottegaveneta.com). Subway: E, V to Fifth Avenue-53rd Street; N, R, W to Fifth Avenue-59th Street. **Open** 10am-6.30pm Mon-Wed, Fri, Sat; 10am-7pm Thur; noon-5pm Sun. **Credit** AmEx, DC, Disc, MC, V.

At this luxe Italian label's largest store worldwide, a dramatic leather-and-steel staircase links the ground floor with a mezzanine. The gargantuan emporium stocks the complete line of shoes and handbags, along with men's and women's apparel available only here.

Chanel

15 E 57th Street, between Fifth & Madison Avenues (1-212 355 5050/www.chanel.com). Subway: E, V to Fifth Avenue-53rd Street; N, R, W to Fifth Avenue-59th Street. **Open** 10am-6.30pm Mon-Wed, Fri; 10am-7pm Thur; 10am-6pm Sat; noon-5pm Sun. **Credit** AmEx, DC, MC, V.

With a façade that resembles the iconic Chanel No.5 perfume bottle, the brand's flagship conjures up the spirit of Madame Coco herself. Fashion architect Peter Marino recently redesigned and enlarged the space for this haul of divine Frenchness. Drop in at Chanel Fine Jewelry (733 Madison Avenue, at 64th Street, 1-212 535 5828) for correspondingly elegant baubles and beads.

Other locations: 139 Spring Street, at Wooster Street, Soho (1-212 334 0055); 737 Madison Avenue, at 64th Street, Upper East Side (1-212 535 5505).

Diane von Furstenberg, the Shop

385 W 12th Street, between Washington Street & West Side Highway (1-646 486 4800/www.dvf. com). Subway: A, C, E to 14th Street; L to Eighth Avenue. **Open** 11am-6pm Mon-Wed, Fri; 11am-8pm Thur; 11am-5pm Sat; noon-5pm Sun. **Credit** AmEx, Disc, MC, V.

Although known for her classic wrap dress (she sold five million of them in the 1970s), indefatigable socialite Diane von Furstenberg has installed much more at this soigné space, which resembles the inside of a jewellery box. Whether you go for ultra-feminine dresses or sporty knits, you'll emerge from the changing room feeling like a princess.

Dolce & Gabbana

825 Madison Avenue, between 68th & 69th Streets (1-212 249 4100/www.dolcegabbana.it). Subway: 6 to 68th Street-Hunter College. **Open** 10am-6pm Mon-Wed, Fri, Sat; 10am-7pm Thur; noon-6pm Sun. **Credit** AmEx, DC, MC, V.

The Italian design team of Domenico Dolce and Stefano Gabbana gives love to Uptowners and Downtowners alike. Visit the smarter Madison Avenue locale (and see how close the Canal Street knock-offs come to the real thing), or shop the West Broadway store for the cheaper D&G line.
Other locations: D&G, 434 West Broadway, between Prince & Spring Streets, Soho (1-212 965 8000).

Donna Karan New York

819 Madison Avenue, between 68th & 69th Streets (1-212 861 1001/www.donnakaran.com). Subway: 6 to 68th Street-Hunter College. **Open** 10am-6pm Mon-Wed, Fri, Sat; 10am-7pm Thur; noon-6pm Sun. **Credit** AmEx, DC, MC, V.

Created around a central garden with a bamboo forest, Donna Karan's upscale flagship store caters to men, women and the home. Make sure you check out the organic café at the nearby DKNY store, as well as Donna-approved reads, clothing, shoes and vintage furniture.
Other locations: DKNY, 655 Madison Avenue, at 60th Street, Upper East Side (1-212 223 3569).

Marc Jacobs

163 Mercer Street, between Houston & Prince Streets (1-212 343 1490/www.marcjacobs.com). Subway: B, D, F, V to Broadway-Lafayette Street; N, R, W to Prince Street; 6 to Bleecker Street. **Open** 11am-7pm Mon-Sat; noon-6pm Sun. **Credit** AmEx, DC, Disc, MC, V.

Men and women get fashion parity at Jacobs's Soho boutique. A separate-but-equal policy rules at the designer's trio of shops on Bleecker Street – men's, women's and accessories – which keep the West Village well kitted-out.
Other locations: Marc by Marc Jacobs, 403-405 Bleecker Street, at 11th Street, Meatpacking District (1-212 924 0026); Marc Jacobs Accessories, 385 Bleecker Street, at Perry Street, Meatpacking District (1-212 924 6126).

Prada

575 Broadway, at Prince Street (1-212 334 8888/ www.prada.com). Subway: N, R, W to Prince Street. **Open** 11am-7pm Mon-Sat; noon-6pm Sun. **Credit** AmEx, Disc, MC, V.

The Rem Koolhaas-designed Soho flagship cemented Prada's status as the label of choice for New York's fashion fleet (yes, you still have to put your name on a waiting list to buy the latest shoe styles). The giant wood Wave structure is the store's focal

Eat, Drink, Shop

Tracy Reese. *See p233.*

point. If you're only interested in the accessories, then skip the crowds at the two larger shops and stop by the small Fifth Avenue location. **Other locations**: 724 Fifth Avenue, at 57th Street, Midtown (1-212 664 0010); 841 Madison Avenue, at 70th Street, Upper East Side (1-212 327 4200).

Ralph Lauren

867 Madison Avenue, at 72nd Street (1-212 606 2100/www.polo.com). Subway: 6 to 68th Street-Hunter College. **Open** 10am-7pm Mon-Wed, Fri, Sat; 10am-8pm Thur; noon-5pm Sun. **Credit** AmEx, DC, Disc, MC, V.

Ralph Lauren spent $14 million turning the old Rhinelander mansion into an Ivy League dream of a superstore: it's filled with oriental rugs, paintings, riding whips, leather club chairs, mahogany and fresh flowers. The young homeboys, skaters and bladers who've adopted Ralphie's togs head straight to Polo Sport across the street.
Other locations: Ralph Lauren Boutique, 380 Bleecker Street, between Charles & Perry Streets, Meatpacking District (1-212 645 5513); Polo Sport, 381 Bleecker Street, between Charles & Perry Streets, Meatpacking District (1-646 638 0684).

Stella McCartney

429 W 14th Street, between Ninth & Tenth Avenues (1-212 255 1556/www.stellamccartney.com). Subway: A, C, E to 14th Street; L to Eighth Avenue. **Open** noon-7pm Mon-Sat; 12.30-6pm Sun. **Credit** AmEx, DC, Disc, MC, V.

Celeb designer McCartney (famously the daughter of Beatle Paul), who won acclaim for her rock-star

Clothes lines For him: L Train

Crossing the city along 14th Street, the L train offers stylish blokes a chance to stock their closets without having to venture too far up- or downtown. Off the Eighth Avenue stop, the Meatpacking District's **DDC Lab** (427 W 14th Street, between Ninth & Tenth Avenues, 1-212 414 5801) has togs that are both fashion- and technology-forward, with chic, futuristic items cut from such materials as antimicrobial fabric and waxed leather. **Buckler** (13 Gansevoort Street, at Hudson Street, 1-212 255 1596) is the flagship of Brit designer Andrew Buckler, who crafts staples such as button-downs, T-shirts and blazers that straddle the line between dressy and casual. Nearby, vintage shop **CherryMen** (17 Eighth Avenue, between Jane & W 12th Streets, 1-212 924 5188; *photo below*) can fulfill a guy's nostalgic needs. As a last stop before getting back on the train, any man worth his weight in denim should hit **Barneys Co-op** (236 W 18th Street, between Seventh

& Eighth Avenues, 1-212 593 7800), which has an extensive collection of jeans. Two stops over, at Union Square, **Paul Smith** (108 Fifth Avenue, at 16th Street, 1-212 627 9770; *see also p238*) is a mecca for dapper Dans who can't get enough of the UK designer's subtly preppy suits and sweaters.

In the East Village, near the First Avenue station, **Odin** (328 E 11th Street, between First & Second Avenues, 1-212 475 0666; *see also p238*) has a host of underground and up-and-coming labels for the grown-up skate rat who appreciates high-quality style. **UnderdogEast** (117 E 7th Street, between First Avenue & Avenue A, 1-212 388 0560) is a luxe shop for modern label-hounds in search of tastefully tailored goods, such as perfectly cut blazers and button-downs.

You'll find some of the most trendsetting men's stores across the river in Williamsburg. Off Bedford Avenue, **Nom de Guerre**'s outer-borough outpost (88 North 6th Street,

between Berry Street & Wythe Avenue, 1-718 387 3363) draws neighbourhood denizens in search of au courant basics. **Yoko Devereaux** (338 Broadway, between Rodney & Keap Streets, 1-718 302 1450) offers streetwear dressed up a notch or two, with sweatshirt-material blazers and soft screen-printed T-shirts. Now call a car (try Northside Car Service, 1-718 387 2222) to help haul away your loot.

collections for Chloé, now showcases pricey lines of glam-sprite womenswear, shoes and accessories at her first stand-alone store.

Tracy Reese
641 Hudson Street, between Gansevoort & Horatio Streets (1-212 807 0505). Subway: A, C, E to 14th Street; L to Eighth Avenue. **Open** 11am-7pm Mon-Wed; 11am-8pm Thur-Sat; noon-7pm Sun. **Credit** AmEx, Disc, MC, V.

With the opening of her eponymous Meatpacking District flagship, apostles of arch-feminine designer Tracy Reese now have a house of worship. The 2,200sq ft of curvaceous walls, twinkly chandeliers and fuchsia cushioned-settees pays tribute to all things girly – much like Reese's threads. **Photo** *p231*.

Boutiques

Annie O
105 Rivington Street, between Essex & Ludlow Streets (1-212 475 3490/www.hotelonrivington.com/annieo.html). Subway: F to Delancey. **Open** 1pm-11pm Tue-Sat; noon-6pm Sun. **Credit** AmEx, MC, V.

Party like a rock star? Now you can shop like one too at Annie O, a music-themed boutique, tucked into the Hotel on Rivington (*see p53*) on the Lower East Side. Shop curator Annie Ohayon – a former music publicist for acts such as Pearl Jam, Lou Reed and the Smashing Pumpkins – handpicks goods spiked with a naughty, rock 'n' roll sensibility. The shop has been quick to garner rave reviews from the local press, and it's easy to see why. **Photo** *p234*.

Clothes lines For her: N/R/W Train

Ladies, let the N/R/W train be your shopping guide. Starting in Park Slope, hit **Diana Kane** (229 Fifth Avenue, between Carroll & President Streets, 1-718 638 6520) near Union Street. It's a great place to stock up on seasonal gear like swimwear, lingerie and fragrances. One stop up the line, at Pacific Street, you'll find **Sir** (360 Atlantic Avenue, between Bond & Hoyt Streets, 1-718 643 6877). Don't be fooled by the masculine moniker – the

popular Brooklyn destination for vintage-inspired threads is strictly for chicks. Next, head into Manhattan and get off at City Hall. No lover of European labels goes more than a few weeks without checking in at downtown discount palace **Century 21** (*see p236*).

Myriad stores, from high-end to low, inhabit the five-block radius around your next stop, Prince Street in Soho. Among the best are **APC** (131 Mercer Street, between Prince & Spring Streets, 1-212 966 9685), which takes well-made basics and adds a French accent, and, a few blocks north, **Nave** (159 Mercer Street, between W Houston & Prince Streets, 1-212 274 1255), for chic, wearable goods like perfect cotton trench coats and distinctive silk-screened Ts.

If it's supercheap, trendy pieces you're after, then get back on the train and head to 34th Street. **Forever21** (50 W 34th Street

at Broadway, 1-212 564 2346), a three-floor megastore, hawks some of the best designer knockoffs around.

Make your way to Fifth Avenue for the best kind of the B-list: Barneys, Bergdorf's and Bendel's. While **Henri Bendel** (*see p229; photo above*) has a new 'beach boutique', complete with summer stock, **Barneys** (*see p228*) is a top spot for cashmere and eveningwear. **Bergdorf Goodman** (*see p229*) just opened a Goyard boutique on the main floor and remains a label-conscious New Yorker's go-to spot. If your stamina is as unlimited as your MetroCard, check out one more great store, at the end of the R line – **Lulu's** (70-34 Austin Street, between 70th Road & 71st Street, 1-718 793 3268) in Forest Hills. It's a haven for premium denim and sleek pieces from the likes of Frankie B and Solo. Now give that card one last swipe and take your new clothes out on the town.

Eat, Drink, Shop

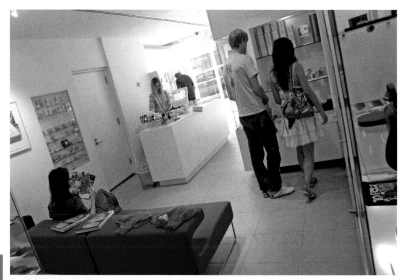

Annie O rocks (and so does her shop). *See p233.*

Bird

430 Seventh Avenue, between 14th & 15th Streets, Park Slope, Brooklyn (1-718 768 4940). Subway: F to 15th Street-Prospect Park. **Open** 11.30am-7pm Mon-Sat; noon-6pm Sun. **Credit** AmEx, Disc, MC, V.
Park Slope's Bird has always been a favourite of neighbourhood girls looking for designer dresses and Ts, but new owner Jennifer Mankins recently made it the spot in Brooklyn for jeans, stocking Chip & Pepper, James Jeans and Wrangler, and more.

Bond 07

7 Bond Street, between Broadway & Lafayette Street (1-212 677 8487). Subway: B, D, F, V to Broadway-Lafayette Street; 6 to Bleecker Street. **Open** 11am-7pm Mon-Sat; noon-7pm Sun. **Credit** AmEx, MC, V.
Selima Salaun, of the famed Le Corset by Selima (*see p237*), has branched out from undies and eyewear to embrace an eclectic mix of clothing (Alice Roi, Colette Dinnigan), accessories and French furniture. Vintage eyewear and bags are also available.

Calypso Christiane Celle

654 Hudson Street, between Gansevoort & W 13th Streets (1-646 638 3000/www.calypso-celle.com). Subway: A, C, E to 14th Street; L to Eighth Avenue. **Open** 11am-7pm Mon-Sat; noon-7pm Sun. **Credit** AmEx, DC, MC, V.
Christiane Celle has created a Calypso empire, of which this new outpost in the Meatpacking District is the crown jewel. Stop by any of the shops for gorgeous slip dresses, suits, sweaters and scarves, many from little-known French designers.
Other locations: throughout the city.

Cantaloup

1036 Lexington Avenue, at 74th Street (1-212 249 3566). Subway: 6 to 77th Street. **Open** 11am-7pm Mon-Sat; noon-6pm Sun. **Credit** AmEx, MC, V.
Finally, a boutique that gives UES girls a reason to skip the trip down to Nolita. Cantaloup is chock-full of emerging labels such as James Coviello and Chanpaul, and it's less picked over than the below-Houston boutiques.
Other locations: 1359 Second Avenue, at 74th Street, Upper East Side (1-212 288 3569).

Comme des Garçons

520 W 22nd Street, between Tenth & Eleventh Avenues (1-212 604 9200). Subway: C, E to 23rd Street. **Open** 11am-7pm Tue-Sat; noon-6pm Sun. **Credit** AmEx, DC, Disc, MC, V.
In this austere store devoted to Rei Kawakubo's architectural designs for men and women, clothing is hung like art in an innovative space that feels like a gallery – well placed in Chelsea.

Elizabeth Charles

639½ Hudson Street, between Gansevoort & Horatio Streets (1-212 243 3201/www.elizabeth-charles.com). Subway: A, C, E to 14th Street; L to Eighth Avenue. **Open** noon-7.30pm Tue-Sat; noon-6.30pm Sun. **Credit** AmEx, MC, V.
Oz native Elizabeth Charles transferred her eponymous shop from the West Village to the fashion nexus of the Meatpacking District last year, allowing for an even greater selection of flirty clothes from designers Down Under. Most labels are exclusive to the store, so chances are you won't see your outfit on anyone else – unless you go to Australia.

Girlshop

819 Washington Street, between Gansevoort & Little W 12th Streets (1-212 255 4985/www.girlshop.com). Subway: L to Eighth Avenue. **Open** 11am-7pm Mon-Wed; 11am-8pm Thur-Sat; noon-7pm Sun. **Credit** AmEx, MC, V.

Girlshop.com's bricks-and-mortar sibling offers instant gratification to shoppers who can now try on hot numbers available online by Keanan Dufty, Cigana, or any of the myriad labels. The perfect alternative for those who fall between two sizes.

Kirna Zabete

96 Greene Street, between Prince & Spring Streets (1-212 941 9656/www.kirnazabete.com). Subway: C, E to Spring Street; R, W to Prince Street. **Open** 11am-7pm Mon-Sat; noon-6pm Sun. **Credit** AmEx, MC, V.

The Nick Dine-designed, futuristic-feeling store stocks avant-garde yet wearable women's clothing and shoes from haute designers like Jean Paul Gaultier and Balenciaga, along with a range of fragrances, and the kind of jeans you probably won't want to do the decorating in.

Opening Ceremony

35 Howard Street, between Broadway & Lafayette Street (1-212 219 2688). Subway: J, M, N, Q, R, W, Z, 6 to Canal Street. **Open** 11am-8pm Mon-Sat; noon-7pm Sun. **Credit** AmEx, MC, V.

Opening Ceremony offers a stylish trip around the world, in a warehouse-size space gussied up with grape-coloured walls and crystal chandeliers. The boutique presents fashions by country (Sweden takes centre stage through September 2007). Buyers cull from couture labels, independent designers, mass-market brands and open-air markets.

Patricia Field

302 Bowery, between Bleecker & Houston Streets (1-212 966 4066/www.patriciafield.com). Subway: C, E to Spring Street. **Open** noon-8pm Mon-Thur, Sun; noon-9pm Fri, Sat. **Credit** AmEx, Disc, MC, V.

Some people celebrate their 40th anniversary with diamonds or extravagant parties. Not Patricia Field. She is commemorating her 40th year in retail with a new boutique. Marking a return to the East Village after closing her seminal 8th Street store over a decade ago in 1996, the two-level Bowery shop is a veritable *This Is Your Life*-style retrospective of the fashion icon's costume-design career. Graffiti by street artist De la Vega, trophies from the sets of *Sex and the City* and *The Devil Wears Prada*, and a neon sign from her now-closed Hotel Venus outpost make lively set dressings for playful garb. In addition to fashion, there's jewellery, lingerie and cosmetics. And for shoppers in need of a makeover or a new hairstyle, there's also a hair and make-up salon.

Pieces

671 Vanderbilt Avenue, at Park Place, Prospect Heights, Brooklyn (1-718 857 7211/www.pieces ofbklyn.com). Subway: 2, 3 to Grand Army Plaza. **Open** 11am-7pm Tue-Thur; 11am-8pm Fri, Sat; 11am-6pm Sun. **Credit** AmEx, MC, V.

At this husband-and-wife-owned store, white-washed brick walls are the backdrop for vibrant clothing and accessories along the lines of Pretty Punk miniskirts, Ant pinstriped dress shirts and Anja Flint clutches. Menswear is also stocked.
Other locations: Pieces of Harlem, 228 W 135th Street, between Adam Clayton Powell Jr Boulevard (Seventh Avenue) & Frederick Douglass Boulevard (Eighth Avenue), Harlem (1-212 234 1725).

Patricia Field.

Eat, Drink, Shop

Pretty designs from the other side of the world, courtesy of **Rebecca Taylor**.

Rebecca Taylor

260 Mott Street, between Houston & Prince Streets (1-212 966 0406/www.rebeccataylor.com). Subway: B, D, F, V to Broadway-Lafayette Street; N, R, W to Prince Street; 6 to Bleecker Street. **Open** noon-6pm daily. **Credit** AmEx, MC, V.

This New Zealand designer's shop is adorned with murals of fairy worlds and butterflies – perhaps the source of inspiration for her whimsical, kittenish dresses and jackets.

Scoop

861 Washington Street, between 13th & 14th Streets (1-212 691 1905/www.scoopnyc.com). Subway: A, C, E to 14th Street; L to Eighth Avenue. **Open** 11am-8pm Mon-Fri; 11am-7pm Sat; noon-6pm Sun. **Credit** AmEx, DC, Disc, MC, V.

Scoop represents the ultimate fashion editor's closet. Clothing from the likes of Juicy Couture, Diane von Furstenberg, Philosophy and others is arranged by hue, not by label. The newest outposts, in the Meatpacking District, have fab finds for both genders at neighbouring stores; hit the Soho shop for women only, the uptown branch if you're after a more classic look for guys and gals. For the menswear store up the street, *see p238*.

Other locations: 532 Broadway, between Prince & Spring Streets, Soho (1-212 925 2886); 1275 Third Avenue, between 73rd & 74th Streets, Upper East Side (1-212 535 5577).

Steven Alan

103 Franklin Street, between Church Street & West Broadway (1-212 343 0692/www.stevenalan.com). Subway: 1 to Franklin Street. **Open** 11.30am-7pm Mon-Wed, Fri, Sat; 11.30am-8pm Thur. **Credit** AmEx, MC, V.

Decorated like an old-school general store, this roomy shop leans slightly in favour of the ladies – the front section is earmarked for hot-chick labels such as Botkier, Christopher Deane and, of course, Steven Alan. The back area does right by the gents, though, with Rogan jeans and items from Filson, an outdoorsmen's line. Don't skip the jewellery up front.

Other locations: 465 Amsterdam Avenue, between 82nd & 83rd Streets, Upper West Side (1-212 595 8451).

TG-170

170 Ludlow Street, between Houston & Stanton Streets (1-212 995 8660/www.tg170.com). Subway: F to Delancey Street; J, M, Z to Delancey-Essex Streets. **Open** noon-8pm daily. **Credit** AmEx, MC, V.

Terri Gillis has an eye for emerging designers: she was the first to carry Built by Wendy and Pixie Yates. Nowadays, you'll find Jared Gold and Liz Collins pieces hanging in her newly expanded store.

Bargains

Century 21

22 Cortlandt Street, between Broadway & Church Street (1-212 227 9092/www.c21stores.com). Subway: R, W to Cortlandt Street. **Open** 7.45am-8pm Mon-Wed, Fri; 7.45am-8.30pm Thur; 10am-8pm Sat; 11am-7pm Sun. **Credit** AmEx, MC, V.

A white Gucci men's suit for $300? A Marc Jacobs cashmere sweater for less than $200? Roberto Cavalli sunglasses for a scant $30? You're not dreaming – you're shopping at Century 21. The prized score is rare but the place is still intoxicating; savings are usually between 25% and 75% off regular prices.

Other locations: 472 86th Street, between Fourth & Fifth Avenues, Bay Ridge, Brooklyn (1-718 748 3266).

Find Outlet

*229 Mott Street, between Prince & Spring Streets
(1-212 226 5167). Subway: N, R, W to Prince
Street; 6 to Spring Street.* **Open** noon-7pm daily.
Credit MC, V.
Skip the sample sales and head to Find Outlet
instead. High-fashion samples and overstock are at
drastically reduced prices (with 50% off, on average), so you can dress like a fashion editor on an editorial assistant's budget.
Other locations: 361 W 17th Street, between
Eighth & Ninth Avenues, Chelsea (1-212 243 3177).

Market NYC

*268 Mulberry Street, between Houston & Prince
Streets (1-212 580 8995/www.themarketnyc.com).
Subway: B, D, F, V to Broadway-Lafayette Street;
N, R, W to Prince Street; 6 to Bleecker Street.*
Open 11am-7pm Sat, Sun. **No credit cards**.
Yes, it's housed in the gymnasium of a church's
youth centre, but this place is no small shakes. Every
weekend, contemporary fashion and accessory
designers hawk their (usually unique) wares here.

Children's clothing

Babybird

*428 Seventh Avenue, between 14th & 15th Streets,
Park Slope, Brooklyn (1-718 788 4506). Subway:
F to Seventh Avenue.* **Open** 10.30am-6.30pm Mon-
Sat; noon-6pm Sun. **Credit** AmEx, MC, V.
An offshoot of the neighbouring Bird (an ultra-cool
store for grown-ups; *see p234*), Babybird is filled
with comfy basics in stylish colours for the kids. We
love the fish tank built into the register counter.

Calypso Enfant

*426 Broome Street, between Crosby & Lafayette
Streets (1-212 966 3234/www.calypso-celle.com).
Subway: 6 to Spring Street.* **Open** 11am-7pm
Mon-Sat; noon-7pm Sun. **Credit** AmEx, MC, V.
Fans of Calypso Christiane Celle (*see p234*) adore
this Francophile children's boutique: the tiny wool
coats look as if they could have been lifted straight
from the pages of a classic children's book.

Sam & Seb

*208 Bedford Avenue, between North 5th & 6th
Streets, Williamsburg, Brooklyn (1-718 486 8300/
www.samandseb.com). Subway: L to Bedford Avenue.*
Open noon-7pm Mon-Wed; noon-8pm Thur, Fri;
11am-8pm Sat; 11am-7pm Sun. **Credit** AmEx, DC,
Disc, MC, V.
For style-conscious procreators who wouldn't dream
of clothing their offspring in generic baby clothes,
Williamsburg's groovy Sam & Seb delivers 1960s-
and '70s-inspired play clothes and funky consignment pieces by local designers, along with silk-
screened Jimi Hendrix and Bob Marley mini-Ts.

Yoya

*636 Hudson Street, between Horatio & Jane
Streets (1-646 336 6844/www.yoyashop.com).
Subway: A, C, E to 14th Street; L to Eighth Avenue.*

Open 11am-7pm Mon-Sat; noon-5pm Sun.
Credit AmEx, Disc, MC, V.
Various Village sensibilities – European, bohemian
and hip – come together in this store, which is aimed
at infants to six-year-olds. Labels such as Erica
Tanov, Temperley for Little People, and Imps &
Elves are available, as well as tiny-size (but not tiny-
priced) Diesel Ts.

Lingerie & swimwear

Most department stores have comprehensive
lingerie and swimwear sections, and Victoria's
Secret shops abound; but the following spots
are special places to go for extra-beautiful
bedroom and beachside wear.

Agent Provocateur

*133 Mercer Street, between Prince & Spring
Streets (1-212 965 0229/www.agentprovocateur.
com). Subway: B, D, F, V to Broadway-Lafayette
Street; N, R, W to Prince Street; 6 to Spring
Street.* **Open** 11am-7pm Mon-Sat; noon-6pm
Sun. **Credit** AmEx, MC, V.
Looking for something to rev up your sweetie's heart-
beat? Then check out this patron saint of provoca-
tive panties. Va-va-voomy bras, garters and bustiers
are dubbed with Bond-girl names. **Photo** *p238.*

Catriona MacKechnie

*400 W 14th Street, between Ninth & Tenth Avenues
(1-212 242 3200). Subway: A, C, E to 14th Street.*
Open 11am-7.30pm Mon-Sat; noon-6pm Sun.
Credit AmEx, MC, V.
Glasgow-born Catriona MacKechnie has turned lingerie into haute couture with her dramatically
decked-out eponymous shop. Along with exclusive
UK labels and the proprietor's own line, MacKechnie
offers custom knicker fittings.

Erès

*621 Madison Avenue, between 58th & 59th Streets
(1-212 223 3550/www.eres.fr). Subway: N, R, W to
Fifth Avenue-59th Street.* **Open** 10am-6pm Mon-Sat.
Credit AmEx, DC, Disc, MC, V.
Paris's reigning queen of sophisticated bathing togs
fits in swimmingly on New York's toniest avenue.
Sunny white walls and serene blond-wood floors
and counters give the merchandise the pedestal
treatment. Precious intimates and colourful bathing
suits are displayed on custom-made hangers, fabric
busts and mannequins.
Other locations: 98 Wooster Street, between Prince
& Spring Streets, Soho (1-212 431 7300).

Le Corset by Selima

*80 Thompson Street, between Broome & Spring
Streets (1-212 334 4936). Subway: C, E to Spring
Street.* **Open** 11am-7pm Mon-Fri; noon-8pm Sat;
noon-7pm Sun. **Credit** AmEx, DC, Disc, MC, V.
In addition to Selima Salaun's slinky designs, this
boudoir-like boutique stocks antique camisoles, vintage silk kimonos, comely lingerie and Victorian-
and Edwardian-inspired corsets.

Agent Provocateur – saucy stuff. *See p237.*

Malia Mills

199 Mulberry Street, between Kenmare & Spring Streets (1-212 625 2311/www.maliamills.com). Subway: 6 to Spring Street. **Open** noon-6pm daily. **Credit** AmEx, MC, V.

Ever since one of her designs made the cover of *Sports Illustrated*'s swimsuit issue a dozen years ago, Malia Mills's swimwear has been a staple for St Bart's bathing beauties. Flip-flops and long, luxurious terry-cloth robes are provided for ladies trying on bikini separates.

Other locations: Malia Mills Outlet, 16th Floor, 263 W 38th Street, between Seventh & Eighth Avenues, Garment District (1-212 354 4200 ext 214).

Mixona

262 Mott Street, between Houston & Prince Streets (1-646 613 0100/www.mixona.com). Subway: B, D, F, V to Broadway-Lafayette Street; N, R, W to Prince Street; 6 to Bleecker Street. **Open** 11am-7.30pm Mon-Fri, Sun; 11am-8pm Sat. **Credit** AmEx, MC, V.

Luxurious under-things by 30 designers are found here, including Christina Stott's leather-trimmed mesh bras and Passion Bait's lace knickers.

Vilebrequin

1070 Madison Avenue, at 81st Street (1-212 650 0353/www.vilebrequin.com). Subway: 6 to 77th Street. **Open** 10am-6pm Mon-Sat; noon-5pm Sun. **Credit** AmEx, DC, MC, V.

Boxer-style swimming trunks (men's only) in five adult styles (plus one for boys) are the mainstay of this St-Tropez-based company's shop. Styles and patterns include seahorses and pinstripes. **Other locations**: 436 West Broadway, at Prince Street, Soho (1-212 431 0673).

Menswear

A

125 Crosby Street, between Houston & Prince Streets (1-212 941 8435). Subway: N, R, W to Prince Street. **Open** 11am-7pm Mon-Fri; noon-7pm Sat; noon-6pm Sun. **Credit** AmEx, DC, MC, V.

When A Atelier dropped women's clothes from its racks last year, it also dropped 'atelier' from its name. Now a sophisticated men's-only store, A distinguishes itself from the high-fashion Soho pack with rarefied labels such as Balenciaga, Cloak and Les Hommes. Score for the boys.

Odin

328 E 11th Street, between First & Second Avenues (1-212 475 0666). Subway: L to First Avenue. **Open** noon-8pm daily. **Credit** AmEx, MC, V.

Gentlemen generally prefer one-stop shopping, and so favour this East Village guys' emporium, which tows the line between boys' street-savvy threads and men's tailored attire – all with an edge, of course.

Paul Smith

108 Fifth Avenue, between 15th & 16th Streets (1-212 627 9770/www.paulsmith.co.uk). Subway: L, N, Q, R, W, 4, 5, 6 to 14th Street-Union Square. **Open** 11am-7pm Mon-Wed, Fri, Sat; 11am-8pm Thur; noon-6pm Sun. **Credit** AmEx, Disc, MC, V.

Paul Smith devotees love this store's raffish English-gentleman look. They're even more partial to the designs and accessories that combine elegance, quality and wit (and some serious price tags).

Scoop Men

873 Washington Street, between 13th & 14th Streets (1-212 929 1244/www.scoopnyc.com). Subway: A, C, E to 14th Street; L to Eighth Avenue. **Open** 11am-8pm Mon-Fri; 11am-7pm Sat; noon-6pm Sun. **Credit** AmEx, DC, Disc, MC, V.

For review, see p236 **Scoop**.

Other locations: 1273 Third Avenue, between 73rd & 74th Streets, Upper East Side (1-212 535 5577).

Seize sur Vingt

243 Elizabeth Street, between Houston & Prince Streets (1-212 343 0476/www.16sur20.com). Subway: B, D, F, V to Broadway-Lafayette Street; N, R, W to Prince Street; 6 to Bleecker Street. **Open** 11am-7pm Mon-Sat; noon-6pm Sun. **Credit** AmEx, Disc, MC, V.

Ready-to-wear men's shirts are available here, but the real draws are the bespoke suits and custom-cut button-downs. Shirts come in Wall Street pinstripes and preppy gingham, with mother-of-pearl buttons and short, square collars. Be sure to check out the fine handkerchiefs too.

Eat, Drink, Shop

Streetwear

A Bathing Ape

91 Greene Street, between Prince & Spring Streets (1-212 925 0222). Subway: N, R to Prince Street. **Open** 11am-8pm Mon-Sat; noon-7pm Sun. **Credit** AmEx, MC, V.

The cult label created by Japanese designer Nigo planted its first US flagship in Soho last spring. Nigo, who has collaborated with Pharrell Williams, among others, devotes most of his shop to BAPE threads, while an upstairs shoe salon housing BAPEsta kicks has made the city's sneaker-hungry masses go ape.

Autumn

436 E 9th Street, between First Avenue & Avenue A (1-212 677 6220/www.autumnskateboarding.com). Subway: L to First Avenue; 6 to Astor Place. **Open** noon-7pm daily. **Credit** AmEx, Disc, MC, V.

Proprietor and amateur skateboarder David Mimms and his wife, Kristen Yaccarino, stock DVS, Emerica, Etnies, iPath, Lakai and Vans for your half-pipe pleasure. Ts and jeans, not to mention scores of boards, are available too.

Brooklyn Industries

162 Bedford Avenue, at North 8th Street, Williamsburg, Brooklyn (1-718 486 6464/www.brooklynindustries.com). Subway: L to Bedford Avenue. **Open** 11am-9pm Mon-Sat; noon-8pm Sun. **Credit** AmEx, Disc, MC, V.

Bags sporting the skyline label and zippered sweat-shirt hoodies with Brooklyn emblazoned across the chest are just the tip of the iceberg here.
Other locations: 286 Lafayette Street, between Prince & Spring Streets, Soho/Little Italy (1-212 219 0862); 206 Fifth Avenue, at Union Street, Park Slope, Brooklyn (1-718 789 2764); 100 Smith Street, at Atlantic Avenue, Boerum Hill, Brooklyn (1-718 596 3986); 184 Broadway, at Driggs, Williamsburg, Brooklyn (1-718 218 9166).

Dave's Quality Meat

7 E 3rd Street, between Bowery & Second Avenue (1-212 505 7551/www.davesqualitymeat.com). Subway: F, V to Lower East Side-Second Avenue. **Open** noon-7pm Mon-Sat; noon-6pm Sun. **Credit** AmEx, Disc, MC, V.

Dave Ortiz – formerly of urban-threads label Zoo York – and professional skateboarder Chris Keefe stock top-shelf streetwear in their wittily designed shop complete with meat hooks and mannequins sporting butchers' aprons. Homemade graphic-print Ts are wrapped in plastic and displayed in a deli case.

Phat Farm

129 Prince Street, between West Broadway & Wooster Street (1-212 533 7428/www.phatfarmstore.com). Subway: C, E to Spring Street; N, R, W to Prince Street. **Open** 11am-7pm Mon-Sat; noon-6pm Sun. **Credit** AmEx, Disc, MC, V.

Def Jam impresario Russell Simmons's classy, conservative take on hip hop couture: phunky-phresh baggy clothing for guys; for gals, the Baby Phat line.

Prohibit NYC

269 Elizabeth Street, between Houston & Prince Streets (1-212 219 1469/www.prohibitnyc.com). Subway: F, V to Lower East Side-Second Avenue. **Open** noon-8pm daily. **Credit** AmEx, MC, V.

City guys can get all their necessities at this spare, polished upscale streetwear boutique, from well-made threads and special-edition sneakers to hair-cuts (with hot-towel treatment; $30) while seated in an apple-red vintage barber's chair.

Recon

359 Lafayette Street, between Bleecker & Bond Streets (1-212 614 8502/www.reconstore.com). Subway: 6 to Bleecker Street. **Open** noon-7pm Mon-Thur, Sun; noon-8pm Fri, Sat. **Credit** AmEx, MC, V.

The joint venture of one-time graffiti artists Stash and Futura, Recon offers graf junkies a chance to wear the work on clothing and accessories.

Stüssy

140 Wooster Street, between Houston & Prince Streets (1-212 274 8855). Subway: N, R, W to Prince Street. **Open** noon-7pm Mon-Fri; 11am-7pm Sat; noon-6pm Sun. **Credit** AmEx, MC, V.

Tricky isn't the only one who wants to be dressed up in Stüssy. Come here for all the skate and surf wear that made Sean Stüssy famous, as well as utilitarian Japanese bags from Headporter.

Supreme

274 Lafayette Street, between Jersey & Prince Streets (1-212 966 7799). Subway: B, D, F, V to Broadway-Lafayette Street; N, R, W to Prince Street; 6 to Spring Street. **Open** 11.30am-7pm Mon-Sat; noon-6pm Sun. **Credit** AmEx, MC, V.

Filled mostly with East Coast brands such as Chocolate, Independent and Zoo York, this skate-wear store also stocks its own line. Look for pieces by Burton and DC Shoe – favourites of skaters like Colin McKay and Danny Way.

Triple Five Soul

290 Lafayette Street, between Houston & Prince Streets (1-212 431 2404/www.triple5soul.com). Subway: B, D, F, V to Broadway-Lafayette Street; N, R, W to Prince Street; 6 to Bleecker Street. **Open** 11am-7pm Mon-Thur, Sun; 11am-7.30pm Fri, Sat. **Credit** AmEx, Disc, MC, V.

Although the label is no longer exclusive to New York, the city can still boast the brand's only stand-alone stores. Find the very necessary hooded sweat-shirts and Ts stamped with the Triple Five logo at this Soho spot.
Other locations: 145 Bedford Avenue, at North 9th Street, Williamsburg, Brooklyn (1-718 599 5971).

Unis

226 Elizabeth Street, between Houston & Prince Streets (1-212 431 5533). Subway: B, D, F, V to Broadway-Lafayette Street; N, R, W to Prince Street; 6 to Bleecker Street. **Open** noon-7pm Mon-Wed, Sun; noon-7.30pm Thur-Sat. **Credit** AmEx, Disc, MC, V.

Good as old

Sick of browsing? Use our foolproof finder to locate those key vintage pieces.

A 1980s CONCERT T

You may be kicking yourself because your Def Leppard Hysteria tour T-shirt went the way of the Salvation Army years ago, yet who could have guessed that it would become such a valuable possession? You can still score retro concert Ts, but be prepared to pay a lot more than you did at the merchandise table back in '87. **Screaming Mimi's** (382 Lafayette Street, between Great Jones & E 4th Streets, 1-212 677 6464; *photo right*) hardy stash includes cheeseball favourites such as New Kids on the Block and Michael Jackson, starting at around $45. At **What Comes Around Goes Around** (351 West Broadway, between Broome & Grand Streets, 1-212 343 9303),

you'll find the Holy Grails of concert Ts, featuring Bruce Springsteen, Prince, Ted Nugent and the Police.

A 1960s COUTURE GOWN

Sure, it's unlikely that you'll be walking the red carpet anytime soon, but that shouldn't stop you from indulging your Hilary Swank-fuelled dreams of finding the perfect vintage evening gown. For high-end couture, do as the film industry does and go to the recently expanded **New York Vintage** (117 W 25th Street, between Sixth & Seventh Avenues, 1-212 647 1107), where you can find Givenchy, Dior, Balenciaga, Chanel and Fortuny. Expect to pay between $500 and $5,000 for the good stuff. Those with deep pockets and discerning

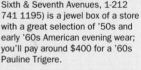

tastes also head to **Resurrection** (217 Mott Street, between Prince & Spring Streets, 1-212 625 1374) for Pucci, YSL and Ossie Clark. **Jim Smiley Vintage Clothing** (2nd Floor, 128 W 23rd Street, between Sixth & Seventh Avenues, 1-212 741 1195) is a jewel box of a store with a great selection of '50s and early '60s American evening wear; you'll pay around $400 for a '60s Pauline Trigere.

A 1920s VENETIAN MIRROR

Your first stop in the hunt should be **Paris Apartment** (70 E 1st Street, between First & Second Avenues, 1-917 749 5089; *photo left*), a luxurious boudoir-size shop decked with Murano-glass chandeliers and glam vanities worthy of Hayworth and Garbo. A pristine scalloped-edge mirror was the East Village shop's recent focal point, and smaller wall mirrors come in regularly. Across town, Greg Ventra and Mark Field, the owners of **Venfield** (392 Bleecker Street, between Perry & W 11th Streets, 1-212 627 5552), make monthly European jaunts to keep their genteel West Village fun house gleaming with Venetian stunners of all sizes – from tabletop prop vanities with floral etchings to rare amber-tinted wall mirrors.

AN ORIGINAL HANS WEGNER CREDENZA

Hans Wegner, who is known for his perfect proportions and fastidious attention to detail, is one of the grandaddies of Danish modern design. 'The Scandinavians use wood flawlessly,' says William Lee, owner of the expertly organised **Modernlink** (35 Bond Street, between Bowery & Lafayette Streets, 1-212 254 1300), the go-to place in Manhattan for mid-century modern furniture. Lee combs through the Danish countryside every few weeks to fill his 3,000-square-foot treasure chest with gold standards, such as the very rare Wegner 'President' sideboard. In Brooklyn, two more especially reliable spots beckon. At **Baxter & Liebchen** (33 Jay Street, at Plymouth Street, Dumbo, Brooklyn, 1-718 797 0630), whose impressive flock of 700 vintage pieces averages a dozen credenzas a week, owner Andrew Kevelson says, 'It is hard to have more than one of a given model. But the most popular pieces – the low rosewood side tables by Wegner – we have all the time'. **Horseman Antiques** (351 Atlantic Avenue, at Hoyt Street, Boerum Hill, Brooklyn, 1-718 596 1048), a cavernous 24,000-square-foot showroom, also has credenzas galore. Half of owner Donald Gianchetta's stock is American, but with an additional 14,000 square feet of retail space in Neptune, New Jersey, Gianchetta confidently says, 'We always have plenty of Hans Wegner'.

A 1940s PEEP-TOE PUMP

Zia Ziprin has made herself the Yoda of the vintage-shoe world, with a wealth of both knowledge and stock. Tucked away on the second floor of a Lower East Side walk-up is her **Girls Love Shoes** (2nd Floor, 85 Hester Street, between Allen & Orchard Streets, 1-917 250 3268), which may have the best selection of vintage kicks in the country: more than 2,000 pairs – some dating to the early 1800s. The archive, which includes the most breathtaking (and fragile) pairs (only for rent), is open by appointment, but the retail store keeps a lot of treasures on hand as well. On 23rd Street in Chelsea, vintage mainstay **The Family Jewels** (130 W 23rd Street, between Sixth & Seventh Avenues, 1-212 633 6020) offers a dramatic array of pristine items often used in fashion shoots and films. Here, you'll find 1920s beaded flapper dresses and '40s bathing suits à la Esther Williams, plus a rainbow of leather jackets, satin bags, printed dresses and glittering sequined sweaters. Allan Pollock and Suzi Kandel, owners of the decade-old Upper West Side institution **Allan & Suzi** (416 Amsterdam Avenue, at 80th Street, 1-212 724 7445), have amassed an impressive collection of vintage platform shoes. Their *Pee-Wee's Playhouse*-esque boutique also has a location in Asbury Park, New Jersey. Here in Manhattan, the racks are crowded with major labels: Yves Saint Laurent, Lacroix and Pucci. There's also tons of jewellery, some from the 1920s.

Korean-American designer Eunice Lee's structured streetwear used to be for boys only, but she let the girls in on the fun in 2003. Both collections are featured in her sleek Nolita boutique, along with Botkier bags and other accessories.

Sneakers

Adidas

610 Broadway, at Houston Street (1-212 529 0081/ www.adidas.com). Subway: N, R, W to Prince Street. **Open** 10am-10pm Mon-Sat; 11am-7pm Sun. **Credit** AmEx, DC, Disc, MC, V.

Inside this 29,500sq ft Soho space – decorated with giant images of athletes – you'll find every imaginable garment associated with the brand, including sportster threads by Stella McCartney.

Alife Rivington Club

158 Rivington Street, between Clinton & Suffolk Streets (1-212 375 8128/http://rivingtonclub.com). Subway: F to Delancey Street; J, M, Z to Delancey-Essex Streets. **Open** noon-7pm daily. **Credit** AmEx, MC, V.

'Sneakers' equal 'religion' in this tiny, out-of-the-way shop, which is arguably the city's main hub for hard-to-get shoes. The store, like its wares, has a rather exclusive vibe: there's no sign, no street number, no indication that the joint even exists from the outside. Look closely and ring the bell to check out the rotating selection of 60 or so styles.

Classic Kicks

298 Elizabeth Street, between Houston & E 1st Streets (1-212 979 9514). Subway: B, D, F, V to Broadway-Lafayette; 6 to Bleecker Street. **Open** noon-7pm Mon-Sat. **Credit** AmEx, MC, V.

One of the more female-friendly sneaker shops, Classic Kicks stocks mainstream and rare styles of Converse, Lacoste, Puma and Vans, to name but a few, for both boys and girls, along with a decent selection of clothes.

Clientele

267 Lafayette Street, at Prince Street (1-212 219 0531). Subway: N, R, W to Prince Street; 6 to Spring Street. **Open** noon-8pm Mon-Sat; noon-7pm Sun. **Credit** AmEx, MC, V.

Set up like an art-gallery display, the kicks line one wall of the minimalist store, and patrons sit on a long wooden bench to admire them.

Vintage & thrift

Goodwill and the Salvation Army are great for vintage finds, but it can take hours of digging to discover a gem. Enter thrift boutiques, where the digging has been done for you. We have listed a wide range here, from the more extravagant shops that cherry-pick vintage YSL and Fiorucci for their racks, to your general T-shirt havens, as well as a few that fall in between.

Allan & Suzi

416 Amsterdam Avenue, at 80th Street (1-212 724 7445/www.allanandsuzi.net). Subway: 1 to 79th Street. **Open** 12.30-7pm Mon-Sat; noon-6pm Sun. **Credit** AmEx, Disc, MC, V.

Models and celebs drop off worn-once Gaultiers, Muglers, Pradas and Manolos here. The platform shoe collection is flashback-inducing and incomparable, as is the selection of vintage jewellery.

Beacon's Closet

88 North 11th Street, between Berry Street & Wythe Avenue, Williamsburg, Brooklyn (1-718 486 0816/ www.beaconscloset.com). Subway: L to Bedford Avenue. **Open** noon-9pm Mon-Fri; 11am-8pm Sat, Sun. **Credit** AmEx, Disc, MC, V.

At this Brooklyn favourite, not only are the prices great, but so is the Williamsburg-appropriate clothing selection.

Other locations: 220 Fifth Avenue, between President & Union Streets, Park Slope, Brooklyn (1-718 230 1630).

D/L Cerney

13 E 7th Street, between Second & Third Avenues (1-212 673 7033). Subway: N, R, W to 8th Street-NYU; 6 to Astor Place. **Open** noon-8pm Tue-Sun. **Credit** AmEx, MC, V.

Specialising in timeless, original designs for stylish fellows, the store also carries menswear from the 1940s to the '60s. Mint-condition must-haves include hats (including some pristine fedoras), ties and shoes. An adjacent shop carries D/L Cerney's new women's line, which also merits a look.

Edith

104 Rivington Street, between Essex & Ludlow Streets (1-212 979 9992). Subway: F to Delancey Street; J, M, Z to Delancey-Essex Streets. **Open** 1-8pm Mon-Fri; noon-8pm Sat, Sun. **Credit** AmEx, MC, V.

Check out one of the city's best collections of (mostly) fine leather bags, not to mention an army of shoes, at this slightly below-street-level shop. There's no trash here – only the cream of the vintage crop. The front rack displays Edith & Daha's own line of clothing.

Foley & Corinna

108 Stanton Street, between Essex & Ludlow Streets (1-212 529 2338/www.foleyandcorinna.com). Subway: F to Delancey Street; J, M, Z to Delancey-Essex Streets. **Open** noon-8pm Mon-Sat; noon-7pm Sun. **Credit** AmEx, MC, V.

Vintage-clothing fiends like Liv Tyler and Donna Karan know they can have it both ways: shoppers freely mix old (Anna Corinna's vintage finds) with new (Dana Foley's original creations, including lace tops, leather-belted pants and sheer wool knits) to compose a truly one-of-a-kind look. Encourage the boy in your life to spiff up at the men's store, just around the corner.

Other locations: Foley & Corinna Men, 143 Ludlow Street, between Rivington & Stanton Streets, Lower East Side (1-212 529 5043).

INA

101 Thompson Street, between Prince & Spring Streets (1-212 941 4757/www.inanyc.com). Subway: C, E to Spring Street. **Open** noon-7pm Mon-Thur, Sun; noon-8pm Fri, Sat. **Credit** AmEx, MC, V.
For the past 11 years, INA on Thompson Street has reigned over the downtown consignment scene. The Soho location features drastically reduced couture pieces, the shop on Prince Street carries trendier clothing, and the Mott Street shop is for men. **Other locations**: 21 Prince Street, between Elizabeth & Mott Streets, Little Italy (1-212 334 9048); 208 E 73rd Street, between Second & Third Avenues, Upper East Side (1-212 249 0014); 262 Mott Street, between Houston & Prince Streets, Soho (1-212 334 2210).

Local Clothing

328 E 9th Street, between First & Second Avenues (1-212 777 3850). Subway: L to Third Avenue. **Open** 8pm Mon-Thur, Sun; noon-9pm Fri, Sat. **Credit** AmEx, Disc, MC, V.
It's funny how vintage never gets old. NYC's latest installment in aged threads is East Village shop Local Clothing, a women's vintage trove that focuses on garb from as far back as the Victorian era up to the first MTV generation.

Marmalade

172 Ludlow Street, between Houston & Stanton Streets (1-212 473 8070/marmaladevintage.com). Subway: F, V to Lower East Side-Second Avenue. **Open** noon-9pm daily. **Credit** AmEx, MC, V.
Marmalade, one of the cutest vintage-clothing stores on the Lower East Side, has some of the hottest 1970s and '80s threads to be found below Houston Street. That slinky cocktail dress or ruffled blouse is tucked amid a selection of well-priced, well-cared-for items. Accessories, vintage shoes and a small selection of men's clothing are also available.

Fashion accessories

Jewellery

Agatha

611 Madison Avenue, at 58th Street (1-212 758 4301/www.agatha.fr). Subway: N, R, W to Fifth Avenue-59th Street; 4, 5, 6 to 59th Street. **Open** 10am-7pm Mon-Sat; noon-6pm Sun. **Credit** AmEx, Disc, MC, V.
The queen of the costume-jewellery joints, Agatha stocks low-priced trinkets that look like a million bucks. Jumbo pearls, oversize rings and graphic, modern designs abound. **Other locations**: 159A Columbus Avenue, between 67th & 68th Streets, Upper West Side (1-212 362 0959).

Alexis Bittar

465 Broome Street, between Greene & Mercer Streets (1-212 625 8340/www.alexisbittar.com). Subway: N, R, W to Prince Street; 6 to Spring Street. **Open** 11am-7pm Mon-Sat; noon-6pm Sun. **Credit** AmEx, MC, V.
A Brooklyn-based designer known for his chunky Lucite and semi-precious stone accessories, Bittar adorned his recently opened boutique with vintage wallpaper and a Victorian lion's-paw table.

Doyle & Doyle

189 Orchard Street, between Houston & Stanton Streets (1-212 677 9991/www.doyledoyle.com). Subway: F, V to Lower East Side-Second Avenue. **Open** 1-7pm Tue, Wed, Fri; 1-8pm Thur; noon-7pm Sat, Sun. **Credit** AmEx, Disc, MC, V.
Whether your taste is art deco or nouveau, Victorian or Edwardian, gemologist sisters Pam and Elizabeth Doyle, who specialise in estate and antique jewellery, will have that intimate, one-of-a-kind piece you're looking for, including engagement and eternity rings.

Fragments

116 Prince Street, between Greene & Wooster Streets (1-212 334 9588/www.fragments.com). Subway: B, D, F, V to Broadway-Lafayette Street; N, R, W to Prince Street. **Open** 11am-7pm Mon-Sat; noon-6pm Sun. **Credit** AmEx, DC, Disc, MC, V.
Over two decades, Fragments owner Janet Goldman has assembled a stable of more than 100 pet jewellery designers, who offer their creations to her before selling them to major stores such as Barneys.

Tiffany & Co

727 Fifth Avenue, at 57th Street (1-212 755 8000/www.tiffany.com). Subway: E, V to Fifth Avenue-53rd Street; F to 57th Street; N, R, W to Fifth Avenue-59th Street. **Open** 10am-7pm Mon-Fri; 10am-6pm Sat; noon-5pm Sun. **Credit** AmEx, DC, Disc, MC, V.
The heyday of Tiffany's was at the turn of the 20th century, when Louis Comfort Tiffany, the son of founder Charles Lewis Tiffany, took the reins and began to create sensational art nouveau jewellery. Today, the design stars are the no-less august Paloma Picasso and Elsa Peretti. Three floors are stacked with precious jewels, silver, watches, porcelain and the classic Tiffany engagement rings. FYI: breakfast is not served.

Shoes

Camper

125 Prince Street, at Wooster Street (1-212 358 1842/www.camper.es). Subway: N, R, W to Prince Street. **Open** 11am-8pm Mon-Sat; noon-6pm Sun. **Credit** AmEx, DC, MC, V.
Dozens of styles from the Spanish-made line of casual shoes are stocked in this large corner store.

Chuckies

1073 Third Avenue, between 63rd & 64th Streets (1-212 593 9898). Subway: F to Lexington Avenue-63rd Street. **Open** 10.45am-7.45pm Mon-Fri; 10.45am-7.30pm Sat; 12.30-7pm Sun. **Credit** AmEx, DC, Disc, MC, V.
An alternative to department stores, Chuckies carries high-profile labels for men and women. Its stock ranges from old-school Calvin Klein and Jimmy Choo to up-and-coming Ernesto Esposito.

Eat, Drink, Shop

Jimmy Choo

645 Fifth Avenue, at 51st Street (1-212 593 0800/ www.jimmychoo.com). Subway: E, V to Fifth Avenue-53rd Street. **Open** 10am-6pm Mon-Wed, Fri, Sat; 10am-7pm Thur; noon-5pm Sun. **Credit** AmEx, MC, V.
Jimmy Choo, famed for conceiving Princess Diana's custom-shoe collection, has conquered America with his six-year-old emporium, which features chic boots, sexy stilettos, curvaceous pumps and kitten-ish flats. Prices start at $450.

Manolo Blahnik

31 W 54th Street, between Fifth & Sixth Avenues (1-212 582 3007). Subway: E, V to Fifth Avenue-53rd Street. **Open** 10.30am-6pm Mon-Fri; 10.30am-5.30pm Sat. **Credit** AmEx, MC, V.
The high priest of timelessly glamorous shoes will put style in your step, kudos on your tootsies – and a deep, deep dent in your wallet.

Otto Tootsi Plohound

137 Fifth Avenue, between 20th & 21st Streets (1-212 460 8650). Subway: N, R, W to 23rd Street. **Open** 11.30am-8pm Mon-Fri; 11am-8pm Sat; noon-7pm Sun. **Credit** AmEx, DC, Disc, MC, V.
One of the best places for the latest shoe styles, Tootsi has a big selection of trendy (and slightly overpriced) imports for women and men.
Other locations: throughout the city.

Food & Drink

There are more than 20 open-air 'greenmarkets', sponsored by city authorities, in various locations on different days. The largest and best known is at Union Square, where small producers of cheese, flowers, herbs, fruits and vegetables hawk their goods on Mondays, Wednesdays, Fridays and Saturdays (8am-6pm). Arrive early, before the prime stuff sells out. For other venues, check with the Council on the Environment of NYC (1-212 788 7476, www.cenyc.org).

Bakeries & cupcakes

Thanks to Magnolia Bakery, cupcakes have become a portable obsession among New Yorkers in recent years; here's where to grab your sugar fix.

Amy's Bread

672 Ninth Avenue, between 46th & 47th Streets (1-212 977 2670/www.amysbread.com). Subway: C, E to 50th Street; N, R, W to 49th Street. **Open** 7.30am-11pm Mon-Fri; 8am-11pm Sat; 9am-6pm Sun. **No credit cards.**
Whether you want sweet (chocolate-chubbie cookies) or savoury (semolina-fennel bread, hefty French sourdough boules), Amy's never disappoints.
Other locations: Chelsea Market, 75 Ninth Avenue, between 15th & 16th Streets, Chelsea (1-212 462 4338).

Billy's Bakery

184 Ninth Avenue, between 21st & 22nd Streets (1-212 647 9956/www.billysbakerynyc.com). Subway: C, E to 23rd Street. **Open** 9am-11pm Mon-Thur, Sun; 9am-midnight Fri, Sat. **Credit** AmEx, Disc, MC, V.
Amid super-sweet retro delights such as coconut cream pie, Hello Dollies and Famous Refrigerator Cake, you'll find friendly service in a setting that will remind you of Grandma's kitchen – or, at least, it will if your grandmother was Betty Crocker.

Magnolia Bakery

401 Bleecker Street, at 11th Street (1-212 462 2572). Subway: 1 to Christopher Street. **Open** noon-11.30pm Mon; 9am-11.30pm Tue-Thur; 9am-12.30am Fri; 10am-12.30am Sat; 10am-11.30pm Sun. **Credit** AmEx, Disc, MC, V.
Part sweet market, part meet market, Magnolia sky-rocketed to fame after featuring on *Sex and the City*, and it's still oven-hot. The pastel-iced cupcakes are much vaunted, but you can also pick up a cup of custardy, Southern-style banana pudding (Brits: think trifle) or a scoop from the summertime ice-cream cart. Then, sweetmeat in hand, join the other happy eaters clogging nearby apartment stoops.

Chocolatiers

Jacques Torres Chocolate Haven

350 Hudson Street, between Charlton & King Streets, entrance on King Street (1-212 414 2462/ www.jacquestorres.com). Subway: 1 to Houston Street. **Open** 9am-7pm Mon, Wed-Fri; 10am-8pm Sat; 11am-7pm Sun. **Credit** AmEx, MC, V.
Walk into Jacques Torres's new glass-walled shop and café, and you'll be surrounded by a Willy Wonka-esque chocolate factory that turns raw cocoa beans into luscious goodies before your very eyes. Sweets for sale range from the sublime (deliciously rich hot chocolate, steamed to order) to the ridiculous (chocolate-covered fortune cookies).
Other locations: Jacques Torres Chocolate, 66 Water Street, between Dock & Main Streets, Dumbo, Brooklyn (1-718 875 9772).

La Maison du Chocolat

1018 Madison Avenue, between 78th & 79th Streets (1-212 744 7117/www.lamaisonduchocolat.com). Subway: 6 to 77th Street. **Open** 10am-7pm Mon-Sat; noon-6pm Sun. **Credit** AmEx, MC, V.
This suave cocoa-brown boutique, the creation of Robert Linxe, packages refined (and pricey) examples of edible Parisian perfection as if they were fine jewellery. A small café serves hot and cold chocolate drinks and a selection of sweets.
Other locations: 30 Rockefeller Plaza, 49th Street, between Fifth & Sixth Avenues (1-212 265 9404).

Richart

7 E 55th Street, between Madison & Fifth Avenues (1-888 742 4278/www.richart-chocolates.com). Subway: E, V to Fifth Avenue-53rd Street. **Open** 10am-7pm Mon-Fri; 10am-6pm Sat. **Credit** AmEx, MC, V.

Object of your confection

Many of us can't stop thinking about our next chocolate fix. Small children dress up in goofy costumes on Halloween once a year to get their hands on some. The same cannot be said of peppermints. No, chocolate is indeed on another level all together – and in recent years Manhattan has seen an explosion of chocolate shops.

Legendary chocolatier Jacques Torres has unveiled his most irresistible creation yet: **Chocolate Haven** (see p244; photo below), an 8,000-square-foot factory that serves as the Manhattan hub for the pastry chef's growing chocolate empire. The space features a cocoa-pod-shaped café overlooking the candy-making facilities, so visitors can indulge in chocolate treats and watch as cocoa beans are transformed into chocolate bars.

Another great sweet boutique is the West Village's **Chocolate Bar** (48 Eighth Avenue, between Horatio & Jane Streets, 1-212 366 1541). The store carries only candies, cookies and brownies from high-end local makers. This is also, as the name suggests, the place to score an updated version of the candy bar. Chocolate Bar has created some worthy options like hefty dark-chocolate bars flavoured liberally with mint or orange. For something bite-sized, check out the shop's Mojito truffle, flavoured with rum, lime and mint. Or a lemon-hazelnut one. Or peanut-butter caramel.

Booze-hounds, on the other hand, will fall head-over-heels for **Chocolat Michel Cluizel**. The French fine-chocolate producer opened his first stateside shop inside the Flatiron's ABC Carpet & Home (888 Broadway, at 19th Street, 1-212 473 3000), and even scored a liquor licence. His 'adult' chocolate bonbons, wrapped in foil, contain the likes of Calvados, Cognac, Cointreau, or morello cherries aged in kirsch. Bite carefully.

If you like candies on your chocolate, check out **Divalicious** (365 Broome Street, between Elizabeth & Mott Streets, 1-212 343 1243; photo below). Here, you'll find chocolate-covered everything – fortune cookies, graham crackers and pretzels, as well as chocolate lollipops and chocolate hearts.

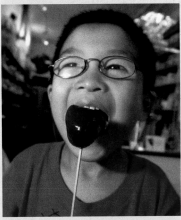

Eat, Drink, Shop

CHAI TEA

EARL GREY TEA

LOVE POTION
(dark chocolate ganache)

CHAMPAGNE KISS
(Rosé Champagne)

French master-chocolatier Michel Richart is an intellectual sensualist, one who's as likely to fill a bonbon with green-tea essence or basil ganache as with the more expected coffee or hazelnuts. His precisely geometric squares are topped with cool graphic patterns – swirls, bubbles, even leopard prints – to indicate the fillings within.

Scharffen Berger
473 Amsterdam Avenue, at 83rd Street (1-212 362 9734/www.scharffenberger.com). Subway: 1 to 86th Street. **Open** *10am-8pm Mon-Thur; 10am-9pm Fri, Sat; 11am-7pm Sun.* **Credit** *AmEx, Disc, MC, V.*
At this bite-sized boutique from the artisanal chocolate maker from Berkeley, California, you'll find gift boxes of remarkable dark ganache-filled treats (in flavours like fresh lemon and sea-salt caramel), jars of chocolate sauce and chocolate-mint lip balm.

Stores

Dean & DeLuca
560 Broadway, at Prince Street (1-212 431 1691/ www.deananddeluca.com). Subway: N, R, W to Prince Street. **Open** *10am-8pm Mon-Sat; 10am-7pm Sun.* **Credit** *AmEx, Disc, MC, V.*
Dean & DeLuca's flagship store (one of only two that offer more than just a fancy coffee bar) provides the most sophisticated (and pricey) selection of speciality food items in the city.
Other locations: throughout the city.

Whole Foods
Concourse level, Time Warner Center, 10 Columbus Circle, at Broadway (1-212 823 9600/www.whole foods.com). Subway: A, B, C, D, 1 to 59th Street-Columbus Circle. **Open** *8am-10pm daily.* **Credit** AmEx, Disc, MC, V.
You'll feel healthier just walking around this veritable cornucopia of fresh food. Gorgeous as well as good for you, Whole Foods is the city's best bet for organic offerings. Take advantage of the well-stocked wine store seven days a week.

Other locations: 4 Union Square South, between Broadway & University Place, Greenwich Village (1-212 673 5388); 250 Seventh Avenue, at 24th Street, Flatiron District (1-212 924 5969).

Zabar's
2245 Broadway, at 80th Street (1-212 787 2000/ www.zabars.com). Subway: 1 to 79th Street. **Open** *8am-7.30pm Mon-Fri; 8am-8pm Sat; 9am-6pm Sun.* **Credit** AmEx, MC, V.
Zabar's is more than just a market – it's a New York City landmark. You might leave the place feeling a little light in the wallet, but you can't beat the top-flight prepared foods. Besides the famous smoked fish and rafts of Jewish delicacies, Zabar's has fabulous selections of bread, cheese and coffee – and an entire floor of well-priced gadgets and housewares.

Sundries

Guss' Pickles
85-87 Orchard Street, between Broome & Grand Streets (www.gusspickle.com). Subway: F to Delancey Street; J, M, Z to Delancey-Essex Streets. **Open** *9.30am-6.30pm Mon-Thur; 9.30am-4pm Fri; 10am-6pm Sun.* **Credit** AmEx, MC, V.
After moving twice in recent years, the Pickle King has settled down, and the complete, delicious array of sours and half-sours, pickled peppers, watermelon rinds and sauerkraut is available to grateful New Yorkers once again.

Russ & Daughters
179 E Houston Street, between Allen & Orchard Streets (1-212 475 4880/www.russanddaughters. com). Subway: F, V to Lower East Side-Second Avenue. **Open** *9am-7pm Mon-Sat; 8am-5.30pm Sun.* **Credit** AmEx, Disc, MC, V.
Russ & Daughters, which has been open for nigh on a century (since 1914, to be precise), sells eight kinds of smoked salmon and many Jewish-inflected Eastern European delectables, along with dried fruits, chocolates and caviar. **Photo** *p247.*

Guss' Pickles.

Russ & Daughters. *See p246.*

Health & Beauty

Beauty & cosmetics

Face Stockholm

110 Prince Street, at Greene Street (1-212 966 9110/ www.facestockholm.com). Subway: N, R, W to Prince Street. **Open** 11am-7pm Mon-Sat; noon-6pm Sun. **Credit** AmEx, MC, V.

In addition to a full line of eyeshadows, lipsticks, blushers and tools, Face offers make-up application lessons to help improve your own technique. **Other locations:** 226 Columbus Avenue, between 70th & 71st Streets, Upper West Side (1-212 769 1420).

John Masters Organics

77 Sullivan Street, between Spring & Broome Streets (1-212 343 9590/www.johnmasters.com). Subway: C, E to Spring Street; N, R, W to Prince Street. **Open** 11am-7pm Mon-Sat. **Credit** AmEx, MC, V.

Organic doesn't get more orgasmic than in John Masters's chic apothecary line. Blood orange and vanilla body wash and lavender and avocado intensive conditioner are just two of the good-enough-to-eat products that you can get to go. **Photos** *p249.*

Kiehl's

109 Third Avenue, between 13th & 14th Streets (1-212 677 3171/www.kiehls.com). Subway: L to Third Avenue; N, Q, R, W, 4, 5, 6 to 14th Street-Union Square. **Open** 10am-7pm Mon-Sat; noon-6pm Sun. **Credit** AmEx, DC, MC, V.

Although it is 154 years old and has recently expanded, this New York institution is still a mob scene. Check out the Motorcycle Room, full of vintage Harleys (the owner's obsession). Try one dab of Kiehl's moisturiser, lip balm or body lotion from the plentiful free samples, and you'll be hooked. **Other locations:** 150 Columbus Avenue, between 66th & 67th Streets, Upper West Side (1-212 799 3438).

MAC

113 Spring Street, between Greene & Mercer Streets (1-212 334 4641/www.maccosmetics.com). Subway: C, E to Spring Street. **Open** 11am-7pm Mon-Wed; 11am-8pm Thur-Sat; noon-7pm Sun. **Credit** AmEx, DC, Disc, MC, V.

Make-up Art Cosmetics is famous for lipsticks and eyeshadows in must-have colours and for offbeat celebrity spokesmodels like RuPaul and kd lang. **Other locations:** throughout the city.

Ricky's

509 Fifth Avenue, between 42nd & 43rd Streets (1-212 949 7230/www.rickys-nyc.com). Subway: B, D, F, V to 42nd Street-Bryant Park; 7 to Fifth Avenue. **Open** 8am-9pm Mon-Fri; 10am-8pm Sat; 10am-7pm Sun. **Credit** AmEx, Disc, MC, V.

Stock up on tweezers and make-up cases that look like souped-up fishing tackle boxes at this mecca for make-up. Ricky's own line, Mattése, is worth a look. **Other locations:** throughout the city.

Perfumeries

Bond No.9

9 Bond Street, between Broadway & Lafayette Street (1-212 228 1940). Subway: B, D, F, V to Broadway-Lafayette Street; 6 to Bleecker Street. **Open** 11am-8pm Mon-Sat; noon-6pm Sun. **Credit** AmEx, MC, V.

Custom-blended bottles of bliss, and scents that pay olfactory homage to New York City – Wall Street, Nouveau Bowery, New Harlem – are available here. Don't worry, there's no Chinatown Sidewalk. **Other locations:** 680 Madison Avenue, at 61st Street, Upper East Side (1-212 838 2780); 897 Madison Avenue, at 73rd Street, Upper East Side (1-212 794 4480).

CB I Hate Perfume

93 Wythe Avenue, between North 10th & 11th Streets, Williamsburg, Brooklyn (1-718 384 6890/ www.cbihateperfume.com). Subway: L to Bedford. **Open** noon-6pm Tue-Sat. **Credit** MC, V.

Contrary to his shop's name, Christopher Brosius doesn't hate what he sells, he just despises the concept. Collaborate with the olfactory genius on a signature scent of your own, or pick up a ready-made splash of quirky scents like Crayon and Rubber Cement; home fragrances include Gathering Apples.

Jo Malone
949 Broadway, at 22nd Street (1-212 673 2220/ www.jomalone.com). Subway: N, R, W to 23rd Street. **Open** 10am-8pm Mon-Sat; noon-6pm Sun. **Credit** AmEx, DC, Disc, MC, V.
British perfumer Jo Malone champions the 'layering' of scents as a way of creating a personalised aroma. Along with perfumes and colognes, her Flatiron District boutique offers candles, skincare products and super-pampering facials. Both treatments and products hit the mark.
Other locations: 946 Madison Avenue, between 74th & 75th Streets (1-212 472 0074).

Salons

New York is the city of fresh starts; and what better way to begin anew than with your hair? Whether you want a full-out makeover, a rock 'n' roll do, or just a trim, there's a salon for you. The stylin' superstars at Frédéric Fekkai Beauté de Provence (1-212 753 9500) and Louis Licari (1-212 758 2090) are top-notch, but they charge hair-raising prices. The following salons offer specialised services – budget, rocker, ethno-friendly – and unique settings for your special NYC cut.

Astor Place Hair Stylists
2 Astor Place, at Broadway (1-212 475 9854). Subway: N, R, W to 8th Street-NYU; 6 to Astor Place. **Open** 8am-8pm Mon-Sat; 9am-6pm Sun. **No credit cards**.
An army of barbers does everything from neat trims to shaved designs. You can't make an appointment; just take a number and wait outside with the crowd. Sunday mornings are quiet. Cuts start at $12; blow-drys, $20; dreads, $75. **Photo** *p250*.

Blow Styling Salon
342 W 14th Street, between Eighth & Ninth Avenues (1-212 989 6282). Subway: A, C, E to 14th Street. **Open** 8am-8pm Mon-Fri; 10am-8pm Sat; noon-6pm Sun. **Credit** AmEx, Disc, MC, V.
Jennifer Denton and Vigdis Boulton's award-winning Meatpacking District spot is scissor-free, focusing instead on pampering head massages and expertly executed blow-outs (from around $40).

John Masters Organics
For listing, see p247.
It's like visiting an intoxicating botanical garden: the organic scalp treatment will send you into relaxed oblivion, and ammonia-free, herbal-based colour treatments will appeal to your inner purist. Cuts or colouring start at $90. **Photos** *p249*.

Laicale
129 Grand Street, between Broadway & Crosby Street (1-212 219 2424). Subway: J, M, N, Q, R, W, Z, 6 to Canal Street. **Open** 11am-8pm Mon-Fri; 10am-6pm Sat; noon-6pm Sun. **Credit** AmEx, MC, V (gratuities accepted in cash only).
Get your locks chopped at this industrial chrome-and-glass hair mecca while the shop's own DJ spins the tunes. Most of the stylists here also work for magazines and runway shows. Cuts start at $75; highlights, $145.

Miwa/Alex Salon
24 E 22nd Street, between Broadway & Park Avenue South (1-212 228 4422/www.miwaalex.com). Subway: N, R, W, 6 to 23rd Street. **Open** 8.30am-5.30pm Mon; 8.30am-7pm Tue-Fri. **Credit** MC, V.
Tucked inside a posh, friendly space in the Flatiron District, Miwa/Alex delivers the sort of smart and unique cut you expect in New York. Cuts start at $65 for women; $50 for men.

Mudhoney
148 Sullivan Street, between Houston & Prince Streets (1-212 533 1160). Subway: C, E to Spring Street. **Open** noon-8pm Tue-Fri; noon-6pm Sat. **No credit cards**.
Don't be surprised if the stylist never removes his orange-tinted sunglasses; you're in the city's premier rock 'n' roll salon. The decor alone – a torture chair, lascivious stained-glass – will make the time in this tiny, attitude-packed place fly by. Cuts start at $75, and attract just as much attention as you want.
Other locations: 7 Bond Street, between Broadway & Lafayette Street, East Village (1-212 228 8128).

Spas

Juvenex
5th Floor, 25 W 32nd Street, between Broadway & Fifth Avenue (1-646 733 1330/www.juvenex spa.com). Subway: B, D, F, N, Q, R, V, W to 34th Street-Herald Square. **Open** 24hrs daily. **Credit** AmEx, Disc, MC, V.
This formerly girls-only 24-hour spa gained a cult following among post-partiers seeking communal detox in its jade igloo sauna. But boys can finally join the fun every night after 9pm. Treatments (unlike the sauna) are private; facials include the Oxygen ($130 for 75 minutes) and the Energizing Ginseng ($105 for 60 minutes). The price of a massage starts from $95.

Nickel
77 Eighth Avenue, at 14th Street (1-212 242 3203/ www.nickelformen.com). Subway: A, C, E to 14th Street; L to Eighth Avenue. **Open** 1-9pm Mon, Sun; 11am-9pm Tue-Fri; 10am-9pm Sat. **Credit** AmEx, Disc, MC, V.
New York's official temple of male grooming offers facials, waxing, massages, manicures and pedicures. The product line includes Washing Machine shower gel and Fire Insurance aftershave, as well as Self-Absorbed suntan oil – for the Narcissus in all of us.

Oasis Day Spa
2nd Floor, 108 E 16th Street, between Union Square East & Irving Place (1-212 254 7722/www.oasisday spanyc.com). Subway: L, N, Q, R, W, 4, 5, 6 to 14th Street-Union Square. **Open** *10am-10pm Mon-Fri; 9am-9pm Sat, Sun.* **Credit** *AmEx, Disc, MC, V.*
The flagship location of this posh wellness sanctuary features everything from hair styling and detoxifying mud wraps to acupuncture. Stressed-out travellers can stop at the JFK branch (Jet Blue Terminal 6, 1-212 254 7722) for manicures, hot shaves or even full-body massages.
Other locations: throughout the city.

Home & Gifts

Children's toys

Kidding Around
60 W 15th Street, between Fifth & Sixth Avenues (1-212 645 6337). Subway: F, V to 14th Street; L to Sixth Avenue. **Open** *10am-7pm Mon-Sat; 11am-6pm Sun.* **Credit** *AmEx, Disc, MC, V.*
Loyal customers frequent this quaint shop for clothing and learning-toys for the brainy baby. The play area in the back will keep your little one occupied while you shop.

Toys 'R' Us Times Square
1514 Broadway, between 44th & 45th Streets (1-800 869 7787). Subway: N, Q, R, W, 42nd Street S, 1, 2, 3, 7 to 42nd Street-Times Square. **Open** *9am-10pm Mon-Sat; 11am-6pm Sun.* **Credit** *AmEx, Disc, MC, V.*
The chain's flagship location is the world's largest toy store – big enough for a 60ft-high Ferris wheel inside and an animatronic tyrannosaur to greet you at the door. Brands rule here: there's an incredible two floors of Barbie paraphernalia, displayed in a life-sized Barbie house, plus a café with its very own sweetshop – Candy Land – that's designed to look like the board game.
Other locations: throughout the city.

Flea markets

Among bargain-hungry New Yorkers, flea-market rummaging is pursued with religious devotion. What better way to walk off that overstuffed omelette from brunch than to explore aisles of old vinyl records, unusual trinkets, vintage linens and funky furniture?

The Garage
112 W 25th Street, between Sixth & Seventh Avenues (no phone). Subway: F, V to 23rd Street. **Open** *sunrise-sunset Sat, Sun.* **No credit cards.**
Designers (and the occasional dolled-down celebrity) hunt regularly – and early – at this flea market inside an emptied parking garage. This spot specialises in old prints, vintage clothing, silver and linens; there's lots of household paraphernalia too.

John Masters Organics *See p247 and p248.*

crucifixes, collectable toys and Mexican Day of the Dead statues: kitsch reigns. Vintage clothing is peppered throughout the store.

Metropolitan Opera Shop
136 W 65th Street, at Broadway (1-212 580 4090/ www.metguild.com/shop). Subway: 1 to 66th Street-Lincoln Center. **Open** 10am-10pm Mon-Sat; noon-6pm Sun. **Credit** AmEx, Disc, MC, V.
This shop, in the Metropolitan Opera House at Lincoln Center, sells CDs and cassettes, opera books, memorabilia and DVDs. Kids aren't forgotten, either: there are plenty of educational CDs.

Pearl River Mart
477 Broadway, between Broome & Grand Streets (1-212 431 4770/www.pearlriver.com). Subway: J, M, N, Q, R, W, Z to Canal Street; 6 to Spring Street. **Open** 10am-7.20pm daily. **Credit** AmEx, Disc, MC, V.
This browse-worthy downtown emporium is filled with all things Chinese: slippers, clothing, gongs, groceries, medicinal herbs, stationery, teapots and all sorts of fun trinkets and gift items.

Home design

ABC Carpet & Home
888 Broadway, at 19th Street (1-212 473 3000/ www.abchome.com). Subway: L, N, Q, R, W, 4, 5, 6 to 14th Street-Union Square. **Open** 10am-8pm Thur; 10am-6.30pm Fri, Sat; noon-6pm Sun. **Credit** AmEx, Disc, MC, V.
At this shopping landmark, the selection of accessories, linens, rugs and reproduction and antique furniture (Western and Asian) is unbelievable; so are the mostly steep prices. For bargains, head to ABC's warehouse outlet in the Bronx.
Other locations: 20 Jay Street, at Plymouth Street, Dumbo, Brooklyn (1-718 643 7400); ABC Carpet & Home Warehouse, 1055 Bronx River Avenue, between Bruckner Boulevard & Westchester Avenue, Bronx (1-718 842 8772).

Las Venus
163 Ludlow Street, between Houston & Stanton Streets (1-212 982 0608). Subway: F, V to Second Avenue. **Open** noon-8pm Mon-Sat; noon-7pm Sun. **Credit** AmEx, Disc, MC, V.
Local hipsters all head to this epicentre of 20th-century pop culture to feed their kitsch furniture fixes. Vintage pieces by the greats – Miller, McCobb, Kagan, among others – are flanked by reproductions and the overall collection creates an artfully cluttered reservoir of affordable finds.
Other locations: Las Venus at ABC, 888 Broadway, at 19th Street, Flatiron District (1-212 473 3000 ext 519).

MoMA Design Store
44 W 53rd Street, between Fifth & Sixth Avenues (1-212 767 1050/www.momastore.org). Subway: E, V to Fifth Avenue-53rd Street. **Open** 10am-6.30pm Mon-Thur, Sat, Sun; 10am-8pm Fri. **Credit** AmEx, MC, V.

Astor Place Hair Stylists. See p248.

Greenflea
Intermediate School 44, Columbus Avenue, at 76th Street. Subway: B, C to 72nd Street; 1 to 79th Street. **Open** 10am-5.30pm Sun. **No credit cards**.
Greenflea is an extensive market that offers rare books, African art, antiques, handmade jewellery, crafts and eatables like vegetables and spiced cider (hot or cold, depending on the season). Visit both the labyrinthine interior and the schoolyard.

Hell's Kitchen Flea Market
39th Street, between Ninth & Tenth Avenues (1-212 243 5343). Subway: A, C, E to 34th Street-Penn Station. **Open** sunrise-sunset Sat, Sun. **No credit cards**.
The huge Annex Antiques Fair & Flea Market on 26th Street lost its lease to a property developer, so many of the vendors packed up and moved to this stretch of road in Hell's Kitchen. Anyone familiar with the mind-boggling array of goods on offer at the former site may likely feel a bit cheated in the new space, but there are treasures to be found and momentum is growing.

Gift shops

Love Saves the Day
119 Second Avenue, at 7th Street (1-212 228 3802). Subway: 6 to Astor Place. **Open** noon-9pm daily. **Credit** AmEx, MC, V.
Yoda dolls, Elvis lamps, ant farms, lurid machine-made tapestries of the Madonna, glow-in-the-dark

The store is as wide-ranging as the museum's collection. State-of-the-art home items on display include casseroles, coffee tables, high-design chairs, lighting, office workstations, kids' furniture, jewellery, calendars and lots of Christmas ornaments. **Other locations**: 81 Spring Street, at Crosby Street, Soho (1-646 613 1367).

Moss

146 Greene Street, between Houston & Prince Streets (1-212 204 7100). Subway: B, D, F, V to Broadway-Lafayette Street; N, R, W to Prince Street; 6 to Bleecker Street. **Open** 11am-7pm Mon-Sat; noon-6pm Sun. **Credit** AmEx, Disc, MC, V.
Proprietor Murray Moss has curated perhaps the most impressive collection of high-design items in the city. Many of the streamlined clocks, curvy sofas and funky household items are kept protected under glass at this temple of contemporary home design. For creativity on a larger scale, stop by his newly opened 'museum' adjacent to the store.

Leisure

Bookstores

Chain stores

Barnes & Noble has a number of megastores, and several feature readings by authors. The smaller Borders chain also provides under-one-roof browsing. Check the phone book for the location nearest to you, and pick up a copy of the weekly *Time Out New York* magazine for listings of readings at bookstores and other venues. *See also pp276-278.*

General interest

192 Books

192 Tenth Avenue, between 21st & 22nd Streets (1-212 255 4022/www.192books.com). Subway: C, E to 23rd Street. **Open** noon-6pm Mon, Sun; 11am-7pm Tue-Sat. **Credit** AmEx, MC, V.
In an era when many an indie bookshop has closed its doors, this youngster, open since 2003, is proving that quirky boutique booksellers can make it after all. Owned and 'curated' by art dealer Paula Cooper and her husband, editor Jack Macrae, 192 offers a strong selection of art books and literature, as well as sections on gardening, history, politics, design, music and memoirs. Regular readings, signings and discussions, some featuring well-known writers, are further good reasons to drop by.

St Mark's Bookshop

31 Third Avenue, between 8th & 9th Streets (1-212 260 7853/www.stmarksbookshop.com). Subway: N, R, W to 8th Street-NYU; 6 to Astor Place. **Open** 10am-midnight Mon-Sat; 11am-midnight Sun. **Credit** AmEx, Disc, MC, V.
Students, academics and art professionals gravitate to this East Village bookseller, which opened in 1977. It maintains strong inventories on cultural theory, graphic design, poetry and film studies, as well as numerous avant-garde journals and 'zines.

Eat, Drink, Shop

Christmas gift lift

Let's face it: sometimes regular department stores and boutiques can be horrendously unimaginative and dull – making holiday gift shopping unbearably tedious. That's where the city's holiday bazaars come in. These sprawling temporary shops are filled with offbeat toys, handmade crafts, and more soap and candles than you ever thought existed. Here's our pick of the bunch.

Holiday Market at Union Square

The goods: Lots of candles and soap, plus toys, ties, clocks and nativity scene sets. Most items are reasonably priced, though some jewellery and imported goods can be quite expensive.
The vibe: Competition for customers is fierce, so vendors are aggressive. Frustration can run high when a group stops in front of a booth, easily causing a bottleneck in the narrow walkways with few escape routes.

Grand Central Terminal Holiday Fair

The goods: You'll find lots of jewellery incorporating silver and/or turquoise at this indoor fair, as well as booths housing unusual (and pricey) gifts from Our Name is Mud, the Czechoslovak-American Puppet Theatre and the American Folk Art Museum. But the biggest draw is a huge selection of Christmas-tree ornaments.
The vibe: Live musicians playing over-the-top Christmas tunes, but the crowd is low-key.

Holiday Market at Columbus Circle

The goods: This one's from the same people who put on the Union Square Market, but it seems to have more diverse merchandise – though the air still hangs thick with soap and candles.
The vibe: Lots of no-nonsense shopping.

Second-hand books

Housing Works Used Book Café

126 Crosby Street, between Houston & Prince Streets (1-212 334 3324/www.housingworksubc.com). Subway: B, D, F, V to Broadway-Lafayette Street; N, R, W to Prince Street; 6 to Bleecker Street. **Open** 10am-9pm Mon-Fri; noon-9pm Sat; noon-7pm Sun. **Credit** AmEx, MC, V.

Housing Works is extraordinarily endearing. The two-level space – which stocks literary fiction, non-fiction, rare books and collectibles – is a peaceful spot for solo relaxation or for meeting friends over coffee or wine. All proceeds go to support services

Season's greetings

During the holidays, these showy shops gussy up their window displays with over-the-top creations of lights, wreaths and other Yuletide fanfare. Have a peek.

Barneys New York

Madison Avenue, at 61st Street (1-212 826 8900). Subway: N, R, W to Fifth Avenue-59th Street; 4, 5, 6 to 59th Street. To 5 Jan.

Bergdorf Goodman

754 Fifth Avenue, at 57th Street (1-212 753 7300). Subway: N, R, W to Fifth Avenue-59th Street. To 5 Jan.

Bloomingdale's

Lexington Avenue, at 59th Street (1-212 705 2000). Subway: N, R, W to Lexington Avenue-59th Street; 4, 5, 6 to 59th Street. To 1 Jan.

Henri Bendel

712 Fifth Avenue, between 55th & 56th Streets (1-212 247 1100). Subway: E, V to Fifth Avenue-53rd Street; N, R, W to Fifth Avenue-59th Street. To 5 Jan.

Macy's

Herald Square, 34th Street, between Sixth & Seventh Avenues (1-212 494 4000). Subway: B, D, F, N, Q, R, V, W to 34th Street-Herald Square; 1, 2, 3 to 34th Street-Penn Station. To 5 Jan.

Saks Fifth Avenue

Fifth Avenue, at 50th Street (1-212 753 4000). Subway: B, D, F, V to 47th-50th Streets-Rockefeller Center. To 31 Dec.

for homeless people living with HIV/AIDS. The premises also hosts an interesting array of events, such as book readings. *See also p277.*

Labyrinth Books

536 W 112th Street, between Amsterdam Avenue & Broadway (1-212 865 1588/www.labyrinthbooks.com). Subway: 1 to 110th Street-Cathedral Parkway. **Open** 9am-10pm Mon-Fri; 10am-8pm Sat; 11am-7pm Sun. **Credit** AmEx, MC, V.

The academic crowd thrives in Labyrinth's rarefied air. You may find remaindered copies of *Heidegger, Coping, and Cognitive Science* or a coffee-table book entitled *Black Panthers 1968.*

Strand Book Store

828 Broadway, at 12th Street (1-212 473 1452/www.strandbooks.com). Subway: L, N, Q, R, W, 4, 5, 6 to 14th Street-Union Square. **Open** 9.30am-10.30pm Mon-Sat; 11am-10.30pm Sun. **Credit** AmEx, DC, Disc, MC, V.

Owned by the Bass family since 1927, the legendary Strand – with its '18 miles of books' – offers incredible deals on new releases, loads of used books, plenty of hard-to-finds and New York City's largest rare book collection. Staff are pretty good at pointing you in the right direction. **Photo** *p253.*

Other locations: Strand, 95 Fulton Street, between Gold & William Streets, Financial District (1-212 732 6070); Strand Kiosk, Central Park, Fifth Avenue, at 60th Street, Upper East Side (1-646 284 5506).

Speciality stores

Books of Wonder

18 W 18th Street, between Fifth & Sixth Avenues (1-212 989 3270/www.booksofwonder.com). Subway: F, V to 14th Street; L to Sixth Avenue; 1 to 18th Street. **Open** 10am-7pm Mon-Sat; noon-6pm Sun. **Credit** AmEx, Disc, MC, V.

It recently moved two doors down and combined forces with the Cupcake Café in late 2004, but the city's only independent children's bookstore still features both the very new (the staff hosted a midnight-madness party to celebrate the release of the last Harry Potter) and the very old (rare and out-of-print editions), plus foreign-language and reference titles, and a special collection of Oz books.

East West

78 Fifth Avenue, between 13th & 14th Streets (1-212 243 5994/www.eastwest.com). Subway: L, N, Q, R, W, 4, 5, 6 to 14th Street-Union Square. **Open** 11am-7pm Mon-Sat; 11am-6.30pm Sun. **Credit** AmEx, Disc, MC, V.

This spiritual titles holder devotes equal space to Eastern and Western traditions, from alternative health and yoga to philosophy.

Forbidden Planet

840 Broadway, at 13th Street (1-212 475 6161/www.fpnyc.com). Subway: L, N, Q, R, W, 4, 5, 6 to 14th Street-Union Square. **Open** 10am-10pm Mon, Tue, Sun; 10am-midnight Wed-Sat. **Credit** AmEx, Disc, MC, V.

Eat, Drink, Shop

Embracing both the pop-culture mainstream and the cult underground, the Planet takes all comics seriously. You'll find graphic novels (Neil Gaiman's *Sandman*, Craig Thompson's *Blankets*), serials (*Asterix, Batman*), and film and TV tie-ins.

Hue-Man Bookstore & Café

2319 Frederick Douglass Boulevard (Eighth Avenue), between 124th & 125th Streets (1-212 665 7400/ www.huemanbookstore.com). Subway: A, B, C, D to 125th Street. **Open** 10am-8pm Mon-Sat; 11am-7pm Sun. **Credit** AmEx, Disc, MC, V.

Focusing on African-American non-fiction and fiction, this superstore-sized Harlem indie also stocks bestsellers and general-interest books.

Mysterious Bookshop

58 Warren Street, between Church & West Broadway Streets (1-212 587 1011/www.mysteriousbookshop. com). Subway: A, C, 1, 2 to Chambers Street. **Open** 11am-7pm daily. **Credit** AmEx, DC, Disc, MC, V.

Devotees of mystery, crime and spy genres will know owner Otto Penzler, both as an editor and from his book recommendations on Amazon.com. His shop holds a wealth of paperbacks, hardcovers and autographed first editions.

Cameras & electronics

When buying expensive electronic gear, it pays to go to a well-known store, where you'll get reliable advice about a device's compatibility with systems in the country in which you plan to use it. For specialised photo processing, we recommend Duggal (www.duggal.com).

Apple Store Fifth Avenue

767 Fifth Avenue, between 58th & 59th Streets (1-212 336 1440/www.apple.com/retail/fifthavenue). Subway: E, V to Fifth Avenue-53rd Street; N, R, W to Fifth Avenue-59th Street. **Open** 24hrs daily. **Credit** AmEx, Disc, MC, V.

Marked by a 32ft-tall glass entrance, the Apple Store Fifth Avenue is NYC's new subterranean mecca for all things Mac. Inside the techie bunker, aisles are lined with test-drive-ready MacBooks, iPods and accessories. The 45ft-long Genius Bar, like the store, is open 24/7, giving insomniacs a place to bring their ailing laptops at two in the morning.
Other locations: 103 Prince Street, at Greene Street, Soho (1-212 226 3126).

B&H

420 Ninth Avenue, at 34th Street (1-212 444 5040/ www.bhphotovideo.com). Subway: A, C, E to 34th Street-Penn Station. **Open** 9am-7pm Mon-Thur; 9am-2pm Fri; 10am-5pm Sun. **Credit** AmEx, Disc, MC, V.

B&H is the ultimate one-stop shop for all your photographic, video and audio needs (including professional audio equipment and discounted Bang & Olufsen products). Be aware that the shop is closed on Friday afternoons, all day Saturday and on Jewish holidays.

Enjoy a flick: **Strand Book Store**. *See p252.*

Gadget repairs

Computer Solutions Provider

Room 202, 261 W 35th Street, between Seventh & Eighth Avenues (1-212 216 9469). Subway: 1, 2, 3 to 34th Street. **Open** 9am-6pm Mon-Fri. **Credit** AmEx, MC, V.

It might not be a sexy name but it delivers exactly what you want, when you want it: specialists in Macs, PCs and related peripherals, these techies can recover lost data and help you through other computer disasters; they even make house calls.

Photo-Tech Repair Service

110 E 13th Street, between Third & Fourth Avenues (1-212 673 8400/www.phototech.com). Subway: L, N, Q, R, W, 4, 5, 6 to 14th Street-Union Square. **Open** 8am-4.45pm Mon, Tue, Thur, Fri; 8am-6pm Wed; 10am-3pm Sat. **Credit** AmEx, Disc, MC, V.

This shop has 18 on-site technicians and guarantees that it can fix your camera regardless of the brand. A rush service is also available.

Music

Classical

Westsider Records

233 W 72nd Street, between Broadway & West End Avenue (1-212 874 1588). Subway: 1, 2, 3 to 72nd Street. **Open** 11am-8pm daily. **Credit** MC, V.

This solidly classical store has traditionally stocked only vinyl, but the 21st century has swept in a wave of CDs. It also carries a sprinkling of jazz records and drama and film books.

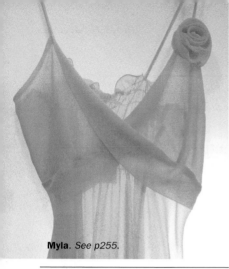

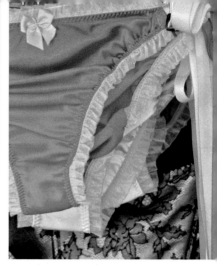

Myla. *See p255*.

Electronica

Dance Tracks

91 E 3rd Street, at First Avenue (1-212 260 8729/ www.dancetracks.com). Subway: F, V to Lower East Side-Second Avenue. **Open** noon-8pm Mon-Fri; noon-8pm Sat; noon-7pm Sun. **Credit** AmEx, Disc, MC, V.

European imports hot off the plane make this store a must. But it also has racks of domestic house, enticing bins of Loft/Paradise Garage classics and private decks on which to sample them.

Hip hop & R&B

Beat Street Records

494 Fulton Street, between Bond Street & Elm Place, Brooklyn (1-718 624 6400/www.beatst.com). Subway: A, C, G to Hoyt-Schermerhorn; 2, 3, 4, 5 to Nevins Street. **Open** 10am-7pm Mon-Sat; 10am-6pm Sun. **Credit** AmEx, Disc, MC, V.

In a block-long basement with two DJ booths, Beat Street proffers the latest vinyl. CDs run from dancehall to gospel, but the 12in singles and new hip hop albums make this the first stop for local DJs.

Fat Beats

2nd Floor, 406 Sixth Avenue, between 8th & 9th Streets (1-212 673 3883/www.fatbeats.com). Subway: A, B, C, D, E, F, V to W 4th Street. **Open** noon-9pm Mon-Sat; noon-6pm Sun. **Credit** MC, V.

Everyone – Beck, DJ Evil Dee, DJ Premier, Mike D, Q-Tip – shops at this tiny Greenwich Village shrine to vinyl for treasured hip hop, jazz, funk and reggae releases; underground magazines (like *Wax Poetics*); and cult flicks (such as *Wild Style*).

Jazz

Jazz Record Center

Room 804, 236 W 26th Street, between Seventh & Eighth Avenues (1-212 675 4480/www.jazzrecord center.com). Subway: C, E to 23rd Street; 1 to 28th Street. **Open** 10am-6pm Mon-Sat. **Credit** Disc, MC, V.

The city's best jazz store stocks current and out-of-print records, books, videos and other jazz-related merchandise. Worldwide shipping is available.

Multigenre

Bleecker Bob's

118 W 3rd Street, between MacDougal Street & Sixth Avenue (1-212 475 9677/www.bleecker bobs.com). Subway: A, B, C, D, E, F, V to W 4th Street. **Open** 11am-1am Mon-Thur, Sun; 11am-3am Fri, Sat. **Credit** AmEx, MC, V.

Come to Bleecker Bob's for hard-to-find new and used music, especially on vinyl. An online ordering service is due imminently.

Etherea

66 Avenue A, between 4th & 5th Streets (1-212 358 1126/www.ethereaonline.com). Subway: F, V to Lower East Side-Second Avenue. **Open** noon-10pm Mon-Thur, Sun; noon-11pm Fri, Sat. **Credit** AmEx, Disc, MC, V.

Etherea stocks mostly electronic, experimental, house, indie and rock CDs.

Mondo Kim's

6 St Marks Place, between Second & Third Avenues (1-212 598 9985/www.kimsvideo.com). Subway: 6 to Astor Place. **Open** 9am-midnight daily. **Credit** AmEx, MC, V.

Each branch of this movie and music mini-chain has a slightly different name but all offer a great selection for collector geeks: electronic, indie, krautrock, prog, reggae, soul, soundtracks and used CDs. **Other locations**: throughout the city.

Other Music

15 E 4th Street, between Broadway & Lafayette Street (1-212 477 8150/www.othermusic.com). Subway: N, R, W to 8th Street-NYU; 6 to Astor Place. **Open** noon-9pm Mon-Fri; noon-8pm Sat; noon-7pm Sun. **Credit** AmEx, MC, V.

This wee audio temple is dedicated to small-label, often imported new and used CDs and LPs. It organises music by arcane categories (for instance, 'La Decadanse' includes lounge, Moog and slow-core soundtracks) and sends out a free weekly email with staffers' reviews of their favourite new releases.

St Marks Sounds

20 St Marks Place, between Second & Third Avenues (1-212 677 3444). Subway: 6 to Astor Place. **Open** noon-9pm Mon-Thur, Sun; noon-10pm Fri, Sat. **No credit cards**.

Housed in two neighbouring storefronts, Sounds is the best bargain on the block for new and used music. The shop at 20 St Marks Place specialises in jazz and international recordings.

Subterranean Records

5 Cornelia Street, between Bleecker & W 4th Streets (1-212 463 8900). Subway: A, B, C, D, E, F, V to W 4th Street. **Open** noon-8pm Mon-Wed; noon-10pm Thur-Sat; noon-7pm Sun. **Credit** MC, V.

Just off Bleecker Street, this shop carries new, used and live recordings, as well as a large selection of imports. Vinyl LPs and 45s fill the basement.

Superstore

Virgin Megastore

52 E 14th Street, at Broadway (1-212 598 4666/ www.virginmega.com). Subway: L, N, Q, R, W, 4, 5, 6 to 14th Street-Union Square. **Open** 9am-1am Mon-Sat; 10am-midnight Sun. **Credit** AmEx, Disc, MC, V.

Besides a huge selection from every genre of music, Virgin Megastore has in-store performances and a great selection of CDs from the UK. Books, DVDs and videos are also available.

Other locations: 1540 Broadway, between 45th & 46th Streets, Theater District (1-212 921 1020).

World music

World Music Institute

Suite 903, 49 W 27th Street, between Broadway & Sixth Avenue (1-212 545 7536/www.worldmusic institute.org). Subway: N, R, W to 28th Street. **Open** 10am-6pm Mon-Fri. **Credit** AmEx, MC, V.

The shop is small, but if you can't find what you're looking for, then WMI's expert, helpful employees can order sounds from the remotest corners of the planet and have them shipped to you, usually within two to four weeks.

Sex shops

Leather Man

111 Christopher Street, between Bleecker & Hudson Streets (1-212 243 5339/www.theleatherman.com). Subway: 1 to Christopher Street. **Open** noon-10pm Mon-Sat; noon-8pm Sun. **Credit** AmEx, Disc, MC, V.

Cock rings, padlocks and sturdy handcuffs beckon from wall-mounted cabinets on the first floor, while

the basement (of course) is where serious bondage apparel is hung. There are also fake penises of every imaginable (and unimaginable) description.

Myla

20 E 69th Street, between Fifth & Madison Avenues (1-212 570 1590). Subway: 6 to 68th Street-Hunter College. **Open** 10am-6pm Mon-Fri. **Credit** AmEx, Disc, MC, V.

London-based naughty-nighties emporium Myla sells elegant boudoir accessories, including tasteful (yet nipple-exposing) 'peephole' bras, silk wrist-ties and blindfolds, plus a handful of sculptural vibrators. **Photos** *p254*.

Toys in Babeland

94 Rivington Street, between Ludlow & Orchard Streets (1-212 375 1701/www.babeland.com). Subway: F, V to Lower East Side-Second Avenue. **Open** noon-10pm Mon-Thur, Sun; noon-11pm Fri, Sat. **Credit** AmEx, MC, V.

At this friendly sex-toy boutique – run by women and skewed towards women, although everyone is welcome if the attitude is right – browsers are encouraged to handle all manner of buzzing, wriggling and bendable playthings. The ladies at Babeland also host frank sex-ed classes (open to all genders and sexualities) whose subjects include, for example, 'Strap-On Seductions'.

Other locations: 43 Mercer Street, between Broome & Grand Streets, Soho (1-212 966 2120).

Specialities & eccentricities

Brooklyn Superhero Supply Company

372 Fifth Avenue, between 5th & 6th Streets, Park Slope, Brooklyn (1-718 499 9884/www.superhero supplies.com). Subway: F, R to 4th Avenue-9th Street. **Open** 11am-5pm daily. **Credit** AmEx, Disc, MC, V.

When he's not busy writing books or publishing his literary journal *McSweeney's*, Dave Eggers defends truth and virtue at this kitschy shop where you can buy anti-matter by the can. But beware: you must take the superhero pledge with every purchase.

Kate's Paperie

561 Broadway, between Prince & Spring Streets (1-212 941 9816/www.katespaperie.com). Subway: N, R, W to Prince Street; 6 to Spring Street. **Open** 10am-7.30pm daily. **Credit** AmEx, Disc, MC, V.

Kate's is the ultimate paper mill. Choose from more than 5,000 kinds of paper by mining the rich vein of stationery, custom-printing services, journals, photo albums and creative, amazingly beautiful gift wrap.

Other locations: throughout the city.

Nat Sherman

500 Fifth Avenue, at 42nd Street (1-212 764 5000/ www.natsherman.com). Subway: B, D, F, V to 42nd Street-Bryant Park; 7 to Fifth Avenue. **Open** 10am-8pm Mon-Fri; 10am-7pm Sat; 11am-5pm Sun. **Credit** AmEx, DC, MC, V.

Eat, Drink, Shop

Just across the street from the New York Public Library, Nat Sherman offers its own brand of slow-burning cigarettes, as well as cigars and related accoutrements, for your smoking pleasure. Flick your Bic in the upstairs smoking room.

Pearl Paint
308 Canal Street, between Broadway & Church Street (1-212 431 7932/www.pearlpaint.com). Subway: J, M, N, Q, R, W, Z, 6 to Canal Street. **Open** 9am-7pm Mon-Fri; 10am-6.30pm Sat; 10am-6pm Sun. **Credit** AmEx, Disc, MC, V.
This huge art- and drafting-supply commissary sells everything you could possibly need to create your own masterpiece.
Other locations: 207 E 23rd Street, between Second & Third Avenues, Gramercy Park (1-212 592 2179).

Quark International
240 E 29th Street, between Second & Third Avenues (1-212 889 1808). Subway: 6 to 33rd Street. **Open** 10am-6.30pm Mon-Fri; noon-5pm Sat. **Credit** AmEx, DC, Disc, MC, V.
Spy wannabes and budding paranoids can buy body armour or high-powered bugs here. The store will also custom-bulletproof your favourite jacket.

Sam Ash Music
160 W 48th Street, between Sixth & Seventh Avenues (1-212 719 2299/www.samashmusic.com). Subway: B, D, F, V to 47th-50th Streets-Rockefeller Center; N, R, W to 49th Street. **Open** 10am-8pm Mon-Sat; noon-6pm Sun. **Credit** AmEx, MC, V.
This octogenarian musical-instrument emporium dominates its midtown block with four contiguous shops. New, vintage and custom guitars of all varieties are available, along with amps, DJ equipment, drums, keyboards, recording equipment, turntables and an array of sheet music.
Other locations: throughout the city.

Sports

Blades, Board & Skate
659 Broadway, between Bleecker & Bond Streets (1-212 477 7350/www.blades.com). Subway: B, D, F, V to Broadway-Lafayette Street; 6 to Bleecker Street. **Open** 10am-9pm Mon-Sat; 11am-7pm Sun. **Credit** MC, V.
The requisite clothing and gear is sold alongside in-line skates, skateboards and snowboards.
Other locations: throughout the city.

Gerry Cosby & Co
3 Pennsylvania Plaza, Madison Square Garden, Seventh Avenue, at 32nd Street (1-212 563 6464/ 1-877 563 6464/www.cosbysports.com). Subway: A, C, E, 1, 2, 3 to 34th Street-Penn Station. **Open** 9.30am-7.30pm daily. **Credit** AmEx, Disc, MC, V.
Cosby has a huge selection of official team wear and other sporting necessities. The store is open during – and until 30 minutes after – evening Knicks and Rangers games, in case you feel like celebrating.

Paragon Sporting Goods
867 Broadway, at 18th Street (1-212 255 8036/ www.paragonsports.com). Subway: L, N, Q, R, W, 4, 5, 6 to 14th Street-Union Square. **Open** 10am-8pm Mon-Sat; 11.30am-7pm Sun. **Credit** AmEx, DC, Disc, MC, V.
Three floors of equipment and clothing for almost every activity (at every level of expertise) make this the New York sports-gear mecca.

Tattoos & piercing

Tattooing was made legal in New York way back in 1997; piercing, however, remains relatively unregulated. *See also p257* **Ink well**.

New York Adorned
For listing, see p257 **Ink well**.
Proprietor Lori Leven hires world-class tattoo artists to wield the needles at her eight-year-old gothic-elegant establishment. Those with low pain thresholds can go for gentler body decorations such as henna tattoos, finery like ethereal white-gold cluster earrings, crafted by Leven, or pieces by a group of emerging body-jewellery designers.

Venus Modern Body Arts
199 E 4th Street, between Avenues A & B (1-212 473 1954). Subway: F, V to Lower East Side-Second Avenue. **Open** 1-9pm Mon-Thur, Sun; 1-10pm Fri, Sat. **Credit** AmEx, Disc, MC, V.
Venus has tattooed and pierced New Yorkers since 1992 – before body art became de rigueur. It also offers a positively enormous selection of jewellery, so you can put diamonds in your navel and platinum in your tongue.

Travel & luggage

Coach
595 Madison Avenue, at 57th Street (1-212 989 0001/www.coach.com). Subway: N, R, W to Fifth Avenue-59th Street. **Open** 10am-8pm Mon-Sat; 11am-6pm Sun. **Credit** AmEx, DC, Disc, MC, V.
Coach's butter-soft leather briefcases, wallets and handbags have always been exceptional, but the Manhattan Coach stores also stock the label's luxurious outerwear collection.
Other locations: throughout the city.

Flight 001
96 Greenwich Avenue, between Jane & W 12th Streets (1-212 691 1001/www.flight001.com). Subway: A, C, E to 14th Street; L to Eighth Avenue. **Open** 11am-8.30pm Mon-Fri; 11am-8pm Sat; noon-6pm Sun. **Credit** AmEx, DC, Disc, MC, V.
Forgotten something or taken greater advantage of New York's shopping than your bags can handle? This one-stop West Village shop carries guidebooks and chic luggage, along with fun travel products such as pocket-size aromatherapy kits. Flight 001's 'essentials' wall features packets of Woolite, mini-dominoes and everything in between.

Ink well

NYC tattoo artists who are making their mark.

Given the acres of inked skin in this town, it's hard to believe that tattooing has only been legal in New York City for the past nine years – a fact celebrated annually at the New York Tattoo Convention (for dates check out www.nyctattooconvention.com). If you're looking to add a little colour to your life, here are four trusted hometown havens – and their star ink masters – who are putting the stereotypes of grungy shop and scary tattooist to rest.

Troy Denning, Invisible NYC

The parlour: Quell any doubts about whether tattooing is an art with a visit to Invisible NYC. Owned by tattoo artist Troy Denning (*photo right*) and his art historian wife Jesse Lee, the shop is equal parts ink parlour and contemporary art gallery.
The artist: At it for more than 15 years, Denning culls from his travels through Europe and Japan to earn his reputation as a master of large-scale Japanese-influenced designs (from $150 per hour).
148 Orchard Street, between Rivington & Stanton Streets (1-212 228 1358/ www.troydenningtattoo.com).

Chris O'Donnell, New York Adorned

The parlour: An East Village mecca for tattoo celebrities and tattooed celebrities alike, NY Adorned's interior recalls a Far East boudoir – a vibe enhanced by the traditional Mendhi henna designs that it offers to those not yet ready to go under the gun.
The artist: A tattoo artist since he was a high-school senior in 1993, O'Donnell is known for refined Japanese-style pieces, Eastern religious and classic Americana designs (from $75 per completed piece). Call ahead: he's often booked months in advance.
47 Second Avenue, between 2nd & 3rd Streets (1-212 473 0007/www.ny adorned.com).

Scott Campbell, Saved Tattoo

The parlour: Hidden within Brooklyn boutique Saved Gallery of Art and Craft, Saved Tattoo, set among antique curios and paintings, has built a solid reputation through word of mouth spread by Williamsburg cognoscenti.

The artist: A fine-art painter, shop owner Campbell – who's known for old-fashioned typography and antique ornamental designs (from $200 per hour) – was recently tapped by Camel to create the traditional tattoo imagery in the tobacco company's latest ad campaign.
82 Berry Street, at North 9th Street, Williamsburg, Brooklyn (1-718 486 0850/ www.savedtattoo.com).

Dave C Wallin, Tattoo Culture

The parlour: With only one house artist, Tattoo Culture provides a temporary home to visiting artists from around the world. Recent guests have included Belgian Daniel DiMattia, a black-work specialist, and Sento, a renowned tattoo artist from Spain.
The artist: A Williamsburg local, house artist Wallin is an illustrator and comic-book artist as well as a tattooist. A saviour to those with only a vague idea of what style they crave, Wallin – who has a diverse portfolio of traditional and tribal designs (from $125 per hour) – is well known for his ability to combine styles.
129 Roebling Street, between North 4th & 5th Streets, Williamsburg, Brooklyn (1-718 218 6532/www.tattooculture.net).

Arts & Entertainment

Festivals & Events

Celebrate good times.

Cultures convene for that summer feeling, at the **Central Park SummerStage**. *See p262.*

There are eight million people living in New York, so you can bet that any day of the week a few hundred of those people are throwing some kind of get-together. Be it a parade, a concert or an art fair, there's a fun event out there for you. Here's a taste of the seasonal goings-on about town. For more events, check out the other chapters in the Arts & Entertainment section or have a look at the Around Town section of *Time Out New York* magazine. Keep in mind that before you set out or plan a trip around an event, it's always wise to call and make sure the fling is still set to swing.

Spring

Armory Show

Piers 90 & 92, Twelfth Avenue, between 50th & 52nd Streets (1-212 645 6440/www.thearmoryshow.com). Subway: C, E to 50th Street. **Dates** 10-13 Mar.
The show that, in 1913, heralded the arrival of modern art in the US has turned into a contemporary art mart.

St Patrick's Day Parade

Fifth Avenue, from 44th to 86th Streets (www.saintpatricksdayparade.com). **Date** 17 Mar.

This massive march is one of the city's longest running annual traditions – it dates from 1762. If you feel like braving huge crowds and potentially nasty weather, you'll see thousands of green-clad merrymakers strutting to the sounds of pipe bands. Celebrations continue late into the night as the city's Irish bars teem with suds-swigging revellers.

Ringling Bros and Barnum & Bailey Circus Animal Parade

34th Street, from the Queens Midtown Tunnel to Madison Square Garden, Seventh Avenue, between 31st & 33rd Streets (1-212 307 7171/www.ringling.com). **Dates** Spring.
Elephants, horses and zebras march through the tunnel and on to the streets of Manhattan in this unmissable spectacle. Stay up late for the midnight parades that open and close the circus's Manhattan run.

Easter Parade

Fifth Avenue, from 49th to 57th Streets (1-212 484 1222). Subway: E, V to Fifth Avenue-53rd Street. **Date** 8 Apr.
Parade is a misnomer for this little festival of creative hat-making. Starting at 11am on Easter Sunday, Fifth Avenue becomes a car-free promenade of gussied-up crowds milling and showing off extravagant bonnets.

Arrive early to secure a prime viewing spot near St Patrick's Cathedral, at 50th Street. After the parade, head to Tavern on the Green (Central Park West, at 67th Street) for the Mad Hatter's Easter Bonnet Contest, where you'll see even more head-covers.

New York International Auto Show
Jacob K Javits Convention Center, Eleventh Avenue, between 34th & 39th Streets (1-800 282 3336/ www.autoshowny.com). Subway: A, C, E to 34th Street-Penn Station. **Dates** 14-23 Apr.
This gearheads' paradise has more than 1,000 autos and futuristic concept cars on display.

New York Antiquarian Book Fair
Park Avenue Armory, Park Avenue, between 66th & 67th Streets (1-212 777 5218/www.sanfordsmith. com). Subway: 6 to 68th Street-Hunter College. **Dates** 20-22 Apr.
Book dealers from around the globe showcase first editions, illuminated manuscripts and all manner of rare and antique tomes; you'll even find original screenplays and shooting scripts.

Tribeca Film Festival
Various Tribeca locations (1-212 941 2400/www. tribecafilmfestival.org). Subway: A, C, 1, 2, 3 to Chambers Street. **Dates** Late Apr.
Organised by neighbourhood resident Robert De Niro, this festival is packed with hundreds of screenings of independent and international films; it's attended by more than 300,000 film fans.

Cherry Blossom Festival
For listing, see p161 Brooklyn Botanic Garden. **Dates** Late Apr/early May.
Nature's springtime blooms adorn the garden's 200-plus cherry trees at this annual festival. Performances, demonstrations and workshops are all part of the fun.

Global Marijuana March
March starts Broadway, at Houston Street, and proceeds to Battery Park (1-212 677 7180). **Date** 5 May.
In addition to being a good place to meet local stoners, this annual march (which takes place during the first weekend in May in cities around the world) aims to raise awareness about marijuana-related issues.

Bike New York: The Great Five Boro Bike Tour
Battery Park to Staten Island (1-212 932 2453/ www.bikenewyork.org). Subway: A, C, J, M, Z, 1, 2, 3 to Chambers Street; R, W to City Hall; 4, 5, 6 to Brooklyn Bridge-City Hall. Then bike to Battery Park. **Date** 6 May.
Thousands of cyclists take over the city for a 42-mile Tour de New York. (Pedestrians and motorists should plan on extra getting-around time.) Advance registration is required. Event organisers suggest the trains listed above, as some subway exits below Chambers Street may be closed to bike-toting cyclists for safety reasons, and bikes are not allowed at the South Ferry (1 train), Whitehall Street (R, W) and Bowling Green (4, 5) stations.

Bryant Park Free Summer Season
Bryant Park, Sixth Avenue, at 42nd Street (1-212 768 4242/www.bryantpark.org). Subway: B, D, F, V to 42nd Street-Bryant Park; 7 to Fifth Avenue. **Dates** May-Aug.
One of the highlights of the park's free entertainment season is the ever-popular Monday night alfresco movie series, but there's plenty of fun in the daylight hours as well. You can catch Broadway-musical numbers as part of the Broadway in Bryant Park series; *Good Morning America* mini-concerts featuring big-name talent; and a variety of readings, classes and public-art projects.

Red Hook Waterfront Arts Festival
Various locations in Red Hook, Brooklyn (1-718 596 2507/www.bwac.org). Travel: A, C, F to Jay Street-Borough Hall, then B61 bus to Van Brunt Street; F, G to Smith-9th Streets, then B77 bus to Van Brunt Street. **Date** Late May/early June.
This rapidly evolving neighbourhood cultural bash includes dance and music performances, along with the Brooklyn Waterfront Artists' Pier Show.

Lower East Side Festival of the Arts
Theater for the New City, 155 First Avenue, between 9th & 10th Streets (1-212 254 1109/ www.theaterforthenewcity.net). Subway: L to First Avenue; 6 to Astor Place. **Dates** 26-28 May.
This celebration of artistic diversity features performances by dozens of theatrical troupes, poetry readings, films and family-friendly programming.

Washington Square Outdoor Art Exhibit
Various streets surrounding Washington Square Park (1-212 982 6255). Subway: A, B, C, D, E, F, V to W 4th Street; R, W to 8th Street-NYU. **Dates** 27-29 May; 3, 4 June; 2-4, 9, 10 Sept.
Exhibitors here show off photography, sculpture, paintings and one-of-a-kind crafts. It's a great way for browsers and buyers to spend an afternoon.

SOFA New York
Seventh Regiment Armory, 643 Park Avenue, at 67th Street (1-800 563 7632/www.sofaexpo. com). Subway: 6 to 68th Street-Hunter College. **Dates** 31 May-3 June.
Browse this giant show of Sculptural Objects and Functional Art, and you might find that perfect conversation piece for your home.

Summer

Met in the Parks
Various locations (1-212 362 6000/ www.metopera.org). **Dates** June.
The Metropolitan Opera stages free opera performances in Central Park and other NYC parks in June every year. Grab a blanket, pack a picnic (no alcohol or glass bottles) and show up in the afternoon to nab a good spot.

Arts & Entertainment

Central Park SummerStage

Rumsey Playfield, Central Park, entrance on Fifth Avenue, at 72nd Street (1-212 360 2777/ www.summerstage.org). Subway: 6 to 68th Street-Hunter College. **Dates** June-Aug.

Rockers, symphonies, authors and dance companies take over the stage at this super-popular, mostly free annual series. Show up early or plan to listen from outside the gates (not such a bad option, if you bring a blanket – and some snacks). Admission is charged for benefit shows and special events. **Photo** *p260*.

Shakespeare in the Park at the Delacorte Theater

For listing, see p348. **Dates** June-Aug.

One of Manhattan's best summertime events – at the Delacorte Theater in Central Park – gets bold-face stars to pull on their tights and take a whack at the Bard.

Museum Mile Festival

Fifth Avenue, from 82nd to 105th Streets (1-212 606 2296/www.museummilefestival. org). **Date** 2nd Tue in June.

For one day each year, nine of the city's major museums open their doors free of charge to the public. You can also catch live music, street performers and other arty happenings along Fifth Avenue.

National Puerto Rican Day Parade

Fifth Avenue, from 44th to 86th Streets (1-718 401 0404). **Date** 2nd Sun in June.

Salsa music blares, and scantily clad revellers dance along the route and ride colourful floats at this freewheeling party celebrating the city's largest Hispanic community.

Broadway Bares

Roseland Ballroom, 239 W 52nd Street, between Broadway & Eighth Avenue (1-212 840 0770/ www.broadwaycares.org). Subway: 1 to 50th Street. **Dates** Mid June.

The new annual fundraiser for Broadway Cares/Equity Fights AIDS is your chance to see some of the Great White Way's hottest bodies sans costumes. Broadway Cares also hosts an annual auction of star-autographed teddy bears ('Broadway Bears') in February, and a show-tune-filled Easter Bonnet Competition in April, as well as several other fun theatre-themed events throughout the year.

JVC Jazz Festival

Various locations (1-212 501 1390/www.festivalproductions.net). **Dates** Mid June.

A direct descendant of the Newport Jazz Festival, this jazz bash is a New York City institution. The festival not only fills Carnegie and Avery Fisher Halls with big draws, but also sponsors gigs in Harlem and downtown clubs.

Mermaid Parade

Coney Island, Brooklyn (1-718 372 5159/ www.coneyisland.com). Subway: D, F, N, Q to Coney Island-Stillwell Avenue. **Date** 23 June.

Decked-out mermaids and mermen of all shapes, sizes and ages share the parade route with elaborate, kitschy floats, come rain or shine. It's the wackiest summer solstice event you'll likely ever witness. Check the website for details, as the parade location varies from year to year.

Gay & Lesbian Pride March

From Fifth Avenue, at 52nd Street to Christopher Street (1-212 807 7433/www.hopinc.org). **Date** 24 June.

Downtown Manhattan becomes a sea of rainbow flags as gays and lesbians from the city and beyond parade down Fifth Avenue in commemoration of the 1969 Stonewall Riots. After the march, there's a massive street fair and a dance on the West Side piers.

Summer Restaurant Week

Various locations (www.nycvisit.com). **Dates** Late June/early July.

Twice a year, for two weeks at a stretch, some of the city's finest restaurants dish out three-course prix-fixe lunches for $20.07; some places also offer dinner for $30.07. (The lunch price reflects the year.) For the full list of participating restaurants, visit the website. You are advised to make reservations well in advance.

Midsummer Night Swing

Lincoln Center Plaza, Columbus Avenue, between 64th & 65th Streets (1-212 875 5766/ www.lincolncenter.org). Subway: 1 to 66th Street-Lincoln Center. **Dates** Late June-mid July.

Lincoln Center's plaza is turned into a giant dancefloor as bands play salsa, Cajun, swing and other music. Each night is devoted to a different dance style; parties are preceded by lessons. *See also p263* **Best foot forward**.

Celebrate Brooklyn! Performing Arts Festival

Prospect Park Bandshell, Prospect Park West, at 9th Street, Park Slope, Brooklyn (1-718 855 7882/www.celebratebrooklyn.org). Subway: F to Seventh Avenue. **Dates** Late June-late Aug.

Outdoor events include music, dance, film and spoken-word acts. Huge crowds flock to the park's bandshell to hear major artists such as They Might Be Giants and Los Lobos. A $3 donation is requested, and admission is charged for a few benefit shows.

Nathan's Famous Fourth of July Hot Dog Eating Contest

Outside Nathan's Famous, corner of Surf & Stillwell Avenues, Coney Island, Brooklyn (www.nathansfamous.com). Subway: D, F, N, Q to Coney Island-Stillwell Avenue. **Date** 4 July.

Competitive eaters gather from all over the world to pig out at the grandaddy of pig-out contests, which has been happening annually in Coney Island for more than a decade.

Macy's Fireworks Display

East River, exact location varies (1-212 494 4495). **Date** 4 July at approximately 9pm.

Best foot forward

Follow these tips for dancing like a pro at Midsummer Night Swing.

Location, location, location

It's a long-standing tradition that couples congregate at the front toward stage right, while singles gather stage left. If you're looking to get your dance card punched, 'the back wall near the production booth is a prime spot,' according to Midsummer producer Wendy Magro. 'It's like a line-up.'

Ladies' choice

It's perfectly acceptable for women to ask men to dance. 'I tend to ask guys I know,'

says Midsummer regular Heidi Rosenau. 'But the more you do it, the more guys you know.'

Just do it

You're expected to accept an invitation to dance – even if your partner is more like Fred Flintstone than Fred Astaire. 'It's bad form to turn someone down,' says Magro.

A thousand pardons

It's important to tread lightly. 'Try not to crash into anyone,' Rosenau says. 'But if you do, apologise right away.'

This world-famous annual fireworks display is the city's star attraction on Independence Day. The pyrotechnics are launched from barges on the East River, so look for outdoor vantage points along the lower FDR Drive (closed to traffic), the Brooklyn and Long Island City waterfronts, or on Roosevelt Island. Keep in mind, however, that spectators are packed like sardines at the prime public spots.

New York Philharmonic Concerts in the Parks
Various locations (1-212 875 5900/www. newyorkphilharmonic.org). **Dates** July-Aug.
The New York Philharmonic has presented a varied classical-music programme in many of New York's larger parks for more than 40 years.

Seaside Summer & Martin Luther King Jr Concert Series
Various locations (1-718 469 1912/www. brooklynconcerts.com). **Dates** July-Aug.
Grab a lawn chair and listen to free pop, funk, soul and gospel at these outdoor concerts in Brooklyn.

P.S.1 Warm Up
For listing, see p170 P.S.1 Contemporary Art Center. **Dates** July-Sept at 3-9pm Sat.
For years, this weekly Saturday-afternoon bash in the museum's courtyard has drawn fashionable types from all over the city to dance, drink beer and relax in a beach-like environment. Local and international DJs and bands provide the soundtrack.

Mostly Mozart
Lincoln Center, Columbus Avenue, between 64th & 65th Streets (1-212 875 5766/www.lincolncenter. org). Subway: 1 to 66th Street-Lincoln Center. **Dates** Late July-Aug.
For more than 35 years, this four-week-long festival has been mounting a packed schedule of works by Mozart and his contemporaries.

Lincoln Center Out of Doors Festival
For listing, see p328 Lincoln Center. **Dates** Aug.
Free dance, music, theatre, opera and more make up this ambitious and family-friendly festival of classic and contemporary works.

New York International Fringe Festival
Various locations (1-212 279 4488/ www.fringenyc.org). **Dates** Aug.
Wacky, weird and sometimes great, Downtown's Fringe Festival shoehorns hundreds of performances into 16 theatre-crammed days.

Harlem Week
Various Harlem locations (1-212 862 8477/ www.harlemdiscover.com). Subway: B, C, 2, 3 to 135th Street. **Dates** Aug.
Get into the groove at this massive street fair, which serves up live music, art and food along 135th Street. Concerts, film, dance, fashion and sports events are on tap all week.

The **New York City Marathon**. *See p265.*

Central Park Zoo Chillout Weekend
Central Park, entrance on Fifth Avenue, at 65th Street (1-212 439 6500/www.wcs.org). Subway: N, R, W to Fifth Avenue-59th Street; 4, 5, 6 to 59th Street. **Dates** Early Aug.
If you're roaming the city's streets during the dog days of August, this two-day party offers the perfect chilly treat. The weekend freeze-fest features penguin and polar-bear talent shows, games, zookeeper challenges and other frosty fun.

Howl!
Various East Village locations (1-212 505 2225/ www.howlfestival.com). **Dates** Last wk in Aug.
Taking its name from the seminal poem by long-time neighbourhood resident Allen Ginsberg, this all-things-East Village fest is a grab bag of art events, films, performance art, readings and much more. A good chance to dip into local life.

Autumn

West Indian-American Day Carnival
Eastern Parkway, from Utica Avenue to Grand Army Plaza, Brooklyn (1-718 467 1797/www.wiadca.org). Subway: 2, 3 to Grand Army Plaza; 3, 4 to Crown Heights-Utica Avenue. **Date** 4 Sept.

The streets come alive with the jubilant clangour of steel-drum bands and the steady throb of calypso and soca music. Mas bands – elaborately costumed marchers – dance along the parade route, thousands move to the beat on sidewalks, and vendors sell Caribbean crafts, clothing, souvenirs and food.

Broadway on Broadway

43rd Street, at Broadway (1-212 768 1560/ www.broadwayonbroadway.com). Subway: N, Q, R, W to 42nd Street; S, 1, 2, 3, 7 to 42nd Street-Times Square. **Date** Early-mid Sept.
Broadway's biggest stars convene in the middle of Times Square to belt out show-stopping numbers. The season's new productions mount sneak previews, and it's all free.

Atlantic Antic

Atlantic Avenue, from Fourth Avenue to Hicks Street, Brooklyn (1-718 875 8993/www.atlantic ave.org). Subway: B, Q, 2, 3, 4, 5 to Atlantic Avenue; D, M, N, R to Pacific Street. **Dates** Mid Sept.
Entertainment, ethnic foods, kids' activities and the World Cheesecake-Eating Contest fill the avenue at this monumental Brooklyn festival.

CMJ Music Marathon & FilmFest

Various locations (1-917 606 1908/ www.cmj.com). **Dates** Mid Sept.
The annual *College Music Journal* schmooze-fest draws thousands of young fans and music-industry types to one of the best showcases for new rock, indie rock, hip hop and electronica acts. The FilmFest, which runs in tandem with the music blow-out, includes a wide range of feature and short films, many music-related.

Feast of San Gennaro

Mulberry Street, from Canal to Houston Streets (1-212 768 9320/www.sangennaro.org). Subway: B, D, F, V to Broadway-Lafayette Street; J, M, N, Q, R, W, Z, 6 to Canal Street. **Dates** Mid Sept.
This massive street fair stretches along the main drag of what's left of Little Italy. Come on opening and closing days to see the marching band of old-timers, or after dark, when sparkling lights arch over Mulberry Street and the smells of frying *zeppole* and sausages hang in the sultry air.

Next Wave Festival

For listing, see p328 Brooklyn Academy of Music. **Dates** Oct-Dec.
The best of the best in the city's avant-garde music, dance, theatre and opera scenes are performed at this lengthy annual affair.

New York Film Festival

Alice Tully Hall, Avery Fisher Hall & Walter Reade Theater at Lincoln Center, Broadway, at 65th Street (1-212 875 5050/www.filmlinc.com). Subway: 1 to 66th Street-Lincoln Center. **Dates** Early-mid Oct.
This uptown institution, founded in 1962, is still a worthy cinematic showcase, packed with premières, features and short flicks from around the globe, plus a stellar list of celebrities for the red-carpet events.

Open House New York

Various locations (1-917 583 2398/ www.ohny.org). **Dates** Early-mid Oct.
Get an insider's view – literally – of the city that even most locals haven't seen. More than 100 sites of architectural interest normally off-limits to visitors throw open their doors and welcome the curious during a weekend of urban exploration. Lectures and educational programmes are also on offer all week.

d.u.m.b.o. art under the bridge

Various locations in Dumbo, Brooklyn (1-718 694 0831/www.dumboartscenter.org). Subway: A, C to High Street; F to York Street. **Dates** Mid Oct.
Dumbo has become a Brooklyn art destination, and this weekend of art appreciation, featuring concerts, forums, a short-film series and in-studio visits, is a popular event.

Village Halloween Parade

Sixth Avenue, from Spring to 22nd Streets (www.halloween-nyc.com). **Date** 31 Oct at 8pm.
The sidewalks at this iconic Village shindig are always packed beyond belief. For the best vantage point, put on a costume and watch from inside the parade (line-up starts at 6.30pm on Sixth Avenue, at Spring Street).

New York City Marathon

Staten Island side of the Verrazano-Narrows Bridge, to Tavern on the Green, in Central Park (1-212 423 2249/www.nycmarathon.org). **Date** Early Nov.
The sight of 35,000 marathoners hotfooting it through all five boroughs over a 26.2-mile course is an impressive one. Scope out a spot somewhere in the middle (the starting and finish lines are mobbed) to get a good view of the herd. **Photo** *p264.*

Macy's Thanksgiving Day Parade & Eve Balloon Blowup

Central Park West, at 77th Street to Macy's, Broadway, at 34th Street (1-212 494 4495/www.macysparade.com). **Date** 23 Nov at 9am.
The stars of this nationally televised parade are the gigantic balloons, the elaborate floats and good ol' Santa Claus. New Yorkers brave the cold night air to watch the rubbery colossi take shape at the inflation area on the night before Thanksgiving (from 77th to 81st Streets, between Central Park West & Columbus Avenue). **Photo** *p266.*

Winter

Radio City Christmas Spectacular

For listing, see p319 Radio City Music Hall.
Dates Nov-early Jan.
The high-kicking Rockettes and an onstage nativity scene with live animals are the attractions at this (pricey) annual homage to the Yuletide season.

The Nutcracker

New York State Theater, Lincoln Center, Columbus Avenue, at 63rd Street (1-212 870 5570/www.nycballet.com). Subway: 1 to 66th Street-Lincoln Center. **Dates** 24 Nov-1st wk in Jan.

Arts & Entertainment

Performed by the New York City Ballet, George Balanchine's fantasy world of fairies, princes and toy soldiers is a family-friendly holiday diversion.

Christmas Tree-Lighting Ceremony
Rockefeller Center, Fifth Avenue, between 49th & 50th Streets (1-212 332 6868/www.rockefeller center.com). Subway: B, D, F, V to 47th-50th Streets-Rockefeller Center. **Date** Late Nov/early Dec.
The crowds can be overwhelming here, even if you stake out a place early. Those who brace them will witness celebrity appearances and pop-star performances. But there's plenty of time during the holiday season to marvel at the giant evergreen.

The National Chorale Messiah Sing-In
Avery Fisher Hall, Lincoln Center, Columbus Avenue, at 65th Street (1-212 333 5333/www.lincolncenter. org/www.nationalchorale.org). Subway: 1 to 66th Street-Lincoln Center. **Dates** Mid Dec.
Hallelujah! Chase those holiday blues away by joining with the National Chorale and hundreds of your fellow audience members in a rehearsal and performance of Handel's *Messiah*. No previous singing experience is necessary, and you can buy the score on site, though advance perusal would help novices to the work.

New Year's Eve Ball Drop
Times Square (1-212 768 1560/www.timessquare bid.org). Subway: N, Q, R, W, 42nd Street S, 1, 2, 3, 7 to 42nd Street-Times Square. **Date** 31 Dec.
Meet up with half a million others and watch the giant illuminated ball descend amid a blizzard of confetti and cheering. Expect freezing temperatures, densely packed crowds, absolutely no bathrooms – and very tight security.

New Year's Eve Fireworks
Naumburg Bandshell, middle of Central Park, at 72nd Street (www.centralparknyc.org). Subway: B, C to 72nd Street; 6 to 68th Street-Hunter College. **Date** 31 Dec.
The fireworks explode at midnight, and you can participate in a variety of evening festivities, including dancing and a costume contest. The best views are from Tavern on the Green (at 67th Street), Central Park West (at 72nd Street) and Fifth Avenue (at 90th Street).

New Year's Eve Midnight Run
Naumburg Bandshell, middle of Central Park, at 72nd Street (1-212 860 4455/www.nyrrc.org). Subway: B, C to 72nd Street; 6 to 68th Street-Hunter College. **Date** 31 Dec.
Start the new year with a four-mile jog through the park. There's also a masquerade parade, fireworks, prizes and a booze-free toast at the halfway mark.

New Year's Day Marathon Poetry Reading
For listing, see p278 Poetry Project.
Date 1 Jan.

Macy's Thanksgiving Day Parade. *See p265.*

Big-name bohemians (Patti Smith, Richard Hell, Jim Carroll) step up to the mic during this free, all-day spoken-word spectacle.

Winter Antiques Show
Seventh Regiment Armory, 643 Park Avenue, between 66th & 67th Streets (1-718 292 7392/ www.winterantiquesshow.com). Subway: 6 to 68th Street-Hunter College. **Dates** 19-28 Jan.
One of the world's most prestigious antiques shows brings together more than 70 American and international dealers.

Winter Restaurant Week
For listing, see p262 Summer Restaurant Week.
Dates Late Jan/early Feb.
Another opportunity to sample delicious gourmet food at soup-kitchen prices (well, almost).

Chinese New Year
Around Mott Street, Chinatown (1-212 966 0100). Subway: J, M, N, Q, R, W, Z, 6 to Canal Street. **Dates** Early Feb.
Gung hay fat choy!, as the greeting goes. Chinatown bustles with energy during the two weeks of the Lunar New Year. Festivities include a staged fireworks display, a dragon parade (which snakes in and out of several restaurants), various performances and delicious food.

Art Show
Seventh Regiment Armory, 643 Park Avenue, between 66th & 67th Streets (1-212 940 8590/ www.artdealers.org). Subway: 6 to 68th Street-Hunter College. **Dates** Mid-late Feb.
Whether you're a serious collector or just a casual art fan, this vast fair is a great chance to peruse some of the world's most impressive for-sale pieces dating from the 17th century to the present.

Arts & Entertainment

Art Galleries

Contemporary art? Where to start?

A contest of concepts at **Barbara Gladstone**. *See p269.*

New York's contemporary art scene is a universe unto itself. New galleries are constantly popping up near established ones, adding to ever-expanding clusters spreading through Manhattan, Brooklyn and Queens. The epicentre of New York's contemporary art surge lies in West Chelsea, where the old and new converge. On one street, you can ride a rickety freight elevator to see a show by bright young talents and then – in a gallery the size of an aeroplane hangar just a half-block away – behold multi-million-dollar sculptures by an art star from the 1960s. Given the number and variety of spaces in this neighbourhood, a comprehensive gallery crawl is easily a full-day endeavour.

Connoisseurs craving visual comfort food should head to the Upper East Side. Art emporiums along Museum Mile are filled with works by the old masters, and prestigious galleries around 57th Street offer an impressive pageant of blue-chip shows. Soho, though no longer the booming art scene it was in the 1980s, still lays claim to some admirable galleries and non-profit spaces, while several progressive dealers have started to set up shop in the nearby Lower East Side. For the past few years, Williamsburg has been a hotbed of artistic activity, and is now a mecca for contemporary art lovers. Even Dumbo, with a handful of art venues along its waterfront, is worth a visit. Eager crowds continue to flock northwards to Long Island City in Queens, particularly for shows at MoMA affiliate P.S.1 (*see p169*). Today – thanks to the pioneering artists and real estate-savvy 'gallerists' who call these areas home – neighbourhoods that once seemed out of the way are now fresh and vital art destinations.

But before you hit the pavement running, be sure to consult *Time Out New York* magazine, for the most reliable and up-to-date listings and reviews, or the Friday and Sunday editions of the *New York Times*. For unopinionated (yet extensive) listings, pick up the monthly *Gallery Guide* (www.galleryguide.org). It's usually available in galleries for free, or for around $3 at newsstands.

Note that galleries are generally closed on Mondays and public holidays (*see p383* **Holidays**), and many are open only on weekdays from May or June to early September – some close for the entire month of August. Summer hours are listed for most venues, but it's always wise to call first before heading out.

Lower East Side

Once a land of pushcarts and pickles, the Lower East Side is currently experiencing a renaissance. For an overview of the scene (which includes artist-run spaces too numerous to mention), take the ELS-LES walking tour (www.elsles.org).
Subway: *F to East Broadway or Delancey Street; F, V to Lower East Side-Second Avenue; J, M, Z to Delancey-Essex Streets.*

ELS-LES (Every Last Sunday on the Lower East Side) Open Studios

Various studios and galleries in the Lower East Side (www.lowereastsideny.com/artwalkparticipant.htm). **Open** 1-7pm last Sun of the mth. **Admission** free, though a donation is suggested.
This is a great way to get a taste of the Lower East Side's rapidly evolving art scene. On the last Sunday of every month, a number of artist- and artisan-run studios in the area open their doors to the public (download a map from the website to find the venues). Participants vary, but ABC No Rio (156 Rivington Street, between Clinton & Suffolk Streets, 1-212 254 3697), Metalstone Gallery (175 Stanton Street, at Clinton Street, 1-212 253 8308) and Zito Studio Gallery (122 Ludlow Street, between Delancey & Rivington Streets, 1-646 602 2338) are likely to be among the art spaces opening their doors to interested members of the public.

Orchard

47 Orchard Street, between Grand & Hester Streets (1-212 219 1061). **Open** 1-6pm Thur-Sun.
The latest addition to the Lower East Side's art scene is a collaborative effort (cohorts include Andrea Fraser, Rebecca Quaytman and Gareth James). While most art galleries focus on developing artists' careers, Orchard's mission is stewardship – both of art history (screening a Michael Asher film unseen since the 1970s, for instance) and political consciousness.

Participant Inc

95 Rivington Street, between Ludlow & Orchard Streets (1-212 254 4334/www.participantinc.org). **Open** noon-7pm Wed-Sun.
Overseen by its curator Lia Gangitano, Participant Inc is a glass-fronted gallery and a Lower East Side hotspot. Expect entertaining, intelligent exhibitions that cross-breed visual and performing arts with literature and new media.

Reena Spaulings Fine Art

371 Grand Street, between Essex & Norfolk Streets (1-212 477 5006/www.reenaspaulings.com). **Open** *Sept-July* noon-6pm Thur-Sun.

What started as artist Emily Sundblad's storefront studio has become – with help from critic and gallery co-founder John Kelsey – Reena Spaulings Fine Art. Since 2004, the establishment has housed conceptual collaborative exhibitions as well as solo shows by up-and-coming artists from the US and Europe. Seth Price, Jutta Koether and Josh Smith are among the artists who have exhibited here.

Rivington Arms

4 E 2nd Street, at Bowery (1-646 654 3213/ www.rivingtonarms.com). **Open** *Sept-July* 11am-6pm Wed-Fri; noon-6pm Sat, Sun.
This intimate storefront space, run by Melissa Bent and Mirabelle Marden (painter Brice Marden's daughter), has attracted both a fashionable crowd of followers and enviable critical kudos.

Soho

The main concentration of Manhattan galleries may have shifted to the western blocks of Chelsea, but a few notables still reside here, and a number of the city's most important non-profit venues continue to make the area a vital stop on the art map.
Subway: *A, C, E, J, M, N, Q, R, W, Z, 1, 6 to Canal Street; B, D, F, V to Broadway-Lafayette Street; N, R, W to Prince Street; 6 to Spring Street.*

Deitch Projects

18 Wooster Street, between Canal & Grand Streets (1-212 343 7300/www.deitch.com). **Open** noon-6pm Tue-Sat.
Jeffrey Deitch is an art-world impresario whose gallery features live spectacles as well as large-scale, sometimes overly ambitious, efforts by artists working in virtually all media. (By comparison, Deitch's original Grand Street site seems small and sedate, but it's the one of his two Soho spaces that we most confidently recommend.) Solo shows, by the likes of Yoko Ono, aim to be both complex and accessible.

Peter Blum

99 Wooster Street, between Prince & Spring Streets (1-212 343 0441/www.peterblumgallery.com). **Open** *Sept-June* 10am-6pm Tue-Fri; 11am-6pm Sat.
This elegant space is manned by a dealer with an impeccable eye and wide tastes. Past exhibitions have run the gamut from drawings by art stars Robert Ryman and Alex Katz to terracotta funerary figures from West Africa and colourful quilts by African-American folk artist Rosie Lee Tompkins.

Ronald Feldman Fine Arts

31 Mercer Street, between Canal & Grand Streets (1-212 226 3232/www.feldmangallery.com). **Open** *Sept-June* by appointment only Mon; 10am-6pm Tue-Sat. *July, Aug* 10am-6pm Mon-Thur; 10am-3pm Fri.
This Soho pioneer has brought us landmark shows of such legendary avant-gardists as Eleanor Antin, Leon Golub and Hannah Wilke. Feldman also regularly takes chances on newer talents like British photographer Keith Cottingham – all to good effect.

Chelsea

Chelsea has the city's highest concentration of galleries; just be advised that it can be hard to see even half the neighbourhood in one day. The subway takes you only as far as Eighth Avenue, so you'll have to walk at least one long block westward to get to the galleries. You can also take the M23 crosstown bus.
Subway: *A, C, E to 14th Street; C, E to 23rd Street; L to Eighth Avenue.*

Alexander & Bonin

132 Tenth Avenue, between 18th & 19th Streets (1-212 367 7474/www.alexanderandbonin.com). **Open** *Sept-June* 10am-6pm Tue-Sat. *July* 10am-6pm Tue-Fri. *Aug* by appointment only.
This long, cool drink of an exhibition space features contemporary painting, sculpture and photography by artists such as Willie Doherty, Mona Hatoum, Rita McBride, Doris Salcedo and Paul Thek.

Andrea Rosen Gallery

525 W 24th Street, between Tenth & Eleventh Avenues (1-212 627 6000/www.andrearosengallery.com). **Open** *Sept-June* 10am-6pm Tue-Sat. *July, Aug* 10am-6pm Mon-Fri.
During the past 17 years, Andrea Rosen has established several major careers: the late Felix Gonzalez-Torres got his start here (the gallery now handles the artist's estate), as did Wolfgang Tillmans, Andrea Zittel and John Currin (who left for the Gagosian Gallery in 2003). Recent additions to the gallery's roster, such as the much-touted young sculptor David Altmejd, promise more of the same high quality to come.

Andrew Kreps Gallery

525 W 22nd Street, between Tenth & Eleventh Avenues (1-212 741 8849/www.andrewkreps.com). **Open** *Sept-June* 10am-6pm Tue-Sat. *July, Aug* 10am-6pm Mon-Fri.
The radicals in Andrew Kreps's adventurous stable of artists include Ricci Albenda, Roe Ethridge, Robert Melee and Ruth Root.

Anton Kern Gallery

532 W 20th Street, between Tenth & Eleventh Avenues (1-212 367 9663/www.antonkerngallery.com). **Open** *Sept-July* 10am-6pm Tue-Sat. *Aug* by appointment only.
The son of artist Georg Baselitz, Kern presents young American and European artists whose installations have provided the New York art scene with some of its most visionary shows. The likes of Kai Althoff, Sarah Jones, Michael Joo, Jim Lambie and David Shrigley all show here.

Barbara Gladstone

515 W 24th Street, between Tenth & Eleventh Avenues (1-212 206 9300/www.gladstonegallery.com). **Open** *Sept-mid June* 10am-6pm Tue-Sat. *Mid June-Labor Day* 10am-6pm Mon-Fri.
Gladstone is strictly blue-chip, with an emphasis on the conceptualist and the daring. Matthew Barney, Sarah Lucas and Anish Kapoor exhibit here.

Bellwether

134 Tenth Avenue, between 18th & 19th Streets (1-212 929 5959/www.bellwethergallery.com). **Open** *Sept-July* 10am-6pm Tue-Sat.
The hot-pink luminous neon sign in the window heralds the arrival of this former Brooklyn stalwart over the river at its street-level digs in Chelsea.

Chelsea remains the epicentre of New York's art scene.

Art attack

Migration to Chelsea's Wild West has now begun in earnest.

On a blustery midweek afternoon last winter, Sheri Pasquarella, a 29-year-old art consultant and private dealer, conducted a tour of the cavernous 27th Street space that housed the Tunnel nightclub until 2001. It was almost empty – and silent, except for the whir of a fashion shoot's cameras off to one side. In a wilder and more chaotic New York in times past, the spot was often filled with drag queens and undulating throngs, even drug-sniffing dogs from the NYPD. However, following a quiet era and that hopeful tour by Pasquarella, it's become a major new attraction for Chelsea gallery-goers.

Six young art gallerists have moved their businesses here from other parts of Chelsea, filling the series of old loading-dock bays along the south side of the former Tunnel site. It's adding up to probably the most concerted effort to expand Chelsea's gallery scene since the art world began abandoning Soho for the west side in the mid 1990s. Intent on creating an instant 'destination block', Pasquarella has led the exodus of dealers in emerging art to an unlikely promised land: a windswept strip of street-level spaces between Eleventh and Twelfth Avenues, under the shadow of the imposing Starrett-Lehigh Building. The tribe that accompanied Pasquarella on this quest – Oliver Kamm Gallery, Foxy Production, Derek Eller Gallery, Clementine Gallery, John Connelly Presents and Wallspace – had moved, in art-world terms, to terra incognita.

'It's totally off the beaten path,' said Connelly, 37 (*pictured*), 'even though it's a block and a half away from Gagosian.' The gallerist, along with Pasquarella, has been a driving force behind the new micro-district.

The Gagosian he speaks of is the Larry Gagosian Gallery (*see p270*), the Everest of Chelsea's art scene, which sits at the corner of West 24th Street and Eleventh Avenue. It has been, until now, the neighbourhood's western boundary. But while the distance Connelly mentioned is a short one, it might as well be a walk to the moon for some capricious art lovers. Still, he said, 'Having a group of young, emerging galleries that have a really good-quality programme, we thought, would be a good draw.'

Pasquarella and Connelly have known each other for three years; when they each went solo following separate gallery gigs, the two decided to look for real estate together.

Setting trends within the art world since 1999, Bellwether represents such promising talents as Ellen Altfest, Adam Cvijanovic and Amy Wilson.

Daniel Reich Gallery

537A W 23rd Street, between Tenth & Eleventh Avenues (1-212 924 4949/www.danielreich gallery.com). **Open** 11am-6pm Tue-Sat. Call for summer hours.

Young gallerist Daniel Reich exhibited works out of his tiny apartment before settling into this current ground-floor space that – despite its white-cube setting – continues to host a group of artists thinking out of the box, like Christian Holstad, Hernan Bas, Delia Gonzalez and Gavin Russom.

David Zwirner

525 W 19th Street, between Tenth & Eleventh Avenues (1-212 727 2070/www.davidzwirner.com). **Open** *Sept-June* 10am-6pm Tue-Sat. *July, Aug* 10am-6pm Mon-Fri.

German expatriate David Zwirner has a head-turning roster of international contemporary artists on his books that includes Marcel Dzama, Toba Khedoori, Chris Ofili, Neo Rauch and Diana Thater. (*See also p274* Zwirner & Wirth.)

Friedrich Petzel Gallery

535 W 22nd Street, between Tenth & Eleventh Avenues (1-212 680 9467/www.petzel.com). **Open** *Sept-June* 10am-6pm Tue-Sat. *July, Aug* 10am-6pm Mon-Fri.

The Friedrich Petzel Gallery represents some of the brightest young stars on the international scene, so you can count on intriguing shows. Sculptor Keith Edmier, photographer Dana Hoey, painter and filmmaker Sarah Morris and installation artists Jorge Pardo and Philippe Parenno all show here.

Gagosian Gallery

555 W 24th Street, between Tenth & Eleventh Avenues (1-212 741 1111/www.gagosian.com). **Open** *Sept-June* 10am-6pm Tue-Sat. *July-Aug* 10am-6pm Mon-Fri.

Larry Gagosian's mammoth (20,000sq ft) contribution to 24th Street's top-level galleries was launched in 1999 with an exhilarating show of Richard Serra sculptures. There's been no slackening since then, with follow-up exhibitions featuring works by Douglas Gordon, Ellen Gallagher, Damien Hirst, Ed Ruscha, Julian Schnabel and Andy Warhol. Another Gagosian Gallery is located uptown (*see p274*).

That's when they came across the Tunnel building and its 11,000-square-feet-worth of loading-dock space. 'It was clear that although the landlord wanted an art-gallery presence, they didn't really have a vision,' Pasquarella said. 'John and I came up with a concept of what to do with that space, and we approached galleries whose personalities would be good "fits" with our own.'

In a sense, the West 27th Street project is a miniature extension of gallery migrations across the city over the past 40 years. Soho, the East Village and Williamsburg would be unimaginable today without the waves of pioneering artists and galleries there. But the process of creating art neighbourhoods as bohemian paradises was ultimately self-defeating, as artists and dealers would end up pricing themselves out of the hot rental markets they created. Chelsea, however, turned out to be different. People took a more dry-eyed approach to building a brave new art world, whereby old garages would be transformed into glitzy showcases for art – and nothing more. Unlike Soho or the East Village, art isn't made in Chelsea for the most part; it's just sold there.

Time will tell whether this new outpost of art will succeed, not just in terms of sales, but in terms of quality.

Several months after the grand opening, which had hundreds of curious art lovers packing the spaces, Connelly assured that people were definitely not shying away from making the trek. 'We have fantastic foot traffic,' he said, 'but it still feels off the track. People say that it feels like Soho in the '80s.' *Visit the galleries on West 27th Street, between Eleventh and Twelfth Avenues.*

Greene Naftali Gallery

8th Floor, 526 W 26th Street, between Tenth & Eleventh Avenues (1-212 463 7770/www.greene naftaligallery.com). **Open** *Sept-June* 10am-6pm Tue-Sat. *July, Aug* 10am-6pm Mon-Fri.
This gallery is worth visiting purely for its wonderful light and spectacular panorama, yet the keen vision of Carol Greene outdoes even the eighth-floor view. Mavericks like sculptor Rachel Harrison and video artist Paul Chan draw rave reviews.

John Connelly Presents

625 W 27th Street, between Eleventh & Twelfth Avenues (1-212 337 9563/www.johnconnelly presents.com). **Open** *Sept-June* 10am-6pm Tue-Sat. *July, Aug* 10am-6pm Mon-Fri.
Connelly, long-time director of the Andrea Rosen Gallery, quickly earned a reputation as one of the most exciting young dealers around after he struck out on his own. In 2006 he and six other Chelsea gallerists moved their enterprises into a string of old loading-dock bays along 27th Street, creating one of the hottest gallery-hopping blocks in the 'hood (*see pp270-271* **Art attack**). Expect provocative works by emerging young artists, with an emphasis on installation.

The Kitchen

512 W 19th Street, between Tenth & Eleventh Avenues (1-212 255 5793/www.thekitchen.org). **Open** noon-6pm Tue-Fri; 11am-7pm Sat.
In its infancy in the early 1970s, the Kitchen (originally located in Soho) provided a safe haven for artists to take risks in the fields of experimental video art and music. Under the direction of Deb Singer since 2004, this non-profit centre for video, music, dance, performance, film and literature continues to house exhilarating avant-garde performances and bold, unpredictable art exhibitions.

Lehmann Maupin

540 W 26th Street, between Tenth & Eleventh Avenues (1-212 255 2923/www.lehmannmaupin. com). **Open** *July-Labor Day* 10am-6pm Tue-Fri. *Aug* by appointment only.
This gallery left its Rem Koolhaas-designed loft in Soho but kept Koolhaas on board when it came to designing its new Chelsea digs, located in a former garage. Epic exhibitions feature hip international artists, the likes of Tracey Emin, Gilbert & George, Teresita Fernandez, Do-Ho Suh and Juergen Teller.

Arts & Entertainment

Paula Cooper. See p273.

Leo Koenig Inc

545 W 23rd Street, between Tenth & Eleventh Avenues (1-212 334 9255/www.leokoenig.com). **Open** 10am-6pm Tue-Sat.

Leo Koenig's father is Kasper Koenig, the internationally known curator and museum director, but Leo has been making a name for himself independently by showcasing cutting-edge American and German talent in his own gallery – Meg Cranston, Torben Giehler and Lisa Ruyter are among the artists he's exhibited here.

Luhring Augustine Gallery

531 W 24th Street, between Tenth & Eleventh Avenues (1-212 206 9100/www.luhring augustine.com). **Open** *Sept-May* 10am-6pm Tue-Sat. *June-Aug* 10am-5.30pm Mon-Fri.

Designed by Richard Gluckman, the area's architect of choice, the Luhring Augustine Gallery features work from an impressive index of contemporary artists, such as British sculptor Rachel Whiteread, Swiss video star Pipilotti Rist, Japanese photographic artist Yasumasa Morimura and Americans Janine Antoni, Larry Clark, Gregory Crewdson and Christopher Wool.

Mary Boone Gallery

541 W 24th Street, between Tenth & Eleventh Avenues (1-212 752 2929/www.maryboone gallery.com). **Open** *Sept-June* 10am-6pm Tue-Sat. *July, Aug* by appointment only.

Mary Boone made her name in the 1980s representing Julian Schnabel, Jean-Michel Basquiat and Francesco Clemente at her renowned Soho gallery. She later moved to Midtown (*see p273*) and, in 2000, added this sweeping space in a former garage in Chelsea, showing established artists like painter David Salle, collage artist Barbara Kruger and figurative artist Eric Fischl alongside the work of young up-and-comers like Kevin Zucker and Hilary Harkness. The size of the space means that large-scale works can be accommodated here.

Matthew Marks Gallery

523 W 24th Street, between Tenth & Eleventh Avenues (1-212 206 0200/www.matthewmarks.com). **Open** *Sept-June* 11am-6pm Tue-Sat. *July, Aug* 11am-6pm Mon-Fri.

The Matthew Marks Gallery was a driving force behind Chelsea's transformation into one of the city's top art destinations, and, with three outposts to its name, it remains one of the neighbourhood's power-houses. The gallery showcases such international talent as Robert Gober, Nan Goldin, Andreas Gursky, Ellsworth Kelly, Brice Marden and Ugo Rondinone. **Other locations:** 521 W 21st Street, between Tenth & Eleventh Avenues (1-212 243 0200); 523 W 24th Street, between Tenth & Eleventh Avenues (1-212 243 0200).

Metro Pictures

519 W 24th Street, between Tenth & Eleventh Avenues (1-212 206 7100/www.metropictures gallery.com). **Open** *Sept-mid June* 10am-6pm Tue-Sat. *Mid June-Labor Day* 10am-6pm Mon-Fri.

The gallery is best known for representing the art-world superstar Cindy Sherman, along with such big contemporary names as multi-media artist Mike Kelley, Robert Longo (known for his works produced using the mediums of photography and charcoal) and the late German artist Martin Kippenberger.

PaceWildenstein Gallery

534 W 25th Street, between Tenth & Eleventh Avenues (1-212 929 7000/www.pace wildenstein.com). **Open** *Sept-May* 10am-6pm Tue-Sat. *June-Aug* 10am-6pm Mon-Thur; 10am-4pm Fri.

In a space designed by the artist Robert Irwin, this welcoming Chelsea branch of the famous 57th Street gallery houses grand-scale shows by major contemporary talents such as Chuck Close, Alex Katz, Sol LeWitt, Robert Rauschenberg, Elizabeth Murray and Kiki Smith. **Other locations:** 545 W 22nd Street, between Tenth & Eleventh Avenues (1-212 989 4258).

Paula Cooper Gallery

534 W 21st Street, between Tenth & Eleventh
Avenues (1-212 255 1105). **Open** *Sept-May*
10am-6pm Tue-Sat. *June-Aug* 9.30am-5pm Mon-Fri.
First in Soho, and early to Chelsea, Paula Cooper
has built up an impressive art temple for worship-
pers of contemporary work. (She has also opened
a second space, located across the street.) The
gallery is best known for minimalist and conceptualist work, including pieces by photographers
Zoe Leonard and Andres Serrano and sculptors
such as Carl Andre, Donald Judd and Sherrie
Levine. You'll also see younger artists who are just
starting to make a name for themselves, like Kelley
Walker and John Tremblay.
Other locations: 521 W 21st Street, between Tenth
& Eleventh Avenues (1-212 255 5247).

Postmasters Gallery

459 W 19th Street, between Ninth & Tenth
Avenues (1-212 727 3323/www.postmasters
art.com). **Open** *Sept-July* 11am-6pm Tue-Sat.
Postmasters Gallery, run by the savvy duo of
Magdalena Sawon and Tamas Banovich, emphasises technologically inflected art (most of which
leans towards the conceptualist) in the form of sculpture, painting, new media and installations from the
likes of Diana Cooper and Christian Schumann.

Robert Miller Gallery

524 W 26th Street, between Tenth & Eleventh
Avenues (1-212 366 4774/www.robertmiller
gallery.com). **Open** *Sept-June* 10am-6pm Tue-
Sat. Call for summer hours.
This former 57th Street stalwart often shows works
by well-established artists that you might expect to
see displayed at a museum rather than in a gallery.
Exhibitors include the likes of painters Lee Krasner,
Alice Neel and Tom Wesselmann, and photogra-
phers Bruce Weber and Diane Arbus.

Sonnabend

536 W 22nd Street, between Tenth & Eleventh
Avenues (1-212 627 1018). **Open** *Sept-July*
10am-6pm Tue-Sat. *Aug* by appointment only.
Sonnabend is a well-established standby in a muse-
um-like space that shows new work by Ashley
Bickerton, Gilbert & George, Candida Höfer, Jeff
Koons, Haim Steinbach and Matthew Weinstein.

57th Street

The home of Carnegie Hall, Tiffany & Co,
Bergdorf Goodman and a number of art
galleries, the area surrounding 57th Street
is a beehive of commercial activity that's
lively, cultivated, chic – and expensive.
Subway: *E, V to Fifth Avenue-53rd Street; F to*
57th Street; N, R, W to Fifth Avenue-59th Street.

Greenberg Van Doren Gallery

7th Floor, 730 Fifth Avenue, at 57th Street (1-212
445 0044/www.gvdgallery.com). **Open** *Sept-May*
10am-6pm Tue-Sat. *June-Aug* 10am-5pm Mon-Fri.

This elegant gallery represents established artists
Jennifer Bartlett and Richard Diebenkorn, as well as
younger talent like painters Benjamin Edwards and
Cameron Martin, video artist Alix Pearlstein plus
photographers Tim Davis and Jessica Craig-Martin.

Marian Goodman Gallery

4th Floor, 24 W 57th Street, between Fifth
& Sixth Avenues (1-212 977 7160/www.marian
goodman.com). **Open** *Sept-June* 10am-6pm Mon-
Sat. *July, Aug* 10am-6pm Mon-Fri.
This well-known space offers a host of renowned
names. Look for artists John Baldessari, Christian
Boltanski, Maurizio Cattelan, Gabriel Orozco,
Gerhard Richter, Thomas Struth and Jeff Wall.

Mary Boone Gallery

4th Floor, 745 Fifth Avenue, between 57th &
58th Streets (1-212 752 2929/www.maryboone
gallery.com). **Open** *Sept-June* 10am-6pm Tue-Sat.
Here, one-time Soho celeb Boone continues to produce hit shows featuring young artists, but her most
prized venue is now her newer gallery in Chelsea (see
p272). The star attractions at both locations are
established players such as Ross Bleckner, Peter
Halley and hip provocateur Damian Loeb.

PaceWildenstein Gallery

2nd Floor, 32 E 57th Street, between Madison
& Park Avenues (1-212 421 3292/www.pace
wildenstein.com). **Open** *Sept-May* 9.30am-6pm
Tue-Sat. *June-Aug* 9.30am-6pm Mon-Fri.
To view shows by a few of the 20th century's most
significant artists, head to this institution on 57th
Street. Here you'll find pieces by such notables as
Chuck Close, Agnes Martin, Pablo Picasso, Ad
Reinhardt, Mark Rothko, Lucas Samaras, Elizabeth
Murray and Kiki Smith. The Pace Prints division at
this location exhibits works on paper by everyone
from old masters to notable contemporaries. And if
you're not content with that, the gallery also deals
in fine ethnic and world art.

The Project

3rd Floor, 37 W 57th Street, between Fifth & Sixth
Avenues (1-212 688 1585/www.elproyecto.com).
Open *Sept-June* 10am-6pm Mon-Fri. Call for
summer hours.
This gallery has been the darling of European critics and curators ever since it opened in 1998,
and its move from Harlem to Midtown has only
increased its keen following. Expect work by
acclaimed young artists, the likes of Julie Mehretu,
Peter Rostovsky and Stephen Vitiello.

Upper East Side

Many galleries on the Upper East Side sell
masterpieces to billionaires. Still, anyone can
look at the exhibited works for free, and some
pieces are treasures that will vanish from public
view for years, if sold to private collectors.
Subway: *6 to 68th Street-Hunter College*
or 77th Street.

Arts & Entertainment

Gagosian Gallery

980 Madison Avenue, at 76th Street (1-212 744 2313/www.gagosian.com). **Open** *Sept-May* 10am-6pm Tue-Sat. *June-Aug* 10am-6pm Mon-Fri.

Long a force to be reckoned with in the world of contemporary art, Larry Gagosian runs pristine temples Uptown and in Chelsea (*see p270*). Featured artists include Francesco Clemente and Richard Serra, plus younger stars like Cecily Brown and Damien Hirst.

Knoedler & Co

19 E 70th Street, between Fifth & Madison Avenues (1-212 794 0550/www.knoedlergallery.com). **Open** *Sept-May* 9.30am-5.30pm Tue-Fri. *June-Aug* 9.30am-5pm Mon-Fri.

Opened in 1846, the oldest gallery in New York exhibits museum-quality post-war work and contemporary artists like Lee Bontecou and John Walker.

Mitchell-Innes & Nash

5th Floor, 1018 Madison Avenue, between 78th & 79th Streets (1-212 744 7400/www.miandn.com). **Open** *Sept-June* 10am-5pm Tue-Sat. *July* 10am-5pm Mon-Fri. Call for Aug hours.

This 12-year-old gallery is run by two former specialists from Sotheby's. The ambitious programme ranges from modern masters like Willem de Kooning to up-and-comers like Kojo Griffin. **Other locations**: 534 W 26th Street, between Tenth & Eleventh Avenues (1-212 744 7400).

Zwirner & Wirth

32 E 69th Street, between Madison & Park Avenues (1-212 517 8677/www.zwirnerandwirth.com). **Open** *Sept-June* 10am-6pm Tue-Sat. *July-Labor Day* 10am-6pm Mon-Fri.

Z&W, located in a renovated townhouse space, exhibits modern and contemporary masters like Dan Flavin, Martin Kippenberger and Bruce Nauman. (*See also p270* **David Zwirner**.)

Harlem

Triple Candie

461 W 126th Street, between Morningside & Amsterdam Avenues (1-212 865 0783/www.triple candie.org). Subway: A, B, C, D, 1 to 125th Street. **Open** noon-5pm Thur-Sun.

This multicultural arts centre brings exhibitions and educational programmes to Harlem's west side.

Brooklyn

Artists who live and work in Brooklyn have created a thriving art scene, with Williamsburg its uncontested hub. (For a printable map of the area's venues, visitwww.williamsburg galleryassociation.com.) While many galleries have migrated to Chelsea after blossoming in the borough, plenty of exceptional spaces have stayed put. Most are open on Sundays and Mondays, when the majority of galleries in Manhattan are closed.

Black & White Gallery

483 Driggs Avenue, between North 9th & 10th Streets, Williamsburg (1-718 599 8775/www.blackandwhiteartgallery.com). Subway: L to Bedford Avenue. **Open** *Sept-July* noon-6pm Mon, Fri-Sun and by appointment.

Gallery founder and director Tatyana Okshteyn is good at finding new talent. At a typical show opening, you can expect to see large-scale installations in the outdoor courtyard, sculpture or paintings throughout the gallery and enthusiastic gallery-goers spilling on to the sidewalk. **Other locations**: 636 W 28th Street, between Eleventh & Twelfth Avenues (1-212 244 3007).

Jack the Pelican Presents

487 Driggs Avenue, between North 9th & 10th Streets, Williamsburg (1-718 782 0183/www.jackthepelicanpresents.com). Subway: L to Bedford Avenue. **Open** *Sept-July* noon-6pm Mon, Thur-Sun.

Jack the Pelican joined the newest wave of Williamsburg galleries in 2003 when partners Don Carroll and Matt Zalla opened this space dedicated to offbeat and edgy art. One recent exhibition involved live-in artists; another featured an installation of the world's largest bowie knife.

Pierogi

177 North 9th Street, between Bedford & Driggs Avenues, Williamsburg (1-718 599 2144/www.pierogi2000.com). Subway: L to Bedford Avenue. **Open** *Sept-July* noon-6pm Mon, Thur-Sun and by appointment.

Pierogi, one of Williamsburg's established galleries, presents the Flat Files, a series of drawers containing works on paper by some 800 artists. Don't pass up the chance to don those special white gloves and handle the archived artwork yourself.

Non-profit spaces

apexart

291 Church Street, between Walker & White Streets (1-212 431 5270/www.apexart.org). Subway: J, M, N, Q, R, W, Z, 6 to Canal Street; 1 to Franklin Street. **Open** *Sept-July* 11am-6pm Tue-Sat.

Founded in 1994 by artist Steven Rand, apexart's inspiration comes from the independent critics, curators and artists selected for its curatorial programme. The work rarely follows prevailing fashions; more often, it anticipates them, with a focus on ideas and on encouraging public dialogue.

Art in General

79 Walker Street, between Broadway & Lafayette Street (1-212 219 0473/www.artingeneral.org). Subway: J, M, N, Q, R, W, Z, 6 to Canal Street. **Open** *Sept-June* noon-6pm Tue-Sat.

Now celebrating its 25th year, this Chinatown oddball has a vigorous resident-artist programme that introduces newcomers – from New York, Europe, Cuba and elsewhere in Latin America – to the public, in a homey, almost familial atmosphere.

The Drawing Center
35 Wooster Street, between Broome & Grand Streets (1-212 219 2166/www.drawingcenter.org). Subway: A, C, E, J, M, N, Q, R, W, Z, 6 to Canal Street. **Open** *Sept-July* 10am-6pm Tue-Fri; 11am-6pm Sat.
This 30-year-old Soho standout, a stronghold of works on paper, assembles critically acclaimed pro-grammes that feature not only soon-to-be art stars but also museum-calibre legends such as James Ensor, Ellsworth Kelly and even Rembrandt.

Grey Art Gallery at New York University
100 Washington Square East, between Washington & Waverly Places (1-212 998 6780/www.nyu.edu/greyart). Subway: A, B, C, D, E, F, V to W 4th Street; N, R, W to 8th Street-NYU. **Open** *Mid Sept-mid July* 11am-6pm Tue, Thur, Fri; 11am-8pm Wed; 11am-5pm Sat.* **Admission** suggested donation $3.
NYU's museum-laboratory holds a multimedia col-lection of nearly 6,000 artworks covering the entire range of visual art. The emphasis here is on the late 19th and 20th centuries.

Momenta Art
72 Berry Street, between North 9th & 10th Streets, Williamsburg, Brooklyn (1-718 218 8058/www.momentaart.org). Subway: L to Bedford Avenue. **Open** *Sept-June* noon-6pm Mon, Thur-Sun.
Momenta is housed in a tiny Brooklyn space, yet it conveys the importance of a serious Chelsea gallery. You'll find solo and group exhibitions from a cross-section of emerging, mainly conceptualist, artists.

SculptureCenter
44-19 Purves Street, at Jackson Avenue, Long Island City, Queens (1-718 361 1750/www.sculpture-center.org). Subway: E, V to 23rd Street-Ely Avenue; G to Long Island City-Court Square; 7 to 45th Road-Court House Square. **Open** 11am-6pm Mon, Thur-Sun.
One of the best places to see work by blossoming and mid-career artists, this gallery is known for its very broad definition of sculpture. The impressive steel-and-brick digs, designed by architect Maya Lin, opened in late 2002.

Smack Mellon Gallery
92 Plymouth Street, between Washington & Main Streets, Dumbo, Brooklyn (1-718 834 8761/www.smackmellon.org). Subway: A, C to High Street; F to York Street. **Open** noon-6pm Wed-Sun.
Avant-garde group shows fill this gallery's new waterfront digs. The recently renovated, 12,000sq ft space has ample room for emerging and mid-career artists to exhibit work in all media.

White Columns
320 W 13th Street, between Hudson & W 4th Streets, entrance on Horatio Street (1-212 924 4212). Subway: A, C, E, 1, 2, 3 to 14th Street; L to Eighth Avenue. **Open** noon-6pm Tue-Sat.
British-born Matthew Higgs – artist, writer and now director and chief curator here at New York's oldest alternative art space – has been getting high

marks for shaking things up by expanding the curatorial focus beyond New York, while staying committed to under-represented artists.

Photography

New York is photo country, no doubt about it. For a comprehensive overview of local exhibitions, look out for the bimonthly directory *Photograph* ($8 at galleries or online at www.photography-guide.com).

Edwynn Houk Gallery
4th Floor, 745 Fifth Avenue, between 57th & 58th Streets (1-212 750 7070/www.houkgallery.com). Subway: N, R, W to Fifth Avenue-59th Street. **Open** *Sept-July* 11am-6pm Tue-Sat. Call for summer hours.
The Edwynn Houk Gallery is a respected specialist in vintage and contemporary photography. Among the artists exhibited are Brassaï, Lynn Davis, Dorothea Lange, Annie Leibovitz, Man Ray and Alfred Stieglitz, each commanding, as you'd expect for talent of this calibre, the very top dollar prices.

International Center of Photography
1133 Sixth Avenue, at 43rd Street (1-212 857 0000/www.icp.org). Subway: B, D, F, V to 42nd Street-Bryant Park; 7 to Fifth Avenue. **Open** 10am-6pm Tue-Thur, Sat, Sun; 10am-8pm Fri. **Admission** $10; $7 seniors, students; free under-12s. Voluntary donation 5-8pm Fri.
In 2001 the International Center of Photography's galleries, once split between midtown and uptown locations, were consolidated in a redesigned build-ing that also accommodates a school and a library (a major archive of photography magazines and thousands of biographical and photographic files). Begun in the 1960s as the International Fund for Concerned Photography, ICP houses work by leg-endary photojournalists Werner Bischof, Robert Capa, David Seymour and Dan Weiner, who were tragically killed on assignment. True to their tradi-tion, news and documentary photography remains an important part of the centre's programme, which also includes contemporary photos and video. Two floors of exhibition space often showcase retrospec-tives devoted to a single artist; more recent shows have focused on the work of Larry Clark, Ralph Eugene Meatyard and André Kertész.

Pace/MacGill
9th Floor, 32 E 57th Street, between Madison & Park Avenues (1-212 759 7999/www.pacemacgill.com). Subway: N, R, W to Lexington Avenue-59th Street; 4, 5, 6 to 59th Street. **Open** *Sept-late June* 9.30am-5.30pm Tue-Fri; 10am-6pm Sat. *Late June-Aug* 9.30am-5.30pm Mon-Thur; 9.30am-4pm Fri.
Pace/MacGill is a well-established gallery that fre-quently shows work by such well-known names as Walker Evans, Robert Frank, Irving Penn and Alfred Stieglitz, in addition to groundbreaking con-temporaries like Chuck Close and Kiki Smith.

Arts & Entertainment

Books & Poetry

Authors prove they can do more than read and write.

Bowery Poetry Club. *See p278.*

On a recent evening in a downtown bar, Lydia Davis, an author known for stories full of comic quirkiness and well-wrought neuroses, treated the packed space to unpublished work. For her fans, it was a thrilling night – a peek into a much-anticipated book (tentatively titled *Good Times and Forbidden Subjects*) that everyone else will have to wait eight months to read. But the audience was treated to more than just Davis's distinctive prose and droll explanations of what inspired her tales. This was the Happy Ending Reading Series, curated by novelist and MC extraordinaire Amanda Stern, who requires all of her literary participants to do something unpredictable. To fulfil that request, Davis had a keyboard on hand to play Bach's Prelude No. 1 in C Major. She even found someone in the audience who could sing – quite beautifully.

The Happy Ending Series is one of the most festive readings in town; you often leave feeling like you've caught a bit of literary history in the making. But it's not the only place in which to see an author read in New York, a city that offers many engaging literary events weekly. Book-related happenings take place in a variety of locations: big bookstore chains, bars, even city parks. It can be fun to catch the bustling literati at crowded events, but you can often see well-known authors at cosy venues too: Joan Didion and James Salter have read at the high-end **92nd Street Y**, yet both have also read at the small independent bookstore **192 Books**.

Whatever type of event you're drawn to, readings are like the rock shows of the book world, providing the opportunity to see your favourite writers in the flesh. Even better, they're a chance to interact with literature in a different way from being alone with a book, since authors tend to add a dimension to their work with their tone and through the Q&A sessions that usually follow. To find out who's reading and where, check out the weekly listings in *Time Out New York*.

See also p109 **Feeling bookish?**

Author appearances

Barnes & Noble

33 E 17th Street, between Broadway & Park Avenue South (1-212 253 0810/www.barnesandnoble.com). Subway: L, N, Q, R, W, 4, 5, 6 to 14th Street-Union Square. **Admission** free.

Many an author touches down at a Barnes & Noble. This Union Square branch offers an especially varied schedule. Recent names include Joyce Carol Oates, Ian McEwan and Michael Cunningham.

Bluestockings

172 Allen Street, between Rivington & Stanton Streets (1-212 777 6028/www.bluestockings.com). Subway: F, V to Lower East Side-Second Avenue. **Admission** suggested donation free-$10. **Credit** AmEx, MC, V.
This self-proclaimed progressive bookstore and café hosts frequent readings and discussions, often on feminist and lesbian themes. Past readers have included graphic novelist Alison Bechdel as well as political writer Michelle Goldberg.

Books of Wonder

18 W 18th Street, between Fifth & Sixth Avenues (1-212 989 3270/www.booksofwonder.net). Subway: F, V to 14th Street; L to Sixth Avenue. **Admission** free.
This is the place to find children's books – both new and old – and to catch events featuring both established and up-and-coming authors.

Half King

505 W 23rd Street, between Tenth & Eleventh Avenues (1-212 462 4300/www.thehalfking.com). Subway: C, E to 23rd Street. **Admission** free.
Co-owned by Sebastian Junger, the author of *The Perfect Storm*, the Half King holds Monday night readings. Recent authors have included Amanda Filipacchi, Elizabeth Gilbert and Junger himself.

Happy Ending Series

Happy Ending, 302 Broome Street, between Eldridge & Forsyth Streets (1-212 334 9676). Subway: F, V to Delancey Street; J, M, Z to Delancey-Essex Streets. **Admission** free.
Hosted by Amanda Stern, these reading events (with musical interludes) take place in a massage parlour turned-watering-hole. The bar setting lends the series a laid-back, convivial vibe. Recent readers that have featured here have included Heather McGowan, Sean Wilsey and David Rakoff.

Housing Works Used Book Café

For listings, see p252. **Admission** free; book donations encouraged.
Both the emerging and the illustrious mingle at the microphone (and in the audience) at this Soho bookstore and café, which has one of the best readings series in the city. What's more, all of the profits from events go towards providing shelter and support services to homeless people living with HIV and AIDS. Visiting authors run the gamut: Gary Shteyngart, Lynne Tillman, Sam Lipsyte, Jonathan Lethem… the list goes on.

Hue-Man Bookstore

2319 Frederick Douglass Boulevard (Eighth Avenue), between 124th & 125th Streets (1-212 665 7400/ www.huemanbookstore.com). Subway: A, B, C, D to 125th Street. **Admission** free.
This spacious Harlem bookstore features frequent readings as well as in-store appearances by authors (Bill Clinton, whose office is nearby, held a signing of his memoirs here), with an emphasis on African-American writers and topics.

KGB

2nd Floor, 85 E 4th Street, between Second & Third Avenues (1-212 505 3360/www.kgbbar.com). Subway: F, V to Lower East Side-Second Avenue; 6 to Astor Place. **Admission** free.
This dark and formerly smoky East Village hangout with an old-school Communist theme runs several top-notch weekly series, featuring NYC writers, poets, fantasy authors and more.

McNally Robinson Bookstore

50 Prince Street, between Lafayette & Mulberry (1-212 274 1160/www.mcnallyrobinson.com). Subway: N, R to Prince Street; 6 to Spring Street. **Admission** free.
McNally Robinson is an excellent new independent bookstore. To cement its reputation, it's inviting a wide range of non-fiction writers and novelists to read in its comfortable café space.

National Arts Club

15 Gramercy Park South, between Park Avenue South & Irving Place (1-212 475 3424/ www.nationalartsclub.org). Subway: 6 to 23rd Street. **Admission** free, except for benefits.
A posh Gramercy Park address, and grand Victorian interiors, make this spot a suitably dramatic setting for gazing upon your literary idol. Lectures and readings are open to the public as space permits; check the website for upcoming events. And be forewarned: at certain readings, business attire is required.

New School University

66 W 12th Street, between Fifth & Sixth Avenues (1-212 229 5353/tickets 1-212 229 5488/www.new school.edu). Subway: F, V to 14th Street; L to Sixth Avenue. **Admission** free-$15; students free. **Credit** AmEx, MC, V.
Mary Karr, Nick Flynn and Anne Carson are a few of the notable writers who have participated in the New School University's wide-ranging readings and literary forums. It's also worth looking out for political discussions and poetry nights.

92nd Street Y

1395 Lexington Avenue, at 92nd Street (1-212 415 5500/www.92y.org). Subway: 6 to 96th Street. **Admission** $16-$35. **Credit** AmEx, MC, V.
Big-name novelists, journalists and poets preside over some grand intellectual feasts here, with talks by critic James Wood, as well as a reading series featuring writers the likes of James Salter, Michael Chabon and Alice Munro. The Biographers/Critics and Brunch events are also popular.

192 Books

192 Tenth Avenue, at 21st Street (1-212 255 4022). Subway: C, E to 23rd Street. **Admission** free.
This independent bookstore offers a wide variety of books, focusing on literary titles and art history. Its reading series is phenomenal, bringing in quality authors, such as novelists Ken Kalfus and Clifford Chase, and poet John Ashbery. **Photo** *p278.*

Having a browse at **192 Books**. See p277.

Poetry Project

St Mark's Church in-the-Bowery, 131 E 10th Street, at Second Avenue (1-212 674 0910/www.poetry project.com). Subway: L to First Avenue; 6 to Astor Place. **Admission** $8; $7 seniors/students. **No credit cards.**

The Project, housed in a beautiful old church, has hosted an amazing roster of poets since its inception way back in 1966, including creative luminaries like the late Ted Berrigan, Patti Smith and Eileen Myles. It also offers workshops, lectures, book parties and an open poetry reading on the first Monday of each month.

Printed Matter

195 Tenth Avenue, at 21st Street (1-212 925 0325/ www.printedmatter.org). Subway: C, E to 23rd Street. Located across the street from 192 Books (*see p277*), this treasure trove of a bookshop doesn't host many readings, but it does have an awesome selection of art books – monographs, biographies, critical studies and much more.

Sunny's Bar

253 Conover Street, between Beard & Reed Streets, Red Hook, Brooklyn (1-718 625 8211). Travel: F, G to Smith-9th Streets, then take the B77 bus to Conover Street. **Admission** $3 donation. **No credit cards.**

Red Hook is becoming a popular neighbourhood, but it still offers a taste of old Brooklyn, and this onetime docker's bar exemplifies this fact. On one Sunday a month, the watering hole invites authors such as Phillip Lopate, Meg Wolitzer and Peter Blauner to share their work.

Spoken word

Most spoken-word events begin with a featured poet or two, before moving on to an open mic. If you'd like to participate, show up a little early and ask for the sign-up sheet. Ensure that you adhere to poetry-slam etiquette: feel free to express approval out loud, but keep criticism to yourself (silence speaks louder than words). For an up-to-date schedule of events throughout the city, check out the Ultimate NYC Poetry Calendar (www.poetz.com/calendar).

Bowery Poetry Club

308 Bowery, between Bleecker & Houston Streets (1-212 614 0505/www.bowerypoetry.com). Subway: B, D, F, V to Broadway-Lafayette Street; 6 to Bleecker Street. **Admission** free-$15. **No credit cards.**

Celebrating the grand oral traditions and cyberific future of poetry, the funky BPC features spoken-word events nightly, with readings and performance in the afternoon. The Urbana National Slam team leads an open mic on Thursdays. **Photo** *p276.*

Cornelia Street Café

29 Cornelia Street, between Bleecker & W 4th Streets (1-212 989 9319/www.corneliastreet cafe.com). Subway: A, B, C, D, E, F, V to W 4th Street. **Admission** free-$6, 1-drink minimum. **Credit** AmEx, MC, V.

This charming West Village restaurant is home to several long-running series of spoken-word events, along with live music and theatre. At the time of writing, the café's basement performance space was devoting nights to Arab-, Greek- and Italian-American writers. The open-mic Pink Pony series is on Fridays (arrive before 6pm to sign up for a slot).

Moth StorySLAM

www.themoth.org.

Better at talking than at writing? The Moth, known for its big-name monthly storytelling shows, also sponsors open slams in various venues. Ten raconteurs get five minutes each to tell a favourite story (no notes allowed!) to a panel of judges.

Nuyorican Poets Café

236 E 3rd Street, between Avenues B & C (1-212 505 8183/www.nuyorican.org). Subway: F, V to Lower East Side-Second Avenue. **Admission** $5-$15. **No credit cards.**

This 30-plus-year-old East Village community arts centre is known for its long history of raucous slams, jam sessions and anything-goes open mics.

SOS: Sunday Open Series

ABC No Rio, 156 Rivington Street, between Clinton & Suffolk Streets (1-212 254 3697/www.abcnorio.org). Subway: F to Delancey Street; J, M, Z to Delancey-Essex Streets. **Show** 3pm Sun. **Admission** $3. **No credit cards.**

Community-based art centre ABC No Rio's long-running Sunday-afternoon open mic promises a welcoming vibe, no time limits and 'no BS'.

Arts & Entertainment

Cabaret & Comedy

Let New York's kings of comedy and cabaret light up your night.

Cabaret

Cabaret singing, as a general rule, happens in little rooms. On the slightly elevated stage of a cosy nightclub, a vocalist stands in front of a microphone, often backed only by the tinkling of a piano; and for the next hour or so, the performer offers the audience a bouquet of evocative songs. In the globalist age, cabaret is a fundamentally local art: a private party in a box – or, in old-school nightclub parlance, a boîte.

Perhaps no other genre offers quite so diverse an array of performers. Hip jazz types, grand old broads, bright young musical-theatre belters, semi-classical recitalists, female impersonators, neo-lounge singers – all share the same crowded rooms. Cabaret today is a confluence of opposites: the heights of polish with the depths of amateurism; the conventional and the unconventional; intense honesty and airy pretense; earnestness and camp.

Manhattan's three fanciest cabarets – the **Café Carlyle**, **Feinstein's at the Regency** and the **Oak Room** at the Algonquin Hotel – are throwbacks to a more elegant, Fred-and-Ginger era of New York nightlife. The men wear jackets, the women are often tastefully bejewelled. This is the New York of Woody Allen movies, where well-heeled daters can take in dinner and a show in one swank package. Neighbourhood clubs such as Danny's Skylight Room and the Hideaway Room@Helen's are less formal and less pricey.

After a rash of closings a few years back, new venues, like the Metropolitan Room and the Laurie Beechman, have popped up all over town.

Cabaret music tends to draw from what's known as the 'Great American Songbook', a vast repertoire of classic tunes by the likes of Cole Porter and the Gershwins, supplemented with songs by such contemporary composers as Joni Mitchell and Rufus Wainwright. The emphasis tends to be on storytelling and lyrical interpretation; the best performers can make each person in the audience feel personally serenaded. More than anything else, cabaret is an act of intimacy, which can make it an excellent option for a romantic evening. The Great American Songbook may be old-fashioned, but until people stop falling in and out of love, it will never be out of date.

Classic nightspots

Café Carlyle

The Carlyle, 35 E 76th Street, at Madison Avenue (1-212 744 1600/reservations 1-800 227 5737/ www.thecarlyle.com). Subway: 6 to 77th Street. **Shows** 8.45pm Mon-Thur; 8.45pm, 10.45pm Fri, Sat. **Cover** Varies, usually $50-$125, sometimes with compulsory dinner. **Credit** AmEx, DC, Disc, MC, V.
This elegant boîte in the Carlyle hotel, with its airy murals by Marcel Vertes, is the epitome of sophisticated New York chic, attracting top-level singers like Eartha Kitt, Barbara Cook and Ute Lemper. Woody Allen sometimes plays clarinet with Eddie Davis and

The Metropolitan Room. *See p281.*

Arts & Entertainment

his New Orleans Jazz Band on Monday nights (call ahead to confirm). Don't dress casually – embrace the high life. To drink in some atmosphere without spending quite so much, try Bemelmans Bar across the hall, which always features an excellent pianist (5.30pm-12.30am Mon-Sat; $20-$25 cover).

Feinstein's at the Regency
Regency Hotel, 540 Park Avenue, at 61st Street (1-212 339 4095/www.feinsteinsattheregency.com). Subway: N, R, W to Lexington Avenue-59th Street; 4, 5, 6 to 59th Street. **Shows** 8.30pm Tue-Thur; 8.30pm, 11pm Fri, Sat. **Cover** $60-$75, $25-$40 food-and-drink minimum. **Credit** AmEx, DC, Disc, MC, V.
Cabaret's crown prince, Michael Feinstein, draws A-list talent to this swank room in the Regency. It's pricey, but you often get what you pay for. Recent performers have included some of the top names in the business: Chita Rivera, Diahann Carroll and Brian Stokes Mitchell, to name just a few.

Oak Room
Algonquin Hotel, 59 W 44th Street, between Fifth & Sixth Avenues (1-212 840 6800/reservations 1-212 419 9331/www.algonquinhotel.com). Subway: B, D, F, V to 42nd Street-Bryant Park; 7 to Fifth Avenue. **Shows** 9pm Tue-Thur; 9pm, 11.30pm Fri, Sat. **Cover** $50-$65, $20 drink minimum; $50 dinner compulsory at 1st Fri and Sat shows. **Credit** AmEx, DC, Disc, MC, V.
This banquette-lined room is the place to enjoy cabaret luminaries like Karen Akers and Andrea Marcovicci, plus rising stars like the luminous Maude Maggart and the formidable jazz singer Paula West. And yes, all you Dorothy Parker fans, it's *that* Algonquin.

Standards

Danny's Skylight Room
Grand Sea Palace, 346 W 46th Street, between Eighth & Ninth Avenues (1-212 265 8130/1-212 265 8133/www.dannysgsp.com). Subway: A, C, E to 42nd Street-Port Authority. **Shows** Times vary. *Piano bar* 8-11pm daily. **Cover** $10-$25, $12-$15 food-and-drink minimum. No cover for piano bar. **Credit** AmEx, DC, Disc, MC, V.
A pastel-hued nook within the Grand Sea Palace on Restaurant Row, Danny's features up-and-comers as well as a few of the more mature cabaret and jazz stand-bys, such as the ageless sprite Blossom Dearie.

Don't Tell Mama
343 W 46th Street, between Eighth & Ninth Avenues (1-212 757 0788/www.donttellmama.com). Subway: A, C, E to 42nd Street-Port Authority. **Shows** Times vary, 2-3 shows per night. *Piano bar* 9pm-4am daily. **Cover** $5-$20 plus 2-drink minimum. No cover for piano bar, but 2-drink minimum. **Credit** AmEx, DC, Disc, MC, V.
Showbiz pros and piano-bar buffs adore this dank but homey Theater District stalwart, where acts range from the strictly amateur to potential stars of tomorrow. The nightly line-up may include pop, jazz and musical-theatre singers, as well as female impersonators, comedians and musical revues.

Duplex
61 Christopher Street, at Seventh Avenue South (1-212 255 5438). Subway: 1 to Christopher Street-Sheridan Square. **Shows** 7pm, 9pm daily. *Piano bar* 9pm-4am daily. **Cover** $5-$25 plus 2-drink minimum. **Credit** AmEx, MC, V.
The Duplex may not have classic glamour, but it's the city's oldest cabaret. Going strong for 50-plus years, it's a good-natured testing ground for new talent.

Hideaway Room @ Helen's
169 Eighth Avenue, between 18th & 19th Streets (1-212 206 0609/www.helensnyc.com). Subway: A, C, E to 14th Street; 1 to 18th Street. **Shows** Times vary, 2-3 shows per night. *Piano bar* 6-10pm daily. *Open mic* 10pm-4am daily. **Cover** $15-$25, $15 food-and-drink minimum. No cover for piano bar. **Credit** AmEx, MC, V.
In addition to the eclectic range of performers – from the leonine Baby Jane Dexter and the legendary Julie Wilson through a panoply of drag queens (this is Chelsea, after all) – this fresh, friendly boîte boasts a piano bar and affordable food.

Ars Nova. *See p281.*

Laurie Beechman Theatre

407 W 42nd Street, at Ninth Avenue (1-212 695 6909/www.theduplex.com). Subway: A, C, E to 42nd Street-Port Authority. **Shows** 7pm, 9.30pm Mon, Fri, Sun. *Open mic* 10.30pm-2am Fri. **Cover** $15-$25 plus 2-drink minimum. **Credit** AmEx, MC, V.

Tucked away beneath the West Bank Café, the city's newest cabaret joint is home to many local favourites, such as Lisa Asher and the irrepressible Brandon Cutrell (who also hosts the After Party, the racy open-mic show-tune on Friday nights).

Metropolitan Room

34 W 22nd Street, between Fifth & Sixth Avenues (1-212 206 0440/www.metropolitanroom.com). Subway: F, R, V, W to 23rd Street. **Shows** Times vary. **Cover** $10-$30 plus 2-drink minimum. **Credit** AmEx, MC, V.

This atmospheric new space, formerly occupied by the Gotham Comedy Club, is quickly establishing itself as Manhattan's mid-level cabaret venue of choice. The very solid line-up of nightclub and musical theatre performers includes jazz legend Annie Ross and the medley-friendly lounge duo Gashole. **Photo** *p279*.

Comedy

The communities surrounding every style of NYC comedy have grown over the past year. The 'alternative' scene is now so popular that its moniker hardly makes sense. But whether you describe its performers as edgy, downtown or indie, you'll find most of them doing characters, sketch and stand-up in the East Village and the Lower East Side. They've drawn so many people to **Rififi**, that the venue is now almost exclusively dedicated to comedy. Of course, the traditional stand-up club circuit is still going strong thanks to a resurgence of comedy fans in the city and new 300-seat venues such as the revamped **Gotham Comedy Club** and the forthcoming Comix. And long-form improvisation is also spreading outward from its birthplace in Chelsea. With four theatres within several blocks of each other, some have dubbed the area the 'Improv District'.

Ars Nova

511 W 54th Street, between Tenth & Eleventh Avenues (1-212 977 1700/www.arsnovanyc.com). Subway: C, E to 50th Street. **Shows** Times vary. **Cover** free-$20. **Average drink** $5. **Credit** AmEx, Disc, MC, V (online tickets only).

There aren't many entertainment options along Tenth Avenue, but one is worth the trek: a jewellery box of a theatre that stages a heady repertory of comedy, cabaret and music shows, in an environment that's focused more on the performance than on the cash register at the bar. The schedule is a little erratic, but the Thursdays at Ten series is always a good bet. **Photo** *p280*.

Carolines on Broadway

1626 Broadway, between 49th & 50th Streets (1-212 757 4100/www.carolines.com). Subway: N, R, W to 49th Street (W weekdays only); 1 to 50th Street. **Shows** Times vary. **Cover** $15-$45 (2-drink minimum). **Average drink** $7. **Credit** AmEx, DC, MC, V.

Even comics who are regulars at the city's other stand-up rooms have to work extra hard to get stage time at this institution. Carolines is the best place to see marquee names, including sitcom-ready stars, faces from the '80s comedy boom and cable-special ravers. You probably won't see anything especially edgy or underground, but tourists looking for something to write home about will leave satisfied.

Chicago City Limits

318 W 53rd Street, between Eighth & Ninth Avenues, ground floor of the Improv (1-212 888 5233/www. chicagocitylimits.com). Subway: C, E to 50th Street. **Shows** 8pm Wed-Fri; 8pm, 10pm Sat. **Cover** $15 plus 2-drink minimum. **Credit** AmEx, Disc, MC, V.

CCL's sketch- and improv-comedy revues play at the New York Improv's second stage. The CCL, which moved from Chicago in 1979, presents topical sketches, songs and audience-inspired improv. The CCL Training Center offers classes and workshops. Explore a different medium on the first Sunday of every month, when the club hosts a short comedy film festival; for details, see www.firstsundays.com.

Comedy Cellar

117 MacDougal Street, between Bleecker & W 3rd Streets (1-212 254 3480/www.comedycellar. com). Subway: A, B, C, D, E, F, V to W 4th Street. **Shows** 9pm, 10.45pm Mon-Thur, Sun; 9pm, 10.45pm, 12.30am Fri; 7.30pm, 9.15pm, 11pm, 12.45am Sat. **Cover** $15 (2-drink minimum). **Average drink** $6. **Credit** AmEx, MC, V.

Claustrophobes, beware: it gets crowded down here, especially on weekends, thanks to the immense popularity of this Village stand-by and its superb bookings. On any given night, you can expect to see Jim Norton and other local greats whose acts are more x-rated than those at Carolines.

Comedy Village

82 W 3rd Street, between Sullivan & Thompson Streets (1-212 477 0130/www.comedyvillage.com). Subway: A, B, C, D, E, F, V to W 4th Street. **Shows** 9.30pm, 11.30pm Mon-Thur, Sun; 8.30pm, 10pm, 12.30am Fri, Sat. **Cover** $20 plus 2-drink minimum Mon-Thur; $25 plus 2-drink minimum Fri, Sat.

PJ Landers runs this intimate, no-frills venue in the spot where the long-standing Boston Comedy Club used to be. You won't see as many big names, but you're still likely to have a good time.

Dangerfield's

1118 First Avenue, between 61st Street & 62nd Streets (1-212 593 1650/www.dangerfields.com). Subway: N, R, W to Lexington Avenue-59th Street; 4, 5, 6 to 59th Street. **Shows** 8.45pm Mon-Thur, Sun; 8.30pm, 10.30pm Fri; 8pm, 10.30pm, 12.30am Sat. **Cover** $12.50-$20. **Average drink** $7. **Credit** AmEx, DC, Disc, MC, V.

The decor at New York's oldest comedy club is still going strong, despite the demise of its namesake, who founded it as a cabaret back in 1969. The space itself may be a little musty, but the comics are young and lively. And while other venues gouge you with a two-drink minimum, the house that Rodney built remains the only stand-up club in town where splurging for the hooch is strictly optional. Respect.

Gotham Comedy Club

208 W 23rd Street, between Seventh & Eighth Avenues (1-212 367 9000/www.gothamcomedy club.com). Subway: F, N, R, V, W to 23rd Street (W weekdays only). **Shows** 8.30pm Mon-Thur, Sun; 8.30pm, 10.30pm Fri; 7.30pm, 9.30pm, 11.30pm Sat. **Cover** $12-$20 (2-drink minimum). **Average drink** $7. **Credit** AmEx, MC, V.
Elegance is a matter of pride at the Gotham, and it's no slouch in the laugh department, either. Jim Gaffigan and Judy Gold are regulars, and late-night surprise visits are common. And now that it's moved into new 300-seat digs, it'll be putting up the kind of headliners otherwise reserved for Carolines (*see p281*).

Laugh Factory

669 Eighth Avenue, between 42nd & 43rd Streets (1-212 586 7829/www.laughfactory.com). Subway: A, C, E to 42nd Street-Port Authority. **Shows** 8.30pm Mon-Thur, Sun; 8.30pm, 11.30pm Fri; 8.30pm, 10.30pm, 12.30am Sat. **Cover** $15-$40 plus 2-drink minimum. **Average drink** $7. **Credit** AmEx, Disc, MC, V.
Although still relatively young, the New York outpost of Jamie Masada's famed LA club has chipped away a place for itself in the scene. The programming varies across three stages from sketch to stand-up and from amateurs to national headliners, such as Kathy Griffin and Jamie Kennedy.

Laugh Lounge NYC

151 Essex Street, between Rivington & Stanton Streets (1-212 614 2500/www.laughloungenyc.com). Subway: F to Delancey Street; J, M, Z to Delancey-Essex Streets. **Shows** 8.30pm and/or 10.30pm Mon-Thur, Sun; 8.30pm, 10.30pm Fri, Sat. **Cover** $10 (2-drink minimum); call for information regarding student discounts. **Average drink** $8. **Credit** AmEx, MC, V.
Anyone looking for a change of pace from the 'herd 'em in, liquor 'em up, herd 'em out' mentality of many stand-up clubs will appreciate the casual friendliness of this newcomer. Expect a mix of fresh faces and circuit regulars behind the mic.

Magnet Theater

254 W 29th Street, between Seventh & Eighth Avenues (1-212 244 8824/www.magnettheater.com). Subway: A, C, E to 34th Street-Penn Station; 1 to 28th Street. **Shows** Times vary. **Cover** free-$7. **Average drink** $4. **No credit cards**.
Modern-day improv guru Armando Diaz and fellow instructors Ed Herbstman and Abby Sher, who all met at Chicago's Improv Olympic while working under the late Del Close (who's credited with creating long-form improv) are behind this new spot. It tends to add a more theatrical feel to its productions.

New York Improv

318 W 53rd Street, between Eighth & Ninth Avenues (1-212 757 2323). Subway: C, E to 50th Street. **Shows** 9pm Mon-Thur, Sun; 9pm, 11pm, midnight Fri, Sat. **Cover** $10-$20 plus 2-drink minimum. **Average drink** $6. **Credit** AmEx, Disc, MC, V.
Once dubbed the 'Yankee Stadium' of comedy clubs, the Improv showcased legends such as Bill Cosby, Andy Kaufman and Robin Williams during its first stint after opening in 1963. After being closed for years, former owners recently opened this basement joint a few blocks from the original, and showcase TV faces and other regulars from the club circuit.

People's Improv Theater

2nd Floor, 154 W 29th Street, between Sixth & Seventh Avenues (1-212 563 7488/www.improv central.com). Subway: 1 to 28th Street. **Shows** Times vary. **Cover** $5-$12. **Average drink** $3 (no alcohol). **No credit cards.**
Expats from the Upright Citizens Brigade Theatre started their rival operation in 2002. The PIT shares Upright Citizens Brigade Theatre's (*see below*) commitment to Chicago-style improv and sketch comedy.

Rififi

Cinema Classics, 332 E 11th Street, between First & Second Avenues (1-212 677 1027/rififinyc.com). Subway: L to First Avenue. **Shows** Times vary. **Cover** free-$5. **No credit cards.**
In the back room of this movie house you'll find almost exclusively indie, underground comedy. The seven weekly recurring variety shows include *Oh hello* (Thur), *Giant Tuesday night of amazing inventions and also there is a game*, and *Invite them up* (Wed) – three of the best shows in town.

Stand-Up New York

236 W 78th Street, at Broadway (1-212 595 0850/ www.standupny.com). Subway: 1 to 79th Street. **Shows** 9pm Mon-Thur, Sun; 8pm, 10pm, midnight Fri, Sat. **Cover** $15-$20 plus 2-menu item minimum. **Average drink** $6. **Credit** AmEx, MC, V.
Since it's a clean, professional room that books a lot of the same comics as its competitors, Stand-Up's biggest plus point is that it has the nabe all to itself. On a good night, you might see Ted Alexandro, Mitch Fatel or Jessica Kirson. On a more typical night, you won't – but you'll still get some solid laughs.

Upright Citizens Brigade Theatre

307 W 26th Street, between Eighth & Ninth Avenues (1-212 366 9176/www.ucbtheatre.com). Subway: E to 23rd Street; 1 to 28th Street. **Shows** Times vary. **Cover** $5-$20. **Average drink** $3. **No credit cards**.
Fans of adventurous improv and sketch comedy flock here in hope of glimpsing a current Saturday Night Live cast member on stage. (People with performance dreams of their own also take classes here.) Don't expect *Whose Line*-style antics: the emphasis is on long-form improv, the character-driven style imported from Chicago's Improv Olympic. Reserve early for Friday's *Stepfathers* show, Saturday's *Mother* and Sunday's *ASSSSCAT 3000*.

Children

Got kids in tow? No problem.

Brace yourself: kids lose their minds here. And who can blame them? The streets pulsate with all walks of life, museums are full of surprises and nights sparkle with a zillion twinkling lights. It's the perfect environment for short attention spans (young and old) so even the most hard to please kid can find something to smile about. Just be forewarned: all this stimulation can overload the circuits of the very young. So take in the sights but, in-between the Empire State Building and the Statue of Liberty, put away the map and have a wander, or park yourself in one of the dozens of playgrounds and let the little tykes blow off some steam.

Naturally, you'll want to take in some of New York's most popular offerings. We've listed spots that cater to the city's little cognoscenti, as well as some traditional fare that has entertained generations of NYC children. To keep up with the child-friendly events happening during your stay, pick up a copy of *Time Out New York Kids*.

Where to stay

Most hotels, especially the big chain hotels, will move a crib or an extra bed into your room in order to accommodate your tot. Ask if this service is available when you book, and check on the size of the room; it is often the case that the hipper the hotel, the smaller the rooms, since most of the trendy places assume that their guests will be out on the town all night. A few places that are especially child-friendly are listed below. For more on hotels, *see pp48-77*.

Holiday Inn Midtown
440 W 57th Street, between Ninth & Tenth Avenues (1-212 581 8100/1-800 465 4329/ www.hi57.com).
The Hell's Kitchen branch of the international chain.

Hotel Beacon
2130 Broadway, between 74th & 75th Streets (1-212 787 1100/1-800 572 4969/ www.beaconhotel.com).
For review, see p75.

Inn on 23rd
131 W 23rd Street, between Sixth & Seventh Avenues (1-212 463 0330/www.innon23rd.com).
For review, see p62.

Roger Smith
501 Lexington Avenue, between 47th & 48th Streets (1-212 755 1400/1-800 445 0277/ www.rogersmith.com).
For review, see p66.

Babysitting

Baby Sitters' Guild
1-212 682 0227/www.babysittersguild.com. **Bookings** 9am-9pm daily. **No credit cards**. Long- or short-term multilingual sitters cost from $20 per hour (four-hour minimum) plus cab fare. Babysitters are available around the clock.

Pinch Sitters
1-212 260 6005. **Bookings** 8am-5pm Mon-Fri. **No credit cards**. Charges are $17 per hour (four-hour minimum), plus the babysitter's cab fare after 9pm ($10 maximum).

Classic kids' New York

Astroland Amusement Park
1000 Surf Avenue, at West 10th Street, Coney Island, Brooklyn (1-718 372 0275/www.astroland. com). Subway: D, F, Q to Coney Island-Stillwell Avenue. **Open** *Mid Apr-mid June* noon-6pm Sat, Sun, weather permitting (plus weekdays during public-school spring break). *Mid June-Labor Day* noon-midnight daily. *Early Sept-early Oct* opens at noon Sat, Sun; closing time depends on weather. **Admission** $2.50-$6 per ride; Mon-Thur and Fri mornings $22.99 per 6hr unlimited-rides session. **Credit** MC, V.
This well-aged, iconic Coney Island amusement park has an appealing grunginess that makes it a welcome alternative to slick, mouse-themed parks. Kids over 54in (137cm) tall can ride the world-famous Cyclone rollercoaster; young ones will prefer the Tilt-a-Whirl or the carousel. Coney Island is being bought by developers and may become America's newest 'family destination' – a cleaned-up clone of itself.

Dinosaurs at the American Museum of Natural History
For listing, see p145 American Museum of Natural History.
Children of all ages request repeat visits to this old-fashioned, exhibit-based museum – especially to see the infamous dinosaur skeletons, the enormous blue whale and, in the colder months, the free-flying butterflies. During the holiday season, look for the Christmas tree decorated with origami ornaments (they include dinosaur shapes, of course). Paper-folders are on hand to help visitors make their own.

The Nutcracker

For listing, see p266.
Generations of New York kids have counted on the New York City Ballet to provide this Balanchine holiday treat. The pretty two-act production features an on-stage snowstorm, a flying sleigh, a one-ton Christmas tree and child-dancers.

Storytelling at the Hans Christian Andersen Statue

Central Park, entrance on Fifth Avenue, at 72nd Street (www.centralparknyc.org). Subway: 6 to 68th Street-Hunter College. **Dates** *June-Sept* 11am-noon Sat. **Admission** free.
Children five and older have gathered for decades at the foot of this climbable statue to hear master storytellers from all over the country.

Temple of Dendur at the Met

For listing, see p139 Metropolitan Museum of Art. The Met can be overwhelming unless you make a beeline for one or two specific galleries. The impressive Temple of Dendur, a real multi-roomed ancient temple with carvings and reliefs (and graffiti), was brought here from Egypt stone by stone, and it's a perennial hit. Also check out the mummies in the Egyptian Room and the medieval arms and armour collection. Pick up a few of the Met's printed *Family Guides* (free at the museum's information desks and available for online download), which give kids the inside scoop on what they're seeing. Note that the Met now opens on most Monday holidays – and provides special children's programming – when many other museums are closed.

Circuses

Each spring, **Ringling Bros and Barnum & Bailey's** three-ring circus (*see p260*) comes to Madison Square Garden, and so do animal-rights picketers. You can't beat the world-famous circus for spectacle, but the one-ring alternatives listed below are more fun.

Big Apple Circus

Damrosch Park, Lincoln Center, 62nd Street, between Columbus & Amsterdam Avenues (1-212 268 2500/www.bigapplecircus.org). Subway: 1 to 66th Street-Lincoln Center. **Dates** Oct-Jan. Call or visit website for schedule and prices. **Credit** AmEx, Disc, MC, V.
New York's travelling circus was founded 29 years ago as an intimate answer to the Ringling Bros extravaganza. The clowns in this non-profit show are among the most creative in the country. The circus performs a special late show on New Year's Eve, at the end of which the audience joins the performers in the ring.

UniverSoul Circus

1-800 316 7439/www.universoulcircus.com. **Dates** Early Apr-late May. Call or visit website for venue, schedule and prices. **Credit** AmEx, DC, Disc, MC, V.
This one-ring 'circus of colour' has the requisite clowns and animals with a twist: instead of familiar circus music, you get hip hop, R&B, salsa – and a morality-tale finale. The group usually appears in Brooklyn's Prospect Park in the spring.

Film

New York International Children's Film Festival

Various venues (1-212 349 0330/www.gkids.com). **Dates** Feb-Mar. Call or visit website for schedule and prices. **Credit** AmEx, MC, V.
This three-week fest is a hot ticket. An exciting mix of shorts and full-length features is presented to everyone from tots to teens. Many of the films are by international indie filmmakers – and not just those who make kids' flicks. Children determine the winners, which are then screened at an awards ceremony.

Tribeca Film Festival

Various Tribeca venues (www.tribecafilmfestival.org). **Dates** 25 Apr-6 May 2007. Visit website for schedule and prices. **Credit** AmEx, MC, V.
Robert De Niro's affair includes two weeks of screenings for kids, both commercial premières and shorts programmes, plus an outdoor street festival.

Museums & exhibitions

Museums usually offer weekend and school-break workshops, as well as interactive exhibitions. Even the very young love exploring the **American Museum of Natural History**; its **Rose Center for Earth and Space** (*see p145*) features exhibits and a multimedia space show within the largest suspended glass cube in the US. Children of all ages will be fascinated by the amazing scale-model *Panorama of the City of New York* at the **Queens Museum of Art** (*see p169*) and by the toy collection at the **Museum of the City of New York** (*see p138*), with teddy bears, games and dolls' houses. At the **American Museum of the Moving Image** (*see p167*), kids mess with *Jurassic Park* sound effects and play with moving-image technology. The **Intrepid Sea-Air-Space Museum** (*see p125*) houses interactive battle-related exhibits on an aircraft carrier. Many art museums offer family tours and workshops that may include sketching in the galleries, notably the **Brooklyn Museum** (*see p161*), the **Metropolitan Museum of Art** (*see p138*) and the **Whitney Museum of American Art** (*see p138*). The **Museum of Modern Art** (*see p127*) also caters to families in its expanded midtown space, with a large variety of programmes, including the Ford Family Programs and Family Art Workshops; MoMA family programmes include admission to the museum – which saves you a bundle.

Storytelling at the Hans Christian Andersen Statue. *See p284.*

Brooklyn Children's Museum

145 Brooklyn Avenue, at St Marks Avenue, Crown Heights, Brooklyn (1-718 735 4400/www.bchildmus. org). Subway: A to Nostrand Avenue; C to Kingston-Throop Avenue; 3 to Kingston Avenue. **Open** *Sept-June* 1-6pm Wed-Fri; 11am-6pm Sat, Sun. *July, Aug* 1-6pm Tue-Fri; 11am-6pm Sat, Sun. Call or visit website for holiday hours. **Admission** $5; free under-1s. **Credit** AmEx, Disc, MC, V.

Founded in 1899, BCM is the world's first museum designed for kids. It has more than 27,000 artefacts in its main collection, including prehistoric fossils and present-day toys from around the world. Hands-on exhibits and live small animals rule the Animal Outpost, and the People Tube (a huge sewer pipe) connects four exhibit floors. On weekends, a free shuttle bus makes a circuit from the Grand Army Plaza subway station to the Brooklyn Museum and this museum. BCM is undergoing major expansion into a new building – the world's first green museum, scheduled to open in 2007; check the website before setting out.

Children's Museum of the Arts

182 Lafayette Street, between Broome & Grand Streets (1-212 941 9198/www.cmany.org). Subway: 6 to Spring Street. **Open** noon-5pm Wed, Fri-Sun; noon-6pm Thur. **Admission** $8. Voluntary donation 4-6pm Thur. **Credit** AmEx, MC, V ($35 minimum).

Kids under seven love this low-key museum, with its floor-to-ceiling blackboards, art computers and vast store of art supplies.

Children's Museum of Manhattan

212 W 83rd Street, between Amsterdam Avenue & Broadway (1-212 721 1234/www.cmom.org). Subway: 1 to 86th Street. **Open** 10am-5pm Wed-Sun. Call for summer and holiday hours. **Admission** $8; $5 seniors; free under-1s. **Credit** AmEx, MC, V.

This children's museum promotes several types of literacy and encourages creativity through its interactive exhibitions and programmes. In the Inventor Center, computer-savvy kids can take any idea they dream up – a flying bike, a talking robot – and design it on-screen using digital imaging.

New York Hall of Science

For listing, see p169.

Known for the 1964 World's Fair pavilion in which it is housed and the rockets from the US space programme that flank it, this discovery-based museum has always been worth a trek for its discovery-based exhibits. Since its massive expansion in 2005, it's become a must for curious kids. The new building houses permanent hands-on exhibits that deal with 21st-century concepts such as networks, the science of sports and, in a massive pre-school-science area, the urban world. From March to December, the 30,000sq ft outdoor Science Playground teaches children the principles of balance, gravity and energy. Other standouts include the first interactive exhibit devoted to maths (designed by Charles and Ray Eames).

Sony Wonder Technology Lab

Sony Plaza, 56th Street, between Fifth & Madison Avenues (1-212 833 8100/www.sonywondertechlab.com). Subway: E, V to Fifth Avenue-53rd Street; N, R, W to Fifth Avenue-59th Street. **Open** 10am-5pm Tue-Sat; noon-5pm Sun; reservations recommended. **Admission** free.

Recently refurbished and expanded, this digital wonderland lets visitors use state-of-the-art technology, over four floors, to play at designing video games, assisting in surgery, editing a TV show and operating robots. A new interactive exhibit even lets visitors rock out in a band. Best for children aged eight and older.

Outdoor places

Battery Park City Parks

Battery Park City, Hudson River, between Chambers Street & Battery Place (1-212 267 9700/www.bpcparks.org). Subway: A, C, 1, 2, 3 to Chambers Street; 1 to Rector Street. **Open** 6am-1am daily. **Admission** free.

Besides watching the boats along the Hudson, kids can enjoy one of New York's best playgrounds, an open field for ball games, Frisbee and lazing, and a park house that has balls, board games and toys for the borrowing. Kids' events are held from May to October (visit the website for a schedule). Don't miss the picnic garden near the Chambers Street entrance, where kids love to interpret (and climb on) sculptor Tom Otterness's *Real World* installation.

Riverbank State Park

Hudson River, at 145th Street (1-212 694 3600). Subway: 1 to 145th Street. **Open** 6am-11pm daily. *Ice skating* Nov-Jan; call for hours. **Admission** free. Rink $1; skate rental $4.

This 28-acre park features a skating rink and other athletic facilities, along with the Totally Kid Carousel (June-Aug), designed by children.

Central Park

Most New Yorkers don't have their own garden – instead, they have public parks. The most popular is Central Park, with places and programmes just for kids. (Visit www.centralparknyc.org for a calendar.) Don't miss the beautiful antique carousel (April to November 10am to 6pm daily; December to April 10am to 4.30pm Saturday and Sunday; $1.25 a ride). The Heckscher Playground (one of 20) will soon boast an up-to-date adventure area.

Central Park Zoo

For listing, see p137.

The stars of this refurbished wildlife centre are the penguins and the polar bear, which live in glass habitats so that visitors can watch their under water antics. The zoo also runs breeding programmes for some endangered species.

Conservatory Water

Central Park, entrance on Fifth Avenue, at 72nd Street. Subway: 6 to 68th Street-Hunter College. **Open** *July, Aug* 11am-7pm Mon-Fri, Sun; 2-7pm Sat, weather permitting. **Admission** free.

Stuart Little Pond, named after EB White's storybook mouse, is a mecca for model-yacht racers. When the boat master is around, rent a remote-controlled vessel ($10 per hr).

Henry Luce Nature Observatory

For listing, see p137.

Inside the Gothic Belvedere Castle, telescopes, microscopes and hands-on exhibits teach kids about the plants and animals living in the park. With ID, you can borrow a Discovery Kit: binoculars, a birdwatching guide and other cool tools.

North Meadow Recreation Center

Central Park, Midpark, at 97th Street (1-212 348 4867/www.centralparknyc.org). Subway: B, C, 6 to 96th Street. **Open** Check website for hours. **Admission** free.

Park visitors with photo ID can check out the Field Day Kit, which includes a Frisbee, Hula-Hoop, jump rope, kickball, and Wiffle ball and bat.

Victorian Gardens

Central Park, Wollman Rink (1-212 982 2229/www.victoriangardensnyc.com). Subway: N, R, W to Fifth Avenue-59th Street. **Open** *Mid May-early Sept* 11am-7pm Mon-Fri; 10am-8pm Sat, Sun. **Admission** $1 per game/ride. $6.50 general admission, $12 unlimited rides weekdays; $7.50 general admission, $14 unlimited rides weekends, holidays. Free admission for children under 36in tall. **No credit cards**.

Central Park's first Disneyesque feature is this nostalgia-themed amusement park geared to young children. The mini-teacup carousel and Rio Grande train are bound to be hits with little kids.

Wollman Rink

For listing, see p338.

Skating in Central Park amid snowy trees, with grand apartment buildings towering in the distance, is a New York tradition, and a classic image of the city. This popular (read: crowded) rink offers lessons and skate rentals, plus a snack bar where you can warm up with hot chocolate.

Performing arts

Adventures of Maya the Bee

45 Bleecker Theater, 45 Bleecker Street, at Lafayette Street (1-212 253 9983/www.45bleecker.com/maya.html). Subway: B, D, F, V to Broadway-Lafayette Street; 6 to Bleecker Street. **Shows** *Oct-June* 11am Sat. **Tickets** $15. **Credit** AmEx, MC, V.

The star of the Culture Project's long-running jazz puppet play is the sweetest little bee that kids are likely to meet. But some of the creatures Maya encounters are not so nice – this is the insect world, after all. Recommended for ages five to nine.

Carnegie Hall Family Concerts
For listing, see p328. **Tickets** $8.
Even kids who profess to hate classical music are usually impressed by a visit to Carnegie Hall. The Family Concert series features first-rate classical, world-music and jazz performers, along with pre-concert workshops and storytelling. Concerts run from autumn through to spring and are recommended for kids aged five to 12.

Family Matters
For listing, see p352 Dance Theater Workshop. **Tickets** $20; $10 children.
Curated by a pair of choreographer parents and geared for children aged three and up (some shows are for pre-teens and teens), Family Matters is a quirky variety show blending art, dance, music and theatre. Call or check the website for a schedule.

Jazz for Young People
For listing, see p322 Jazz at Lincoln Center.
These participatory concerts, held at Jazz at Lincoln Center's smart new digs and modelled on the New York Philharmonic Young People's Concerts, are led by the trumpeter and all-round jazz great Wynton Marsalis.

Kids'n Comedy
Gotham Comedy Club, 208 W 23rd Street, between Seventh & Eighth Avenues (1-212 877 6115/ www.kidsncomedy.com). Subway: F, N, R, V, W to 23rd Street. **Shows** Call or visit website for schedule; reservations required. **Tickets** $15 plus 1-drink minimum. **Credit** AmEx, MC, V.
Kids'n Comedy has a stable of funny kids, aged nine to 17, who deliver their own stand-up material, much of it mined from the homework-sucks vein (and some lines clearly culled from Daddy's last cocktail party).

Little Orchestra Society
Various venues (1-212 971 9500/www.little orchestra.org). **Tickets** $12-$50. **Credit** MC, V.
Since 1947 this orchestra has presented classical concerts for kids, including the popular interactive *Peter and the Wolf* for pre-schoolers and December's spectacular *Amahl and the Night Visitors*.

New Victory Theater
For listing, see p348. **Tickets** $10-$50.
As New York's only full-scale young people's theatre, the New Victory presents international theatre and dance companies at junior prices. Shows often sell out well in advance, so reserve seats early.

New York Theatre Ballet
Florence Gould Hall, 55 E 59th Street, between Madison & Park Avenues (1-212 355 6160/ www.nytb.org). Subway: N, R, W to Lexington Avenue-59th Street; 4, 5, 6 to 59th Street. **Tickets** $30; $25 under-12s. Tickets also available through Ticketmaster. **Credit** AmEx, MC, V.
Enjoy one-hour adaptations of classic ballets such as *The Nutcracker*. The interactive *Carnival of the Animals* teaches the audience basic dance moves, and *Alice in Wonderland* is a vaudeville-style romp.

Swedish Cottage Marionette Theater
Central Park West, at 81st Street (1-212 988 9093). Subway: B, C to 81st Street-Museum of Natural History. **Shows** Oct-June 10.30am, noon Tue-Fri; 1pm Sat. *July, Aug* 10.30am, noon Mon-Fri. **Tickets** $6; $5 children. **No credit cards**.
Reservations are essential at this intimate theatre, located in an old Swedish schoolhouse run by the City Parks Foundation.

Theatreworks/NYC
Lucille Lortel Theatre, 121 Christopher Street, between Bleecker & Hudson Streets (1-212 647 1100/www.theatreworksusa.org). Subway: 1 to Christopher Street. **Shows** Nov, Dec, Mar, Apr, July, Aug. **Tickets** $35. **Credit** AmEx, MC, V.
Over 45 years, the travelling company Theatreworks/ USA has developed a reputation for producing dependable, if somewhat bland, mostly musical adaptations of kid-lit classics. The company finally formed a New York arm in 2005. Based at the legendary Lortel Theatre, it promises to uphold the Theatreworks tradition, but with better production values.

Urban Word NYC
Various venues (www.urbanwordnyc.org).
A DJ hosts poetry slams and open mics for 'the next generation'. Teens bring their own (uncensored) poems and freestyle rhymes or give props to other kids performing theirs.

Sports & activities

For bicycling, horseback riding and ice skating, *see pp333-339.*

Chelsea Piers
Piers 59-62, W 17th through 23rd Streets, at Eleventh Avenue (1-212 336 6666/www.chelsea piers.com). Subway: C, E to 23rd Street.
A roller rink, gym, pool, toddler gym, extreme-skating park, ice-skating rinks, batting cages and rock-climbing walls are all found in this vast complex. The Flip 'n' Flick programme (occasional Saturdays, 7-11pm) allows parents a night off while the kids enjoy athletic activities and a movie. *See also p336.*

Downtown Boathouse
Riverside Park South Pier, at 72nd Street & Hudson River (1-646 613 0740/www.downtown boathouse.org). Subway: 1, 2, 3 to 72nd Street. **Open** *15 May-15 Oct* 10am-5pm daily.
From 15 May to 15 October, weather permitting, this volunteer-run organisation offers free kayaking on weekends. All trips are offered on a first-come, first-served basis, and you must be able to swim. **Other location**: Pier 96, at 56th Street & Hudson River, Midtown.

Sydney's Playground
66 White Street, between Broadway & Church Street (1-212 431 9125/www.sydneysplayground.com). Subway: J, M, N, Q, R, W, Z, 6 to Canal Street.

Arts & Entertainment

Go ask Alice

Some say that this city is no place for
children – but where else in the world can
kids say they've visited Wonderland?
No doubt Alice's supporting cast, the Red
Queen, the March Hare and the Caterpillar,
would agree that the city is wondrous.
Indeed, along with Alice, they're all here:
around corners, behind doors, in parks
and teahouses and even underground.

DOWN THE RABBIT HOLE

Subway riders might like *Alice's Adventures
in Wonderland*'s original title, *Alice's
Adventures Under Ground*. When author
Lewis Carroll (a professor of mathematics
as well as an author) sent Alice falling down
the White Rabbit's hole, he was puzzling
over a hotly debated scientific problem of
the time: what would happen if one were to
travel straight through the centre of the earth?
Young subway riders can ponder the same
question as they descend deep into the
bowels of Manhattan. Distract them with a
view of Liliana Porter's four mosaic murals
(*photo far right*) at the 50th Street-Seventh
Avenue station. Created for the MTA's Arts
for Transit programme, the murals are
collectively titled *Alice: the Way Out*.
50th Street & Eighth Avenue subway stop.

THE POOL OF TEARS

Why does the storybook Alice cry a river?
Maybe it's not (as Carroll suggests) because
she's grown too large to fit through the door,
but because her fingers are being grabbed
by every pipsqueak who wants to ascend

to the top of her mushroom perch. The
burnished fingers belong to sculptor José
de Creeft's famous 11-foot-tall climbable
Alice statue (*photo above*), near Central
Park's Conservatory Water. Known as the
Margarita Delacorte Memorial, the bronze was
dedicated in 1959 by philanthropist and Dell
Press founder George Delacorte, as a tribute
to his wife, who was an ardent Carroll reader.
Central Park, at 76th Street, near Fifth Avenue.

Open *Sept-May* 10am-6pm daily. *Memorial Day-
Labor Day* 10am-6pm Mon-Fri. **Admission** $13 for
1st child with adult; $6 each additional child/adult.
Credit AmEx, Disc, MC, V.
For kids five and under, this huge indoor play space
resembles a streetscape, complete with a multilevel
'climbing city', a 'roadway' for ride-on toys and a café.

Trapeze School New York

For listing, see p339.
Kids over six can fly through the air with the greatest
of ease. (You can also just stop along the esplanade and
watch.) Under 12s must be accompanied by an adult.

Willy Bee's Family Lounge

*302 Metropolitan Avenue, between Driggs Avenue
& Roebling Street, Williamsburg, Brooklyn (1-718
599 3499/www.willybees.com). Subway: L to Bedford
Avenue.* **Open** 9am-7pm Mon-Thur; 9am-8pm Fri;
10am-8pm Sat; 10am-6pm Sun. **Credit** MC, V.

NYC's hippest neighbourhood, across the river
from the Lower East Side, has started turning into
baby-central as its artsy residents couple and pro-
create. Visit for a blast of alternakid culture and a
pit stop at Willy Bee's café and play space, a
favourite hangout for local parents. Sip wine while
the children check out the toys or mess around in
the backyard with their new found friends.

Tours

ARTime

1-718 797 1573. **Open** *Oct-June* 11am-12.30pm
1st Sat of mth. **Admission** $25 per parent-child
pair, $5 each additional child. **No credit cards**.
Since 1994 art historians with backgrounds in education have led monthly contemporary-art tours of
Chelsea galleries for groups of kids aged five to
ten (and their parents).

Arts & Entertainment

Less than a five-minute walk north, in the James Michael Levin Playground, is Central Park's best-kept secret – another Alice sculpture. Fredrick Roth's chunky concrete Loeb Memorial Fountain (named in honour of child-welfare advocate Sophie Loeb) has been a park fixture since 1936, when it was installed as a drinking fountain. In 1987 it was refitted as a sprinkler and moved to the Levin Playground. Alice looks quite monumental flanked by the mean-looking Duchess and the Mad Hatter.
Central Park at 77th Street near Fifth Avenue.

MURDERING TIME

For Alice lit, there's no better place than the Strand Book Store (*see p252*). In a brilliant manifestation of Carrollian un-logic, red directional arrows and floating question marks hang every which way, above eight miles of books. Head for the children's section, where an entire bottom shelf of lovely and inexpensive Alice editions, from Arthur Rackham's *Art Nouveau Alice* to *The Best of Lewis Carroll*, is available. *828 Broadway, at 12th Street.*

ALICE'S RESTAURANT?

This Manhattan spot offers tea parties worthy of the Mad Hatter. 'My sister and I have an Alice obsession,' admits Haley Fox, co-owner with her sister Lauren of the whimsical **Alice's Tea Cup**

(*see p211*). 'We wanted to host the quintessential tea party, but not necessarily like the Waldorf's. Ours is less pinky-up; it's come as you are.' The café is far from ordinary, however: waitresses wear butterfly wings and the walls are covered in murals inspired by Alice illustrator John Tenniel and Lauren Berley's photographs of a punked-out Alice. (Berley took the pictures in front of the Central Park sculpture.) Quirky Alice collectibles fill the front room, which doubles as a boutique and take-out counter. Diners choose between a cup of 'wee tea', a 'nibble' (actually a three-tiered tea service) and the blowout 'Jabberwock', a tea and sandwich smörgåsbord.
102 W 73rd Street, at Columbus Avenue (1-212 799 3006).

Arts & Entertainment

Confino Family Apartment Tour

For listing, see p107 Lower East Side Tenement Museum.
A weekly interactive tour teaches children aged five to 14 about immigrant life in the early 20th century. Kids play games and handle knick-knacks from the era.

Zoos

Bronx Zoo

Bronx River Parkway, at Fordham Road (1-718 367 1010/www.bronxzoo.org). Subway: 2, 5 to West Farms Square-East Tremont Avenue. **Open** *Apr-Oct* 10am-5pm Mon-Fri; 10am-5.30pm Sat, Sun, holidays. *Nov-Mar* 10am-4.30pm daily. **Admission** *Apr-Oct* $12; $9 seniors, children; free under-2s. *Nov-Mar* $8; $6 seniors, children; free under-2s. Voluntary donation Wed. (Some rides and exhibitions are extra.) **Credit** AmEx, DC, Disc, MC, V.

Inside the Bronx Zoo is the Bronx Children's Zoo, with lots of domesticated critters to pet, plus exhibits that show the world from an animal's point of view. Beyond the Children's Zoo, camel rides (Apr-Oct) and sea-lion feedings (11am and 3pm) are other can't-miss attractions for visitors with kids. *See also p175.*

New York Aquarium

610 Surf Avenue, at West 8th Street, Coney Island, Brooklyn (1-718 265 3474/www.nyaquarium.com). Subway: D to Coney Island-Stillwell Avenue; F, Q to W 8th Street-NY Aquarium. **Open** Visit website for hours. **Admission** $11; $7 seniors, 2-12s; free under-2s. **Credit** AmEx, Disc, MC, V.
Like the rest of Coney Island, this aquarium is a little shabby, but kids enjoy seeing the famous beluga whale family, the scary sharks and the entertaining sea-lion show – and then taking a stroll along the Coney Island boardwalk.

Clubs

New Yorkers have gotta fight for their right to party.

The bigger the better? Not necessarily, but **Avalon** does its best. See *p291*.

New Yorkers may be reluctant to admit it, but their otherwise great city is currently engaged in an uneasy relationship with clubland. It started back in the early 1990s, when Mayor Rudolf Giuliani had a seemingly monomaniacal distaste for any kind of nightlife. During those dark days, dance clubs faced continual harassment from the authorities, who often cited the bizarre anti-dancing cabaret laws (a relic from the 1920s) when ticketing nightspots for various violations. While the situation today may not be as dire as it was, clubs still seem to be singled out by the present powers that be. Take, for example, a recent City Council proposal to mandate pricey security cameras at all club entrances and exits, as well as requiring clubs to have electronic ID scanners to reduce underage drinking. Sure, this might seem reasonable on the face of it – until you learn that the proposal, which would cost each venue thousands of dollars, only applies to dance clubs, not to rock venues or other drinking establishments. If that type of

blatant hostility weren't enough, consider the other main lasso strangling poor helpless dance clubs – the ever-surging real-estate market, which has raised club rents to the point where many venues are afraid to take a chance on any music more challenging than top 40 hip hop and dance pop, for fear of alienating the mainstream. And, while we're at it: God help anyone who wants to sit down in a club these days – you'll have to fork over a king's ransom for liquor in a velvet roped 'bottle-service' area.

Thankfully, the ghosts of clubs past that partied at the Loft, Studio 54, Paradise Garage, Pyramid, Sound Factory and Twilo linger on. Sure, it's unlikely that we'll ever see a return to the scene's glory days, when the city could lay claim to being one of the world's best nightlife spots, but there's still plenty of good times to be had in clubland every night of the week here, if you know where to look (*see p294* **Boogie off-nights**). **Element** (*see p291*), in an old bank on the Lower East Side, is the latest nightlife

Arts & Entertainment

offering that's revving up the city's heartbeat. Underground-house and techno heads can groove at venues such as **Sullivan Room** (see p294) and **Cielo** (see below); even the megaclubs have been scheduling dubstep or electro-disco nights on occasion.

A few bright spots keep the clubland buzz kill at bay. The Meatpacking District's **APT** (see p295) regularly scores some of the world's best spinners to play at what's essentially nothing more fancy than a bar with a sound system, albeit a really killer sound system. There's the rollicking rock 'n' roll circus **Motherfucker** (see p296), a roving party that is regularly touted as the world's best – why not decide for yourself? P.S.1's **Warm Up** (see p296), a weekly summertime soirée held in a courtyard at a Queens museum, attracts thousands of kids who like nothing better than to boogie down to some pretty twisted DJs. And if you're really lucky, you might even hear about an illegal warehouse party hidden away in the outer boroughs – though you'd better hope the cops don't hear about it too.

Clubs

Avalon
660 Sixth Avenue, at 20th Street (1-212 807 7780/ www.nyavalon.com). Subway: F, V, R, W to 23rd Street. **Open** 10pm-6am Fri-Sun. **Cover** $25. **Average drink** $9.
Though many of the city's big clubs suffer from a conservative music policy, at least Avalon – the erstwhile Limelight – is making the effort to occasionally feature interesting beats, with the likes of techno wizard Robert Hood and Death in Vegas's Richard Fearless dropping by for a date on the decks. **Photos** p290.

Cielo
18 Little W 12th Street, between Ninth Avenue & Washington Street (1-212 645 5700/www.cielo club.com). Subway: A, C, E to 14th Street; L to Eighth Avenue. **Open** 10pm-4am daily. **Cover** $5-$20. **Average drink** $10.
You'd never guess from the Paris Hilton wannabes in the neighbourhood that the attitude inside this exclusive club is close to zero. Grab a cocktail from the bar, then move to the sunken dancefloor where hip-to-hip crowds gyrate to deep beats from top DJs, including NYC old-schoolers François K, Tedd Patterson and Little Louis Vega, as well as international spinners of all sorts. The club, which features a crystal-clear sound system, has won a bevy of 'best club' awards in its four years of existence – and deserves them all.

Club Shelter
150 Varick Street, at Vandam Street (1-646 862 6117/www.clubshelter.com). Subway: 1 to Houston Street. **Open** 11pm-noon Sat. **Cover** $15-$20. **Average drink** $6.

This address has been home to a variety of nightspots over the years. The current beloved incarnation is Shelter (and before Shelter, it was Club Standard), the city's longest-running house 'n' classics party. The Saturday-night no-attitude dance marathon is a New York institution that's been around in one form or another for some 15 years, and which continues to draw a wild-looking agglomeration of people to the dark, sweaty dancefloor. Timmy Regisford, the resident DJ for the Shelter shindig hypnotises dancefloor denizens week after week – many disciples stay until the music stops sometime on Sunday afternoon.

Copacabana
560 W 34th Street, at Eleventh Avenue (1-212 239 2672/www.copacabanany.com). Subway: A, C, E to 34th Street-Penn Station. **Open** 6pm-3am Tue; 11pm-5am Thur-Sat. **Cover** $5-$30. **Average drink** $9.
Good-looking Latinos – and the sexy mamas who love them – pack the Copa's 48,000sq ft to dance through the night. Live bands play upstairs (including salsa clásica giants such as Tito Nieves and El Gran Combo) with synchronised showgirls and boys shaking the large dancefloor, while downstairs is thumping house music. Women show off their curves; men tend to sport suits and ties. Dozens of bartenders are available, but with this large a crowd, it's probably prudent to arrive with a full tank. Occasional hip hop and R&B sounds are featured in the club's side rooms.

Crobar
530 W 28th Street, between Tenth & Eleventh Avenues (1-212 629 9000/www.crobar.com). Subway: C, E to 23rd Street. **Open** 10pm-7am Thur-Sat. **Cover** $20-$30. **Average drink** $9.
Getting past the front door can be exasperating, but it's worth the drama. The decor and atmosphere at NYC's most mega of megaclubs carry you back to a time when it was easy to get lost inside a nitery. That's because this New York outpost of the nightlife chain is massive. A stellar sound system – and the beats of such crowd-rocking DJs as Sander Kleinenberg, David Morales and Victor Calderone – keeps the dancefloor packed. (Other nights feature far less noteworthy DJs; if you care at all about the music you're dancing to, it pays to check the schedule.) Skybox-style VIP booths offer perfect people-watching perches; smaller, tucked-away lounge areas allow for intimate private moments – although that luxury comes at a price, since these are reserved for those willing to plunk down $330 or more for a bottle. But even for the hoi polloi, there's more than enough sensory overload here to entertain.

Element
225 E Houston Street, at Essex Street (1-212 254 2200/www.elementny.com). Subway: F, V to Lower East Side-Second Avenue. **Open** 10pm-4am Fri, Sat. Call for events on other nights. **Cover** $10-$20 (cash only). **Average drink** $9.

A former bank, goth hotspot and studio of Jasper Johns, this hulking space offers a massive dancefloor encircled by a perfect-view balcony, a mellow VIP area and a cool underground vault. Watch out for nights dedicated to soul, house and new-wave sounds, plus some Saturday-night queer action with a party called, appropriately enough, Bank. It's where you'll find all of the downtown creatures of the night, from Amanda Lepore to Larry Tee and the gang. Be sure to check out the downstairs lounge, Vault, which features underground sounds of all sorts.

Happy Valley

14 E 27th Street, between Fifth & Madison Avenues (1-212 481 2628/www.happyvalleynyc.com). Subway: R, W to 23rd Street. **Open** 10.30pm-4am Tue, Thur-Sat. **Cover** varies. **Average drink** $8.

The newish Happy Valley features a vaguely retro look; with its DJ booth ensconced in a giant disco ball and giant girlie legs propped up behind the main bar, it's somehow reminiscent of '80s hotspots like Danceteria. So it's fitting that party princess Susanne Bartsch, someone who practically defined the wild late '80s scene, has taken control of Tuesday nights, for an electrorocky affair where polysexual club kids young and old don their finest garb for one of NYC's most showy hoedowns. The other nights, more prosaic in both music and crowd, fade in comparison.

Lotus

409 W 14th Street, between Ninth Avenue & Washington Street (1-212 243 4420/www.lotus newyork.com). Subway: A, C, E to 14th Street; L to Eighth Avenue. **Open** 10pm-4am Tue-Sun. **Cover** $20. **Average drink** $8.

Though a few years past its pioneer days, this chi-chi model-infested club is still a central hotspot. The triple-tiered, Asian-accented space, with an over-looking balcony, allows for prime people-watching opportunities. Sample delicate hors-d'oeuvres and fresh watermelon Martinis at the bar, or turn up late with your best-dressed buddies and throw down a few hundred bucks on a few bottles. A contingent of downtown hipsters comes for the Friday night GBH affair; the rest of the week, expect tall girls, guys with thinning hair and plenty of Eurotrash.

Love

40 W 8th Street, at MacDougal Street (1-212 477 5683/www.musicislove.net). Subway: A, B, C, D, E, F, V to W 4th Street; R, W (weekdays only) to 8th Street-NYU. **Open** 10pm-4am Wed-Sat; 5pm-1am Sun. **Cover** $10-$15. **Average drink** $6.

Love, a relatively new addition to the city's clubbing landscape, is an anomaly; its focus is squarely on the music (mostly of the deep-house variety) and on building a scene. It's hardly a revolutionary concept, but in today's nightlife world of going for the quick buck, Love stands out from the crowd. The main room is a sparsely furnished bare box, but the DJ line-up is pretty impressive – names on the level of the Greenskeepers' James Curd and Body & Soul's Joe Claussell have all graced the decks here – and the sound system is one of New York's finest.

Marquee

289 Tenth Avenue, between 26th & 27th Streets (1-646 473 0202). Subway: C, E to 23rd Street. **Open** 10pm-4am Tue-Sat. **Cover** $20. **Average drink** $9.

The owners tore the roof off a former garage, and custom-made everything here: the vaulted ceiling, the glass-beaded chandelier, the leather place mats, even the champagne buckets. The centrepiece is a spectacular double-sided staircase that leads to a mezzanine level, where a glass wall overlooks the

Element. *See p291.*

action below. The club accommodates up to 600 people, but despite having been around for a couple of years, this spot is still so hot (the bartenders too) that you'll have trouble getting past the velvet rope. Don't expect much musically, though – as with many places where the scene trumps the tunes, it's largely middle-of-the-road fare. FYI: Christina Aguilera and Paris Hilton both had their album release parties here.

Pacha
618 W 46th Street, between Eleventh & Twelfth Avenues (1-212 209 7500/www.pachanyc.com).
Open 5pm-4am Thur; 10pm-6am Fri, Sat.
Cover $20-$25. **Average drink** $9.
The worldwide glam-clubbing chain Pacha, with outposts in nightlife hotspots such as Ibiza, London and Buenos Aires, has finally hit the US market with its swanky NYC outpost helmed by superstar spinner Erick Morillo. The spot attracts heavyweights ranging from local hero Danny Tenaglia to big-time visiting jocks such as Timo Maas and Josh Wink, but like most big clubs, it pays to check the line-up ahead if you're into underground beats: the space has been known in the past to book overtly commercial spinners. **Photos** *p295.*

Pyramid
101 Avenue A, between 6th & 7th Streets (1-212 228 4888). Subway: F, V to Lower East Side-Second Avenue; L to First Avenue; 6 to Astor Place. **Open** 10pm-4am daily. **Cover** free-$15. **Average drink** $7.
In a clubbing era that's long gone, the Pyramid was a cornerstone of forward-thinking queer club culture. In what could be considered a sign of the times, the venue's sole remaining gay soirée is Friday night's non-progressive '80s dance-fest, 1984. Otherwise, the charmingly decrepit space features

the long-running drum 'n' bass bash Konkrete Jungle, as well as an interesting rotating roster of goth and new-wave affairs.

Sapphire
249 Eldridge Street, between Houston & Stanton Streets (1-212 777 5153/www.sapphirenyc.com). Subway: F, V to Lower East Side-Second Avenue.
Open 7pm-4am daily. **Cover** $5. **Average drink** $5.
The bare walls and minimal decorations are as raw as it gets – and not particularly appealing – yet the energetic, unpretentious crowd is oblivious to the aesthetic. A dance crowd packs the place every night of the week. Various nights feature house, hip hop, reggae and disco.

Spirit
530 W 27th Street, between Tenth & Eleventh Avenues (1-212 268 9477/www.spiritnewyork.com). Subway: C, E to 23rd Street. **Open** 10pm-4am Fri, Sat. **Cover** free-$30. **Average drink** $8.
Spirit hasn't yet come close to filling the void left when superclub Twilo (and before that, the original Sound Factory) departed this sacred ground. The New York outpost of a successful Dublin venture, this is a one-stop nightlife complex with a restaurant, live performance space and dance club. One miscalculation has already flopped here: the strange hippie vibe of the Mind Lounge (tarot readings, massages, psychic sessions) scared off night crawlers, as did its high prices. So Spirit took the predictable route and hired mainstream promoters and DJs who play generic house and hip hop to a generic trendy bunch. Things have gotten a touch better of late, though, with the Made Event crew occasionally taking the space over to feature DJs the calibre of prog-tech spinner Lee Burridge (from the UK's Tyrant bash) and minimal house maven Richie Hawtin.

Subtonic Lounge at Tonic

107 Norfolk Street, between Delancey & Rivington Streets (1-212 358 7501/www.tonicnyc.com). Subway: F to Delancey Street; J, M, Z to Delancey-Essex Streets. **Open** 7.30pm-2am Thur-Sat. **Cover** free-$12. **Average drink** $6.

Subtonic Lounge, the unadorned basement of the Lower East Side's avant-bohemian Tonic (*see p320*) performance space, features the Friday night Bunker bash, where DJs spin a myriad of underground beats ranging from challenging IDM to straight-up techno. The sound system might not be all that, but the party throwers and the patrons (who rest on banquettes inside giant, ancient wine casks) make up for it with sheer exuberance.

Sullivan Room

218 Sullivan Street, between Bleecker & W 3rd Streets (1-212 252 2151/www.sullivanroom.com). Subway: A, B, C, D, E, F, V to W 4th Street. **Open** 10pm-4am Mon, Tue, Thur-Sat. **Cover** $5-$15. **Average drink** $8.

Where's the party? It's right here in this unmarked subterranean space, which hosts some of the best deep-house, tech-house and breaks bashes the city has to offer. It's an utterly unpretentious club, with little of the glitz of bigger clubs – but hell, all you really need are some thumpin' beats and a place to move your feet, right?

Webster Hall

125 E 11th Street, between Third & Fourth Avenues (1-212 353 1600/www.webster-hall.com). Subway: L, N, Q, R, W, 4, 5, 6 to 14th Street-Union Square. **Open** 10pm-5am Thur-Sat. **Cover** free-$30. **Average drink** $6.

Should you crave the sight of big hair, muscle shirts and gold chains, Webster Hall offers all that and, well, not much more. The grand four-level space, built in the 1800s as a dance hall, is nice enough, and the DJs aren't bad (disco, hip hop, soul, Latin, progressive house or pop hits), but it's hard to forget who you're sharing the dancefloor with. Wet T-shirt and striptease contests also feature.

Boogie off-nights

If weekend crowds get you down, hit these alternative parties.

Monday at Deep Space

Boutique club Cielo (*see p291*) hosts the transcendentally talented François K's night dedicated to dubbed-out vibes and abstract grooves, with everything from bossa nova to techno intoxicating a dancefloor packed with underground-music junkies. It's not for nothing that this soirée regularly receives the clubbing industry's 'Best Party' awards. *For more info, visit www.deepspacenyc.com.*

Tuesday at Camouflage

The motto of this long-running affair is 'drum 'n' bass for mature audiences', meaning the bash is geared towards those with sophisticated taste in rapid-fire breakbeats. But that doesn't imply that Camouflage is sedate – especially when the crew manages to entice the likes of visiting superstars Shy FX and Fabio to visit the fête's petite East Village home, Sin Sin. *Visit www.camonyc.com.*

Wednesday at Roots

It's back to Cielo (*see above; photo right*) for this soulful-house hoedown, with two of the world's pre-eminent practitioners of the sound – Masters at Works' Louis Vega and Blaze's Kevin Hedge – pumping out their heartfelt tunes. And New York clubbers like to complain that they have nothing to do... *Visit www.cieloclub.com.*

Sunday at APT

DJ Angola uses left-of-centre syncopation to work the crowd on APT's (*see p295*) cushy street-level spot, while Chez Music's Neil Aline holds it down with deep house in the basement. They're both great spinners, but it's the crowd – trannies in full regalia, blotto scenester types, slumming-it trust-funders – that's made this weekly winging Gotham's most debased off-night bash. *Visit www.aptwebsite.com.*

Lounges & DJ bars

Pacha. *See p293.*

APT
*419 W 13th Street, between Ninth Avenue &
Washington Street (1-212 414 4245/www.apt
website.com). Subway: A, C, E to 14th Street;
L to Eighth Avenue.* **Open** 7pm-4am daily.
Cover varies. **Average drink** $9.
Kicking back in APT's formerly exclusive street-level
space (the chill design is by India Mahdavi) is like
being at an impromptu party in some trust-fund
baby's Upper East Side townhouse. Down below, people looking for the perfect beat gather in a minimalist, fake-wood-panelled rectangular room. The space
features an amazing array of DJs; top spinners such
as locals DJ Spun and the Negroclash crew, and superstars like cosmic-disco dons the Idjut Boys and house-
music hero Tony Humphries regularly regale the
tipplers with a wide range of underground sounds.

Slipper Room
*167 Orchard Street, at Stanton Street (1-212 253
7246/www.slipperroom.com). Subway: F, V to Lower
East Side-Second Avenue.* **Open** 8pm-4am Tue-Sat.
Average drink $8.
New York City has a healthy neo-burlesque scene,
and the petite Slipper Room is, if not at that scene's
nexus, pretty darn near it. Many of the Victorian-
looking venue's happenings, notably Friday's Hot
Box hoedown, feature plenty of bump-and-grind
action, with DJs spinning the appropriate beats; the
occasional live band completes the picture.

Triple Crown
*108 Bedford Avenue, at North 11th Street,
Williamsburg, Brooklyn (1-718 388 8883/
www.triplecrownpage.com). Subway: L to Bedford
Avenue.* **Open** 6pm-4am daily. **Average drink** $8.
Since its autumn '04 opening, the sleek Williamsburg
lounge Triple Crown has managed to rise to the top
of the city's hip hop venues. Granted, the competition for that status isn't exactly fierce, but when
you regularly score spinners on the level of Rob
Swift from the X-Ecutioners, A Tribe Called Quest's
Ali Shaheed Muhammad and old-school legend
Schoolly D, you're obviously doing something right.

Roving & seasonal parties

New York has a number of peripatetic and
season-specific shindigs. Nights, locations
and prices vary, so call, email or hit the
websites for the latest updates.

Cooper-Hewitt Summer Sessions: Design + DJs + Dancing
For listing, see p138 Cooper-Hewitt, National Design
Museum. **Open** *July, Aug* 6-9pm Fri. **Cover** $10
(includes museum admission). **Average drink** $8.
In the warmer months, the city's premier design
museum hosts after-work outdoor revelry, but
these aren't garden parties in the traditional sense.
DJs ranging from local funksters to international

Arts & Entertainment

superstars work the crowd with all manner of underground beats. Still, the vibe is a lot more genteel than the similar P.S.1 Warm Up party (*see below*).

Giant Step
www.giantstep.net.
Giant Step parties have been among the best of the nu-soul scene the early '90s – back before there was a nu-soul scene. Sadly, the gang doesn't throw as many fêtes as it once did, now preferring to concentrate on live shows and record promotions. But on the rare occasion that Giant Step does decide to pack a dancefloor, you'd be a fool to miss it: the music is always great, and the multicultural crowd gorgeous.

Motherfucker
www.motherfuckernyc.com.
This roaming, polysexual trash fest, which is helmed by veteran NYC scenesters Justine D, Michael T, Georgie Seville and Johnny T, is generally considered the best bash going in town right now. Held on the eves of major holidays at an array of the city's biggest clubs, it features Justine, Michael and guests spinning an anarchic mix of sleazed-out electro, new wave and disco, plus the most utterly deviant menagerie of club freaks that you're likely to come across nowadays. In many ways, it's a throwback to the glory days of New York's once-decadent clubbing scene.

P.S.1 Warm Up
P.S.1 Contemporary Art Center, 22-25 Jackson Avenue, at 45th Road, Jackson Heights, Queens (1-718 784 2084/www.ps1.org). Subway: E, V to 23rd Street-Ely Avenue; G to 21st Street-Jackson Avenue; 7 to 45th Road-Court House Square.
Open *July-Sept* 2-9pm Sat. **Cover** $8 (includes museum admission). **Average drink** $5.
Back in 1997, who could have guessed that the courtyard of the Museum of Modern Art-affiliated P.S.1 Contemporary Art Center would play host to some of the most anticipated, resolutely underground clubbing events in the city? Since the Warm Up series kicked off that year, summer Saturdays truly haven't been the same. Thousands of dance-music fanatics pack the space, swigging beer, dancing and generally making a mockery of the soirée's arty setting. The sounds range from spiritually inclined soul to full-bore techno, spun by local and international stars.

Turntables on the Hudson
1-212 560 5593/www.turntablesonthehudson.com.
This ultra-funky affair has a permanent Friday home at the Lightship Frying Pan (Pier 63, Twelfth Avenue, at 23rd Street, 1-212 989 6363), but it pops up all over the place on other nights of the week. DJs Nickodemus, Mariano and their guests do the dub-funky, world-beat thing, and live percussionists add to the flavour. As good as it gets.

How *not* to get kicked out
NYC bouncers' tips for staying on their good sides.

Don't smoke
Don't spark up in front of security, whether you're smoking tobacco or a cigarette of a 'funny' variety. 'It's amazing how many people think it's OK to light up,' a stoic club-security man says. 'It's not.'

Curtail the bathroom antics
Squeezing more than one body into a bathroom stall is a big no-no. 'I don't care what you're doing in there,' one bouncer tells us. 'I'm gonna pound on that door until you're not doing it any more.'

Don't try to score off the bouncer
For some reason, a lot of people assume that bouncers double as drug vendors. You may not get kicked out for asking a bouncer for illicit substances, but you'll surely go on his shit list.

The bribes won't work
Don't assume that cosying up to the security staff will grant you any special status. To avoid waiting in line, for instance, 'women promise to flash their tits and men offer cash,' a Meatpacking District bouncer says. 'Unfortunately, I can't do anything for them. So no tits and no tips.'

Men: respect the ladies
Bouncers tend to be very protective of their female co-workers, almost as if they're playing the role of big brother. A patron's drunken, slobbering pick-up attempt just may result in an early exit.

No name-dropping
Never allow the phrase 'don't you know who I am?' to leave your lips. Name-droppers are a security professional's pet peeve.

Follow instructions
When the night is over and the bouncer bellows that it's time to leave, that's not just a suggestion. 'Everyone who works at the club is tired and wants to go home,' says a particularly hulking bouncer. 'Don't they realise that we're people too?' Listen to what the man says!

Arts & Entertainment

Film & TV

Cinema city.

New York loves to hog the spotlight. And why not, we ask? There's simply no location as iconic – from the classic art deco spires of the Chrysler Building to the earthy façades of outer-borough pizzerias. There's always a scene in the making, and your tour of the city will undoubtedly bring to mind some of the greats, like *King Kong*, *Annie Hall* and *Do the Right Thing*. Let's not forget the small screen, too: crane your neck with the rest of the gathering crowd in Times Square and you can wave your way on to MTV's *Total Request Live*.
    See also pp37-39.

Film

It's easy to fall into hyperbole, but in this case it's true: New York offers the serious movie lover an unparalleled choice. Glitzy multiplexes show the latest Hollywood releases, but the city's pride is its dozens of art-house cinemas and museums, slaking the thirst of even the most esoteric tastes. Prestigious festivals and retrospectives pepper the schedule year-round. For current listings, check daily newspapers, or pick up an issue of *Time Out New York*.

Art & revival houses

Angelika Film Center
18 W Houston Street, at Mercer Street (1-212 995 2000/www.angelikafilmcenter.com). Subway: B, D, F, V to Broadway-Lafayette Street; N, R, W to Prince Street; 6 to Bleecker Street. **Tickets** $10.75; $7 seniors, under-12s. **Credit** AmEx, MC, V.
The six-screen Angelika emphasises independent fare, both American and foreign. The complex is a zoo on weekends, so come extra early or visit the website to buy advance tickets.

BAM Rose Cinemas
For listing, see p328 Brooklyn Academy of Music. **Tickets** $10; $7 students (Mon-Thur only), seniors, children (weekdays). **Credit** AmEx, MC, V.
Brooklyn's premier art-film venue does double duty as a repertory house for well-programmed classics and a first-run multiplex for independent films.

Cinema Village
22 E 12th Street, between Fifth Avenue & University Place (1-212 924 3363/www.cinemavillage.com). Subway: L, N, Q, R, W, 4, 5, 6 to 14th Street-Union Square. **Tickets** $10; $7.50 students; $5.50 seniors, under-13s. **Credit** MC, V.

This three-screen cinema specialises in American indie flicks and foreign movies. Check out the subway turnstile that admits ticket-holders to the lobby.

Film Forum
209 W Houston Street, between Sixth Avenue & Varick Street (1-212 727 8110/www.filmforum. com). Subway: 1 to Houston Street. **Tickets** $10; $5 seniors, under-12s (senior discount before 5pm Mon-Fri).* **Credit** Cash only at box office; AmEx, MC, V on website.
Though seats and sight lines leave something to be desired, this three-screen art theatre presents great documentaries, new and repertory films and a cute crowd of budding NYU auteurs and film geeks.

IFC Center
323 Sixth Avenue, at 3rd Street (1-212 924 7771/ www.ifccenter.com). Subway: A, B, C, D, E, F, V to W 4th Street. **Tickets** $10.75; $7 seniors, under-12s. **Credit** AmEx, MC, V.
The long-darkened Waverly has risen again as a modernised three-screen art house, showing the latest indie hits, choice midnight cult items and the occasional foreign classic. A high-toned café provides sweets, lattes and substantials; and you might rub elbows with the talent on screen, since many come to introduce their work on opening night.

The ImaginAsian
239 E 59th Street, between Second & Third Avenues (1-212 371 6682/www.theimaginasian.com). Subway: N, R, W to Lexington Avenue-59th Street; 4, 5, 6 to 59th Street. **Tickets** $9; $6 seniors, under-12s. **Credit** MC, V.
Since its 2004 rechristening, this 300-seat movie palace has faithfully devoted itself to all things Asian or Asian-American. Typical fare includes jolting J-horror freakouts, cutting-edge Korean dramas and the latest dance moves bustin' outta Bollywood.

Landmark's Sunshine Cinema
143 E Houston Street, between First & Second Avenues (1-212 330 8182/1-212 777 3456). Subway: F, V to Lower East Side-Second Avenue. **Tickets** $10.75; $7 seniors. **Credit** AmEx, MC, V.
A beautifully restored 1898 Yiddish theatre has become one of New York's snazziest art houses, presenting some of the finest new independent cinema in air-conditioned luxury. **Photo** *p299.*

Leonard Nimoy Thalia
Symphony Space, 2537 Broadway, at 95th Street, entrance on 95th Street (1-212 864 5400/ www.symphonyspace.org). Subway: 1, 2, 3 to 96th Street. **Tickets** $10; $8 seniors, students. **Credit** AmEx, MC, V.

The famed Thalia art house – featured in *Annie Hall* – was recently rebuilt. It's more comfortable now, and still offers retrospectives of foreign classics, but with more cutting-edge stuff thrown into the mix.

Paris Theatre
4 W 58th Street, between Fifth & Sixth Avenues (1-212 688 3800/1-212 777 3456). Subway: F to 57th Street; N, R, W to Fifth Avenue-59th Street. **Tickets** $10; $6 seniors, children. **Credit** Cash only at box office; AmEx, MC, V on website.
Near the Plaza Hotel, this posh cinema is de rigueur for cinéastes who love foreign-language films.

Quad Cinema
34 W 13th Street, between Fifth & Sixth Avenues (1-212 255 8800/www.quadcinema.com). Subway: F, V to 14th Street; L to Sixth Avenue. **Tickets** $10; $7 seniors, 5-12s. **Credit** Cash only at box office; AmEx, MC, V on website.
Four small screens (in Downtown's first multiplex) show a range of foreign and American independents, as well as documentaries, many dealing with gay sexuality and politics. Note that under-fives are not admitted.

Two Boots Pioneer Theater
155 E 3rd Street, between Avenues A & B (1-212 591 0434/www.twoboots.com). Subway: F, V to Lower East Side-Second Avenue. **Tickets** $9; $6.50 seniors, students & children. **Credit** AmEx, Disc, MC, V.
Phil Hartman, founder of the Two Boots pizza chain, also runs this East Village alternative film centre, which shows an assortment of newish indies, horror revivals and themed festivals.

Museums & societies

Anthology Film Archives
32 Second Avenue, at 2nd Street (1-212 505 5181/ www.anthologyfilmarchives.org). Subway: F, V to Lower East Side-Second Avenue. **Tickets** $8; $7 seniors, students. **No credit cards.**
Set in a crumbling landmark building, Anthology is a fiercely independent cinema showcasing foreign and experimental film and video. Its first offering, in 1970, was a typewritten manifesto.

Brooklyn Museum
For listing, see p161.
The eclectic roster at Brooklyn's stately palace of fine arts concentrates on offbeat foreign films and smart documentaries.

Film Society of Lincoln Center
Walter Reade Theater, Lincoln Center, 165 W 65th Street, between Broadway & Amsterdam Avenue, plaza level above Alice Tully Hall (1-212 875 5601/ www.filmlinc.com). Subway: 1, 9 to 66th Street-Lincoln Center. **Tickets** $10; $7 students; $5 seniors (before 6pm Mon-Fri), 6-12s. **Credit** Cash only at box office; MC, V on website.
The FSLC was founded in 1969 to support filmmakers and promote contemporary film and video. It operates the Walter Reade Theater, a state-of-the-art venue in Lincoln Center with the city's most comfortable cinema seats and best sight lines. Programmes are usually thematic with an international perspective. In autumn, the Society hosts the New York Film Festival (*see p265*).

IMAX Theater
For listing, see p145 American Museum of Natural History.
The IMAX screen is an eye-popping four storeys high; child-friendly movies explore the myriad wonders of the natural world.

Metropolitan Museum of Art
For listing, see p138.
The Met offers a programme of documentaries on art – many relating to current museum exhibitions – that are screened in the Uris Center Auditorium (near the 81st Street entrance).

Museum of Modern Art
For listing, see p127.
The city's smartest destination for superb programming of art films and experimental work, drawing from a vast vault that's second to none.

Museum of Television & Radio
For listing, see p127.
The museum's collection includes thousands of TV programmes that can be viewed at private consoles.

Museum of the Moving Image
For listing, see p167.
Moving Image, the first American museum devoted solely to the art of motion pictures, puts on an impressive schedule of more than 700 films a year, many of which are organised into some of the most creatively curated series in the city.

Foreign-language films

Many of the institutions listed above also screen films in languages other than English.

Asia Society & Museum
For listing, see p138.
See works from China, India and other Asian countries, as well as Asian-American productions.

French Institute Alliance Française
For listing, see p328 Florence Gould Hall.
FIAF shows French and francophone movies.

Goethe-Institut New York
For listing, see p138.
Screens German films in various locations around the city, as well as in its own opulent auditorium.

Japan Society
For listing, see p132.
The society organises a carefully chosen schedule of current and classic Japanese fare.

Landmark's Sunshine Cinema.
See p297.

Film festivals

Each spring, MoMA and the Film Society of Lincoln Center (FSLC) sponsor the highly regarded **New Directors/New Films** series, presenting works by on-the-cusp filmmakers from around the world. The FSLC, together with Lincoln Center's *Film Comment* magazine, also puts on the popular **Film Comment Selects** series, which allows the magazine's editors to showcase their favourite movies that have yet to be distributed in the US. Plus, every September and October, the FSLC hosts the prestigious **New York Film Festival** (*see p265*). The **New York Independent Film & Video Festival** (www.nyfilmvideo.com) lures cinéastes twice yearly, in April and November. Every April, Robert De Niro rolls out his **Tribeca Film Festival** (*see p261*), which has established itself as a serious destination for film lovers. The **New York Lesbian & Gay Film Festival** is in early June (1-212 571 2170, www.newfestival.org). January brings the annual **New York Jewish Film Festival** (1-212 875 5600) to Lincoln Center's Walter Reade Theater.

TV

Studio tapings

The Daily Show with Jon Stewart
513 W 54th Street, between Tenth & Eleventh Avenues (1-212 586 2477/www.comedycentral. com/dailyshow). Subway: C, E to 50th Street. **Tapings** 5.30pm Mon-Thur.
Reserve tickets at least three months ahead by phone, or call at 11.30am on the Friday before you'd like to attend and see if there's a cancellation. You must be at least 18 and have a photo ID.

Late Night with Conan O'Brien
30 Rockefeller Plaza, Sixth Avenue, between 49th & 50th Streets (1-212 664 3056/www.nbc.com/conan). Subway: B, D, F, V to 47th-50th Streets-Rockefeller Center. **Tapings** 5.30pm Tue-Fri.

Call at least three months in advance for tickets. A small number of same-day standby tickets are distributed at 9am (49th Street entrance); one ticket per person. You must be at least 16 and have a photo ID.

Late Show with David Letterman
1697 Broadway, between 53rd & 54th Streets (1-212 975 1003/www.lateshowaudience.com). Subway: B, D, E to Seventh Avenue. **Tapings** 5.30pm Mon-Wed; 5.30pm, 8pm Thur.
Seats can be hard to come by. Try requesting tickets for a specific date by filling out a form on the show's website. You may also be able to get a standby ticket by calling 1-212 247 6497 at 11am on the day of taping. You must be 18 and have a photo ID.

Saturday Night Live
30 Rockefeller Plaza, Sixth Avenue, between 49th & 50th Streets (1-212 664 3056/www.nbc.com/snl). Subway: B, D, F, V to 47th-50th Streets-Rockefeller Center. **Tapings** Dress rehearsal at 8pm; live show at 11.30pm.
Tickets are notoriously difficult to snag, so don't get your hopes up. The season is assigned by lottery every autumn. Send an email to snltickets@nbc.com anytime during August, or try the standby ticket lottery on the day of the show. Line up by 7am under the NBC Studio marquee (50th Street, between Fifth & Sixth Avenues). You must be at least 16.

Tours

These tours sell out, so reserve in advance.

Kramer's Reality Tour
The Producers Club, 358 W 44th Street, between Eighth & Ninth Avenues (1-800 572 6377/ www.kennykramer.com). Subway: A, C, E to 42nd Street-Port Authority. **Tours** 11.45am Sat, Sun (holiday weekends only); reservations required. **Tickets** $40. **Credit** AmEx, Disc, MC, V.
Kenny Kramer (yes, the guy who inspired the *Seinfeld* character) takes you to many of the show's locations on his tour bus. The tours have been running since 1996, and each one lasts three hours.

Sex and the City Tour
Meet at Pulitzer Fountain, near the Plaza Hotel, Fifth Avenue, between 58th & 59th Streets (1-212 209 3370/www.sceneontv.com). Subway: N, R, W to Fifth Avenue-59th Street. **Tours** 11am Mon-Fri; 10am, 11am, 3pm Sat; 10am, 11am, 3pm Sun. **Tickets** $35. **Credit** MC, V.
The show has long since wrapped, but it lives on in syndication and, apparently, on this tour, which takes you to more than 35 sites.

The Sopranos Tour
Meet at the giant button sculpture, Seventh Avenue, at 39th Street (1-212 209 3370/www.sceneontv.com). Subway: N, Q, R, W to 42nd Street; S, 1, 2, 3, 7, 9 to 42nd Street-Times Square. **Tours** 2pm Sat, Sun. **Tickets** $40. **Credit** MC, V.
A bus takes you to New Jersey to check out Tony's haunts, from the Bada Bing! to Pizzaland.

Arts & Entertainment

Gay & Lesbian

NYC and LGBT make for a perfect match.

I'm not moving till I've finished this chapter... **Oscar Wilde Bookshop**. *See p301.*

There's a reason why small-town queers the world over are wowed by a feeling of joyous freedom while visiting NYC; by the time they add up the myriad options that exist *specifically for* the lesbian, gay, bisexual and transgender (LGBT) community, they wish they could extend their stay by a few weeks. The city has queer clubs, eateries, stores, bars, events, publications, neighbourhoods and a handful of politicians; why, even the City Council Speaker Christine Quinn – otherwise known as the second most-influential politician in the city (after the mayor) – is an out and feisty lesbian.

Furthermore, this is a city that's home to not one gay scene, but a slew. You'll find niches for all – from steroid-pumped circuit boys and inked-up rocker dykes to politically active trannyfags and settled-down parents who haven't been to a club or protest in years. There's a community for everyone, every day of the week, in all five boroughs, whether at a park or in a club or on the TV or radio.

It's no accident that New York is such a homo haven, of course. For starters, it is the home of the 1969 Stonewall Riots in the West Village – the event credited with jump-starting the modern gay-rights movement. Gay history has been made here ever since. NYC is the place that launched publications from *OutWeek* to *Out,* pop-culture icons from the Village People to Junior Vasquez and important activist organisations from ACT UP to Queer Nation. The city's dwellers also have no shortage of queer role models, including politicians, artists, performers, writers and activists. Even the laws here foster a healthy queer existence, criminalising anti-gay violence, forbidding discrimination in the workplace and affording same-sex couples comprehensive domestic partnership rights; the city has continued to fall short when it comes to equal marriage rights, however, with the state's highest court declaring gay marriage illegal in July 2006 after a lengthy court battle.

Also, it must be noted that anti-gay harassment incidents do happen here – a frustrating reality that was underscored most recently by the attack on nightclub personality Kevin Aviance in the East Village in 2006. Use common sense when walking home late at night, take in your surroundings and be sure to report any incidents to the Anti-Violence Project (*see p303*).

As an out-of-towner who's short on time but long on desire to get a taste of the gay scene that's right for you, make a beeline to the **Lesbian, Gay, Bisexual & Transgender Community Center** (see p302). It's a great first-stop, as the information desk attendant will be happy to supply you with an informative visitor's packet, as well as a schedule listing the gatherings of more than 300 groups that use the facility, from the Lesbian Sex Mafia to the New York Association for Gender Rights Advocacy (NYAGRA). Its racks of fliers and publications upstairs contain details of practically every queer group venue and event in the entire city.

The biggest queer event, the annual **Gay Pride Week**, takes place in June. LGBT folks flock here from around the world to revel in queer fun by attending a swirl of parties and performances, and by joining a half-million or so spectators and participants at the Pride March (see p262). Other summer events include the popular **NewFest** gay film festival, held in mid June, and two July theatre festivals – the Fresh Fruit Festival and HOT! The Annual NYC Celebration of Queer Culture. But rest assured that you'll find gay drama in this town anytime, anyplace.

Books & media

The number of gay bookstores has dropped significantly in recent years – victims of Barnes & Noble, Amazon.com and other inclusive sellers. Still, the following two reliable indie shops remain great places to browse or buy.

Bluestockings

172 Allen Street, between Rivington & Stanton Streets (1-212 777 6028/www.bluestockings.com). Subway: F, V to Lower East Side-Second Avenue. **Open** noon-10pm Mon-Fri; 10am-10pm Sat, Sun. **Credit** AmEx, MC, V.

This former feminist bookseller now bills itself more broadly as a radical bookstore, fair-trade café and activist resource centre. It continues to stock a load of LGBT writings and erotica, and regularly hosts queer events including trans-politics forums, dyke knitting circles and women's open-mic nights.

Oscar Wilde Bookshop

15 Christopher Street, between Sixth & Seventh Avenues (1-212 255 8097/www.oscarwildebooks. com). Subway: 1 to Christopher Street-Sheridan Square. **Open** 11am-7pm daily. **Credit** AmEx, Disc, MC, V.

Purportedly the world's first gay bookstore (it opened four decades ago, in 1967), Oscar Wilde is small on size but big on atmosphere. Come for the history, the friendly and knowledgeable staff, the picturesque neighbourhood, and the new and used books and queer magazines. Keep an eye out for first-edition classics too. **Photo** p300.

Publications

Time Out New York's Gay & Lesbian section offers a lively weekly guide to city happenings. Both of New York's weekly gay entertainment magazines – *HX* and *Next* – include extensive boycentric information on bars, clubs, restaurants, events, group meetings and sex parties. The monthly *Go NYC* – 'a cultural road map for the city girl' – gives the lowdown on the lesbian scene. The newspaper *Gay City News* provides feisty political coverage with an activist slant; its arch-rival, the *New York Blade* (now published by *HX*), focuses on queer politics and news. All are free and widely available in street boxes or at gay and lesbian bars and bookstores. *MetroSource* ($4.95) is a bimonthly glossy with a guppie slant and tons of listings.

Television & radio

After a flurry of queer networks stormed the cable waves in 2005, only two remain: Logo, from the folks behind MTV, and the on-demand Here! TV, both offering a cornucopia of feature films, talk shows and documentaries. Both are available around the clock via the local Time Warner Cable provider. And then there's the fabulous Manhattan Neighborhood Network (MNN), the public-access station that allows New Yorkers of all stripes to have their very own programmes. There are plenty of queer ones in the mix, with the *Gay USA* news programme, the nightlife-centric *ADD-TV* pastiche and the long-running *Dyke TV* among the standouts (though programming varies depending on the cable company, so you may not be able to watch these shows on a hotel TV). *HX* and *Next* provide the most current gay-TV listings. You can also catch frequent reruns of *Will & Grace*, late at night, on channel 11 or *The L Word* on Showtime. On the radio, NYC's community-activist station, WBAI-FM 99.5, features the progressive gay talk show *Out-FM* on Mondays at 11am. Sirius satellite radio, meanwhile, offers the 24/7 *OutQ* on channel 106, with programming from such New York personalities as Michelangelo Signorile, Frank DeCaro and Larry Flick.

Centres & helplines

Gay & Lesbian Switchboard of New York Project

1-212 989 0999/www.glnh.org. **Open** 4pm-midnight Mon-Fri; noon-5pm Sat.

This phone service offers excellent peer counselling, legal referrals, details on gay and lesbian organisations, and information on bars, restaurants and

Up on the deck at **Cattyshack**. *See p307.*

hotels. Outside New York (but within the US), callers can use the toll-free Gay & Lesbian National Hotline (1-888 843 4564).

Gay Men's Health Crisis
119 W 24th Street, between Sixth & Seventh Avenues (1-212 367 1000/AIDS advice hotline 1-212 807 6655/www.gmhc.org). Subway: F, V, 1 to 23rd Street. **Open** *Hotline* 10am-6pm Mon-Fri; noon-3pm Sat; recorded information in English and Spanish at other times. *Office* 10am-6pm Mon-Fri.

GMHC was the world's first organisation dedicated to helping people with AIDS. Its threefold mission is to push for better public policies; to educate the public to prevent the further spread of HIV; and to provide services and counselling to people living with HIV. Support groups usually meet in the evening.

Lesbian, Gay, Bisexual & Transgender Community Center
208 W 13th Street, between Seventh & Eighth Avenues (1-212 620 7310/www.gaycenter.org). Subway: A, C, E, 1, 2, 3 to 14th Street; L to Eighth Avenue. **Open** 9am-11pm daily.

Activist organisations ACT UP and GLAAD both started here. It provides info for gay tourists; political, cultural, spiritual and emotional support; and a meeting space for 300-odd groups. The National Museum & Archive of Lesbian & Gay History and the Pat Parker/Vito Russo Library are housed here.

Lesbian Herstory Archives
484 14th Street, between Eighth Avenue & Prospect Park West, Park Slope, Brooklyn (1-718 768 3953/ www.lesbianherstoryarchives.org). Subway: F to 15th Street-Prospect Park. **Open** times vary. Call or visit website for more information.

Located in Brooklyn's Park Slope neighbourhood, the Herstory Archives contain more than 20,000 books (cultural theory, fiction, poetry, plays), 1,600 periodicals and assorted memorabilia. The cosy brownstone also hosts occasional film screenings, readings and social gatherings, plus an annual open house held in late June.

Michael Callen-Audre Lorde Community Health Center
356 W 18th Street, between Eighth & Ninth Avenues (1-212 271 7200/www.callen-lorde.org). Subway: A, C, E to 14th Street; L to Eighth Avenue; 1 to 18th Street. **Open** 8.30am-8pm Mon; 8.30-11.30am, 2.30-8pm Tue; 12.30-8pm Wed; 9am-4.30pm Thur, Fri.

This is the country's largest health centre primarily serving the gay, lesbian, bisexual and transgender community. It offers comprehensive medical care, HIV treatment, STD screening and treatment, mental health services, peer counselling as well as free adolescent services (including a youth hotline, on 1-212 271 7212).

NYC Gay & Lesbian Anti-Violence Project
Suite 200, 240 W 35th Street, between Seventh & Eighth Avenues (24hr bilingual hotline 1-212 714 1141/1184/www.avp.org). Subway: A, C, E, 1, 2, 3 to 34th Street-Penn Station. **Open** 10am-8pm Mon-Thur; 10am-6pm Fri.
The Project works with local police to provide support to victims of anti-queer crime, plus volunteers who offer advice on seeking help from police. Long- and short-term counselling services are available.

Sylvia Rivera Law Project
1-212 337 8550/www.srlp.org.
Call for information on special trainings and workshops provided by SRLP, named after civil-rights pioneer and Stonewall uprising veteran Sylvia Rivera. The project provides free legal services to transgender, intersex and gender-nonconforming people of colour with low incomes.

Trevor Project
24hr hotline 1-866 488 7386/www.thetrevor project.org.
Operating on the belief that 98% of all teen suicides are preventable, the Trevor Project runs a hotline for LGBT youth who are desperately seeking a reason to live. Gay teens are three times more likely to attempt suicide than their heterosexual peers. The folks on the other end of this phone line want to put an end to that statistic.

Queer perspective

Sure, every neighbourhood has gay residents, but only a select few deserve to be deemed 'gaybourhoods'. The big daddy of them all is Chelsea, where hot, upwardly mobile men strut and cruise along the runway-like Eighth Avenue between 14th and 23rd Streets. The strip is positively bulging with muscled queens, as well as sleek boutiques, gyms, lounges and eateries. The 'hood is also headquarters for *HX*, and you'll find copies of the nightlife guide in street boxes on practically every corner.

Some would argue that Chelsea has started to slip from its place at the top, though, as nearby Hell's Kitchen, or Clinton – located just to the north – has rapidly gained gay ground. Positioned conveniently near to Manhattan's Theater District, Hell's Kitchen is where you'll find an exploding number of gay-geared eateries, boutiques and bars – most notably the new and instantly hopping **Vlada** (*see p306*).

If these 'hoods, in all their clonish glory, leave you a bit bored, head Downtown, where more diverse gaybourhoods await. An edgier crowd of boys, dykes, drag queens and transfolks reign in the East Village, home to a vast network of bars and clubs that cater to queers who prefer the Scissor Sisters and pierced septums to Kristine W and fake tans.

Across town, on Christopher Street in the **West Village**, you'll find the historic heart of gay New York. It's home to the legendary **Stonewall** (*see p305*), friendly piano bars, stores full of pink-triangle key chains and a healthy number of gay and lesbian bars. Though the historic cruising spot of the Christopher Street Pier has been remodelled in recent years, from crumbling concrete strip to pretty landscaped park, it still draws gaggles of African-American and Latino gay youths, much to the chagrin of older (and wealthier) gay folks who live in the nearby townhouses and condo towers.

Beyond Manhattan's borders, Brooklyn's tree-lined **Park Slope** is a long-time enclave for lesbians and gay men – especially settled-down types with kids and real careers, as the affordable-rent days that started the whole dyke settlement are long gone. During the first weekend in June, the Slope hosts the annual **Brooklyn Pride March**, a (very) scaled-down version of Manhattan's parade. Brooklyn's hipster Williamsburg neighbourhood is also home to a large queer population, this one closely resembling the tattooed masses of the East Village.

Other boroughs have less pronounced gay scenes, with the most visible one found in Jackson Heights, Queens, home to several LGBT bars and clubs and a large South American queer population. Chueca (69-04 Woodside Avenue, at 69th Street, 1-718 424 1171) is a hopping spot for salsa-dancing lesbian couples. And the **Queens Pride March**, held in Jackson Heights in mid June, is a less corporate and more ethnically diverse version of the main Pride event in Manhattan.

Sex parties are, of course, part of any gay scene, and New York's is no exception. Men of all ages, shapes and sizes frequent fetish bars and clubs, like the **Eagle** (*see p306*) in Chelsea, as well as numerous private sex and fetish parties (see *HX* magazine for thorough listings). Gay Male S/M Activists (www.gmsma.org) holds frequent parties and workshops on kinky play, with its star attraction the annual Folsom Street East festival held in June in the Meatpacking District. Libidinous lesbians should head to one of the friendly, dyke-owned Toys in Babeland (*see p255*) boutiques, which hold occasional workshops on topics from female ejaculation to anal pleasure, or to the wild women's sex party Submit (1-718 789 4053), where a den of slings, shower rooms and handcuffs awaits you monthly. Similarly, the monthly SPAM: Sex Party and More is a Brooklyn-based underwear soirée that welcomes dykes, fags, trannies, bis – anyone except for straight folks, basically.

The Eagle. See p306.

Where to stay

Chelsea Mews Guest House
344 W 15th Street, between Eighth & Ninth Avenues (1-212 255 9174). Subway: A, C, E to 14th Street; L to Eighth Avenue. **Rates** $100-$320 single/double. **No credit cards.**
Built in 1840, this guesthouse caters to gay men. Rooms are comfortable and well furnished and, in most cases, have semi-private bathrooms. A laundry service and bicycles are complimentary. The creepily named Anne Frank Suite has two twin beds and a private bathroom.

Chelsea Pines Inn
317 W 14th Street, between Eighth & Ninth Avenues (1-212 929 1023/1-888 546 2700/www.chelsea pinesinn.com). Subway: A, C, E to 14th Street; L to Eighth Avenue. **Rates** (incl breakfast) $109-$219 single/double. **Credit** AmEx, DC, Disc, MC, V.
On the border of Chelsea and the West Village, Chelsea Pines welcomes gay guests of all persuasions. The 25 rooms are clean and comfortable; most have private bathrooms, and all include a radio, TV, free WiFi and refrigerator.

Colonial House Inn
318 W 22nd Street, between Eighth & Ninth Avenues (1-212 243 9669/1-800 689 3779/www.colonialhouseinn.com). Subway: C, E to 23rd Street. **Rates** (incl breakfast) $85-$130 single/double with shared bath; $125-$150 single/double with private bath (higher on weekends). **Credit** MC, V.

This beautifully renovated 1850s townhouse sits on a quiet street in Chelsea. Run by, and primarily for, gay men, it's a great place to stay, even if some of the less expensive rooms are a bit snug. Bonuses: a fireplace in three of the deluxe rooms, a rooftop deck for all (nude sunbathing allowed) and an owner, Mel Cheren, famous in the dance-music world as the CEO of West End Records and financial backer of the legendary Paradise Garage.

East Village B&B
244 E 7th Street, between Avenues C & D (1-212 260 1865). Subway: F, V to Lower East Side-Second Avenue. **Rates** (incl breakfast) $100 single; $120 double; $300 apartment. **No credit cards.**
This lesbian-owned gem is tucked into a turn-of-the-20th-century apartment building on a quiet East Village block. The recently remodelled space has gleaming wood floors and exposed brick, plus an eclectic art collection. The bedrooms are done up in bold colours, one of the bathrooms has a small tub and the living room has a TV and CD player.

Incentra Village House
32 Eighth Avenue, between Jane & W 12th Streets (1-212 206 0007/www.incentravillage.com). Subway: A, C, E to 14th Street; L to Eighth Avenue. **Rates** $149-$269. **Credit** AmEx, MC, V.
Two cute 1841 townhouses in the West Village make up this recently renovated guesthouse run by gay men. The spacious rooms have private bathrooms and kitchenettes; some have working fireplaces. A 1939 Steinway baby-grand piano graces the parlour.

Ivy Terrace
230 E 58th Street, between Second & Third Avenues (1-516 662 6862/www.ivyterrace.com). Subway: N, R, W to Lexington Avenue-59th Street; 4, 5, 6 to 59th Street. **Rates** (incl breakfast) $180-$300 single/double; $1,300-$1,600 weekly. **Credit** AmEx, MC, V.
This lovely lesbian-run B&B sits on the same block as boy haunts OW Bar and the Townhouse. The three cosy rooms feature wood floors and lacy bedspreads on old-fashioned sleigh beds. Owner Vinessa Milando (who runs the inn with partner and lesbian-party promoter Sue Martino) provides breakfast each morning. You're also free to create your own meals: each room has a gas stove and a full-size fridge.

Bars

Most gay bars in New York offer drinks specials, happy hours and colourful theme nights; some have hot-body contests, live performances and go-go boys (dyke bars, of course, usually have pool tables). This past year has brought a sleek new boys' lounge, Vlada, to Hell's Kitchen; grungy-cool boys' hang EasternBloc to the East Village; a hip new girls' party at Nowhere; and, sadly, the demise of East Village favourite Starlight. If you wind up at a place that doesn't feel like your scene, don't fret – there are plenty of others just a few twirls away.

Lower East Side & East Village

Boysroom
*211 Avenue A, at 13th Street (www.tripwithus.
com). Subway: L to First Avenue.* **Open** 10pm-
4am daily. **Cover** $5-$10. **Average drink** $7.
No credit cards.
After a year's closure, this dark, sex-vibe lounge
from downtown creature of the night Misstress
Formika – DJ, drag queen and hostess with the
mostest – has returned to inhabit a new space just
up the street from its old one. Pile in for the young
crowds, amateur go-go contests and porn, which is
piped in on mounted TV screens. Expect a different
theme (all cruise-oriented) every night.

The Cock
*29 Second Avenue, at 2nd Street (no phone).
Subway: F, V to Lower East Side-Second Avenue.*
Open 4pm-4am daily. **Cover** $5-$10. **Average
drink** $7. **No credit cards**.
This wonderfully dark and sleazy fag-rock spot has
nightly soirées featuring lots of cruising, cocktail-
guzzling and heavy petting among the rail-thin,
messy-haired young boys.

EasternBloc
*505 E 6th Street, between Avenues A & B (1-212
777 2555/www.easternblocnyc.com). Subway: F, V
to Lower East Side.* **Open** 7pm-
4am daily. **Cover** free-$5. **Average drink** $7.
No credit cards.
This cool, new little space has a red-scare Commie
feel – in the sexiest of ways, with TV screens that
show Bettie Page films, and Soviet-era posters.
Bartenders are cuties, and nightly themes range
from Brüt Thursdays, for tough daddies and those
who love them, to Outlaw Saturdays, a go-go-stud-
laden night of fabulous filth.

Mo Pitkin's House of Satisfaction
*34 Avenue A, between 2nd & 3rd Streets (1-212
777 5660). Subway: F, V to Lower East Side-Second
Avenue.* **Open** 5pm-4am daily. **Average drink**
$6. **Credit** AmEx, MC, V.
A new hotspot, Mo's is a multi-space entity that
offers a straight-up cocktail lounge, cabaret space
and eaterie. Its crowd is mixed but very queer,
thanks to shows and events from downtown faves
like drag king Murray Hill, rockin' drag queen Lisa
Jackson, comedians Mintyfresh and weekly drag
bingo tournaments.

Nowhere
*322 E 14th Street, at First Avenue (1-212 477
4744). Subway: L to First Avenue.* **Open** 3pm-
4am daily. **Average drink** $5. **No credit cards**.
A friendly, spacious bar, from the same folks who
run the nearby Phoenix (447 E 13th Street, between
First Avenue & Avenue A, 1-212 477 9979). Nowhere
attracts attitude-free crowds filled with everyone
from dykes to bears, thanks to a fun line-up of theme
nights. Thursday nights belong to the ladies.

West Village

Chi Chiz
*135 Christopher Street, at Hudson Street (1-212
462 0027). Subway: 1 to Christopher Street-Sheridan
Square.* **Open** 3pm-4am daily. **Average drink** $5.
No credit cards.
This hotspot for men of colour, just steps from the
Christopher Street Pier, is a cruisy kind of place.
Swarms form at Monday night's karaoke, and both
Tuesday's She-Chiz Ladies' Night and Thursday's
evening pool tournaments are equally popular.

Cubbyhole
*281 W 12th Street, at 4th Street (1-212 243
9041). Subway: A, C, E to 14th Street; L to Eighth
Avenue.* **Open** 4pm-2am Mon-Wed; 4pm-4am Thur,
Fri; 2pm-4am Sat, Sun. **Average drink** $6.
No credit cards.
This friendly lesbian spot is always chock-full of flir-
tatious girls, with the standard set of Melissa
Etheridge or kd lang blaring in the background.
Chinese paper lanterns, tissue-paper fish and old
holiday decorations emphasise the welcoming
home-made charm – as do the many dyke-friendly
gay boys and straight folks who are often found bel-
lying up to the bar.

Henrietta Hudson
*438 Hudson Street, at Morton Street (1-212 924
3347/www.henriettahudson.com). Subway: 1 to
Christopher Street-Sheridan Square.* **Open** 4pm-
4am Mon-Fri; 1pm-4am Sat, Sun. **Average drink**
$6. **Credit** AmEx, MC, V.
A long-time, beloved lesbian bar, Henrietta Hudson
is a glammy lounge that attracts young hottie
girls from all over the New York area, especially the
nearby burbs. Every night's a different DJed party,
with Mamacita, Naughty Girl and Hump among the
fancifully named options.

Monster
*80 Grove Street, at Sheridan Square (1-212 924
3558). Subway: 1 to Christopher Street-Sheridan
Square.* **Open** 4pm-4am Mon-Fri; 2pm-4am Sat, Sun.
Average drink $5. **No credit cards**.
Upstairs, locals gather to sing show tunes in the piano
lounge. (And, honey, you haven't lived till you've witnessed a bunch of tipsy queers belting out the best of
Broadway.) The downstairs disco caters to a young
outer-borough crowd just itchin' for a bit of fun.

Stonewall
*53 Christopher Street, between Seventh Avenue
South & Waverly Place (1-212 463 0950).
Subway: 1 to Christopher Street-Sheridan Square.*
Open 4pm-4am daily. **Average drink** $6.
No credit cards.
This is the gay landmark, next door to the actual
location of the 1969 gay rebellion against police
harassment. For years, the joint was a snore but
lately it's had an infusion of sexy shenanigans, such
as go-go boys, strip contests and nights that are
reserved for Latino boys.

Vlada.

Chelsea

Barracuda

275 W 22nd Street, between Seventh & Eighth Avenues (1-212 645 8613). Subway: C, E to 23rd Street. **Open** 4pm-4am daily. **Average drink** $6. **No credit cards**.

This long-time staple is friendlier and more comfortable than the neighbourhood competition. It's got a traditional, low-lit bar up front and a frequently redecorated lounge in the back. Drag-queen celebrities perform throughout the week, and, take note: there's never a cover charge.

The Eagle

554 W 28th Street, between Tenth & Eleventh Avenues (1-646 473 1866/www.eaglenyc.com). Subway: C, E to 23rd Street. **Open** 10pm-4am Mon-Sat; 5pm-4am Sun. **Average drink** $5. **No credit cards**.

A must for leather lovers, the Eagle is a fetish bar that hosts beer blasts, foot-worship fêtes, leather soirées and simple nights of pool playing and cruising. What more could you ask for? *Photo p304*.

Gym

167 Eighth Avenue, at 18th Street (1-212 337 2439/www.gymsportsbar.com). Subway: A, C, E to 14th Street; L to Eighth Avenue. **Open** 4pm-4am daily. **Average drink** $7. **No credit cards**.

This popular spot is all about games – of the actual sporting variety, that is. Catch theme parties that revolve around gay sports leagues, plus pool tables, video games and pro events from rodeo competitions to figure skating (everyone's favourite) shown on big-screen TVs.

XES Lounge

157 W 24th Street, between Sixth & Seventh Avenues (1-212 604 0212/www.xesnyc.com). Subway: F, V, 1 to 23rd Street. **Open** 4pm-4am daily. **Average drink** $7. **Credit** AmEx, MC, V.

This fun, neighbourhood-style spot has exposed brick walls, metal coffee tables, Eames chairs, a patio with Japanese maples, Philippe Starck furniture and a much-appreciated smoking-allowed policy. Catch theme parties and drag shows on weekends.

Midtown

OW Bar

221 E 58th Street, at Second Avenue (1-212 355 3395). Subway: N, R, W to Lexington Avenue-59th Street; 4, 5, 6 to 59th Street. **Open** 4pm-4am Mon-Sat; 2pm-4am Sun. **Average drink** $6. **Credit** AmEx, Disc, MC, V.

Oscar Wilde's initials adorn this East Side watering hole. In addition to the cosy lounge area, jam-packed digital jukebox and lovely patio, there are frequent drag and cabaret performances. Expect a friendly, neighbourhood feel.

Therapy

348 W 52nd Street, between Eighth & Ninth Avenues (1-212 397 1700). Subway: C, E to 50th Street. **Open** 5pm-2am Mon-Wed, Sun; 5pm-4am Thur-Sat. **Average drink** $7. **Credit** AmEx, MC, V.

Therapy is just what the analyst ordered: the minimalist, dramatic two-level space offers performances by bona fide Broadway stars, clever cocktails including the Freudian Sip and, of course, a crowd of beautiful boys. You'll even find good grub here.

Vlada

331 W 51st Street, between Eighth & Ninth Avenues (1-212 974 8030/www.vladabar.com). Subway: C, E to 50th Street. **Open** 4pm-4am Tue-Sun. **Average drink** $6. **Credit** AmEx, MC, V.

This sleek new addition to Hell's Kitchen is a narrow, modern and hyper-stylish lounge that attracts scores of handsome men for infused-vodka cocktails, nibbly bits like foie gras ravioli and tuna tartare and entertainment spanning drag shows to stand-up.

This hoppin', bi-level space is all industrial-chic, spare-design charm. It's a full-time lesbian joint, courtesy of former Meow Mix cat Brooke Webster, and its theme nights, excellent DJs and breezy roof deck have been bringing in the crowds, from Brooklyn, downtown Manhattan and beyond. **Photo** *p302*.

Excelsior
390 Fifth Avenue, between 6th & 7th Streets, Park Slope (1-718 832 1599). Subway: M, R to Union Street. **Open** 6pm-4am Mon-Fri; 2pm-4am Sat, Sun. **Average drink** $7. **No credit cards**.
Refined Excelsior, bathed in red, black and chrome, has a spacious deck out back, a beautiful garden, an eclectic jukebox and an excellent selection of beers on tap. The boys are cute, local and friendly.

Ginger's Bar
363 Fifth Avenue, between 5th & 6th Streets, Park Slope (1-718 788 0924). Subway: M, R to Union Street. **Open** 5pm-4am Mon-Fri; 2pm-4am Sat, Sun. **Average drink** $6. **No credit cards**.
The front room of Ginger's, with its dark-wood bar, looks out on to a bustling street. The back, which has an always-busy pool table, evokes a rec room. Come summertime, the patio feels like a friend's yard. This congenial local hang is full of all sorts of dykes, many with their dogs – or favourite gay boys – in tow.

Metropolitan
559 Lorimer Street, at Metropolitan Avenue, Williamsburg (1-718 599 4444). Subway: G to Metropolitan Avenue, L to Lorimer Street. **Open** 3pm-4am daily. **Average drink** $5. **No credit cards**.
The hipster enclave of Williamsburg has its fair share of queers, and this is its sole gay stand-by. Stop in to refresh with an icy brew while you're tooling around the neighbourhood; you'll find a mellow crowd (featuring lots of beards – of the facial-hair variety), video games, a patio and drinks specials galore. **Photo** *p309*.

Uptown

Candle Bar
309 Amsterdam Avenue, at 74th Street (1-212 874 9155). Subway: 1, 2, 3 to 72nd Street. **Open** 2pm-4am daily. **Average drink** $5. **No credit cards**.
An Upper West Side mainstay, Candle Bar is a small, cruisy, neighbourhood kind of place, with regulars and a well-used pool table. Catch nightly drink specials, from Buds to potent Margaritas.

No Parking
4168 Broadway, between 177th Street & 178th Streets (1-212 923 8700). Subway: 1, 2, 3 to 168th Street. **Open** 4pm-4am daily. **Average drink** $6. **No credit cards**.
If you're feeling frisky, head straight to No Parking in Washington Heights, where a beefy doorman frisks you before entering. Don't be scared, though: the only pistols these cute locals are packing are the fun kind. The bar also boasts a crew of awesome R&B, disco and hip hop video-DJs.

Suite
992 Amsterdam Avenue, at 109th Street (1-212 222 4600/www.suitenyc.com). Subway: 1, 2, 3 to 110th Street. **Open** 4pm-4am daily. **Average drink** $5. **No credit cards**.
Suite opened in the summer of 2005 and offers a relaxed, comfortable atmosphere for local gay resident and Columbia students alike. Nightly drag performances have a fun, let's-put-on-a-show feeling.

Brooklyn

Cattyshack
249 Fourth Avenue, between Carroll & President Streets, Park Slope (1-718 230 5740). Subway: M, R to Union Street. **Open** 2pm-4am Mon-Fri; noon-4am Sat, Sun. **Average drink** $7. **No credit cards**.

Clubs

A number of New York clubs have gay parties or gay nights. For more clubs, plus additional information about some of those listed below, *see pp290-296*.

Dance clubs & parties

Alegria
Crobar, 530 W 28th Street, between Tenth & Eleventh Avenues (1-212 629 9000/www.alegria events.com). Subway: C, E to 23rd Street. **Open** 11pm-4am Mon, Thur-Sun. **Cover** $50-$70. **Average drink** $9. **Credit** AmEx, DC, Disc, MC, V.
Ric Sena's frequent special event, landing in Crobar every couple of months or so – with extra events around Pride time – has grown into one of the most popular dance parties on the circuit. Go for the awe-inspiring space, sea of shirtless muscle boys and top-notch music from DJs like Tony Moran and Abel.

Arts & Entertainment

Element

225 E Houston Street, at Essex Street (1-212 254 2200/www.elementnyc.com). Subway: F, V to Lower East Side–Second Avenue. **Open** 10pm-4am Fri, Sat (check website for other nights). **Cover:** $10-$20. **Average drink** $8.

A former bank, this hulking East Village space provides some Saturday-night queer times with a party called, appropriately enough, Bank. It's where you'll find all of the downtown creatures of the night, from Amanda Lepore to Larry Tee and the gang.

Lovergirl

Speeed, 20 W 39th Street, between Fifth & Sixth Avenues (1-212 252 3397). Subway: B, D, F, V to 42nd Street–Bryant Park; 7 to Fifth Avenue. **Open** 10pm-5am Sat. **Cover** $10-$15. **Average drink** $6. **No credit cards.**

Lovergirl, a popular women's party, takes advantage of Club Shelter's dynamite sound system and state-of-the-art lighting. The multiracial crowd, which doesn't start flowing in until after midnight, enthusiastically shakes it to hip hop, R&B, funk, reggae and Latin music, while ultra-sexy go-go gals sport the latest in fashionable G-strings.

Mr Black

643 Broadway, at Bleecker Street (1-212 253 2560/ www.mrblacknyc.com). Subway: B, D, F, V to Broadway-Lafayette Street. **Open** 9pm-4am daily. **Average drink** $6. **No credit cards.**

A friendly, alternative dance den that sits on the edge of the East Village, West Village and Soho, this is a new space that's creating lots of buzz by its varied party nights. Catch House of Stank on Wednesdays, with underground house, classics and 'bitch tracks', and Boys Gone Wild on Saturdays with crazy host Jonny McGovern. Its vibe is wacky, edgy, young and creative.

Face facts: Keo Nozari

What do the disco era's Village People, 1990s dancefloor sensation Deee-Lite, supermodel RuPaul, pop stars the Scissor Sisters and art-soul singer Antony have in common? They all launched their musical careers in New York's gay nightlife scene, that's what, and, after creating a buzz with the locals, managed to achieve worldwide popularity. The Scissor Sisters have been this decade's biggest such musical success story so far: their debut album in 2004 was a huge hit, selling over a million-and-a-half copies worldwide.

Now plenty of other New York acts are eager to follow in their footsteps, including

Keo Nozari, who shares a passion for dance music, as well as nightclub connections, a queer fan base and major doses of talent.

'I think the real deals shine through in the end,' says Nozari, who has reason to toot his own horn. The singer, who is also a DJ at Therapy (*see p306*) and other gay hangouts, has generated a strong buzz for his self-released debut album, *Late Nite VIP*, which hit music stores in late 2005. *Billboard* compared Nozari's soaring singing style to that of a young George Michael, and cited *Late Nite*'s 'electro-funk-fuelled pop sound' as being on a par with the work of writer-producer Stuart Price (Madonna's *Confessions on a Dancefloor*) and Janet Jackson's longtime collaborators Jimmy Jam and Terry Lewis.

Like Jam, Lewis and also Prince (another of the singer's musical idols), Nozari – who's half French and half Persian – grew up a non-blond in mostly Nordic Minnesota. Ten years ago, he entered NYU to study music technology. 'Yes, I came with pop-star aspirations,' he admits. His cute-as-a-boybander looks and upbeat personality couldn't have hurt these aspirations, yet Nozari's proven himself adept at crafting heartfelt and catchy lyrics about love, romance and other travails on such songs as 'Question of Monogamy' and 'Super Fluidity'. Some critics might dismiss his work as bubblegum pop, but Nozari says he goes for a balance: 'My music rides that tricky line between frothy pop tunes and deeply introspective songwriting.'
For further info, see www.keonozari.com.

Metropolitan. See p307.

Motherfucker

www.motherfuckernyc.com.
If rock 'n' roll is your thing, you'll want to check out Motherfucker, the wildly popular polysexual dance party that takes place about seven times a year, rarely at the same venue. Its Independence Day blowout is particularly popular. *See also p296.*

Saint at Large

1-212 674 8541/www.saintatlarge.com.
The now-mythical Saint was one of the first venues where New York's gay men could enjoy dancefloor freedom. The club closed, but the clientele keeps the memory alive with a huge and très important annual circuit party: the fetishy Black Party, with mind-blowing themes that revolve around kink and sex shows. The White Party, its angelic answer, has been on hold for a couple of years, but check the website for updates on its buzzed-about reappearance.

Shescape

Various venues, see website for schedule (www. shescape.com). Subway: F, V to 23rd Street. **Open** 8pm-4am Sat, Sun. **Cover** $5. **Average drink** $7. **No credit cards.**
The Shescape crew has been offering some of the hottest lesbian bashes around since the 1970s. The best time to join the party is on one of its infamous special events – on Thanksgiving Eve, Pride weekend and New Year's Eve, among other times.

Splash

50 W 17th Street, between Fifth & Sixth Avenues (1-212 691 0073/www.splashbar.com). Subway: F, V to 14th Street; L to Sixth Avenue. **Open** 4pm-4am Mon-Thur, Sun; 4pm-5am Fri, Sat. **Cover** $5-$20. **Average drink** $7. **No credit cards.**

This Chelsea institution offers a large dance space as well as the famous onstage showers, where hunky go-go boys get wet and wild. The supermuscular bartenders here seem bigger than ever. Nationally known DJs rock the house, local drag celebs give good face, and in-house VJs flash eclectic snippets of classic musicals and videos.

Restaurants & cafés

Same-sex couples holding hands across a candlelit table are pretty commonplace in this city. But if you'd like to be certain you'll be in the gay majority when you dine, then check out the following places where it's the straight folks who get the second glances.

Better Burger NYC

178 Eighth Avenue, at 19th Street (1-212 989 6688). Subway: C, E to 23rd Street; 1 to 18th Street. **Open** 11am-midnight Mon-Thur, Sun; 11am-1am Fri, Sat. **Average burger** $6. **Credit** AmEx, MC, V.
Gayest burger joint ever! It's also the healthiest. But don't worry: the menu – which includes lean patties of beef, turkey or soya – is as delicious as the hunky clientele. And although it is a fast-food joint, it's a classy one, listing organic beers and wines to go with your burger, as well as air-baked fries and house-made ketchup. Yum!

Counter

105 First Avenue, between 6th & 7th Streets (1-212 982 5870). Subway: F, V to Lower East Side-Second Avenue. **Open** 5pm-midnight Mon-Fri; 11am-1am Sat, Sun. **Average main course** $15. **Credit** AmEx, MC, V.

This hip, lesbian-owned East Village spot takes vegetarian cuisine to a whole new level, adding a wine bar with a dozen organic offerings. Pair a glass or two with one of the lip-smackin' vegan tapas, or try bigger eats, such as portobello au poivre or curried plantain dumplings drizzled in coconut sauce. Brunch is served on weekends.

Cowgirl

519 Hudson Street at 10th Street (1-212 633 1133/ www.cowgirlnyc.com). Subway: 1 to Christopher Street-Sheridan Square. **Open** 10am-11pm Mon-Thur, Sun; 10am-midnight Fri, Sat. **Average main course** $13. **Credit** AmEx, MC, V.

Formerly Cowgirl Hall of Fame, this West Village spot has a big lesbian following. Blame the chicken-fried steak, the house Margaritas, the Patsy Cline theme or the close proximity to Henrietta Hudson and Rubyfruit's. Whatever. It's just a straight-up good time, with solid cowgirl-fare to boot.

Diner 24

102 Eighth Avenue, at 15th Street (1-212 242 7773). Subway: A, C, E to 14th Street; L to Eighth Avenue. **Open** 11am-6am Mon-Fri; 11am-8am Sat, Sun. **Average main course** $15. **Credit** AmEx, Disc, MC, V.

Your company here depends on what time of day you saunter in for the delicious comfort food. Weekday lunchtimes bring local office workers with cute local guys nursing coffees, while weekend mornings bring in the party boys who have been out all night. Saturday at midnight is a treat, as rotating drag queens (with Candis Cayne and Shequida as recent examples) offer a side of performance to go with your mac 'n' cheese.

Elmo

156 Seventh Avenue, between 19th & 20th Streets (1-212 337 8000/http://elmorestaurant.com). Subway: 1 to 18th Street. **Open** 11am-midnight Mon-Thur; 11am-2am Fri, Sat; 10am-midnight Sun. **Average main course** $14. **Credit** AmEx, Disc, MC, V.

This spacious, brightly decorated eaterie has good, reasonably priced food and a bar that offers a view of the dining room, which is jammed with guys in clingy tank tops – regardless of the weather. And then there's the fun basement lounge, which hosts frequent readings, comedy and drag shows, plus the occasional chic-lesbian soirée.

Foodbar

149 Eighth Avenue, between 17th & 18th Streets (1-212 243 2020). Subway: 1 to 18th Street. **Open** 11am-midnight daily. **Average main course** $15. **Credit** AmEx, Disc, MC, V.

Foodbar's globally influenced American menu will get your mouth watering, if the customers haven't already. Balsamic-glazed roasted chicken, a Moroccan salad and steak au poivre, and big-brunch omelettes are each entirely satisfying. Servers are efficient and coquettish – a combination we happen to treasure. It's a classic Chelsea hang.

44 & X Hell's Kitchen

622 Tenth Avenue, at 44th Street (1-212 977 1170). Subway: A, C, E to 42nd Street-Port Authority. **Open** 5.30pm-midnight Mon-Wed; 5.30pm-12.30am Thur, Fri; 11.30am-12.30am Sat, Sun. **Average main course** $20. **Credit** AmEx, MC, V.

Fabulous queens pack out the sleek dining space that was one of the first bright spots on quickly gentrifying Tenth Avenue. It's situated alongside the Theater District and the Manhattan Plaza high-rises, home to thousands of artistes. Oh, and the food's great, too. Average sandwich $5.75. **No credit cards** like creamy mac 'n' cheese, and American specialities like filet mignon. It's the perfect post-theatre or pre-club pit stop.

Java Boy/View Bar

232 Eighth Avenue, at 22nd Street (1-212 929 2243). Subway: C, E to 23rd Street. **Open** 7am-4am daily. **Average sandwich** $5.75. **No credit cards.**

With Big Cup – the quintessential Chelsea coffee-bar – now no longer, View Bar has stepped in to fill the caffeine need. It offers cups of joe and wireless service by day, and above-average joes drinking cocktails by night. The view on to the Eighth Avenue runway is perfect too.

Lips

2 Bank Street, at Greenwich Avenue (1-212 675 7710). Subway: 1, 2, 3 to 14th Street. **Open** 5.30pm-midnight Mon-Thur; 5.30pm-1am Fri, Sat; 11.30am-4pm, 5.30-11pm Sun. **Average main course** $18. **Credit** AmEx, DC, MC, V.

This festive restaurant certainly does generate an enjoyable, jovial atmosphere: the drag-queen waitstaff serve tasty meals and perform for very enthusiastic patrons. Midweek events tend to be a lot gayer than the weekends, when scores of shrieking straight chicks descend on the place for their bachelorette parties. The Sunday brunch ($15, including copious alcohol) is quite a show.

Rubyfruit Bar & Grill

531 Hudson Street, between Charles & Washington Streets (1-212 929 3343). Subway: 1 to Christopher Street-Sheridan Square. **Open** 2pm-4am Mon-Thur; 3pm-4am Fri, Sat; 11.30am-2am Sun. **Average main course** $20. **Credit** AmEx, DC, Disc, MC, V.

The food is good, but it's not the main selling point at this dedicated lesbian restaurant and bar. An eclectic mix of music and congenial customers make for a great place for fun-loving, old-school dykes.

Superfine

126 Front Street, between Jay & Pearl Streets, Dumbo, Brooklyn (1-718 243 9005). Subway: F to York Street. **Open** 11.30am-3pm, 6-11pm Tue-Thur; 11.30am-3pm, 6pm-4am Fri; 2.30pm-4am Sat; 11.30am-2am Sun. **Average main course** $15. **Credit** AmEx, MC, V.

Owned by a couple of super-cool dykes, this spacious eaterie, bar and art gallery serves seasonal Mediterranean cuisine in its hip space. The mellow vibe and pool table draw a mixed, local crowd. The south-western themed brunches are delicious.

Music

New York's music scene hits all the right notes.

Popular

Depending on the year, people alternately lament the moribund state of New York's music scene, or boast triumphantly of its global dominance. The truth of the matter is that an undeclared music festival takes place in the city nearly every night of the week, with innumerable acts of untold genres sprawling out across Manhattan and Brooklyn. Plan accordingly and you can catch more than one world-class show in a single night.

Keep in mind that bigger is not always better. While no sweeping American tour is complete without a Manhattan stop – whether that means Madonna's latest schlep through **Madison Square Garden** or indie hotshots Tapes 'n Tapes filling **Bowery Ballroom** – what makes New York concert-going so unique is the never-ending supply of upstarts, hopefuls and local weirdos. These performances can be more exciting, intimate and, yes, affordable. Nellie McKay and Regina Spektor, for instance, were both discovered playing for tip money at the tiny **Sidewalk Café**, an East Village spot that's free but for a modest drink minimum.

For larger seated shows, the iconic theatres uptown cannot be beat. The palatial art deco totem **Radio City Music Hall**, Harlem's decaying benchmark the **Apollo Theater**, and **Carnegie Hall** all lend historic import to even tedious performances. For smaller shows, the best bets lie across Downtown Manhattan and select neighbourhoods in Brooklyn. Rock music dominates the Lower East Side and Williamsburg, while a smattering of cosy jazz clubs thrive in Greenwich Village. And you don't have to look far for hip hop, soul, blues, folk, world music and everything in between.

To help navigate the scene, we've organised the city's most active and notable venues by genre. Note to the anal: these categories are loose. Many spots will feature scraggly rock one night and jazz the next, or skip from Brazilian music to folk in a single evening. And be prepared to linger: if a listing says a favourite band is going on at 11pm, you might wait till midnight or later. A valid photo ID proving that you're 21 or over is essential, not only to drink but, often, just to get in (a passport or a driver's licence are best).

NYC bouncers have heard it all, and they're impervious to excuses (*see p296* **How** *not* **to get kicked out**); grey hair does not always prove one's adulthood. (Wrinkles and a walking frame might do the trick, though.) Tickets are usually available from clubs in advance and at the door. A few small and medium-size venues also sell advance tickets through local record stores. For larger events, it's wise to buy through Ticketmaster (*see p383*) on the web, over the phone or at one of the outlets located throughout the city. Tickets for some events are available from Ticket Web (www.ticketweb.com). You can also buy them online from websites of specific venues (URLs are included in venue listings where available). And remember to call ahead for information and show times, which often change without notice.

Arenas

Continental Airlines Arena
For listing, see p333 Meadowlands Sports Complex. New Jersey's answer to Madison Square Garden recently played host to the likes of U2, Bruce Springsteen and Pearl Jam. Oldies showcases and radio-sponsored pop and hip hop extravaganzas also take place here.

Madison Square Garden
For listing, see p333.
Madison Square Garden, one of the world's most famous arenas, is where the biggest acts – Prince, Mariah, Beastie Boys – come out to play. Whether you can see them well depends a lot on your seat, or your binoculars.

Nassau Veterans Memorial Coliseum
For listing, see p333.
Long Island's arena hosts mainstream acts like Bon Jovi and Aerosmith, punctuated by occasional teen-pop sock hops (*American Idol* Live!) and garish Bollywood showcases.

Rock, pop & soul

Ace of Clubs
9 Great Jones Street, at Lafayette Street (1-212 677 6963/www.aceofclubsnyc.com). Subway: B, D, F, V to Broadway-Lafayette Street; 6 to Bleecker Street. **Shows** Doors open at 7pm. **Cover** $5-$12. **No credit cards**.

CityParks
Foundation
People + Parks

Central Park
SummerStage

Free music, dance, word, and film in the
heart of New York City all summer long.

Performance Central

Free

Visit www.SummerStage.org or call (212) 360-2777

All this shoebox of a space had needed the past few years was a booker with some taste. Ask and ye shall receive, as early in 2005 it morphed from the old Under Acme into Ace of Clubs, bringing in a diverse mix of mostly local rock (the Giraffes), blues (Corey Harris) and progressive jazz (the Jazz Passengers' Bill Ware and his Urban Vibes project). The location is as central as they come, and if you need a bite, the restaurant Acme should satisfy your soul-food cravings.

Apollo Theater

253 W 125th Street, between Adam Clayton Powell Jr Boulevard (Seventh Avenue) & Frederick Douglass Boulevard (Eighth Avenue) (1-212 531 5305/www. apollotheater.com). Subway: A, B, C, D, 1 to 125th Street. **Box office** 10am-6pm Mon, Tue, Thur, Fri; 10am-8.30pm Wed; noon-6pm Sat. **Tickets** $20-$100. **Credit** AmEx, DC, Disc, MC, V.

Visitors might think they know Harlem's venerable Apollo from TV's *Showtime at the Apollo*, but as the saying goes, the small screen adds about 10lb. Inside, the elegant yet lived-in theatre – still the city's home of R&B and soul music – is actually quite cosy. Known for launching the careers of Ella Fitzgerald, Michael Jackson and D'Angelo, to name just a few, the Apollo continues to bring in veteran talent like Aretha Franklin as well as special performances by younger artists – when Gorillaz took its live *Demon Days* spectacle from Manchester to the States, this is the theatre Mr Albarn selected.

Arlene's Grocery

95 Stanton Street, between Ludlow & Orchard Streets (1-212 995 1652/www.arlenesgrocery.net). Subway: F to Delancey Street; J, M, Z to Delancey-Essex Streets. **Open** 6pm-4am daily. **Cover** $7. **Credit** AmEx, MC, V.

A divey mid-level rung on the local-band ladder, Arlene's can pack as many as six rock acts a night, often adding afternoon shows on Saturdays. Monday night's live-band karaoke is an institution, even if the band that started it all has moved on. A lively spot in the liveliest of neighbourhoods.

Avalon

662 Sixth Avenue, at 20th Street (1-212 807 7780). Subway: F, V, R, W to 23rd Street. **Open** 10pm-7am Fri-Sun. **Cover** $14-$25. **No credit cards**.

Avalon is housed in an old Gothic building in Chelsea; years ago, it was a church. Yet perhaps more holy to some is its status as the former site of the famed dance club Limelight. The club still hosts dance acts, but packs in rock shows with bands like Pelican, the New York Dolls and Islands.

BB King Blues Club & Grill

237 W 42nd Street, between Seventh & Eighth Avenues (1-212 997 4144/www.bbkingblues.com). Subway: A, C, E to 42nd Street-Port Authority; N, Q, R, W to 42nd Street; S, 1, 2, 3, 7 to 42nd Street-Times Square. **Box office** 11am-midnight daily. **Tickets** $12-$150. **Credit** AmEx, DC, Disc, MC, V.

The location and appearance might suggest that this place is geared to tourists, but BB's joint in Times Square plays host to one of the widest varieties of music in town: cover bands and soul tributes fill the gaps between big-name bookings such as Ralph Stanley, Lee 'Scratch' Perry and James Brown. Lately, the club has also proved a viable space for extreme metal bands (Napalm Death, Obituary, Hate Eternal) and neo-soul and hip hop acts (such as Angie Stone, GZA/Genius and even Kool Keith). For many shows, the best seats

Rock out

Make your rock star fantasy a reality – for a night, at least – at one (or more) of New York's keenly attended live karaoke joints. The bands at the following places know an insane number of songs, and do their best to follow a singer, no matter how high he or she launches into the stratosphere. Days and times often change; call ahead before heading out to sign your name up.

A&M Roadhouse

57 Murray Street, between Church Street & West Broadway (1-212 385 9005/ www.humankaraoke.com). Alternate Fridays at 9pm. Average wait to sing: two hours.

Arlene's Grocery

95 Stanton Street, between Ludlow & Orchard Streets (1-212 995 1652). Mondays at 10pm. Average wait: one hour.

Hank's Saloon

46 Third Avenue, at Atlantic Avenue, Boerum Hill, Brooklyn (1-718 625 8003). Alternate Mondays at 10pm. Average wait: 30 minutes.

Kenny's Castaways

157 Bleecker Street, between Sullivan & Thompson Streets (1-212 979 9762). Sundays at 8pm. Average wait: 15 minutes.

Lucky Cat

245 Grand Street, between Driggs Avenue & Roebling Street, Williamsburg, Brooklyn (1-718 782 0437). Mondays at 9.30pm. Average wait: 15 minutes.

Magnetic Field

97 Atlantic Avenue, between Henry & Hicks Streets, Brooklyn Heights (1-718 834 0069/ www.magneticbrooklyn.com). Alternate Thursdays at 8pm. Average wait: 20 minutes.

Joe's Pub. See p316.

are at the dinner tables at the front, but the menu prices are steep. (And watch out for drink minimums.) The Harlem Gospel Choir buffet brunch, on Sundays, raises the roof, while live classic-rock, jazz and blues groups play for free most nights at Lucille's Bar & Grill, the restaurant named after King's cherished guitar.

Beacon Theatre
2124 Broadway, at 74th Street (1-212 496 7070). Subway: 1, 2, 3 to 72nd Street. **Box office** 11am-7pm Mon-Fri; noon-6pm Sat. **Tickets** $15-$175. **No credit cards**.
This spacious Upper West Side theatre hosts a variety of popular acts, from Bob Dylan to Anthony Hamilton – and once a year, the Allman Brothers take over the place for a lengthy residency. While the theatre's sound and vastness can be daunting to performer and audience alike, the gaudy, gilded interior and uptown location make you feel like you're having a real night out on the town.

Bowery Ballroom
6 Delancey Street, between Bowery & Chrystie Street (1-212 533 2111/www.boweryballroom.com). Subway: J, M, Z to Bowery; 6 to Spring Street. **Box office** at the Mercury Lounge, *see p317*. **Tickets** $13-$40. **Credit** AmEx, MC, V (bar only).
Probably the best venue in the city for seeing indie bands (either on the way up or holding their own), the Bowery nonetheless manages to bring in a diverse range of artists from in town and around the world, as well as offering a clear view and loud, bright sound from just about any spot. Past bookings have included the Fiery Furnaces, Tom Verlaine, the Boredoms and Tilly and the Wall. Not into an opening band? The spacious downstairs lounge is a great place to relax and socialise between (or during) sets.

Bowery Poetry Club
308 Bowery, at Bleecker Street (1-212 614 0505/ www.bowerypoetry.com). Subway: B, D, F, V to Broadway-Lafayette Street; 6 to Bleecker Street. **Shows** Check website for schedule. **Cover** $3-$10. **Credit** AmEx, MC, V (bar only).
The name of this colourful joint on the Bowery reveals its roots in the poetry slam scene, but it's also the truest current iteration of the East Village's legendary arts scene: all kinds of jazz, folk, hip hop and improv theatre acts can be found here routinely; if you have a taste for the bizarre and don't offend easily, keep your eyes peeled for anything from the Jollyship to the Whiz-Bang musical-puppet crew. The BPC offers a range of sandwiches and hot and cold drinks – and there are generally seats available to rest one's weary feet.

Cake Shop
152 Ludlow Street, between Rivington & Stanton Streets (1-212 253 0036/www.cake-shop.com). Subway: F, V to Lower East Side-Second Avenue. **Shows** Doors open at 8pm. **Cover** $6-$8. **No credit cards**.
This narrow, stuffy but clean basement space gets points for much more than its keen indie-rock bookings, often handled by the busy underground booker known as Todd P. For one thing, it's located in the heart of the Lower East Side, between Pianos (*see p318*) and the Living Room (*see p317*) on Ludlow Street. What's more, it sells pastries and coffee upstairs. Better still (for late-night music junkies, at least), the brightly lit back room on street level sells used vinyl and CDs, as well as a smattering of new releases, DVDs and other record-store ephemera.

Canal Room
285 West Broadway, at Canal Street (1-212 941 8100/ www.canalroomlive.com). Subway: A, C, E, 1 to Canal Street. **Box office** 10am-6pm Mon-Fri; noon-6pm Sat. **Tickets** $7-25. **Credit cards** AmEx, DC, MC, V.

A medium-size club at the northern tip of Tribeca, the Canal Room hosts DJ nights as well as concerts. There's good variety here, from singer-songwriters (Todd Snider, Erin McKeown) to lounge fare (Nouvelle Vague). And every Sunday, the club hosts a reggae party, Reminisce Reggae Sundays. When shows are packed, things can get uncomfortable and the door people tend to be a bit uptight, but you can't go wrong with many of the bookings.

Continental

25 Third Avenue, at St Marks Place (1-212 529 6924/www.continentalnyc.com). Subway: N, R, W to 8th Street-NYU; 6 to Astor Place. **Shows** Doors open at 4pm. **Cover** free-$10. **No credit cards.**
Continental lies just up the road from CBGB (which, at the time of writing, was facing eviction from its long-time East Village spot); and if there's a club to replace that venue, it's this one – not, unfortunately, the CBGB of 1977, as much as the CBGB of 2001: Continental mostly champions sound-alike thrashers who are nameless, albeit competent and very loud. The Continental is among the best rock clubs in the city for drinking: a titillating sign above the bar reads 'Five shots of anything – $10'. The place also smells strongly from the McDonald's next door. Punk forefather Cheetah Chrome and Boston's the Real Kids still pop in for gigs now and then, but the real draw is Monday's Original Punk/Metal Karaoke Band, which will help you live out your rock 'n' roll dreams. All-ages gigs on weekend afternoons are a long-standing tradition.

The Delancey

168 Delancey Street, at Clinton Street (1-212 254 9920/www.thedelancey.com). Subway: F to Delancey Street; J, M, Z to Delancey-Essex Streets. **Shows** Doors open at 8pm. **Cover** $6-$10. **No credit cards.**
Spitting distance from the Williamsburg Bridge (even if you're a lousy spitter) is the Delancey. When it opened shop a couple of years back, the club seemed set to become one of those insufferably trendy hotspots that beautiful people dance in and ugly people blog about. Yet as New York's rock scene mellowed out, so too did the Delancey, leaving its snug basement space less intimidating than people might assume. When the weather's nice, the draw isn't the music so much as the outdoor roof space, with beautiful views of the bridge.

Don Hill's

511 Greenwich Street, at Spring Street (1-212 219 2850/www.donhills.com). Subway: C, E to Spring Street; 1 to Canal Street. **Shows** Doors open at 7.30pm. **Cover** free-$10. **Credit** AmEx, DC, Disc, MC, V.
This somewhat scuzzy, boxy space is no longer a good bet for new live bands. Saturday night's MisShapes party, though, features local DJs playing an eclectic mix, and (occasional) Wednesday's glam-punk bonanza Röck Cändy is always a fun night – especially if you like cheap beer.

Galapagos Art Space

70 North 6th Street, between Kent & Wythe Avenues, Williamsburg, Brooklyn (1-718 782 5188/www.galapagosartspace.com). Subway: L to Bedford Avenue. **Shows** times vary. **Cover** free-$7. **No credit cards.**
A roomy Williamsburg art and performance space that's famed for the dark pool at its entrance focuses on Brooklyn artists, but its mix of music, performance art, readings and film screenings doesn't discriminate. Burlesque and vaudeville nights are weekly staples, while the Mekons have stopped by for readings and art events.

Hammerstein Ballroom

Manhattan Center, 311 W 34th Street, between Eighth & Ninth Avenues (1-212 279 7740/ www.mcstudios.com). Subway: A, C, E to 34th Street-Penn Station. **Box office** noon-5pm Mon-Sat. **Tickets** $10-$50. **Credit** AmEx, MC, V.
Patrons can at times be treated like cattle here and the drinks prices are among the most outlandish in town – upwards of ten bucks for a cheap cocktail in a plastic cup! – but this cavernous space regularly draws big performers in the limbo between club and arena shows. Unless you're on the floor (there is no general admission here), the stage might seem a distant illusion. But the once-poor sound quality has been rectified and the environment itself – dramatic vaulted balconies hanging over a raucous floor – captures that big-show excitement.

Hiro Ballroom at Maritime Hotel

371 Ninth Avenue, at the corner of 16th Street (1-212 625 8553/www.themaritimehotel.com/hiro Ballroom.html). Subway: A, C, E to 14th Street; L to Eighth Avenue. **Open** 10pm-4am Thur-Sun. **Cover** $10-$35. **Credit** AmEx, MC, V.
Hiro Ballroom reeks of Manhattan chic, with a flamboyant Sushi-bar-of-tomorrow atmosphere – a place in which James Bond might feel comfortable checking out a band. Concerts here are scarce – DJ nights are more common – which is unfortunate: the hotel space is a glamorous setting to see a musician, be it Daniel Lanois or Secret Machines. And it feels much fancier than the price of admission suggests.

The Hook

18 Commerce Street, between Dwight & Richards Streets, Red Hook, Brooklyn (1-718 797 3007/ www.thehookmusic.com). Subway: F, G to Carroll Street. **Open** Show days 8.30pm-4am. **Cover** $8-$15. **No credit cards.**
How do you survive as a nightclub in a remote spot? Do like the Hook and bring in a steady stream of must-see bands, from touring outfits (Ted Leo + Pharmacists, Sonic Boom) to small festivals (the annual No Fun Festival, emerging artist showcase Emergenza). The spacious club has a long bar, a wide-open floor, an easygoing vibe and a huge area out back for smokers. Even though the Red Hook area has been on the rise, the Hook itself – on a lonely block of warehouses – is still a destination venue. And barring the nights that the club runs a shuttle

Northsix. *See p318.*

service from the nearest subway, it can be kind of creepy getting there and back – bring a cab number to get home. *See also p158* **Get hooked**.

Irving Plaza
17 Irving Place, at 15th Street (1-212 777 6800/ www.irvingplaza.com). Subway: L, N, Q, R, W, 4, 5, 6 to 14th Street-Union Square. **Box office** noon-6.30pm Mon-Fri; 1-4pm Sat. **Tickets** $10-$60. **Credit** AmEx.
With the rise of clubs like Webster Hall and Warsaw, Irving Plaza has lost its monopoly on concerts by mid-sized touring bands. Yet it's still the place where Jack White goes to debut the Raconteurs or Clap Your Hands Say Yeah plays its big New Year's Eve gig. And from the parlour-lit lounge downstairs to the shadowy corners of the balconies, this pleasantly worn old ballroom whispers of New York's rock past.

Joe's Pub
The Public Theater, 425 Lafayette Street, between Astor Place & E 4th Street (1-212 539 8770/www. joespub.com). Subway: N, R, W to 8th Street-NYU; 6 to Astor Place. **Box office** 1-6pm Mon, Sun; 1-7pm Tue-Sat. **Tickets** $12-$30. **Credit** AmEx, MC, V.
Probably the city's premier small spot for sit-down audiences, Joe's Pub brings in impeccable talent of all genres and national origins. It often gets artists ahead of the curve: acts like Nouvelle Vague and Nellie McKay will play here months before taking their act to much larger rooms. While some well-established names such as Del McCoury, Malian blues nomads Tinariwen and Bobby Bare have played here recently, Joe's also provides a stage for up-and-coming singers (Death Vessel, Elvis Perkins). It's one of the only clubs where something interesting is likely to be happening at some point in any night. A small but solid menu and deep bar selections seal the deal. **Photo** *p314.*

Knitting Factory
74 Leonard Street, between Broadway & Church Street (1-212 219 3132/www.knittingfactory.com). Subway: A, C, E to Canal Street; 1 to Franklin Street. **Box office** 4-11pm Mon-Sat; 2-11pm Sun. **Tickets** $5-$20. **Credit** AmEx, MC, V.
This three-floor circus was once known as NYC's downtown home of avant-garde jazz, but a couple of ownership changes later and jazz is scarce (other than the occasional Bad Plus gig). What you will find is a woolly mix of top-shelf indie acts (the Fall, Art Brut, the Howling Hex), metal (Otep, Pelican, Soilent Green) and locals (Blood on the Wall, Oneida), with a smattering of decent hip hop and college-campus-calibre fillers. The smaller Tap Bar and claustrophobic Old Office, both under the main room (and with separate admissions), often have good DJs tucked in among the busy flow of bands.

Lakeside Lounge
162 Avenue B, between 10th & 11th Streets (1-212 529 8463/www.lakesidelounge.com). Subway: L to First Avenue; N, Q, R, W, 4, 5, 6 to 14th Street-Union Square. **Shows** 9.30pm or 10pm. **Cover** free. **Credit** AmEx, MC, V (bar only).
Because this comfortable East Village joint is co-owned by guitarist and producer Eric Ambel, the roadhouse and roots acts that come through tend to be fun. Local country-tinged talents appear often – and bigger names like Amy Rigby will stop by. The bar, the jukebox and the photo booth are all attractions of their own – and there's never a cover charge.

Lit Lounge
93 Second Avenue, between 5th & 6th Streets (1-212 777 7987/www.litloungenyc.com). Subway: F, V to Lower East Side-Second Avenue; 6 to Astor Place. **Shows** 9pm. **Cover** free-$5. **Credit** AmEx, MC, V (bar only, $20 minimum).

This likeable, if airflow-challenged, dungeon offers a stream of earnest, noisy young indie bands. It's a small room and, with a few exceptions, generally brings in small bands. The location makes it easy to swing into – and back out, if you're hitting the town.

Living Room

154 Ludlow Street, between Rivington & Stanton Streets (1-212 533 7235/www.livingroomny.com). Subway: F to Lower East Side-Second Avenue; J, M, Z to Delancey-Essex Streets. **Open** 6pm-2am Mon-Thur, Sun; 3pm-4am Fri, Sat. **Cover** free; 1-drink minimum. **No credit cards**.

Many local clubs try to lay claim to being the place where Norah Jones got her start, but the Living Room is really it (she even donated a piano as a way of saying thanks). Still, that was in the venue's old (and drab) location; since moving to the Lower East Side's version of Main Street, the stream of singer-songwriters that fill the schedule here has taken on a bit more gleam, and the warmly lit environs seem to be always bustling. In recent years, performers like Karen Ann and Ane Brun have stopped here before moving on to larger local spaces.

Maxwell's

1039 Washington Street, at 11th Street, Hoboken, NJ (1-201 798 0406/www.maxwellsnj.com). Travel: PATH train to Hoboken, then take a cab, the Red Apple bus or NJ Transit 126 bus to 12th Street. **Box office** Visit website for hours. **Tickets** $7-$20. **Credit** AmEx, Disc, MC, V.

The trip out to Maxwell's can be a hassle, but the 15-minute walk from the PATH train – not unpleasant if the weather's on your side – can make you feel like you're in small-town America. The restaurant in front is big and friendly, and for dessert, you can feast on indie rock fare from popular artists like the

Raveonettes and the Waco Brothers as well as a slew of garage acts (Holly Golightly, the Black Lips). Hometown heroes Yo La Tengo stage their more or less annual Hanukkah shows at this area institution.

Mercury Lounge

217 E Houston Street, between Essex & Ludlow Streets (1-212 260 4700/www.mercuryloungenyc.com). Subway: F, V to Lower East Side-Second Avenue. **Shows** Daily, times vary. **Box office** noon-7pm Mon-Sat. **Cover** $8-$15; some shows require advance tickets. **Credit** AmEx, DC, Disc, MC, V (bar only).

The unassuming, boxy Mercury Lounge is both an old standby and pretty much the No.1 indie rock club in town, with solid sound and sight lines (and a cramped bar in the front room). With four-band bills almost every night, you can catch plenty of locals (the Essex Green, the Rogers Sisters) and touring bands (Heartless Bastards, Black Mountain) in the course of just one week. Only two caveats: bills can seem stylistically haphazard, and the set times are regularly later than advertised. Note that some of the spot's bigger shows sell out in advance, mainly through online sales.

Mo Pitkin's House of Satisfaction

34 Avenue A, between 2nd & 3rd Streets (1-212 777 5660/www.mopitkins.com). Subway: F, V to Lower East Side-Second Avenue. **Shows** daily, times vary. **Box office** Advance tickets available through www.ticketweb.com. **Cover** $8-$15 (most shows with 1-drink minimum). **Credit** AmEx, MC, V.

Opened in 2005 by brothers Phil and Jesse Hartman (the former co-owns local pizza institution Two Boots; the latter is a musician known for his work as Laptop), Mo Pitkin's is an only-in-Manhattan type of joint. On the first floor lies a great Jewish-Latino restaurant and bar. Above is a cabaret space

Pete's Candy Store. *See p318.*

Southpaw.

featuring all sorts of comedy and music, including upcoming singer-songwriters (Christina Courtin), roots artists (Tarbox Ramblers), and that very New York in-between (the Trachtenburg Family Slideshow Players). It's a great addition to the city's entertainment landscape – and the latkes (Jewish pancakes) are among the best in town.

New Jersey Performing Arts Center

1 Center Street, at the waterfront, Newark, NJ (1-888 466 5722/www.njpac.org). Travel: PATH train to Newark, then take the Loop shuttle bus to NJPAC. **Box office** noon-6pm Mon-Sat; 10am-3pm Sun. **Tickets** $12-$100. **Credit** AmEx, Disc, MC, V.
Visible from Manhattan (and quite easy to get to, too), NJPAC offers up legends of disco (Donna Summer) and Broadway stars in cabaret performances (Brian Stokes Mitchell), plus crowd pleasing swing and soul music. The summer is chock-full of outdoor entertainment geared to families.

Nokia Theatre Times Square

1515 Broadway, at 44th Street (1-212 307 7171). Subway: N, Q, R, W to 42nd Street; S, 1, 2, 3, 7 to 42nd Street-Times Square. **Box office** 4-11pm daily (advance online purchase recommended). **Tickets** $20-$40. **Credit** AmEx, MC, V.
This large Times Square corporate club begs for character – it has a cookie-cutter aura that would befit a suburban mega-mall – but finds redemption in its creature comforts. The sound and sight lines are both good and well planned, and there's even (gasp!) edible food. Those who wish to look into a musician's eyes can stand in the ample front section, while foot-weary fans can sit in the movie theatre-like section at the back of the room. It's a comfortable place to see a well-known band that hasn't (yet) reached stadium-filling fame: Belle & Sebastian, Morcheeba, Anthrax and Damian 'Jr Gong' Marley have all made the space their own, if just for a night.

Northsix

66 North 6th Street, between Kent & Wythe Avenues, Williamsburg, Brooklyn (1-718 599 5103/ www.northsix.com). Subway: L to Bedford Avenue. **Box office** 4-11pm daily (advance online purchase recommended). **Tickets** $6-$18. **Credit** AmEx, Disc, MC, V (advance purchases only).
One of Williamsburg's top music spots, Northsix does a great job of pleasing trendy locals and music fans who might otherwise steer clear of the area. Easily accessible via the L train, this warehouse-like space has hosted indie stars Serena-Maneesh and Beirut, as well as luminaries like Jonathan Richman and the reformed MC5. It's also one of the few clubs where you can still hear live hip hop (mainly from underground acts, like the Definitive Jux label). **Photo** *p316.*

Pete's Candy Store

709 Lorimer Street, between Frost & Richardson Streets, Williamsburg, Brooklyn (1-718 302 3770/ www.petescandystore.com). Subway: L to Lorimer Street. **Open** 5pm-2am Mon-Wed, Sun; 5pm-4am Thur-Sat. **Cover** Free. **No credit cards.**

An overlooked gem of a venue, tucked away in an old candy shop situated in an obscure corner of Williamsburg. Pete's is gorgeous, tiny and always free. The performers are generally unknown and the crowds can be thin, but it can be a romantic, comfortable place to catch a singer-songwriter. **Photo** *p317.*

Pianos

158 Ludlow Street, between Rivington & Stanton Streets (1-212 505 3733/www.pianosnyc.com). Subway: F to Delancey Street; J, M, Z to Delancey-Essex Streets. **Shows** around 8pm. **Box office** 3pm-4am daily. **Cover** free-$12. **Credit** AmEx, DC, MC, V.
On a Saturday night, Pianos can seem like either the centre of New York or the ninth circle of hell, depending on your tastes. But there's no denying that this style-conscious bar-cum-club brings in a weird, wild mix; one night you'll get trendy local bands (this is where Clap Your Hands Say Yeah really started clapping), the next you might get Prince Paul. The sound is often lousy and the room uncomfortably mobbed, but like it or not, there are always good reasons to go back. The emerging talent booked in the charming, free upstairs lounge is often a good bet.

Radio City Music Hall

1260 Sixth Avenue, at 50th Street (1-212 247 4777/ www.radiocity.com). Subway: B, D, F, V to 47th-50th Streets-Rockefeller Center. **Box office** 10am-8pm Mon-Sat; 11am-8pm Sun. **Tickets** $25-$125. **Credit** AmEx, MC, V.
Few rooms scream 'New York City!' more than this gilded hall, which has recently drawn Ben Folds, the Roots and R Kelly as headliners. The greatest challenge for any performer is not to get

upstaged by the awe-inspiring art deco surroundings – but these same surroundings lend historic heft to even the flimsiest showing.

Roseland

239 W 52nd Street, between Broadway & Eighth Avenue (1-212 247 0200/www.roselandballroom. com). Subway: B, D, E to Seventh Avenue; C to 50th Street. **Box office** at Irving Plaza, *see p316.* **Tickets** $17-$75. **No credit cards.**
Roseland is a slightly depressing Times Square club that's bigger than Irving Plaza and smaller than the Hammerstein Ballroom. As at any large club, you'll find any artist who can fill the room performing here, with past acts including the Arctic Monkeys and Youssou N'Dour.

Sidewalk Café

94 Avenue A, at 6th Street (1-212 473 7373). Subway: F, V to Lower East Side-Second Avenue; 6 to Astor Place. **Shows** around 7.30pm. **Cover** free; 2-drink minimum. **Credit** AmEx, MC, V (bar only).
Despite its cramped and awkward layout, the Sidewalk café is the undisputed focal point of the city's anti-folk scene – though that category means just about anything from piano pop to wry folk. Nellie McKay, Regina Spektor and the Moldy Peaches all started here; Monday's Antihootenanny with anti-folk capo Lach is an institution.

Sin-é

150 Attorney Street, between Houston & Stanton Streets (1-212 388 0077/www.sin-e.com). Subway: F to Delancey Street; J, M, Z to Delancey-Essex Streets. **Open** 7.30pm-1am daily. **Cover** $7-$20. **No credit cards.**

Immortalised by a Jeff Buckley live recording (made at an earlier incarnation), this unassuming little Lower East Side space mainly schedules local indie bands, many more earnest than good. One nice aspect is that, while close enough to walk to Ludlow Street, down here things are quite peaceful and untrafficked.

S.O.B.'s

204 Varick Street, at Houston Street (1-212 243 4940/www.sobs.com). Subway: 1 to Houston Street. **Box office** 11am-6pm Mon-Sat. **Tickets** $10-$25. **Credit** AmEx, DC, Disc, MC, V (food and bar only).
The titular sounds of Brazil are just some of many global genres that keep this Tribeca spot hopping. Hip hop, soul, reggae and Latin beats figure into the mix, with Seu Jorge, Zap Mama, Vivian Green and Hugh Masekela each appearing of late. Careful at the bar – drinks are very highly priced. But the sharp-looking clientele doesn't seem to mind.

Southpaw

125 Fifth Avenue, between Sterling & St Johns Places, Park Slope, Brooklyn (1-718 230 0236/ www.spsounds.com). Subway: B, Q, 2, 3, 4, 5 to Atlantic Avenue; D, M, N, R to Pacific Street. **Shows** Times vary. **Tickets** $7-$20. **No credit cards.**
Another cool space that's far enough out of Manhattan to ensure you'll never come just to chill out, but only to see someone specific. Which is hardly a problem, since the calendar welcomes prime outfits that would play in slightly larger Manhattan rooms, including Sharon Jones and the Dap-Kings, Prefuse 73, the Coup and Howe Gelb. Like its Park Slope neighbourhood, Southpaw tends to draw cool, mellow audiences, and with all this elbow room, getting to the (huge!) bar is hardly an issue.

Theater at Madison Square Garden

Seventh Avenue, between 31st & 33rd Streets (1-212 465 6741/www.thegarden.com). Subway: A, C, E, 1, 2, 3 to 34th Street-Penn Station. **Box office** noon-6pm Mon-Sat. **Tickets** vary. **Credit** AmEx, DC, Disc, MC, V.

This smaller space within the Garden has better sound than the arena. The Theater has hosted world-music celebrations, as well as mainstream hip hop and the annual music festival known as the Jammys.

Tonic

107 Norfolk Street, between Delancey & Rivington Streets (1-212 358 7503/www.tonicnyc.com). Subway: F to Delancey Street; J, M, Z to Delancey-Essex Streets. **Shows** Doors open at 7.30pm. **Cover** $5-$40. **No credit cards.**

After nearly closing shop a couple of years back, Tonic hurtles on as the home of New York's avant-garde, creative and experimental music scenes. On any night you might find challenging experimenters (Tim Barnes, Okkyung Lee or members of Sonic Youth), folkies old and new (Michael Hurley, Entrance) or local rock talent (Cordero, Jennifer O'Connor). In Subtonic (*see p294*), the basement lounge, guests can loll around on banquettes built into giant former wine casks on weekends, as DJs spin hip and edgy sounds, new and old.

Town Hall

123 W 43rd Street, between Sixth & Seventh Avenues (1-212 997 1003/www.the-townhallnyc. org). Subway: B, D, F, V to 42nd Street-Bryant Park; N, Q, R, W to 42nd Street; S, 1, 2, 3, 7 to 42nd Street-Times Square. **Box office** noon-6pm Mon-Sat. **Tickets** $15-$85. **Credit** AmEx, MC, V ($1 surcharge).

Acoustics at the 'people's auditorium' are superb, and there's no doubting the gravitas of Town Hall's surroundings. The Fiery Furnaces, Cat Power and T Bone Burnett have each put on shows here in recent times, and the Broadway by the Year series brings in the best standards and stars from the nearby Great White Way.

Dropping bombs

A Brooklyn-based hip hop crew that's keeping it real.

The term 'Brooklyn rapper' might call to mind illustrious former drug peddlers such as Jay-Z and the Notorious BIG. But Baje One and Krayo, two members of the borough's mostly white hip hop crew **Nuclear Family**, are just normal dudes. 'Most neighbourhoods have a few drug dealers, but listening to mainstream hip hop, you'd think it was everyone,' Krayo says over a BLT. 'Where's the regular guy?'

It's a good question, and Nuclear Family is answering it. The seven-member collective of long-time friends ranging in age from 24 to 29, came together as teenagers in the mid 1990s to create a platform for their various musical projects, all focused on innovative beats and rhymes about everyday life. They're not flashy like Diddy, preachy like Kweli or whiny like Eminem. They're wacky, even a little dorky, and have their own down-to-earth style that captures the concerns of the average schmo. 'Some artists want to be so hip hop,' says Baje One (real name Mike Tumbarello). 'They end up in this narrow mould, neglecting the really interesting parts of their lives.' He turns to Krayo (aka Justin Cox) for back-up. 'Look,' Krayo says, 'there is a part of me that smokes blunts and drinks 40s, but I wouldn't write a whole record about that corny shit.'

Nuclear Family's latest offshoot, Junk Science, made up of Baje One and old friend DJ Snafu (James Christensen), furthers the crew's philosophy with the recently released album *Feeding Einstein*. The raps – which feature contributing artists – are mostly on day-to-day matters like work and money problems, and *Einstein* carries a geek factor true to its moniker.

'People talk about preserving hip hop,' Krayo says. 'But we're too young to remember when it started.' Baje One chimes in: 'The way to preserve it is to do something new with it. Don't try to do what you hear on the radio.' He points to a framed poem by an elementary-school student hanging on the wall, which reminds him of the dangers of conformity; 'Music has changed me,' it reads. 'I dream about being 50 Cent.' Baje One shakes his head. 'How fucked up is that?'

Carnegie Hall. *See p322.*

Trash

256 Grand Street, between Driggs Avenue & Roebling Street, Williamsburg, Brooklyn (1-718 599 1000/www.thetrashbar.com). Subway: L to Bedford Avenue. **Shows** Doors open at 8pm. **Cover** $6-$8. **No credit cards.**
Formerly Luxx, one of Brooklyn's central locations for the late genre known as Electroclash, this slightly grubby club tore down the glitzy wallpaper in 2005, and returned to booking fun rock in its blisteringly loud, red-lit back room. Two bars and a front room with a pool table make Trash a happening place to, you know, get trashed.

Warsaw at the Polish National Home

261 Driggs Avenue, at Eckford Street, Greenpoint, Brooklyn (1-718-387-0505/www.warsawconcerts. com). Subway: G to Nassau Avenue. **Box office** Tickets for sale at the bar 6pm-midnight Tue-Sun. **Tickets** $15 and up. **Credit** AmEx, MC, V.
Warsaw is a nice mid-size venue in Greenpoint. The sound isn't fantastic and getting here from Manhattan can be a chore (the best bet is to take the L train to Bedford Avenue and then walk). For Brooklynites, however, the club offers a good chance to see bands like the Walkmen or Liars without leaving the borough.

Webster Hall

125 E 11th Street, between Third & Fourth Avenues (1-212 353 1600/www.websterhall.com). Subway: L to Third Avenue; N, Q, R, W, 4, 5, 6 to 14th Street-Union Square. **Shows** Visit website for hours. **Tickets** free-$30. **Credit** AmEx, DC, MC, V.
Even if the bookings come in at a relative trickle, the addition of Webster Hall to the local scene provides a great-sounding alternative for bands (not to men-

tion fans) who might have had their fill of comparably sized Irving Plaza. The folks who run Bowery Ballroom and Mercury Lounge provide the bookings here, which is why the schedule features bands that have grown out of those rooms (the Flaming Lips, the Fiery Furnaces, Iron and Wine). As indie rock grows in popularity, its performance spaces are ballooning – which is all well and good, but be sure to show up early if you want to see much.

Jazz & experimental

Barbès

376 9th Street, at Sixth Avenue, Park Slope, Brooklyn (1-718 965 9177/www.barbes brooklyn.com). Subway: F to Seventh Avenue. **Tickets** free-$8. **Credit** Disc, MC, V (bar only).
Show up early if you want to get into Park Slope's global-bohemian club (and you do) – it's tiny. This boîte, run by musically inclined French expats, brings in jazz of the traditional swing and more daring stripes, plus world-music-derived hybrids (Las Rubias del Norte) and acts that are often uncategorisable (One Ring Zero).

Birdland

315 W 44th Street, between Eighth & Ninth Avenues (1-212 581 3080/www.birdlandjazz.com). Subway: A, C, E to 42nd Street-Port Authority. **Box office** Reservations required; call venue. **Tickets** $20-$50, $10 food and drink minimum. **Credit** AmEx, DC, Disc, MC, V.
The name means jazz, but, perhaps in deference to its Theater District digs, Birdland is also a prime destination for cabaret. The jazz names that pass through are unimpeachable (Kurt Elling, Jim Hall, Paquito D'Rivera) and the cabaret stars glowing

Arts & Entertainment

(Christine Andreas, Christine Ebersole). Residencies are among the better ones in town (the Chico O'Farrill Afro-Cuban Jazz Orchestra owns Sundays and David Ostwald's Louis Armstrong Centennial Band hits on Tuesdays; Mondays find cabaret's waggish Jim Caruso and his Cast Party).

Blue Note

131 W 3rd Street, between MacDougal Street & Sixth Avenue (1-212 475 8592/www.bluenote. net). Subway: A, B, C, D, E, F, V to W 4th Street. **Box office** Call or visit website for reservations. **Tickets** $10-$65, $5 food and drink minimum. **Credit** AmEx, DC, MC, V.

On a bustling, slightly seedy block sits the Blue Note, which prides itself on being 'the jazz capital of the world'. Bona fide musical titans (Cecil Taylor, Abbey Lincoln) rub up against hot young talents (Matthew Shipp, Jason Lindner) on the calendar, while the tables in the club get patrons rubbing up against each other. The Late Night Groove series and the Sunday brunches are the best bargain bets.

Carnegie Hall

For listing, see p328.
Carnegie Hall means the big time. In recent years Zankel Hall – a state-of-the-art 599-seat subterranean theatre – has greatly augmented Carnegie's pop, jazz and world-music offerings. Between them both, the complex has welcomed Dave Brubeck, Wayne Shorter, Brad Mehldau and Fred Hersch of late, among many other high-wattage names. **Photo** *p321.*

Cornelia Street Café

29 Cornelia Street, between Bleecker & W 4th Streets (1-212 989 9319/www.corneliastreetcafe. com). Subway: A, B, C, D, E, F, V to W 4th Street. **Cover** $8-$12, $6 drink minimum; doors open at 9pm. **Credit** AmEx, DC, MC, V.

Upstairs is a cosy little Greenwich Village eaterie. Go downstairs and you'll find an even cosier music space that hosts adventurous jazz, poetry, world music and folk. Regular mini-festivals spotlight blues, songwriters and new concert-theatre works.

Iridium Jazz Club

1650 Broadway, at 51st Street (1-212 582 2121/ www.iridiumjazzclub.com). Subway: 1 to 50th Street. **Box office** Reservations recommended; call venue. **Tickets** $25-$35, $10 food/drink minimum. **Credit** AmEx, DC, Disc, MC, V.

One of the nicer places to dine while being hit with top-shelf jazz, both from household names and cats who are more for insiders, Iridium is located smack bang in the middle of Broadway's bright lights. Recent guests include Art Ensemble of Chicago, Mose Allison, and Archie Shepp and Roswell Rudd. Monday nights belong to wise-cracking guitar legend Les Paul; Tuesdays mean the Mingus Big Band.

55 Bar

55 Christopher Street, between Seventh Avenue South & Waverly Place (1-212 929 9883/www.55 bar.com). Subway: 1 to Christopher Street-Sheridan

Square. **Shows** Doors open 5.30pm Fri, Sat; 9.30pm Sun. **Cover** free-$15. **No credit cards.**
Though tiny (oh, call it intimate), this Prohibition-era dive is now one of New York's most artist friendly rooms, thanks to its knowledgeable, appreciative audience. You can catch emerging talent almost every night at the free-of-charge early shows, while late sets regularly feature established artists, including Chris Potter and Mike Stern.

Jazz at Lincoln Center

Broadway, at 60th Street (1-212 258 9595/ www.jazzatlincolncenter.org). Subway: A, B, C, D, 1 to 59th Street-Columbus Circle. **Shows** 7.30pm, 9.30pm. **Box office** Call for reservations. **Tickets** $10-$30 plus food and drink minimums; call for details. **Credit** AmEx, MC, V.

Seductively lit, decorated with elegant photography and blessed with clear sight lines and a gorgeous view of 59th Street and Central Park South, Dizzy's Club Coca-Cola: Jazz at Lincoln Center might be a Hollywood cinematographer's ideal vision of what a Manhattan jazz club ought to be. The swanky, intimate club – a regular hang for some of the most outstanding players in the business – is a class act in all but its clunky, commercialised name. **Photo** *p323.*

Jazz Gallery

290 Hudson Street, between Dominick & Spring Streets (1-212 242 1063/www.jazzgallery.org). Subway: C, E to Spring Street. **Shows** 9pm, 10.30pm. **Box office** Reservations strongly recommended; call venue. **Tickets** $12-$15. **No credit cards.**

The fact that there's no bar here should be a tip-off: the Jazz Gallery is a place to witness true works of art, from the sometimes-obscure but always interesting jazzers who play the club (Henry Threadgill, Steve Coleman) to the photos and arte-facts displayed on the walls. The tiny room's acoustics are sublime.

Jazz Standard

116 E 27th Street, between Park Avenue South & Lexington Avenue (1-212 576 2232/www.jazz standard.com). Subway: 6 to 28th Street. **Box office** Call for reservations. **Tickets** $15-$30. **Credit** AmEx, DC, Disc, MC, V.

The room's airy, multi-tiered floor plan makes for splendid sight lines to match the sterling sound quality, and in keeping with the rib-sticking chow offered upstairs (at restaurateur Danny Meyer's Blue Smoke barbecue joint), the jazz is often of the groovy, hard-swinging variety, with musicians such as pianist Vijay Iyer and tenorist David Murray. Pianist Fred Hersch's annual series of duets is a delight.

Lenox Lounge

288 Malcolm X Boulevard (Lenox Avenue), between 124th & 125th Streets (1-212 427 0253/ www.lenoxlounge.com). Subway: 2, 3 to 125th Street. **Shows** 9pm, 10.30pm, midnight (subject to change; call ahead to check). **Cover** $5-$20 plus 2-drink minimum. **Credit** Disc, MC, V.

Jazz at Lincoln Center. *See p322.*

This classy art deco lounge in Harlem once hosted Billie Holiday and has drawn stars since the late '30s. Saxist Patience Higgins's Sugar Hill Jazz Quartet jams into the wee hours on Mondays. *See also p225.*

Merkin Concert Hall
For listing, see p328.
Just north of Lincoln Center is this home for classical and jazz composers. Merkin's polished digs also provide an intimate setting for chamber music and jazz, folk, cabaret and experimental performers. The New York Guitar Festival mounts elaborate multi-artist tribute concerts that feature the cream of the six-string crop; other series include the New York Festival of Song, WNYC's New Sounds Live and Broadway Close Up.

92nd Street Y
1395 Lexington Avenue, at 92nd Street (1-212 415 5500/www.92y.org). Subway: 6 to 92nd Street.
Box office 9am-9pm Mon-Thur; 9am-5pm Fri; 6-9pm Sat. **Tickets** $20 and up. **Credit** AmEx, MC, V.
Best known for the series Jazz in July (now directed by pianist Bill Charlap) and Lyrics & Lyricists, the uptown Y's schedule extends to gospel, mainstream jazz and singer-songwriters. The small, handsome theatre provides a fine setting for the sophisticated fare that's offered here.

Smoke
2751 Broadway, between 105th & 106th Streets (1-212 864 6662/www.smokejazz.com). Subway: 1 to 103rd Street. **Shows** 9pm, 11pm, 12.30am Mon-Sat; 6pm Sun. **Cover** free, $10 drink minimum Mon-Thur, Sun; $15-$25 Fri, Sat. **Credit** Disc, MC, V.
Not unlike a swanky living room, Smoke is a classy little joint that acts as a haven for local jazz legends and touring artists looking to play an intimate space.

Early in the week, evenings are themed: on Sunday, it's Latin jazz; Tuesday, organ jazz. On weekends, internationally renowned jazzers (Hilton Ruiz, Tom Harrell, Eddie Henderson) hit the stage, relishing the opportunity to play informal gigs uptown.

The Stone
Avenue C, at 2nd Street (no phone/www.thestone nyc.com). Subway: F, V to Lower East Side-Second Avenue. **Shows** Doors open at 8pm; closed Mon. **Cover** $10. **No credit cards**.
Don't call sax star John Zorn's non-profit venture a 'club'. You'll find no food or drinks here, and no nonsense, either – the Stone is an art space dedicated to 'the experimental and the avant-garde'. If you're down for some rigorously adventurous sounds – Anthony Coleman, Okkyung Lee, Tony Conrad, and the ever-shifting constellation of sterling players that live here and pass through – Zorn has made it easy: no advance ticket sales; all ages are admitted (kids 19 and under get discounts); and the bookings are left to a different artist-cum-curator each month.

Sweet Rhythm
88 Seventh Avenue South, between Bleecker & Grove Streets (1-212 255 3626/www.sweetrhythmny.com). Subway: 1 to Christopher Street-Sheridan Square. **Shows** 8pm, 10pm Mon-Thur, Sun; 8pm, 10pm, midnight Fri, Sat. **Cover** $10-$25 ($10 minimum per person per set). **Credit** AmEx, DC, MC, V.
In the same location as the legendary Sweet Basil you'll now find Sweet Rhythm. More of a destination to see a particular artist than a hangout (due to the uninviting seating plan). While a variety of jazz sounds dominates (swing, standards, bop) and big names such as Sonny Fortune and Rashied Ali still

drop in occasionally (not to mention Jane Ira Bloom and Carl Allen), blues and world music are also to hand. Tuesday nights are devoted to vocalists.

Swing 46

349 W 46th Street, between Eighth & Ninth Avenues (1-212 262 9554/www.swing46.com). Subway: A, C, E to 42nd Street-Port Authority. **Shows** 9.30pm. **Cover** $5-$12. **Credit** AmEx, DC, Disc, MC, V.
Swing isn't a trend at this supper club – whether peppy or sappy, these cats mean it. Bands (with names like the Flying Neutrinos and the Flipped Fedoras) that jump, jive and wail await you, so be sure to wear your dancin' shoes. Dance lessons are available for the inexperienced.

Tonic

For listing, see p320.

Village Vanguard

178 Seventh Avenue South, at Perry Street (1-212 255 4037/www.villagevanguard.com). Subway: A, C, E, 1, 2, 3 to 14th Street; L to Eighth Avenue. **Shows** 9pm, 11pm Mon-Thur, Sun; 9pm, 11pm, 12.30am Fri, Sat. **Tickets** $20 plus $10 drink minimum; call or visit website for reservations. **Credit** AmEx, MC, V (online purchases only).
Over 70 years old and still going strong, the Village Vanguard is one of New York's real jazz meccas. History surrounds you here: John Coltrane, Miles Davis and Bill Evans have all grooved in this hallowed hall, and the walls are lined with photos and artefacts. The big names, old and new, continue to fill the Vanguard's line-up, and the 16-piece Vanguard Jazz Orchestra has been the Monday night regular for almost 40 years. Reservations are strongly recommended, and note that the Vanguard takes only cash or travellers' cheques at the door.

Zebulon

258 Wythe Avenue, between Metropolitan Avenue & North Third Street, Williamsburg, Brooklyn (1-718 218 6934/www.zebuloncafeconcert.com). Subway: L to Bedford Avenue. **Shows** Doors open at 4pm. **Cover** free. **Credit** AmEx.
For years people have been talking about Williamsburg as NYC's leading hipster enclave. But how hip could it have been without a killer jazz spot like Zebulon? Emphasising young firebrands (like Gold Sparkle Band and Tyshawn Sorey) over the establishment, Zebulon also welcomes the daring wing of the local rock scene (such as the great singer-songwriter Hannah Marcus). While the café opens in the afternoon, don't expect live music till closer to 10pm.

Blues, country & folk

BB King Blues Club & Grill

For listing, see p313.

Paddy Reilly's Music Bar

519 Second Avenue, at 29th Street (1-212 686 1210/www.paddyreillys.com). Subway: 6 to 28th
Street. **Shows** 9.30pm Mon-Thur; 10.30pm Fri, Sat; 4-8pm Sun. **Cover** $5-$7. **Credit** AmEx, Disc, MC, V.
Patrons flock to this Gramercy institution for the silky Guinness, the house's only draft; but they stay for the lively Irish folk and rock acts that bring the room to life. Popular pub-rockers the Prodigals are regulars on Fridays, and the rest of the weekend features Irish-rock and traditional jam sessions.

Rodeo Bar & Grill

375 Third Avenue, at 27th Street (1-212 683 6500/www.rodeobar.com). Subway: 6 to 28th Street. **Shows** 10pm Mon-Sat; 9pm Sun. **Cover** free. **Credit** AmEx, DC, Disc, MC, V (bar only).
The unpretentious crowd and roadhouse atmosphere, not to mention the lack of a cover charge, make the Rodeo the city's best roots club, with a steady stream of rockabilly, country and related sounds. Rockabilly filly Rosie Flores is a regular, and bluegrass scion Chris Scruggs has visited from Nashville to play his '50s-style rock. Watch out for the peanut shells spread across the floor, and the frat boys from the (dreaded) Murray Hill 'hood.

Latin, reggae & world

BAMcafé at Brooklyn Academy of Music

For listing, see p327 Brooklyn Academy of Music.
Among the cornucopia of live-entertainment programmes found at BAM is the BAMcafé above the lobby, which comes to life on weekend nights with country, spoken word, hip hop, world music and more, by performers such as Son de Madre and Manze. The NextNext series, which began in 2002, focuses on performers in their 20s.

Canal Room

For listing, see p314.

Copacabana

560 W 34th Street, between Tenth & Eleventh Avenues (1-212 239 2672/www.copacabanany. com). Subway: A, C, E to 34th Street-Penn Station. **Cover** $10-$40, $30 at tables; doors open 6pm Tue; 11pm Fri, Sat. **Credit** AmEx, Disc, MC, V.
The city's most iconic destination for Latin music has now become a fully fledged party palace. It's still a prime stop for salsa, cumbia and merengue, but in addition to booking world-renowned stars (Ruben Blades, El Gran Combo, and Tito Nieves with Conjunto Clasico), the Copa now has an alternative nook called the House Room, where dancers can spin to disco, house and Latin freestyle.

Nublu

62 Avenue C, between 4th & 5th Streets (no phone/ www.nublu.net). Subway: F, V to Lower East Side-Second Avenue. **Shows** Doors open at 8pm. **Cover** $5-$10. **No credit cards.**
Inversely proportional to its size – not to mention the seemingly out-of-the-way location deep in Alphabet City – has been Nublu's prominence on the local globalist club scene. A pressure cooker

Nublu. *See p325.*

of creativity, Nublu gave rise to the Brazilian Girls, who started jamming at one late-night session and haven't stopped yet, as well as starting NYC's romance with the northern Brazilian style *forró*. Even on weeknights, events usually start no earlier than 10pm and can run into the wee hours – but if you show up early (and find the unmarked door), the bar is well stocked with wine selections, among other beverages, and the staff as warm as the music.

S.O.B.'s
For listing, see p319.

Zinc Bar
90 W Houston Street, between La Guardia Place & Thompson Street (1-212 477 8337/www.zinc bar.com). Subway: A, B, C, D, E, F, V to W 4th Street. **Open** 6pm-3.30am daily. **Cover** $5. **Credit** AmEx, DC, Disc, MC, V (bar only).
Located where Greenwich Village meets Soho, Zinc Bar is the place to hoot and holler with diehard night owls. The after-hours atmosphere is enhanced by a cool mix of African, flamenco, jazz and samba bands.

Summer venues

Castle Clinton
Battery Park, Battery Place, at State Street (1-212 835 2789). Subway: R, W to Rector Street; 1 to South Ferry; 4, 5 to Bowling Green. **Tickets** free.
One of the nicest views in all of Manhattan is found at its bottom tip, in the heart of Battery Park. This historic fort welcomes established stars whenever the weather is warm, with special events often found on 4 and 14 July. Lyle Lovett, Mates of State, Okkervil River and the Dave Holland Quartet have

all performed for free in the evening air here, but note: tickets do have to be picked up in person on the day of a show, and they always go fast.

Central Park SummerStage
For listing, see p262.
Now in its 21st year, the City Parks Foundation fills summers in the park with just about every sound under the sun. This New York institution has an ear for world music of all types – MIA, Seu Jorge and Amadou and Mariam have all played in recent years – as have Bonnie Raitt, Matthew Shipp and Lady Sovereign. Many of the shows are free, with a handful of high-priced benefits covering for them.

Giants Stadium
For listing, see p333 Meadowlands Sports Complex.
At New Jersey's Giants Stadium you can catch Hot97's annual Summer Jam, one of the biggest hip hop shows in the country, as well as other biggies like the Rolling Stones and Bruce Springsteen.

Lincoln Center Plaza
For listing, see p328 Lincoln Center.
Lincoln Center's multi-tiered floor plan allows for several outdoor stages in one sprawling facility, but the most popular venues are the North Plaza, which houses the well-loved Midsummer Night Swing dance concerts (*see p262*), and the Damrosch Park Bandshell, which rolls out the red carpet for the likes of sax icon Sonny Rollins. When the weather's hot, a wide variety of music from around the world creates a rich global feast.

Nikon at Jones Beach Theatre
Jones Beach, Long Island (1-516 221 1000/ www.tommyhilfigerjonesbeach.com). Travel: LIRR from Penn Station, Seventh Avenue at 32nd Street,

to Freeport, then take the Jones Beach bus. **Box office** 10am-9pm Mon (show days); 10am-6pm Tue-Sat; noon-6pm Sun; open till 9pm show days. **Tickets** $30-$135. **Credit** AmEx, MC, V.

It's a long haul, especially if you don't have your own wheels, and the sound is generally indifferent. Still, you can't beat the open-air setting at this beachside amphitheatre (which before switching sponsors was known as Tommy Hilfiger at Jones Beach Theater). From July to September, the biggest tours stop here, including package shows like Ozzfest and Projekt Revolution, as well as veterans such as Tom Petty, younger singers like Fiona Apple and soul stars both current (Erykah Badu) and classic (Anita Baker).

Prospect Park Bandshell

For listing, see p262 Celebrate Brooklyn! Performing Arts Festival.

Prospect Park Bandshell is to Brooklynites what Central Park SummerStage is to Manhattanites: the place to hear cool tunes in the great outdoors. Adventurous programming for the summer's Celebrate Brooklyn! Performing Arts Festival (*see p262*) runs the global gamut, from exotic (Africa Day) to less so (Canada Day). Of course, everything from blues titans (Bettye LaVette and Charlie Musselwhite) and Latin sounds (Eddie Palmieri, Milly Quezada) to classic movie-and-music pairings round out the calendar. Even Prince has stopped by.

Classical

The buzz in New York City's classical music community is largely focused upon its two major opera houses: the **Metropolitan Opera**, under the leadership of new general manager Peter Gelb, has increased its emphasis on bold, new productions and directors with fresh ideas – some of them imported from worlds of dance and film – while continuing its long-held tradition of presenting the world's biggest stars. Meanwhile, **New York City Opera** faces the departure of its general manager, Paul Kellogg, in June 2007, not to mention the looming threat of a more innovative Met. Elsewhere, it's business as usual: **Carnegie Hall**, on Clive Gillinson's watch, continues to balance solid traditional values in the venerable Issac Stern Auditorium with an eclectic breadth of programming downstairs in Zankel Hall. And whatever the critics may have to say about veteran conductor Lorin Maazel's tenure at the **New York Philharmonic**, there's virtually no question that the orchestra is playing at its highest level in years. And all over the city, a thousand flowers continue to bloom: **Gotham Chamber Opera** has arisen to fill a vital if specialised niche in the repertoire, while the newly opened **Gilder Lehrman Hall** provides

an elegant oasis of intimacy in this roaring, bustling metropolis. The standard New York concert season lasts from September to June, but there are plenty of off-season events and performances. In summer, box office hours may change so call ahead or check websites for times.

Tickets

You can buy tickets directly from most venues, whether by phone, online or at the box office. However, a surcharge is generally added to tickets not bought in person. For more ticket information, *see p382.*

CarnegieCharge

1-212 247 7800/www.carnegiehall.org. **Box office** By phone 8am-8pm daily. **Fee** $6 surcharge per ticket. **Credit** AmEx, DC, Disc, MC, V.

Centercharge

1-212 721 6500. **Box office** By phone 10am-8pm Mon-Sat; noon-8pm Sun. **Fee** $5.50 surcharge per ticket. **Credit** AmEx, Disc, MC, V.

Centercharge sells tickets for events at Alice Tully Hall, Avery Fisher Hall and the Juilliard School, as well as for the Lincoln Center Out of Doors Festival.

Metropolitan Opera

1-212 362 6000/www.metoperafamily.org/met opera/home.aspx. **Box office** By phone 10am-8pm Mon-Sat; noon-6pm Sun. **Fee** $5.50 surcharge per ticket. **Credit** AmEx, Disc, MC, V.

The Met sells tickets for performances held in its opera house (*see p329*), including those of the resident American Ballet Theatre.

Backstage passes

Curious music lovers can go behind the scenes at several of the city's major concert venues. Backstage at the Met (1-212 769 7020, www.met operafamily.org/education/calendar/backstage. aspx) shows you around the famous house during the opera season, which runs from September to May; Lincoln Center Tours (1-212 875 5350) escorts you inside Avery Fisher and Alice Tully Halls, as well as the New York State Theater; Carnegie Hall (1-212 247 7800) guides you through what is perhaps the world's most famous concert hall. For a $15 fee, you may also sit in on rehearsals of the New York Philharmonic (1-212 875 5656), usually held on the Thursday before a concert.

Concert halls

Brooklyn Academy of Music

30 Lafayette Avenue, between Ashland Place & St Felix Street, Fort Greene, Brooklyn (1-718 636 4100/www.bam.org). Subway: B, Q, 2, 3, 4, 5 to Atlantic Avenue; C to Lafayette Street; D, M, N,

R to Pacific Street; G to Fulton Street. **Box office** noon-6pm Mon-Sat; noon-4pm Sun (show days). **Admission** varies. **Credit** AmEx, MC, V.

America's oldest academy for the performing arts continues to present some of the freshest and most adventurous programming in the city. Every autumn and winter, the Next Wave Festival provides an overview of avant-garde music, dance and theatre, while spring brings lauded European opera productions to town. The BAM Harvey Theater, located nearby, offers a smaller, more atmospheric setting for new creations by composers such as Tan Dun and Meredith Monk, as well as innovative stagings of baroque opera. Meanwhile, the resident Brooklyn Philharmonic Orchestra continues to provide innovative programming under the direction of its ambitious young conductor, Michael Christie.

Carnegie Hall

154 W 57th Street, at Seventh Avenue (1-212 247 7800/www.carnegiehall.org). Subway: N, Q, R, W to 57th Street. **Box office** 11am-6pm Mon-Sat; noon-6pm Sun. **Admission** varies. **Credit** AmEx, DC, Disc, MC, V.

The stars – both soloists and orchestras – in the classical music firmament continue to shine most brightly in the Isaac Stern Auditorium, inside this renowned concert hall. Still, it's the spunky upstart Zankel Hall that has generated the most buzz; the below-street-level space offers an eclectic mix of classical, contemporary, jazz, pop and world music. Next door, Weill Recital Hall hosts intimate concerts and chamber music programmes.

Florence Gould Hall

French Institute Alliance Française, 55 E 59th Street, between Madison & Park Avenues (1-212 355 6160/www.fiaf.org). Subway: N, R, W to Fifth Avenue-59th Street; 4, 5, 6 to 59th Street. **Box office** 11am-7pm Tue-Fri; 11am-3pm Sat. **Admission** $10-$35. **Credit** AmEx, MC, V.

Programming in this small, comfortable hall has a decidedly French tone, in both artists and repertoire.

Merkin Concert Hall

Kaufman Center, 129 W 67th Street, between Broadway & Amsterdam Avenue (1-212 501 3330/ www.kaufman-center.org). Subway: 1 to 66th Street-Lincoln Center. **Box office** noon-7pm Mon-Thur, Sun; noon-4pm Fri. **Admission** $10-$50. **Credit** AmEx, MC, V (advance purchases only).

Tucked on a side street in the shadow of Lincoln Center, this unimposing gem of a concert hall offers a robust mix of early music and avant-garde programming, plus an increasing amount of jazz, folk and some more eclectic fare. Regular performances sponsored by WNYC-FM afford opportunities for casual interaction with composers and performers.

New Jersey Performing Arts Center

For listing, see p318.

It only takes around 15 or 20 minutes to reach Newark's sumptuous performing arts complex from Midtown, and the rewards are well worth the trip. Tickets for big-name acts that are sold out at Manhattan venues can often be found here, and performances may be slightly different to those in concurrent Gotham gigs.

92nd Street Y

For listing, see p323.

The YMCA has always stood for solidly traditional orchestral, solo and chamber masterpieces. But it also fosters the careers of young musicians and explores European and Jewish-American music traditions, with innovative, far-reaching results.

Lincoln Center

Built in the 1960s, this massive complex is the nexus of Manhattan's performing arts scene. Lincoln Center hosts lectures and symposia in the Rose Building, in addition to events in the main halls: Alice Tully Hall, Avery Fisher Hall, Metropolitan Opera House, New York State Theater, and the Vivian Beaumont and Mitzi E Newhouse Theaters. Also situated here are the Juilliard School (*see p332*) and the Fiorello H La Guardia High School of Music & Art and Performing Arts (108 Amsterdam Avenue, between 64th & 65th Streets, www.laguardiahs.org), which frequently hosts professional performances.

Big stars like Valery Gergiev, Sir Colin Davis and the Emerson Quartet are Lincoln Center's meat and potatoes, but lately the great divide between the flagship Great Performers season and the relatively audacious, multidisciplinary Lincoln Center Out of Doors Festival (*see p264*) has begun to narrow, thanks to fresher programming. Even the Mostly Mozart festival (*see p264*), a long-time summer staple, has begun drawing a younger, hipper crowd with its progressive bookings and innovative artistic juxtapositions.

Lincoln Center

Columbus Avenue, at 65th Street (1-212 546 2656/www.lincolncenter.org). Subway: 1 to 66th Street-Lincoln Center.

This is the main entry point for Lincoln Center, but the venues that follow are spread out across the square of blocks from 62nd to 66th Streets, between Amsterdam and Columbus Avenues.

Alice Tully Hall

1-212 875 5050. **Box office** 11am-6pm Mon-Sat; noon-8pm Sun. **Admission** free-$75. **Credit** AmEx, Disc, MC, V.

Home to the Chamber Music Society of Lincoln Center (1-212 875 5788, www.chambermusicsociety. org), Alice Tully Hall somehow manages to make its auditorium of 1,096 seats feel cosy. It has no centre aisle, and the seating offers decent legroom. Its Art of the Song series is among Lincoln Center's most inviting offerings.

Metropolitan Opera House.

Avery Fisher Hall

1-212 875 5030. **Box office** 10am-6pm Mon-Sat; noon-6pm Sun. **Admission** $20-$114. **Credit** AmEx, Disc, MC, V.

This handsome, comfortable 2,700-seat hall is the headquarters of the New York Philharmonic (1-212 875 5656, www.nyphilharmonic.org), the country's oldest symphony orchestra (founded in 1842) and one of its finest. The sound, which ranges from good to atrocious depending on who you ask, stands to be improved. Inexpensive early-evening 'rush hour' concerts and open rehearsals are presented on a regular basis. The Great Performers series features top international soloists and ensembles.

Metropolitan Opera House

1-212 362 6000/www.metopera.org. **Box office** 10am-8pm Mon-Sat; noon-6pm Sun. **Admission** $25-$320. **Credit** AmEx, Disc, MC, V.

The Met is the grandest of the Lincoln Center buildings, so it's a spectacular place to see and hear opera. It hosts the Metropolitan Opera from September to May, and major visiting companies during the summer. Opera's biggest stars (think Domingo, Fleming and Gheorghiu) appear here regularly, and artistic director James Levine has turned the orchestra into a true symphonic force. Audiences are knowledgeable and fiercely partisan, with subscriptions remaining in families for generations. Still, the Met has become more inclusive; digital English-language subtitles, which appear on screens affixed to railings in front of each seat, are convenient for the novice and unobtrusive to their more seasoned neighbour. Tickets are expensive, and unless you can afford good seats, the view won't be great; standing room-only tickets start at $15, and you'll have to queue on Saturday morning to buy them. At least you'll be able to see the eye-popping, gasp-inducing sets (by directors such as Zeffirelli) that remain the gold standard here.

New York State Theater

1-212 870 5570. **Box office** 10am-7.30pm Mon; 10am-8.30pm Tue-Sat; 11.30am-7.30pm Sun. **Admission** $16-$120. **Credit** AmEx, DC, Disc, MC, V.

NYST houses the New York City Ballet (www.nycballet.com) as well as the New York City Opera (www.nycopera.com). The opera company has tried to overcome its second-best reputation by being both ambitious and defiantly populist. Rising young American singers often take their first bows at City Opera (many of them eventually make the trek across the plaza to the Met), where casts and productions tend to be younger and sexier than those of its more patrician counterpart. Known for its fierce commitment to the unconventional – from modern American works and musical-theatre productions to intriguing Handel stagings and forgotten *bel canto* gems – City Opera is considerably cooler than its neighbour and about half the price. But truly splashy grand spectacle remains the province of the Met.

Walter Reade Theater

1-212 875 5600/www.filmlinc.com. **Box office** noon-6pm Mon-Fri; 30mins before shows Sat, Sun. **Admission** $10; $7 students; $6 members; $5 6-12s. **No credit cards**. For tickets by phone, call 1-212 496 3809.

This theatre's acoustics are less than fabulous; still, the Great Performers series offers Sunday morning events fuelled by pastries and hot beverages sold in the lobby, and composer-lecturer Robert Kapilow's What Makes It Great? series provides an entertaining introduction to major classical works.

Opera

The Metropolitan Opera and the New York City Opera may be the leaders of the pack, but they're hardly the only game in town. Feisty upstarts and long-standing grass-roots companies ensure that Manhattan's operaphiles are among the best served in the world. Call the organisations or visit their websites for information on ticket prices, schedules and venue. Music schools (*see p332*) also have regular opera programmes.

Amato Opera Theater

319 Bowery, at 2nd Street (1-212 228 8200/ www.amato.org). Subway: B, D, F, V to Broadway-Lafayette Street; 6 to Bleecker Street. **Admission** $30; $25 seniors, students, children. **Credit** AmEx, Disc, MC, V.

Music

Arts & Entertainment

New York's beloved mom-and-pop opera shop offers charming, fully staged productions in a theatre that's only 20ft wide – it's almost like watching opera in your living room. The casting can be inconsistent, but many well-established singers have performed here.

American Opera Projects

South Oxford Space, 138 South Oxford Street, between Atlantic Avenue & Hanson Place, Fort Greene, Brooklyn (1-718 398 4024/www.opera projects.org). Subway: B, Q, 2, 3, 4, 5 to Atlantic Avenue; C to Lafayette Avenue; D, M, N, R to Pacific Street; G to Fulton Street. **Admission** varies. **No credit cards.**

American Opera Projects is not so much an opera company as a living, breathing workshop that allows you the opportunity to follow a new work from gestation to completion.

Dicapo Opera Theatre

184 E 76th Street, between Lexington & Third Avenues (1-212 288 9438/www.dicapo.com). Subway: 6 to 77th Street. **Admission** $47.50. **Credit** MC, V.

This top-notch chamber-opera troupe benefits from City Opera-quality singers performing in a delightfully intimate setting in the basement of St Jean Baptiste Church.

Gotham Chamber Opera

Harry de Jur Playhouse, 466 Grand Street, at Pitt Street (1-212 598 0400/www.gothamchamber opera.org). Subway: B, D to Grand Street; F to East Broadway. **Admission** $30-$65. **Credit** AmEx, MC, V.

The newest addition to NYC's lyrical firmament, this fine young company specialises in chamber opera:

not scaled-down versions of big-stage classics, but rather those rarely staged shows specifically designed for smaller forces in intimate settings.

New York Gilbert & Sullivan Players

www.nygasp.org.

Is Victorian camp your vice? This troupe presents a rotating schedule of the Big Three (*HMS Pinafore*, *The Mikado* and *The Pirates of Penzance*), plus lesser-known G&S works. The annual New Year's Eve Champagne Gala is at Symphony Space (*see p331*).

Other venues

Bargemusic

Fulton Ferry Landing, between Old Fulton & Water Streets, Dumbo, Brooklyn (1-718 624 2083/www.bargemusic.org). Subway: A, C to High Street; F to York Street. **Admission** $25-$40. **Credit** MC, V.

This former coffee-bean barge presents four chamber concerts a week – and a great view of the Manhattan skyline. It's a magical experience, but wrap up in winter. When the weather warms, you can enjoy a drink on the upper deck during the concert's intermission.

Frick Collection

For listing, see p139.

Concerts in the Frick Collection's elegantly appointed concert hall are a rare treat, generally featuring lesser-known but nonetheless world-class performers. After holding the line for free concerts far longer than expected, the Frick finally imposed a $20 ticket charge in 2005; ironically, however, this might make it easier to get tickets, which were routinely snatched

Don't miss | Ring Cycle

In the world of opera, one central pillar of the repertoire looms taller than all others: Richard Wagner's *Der Ring des Nibelungen*, a massive, four-night cycle in which mythological gods, fearsome giants and star-crossed warriors fall prey to all-too-human passions and weaknesses. In New York City, a traditional production at the Metropolitan Opera has held the stage since 1987. But in July 2007 the Lincoln Center Festival presents a new vision of the saga, created in 2003 for Russia's most revered troupe, the Kirov Opera of the Mariinsky Theatre in St Petersburg. Two complete *Ring* cycles – one of them in four consecutive evenings, as the composer intended – will be conducted by the troupe's artistic and general director, Valery Gergiev, who is one of the world's foremost conductors.

According to festival director Nigel Redden, the designers of the Kirov *Ring* conceived their colourful vision of Wagner's epic by drawing on a wealth of ancient sources. 'It is a very contemporary *Ring*, which draws from many different aspects of world culture,' he explains. 'Gergiev and designer George Tsypin have drawn on ideas from Russian, Caucasian and especially Scythian folk mythology, but there are traces of voodoo and African elements, and a monumental pre-Christian European element. It is a radically different *Ring* from the Met's traditional production.'

The production has drawn mixed reviews from critics worldwide. Audiences have been less ambivalent: tickets for a Kirov *Ring Cycle* at the Wales Millennium Centre in 2005 sold out in four hours. Planning ahead is essential.

For tickets, visit www.lincolncenter.org.

up by members before the public even had a chance. Concerts are also broadcast live in the Garden Court, where tickets are not required.

Kaye Playhouse
Hunter College, 68th Street, between Park & Lexington Avenues (1-212 772 4448/www. kayeplayhouse.hunter.cuny.edu). Subway: 6 to 68th Street-Hunter College. **Box office** noon-6pm Mon-Sat. **Admission** $10-$70. **Credit** AmEx, MC, V.
Named after its benefactors – comedian Danny Kaye and his wife Sylvia – this refurbished theatre offers an eclectic programme of professional music and dance performances.

Kitchen
For listing, see p352.
A meeting place for the avant-garde in music, dance and theatre for more than 30 years, the Kitchen has played a less prominent role in the local scene during recent seasons. Still, edgy art can be found here, and prices range from free to $25.

Kosciuszko Foundation
15 E 65th Street, at Fifth Avenue (1-212 734 2130/ www.thekf.org). Subway: F to Lexington Avenue-63rd Street; 6 to 68th Street-Hunter College. **Admission** $15-$30. **Credit** MC, V.
This East Side townhouse hosts a chamber music series with a mission: each programme usually features at least one work by a Polish composer. You're less likely to choke on Chopin than to hear something novel by Paderewski or Szymanowski.

Gilder Lehrman Hall
Morgan Library & Museum, 225 Madison Avenue, at 36th Street (1-212 685 0008/www.themorgan. org). Subway: 6 to 33rd Street. **Admission** varies. **Credit** MC, V.
The latest arrival on the New York concert-music scene, this elegant little gem of a concert hall seats between 236 and 295 people: perfect for song recitals and chamber groups. The St Luke's Chamber Ensemble and Glimmerglass Opera were among the first groups to establish a presence here.

Metropolitan Museum of Art
For listing, see p139.
When it comes to established virtuosos and revered chamber ensembles, the Met's programming is consistently rich and full (and ticket prices are correspondingly high). The museum has also established a youthful resident ensemble, Metropolitan Museum Artists in Concert. Seasonally inspired early music concerts are held uptown in the stunning Fuentidueña Chapel at the Cloisters (*see p153*).

Miller Theatre at Columbia University
Broadway, at 116th Street (1-212 854 7799/ www.millertheatre.com). Subway: 1 to 116th Street-Columbia University. **Box office** noon-6pm Mon-Fri. *Show days* 2 hrs before performance. **Admission** $20; $12 students. **Credit** AmEx, MC, V.

Columbia's Miller Theatre has single-handedly made contemporary classical music sexy in New York City. The credit belongs to executive director George Steel, who proved that presenting challenging fare by composers such as Ligeti, Birtwistle and Zorn in a casual, unaffected setting could attract a young audience – and hang on to it. Miller's early music offerings, many of which are conducted by Steel, are also exemplary.

New York Public Library for the Performing Arts
For listing, see p146.
The library's Bruno Walter Auditorium regularly hosts free recitals, solo performances and lectures.

Symphony Space
2537 Broadway, at 95th Street (1-212 864 5400/ www.symphonyspace.org). Subway: 1, 2, 3 to 96th Street. **Box office** noon-6pm Tue-Sat. **Admission** varies ($2 surcharge per order). **Credit** AmEx, MC, V.
Despite its name, Symphony Space provides programming that is anything but symphony-centric: recent seasons have featured saxophone quartets, Indian classical music and politically astute performances of Purcell's *Dido and Aeneas*. The annual Wall to Wall marathons serve up a full day of music – free of charge – focusing on a particular composer, from Bach to Sondheim.

Tenri Cultural Institute
43A W 13th Street, between Fifth & Sixth Avenues (1-212 645 2800/www.tenri.org). Subway: F, V to 14th Street; L to Sixth Avenue; L, N, Q, R, W, 4, 5, 6 to 14th Street-Union Square. **Admission** varies. **No credit cards.**
A non-profit organisation devoted to promoting the Japanese language and appreciation of international art, Tenri also regularly hosts concerts by New York's leading contemporary music ensembles, such as the American Modern Ensemble and counter)induction, in its clean, cosy gallery space.

Tishman Auditorium
New School University, 66 W 12th Street, at Sixth Avenue (1-212 243 9937/Box office 1-212 229 5488). Subway: F, V to 14th Street; L to Sixth Avenue. **Admission** free-$15. **No credit cards.**
The New School's modestly priced Schneider Concerts chamber series features up-and-coming musicians. Established artists also play here – for a fraction of the prices charged elsewhere.

Churches
From sacred to secular, a thrilling variety of music is performed in New York's churches. Superb acoustics, out-of-this-world choirs and serene surroundings make these houses of worship particularly attractive venues. A bonus is that some concerts are free or very cheap.

Cathedral Church of St John the Divine

1047 Amsterdam Avenue, at 112th Street (1-212 316 7540/www.stjohndivine.org). Subway: B, C, 1 to 110th Street-Cathedral Parkway. **Tickets** Call or visit website for details **Admission** varies. **Credit** AmEx, Disc, MC, V.

The stunning neo-Gothic, 3,000-seat sanctuary provides a heavenly atmosphere for the church's own choir, as well as visiting ensembles. Acoustics, however, are murky.

Christ & St Stephen's Church

120 W 69th Street, between Columbus Avenue & Broadway (1-212 787 2755/www.csschurch. org). Subway: 1, 2, 3 to 72nd Street. **Admission** varies. **No credit cards.**

This small, pleasant West Side church offers one of the most diverse concert rosters in the city.

Church of St Ignatius Loyola

980 Park Avenue, at 84th Street (1-212 288 2520/www.saintignatiusloyola.org). Subway: 4, 5, 6 to 86th Street. **Admission** $10-$40. **Credit** AmEx, Disc, MC, V.

The Sacred Music in a Sacred Space series is a high point of Upper East Side music culture. Lincoln Center also holds concerts here, capitalising on the church's fine acoustics and prime location.

Church of the Ascension

12 W 11th Street, between Fifth & Sixth Avenues (1-212 358 1469/www.voicesofascension.org). Subway: N, R, W to 8th Street-NYU. **Admission** $10-$50. **Credit** MC, V (advance purchases only).

There's a first-rate professional choir, the Voices of Ascension, at this little Village church. You can catch the choir at Lincoln Center on occasion, but home turf is the best place to hear it.

Corpus Christi Church

529 W 121st Street, between Amsterdam Avenue & Broadway (1-212 666 9266/www.mb1800.org). Subway: 1 to 116th Street-Columbia University. **Admission** varies. **Credit** MC, V.

Fans of early music can get their fix from Music Before 1800, a series that regularly imports the world's leading antiquarian artists and ensembles.

St Bartholomew's Church

109 E 50th Street, between Park & Lexington Avenues (1-212 378 0248/www.stbarts.org). Subway: E, V to Lexington Avenue-53rd Street; 6 to 51st Street. **Admission** varies. **Credit** AmEx, MC, V.

This magnificent church hosts the Summer Festival of Sacred Music – one of the city's most ambitious choral music series – and fills the rest of the year with performances by resident ensembles and guests.

St Thomas Church Fifth Avenue

1 W 53rd Street, at Fifth Avenue (1-212 757 7013/ www.saintthomaschurch.org). Subway: E, V to Fifth Avenue-53rd Street. **Admission** $15-$70. **Credit** AmEx, MC, V.

The country's only fully accredited choir school for boys keeps the great Anglican choral tradition alive and well in New York. St Thomas's annual performance of Handel's *Messiah* is a must-hear that's well worth the rather steep ticket price.

Trinity Church/St Paul's Chapel

Trinity Church, Broadway, at Wall Street; St Paul's Chapel, Broadway, at Fulton Street (1-212 602 0747/www.trinitywallstreet.org). Subway: R, W to Rector Street; 4, 5 to Wall Street. **Admission** *Concerts at One series* $2 donation. **No credit cards.**

Historic Trinity, situated in the heart of the Financial District, plays host to the inexpensive Concerts at One series. Performances are held (at 1pm) on Mondays at St Paul's Chapel, and on Thursdays at Trinity Church.

Schools

The **Juilliard School** and the **Manhattan School of Music** are renowned for their talented students, faculty and artists in residence, all of whom regularly perform for free or at low cost. Lately, **Mannes College of Music** has made great strides to rise to the same level. Noteworthy music and innovative programming can also be found at several other colleges and schools in the city.

Juilliard School

60 Lincoln Center Plaza, Broadway, at 65th Street (1-212 769 7406/www.juilliard.edu). Subway: 1 to 66th Street-Lincoln Center. **Admission** usually free.

NYC's premier conservatory stages weekly concerts by student soloists, orchestras and chamber ensembles, as well as elaborate opera productions that can often rival many professional presentations.

Manhattan School of Music

120 Claremont Avenue, at 122nd Street (1-212 749 2802 ext 4428/www.msmnyc.edu). Subway: 1 to 125th Street. **Admission** usually free.

The Manhattan School of Music offers masterclasses, recitals and off-site concerts by its students, faculty and visiting professionals. The American String Quartet, which has been in residence here since 1984, gives concerts regularly, while the Augustine Guitar Series includes recitals by top soloists.

Mannes College of Music

150 W 85th Street, between Columbus & Amsterdam Avenues (1-212 5800210/www. mannes.edu). Subway: B, C, 1 to 86th Street. **Admission** usually free.

In addition to student concerts and faculty recitals, Mannes also mounts ambitious, historically themed concert series; the summer is given over to festivals and workshops for instrumentalists. Most of these events provide affordable performances by some of the world's leading musicians.

Sport & Fitness

New York City's religion.

Couch potatoes (you know who you are), welcome to spectator sport bliss. New York has two pro football teams, three pro hockey teams, three pro basketball teams, and two major league and two minor league baseball teams all just waiting to be cheered on (by you – plus a few thousand fanatical fans). More of a show-off, are you? Well, no bench-warming for you. New York City is packed to the gills with a huge variety of ways to get your muscles burning: kayak on the Hudson, go ice skating at Rockefeller Center, swing a golf club at Chelsea Piers, ride a horse in Central Park or pedal a bike along park trails in any of the five boroughs. Or, if you want to celebrate the fact that you can touch your toes, by all means check out one of the dozens of yoga studios.

Spectator sports

Major venues

All advance tickets for events at these venues are sold through Ticketmaster (*see p383*).

Madison Square Garden
Seventh Avenue, between 31st & 33rd Streets (1-212 465 6741/www.thegarden.com). Subway: A, C, E, 1, 2, 3 to 34th Street-Penn Station. **Open** *Box office* 9am-6pm Mon-Fri; 10am-6pm Sat; noon-1hr after event begins Sun. **Tickets** $25-$350. **Credit** AmEx, DC, Disc, MC, V.

Meadowlands Sports Complex
East Rutherford, NJ (1-201 935 3900/www.meadow lands.com). Travel: NJ Transit Meadowlands Sports Complex bus from Port Authority Bus Terminal. **Open** *Box office* 11am-6pm Mon-Sat; 2hrs prior to event Sun. **Tickets** from $25. **No credit cards** for Giants and Jets games and Meadowlands Racetrack. All other events: AmEx, DC, Disc, MC, V.
Continental Airlines Arena, Giants Stadium and the Meadowlands Racetrack are part of this massive multi-venue complex across the river. All are serviced by the same bus.

Nassau Veterans Memorial Coliseum
1255 Hempstead Turnpike, Uniondale, Long Island (1-516 794 9303/www.nassaucoliseum. com). Travel: LIRR (www.lirr.org) train from Penn Station to Hempstead, then N70, N71 or N72 bus. **Tickets** from $25. **Credit** AmEx, Disc, MC, V.

Baseball

New York City is home to two major league teams – the Yankees and the Mets – and each one has a distinct personality (and fan base). The American League's Yankees are the team with the rich history (think Babe Ruth, Mickey Mantle), the long list of championships and a payroll that would bankrupt a small country. Fans can only hope that the rash of injuries that plagued players in 2006 won't resurface in 2007. The National League's Mets are the relatively new kids on the block: they came along in 1961 to fill the gap that was created after the working-class favourite Brooklyn Dodgers moved to Los Angeles in 1958. The club's scruffy underdog personality keeps many fans rooting for it (fruitlessly, on the whole) year after year. Although – shocker – in 2006, the souvenir jersey of David Wright, Mets' third baseman, out-sold that of Yankees' golden boy Derek Jeter for the first time.

Minor league excitement returned in 2001, when the Staten Island Yankees and the Brooklyn Cyclones (the Mets' minor league team) opened new ballparks with wonderful cityscape settings.

Brooklyn Cyclones
KeySpan Park, 1904 Surf Avenue, between West 17th & 19th Streets, Coney Island, Brooklyn (1-718 449 8497/www.brooklyncyclones.com). Subway: D, F, Q to Coney Island-Stillwell Avenue. **Open** *Box office* 10am-4pm Mon-Sat. **Tickets** $5-$12. **Credit** AmEx, Disc, MC, V.

New York Mets
Shea Stadium, 123-01 Roosevelt Avenue, at 126th Street, Flushing, Queens (1-718 507 8499/ www.mets.com). Subway: 7 to Willets Point-Shea Stadium. **Open** *Box office* 9am-5.30pm Mon-Fri; 9am-2pm Sat, Sun. **Tickets** $5-$70. **Credit** AmEx, Disc, MC, V.

New York Yankees
Yankee Stadium, River Avenue, at 161st Street, Bronx (1-718 293 6000/www.yankees.com). Subway: B, D, 4 to 161st Street-Yankee Stadium. **Open** *Box office* 9am-5pm Mon-Sat; 10am-4pm Sun; and during games.* **Tickets** $10-$110. **Credit** AmEx, Disc, MC, V.

Staten Island Yankees
Richmond County Bank Ballpark, 75 Richmond Terrace, at Bay Street, Staten Island (1-718 720 9200/www.siyanks.com). Travel: Staten Island Ferry

Arts & Entertainment

Catch a piece of the action at Long Island's **Belmont Park**. *See p335.*

to St George Terminal. **Open** *Box office* 9am-6pm Mon-Fri; 10am-6pm Sat; and during games. **Tickets** $9, $10. **Credit** AmEx, Disc, MC, V.

Basketball

Both of the area's NBA teams – the New York Knicks and the New Jersey Nets – are in what could tactfully be described as 'rebuilding phases'. After a few years near the top of the Eastern Conference, the Nets are hoping to make the finals again by pairing younger players with star guard Jason Kidd. The Knicks, the true New York home team, continue to stumble, and 2006's coaching troubles surely haven't helped matters. Watching either squad in its home arena can be an exciting way to spend a night, and tickets are easier to come by these days. The Knicks play at Madison Square Garden; many seats are filled with basketball diehards (like Spike Lee), while Nets games (at the Continental Airlines Arena in New Jersey) are more family-friendly. For real excitement, and better overall gamesmanship, check out college teams in the Big East Tournament or the National Invitation Tournament – both take place in March 2007 at Madison Square Garden. The ladies of the WNBA's New York Liberty hold court at MSG in the summer.

New Jersey Nets
Continental Airlines Arena (for listing, see p333 Meadowlands Sports Complex*). 1-800 765 6387/www.njnets.com.* **Tickets** $15-$150.

New York Knicks
Madison Square Garden (for listing, see p333). www.nyknicks.com. **Tickets** $34-$115.

New York Liberty
Madison Square Garden (for listing, see p333). www.nyliberty.com. **Tickets** $10-$65.

Boxing

Church Street Boxing Gym
25 Park Place, between Broadway & Church Street (1-212 571 1333/www.nyboxinggym.com). Subway: 2, 3 to Park Place; 4, 5, 6 to Brooklyn Bridge-City Hall. **Open** Call or visit website for schedule. **Tickets** $20-$30. **No credit cards**.
Church Street is a workout gym and an amateur boxing venue located in an atmospheric cellar downtown. Evander Holyfield, Mike Tyson and other heavy-hitters have trained here before Garden matches. About ten times a year, on Fridays, the gym hosts white-collar bouts.

Gleason's Gym
83 Front Street, between Main & Washington Streets, Dumbo, Brooklyn (1-718 797 2872/ www.gleasonsgym.net). Subway: F to York Street. **Open** Call or visit website for schedule. **Tickets** $15. **Credit** DC, Disc, MC, V.
Although it occupies an undistinguished second-floor warehouse space in a now-groovy neighbourhood, Gleason's is the professional boxer's address in New York. The 'sweet scientists' who have trained at the city's most storied gym include Muhammad Ali and Jake (*Raging Bull*) La Motta. Monthly white-collar fights draw doctors, lawyers and stockbrokers – in and out of the ring.

Madison Square Garden
For listing, see p333. **Tickets** $30-$305.
Once the country's premier boxing venue, the Garden still hosts some pro fights plus the city's annual Golden Gloves amateur championships.

Dog show

Westminster Kennel Club Dog Show

Madison Square Garden (for listing, see p333).
www.westminsterkennelclub.org. **Tickets** $40-$95.
Dates Feb.
America's most prestigious dog show prances into Madison Square Garden each February. One of the oldest 'sporting' events in the country, it's your chance to see some of the most beautiful, well-trained pooches on the planet compete for the coveted Best in Show trophy – and tasty dog treats.

Football

Every Sunday from September to January, New Yorkers get religious… about football. The city, uniquely, lays claim to two NFL teams, and the Giants and the Jets have equally rabid followings – so rabid that every home game for both squads is officially sold out. But the teams sometimes release a few seats (generally, those that weren't claimed by the visiting team) on the day of the game. Call for availability on the Friday before kick-off. You can also try your luck on eBay or with a scalper (risky; tickets may be counterfeit). Fans of the fast-paced, high-scoring Arena Football League should head out to Nassau Coliseum to see the New York Dragons, who play from February through to May.

New York Dragons

Nassau Veterans Memorial Coliseum (for listing, see p333). 1-866 235 8499/www.newyorkdragons.com. **Tickets** $15-$110.

New York Giants

Giants Stadium (for listing, see p333 Meadowlands Sports Complex). 1-201 935 8222/www.giants.com. **Tickets** $65-$85.

New York Jets

Giants Stadium (for listing, see p333 Meadowlands Sports Complex). 1-516 560 8100/www.newyork jets.com. **Tickets** $60-$80.

Hockey

The National Hockey League's celebrated return in 2006 (after failed contract negotiations the year before cancelled the whole season) should mean the 2007 season is a sure bet. Check newspapers for the schedule. The formerly powerful New York Rangers have repeatedly failed to make the play-offs for an uncomfortable number of seasons. The upstart New Jersey Devils have captured three Stanley Cups in the last 11 years and always play an exciting, hard-nosed brand of hockey. The New York Islanders skate at the

suburban Nassau Coliseum on Long Island. Tickets for all three teams are on sale throughout the season, which runs from October to April.

New Jersey Devils

Continental Airlines Arena (for listing, see p333 Meadowlands Sports Complex). www.newjersey devils.com. **Tickets** $20-$90.

New York Islanders

Nassau Veterans Memorial Coliseum (for listing, see p333). www.newyorkislanders.com. **Tickets** $25-$175.

New York Rangers

Madison Square Garden (for listing, see p333). www.newyorkrangers.com. **Tickets** $23-$630.

Horse racing

There are three major racetracks situated near Manhattan: thoroughbreds run at Aqueduct, Belmont and the Meadowlands. If you don't want to trek all the way to Long Island or New Jersey, then catch the action (and the seedy atmosphere) at any off-track betting (OTB) parlour (check the *Yellow Pages* for locations).

Aqueduct Racetrack

110-00 Rockaway Boulevard, at 110th Street, Jamaica, Queens (1-718 641 4700/www.nyra.com/ aqueduct). Subway: A to Aqueduct Racetrack. **Races** *Thoroughbred* Oct-May Wed-Sun. **Admission** *Clubhouse* $2; *grandstand* $1. Free 2 Jan-7 Mar. **No credit cards.**
The Wood Memorial, a test run for promising three-year-olds, is held each spring. And yes, betting is legal at all New York tracks.

Belmont Park

2150 Hempstead Turnpike, Elmont, Long Island (1-516 488 6000/www.nyra.com/belmont). Travel: from Penn Station, Seventh Avenue at 32nd Street, take LIRR (www.lirr.org) to Belmont Park. **Races** *Thoroughbred* May-July, Sept, Oct Wed-Sun. **Admission** *Clubhouse* $5; *grandstand* $2. **No credit cards.**
This big beauty of an oval is home to the third and longest leg of US horse racing's Triple Crown, the mile-and-a-half Belmont Stakes, which will be held in June in 2007. **Photo** *p334.*

Meadowlands Racetrack

For listing, see p333 Meadowlands Sports Complex. 1-201 843 2446/www.thebigm.com. **Races** *Thoroughbred* Oct, Nov; *harness* Nov-Aug; check website for schedule. **Admission** *Clubhouse* $3; *grandstand* $1. **No credit cards.**
Meadowlands Racetrack offers both harness (trotting) and thoroughbred racing. Top harness racers compete for more than $1 million in the prestigious Hambletonian, which is held on the first Saturday of August.

Arts & Entertainment

Soccer

The Brits call it football; many Americans call it boring. Still, in a city that's home to such a large immigrant population, footy commands a huge number of fans. You'll find pick-up games in many city parks, and the pro MetroStars play across the river at Giants Stadium, which also occasionally hosts top European teams (such as Manchester United) for exhibition games in front of tens of thousands of crazed fans. Check www.meadowlands.com for the schedule.

MetroStars

Giants Stadium (for listing, see p333 Meadowlands Sports Complex*). 1-888 463 8768/www.metro stars.com.* **Tickets** $18-$38.

Tennis

US Open

USTA National Tennis Center, Flushing Meadows-Corona Park, Queens (1-866 673 6849/www. usopen.org). Subway: 7 to Willets Point-Shea Stadium. **Tickets** $22-$120. **Credit** AmEx, MC, V. Tickets go on sale late in the spring for this late-summer grand-slam thriller, which the USTA says is the highest-attended annual sporting event in the world. Check the website for match schedules.

Active sports

A visit to New York means a lot of watching: watching plays, watching concerts, watching that weird cowboy guy who plays guitar in his underwear in Times Square. But if you get a hankering to do something yourself, then the city won't let you down.

All-in-one sports centre

Chelsea Piers

Piers 59-62, W 17th through to 23rd Streets, at Eleventh Avenue (1-212 336 6666/www.chelsea piers.com). Subway: C, E to 23rd Street. **Open** times vary; call or visit website.
This massive sports complex, which occupies a six-block stretch of riverfront real estate, offers just about every popular recreational activity, in a bright, clean, well-maintained facility. Would-be Tigers can practise their swings at the Golf Club (Pier 59, 1-212 336 6400); bowlers can set up their pins at the AMF Lanes (between Piers 59 and 60, 1-212 835 2695). Ice-skaters spin and glide at the Sky Rink (Pier 61, 1-212 336 6100). Rather skate on wheels? Hit the Roller Rink and Skate Park (Pier 62, 1-212 336 6200). The Field House (Pier 62, 1-212 336 6500) has a toddler adventure centre, a rock-climbing wall, a gymnastics training centre, batting cages, basketball courts, indoor playing fields and more. At the Sports Center (Pier 60, 1-212 336 6000) gym,

you'll find classes in everything from triathlon training to hip-hop dance. Hours and fees vary; call or consult the website for more information.

Bicycling

Hundreds of miles of paths make it easy for the recreational biker to get pretty much anywhere in New York. Construction continues on the paths that run alongside the East and Hudson Rivers, and it will soon be possible for riders to completely circumnavigate the island of Manhattan. Visitors can either take a DIY trip using rental bikes and path maps or go on organised rides. A word of caution: cycling in the city is a serious business. Riders must stay alert and abide by traffic laws, especially because drivers and pedestrians often don't. If you keep your ears and eyes open – and wear a helmet – you'll enjoy an adrenaline-pumping ride. Or forget the traffic and just take a spin through one of the city's many parks, including Central and Prospect Parks.

Bike-path maps
Department of City Planning Bookstore

22 Reade Street, between Broadway & Elk Street (1-212 720 3667). Subway: J, M, Z to Chambers Street; R, W to City Hall; 4, 5, 6 to Brooklyn Bridge-City Hall. **Open** 10am-4pm Mon-Fri.
The city's Bicycle Master Plan includes nearly 1,000 miles of cycling lanes. Free annual updates are available at this shop or at www.nyc.gov.
Transportation Alternatives *Suite 127, 10th Floor, W 26th Street, between Sixth & Seventh Avenues (1-212 629 8080/www.transalt.org). Subway: B, D, F, N, Q, R, V, W to 34th Street-Herald Square; 1, 2, 3 to 34th Street-Penn Station.* **Open** 9.30am-6pm Mon-Fri.
Transportation Alternatives (TA) is a non-profit citizens' group that lobbies for more bike-friendly streets. You can pop into the office to get free maps, or download them from the website.

Bike rentals
Gotham Bike Shop *112 West Broadway,*

between Duane & Reade Streets (1-212 732 2247/ www.gothambikes.com). Subway: A, C, 1, 2, 3 to Chambers Street. **Open** 10am-6.30pm Mon-Wed, Fri, Sat; 10am-7.30pm Thur; 10.30am-5pm Sun.
Fees $10/hr; $30/24hrs (includes helmet). **Credit** AmEx, MC, V (credit card and ID required for rental). Rent a sturdy set of wheels from this shop and ride the short distance to the Hudson River esplanade.
Loeb Boathouse *Central Park, entrance on Fifth Avenue, at 72nd Street (1-212 517 2233/ www.centralparknyc.org). Subway: 6 to 68th Street-Hunter College.* **Open** 10am-6pm daily, weather permitting. **Fees** $6-$21 per hr (includes helmet). **Credit** AmEx, MC, V (credit card and ID required for rental).
If you want to cruise through Central Park, this is your place, with more than 100 bikes available.

Metro Bicycles *1311 Lexington Avenue, at 88th Street (1-212 427 4450/www.metrobicycles. com). Subway 4, 5, 6 to 86th Street.* **Open** 9.30am-6.30pm daily. **Fees** $7hr; $35day. **Credit** AmEx, Disc, MC, V.

Trek and Fisher bikes are available to hire by the day; check Metro's website or call for additional locations in Manhattan.

Organised bike rides

Bike the Big Apple *1-201 837 1133/ www.bikethebigapple.com.*

Tag along with a tour company that combines biking with sightseeing. Trips include a Lower East Side and Brooklyn ride that makes stops at chocolate and beer factories.

Fast & Fabulous *1-212 567 7160/ www.fastnfab.org.*

This 'queer and queer-friendly' riding group leads tours throughout the year, usually meeting in Central Park and heading out of the city.

Five Borough Bicycle Club *1-212 932 2300 ext 115/www.5bbc.org.*

This local club always offers a full slate of leisurely rides around the city, as well as jaunts that head further afield, for more experienced riders. Best of all, most trips are free.

Time's Up! *1-212 802 8222/www.times-up.org.*

An alternative-transportation advocacy group, Time's Up! sponsors rides year-round, including Critical Mass, in which hundreds of cyclists and skaters meet at Union Square Park (7pm on the last Friday of every month) and go tearing through the city, often ending up in Greenwich Village.

Bowling

Bowlmor Lanes

110 University Place, between 12th & 13th Streets (1-212 255 8188/www.bowlmor.com). Subway: L, N, Q, R, W, 4, 5, 6 to 14th Street-Union Square. **Open** 11am-3am Mon; 11am-2am Tue-Thur; 11am-4am Fri, Sat; 11am-1am Sun. **Fees** $7.95-$9.25 per person per game; $5 shoe rental. Under-21s not admitted after 5pm Tue-Sun. **Credit** AmEx, MC, V.

Renovation turned a seedy but historic Greenwich Village alley (Richard Nixon bowled here) into a hip downtown nightclub. Monday evening's Night Strike features glow-in-the-dark pins and a techno-spinning DJ in addition to unlimited bowling from 10pm to 3am ($20 per scenester; includes shoes).

Harlem Lanes

See p150.

Gyms

Many gyms offer single-day membership. If you can schedule a workout during off-peak hours (instead of just before or after the workday), you likely won't have to compete for time on the machines. Call for class details.

Crunch

623 Broadway, between Bleecker & Houston Streets (1-212 420 0507/1-888 227 8624/www.crunch.com). Subway: B, D, F, V to Broadway-Lafayette Street; 6 to Bleecker Street. **Open** 6am-10pm Mon-Fri; 9am-7pm Sat, Sun. **Fees** *Day pass* $24. **Credit** AmEx, DC, Disc, MC, V.

For a downtown feel without the downtown attitude, Crunch wins hands down. Most of the ten New York locations feature NetPulse cardio equipment, which lets you surf the web or watch a personal TV while you exercise. Visit Crunch's website for other locations.

New York Sports Club

151 E 86th Street, between Lexington & Third Avenues (1-800 301 1231/www.nysc.com). Subway: 4, 5, 6 to 86th Street. **Open** 5.30am-11pm Mon-Thur; 5.30am-10pm Fri; 8am-9pm Sat, Sun. **Fees** *Day pass* $25. **Credit** AmEx, MC, V.

A day membership at New York Sports Club includes aerobics classes and access to the weights room, cardio machines, steam room and sauna. The 62nd and 86th Street branches feature squash courts. Visit the website for other gym locations.

Horseback riding

Claremont Riding Academy

175 W 89th Street, between Columbus & Amsterdam Avenues (1-212 724 5100). Subway: 1 to 86th Street. **Open** 6.30am-8pm Mon-Fri; 8am-5pm Sat, Sun. **Fees** $55/hr; *lessons* $65 for 30mins or 3 lessons for $165. **Credit** MC, V.

Beginners use an indoor arena while experienced riders can take a leisurely canter along six miles of trails in Central Park. Be prepared to prove your English-saddle-mounted mettle: Claremont subjects all riders to an interview to determine their level of experience.

Kensington Stables

51 Caton Place, at East 8th Street, Kensington, Brooklyn (1-718 972 4588/www.kensington stables.com). Subway: F to Fort Hamilton Parkway. **Open** 10am-sunset. **Fees** *Guided trail ride* $25/hr; *private lessons* $45/hr. Reservations suggested. **Credit** AmEx, Disc, MC, V.

The paddock is small, but miles of lovely riding trails wind through Prospect Park (*see p160*), particularly in the Ravine, which was designed to be seen from horseback.

Ice skating

Lasker Rink

Central Park, midpark, between 106th & 108th Streets (1-212 534 7639/www.centralparknyc. org). Subway: B, C to 110th Street. **Open** Nov-Mar 10am-3.45pm Mon, Wed, Thur; 10am-10pm Tue, Fri; 12.30-10pm Sat; 12.30-4.30pm Sun. **Fees** $4.50; $2.25 children. *Skate rental* $4.75. **Credit** MC, V.

This neighbourhood rink has two skating areas: one is for high-school hockey teams while the other is for the average joe.

Rockefeller Center Ice Rink

1 Rockefeller Plaza, from 49th to 50th Streets, between Fifth & Sixth Avenues (1-212 332 7654/ www.therinkatrockcenter.com). Subway: B, D, F, V to 47-50th Streets-Rockefeller Center. **Open** Oct-Apr; call or visit website for hours. **Fees** $14-$17; $7-$12 under-12s. *Skate rental* $8-$10. **Credit** AmEx, Disc, MC, V.

Easily among the city's most recognisable tourist attractions, Rockefeller Center's rink, under the giant statue of Prometheus, is spot-on for atmosphere – but pretty bad for elbow room. The rink opens with an energetic ice show in mid October but attracts the most visitors when the towering Christmas tree is lit.

Wollman Rink

Central Park, midpark at 62nd Street (1-212 439 6900/www.wollmanskatingrink.com). Subway: N, R, W to Fifth Avenue-59th Street. **Open** *Late Oct-Mar* 10am-2.30pm Mon, Tue; 10am-9pm Wed, Thur, Sun; 10am-11pm Fri, Sat. **Fees** *Mon-Thur* $8.50; $4.25 children; *Fri-Sun* $11; $4.50 children. *Skate rental* $4.75. **No credit cards.**

Less crowded – especially after the holidays – than Rock Center, the rink offers a lovely setting beneath the trees of Central Park.

In-line skating

In-line skating is very popular in New York: the choking traffic makes it practical, and the landscape makes it pleasurable (a beautiful paved loop circumnavigates Central Park; bike paths run along the Hudson River). Join a group skate, or go it alone. The gear shop Blades, Board & Skate (120 W 72nd Street, between Columbus & Amsterdam Avenues, 1-212 787 3911) rents by the day ($20).

Empire Skate Club of New York

PO Box 20070, London Terrace Station, New York, NY 10011 (1-212 774 1774/www.empireskate.org). This club organises in-line and roller skating events throughout the city, including island-hopping tours and night-time rides such as the Thursday Evening Roll: skaters meet from May to October at Columbus Circle (Broadway, at 59th Street, south-west corner of Central Park) at 6.45pm.

Kayaking

Kayaking is a great way to explore New York Harbor and the Hudson River. Given the tricky currents, the tidal shifts and the hairy river traffic, it's best to go on an organised excursion.

Downtown Boathouse

Pier 96, Clinton Cove Park, 56th Street & Westside Highway (1-646 613 0375/www.downtownboat house.org). Subway: A, C, E, 1, 9 to Columbus Circle. **Open** *June-Aug* 5-7pm Mon-Fri; 9am-6pm Sat, Sun, holidays. *Classes* 6-8pm Wed. **Fee** free.

Weather permitting, this volunteer-run organisation offers free kayaking (no appointment necessary) in front of the boathouses, at two locations. It also offers free Wednesday evening classes and three-hour guided kayak trips on weekend mornings. All trips are offered on a first-come, first-served basis; you must be able to swim.
Other locations: Riverside Park promenade, 72nd Street.

Manhattan Kayak Company

Pier 63 Maritime, Twelfth Avenue, at 23rd Street (1-212 924 1788/www.manhattankayak. com). Subway: C, E to 23rd Street. **Open** Call or visit website for schedule and prices. **Credit** AmEx, Disc, MC, V.

Run by veteran kayaker Eric Stiller, who once paddled halfway around Australia, Manhattan Kayak offers beginner to advanced classes and tours. Adventures include the Sushi Tour ($100 per person), in which the group paddles to Edgewater, New Jersey, to dine at a sushi restaurant.

Running

The path ringing the Central Park reservoir is probably the most popular jogging trail in the entire city, but dozens of parks and paths are waiting to be explored. Just tie on a cushy pair of sneakers and go where your feet lead you.

New York Road Runners

9 E 89th Street, between Fifth & Madison Avenues (1-212 860 4455/www.nyrrc.org). Subway: 4, 5, 6 to 86th Street. **Open** 10am-8pm Mon-Fri; 10am-5pm Sat; 10am-3pm Sun. **Fees** Call or visit website. **Credit** AmEx, MC, V.

Hardly a weekend passes without some sort of run or race sponsored by the NYRR, which is responsible for the New York City Marathon. Most races take place in Central Park and are open to the public. The club also offers classes and clinics.

NYC Hash House Harriers

1-212 427 4692/www.hashnyc.com. **Fees** $15 (covers food and beer after the run).

This energetic, slightly wacky group has been running in the Big Apple for more than 20 years and always welcomes newcomers. A 'hash' is part training run, part scavenger hunt, part keg party. The participants follow a three- to five-mile trail that a member (called 'the hare') marks with chalk or other visual clues. After the exercise, the group retires to a local watering hole for drinks and grub.

Swimming

The Harlem, Vanderbilt and West Side YMCAs (www.ymcanyc.org) have decent-sized pools (plus day passes), as do some private gyms. Many hotel pools provide day-pass access as well. The city of New York maintains several Olympic-sized (and plenty of smaller) facilities. Its outdoor pools are free of charge and open from late June to Labor Day: Hamilton Fish (Pitt Street, between Houston & Stanton Streets, 1-212 387 7687); Asser Levy Pool (23rd Street, between First Avenue & FDR Drive, 1-212 447 2020); Tony Dapolito Recreation Center (Clarkson Street, at Seventh Avenue South, 1-212 242 5228). Recreation Center 54 (348 54th Street, between First & Second Avenues,

1-212 754 5411) has an indoor pool. For more information, call New York Parks & Recreation (1-212 639 9675, www.nycgovparks.org).

Tennis

From April through to November, the city maintains excellent municipal courts throughout the five boroughs. Single-play (one-hour) tickets cost $8. For a list of city courts, visit www.nycgovparks.org.

Trapeze

Trapeze School New York

Hudson River Park, between Canal & Vestry Streets (1-917 797 1872/www.trapezeschool.com). Subway: 1 to Canal Street. **Open** May-Nov, weather permitting. **Fees** 2hr class $47-$75, plus $22 one-time application fee. **Credit** AmEx, Disc, MC, V.

Sarah Jessica Parker did it on an episode of *Sex and the City* a few years ago, so it must be cool. Set in a large, cage-like construction on the bank of the Hudson River (a tent for year-round operation is in the works at Pier 40), the school teaches those aged six and upwards to fly through the air with the greatest of ease. You can also watch while a loved one has a fling.

Yoga

Laughing Lotus Yoga Center

3rd Floor, 59 W 19th Street, between Fifth & Sixth Avenues (www.laughinglotus.com). Subway: F, N, R, V, W to 23rd Street. **Open** Call or check website for schedule. **Fees** Single class $10-$15. **Credit** AmEx, Disc, MC, V.

These roomy Chelsea digs accommodate a kind of yogic community centre that has weekly holistic workshops, classes and an in-house tarot reader and astrologist. Among the regular offerings: midnight yoga, reflexology and absolute-beginner classes.

Levitate Yoga

3rd Floor, 780 Eighth Avenue, between 47th & 48th Streets (1-212 974 2288/www.levitateyoga.com). Subway: C, E to 50th Street. **Open** Call or visit website for schedule. **Fees** Single class $18; $12 students. **Credit** AmEx, MC, V.

This modern-looking studio caters to beginners, tourists from nearby hotels, and casts and crews performing at nearby theatres. In the warmer months, special classes are held on the 2,000sq ft rooftop terrace.

Om Yoga Center

6th Floor, 826 Broadway (above Strand Bookstore), between 12th & 13th Streets (1-212 254 9642/ www.omyoga.com). Subway: L, N, Q, R, W, 4, 5, 6 to 14th Street-Union Square. **Open** Call or visit website for schedule. **Fees** Single class $18. **Credit** AmEx, Disc, MC, V.

Cyndi Lee's famed yoga spot offers all-level, flowing-style *vinyasa* yoga classes with a focus on alignment.

Arts & Entertainment

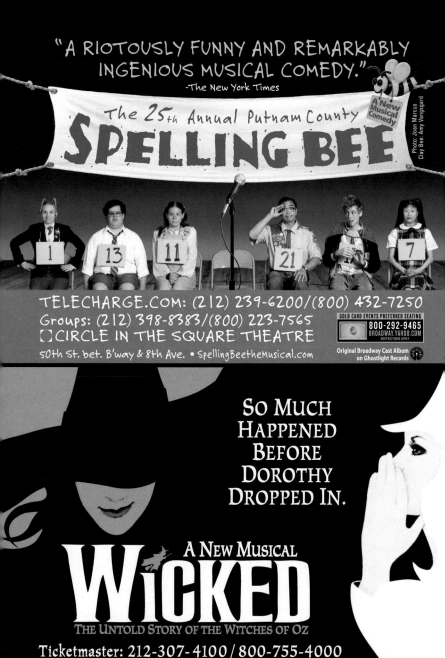

Theatre & Dance

No need for stage fright in a city with so many choices.

Theatre

Judging by box office figures alone, Broadway is booming. In the 2005-06 season, more than 12 million theatre-goers spent a total of $861 million on various attractions along the 'Main Stem'. And if established new works are a worthy yardstick, the industry known as the 'fabulous invalid' has been feeling particularly fab lately. Musicals from the last couple of seasons are still enjoying healthy runs. And non-musical plays – that truly endangered species in the Broadway ecology – still pop up. In recent years, plays such as *Doubt* and *The History Boys* (an English import) have been critical and commercial hits. There are several reasons for the uptick in business and popularity of the Broadway 'brand'. First of all, it's a great time for the American musical comedy. Fast, irreverent and, dare we say, hip tuners such as *Avenue Q, The 25th Annual Putnam County Spelling Bee* and *Monty Python's Spamalot* are not just for Broadway fanatics, enjoying broad appeal. Those who want a little more heart with their show-stoppers have made an astounding success of *Wicked*, the girl-power musical 'prequel' to *The Wizard of Oz*. For all the advance sales and lucre, however, the question remains: is Broadway really the place to see the best

theatre in New York? The answer is complicated. To be sure, producers and creative teams make concessions to the tourist, shying away from material perceived as too controversial or even too 'New Yorky'. However, one can't underestimate the power of spectacle and professional showbiz as perfected by the 'Great White Way' (another traditional moniker for Broadway, derived from the concentration of electric signs announcing shows and stars in white lights). There are also perennial family-friendly draws such as *The Lion King* and *Mary Poppins*, delirious musical comedies like *The Producers* and *Hairspray*, and top-drawer dramas and revivals from Manhattan Theatre Club and the Roundabout Theatre Company. The savvy and intrepid theatre-goer, however, will know to look past the glittering lights of Broadway and to seek out the best new theatrical offerings that take place further downtown. From Midtown's landmark palaces to Downtown's funky Off Broadway and Off-Off Broadway spaces, there is a place – and a show – to suit every taste.

GET YOUR TICKETS HERE
If you have a major credit card, then buying Broadway tickets is simply a matter of picking up the phone. Nearly all Broadway and Off Broadway shows are served by one of the city's 24-hour ticketing agencies, which are

Face facts: Cherry Jones

No other actor speaks on stage like two-time Tony winner Cherry Jones, with each word carefully measured out and administered with loving precision. And no one listens quite like her, either: a great Jones performance includes important intervals of silence, with flashes of thought that illuminate her deceptively serene features. Whether playing a naïve young woman destroyed by romance (*The Heiress*), the sidelined mother of an atomic family in fission (*Flesh and Blood*) or a stern, self-righteous nun (*Doubt*), Jones is a model of emotional intelligence: a worthy heiress to Helen Hayes as First Lady of the American Stage.

Arts & Entertainment

THAT SHOW YOUR NEIGHBOR LOVES.

The DROWSY Chaperone

THE FUNNIEST MUSICAL ON BROADWAY.

WINNER!
BEST MUSICAL!
NY DRAMA CRITICS' CIRCLE &
DRAMA DESK AWARDS

WINNER!
5 TONY AWARDS
INCLUDING BEST MUSIC, BEST BOOK &
BEST FEATURED ACTRESS!

listed in the shows' print advertisements or in the capsule reviews that run each week in *Time Out New York*. The venues' information lines can also refer you to ticket agents sometimes by merely transferring your call (for additional ticketing info, *see p382*). Theatre box offices usually charge a small fee for phone orders.

Some of the cheapest tickets on Broadway are 'rush' tickets (tickets purchased the day of a show at the theatre's box office), which cost an average of $25 – but not all theatres offer these, and some reserve them for students. A few theatres distribute rush tickets through a lottery, usually held two hours before the performance. If a show is sold out, it's worth waiting for standby tickets just before curtain time. Tickets are slightly cheaper for matinées (typically on Wednesdays, Saturdays and Sundays) and previews, and for students or groups of 20 or more. For discount seats, your best bet is TKTS (*see p382*), where you can get tickets on the day of the performance for as much as 75 per cent off the face value. Arrive early to beat, or at least get a jump on, the long lines. TKTS also sells matinée tickets the day before a show. (Beware of scam artists trying to sell tickets to those waiting in line: their tickets are often fake.) You should consider purchasing a set of vouchers from the Theatre Development Fund if you're interested in seeing more than one Off-Off Broadway show or dance event.

Theatre Development Fund

1501 Broadway, between 43rd & 44th Streets (1-212 221 0885 ext 251/www.tdf.org). Subway: N, Q, R, W to 42nd Street; S, 1, 2, 3, 7 to 42nd Street-Times Square. **Open** 10am-6pm Mon-Fri. **No credit cards**.

For $28 TDF offers a book of four vouchers that can be purchased only at its office by visitors who bring their passport or out-of-state driver's licence, or by students and residents on the TDF mailing list. Each voucher is good for one admission to an Off-Off Broadway theatre, dance or music event at venues such as the Atlantic Theater Company, the Joyce, the Kitchen, Performance Space 122 and many more. TDF's NYC/Onstage service (1-212 768 1818) provides information by phone on all events in town.

Broadway

Technically speaking, 'Broadway' is the Theater District that surrounds Times Square on either side of Broadway (the actual avenue), mainly between 41st and 53rd Streets. This is where you'll find the grand theatres that were built largely between 1900 and 1930. Officially, 38 are designated as being part of Broadway – full-price tickets at one of them

can cost more than $100. The big shows are hard to ignore; high-profile revivals and new blockbusters announce themselves from giant billboards and drench the airwaves with radio advertisements. Still, there's more to Broadway than splashy musicals and flashy pop spectacles. In recent years, provocative dramas like *Doubt* and hipster comedies such as *Avenue Q* have had remarkable success, as have revivals of American classics such as Lorraine Hansberry's *A Raisin in the Sun* and Eugene O'Neill's *Long Day's Journey into Night*.

The Roundabout Theatre Company (American Airlines Theatre, 227 W 42nd Street, between Seventh & Eighth Avenues, 1-212 719 1300; Studio 54, 254 W 54th Street, between Broadway & Eighth Avenue) is critically acclaimed for putting on classics that feature all-star casts; it was also the force behind the brilliant revival of *Assassins* by Stephen Sondheim and John Weidman in 2004. You can subscribe to the Roundabout's full season or buy single tickets, if they're available.

Broadway (Theater District)

Subway: *C, E, 1 to 50th Street; N, Q, R, W to 42nd Street; S, 2, 3, 7 to 42nd Street-Times Square.*

Long-running shows

Straight (non-musical) plays can provide some of Broadway's most stirring experiences, but they're less likely than musicals to enjoy long runs. If you aren't in search of song, check *Time Out New York* for current listings and reviews of new or revived dramatic plays.

Avenue Q

Golden Theater, 252 W 45th Street, between Broadway & Eighth Avenue (1-212 239 6200/ www.avenueq.com). Subway: A, C, E to 42nd Street-Port Authority. **Box office** 10am-8pm Mon-Sat; noon-7pm Sun. **Tickets** $21-$96. **Shows** 8pm Tue-Fri; 2pm 8pm Sat; 2pm, 7pm Sun. *Length* 2hrs 15mins. 1 intermission. **Credit** AmEx, DC, Disc, MC, V.

Mixing puppets and live actors with irreverent jokes and snappy songs, this clever, good-hearted musical comedy was a surprise hit. It garnered several 2004 Tonys, including Best Musical.

Chicago

Ambassador Theatre, 219 W 49th Street, between Broadway & Eighth Avenue (1-212 239 6200). Subway: N, R, W to 49th Street; 1 to 50th Street. **Tickets** $58-$111. **Shows** 7pm Tue; 2pm, 8pm Wed; 8pm Sat; 2pm, 8pm Thur, Fri; 6.30pm Sun. *Length* 2hrs 30mins. 1 intermission. **Credit** AmEx, MC, V.

This snappy 1975 John Kander-Fredd Ebb-Bob Fosse show tells the dark saga of chorus girl Roxie Hart, who murders her lover, avoids prison and, with the help of a huckster lawyer, becomes a musical

Arts & Entertainment

Jersey Boys, at the August Wilson Theatre. *See p345*.

star. Director Walter Bobbie and choreographer Ann Reinking's minimalist strip-club aesthetic panders to some abstract lust, but the story is wicked fun and the brassy score infectious.

The Color Purple
Broadway Theatre, 1681 Broadway, at 53rd Street (1-212 239 6200). Subway: N, R, W to 49th Street; 1 to 50th Street. **Tickets** $26.25-$101.25. **Shows** 2pm, 8pm Wed, Sat; 8pm Thur, Fri; 2pm, 7.30pm Sun. *Length* 2hrs 40mins. 1 intermission. **Credit** AmEx, MC, V.
Marsha Norman's adaptation retains as much of Alice Walker's bestselling 1982 novel as could reasonably be expected; the nearly sung-through score, crafted by a trio of seasoned pop songwriters, bobs along in a pleasant, mildly funky R&B groove.

Hairspray
Neil Simon Theatre, 250 W 52nd Street, between Broadway & Eighth Avenue (1-212 307 4100/ www.hairsprayonbroadway.com). Subway: C, E, 1 to 50th Street. **Box office** 10am-8pm Mon-Sat; noon-6pm Sun. **Tickets** $75-$110. **Shows** 7pm Tue; 2pm, 8pm Wed, Sat; 8pm Thur, Fri; 3pm Sun. *Length* 2hrs 35mins. 1 intermission. **Credit** AmEx, DC, Disc, MC, V.
John Waters's classic kitsch film about a big girl with big hair and an ambition to dance, has become an eye-popping song-and-dance stage extravaganza (with an original score by Marc Shaiman) that is bigger, brighter, more satirical and much funnier than the original version. **Photo** *p347*.

Jersey Boys
August Wilson Theatre, 245 W 52nd Street, between Broadway & Eighth Avenues (1-212 239 6200). Subway: C, E, 1 to 50th Street. **Tickets** $80-$110. **Shows** 7pm Tue; 2pm, 8pm Wed, Thur, Sat; 8pm Fri; 3pm Sun. *Length* 2hrs 15mins. 1 intermission. **Credit** AmEx, Disc, MC, V.
The Broadway musical finally does right by the jukebox with this nostalgic behind-the-music tale, presenting the Four Seasons' infectiously energetic 1960s tunes (including 'Walk Like a Man' and 'Big Girls Don't Cry') as they were intended to be performed. A dynamic cast under the sleek direction of Des McAnuff (*700 Sundays*) ensures that Marshall Brickman and Rick Elice's script feels canny instead of canned. **Photos** *p344*.

The Producers
St James Theatre, 246 W 44th Street, between Seventh & Eighth Avenues (1-212 239 6100/ www.producersonbroadway.com). Subway: N, Q, R, W to 42nd Street; S, 1, 2, 3, 7 to 42nd Street-Times Square. **Box office** 10am-8pm Mon-Sat; noon-6pm Sun. **Tickets** $31-$111. **Shows** 7pm Tue; 2pm, 8pm Wed, Sat; 8pm Thur, Fri; 3pm Sun. *Length* 2hrs 45mins. 1 intermission. **Credit** AmEx, DC, Disc, MC, V.
Mel Brooks's ode to tastelessness mixes Broadway razzamatazz with Borscht Belt humour. Original stars Nathan Lane and Matthew Broderick left the cast, but the show still delivers plenty of laughs.

Wicked
Gershwin Theatre, 222 W 51st Street, between Broadway & Eighth Avenue (1-212 307 4100). Subway: C, E, 1 to 50th Street. **Box office** 10am-8pm Mon-Sat; noon-6pm Sun. **Tickets** $50-$110. **Shows** 7pm Tue; 2pm, 8pm Wed, Sat; 8pm Thur, Fri; 3pm Sun. *Length* 2hrs 45mins. 1 intermission. **Credit** AmEx, DC, Disc, MC, V.
Based on novelist Gregory Maguire's 1995 riff on *The Wizard of Oz* mythology, *Wicked* provides a witty prequel to the classic children's book and movie. At the time of writing, Joe Mantello's sumptuous production starred Kate Reinders and Edin Espinosa as young versions of Glinda the Good Witch and the Wicked Witch of the West.

Off Broadway

As the cost of mounting a show on Broadway continues to soar, many serious playwrights are opening their shows in the more adventurous (and less financially demanding) Off Broadway houses. Off Broadway theatres have between 200 and 500 seats, and tickets usually run from $20 to $70. Below are some of our favourite long-running shows, followed by a few of the best theatres and repertory companies.

Long-running shows

Altar Boyz
Dodger Stages, 340 W 50th Street, between Eighth & Ninth Avenues (1-212 239 6200). Subway: C, E, 1 to 50th Street. **Box office** 1-6pm Mon, Sun; 1-7.30pm Tue-Sat. **Tickets** $25-$75. **Shows** 8pm Mon, Tue, Thur, Fri; 2pm, 8pm Sat; 3pm, 7pm Sun. *Length* 1hr 30mins. No intermission. **Credit** AmEx, MC, V.
The Altar Boyz sing about Jesus in the unlikely idiom of boy-band pop, complete with five-part harmony, synchronised steps and prefab streetwise posturing. Mad props where mad props are due: the show's young stars really work their crosses off.

Blue Man Group
Astor Place Theater, 434 Lafayette Street, between Astor Place & E 4th Street (1-212 254 4370/www. blueman.com). Subway: N, R, W to 8th Street-NYU; 6 to Astor Place. **Box office** noon-7.45pm daily. **Tickets** $65-$75. **Shows** 8pm Tue-Thur; 7pm, 10pm Fri; 4pm, 7pm, 10pm Sat; 2pm, 5pm, 8pm Sun. *Length* 2hrs. No intermission. **Credit** AmEx, DC, Disc, MC, V.
Three men with extraterrestrial imaginations (and head-to-toe blue body paint) carry this long-time favourite – a show that's as smart as it is ridiculous.

Stomp
Orpheum Theater, 126 Second Avenue, between St Marks Place & E 7th Street (1-212 477 2477). Subway: N, R, W to 8th Street-NYU; 6 to Astor Place. **Box office** 1-7pm Tue-Fri. **Tickets** $37-$65. **Shows** 8pm Tue-Fri; 7pm, 10.30pm Sat; 3pm, 7pm Sun. *Length* 1hr 30mins. No intermission. **Credit** AmEx, MC, V.

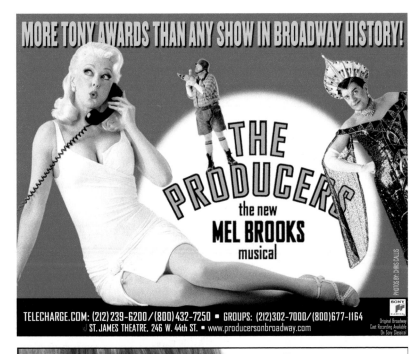

Hairspray still holds its place on Broadway. *See p345.*

This show is billed as a 'percussion sensation' because there's no other way to describe it. Using garbage-can lids, buckets, brooms, sticks and just about anything they can get their hands on, these aerobicised dancer-musicians make a lovely racket.

Repertory companies & venues

Atlantic Theater Company
336 W 20th Street, between Eighth & Ninth Avenues (Telecharge 1-212 239 6200/www.atlantic theater.org). Subway: C, E to 23rd Street. **Box office** 6-8pm Tue-Fri; noon-2pm, 6-8pm Sat; 1-3pm Sun. **Credit** AmEx, Disc, MC, V.
Created in 1985 as an offshoot of acting workshops taught by playwright David Mamet and film star William H Macy, this dynamic theatre has presented nearly 100 plays, including Martin McDonagh's *The Lieutenant of Inishmore* and Duncan Sheik and Steven Sater's *Spring Awakening*. Both productions transferred to Broadway in the 2006-07 season.

Brooklyn Academy of Music
For listing, see p328.
Brooklyn's grand old opera house (along with the Harvey Theater, two blocks away on Fulton Street) stages the multidisciplinary Next Wave Festival (*see p265*); in 2005 it included avant-garde composer Philip Glass's *Orion* and Brit director Edward Hall's all-male rendition of Shakespeare's *Winter's Tale*.

Classic Stage Company
136 E 13th Street, between Third & Fourth Avenues (Ticket Central 1-212 677 4210/www. classicstage.org). Subway: L, N, Q, R, W, 4, 5, 6 to 14th Street-Union Square. **Box office** noon-5pm Mon-Fri. **Credit** AmEx, MC, V.
From Greek tragedies to medieval mystery plays, the Classic Stage Company (under the tutelage of artistic director Brian Kulick) makes the old new again with open rehearsals, staged readings and full-on productions.

59E59
59 E 59th Street, between Madison & Park Avenues (1-212 279 4200/www.59e59.org). Subway: N, R, W to Lexington Avenue-59th Street; 4, 5, 6 to 59th Street. **Box office** noon-7pm daily. **Credit** AmEx, MC, V.
This chic new state-of-the-art East Side venue, which comprises an Off Broadway space and two smaller theatres, made a splash in its first year with the Brits Off Broadway festival. The Off Broadway company Primary Stages now makes its home here. The three theatres are for not-for-profit productions.

Irish Repertory Theatre
132 W 22nd Street, between Sixth & Seventh Avenues (1-212 727 2737/www.irishrepertory theatre.com). Subway: F, V, 1 to 23rd Street. **Box office** 10am-6pm Mon-Fri; 11am-6pm Sat, Sun. **Credit** AmEx, MC, V.

This Chelsea company puts on compelling shows by Irish playwrights. Past productions include Frank McCourt's *The Irish and How They Got That Way* and Enda Walsh's *Bedbound*.

Lincoln Center Theater

For listing, see p328.
The majestic Lincoln Center Theater complex includes two amphitheatre-style drama venues: the 1,138-seat Vivian Beaumont Theater (the Broadway house) and the 338-seat Mitzi E Newhouse Theater (Off Broadway). Expect polished, often star-studded productions of classic plays (such as *Henry IV* featuring Kevin Kline and Ethan Hawke) and new musicals (Adam Guettel's *The Light in the Piazza*). The organisation also commands the considerable resources to mount Tom Stoppard's epic, three-play study of Russian history, *The Coast of Utopia*, in autumn 2006. LCT's founding policy ensures that ticket prices are kept reasonable, averaging $50.

Manhattan Theatre Club

City Center, 131 W 55th Street, between Sixth & Seventh Avenues (1-212 581 1212/Telecharge 1-212 239 6200/www.mtc-nyc.org). Subway: B, D, E to Seventh Avenue. **Box office** 11am-5pm Mon, Sun; noon-7pm Tue-Sat. **Credit** AmEx, DC, Disc, MC, V.
Manhattan Theatre Club has a history of sending young playwrights to Broadway, as seen with successes like John Patrick Shanley's *Doubt*. The club's two theatres are located in the basement of City Center. The 275-seat Stage I Theater features four plays a year; the Stage II Theater offers works in progress, workshops and staged readings, as well as full-length productions. MTC also has a Broadway home in the renovated Biltmore Theatre (261 W 47th Street, between Broadway & Eighth Avenue; tickets from Telecharge, 1-212 239 6200).

New Victory Theater

209 W 42nd Street, between Seventh & Eighth Avenues (1-646 223 3020/Telecharge 1-212 239 6200/www.newvictory.org). Subway: N, Q, R, W to 42nd Street; S, 1, 2, 3, 7 to 42nd Street-Times Square. **Box office** 11am-5pm Mon, Sun; noon-7pm Tue-Sat. **Credit** AmEx, MC, V.
The New Victory is a perfect symbol for the transformation of Times Square. Built in 1900 by Oscar Hammerstein II, Manhattan's oldest theatre became a strip club and adult cinema in the '70s and '80s. Renovated by the city in 1995, the building now features a full season of family-friendly plays.

New World Stages

340 W 50th Street, between Eighth & Ninth Avenues (1-646 871 1730/www.dodgerstages.com). Subway: C, E, 1 to 50th Street. **Box office** 1-6pm Mon, Sun; 1-7.30pm Tue-Sat. **Credit** AmEx, MC, V.
Formerly a movie multiplex, this new centre boasts a shiny, space-age interior and five gorgeous, fully renovated theatres presenting everything from the campy horror tuner *Evil Dead: The Musical* to world premières of new musicals, like *Altar Boyz*. Dodger

Theatrical, an organisation that produces Broadway shows, is behind this $20 million undertaking, which is one of the biggest in recent theatre history.

New York Theatre Workshop

79 E 4th Street, between Bowery & Second Avenue (1-212 460 5475/www.nytw.org). Subway: F, V to Lower East Side-Second Avenue; 6 to Astor Place. **Box office** 1-6pm Tue-Sun.
Credit AmEx, MC, V.
Founded in 1979, the New York Theatre Workshop works with emerging directors eager to take on challenging pieces. Besides plays by the likes of Caryl Churchill (*Far Away, A Number*) and Tony Kushner (*Homebody/Kabul*), this company also premièred *Rent*, Jonathan Larson's Pulitzer Prize-winning musical, which still packs 'em in on Broadway.

Playwrights Horizons

416 W 42nd Street, between Ninth & Tenth Avenues (Ticket Central 1-212 279 4200/ www.playwrightshorizons.org). Subway: A, C, E to 42nd Street-Port Authority. **Box office** noon-8pm daily. **Credit** AmEx, MC, V.
More than 300 important contemporary plays have premièred here, including dramas such as *Driving Miss Daisy* and *The Heidi Chronicles*. Recent seasons have included works by Adam Rapp (*Essential Self-Defense*) and a musical version of *Grey Gardens*.

Public Theater

425 Lafayette Street, between Astor Place & E 4th Street (1-212 539 8500/Telecharge 1-212 239 6200/www.publictheater.org). Subway: N, R, W to 8th Street-NYU; 6 to Astor Place. **Box office** 1-6pm Mon, Sun; 1-7.30pm Tue-Sat.
Credit AmEx, MC, V.
Founded by the late Joseph Papp and dedicated to the work of new American playwrights and performers, this Astor Place landmark is also known for its Shakespeare productions (*see below* Shakespeare in the Park). The building houses five stages and the cabaret space Joe's Pub. The Public recently recruited Oskar Eustis (formerly of the Trinity Repertory Company in Providence, Rhode Island) to serve as the new artistic director.

Second Stage Theatre

307 W 43rd Street, at Eighth Avenue (1-212 246 4422/www.secondstagetheatre.com). Subway: A, C, E to 42nd Street-Port Authority. **Box office** noon-6pm Tue-Sun. **Credit** AmEx, MC, V.
Now located in a beautiful Rem Koolhaas-designed space near Times Square, Second Stage produces the works of new American playwrights, including the New York premières of Mary Zimmerman's *Metamorphoses* and Lisa Loomer's *Living Out*.

Shakespeare in the Park at the Delacorte Theater

Park entrance on Central Park West, at 81st Street, then follow the signs (1-212 539 8750/ www.publictheater.org). Subway: B, C to 81st Street-Museum of Natural History.

The Delacorte Theater in Central Park is the fair-weather sister of the Public Theater (*see above*). When not producing Shakespeare in the East Village, the Public offers the best of the Bard outdoors during the New York Shakespeare Festival (June-Sept). Tickets are free (two per person); they're distributed at both theatres at 1pm on the day of the performance. Around 9am is normally a good time to begin waiting, though the line can start as early as 6am when big-name stars are on the bill.

Vineyard Theatre

108 E 15th Street, at Union Square East (1-212 353 0303/box office 1-212 353 0303/www.vineyard theatre.org). Subway: L, N, Q, R, W, 4, 5, 6 to 14th Street-Union Square. **Box office** 10am-6pm Mon-Fri. **Credit** AmEx, MC, V.
This theatre near Union Square produces excellent new plays and musicals including the downtown cult hit *[title of show]* (yes, that's its actual name) and the Tony Award-winning Broadway hit *Avenue Q* (*see p343*).

Off-Off Broadway

Technically, 'Off-Off Broadway' denotes a show that is presented at a theatre with fewer than 100 seats and created by artists who aren't necessarily card-carrying union pros. It's where some of the most daring writers and performers create their edgiest work. The New York International Fringe Festival (1-212 279 4488, www.fringenyc.org), held every August, is a great way to catch the wacky side of theatre. The cheekily named National Theater of the United States of America (www.ntusa.org), Radiohole (www.radiohole. com) and the International WOW Company (www.internationalwow.org) are troupes that consistently offer inspired, envelope-pushing work. But Off-Off Broadway – where tickets run from $10 to $25 – is not restricted to experimental or solo shows. You can also see classical works and more traditional plays staged by companies such as the Mint Theater (3rd Floor, 311 W 43rd Street, between Eighth & Ninth Avenues, 1-212 315 0231, www.mint theater.org) and at venues like HERE and Performance Space 122 (for both, *see below*).

Repertory companies & venues

The Brick

575 Metropolitan Avenue, between Lorimer Street & Union Avenue, Williamsburg, Brooklyn (1-718 907 3457/www.bricktheater.com). Subway: G to Metropolitan Avenue; L to Lorimer Street. **Box office** opens 15mins prior to curtain. **No credit cards.**
This chic, brick-lined venue in Williamsburg presents a variety of experimental work. Last summer it made a joyful noise with the campy, outrageous Moral Values Festival.

Flea Theater

41 White Street, between Broadway & Church Street (1-212 226 2407/www.theflea.org). Subway: A, C, E, J, M, N, Q, R, W, Z, 1, 6 to Canal Street. **Box office** noon-6pm Mon-Sat. **Credit** AmEx, MC, V.
Founded in fashionable Tribeca in 1997, Jim Simpson's cosy, well-appointed venue has presented both avant-garde experimentation (the work of Mac Wellman) and politically provocative satires (mostly by AR Gurney).

HERE

145 Sixth Avenue, at Broome Street (1-212 647 0202/Smarttix 1-212 868 4444/www.here.org). Subway: C, E to Spring Street. **Box office** 4-10pm daily. **Credit** AmEx, MC, V.
Containing three intimate performance spaces, an art gallery and a chic café, this lovely Tribeca arts complex, dedicated to non-profit arts enterprises, has hosted a number of exciting companies. It was the launching pad for such well-known shows as Eve Ensler's *Vagina Monologues*.

Performance Space 122

150 First Avenue, at 9th Street (1-212 477 5288/ www.ps122.org). Subway: L to First Avenue; 6 to Astor Place. **Box office** 11am-6pm daily. **Credit** AmEx, MC, V.
One of New York's most interesting venues, this non-profit arts centre presents experimental dance, performance art, music, film and video. Eric Bogosian, Whoopi Goldberg, John Leguizamo and others have developed projects here; of more street-level interest is the monthly bloggers' night. Australian trendsetter Vallejo Gantner recently took over as artistic director of this downtown institution, promising to make its programming more international in flavour. The dance programming is also worthy of note; *see p352.*

Dance

Home to the world's foremost dance companies and untold numbers of independent, cutting-edge choreographers, New York is a testament to the endless ways that the human body can get its moves on. The city is the base for the companies of such famous modern dance luminaries as Martha Graham, Alvin Ailey, Merce Cunningham and Trisha Brown. For the classically minded, the **New York City Ballet** (NYCB) offers both innovative new works by its resident choreographer Christopher Wheeldon and the unparalleled repertory of George Balanchine, who established the prestigious School of American Ballet in 1934, and whose choreography transformed ballet in the 20th century. New York is a virtually essential stop for national and international company tours, and, partly for this reason, its audiences tend to be both knowledgeable and enthusiastic.

In a city where, in the 1960s, the Judson Dance Theater spawned the 'postmodern' movement that changed the face of modern dance, experimentation is still alive; a host of venues showcase exceptional artists such as John Jasperse, Jennifer Monson, Neil Greenberg and Gina Gibney, and there are many incubators for new talent. The World Music Institute presents a variety of ethnic dance at venues like **Symphony Space** and **City Center**, and the **Japan Society** (*see p132*) is a goldmine for discovering both avant-garde voices and the purity of traditional dance.

Some choreographers take you out of the theatre altogether with 'site-specific' works, such as those by Noemie Lafrance, who has staged performances in a clocktower, parking garage and, most recently, the massive (and empty) McCarren Park public pool in Williamsburg/Greenpoint.

There are two major dance seasons – March to June, and October to December. The spring season is particularly busy: start with Paul Taylor's consistently brilliant company in March, then grab your seats for the spring programmes of the **American Ballet Theatre** (ABT) and NYCB. That's not to say that dance is dead from July to September; indeed, summer is a great time to catch smaller modern-dance troupes and outdoor performances at the open-air **Central Park SummerStage** (*see p352*), the **Lincoln Center Out of Doors Festival** (*see p264*) and the **River to River Festival** (*see p91*) in lower Manhattan.

If you too yearn to unleash your creative bodily expression, there are dozens of dance schools (some affiliated with major companies) that offer classes in everything from ballet to contact improv to Afro-Caribbean and Haitian dance. Information about classes and workshops is listed in *Time Out New York* magazine. You can call ahead for a schedule, but walk-ins are welcome at most spaces.

Traditional venues

Brooklyn Academy of Music
For listing, see p328.
BAM, which showcases superb local and out of town companies, is one of New York's most prominent cultural institutions. The 2,100-seat Howard Gilman Opera House, with its Federal-style columns and carved marble, is a stunning dance venue. The Mark Morris Dance Group generally performs here in the spring. The 1904 Harvey Theatre (651 Fulton Street, between Ashland & Rockwell Places, Fort Greene, Brooklyn), formerly the Majestic, has hosted choreographers such as John Jasperse and Sarah Michelson. Yearly events include the DanceAfrica Festival, which is held every Memorial Day week-

end and will celebrate its 30th anniversary in 2007; in October, BAM's Next Wave Festival highlights established and experimental dance groups.

City Center
131 W 55th Street, between Sixth & Seventh Avenues (1-212 581 7907/www.nycitycenter.org). Subway: B, D, E to Seventh Avenue; F, N, Q, R, W to 57th Street. **Tickets** $15-$110. **Credit** AmEx, MC, V ($4.75 per-ticket surcharge).
Before the creation of Lincoln Center changed the cultural geography of New York, this was the home of the American Ballet Theatre, the Joffrey Ballet and the New York City Ballet. City Center's lavish decor is golden – as are the companies that pass through here. You can count on superb performances by the ABT in the autumn, the Alvin Ailey American Dance Theater in December, the Paul Taylor Dance Company in the spring and others throughout the year.

Joyce Theater
175 Eighth Avenue, at 19th Street (1-212 242 0800/www.joyce.org). Subway: A, C, E to 14th Street; 1 to 18th Street; L to Eighth Avenue. **Tickets** $30-$45. **Credit** AmEx, DC, Disc, MC, V.
This intimate space, formerly a cinema, is one of the finest theatres in town. Of the 472 seats at the Joyce, there's not a single bad one. Companies and choreographers who present work here, including the Ballet Hispanico, David Parsons and Doug Varone, tend to be more traditional than experimental. In 2007 look for DanceBrazil in February and Pilobolus Dance Theatre in July. During the summer, when many theatres are dark, the Joyce continues its programming. At Joyce Soho, emerging companies present work nearly every weekend.
Other locations: Joyce Soho, 155 Mercer Street, between Houston & Prince Streets, Downtown (1-212 334 7479).

Metropolitan Opera House
For listing, see p329.
A range of international companies, from the Paris Opera Ballet to the Kirov Ballet, perform at the Met. In the spring, this majestic space is home to the American Ballet Theatre, which presents full-length traditional story ballets, as well as contemporary classics by Frederick Ashton and Antony Tudor. The acoustics are wonderful, but the theatre is immense: get as close to the stage as you can afford.

New York State Theater
Lincoln Center, 64th Street, at Columbus Avenue (1-212 870 5570/www.nycballet.com). Subway: 1 to 66th Street-Lincoln Center. **Tickets** $20-$99. **Credit** AmEx, DC, Disc, MC, V.
The neo-classical New York City Ballet headlines at this opulent theatre, which Philip Johnson designed to resemble a jewellery box. NYCB has two seasons: winter begins just before Thanksgiving and features more than a month of performances of George Balanchine's magical *Nutcracker*; the season continues to the end of February with repertory

Arts & Entertainment

performances. The nine-week spring season usually begins in April. The best seats are in the first ring, where the music comes through loud and clear and, even better, you can enjoy the dazzling patterns of the dancers. The works are by Balanchine (the 89ft-by-58ft stage was built to his specifications); Jerome Robbins; Peter Martins, the company's ballet master in chief; and resident choreographer Christopher Wheeldon, whose work has injected the troupe with new life. Weekly cast lists are available online or at the theatre.

Alternative venues

Aaron Davis Hall
City College, Convent Avenue, at W 135th Street (1-212 650 7100/www.aarondavishall.org). Subway: 1 to 137th Street-City College. **Tickets** $15-$35. **Credit** AmEx, MC, V.
Performances at this Harlem centre celebrate African-American life and culture. Companies that have graced the modern, spacious theatre include the Bill T Jones/Arnie Zane Dance Company and the Alvin Ailey junior company, Ailey II.

Brooklyn Arts Exchange
421 Fifth Avenue, at 8th Street, Park Slope, Brooklyn (1-718 832 0018/www.bax.org). Subway: F, M, R to Fourth Avenue-9th Street. **Tickets** $8-$15. **No credit cards**.
Brooklyn Arts Exchange, a multi-arts non-profit organisation, presents a variety of dance concerts by emerging choreographers. There are also performances just for children.

Central Park SummerStage
For listing, see p262.
This outdoor dance series runs during the heat of summer. Temperatures can get steamy, but at least you're outside. Count on seeing traditional and contemporary dance; arrive early to secure a spot close to the stage.

Dance New Amsterdam (DNA)
280 Broadway, at Chambers Street (1-212 625 8369/www.dnadance.org). Subway: R, W to City Hall. **Tickets** $10-$25. **Credit** MC, V.
In 2006 the former Dance Space Center moved downtown into the historic Sun Building, changed its name to Dance New Amsterdam and got to work boosting its rep as a performance space. Its new 135-seat theatre hosts about 50 performances a year, from groups like the Sean Curran Company and Urban Bush Women.

Dance Theater Workshop
Bessie Schönberg Theater, 219 W 19th Street, between Seventh & Eighth Avenues (1-212 924 0077/www.dtw.org). Subway: 1 to 18th Street. **Tickets** $12-$25. **Credit** AmEx, Disc, MC, V.
DTW, led by Cathy Edwards, hosts work by contemporary choreographers, both local and foreign. This space features a 194-seat theatre, two dance studios and an artists' media lab.

Danspace Project
St Mark's Church in-the-Bowery, 131 E 10th Street, at Second Avenue (1-212 674 8194/www.danspace project.org). Subway: L to Third Avenue; 6 to Astor Place. **Tickets** $12-$20. **No credit cards**.
This gorgeous, high-ceilinged sanctuary for downtown dance is at its most sublime when the music is live. The choreographers who take on the four-sided performance space tend towards pure movement rather than technological experimentation.

Galapagos Art Space
For listing, see p315.
This casual Brooklyn club, which plays host to all sorts of creative types, often showcases movement-based performances, among them a burlesque evening on Mondays.

The Kitchen
512 W 19th Street, between Tenth & Eleventh Avenues (1-212 255 5793/www.thekitchen.org). Subway: A, C, E to 14th Street; L to Eighth Avenue. **Tickets** $5-$15. **Credit** AmEx, MC, V.
Although best known as an avant-garde theatre space, the Kitchen also offers experimental dance by inventive, often provocative artists. Choreographers Sarah Michelson and Dean Moss have worked here.

Merce Cunningham Studio
11th Floor, 55 Bethune Street, between Washington & West Streets (1-212 691 9751/www.merce.org). Subway: A, C, E to 14th Street; L to Eighth Avenue. **Tickets** $10-$30. **No credit cards**.
Located in the Westbeth complex on the edge of the West Village, the Cunningham Studio is rented to independent choreographers. As a result, performance quality varies, but some shows are wonderful. The stage and seating area are in a large dance studio; be prepared to take off your shoes – and possibly to sit on the floor, if there's a good crowd.

Movement Research
Judson Church, 55 Washington Square South, at Thompson Street (1-212 539 2611/www.movement research.org). Subway: A, B, C, D, E, F, V to W 4th Street. **Tickets** free.
This free weekly performance series is a great place to check out up-and-coming artists and experimental works. Held every Monday, from September to May, in the renovated, 115-year-old Judson Memorial Church.

Performance Space 122
For listing, see p349.
An assortment of up-and-coming choreographers presents unconventional new works at what was once an abandoned public school. Artists such as Ron Brown and Doug Varone started out here.

Symphony Space
For listing, see p331.
The World Music Institute hosts traditional dancers from around the world, while the regular season features various contemporary choreographers.

Arts & Entertainment

Maria Kowroski performs with the **New York City Ballet**. *See p349.*

Trips Out of Town

Harriman State Park. *See p359.*

Day Trips

Take a break from the streets and skyscrapers on one of these easy getaways.

Of course you want to soak up every last watt of bright lights our big city has to offer. But even New Yorkers crave a little downtime – how else do you think they recharge their batteries for life in the rat race? For many (especially first-time visitors), the attractions of New York City far outshine those of the surrounding area. Still, it is fun to get out of town and see what the hinterland has to offer. Whether you prefer hiking, sunbathing at the beach, or losing your lunch on a rollercoaster, you'll find plenty of options within just a few hours (or less) from NYC. Many getaway spots are accessible by public transport; avoid the high car-rental rates (and nightmare traffic in and out of town) by relaxing on a bus, train or ferry.

GENERAL INFORMATION

NYC & Company, the New York visitors and convention bureau (*see p386* Websites), has many brochures on out-of-town excursions. Look for special packages if you're planning to spend a few days away. The *New York Times*' Sunday travel section carries advertised deals for transport and accommodation. *Time Out New York* magazine's annual Summer Getaways issue will also point you in the right direction.

TRANSPORT

We've included information on how to reach all listed destinations from New York City. Metro-North and the Long Island Rail Road, or LIRR (*see p369*), are the two main commuter-rail systems. Both offer theme tours in the summer. Call the Port Authority Bus Terminal (*see p367*) for information on all bus transport from the city. For a more scenic route, travel by water: NY Waterway (*see p88*) offers services to areas outside Manhattan. For more information on airports, buses, car rental and trains, *see pp366-370*.

Chill out

Mayflower Inn & Spa

It didn't surprise us to find a copy of John Milton's *Paradise Lost* in the poetry section of the library at Adriana and Robert Mnuchin's Mayflower Inn in Washington, Connecticut: nearly everything about the ritzy property's new 20,000-square-foot Destination Spa is Edenic. In between treatments, exercise classes

and wellness seminars, guests knock about the gorgeously landscaped grounds, wear matching nude-looking tan sweat suits and, of course, eat divine organic produce. The closing ceremony to each five-day session even features a banishing of personal demons by way of writing them on paper slips, which are tossed into a fire.

Of course, there are differences between this paradise and the one inhabited by Adam and Eve. For one, the Sunday-to-Friday session is exclusively for women (weekend stays are co-ed). The original wasn't within two hours of New York City, and God didn't charge $6,700 per person to frolic in the garden. Then again, God also didn't offer unlimited spa treatments. Yes, you can have as many massages, facials, body scrubs and energy therapies as your muscles, face, epidermis and chakras can pack into five days. The other two aspects of the Mayflower's triangle of wellness experiences – fitness classes and mind-spirit seminars – are also offered, smörgåsbord-style. Each daily schedule features two exercise options – which may include Mayflower Yoga for Flexibility, Cardio Circuit, Aquatic Ballet and Pilates, among others – at 9am, 10am and 11am. The afternoon schedule is similar, but lists workshop titles such as Dream Interpretation, the Zen of Archery and Hypnotherapy. Hiking excursions, canoeing, tennis and golf are also available. And when you tire of appointments, you can lounge in the whirlpool, read in the library, wander through the waist-high maze of hedges or meditate your way through a granite and grass labyrinth.

Guests choose at the start of their stay whether they want to bond with others or stray from the pack. Itineraries are tailored to personal goals such as getting fit, sleeping better, losing weight or alleviating nutritional concerns. But all of those things should happen no matter what your focus is. The property exudes serenity and the experience, unlike nearby Canyon Ranch, is intimate; capacity is only 28 people. The staff are accommodating, the instructors are knowledgeable, and Adriana Mnuchin and daughter Lisa Hedley are involved and gracious hosts. The rooms, housing elevated four-poster beds, showers and bathtubs, are the epitome of comfort. The all-inclusive health-conscious cuisine is satiating and delicious.

The only unattractive aspect, in fact, is the steepness of the price tag. But to the clientele, about half of whom are New Yorkers, money isn't a roadblock to well-being. And if they are chastising themselves – for that or anything else – five days at the Destination Spa should correct it. It's about shedding original guilt and 'giving yourself permission to enjoy the experience,' Hedley says, in the welcoming Stretch and Release class. In other words, you'll never leave the garden full of shame.

Mayflower Inn & Spa

118 Woodbury Road, route 47, Washington, CT (860 868 9466/www.mayflowerinn.com). 5-day session $6,700 or $6,200 each for 2 if sharing a room; special weekend stay $1,850-$2,310; special mini sessions occasionally available. **Getting there**: For this trip, it's best to rent a car. Check www.mayflowerinn.com for driving directions.

Art star

Dia:Beacon

Take a model example of early 20th-century industrial architecture. Combine it with some of the most ambitious and uncompromising art of the past 50 years. What do you get? One of the finest, most luxuriant aesthetic experiences on earth. Indeed, for the 24 artists whose work is on view, and for the visiting public, Dia:Beacon, Dia Art Foundation's new outpost in the Hudson Valley, is nothing short of a blessing.

Despite its cavernous Chelsea galleries (*see p117* Dia:Chelsea), Dia has never had adequate space to put its hugely scaled collection on permanent display. Its founders, Heiner Friedrich and his wife, Philippa de Menil, an heir to the Schlumberger oil fortune, acquired much of their holdings in the 1960s and '70s. They had a taste for the minimal, the conceptual and the monumental, and supported artists with radical ideas about what art was, what it could do and where it should happen. Together with others of their generation, the Dia circle (Robert Smithson, Michael Heizer, Walter De Maria, Donald Judd and Dan Flavin) made it difficult to consider a work of art apart from its context – be it visual, philosophical or historical – ever again. Thanks to the institution's current director Michael Govan, curator Lynne Cooke and board chairman Leonard Riggio (founder and chairman of Barnes & Noble, Inc), that context is now the biggest contemporary art museum in the world.

An 80-minute train ride from Grand Central, Dia:Beacon sits on a 31-acre tract overlooking the Hudson River. The 300,000-square-foot complex of three brick buildings was erected in 1929 as a box-printing factory for snack-manufacturing giant Nabisco (National Biscuit Company). No less than 34,000 square feet of north-facing skylights provide almost all of the illumination within. Nowhere does that light serve the art here better than in the immense gallery where 72 of the 102 canvases that make

Heaven is a place called **Mayflower Inn & Spa**. *See p356.*

Trips Out of Town

up Andy Warhol's rarely exhibited *Shadows* (1978-9) hang end to end like a mesmerising series of solar flares.

What really sets the Dia:Beacon experience apart, however, is its confounding intimacy. The design of the galleries and gardens by California light-and-space artist Robert Irwin, in collaboration with the Manhattan architectural collective OpenOffice, seems close to genius. Not only does it make this enormous museum feel like a private house, it allows Cooke to draw correspondences between artworks into an elegant narrative of connoisseurship.

Dia:Beacon

Reggio Galleries, 3 Beekman Street, Beacon, NY (1-845 440 0100/www.diabeacon.org). **Open** *14 Apr-17 Oct* 11am-6pm Mon, Thur-Sun. *21 Oct-10 Apr* 11am-4pm Mon, Fri-Sun. **Admission** $10; $7 seniors, students; free under-12s. **Credit** AmEx, MC, V. **Getting there**: Metro-North trains service the Beacon station, and discount rail and admission packages are available (www.mta.info).

Beach day

Sandy Hook

One thing you should know about Sandy Hook: there's a nude beach at its north end (it's called Gunnison Beach, and it's located at parking lot G, in case you're curious). Sure, the swinger set there compels boaters with binoculars to anchor close to shore, and it's also home to a cruisy gay scene – but there's much more to this 1,665-acre natural wonderland than sunbathers in the buff. Along with seven miles of dune-backed ocean beach, the Gateway National Recreation Area is home to the nation's oldest lighthouse (the only one remaining from colonial times), as well as extensive fortifications from the days when Sandy Hook formed the outer line of defence for New York Harbor. Natural areas like the Maritime Holly Forest attract an astounding variety of birds. In fact, large stretches of beach are closed in summer to allow the endangered piping plover a quiet place to mate. The park really does offer a bit of everything – including surfers catching waves within sight of the Manhattan skyline.

With all that the expansive Hook has to offer, it's a bit like having an island getaway at NYC's doorstep. There's even a cool way to get there: rather than take to the roads and their hair-tearing traffic only to find at the end of the drive that the parking lots are full, hop the ferry boat from Manhattan, and turn an excursion to the beach into a scenic mini-cruise. Once you dock at Fort Hancock after the one-hour crossing, it's a short walk to most of the beaches; and if you've still got energy for more, shuttle buses will transport you to any one of the other six strands along the peninsula.

As you'd expect, typical waterside snacks like hot dogs are available at concession stands, which can be found at each of the beach areas. But for more ambitious grub, like Caesar salad with grilled tuna, head to the Seagull's Nest (1-732 872 0025), the park's one restaurant; it's

Dia:Beacon. *See p357.*

located at Area D, about three miles south of the ferry dock. Blanket picnics in the sand are permitted, so a great tip is to bring along goodies for dining alfresco. There are tables and grills for barbecues at Guardian Park at the south end of Fort Hancock.

If baking and eating in the sun all day doesn't appeal to you, there are plenty of historic sites worth exploring other than the lighthouse. The Fort Hancock Museum is located in one of the elegant century-old officer's houses that form an arc facing Sandy Hook Bay, and the abandoned forts make for an interesting day of sightseeing.

Sandy Hook Gateway National Recreation Area

1-732 872 5970/www.nps.gov/gate.
Getting there: Take the ferry. Board weekdays and weekends (June to Labor Day) from W 34th Street at Hudson River or at Pier 11 in the Financial District (at the eastern end of Wall Street). Contact Sea Streak (1-800 262 8743, www.seastreak.com) for reservations and departure times. The return boat leaves at 4.30pm. **Fares** $33. **Travel time** 55mins.

Hit the trail

The city's parks are great places for hanging out, but if you are hankering for a *real* fresh-air escape, you need to be more than a few blocks away from Times Square. These three nearby day hikes will satisfy your desire for nature. When heading out, be sure to take bottled water and energy-producing snacks.

Breakneck Ridge

The trek at Breakneck Ridge is a favourite of many local hikers for its accessibility, variety of trails and awe-inspiring views of the Hudson Valley. The head is roughly a two-mile walk along the highway from the Cold Spring stop on Metro-North's Hudson line (on weekends the train stops closer to the trail at the Breakneck Ridge stop). You'll find the start of the trail on the river's eastern bank, atop a tunnel that was drilled out for Route 9D; it's marked with small white paint splotches (called blazes in hiking parlance) on nearby trees. Be advised: Breakneck got its name for a reason. The initial trail ascends 500 feet in a mile and a half and gains another 500 feet by a series of dips and rises over the next few miles. The hike is not recommended if you're not in good shape. If you do choose this path, there are plenty of dramatic overlooks where you can rest, refuel with water and a snack, and stretch out on a rock. After the difficult initial climb, Breakneck Ridge offers options for all levels of hikers. Several crossings in the first few miles provide alternative routes

Sandy Hook. See p358.

down. Maps of all the paths, which are clearly marked with differently coloured blazes along the way, are available from the New York-New Jersey Trail Conference. Depending on your trail choices, you can spend anywhere from two hours to a full day hiking Breakneck. For trail information and to obtain a map (strongly advised), contact the New York-New Jersey Trail Conference: 1-201 512 9348, www.nynjtc.org.
Getting there: Take the Metro-North Hudson train from Grand Central to the Cold Spring stop. You can get closer to the start of the trail by catching the line's early train to the Breakneck Ridge stop, Sat & Sun only 7.51am and 8.51am. Return trains at 4.44pm and 6.55pm. **Fares** $20 round trip, off-peak. Contact the MTA for schedules (www.mta.nyc.info).

Harriman State Park

Just across the Hudson and south-west of the sprawling campus of West Point is Harriman State Park. You can access its more than 200 miles of trails and 31 lakes – many of which you can swim in – from stops on the Metro-North Port Jervis line. Of the trail options, our favourite is the Triangle Trail, an eight-mile jaunt beginning just past the parking lot at Tuxedo station – about an hour from Penn Station. Triangle leads up steadily more than 1,000 feet towards the summit of Parker Cabin Mountain before turning south to offer views of

Trips Out of Town

All aboard!

Take a ferry up the Hudson River to these opulent historic mansions.

Kykuit

Neatly perched atop a hill in Westchester County, Kykuit (*pictured*), the Rockefeller family's stately manor, and its elaborately landscaped grounds resemble a miniature Versailles. The estate had been off-limits to the public for almost 80 years, but today a network of ferries and trains travelling from Manhattan rendezvous with buses that carry passengers to Kykuit; tours are held in conjunction with historic Philipsburg Manor in nearby Sleepy Hollow. (You'll be familiar with the village's name from Tim Burton's 1999 eponymous film, which was based on a story by Washington Irving.) It may be true that a Kykuit visit isn't the cheapest way to spend a day, but the chance to inspect one of the region's most remarkable interiors and get a glimpse into the lives of an incredibly influential American family really is priceless.

The ferry docks at a pier at Sleepy Hollow and the transition from ferry to bus generally goes smoothly, but some passengers may find themselves standing during the short ride to Philipsburg. Once there, visitors have about an hour in which to explore the compound, which has been restored to resemble a working 18th-century farm, complete with animals and all.

The portals to Kykuit, the Rockefeller family's primary dwelling until the 1980s, first opened to the public in 1992. The two-hour tour of the house and galleries snakes through eight of the boxy Italianate mansion's 40 rooms. Art on display includes stunning Ming vases, sculptures by Rodin and Giacometti and a dozen or so Picasso tapestries. At midpoint the tour spills into the Beaux Arts garden abutting the house;

from the back terrace, verdant hills unfurl towards the Hudson like an Asher B Durand landscape. After descending into a basement-chamber-turned-art-gallery, tour groups head to the coach house – a shrine of sorts for about 30 vintage carriages and automobiles, which have been accumulated by the family over the years. Motorised vehicles on display include a Ford Model S Roadster from 1907, a 1924 Model T and Nelson Rockefeller's spectacular bulletproof black limousine.

Metro-North offers a less costly round-trip package to Sleepy Hollow and Kykuit – allowing visits to Philipsburg, Washington Irving's old home of Sunnyside and railroad baron Jay Gould's Gothic Revival Lyndhurst Castle – but the view from a train rarely compares with the ferry's stunning view of the scenery that lines the Hudson River. Once the boat glides beneath the George Washington Bridge, the apartment complexes start to disappear from the Palisades. And on the return trip, the hazy apparition on the horizon sharpens into yet another (at least partially) Rockefeller production: Manhattan's forest of skyscrapers.

Kykuit

Pocantico Hills, Tarrytown (1-914 631 9491/ www.hudsonvalley.org). **Open** *May-early Nov* 9am-3pm Mon, Wed-Sun. **Admission** $22; $20 seniors; $18 children; not recommended for children under 10. **Credit** MC, V.
Getting there: NY Waterway runs ferries that include admission and buses to Philipsburg Manor and the Kykuit house and galleries tour in the ticket prices. (May-Nov Sat, Sun, 1-800 533 3779, www.nywaterway.com). If you prefer to travel by land, you can take the train: Metro-North offers a round-trip and admission package.

lakes Skenonto and Sebago. From there, it heads down steadily, steeply at times, and ends, after a little more than five miles, at a path marked with red dashes on white. It's a long distance to cover, but the terrain is varied and peaceful. Also, there are intersecting short cuts you can take back to the trailhead. On a hot day, however, the best detour is a dip in one of the lakes and a nap in the sun.
Getting there: Take the Metro-North/NJ Transit Port Jervis train, Penn Station to Tuxedo line (with a train switch in Secaucus, NJ). **Fares** $20 round trip, off-peak. Contact the MTA for schedules

(www.mta.nyc.info). For park information and maps of all the trails in Harriman State Park, contact the New York-New Jersey Trail Conference (1-201 512 9348, www.nynjtc.org); or Harriman State Park (1-845 786 2701, www.nysparks.state.ny.us).

Otis Pike Wilderness

If you're looking for ocean views and a less aggressive hike, Fire Island's Otis Pike Wilderness Area is the trek for you. Though it's an hour and a half on the LIRR from Penn Station to Patchogue, followed by a 30-minute

Other destinations

Several other magnificent historic homes (and their sprawling estates) dot the hills overlooking the Hudson River. The Historic Hudson Valley (1-914 631 8200, www.hudson valley.org) maintains many of these sites, which are open to the public throughout much of the year.

Lyndhurst Castle

635 South Broadway, Tarrytown, NY (1-914 631 4481/www.lyndhurst.org). **Open** *Mid Apr-Oct* 10am-5pm Tue-Sun, Mon holidays. *Dec-mid Apr* 10am-4.15pm Sat, Sun, Mon holidays. **Admission** $10; $9 seniors; $4 12-17s; free under-12s. *Grounds only* $4. **No credit cards**.

Several notable figures have called this Gothic Revival mansion 'home', including former New York City mayor William Paulding and Jay Gould. The interior is sumptuously decorated and lovingly maintained. **Getting there**: NY Waterway runs ferries that include admission and bus to Lyndhurst Castle (May-Nov Sat, Sun, 1-800 533 3779, www.ny waterway.com). Ferry departs at 10.30am at Pier 78 (at 38th Street). **Fares** $49; $25 children. If you prefer to travel by land, you can take the train: from Grand Central, the estate is a scenic 40-minute trip by Metro-North (Hudson line) to Tarrytown and a five-minute taxi ride from the train station.

Sunnyside

West Sunnyside Lane, off Route 9, Tarrytown, NY (1-914 591 8763/www.hudsonvalley.org). **Open** *Mar* 10am-3pm Sat, Sun. *Apr-Oct* 10am-5pm Mon, Wed-Sun. *Nov, Dec* 10am-4pm Mon, Wed-Sun. **Admission** $10; $9 seniors; $6 5-17s; free under-5s. **No credit cards**.

Author Washington Irving renovated and expanded his 18th-century Dutch Colonial cottage in Tarrytown, adding a stepped-gable entrance and a Spanish-style tower (*photo below*).

Getting there: NY Waterway runs ferry services that include cottage admission and buses to Sleepy Hollow's Sunnyside and Philipsburg Manor (May-Nov Sat, Sun, 1-800 533 3779, www.nywaterway.com). Ferry departs at 10.30am at Pier 78 (at 38th Street). **Fares** $46; $25 children. If you prefer to travel by land, you can take the train: Metro-North (*see p369*).

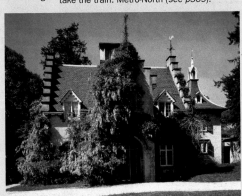

ferry ride to the Watch Hill Visitor Center, Otis Pike's pristine beaches and wildlife are worth the journey. The stretch of preserved wilderness from Watch Hill to Smith Point is home to deer, rabbits, foxes and numerous types of seabirds, including the piping plover, which nests during the summer. Be sure you stay out of the plovers' nesting grounds, which are marked with signs, and don't feed any wildlife you see along the way.

Fire Island is completely flat, apart from a few sand dunes, though trolling the beaches and sandy paths can be slow going. After traversing the boardwalk leading from the Watch Hill Center, hike along Burma Road, a path that runs across the entire island, and in seven miles you'll arrive at the Wilderness Visitor Center at Smith Point.

For a more scenic 14-mile loop, you can hike out along Burma Road and take a different route back along the shoreline – just make sure you stay on the most-travelled paths in order to minimise your effect on the area's fragile ecosystem.

Trips Out of Town

City Island. *See p363.*

Getting there: LIRR Montauk Line, Penn Station to Patchogue. Fares $19 round trip: call 1-718 217 5477. The Davis Park Ferry from Patchogue to Watch Hill is $14 round trip; call 1-631 475 1665 for schedules (May-Oct). For Otis Pike information, contact Fire Island National Seashore (1-631 289 4810, www.nps.gov/fiis).

New England in New York

City Island

Out here, you've got your clam diggers and you've got your mussel suckers. Clam diggers are those folks who were born on City Island – the 1.5-by-1-mile spit of land that lies off the north-east coast of the Bronx on Long Island Sound. Mussel suckers are everybody else.

Today, the number of clam diggers is dwindling. But the small-town feel on City Island – like a tiny New England fishing village in New York City – survives. This is despite the legions of off-islanders who cross the bridge from Pelham Bay Park each weekend to inhale fried clams at one of the restaurants lining City Island Avenue before dashing back to the city. Buffered from the rest of New York by the expanse of Pelham Bay Park, this community of 4,500 feels preserved in amber. There's even a City Island accent: a unique blend of Bronx squonk and New England bray.

The **City Island Nautical Museum** (190 Fordham Street, between Minnieford & King Avenues, 1-718 885 0008, open 1-5pm Sun only), housed in a quaint former schoolhouse, is stocked with model ships, Revolutionary War artefacts and tributes to such local heroes as Ruby Price Dill, the island's first kindergarten teacher. It also has a room devoted to the island's past as a centre of maritime activity. In its heyday, around World War II, City Island was home to no fewer than 17 shipyards. Seven America's Cup-winning yachts were built on the island (and, residents inevitably add, the Cup was lost in 1983 – the very year they stopped building the boats here).

There are still several yacht clubs in operation on these shores and a few sailmakers in the phone book, but City Islanders are more likely to head into Manhattan for work nowadays. Few commercial fishermen are left, though you'd hardly guess it walking into the **Boat Livery** (663 City Island Avenue, at Sutherland Street, 1-718 885 1843) – a bait-and-tackle shop and bar that's changed so little over the past decades that the 'updated' boat-rental prices painted next to the door still read '$2 per day'. The bar, which is dripping with fishing paraphernalia and old Christmas lights, is locally known as the Worm Hole; it serves beer in plastic cups that you can take out to the dock

and drink while you watch the rented boats as they return to shore at sunset.

In summer, City Island is also worth an evening trip. With crab shanties on every corner and boats in the background, the small maritime community exudes a striking Nantucket charm. On Belden Point are **Johnny's Reef** (2 City Island Avenue, 1-718 885 2086) and **Tony's Pier Restaurant** (1 City Island Avenue, 1-718 885 1424); both have outdoor seating areas, and Johnny's Reef has telescopes too. Grab a couple of beers and a basket of fried clams, sit at one of the picnic benches and watch the boats sail by. On Wednesday evenings from mid May to mid September the island offers yacht races: the Eastchester Bay Wednesday Series.
Getting there: Take the 6 train to Pelham Bay Park and transfer to the Bx29 bus, which takes you to City Island.

Theme-park larks

Six Flags Great Adventure

If you like adrenaline-pumping rides and deep-fried junk food, with a lot of shirt-soaking water rides thrown in for good measure, then we have the theme park for you – **Six Flags Great Adventure**. In 2005 Great Adventure heralded the opening of the 'fastest and tallest rollercoaster on Earth', Kingda Ka. Not for the faint of heart, this monster hurls riders 456 feet into the sky at speeds up to 128 miles per hour. (Psst! We hear that the best way to experience this thrilling ride is to eat a few burgers right before you go on and sit in the very front car.)

Whatever rides you choose, it's best to start slowly. You'll need to build courage (and stomach) for the more turbulent attractions to come. A good place to begin is on the huge Ferris wheel, which affords a bird's-eye view of all the main attractions. Swinging from a basket 150 feet in the air, you can scope out the goods on offer: 12 rollercoasters lie in wait for you, not to mention the various spin and puke rides, like Spinmeister and Taz Twister. Follow up the Ferris wheel with a jaunt on Skull Mountain, an in-the-dark rollercoaster (think Disney World's Space Mountain, only smaller). Runaway Train is another coaster with training wheels. Or if you're feeling wimpy, just take a spin on the carousel.

Food is central to Great Adventure, so you should indulge in a corn dog and some cheese fries during a break from the rides. Post-digestion, it's time for the biggies. On the less scary side, there's Rolling Thunder, a wooden coaster that reminds New Yorkers of Coney Island's Cyclone; it's fun but bumpy. Next up,

Trips Out of Town

try the Great American Scream Machine, which has more loops than a Slinky toy. Medusa, a 61mph 'floorless' coaster (the seats are designed so that you're strapped in, but your feet dangle in the air) that plunges from a full 13 storeys in the sky is a hoot. There's also the Chiller, a terrifying-looking coaster that goes both forward and back. Afterwards, you can opt for a hot funnel cake, a sweet way to refuel after a full eight hours of adrenaline surge and burn.

Six Flags Great Adventure

Route 537, Jackson, NJ (1-732 928 1821).
Getting there: NJ Transit buses service Great Adventure daily. Buses leave Port Authority at 9.30am, returning at 8.30pm (sharp!). Call 1-800 772 2222. A round-trip ticket ($50) includes park admission.

A mood for food

Culinary Institute of America

If you're the type of person who rips the recipes out of glossy food magazines and prowls fancy kitchen-supply stores on Sunday afternoons, but you hardly ever so much as crack an egg, you might need a stint at the Culinary Institute of America. Of course, no one's suggesting that you actually change your ways by enrolling in a cooking school. But if you're a food lover, a great place to spend a day is on the CIA campus in Hyde Park, where just one afternoon can fulfil all sorts of epicurean fantasies.

Sprawled over 150 hilly and beautiful acres that overlook the Hudson River, this is the country's oldest culinary college, and also a monument to the romance of the cooking life. The academy once housed a seminary, and as a result the lush campus retains a wonderful sense of calm and serenity.

Although the 2,500 full-time students here pay up to $20,000 a year for the privilege, you can get in on the action for just $5 – not much more than an issue of *Saveur*. The price buys you a tour through Roth Hall, which contains the majority of the campus's 38 kitchens and three of its four restaurants. On Mondays (10am and 4pm), Wednesdays and Thursdays (4pm), enthusiastic student guides take you past the fragrant kitchens, where aspiring chefs work on buttery sauces, vegetable sautées, roast meats and chocolate sculptures. Roth Hall was clearly designed with the voyeur in mind, with windows to the instructional kitchens facing the hallways.

And if this isn't enough, diehard foodies can enroll in a Saturday class. You can choose from a wide range of topics listed on the CIA website. These six-hour classes will set you back about $165 – but just think of all the money you'll save when you start cooking at home instead of eating out.

When you call to sign up for a tour, it's a good idea to book a table at one of the school's four public restaurants: St Andrews Café (serving up grilled meats and fish; vegetarian entrées), Caterina de Medici (perfect for Italian food), American Bounty (for an upscale American menu) or the Escoffier Restaurant (elegant classical French cuisine). The food alone makes a meal here almost worth the trip – with the walking tour as an added bonus. The school also has a no reservation-required place: the Apple Pie Bakery – perfect for a yummy sweet treat. If you are visiting between January and March, or September and early December, ask about the CIA Dining Series – a selection of lectures and tastings that are sure to inspire.

The restaurants stay open for dinner, but by the time the evening rolls around, you'll be ready to board the train back home to get a headstart filling out that CIA application form you picked up on your tour.

Culinary Institute of America

1946 Campus Drive, Hyde Park, NY (1-845 471 6608/www.ciachef.edu).
Getting there: Take a Metro-North train from Grand Central to Poughkeepsie ($26 round trip, off-peak). A cab ride from Poughkeepsie station to the CIA costs $7. (There's almost always a cab or two waiting at the station's taxi stand.)

Six Flags Great Adventure.
See p363.

Directory

Directory

Getting to & from NYC

By air

Airlines

Air Canada *1-800 361 5373/ www.aircanada.ca.*
American Airlines *1-800 433 7300/www.aa.com.*
British Airways *1-800 247 9297/www.britishairways.com.*
Delta Air Lines *1-800 221 1212/www.delta.com.*
JetBlue Airways *1-800 538 2583/www.jetblue.com.*
Northwest/KLM *1-800 225 2525/www.nwa.com.*
United Airlines *1-800 241 6522/www.united.com.*
US Airways *1-800 428 4322/www.usairways.com.*
Virgin Atlantic *1-800 862 8621/www.virgin-atlantic.com.*

To & from the airport

For a list of transport services between New York City and its major airports, call 1-800 247 7433. Public transport is the cheapest method, but it can be both frustrating and time-consuming. None of the airports is particularly close or convenient. Private bus or van services are usually the best bargains. Medallion (city-licensed) yellow cabs, which can be flagged on the street or picked up at designated locations at airports, are more expensive but take you all the way to your destination for a fixed, zoned price, with any tolls on top. (Not so in reverse.) You may also reserve a car service in advance to pick you up or drop you off (*see p369* Taxis & car services). Although it is illegal, many car-service drivers and unlicensed 'gypsy cabs' solicit riders around the baggage-claim areas. Avoid them.

Bus services

New York Airport Service

1-212 875 8200/www.nyairport service.com. Call or visit website for schedule.
Buses operate frequently between Manhattan and both JFK (one way $15/round trip $27) and La Guardia ($12/$21), from early morning to late at night, with stops near Grand Central Terminal (Park Avenue, between 41st & 42nd Streets), near Penn Station (33rd Street, at Seventh Avenue), inside the Port Authority Bus Terminal (*see p367* By bus) and outside a number of midtown hotels (for an extra charge). Buses also operate from JFK to La Guardia (one way $13).

Olympia Trails/ Coach USA

1-212 964 6233/1-877 894 9155/ www.olympiabus.com. Call or visit website for schedule.
Olympia operates between Newark Airport and Manhattan, stopping outside Grand Central Station (41st Street, between Park & Lexington Avenues), and inside Port Authority. The fare is $14 one way (round trip $23); buses leave every 15-20mins, day and night.

SuperShuttle

1-212 209 7000/www.super shuttle.com. 24hrs daily.
Blue SuperShuttle vans offer door-to-door service between NYC and the three major airports. Allow extra time to catch your flight, as vans will be picking up other passengers. The fare varies from $13 to $22, depending on pickup location and destination. Always call to confirm.

Airports

Three major airports service the New York City area, plus the smaller MacArthur Airport on Long Island, served by domestic flights only.

John F Kennedy International Airport

1-718 244 4444/www.panynj.gov.

At $2, the bus and subway link from JFK is dirt cheap but it can take up to two hours to get to Manhattan. At the airport, look for the yellow shuttle bus to the Howard Beach station (free), then take the A train to Manhattan. Thankfully, JFK's AirTrain now offers faster service between all eight airport terminals and the A, E, J and Z subway lines, as well as the Long Island Rail Road, for $5. Visit www.airtrainjfk.com for more information. Private bus and van services are a good compromise between value and convenience (*see above* Bus services). A medallion yellow cab from JFK to Manhattan will charge a flat $45 fare, plus toll (varies by route, but usually $4) and tip (if service is fine, give at least $5). Although metered (not a flat fee), the fare to JFK from Manhattan will be about the same cost. Check out www.nyc.gov/taxi for the latest cab rates.

La Guardia Airport

1-718 533 3400/www.panynj.gov.
Seasoned New Yorkers take the M60 bus ($2), which runs between the airport and 106th Street, at Broadway. The ride takes 40mins to an hour (depending on traffic) and runs from 4.30am to 1.30am daily. The route crosses Manhattan at 125th Street in Harlem. Get off at Lexington Avenue for the 4, 5 and 6 trains; at Malcolm X Boulevard (Lenox Avenue) for the 2 and 3; or at St Nicholas Avenue for the A, B, C and D trains. You can also disembark on Broadway at 116th or 110th Street for the 1 and 9 trains. Less time-consuming options: private bus services cost around $14; taxis and car services charge about $28, plus toll and tip.

MacArthur Airport

1-631 467 3210/www.mac arthurairport.com.
Some flights into this airport in Islip, Long Island, may be cheaper than flights into those above. Getting to Manhattan, of course, 50 miles away, will take longer and be more expensive, unless you take the LIRR. Fares are generally $13 and a shuttle from the airport to the train station is $5. For car service Colonial Transportation (1-631-589 3500) will take up to four people to Manhattan for $143, including tolls and tip.

Newark Liberty International Airport

1-973 961 6000/www.newark airport.com.
Even though it's in next-door New Jersey, Newark still has good mass transit access to NYC. The best bet is a 40min, $11.55 trip by the New Jersey Transit to or from Penn Station. The airport's monorail, AirTrain Newark (www.airtrainnewark.com), is now linked to the NJ Transit and Amtrak train systems. For inexpensive buses, see bus services below. A car service or taxi will run at about $45, plus toll and tip.

By bus

Buses are an inexpensive means of getting to and from New York City, though the ride takes longer and is sometimes uncomfortable. Buses are particularly useful if you want to leave in a hurry; many don't require reservations. Most out-of-town buses come and go from the Port Authority Bus Terminal.

Bus stations

George Washington Bridge Bus Station

4211 Broadway, between 178th & 179th Streets (1-212 564 8484/ www.panynj.gov). Subway: A, 1 to 181st Street.
A few bus lines that serve New Jersey and Rockland County, New York, use this station.

Port Authority Bus Terminal

625 Eighth Avenue, between 40th & 42nd Streets (1-212 564 8484/ www.panynj.gov). Subway: A, C, E to 42nd St-Port Authority.
This somewhat unlovely terminus is the hub for many transportation companies offering commuter and long-distance bus services to and from New York City. If you have an early departure, bring your own breakfast, as the concessions don't open until around 7am. As with any transport terminal, watch out for petty criminals, especially late at night.

Long-distance lines

Greyhound Trailways

1-800 229 9424/www.greyhound. com. **Open** 24hrs daily. **Credit** AmEx, DC, Disc, MC, V.

Greyhound offers long-distance bus travel to destinations across North America.

New Jersey Transit

1-800 772 2222/www.njtransit.com. Call or visit website for schedules. **Credit** MC, V.
NJT provides bus service to nearly everywhere in the Garden State and some destinations in New York State; most buses run around the clock.

Peter Pan

1-800 343 9999/www.peterpanbus. com. **Open** 24hrs daily. **Credit** MC, V.
Peter Pan runs extensive service to cities across the North-east; its tickets are also valid on Greyhound.

By car

If you drive to the city, you may encounter delays at bridge and tunnel crossings (check www.nyc.gov and www.panynj.gov before driving in). Tune your car radio to WINS (1010 on the AM dial) for up-to-the-minute traffic reports. Delays can run anywhere from 15 minutes to two hours – plenty of time to get your money out for the toll ($4 is average). It makes sense, of course, to time your arrival and departure against the commuter flow.

For driving in the city, *see p370.*

Parking

We recommend that if you drive to NYC, you should head for a garage, park your car and leave it there. Parking on the street is problematic and car theft is not unheard of. Garages are plentiful but expensive. If you want to park for less than $15 a day, try a garage outside Manhattan and take public transport into the city. Listed below are Manhattan's better deals. For other options, see the Yellow Pages.

Central Kinney System

www.centralparking.com. **Open** 24hrs daily, most locations. **Credit** AmEx, MC, V.
One of the city's largest parking companies, Kinney is accessible and reliable, though not the cheapest in town. Rates vary, so call for prices.

GMC Park Plaza

1-212 888 7400. **Open** 24hrs daily, most locations. **Credit** AmEx, MC, V.
GMC has more than 70 locations in the city. At $28 overnight, including tax, the one at 407 E 61st Street, between First and York Avenues (1-212 838 4158) is one of the least expensive.

Icon Parking

www.iconparking.com. **Open** 24hrs daily, most locations. **Credit** AmEx, MC, V.
Choose from more than 160 locations via the website to guarantee a spot and price ahead of time.

Standard Parking

Pier 40, West Street, at W Houston Street (1-800 494 7007). **Open** 24hrs daily. **Rates** $16 for 12hrs. **Credit** AmEx, MC, V.
Mayor Parking, another of the city's large chains, offers indoor and outdoor parking. Call for information and for other locations.

By train

America's national rail service is run by Amtrak. Nationwide routes are slow, infrequent and unreliable (if characterful), but there are some good fast services linking the eastern seaboard cities. For commuter rail services, *see p369.*

Train stations

Grand Central Terminal

From 42nd to 44th Streets, between Vanderbilt & Lexington Avenues. Subway: 42nd Street S, 4, 5, 6, 7 to 42nd Street-Grand Central.
Grand Central is home to Metro-North, which runs trains to more than 100 stations throughout New York State and Connecticut. Schedules are available at the terminal. As well as one of New York's loveliest buildings, it's a big retail centre with some excellent eating and drinking venues, including the famous Oyster Bar.

Penn Station

31st to 33rd Streets, between Seventh & Eighth Avenues. Subway: A, C, E, 1, 2, 3 to 34th Street-Penn Station.
Amtrak, Long Island Rail Road and New Jersey Transit trains depart from this terminal, which has printed schedules available.

Directory

Getting Around

Orientation

Manhattan is divided into three major sections: Downtown, which includes all neighbourhoods south of 14th Street; Midtown, roughly the area between 14th and 59th Streets; and Uptown, north of 59th Street.

Generally, avenues run north-south along the length of Manhattan. They are always parallel to one another and are logically numbered, with a few exceptions, such as Broadway, Columbus and Lexington Avenues. Manhattan's centre is Fifth Avenue, so all buildings located east of it will have 'East' addresses, with numbers getting higher towards the East River, and those west of it will have 'West' numbers that get higher towards the Hudson River. Streets are also parallel to one another, but they run east to west, or crosstown, and are numbered, from 1st Street up to 220th Street.

The neighbourhoods of lower Manhattan – including the Financial District, Tribeca, Chinatown and Greenwich Village – were settled prior to urban planning and can be confusing to walk through. Their charming lack of logic makes frequent reference to a map essential.

Public transport

Changes to subway and bus schedules can occur at the last minute, so pay attention to the posters on subway station walls and any announcements you may hear in trains and on subway platforms.

Metropolitan Transportation Authority (MTA)
Travel info 1-718 330 1234/ updates 1-718 243 7777/ www.mta.info.

The MTA runs the subway and bus lines, as well as a number of alternative commuter services to points outside Manhattan. You can get news of service interruptions and download the most current MTA maps from the website. Be warned: backpacks and handbags may be subject to random searches.

City buses

MTA buses are fine… if you're not in a hurry, or just using them for sightseeing. They are white and blue and display a digital destination sign on the front, along with a route number preceded by a letter (M for Manhattan). The $2 fare is payable with a **MetroCard** (*see below*) or exact change (coins only; no pennies). MTA's express buses usually head to the outer boroughs for a $5 fare.

MetroCards allow automatic transfers from bus to bus and between buses and subways. If you pay cash, and you're travelling uptown or downtown and want to go crosstown (or vice versa), ask the driver for a transfer when you get on – you'll be given a ticket for use on the second leg of your journey, valid for two hours. Maps are posted on most buses and at all subway stations; they're also available from NYC & Company (*see p383* Tourist information). The Manhattan bus map is reprinted in this guide (*see p413*). All buses are equipped with wheelchair lifts. Contact the MTA for further information.

Subways

The subway is the fastest way to get around town during the day, and it's far cleaner and safer than it was 20 years ago. The city's system is one of the world's largest and cheapest: $2 will get you from the depths of Brooklyn to the furthest reaches of the Bronx and anywhere in between (though the subway doesn't service Staten Island). Trains run around the clock, but with sparse service and fewer riders at night, it's advisable (and usually quicker) to take a cab after 10pm.

Ongoing improvements have resulted in several changes. This guide provides the most current subway map at press time (*see pp414-415*); you can also ask MTA workers in service booths for a free copy.

To ensure safety, don't stand near the edge of the platform. Late at night and early in the morning, board the train from the designated off-peak waiting area, usually near the middle of the platform; this area is more secure than the ends of the platforms or the outermost cars, which are often less populated at night. Standard urban advice: hold your bag with the opening facing you, keep your wallet in a front pocket and don't wear flashy jewellery. Remember that petty crime increases during the holidays.

METROCARDS

To enter the subway system, you need a MetroCard (it also works on buses), which you can buy from a booth in the station or from one of the brightly coloured MetroCard vending machines, which accept cash, debit and credit cards (AmEx, Disc, MC, V), as well as the NY Convention & Visitors Bureau, the New York Transit Museum in Brooklyn, and many hotels. Free transfers between buses and subways are available only with a **MetroCard**.

There are two types of metro card: pay-per-use and unlimited-ride. Up to four people can use a pay-per-use card, which is sold in denominations from $4 (two trips) to $80. A $20 card offers 12 trips for the price of 10. If you're planning to use the subway or buses often, an unlimited-ride MetroCard is great value. These cards are offered in three amounts: a one-day Fun Pass ($7, available at station vending machines but not at booths), a seven-day pass ($24) and a 30-day pass ($76). These are good for unlimited rides, but you can't share a card with your travel companions, since you can only swipe it once every 18 minutes at a given subway station or on a bus.

SUBWAY LINES

Trains are identified by letters or numbers and are colour-coded according to the line on which they run. Stations are most often named after the street on which they're located. Entrances are marked with a green globe (open 24 hours) or a red globe (limited hours). Many stations have separate entrances for the uptown and downtown platforms – look before you pay.

Local trains stop at every station on the line; express trains make major-station stops only.

Train

The following commuter trains service NY's hinterland.

Long Island Rail Road

1-718 217 5477/www.lirr.org.
LIRR provides rail service from Penn Station, Brooklyn and Queens.

Metro-North

1-212 532 4900/1-800 638 7646/www.mnr.org.
Commuter trains service towns north of Manhattan and leave from Grand Central Terminal.

New Jersey Transit

1-973 762 5100/1-800 772 2222/ www.njtransit.com.
Service from Penn Station reaches most of New Jersey, some points in New York State and Philadelphia.

PATH Trains

1-800 234 7284/www.pathrail.com.
PATH (Port Authority Trans-Hudson) trains run from six stations in Manhattan to various places across the Hudson River in New Jersey, including Hoboken, Jersey City and Newark. The system is fully automated, and entry costs $1.50. You need change or crisp bills for the ticket machines, and trains run 24 hours a day. Manhattan PATH stations are marked on the subway map (*see p416*).

Taxis & car services

Taxicabs

Yellow cabs are hardly ever in short supply – except, of course, at rush hour and in nasty weather. Use only yellow medallion (licensed) cabs; avoid unregulated gypsy cabs. If the centre light on top of the taxi is lit, that means the cab is available and should stop if you flag it down. Jump in and then tell the driver where you're going. (New Yorkers generally give cross-streets rather than addresses.)

Taxis carry up to four people for the same price: $2.50 plus 40¢ per fifth of a mile, with an extra 50¢ charge from 8pm to 6am and a $1 surcharge during rush hour (weekdays from 4pm to 8pm). The average fare for a three-mile ride is $9-$11, depending on the time of day and on traffic (the meter adds another 20¢ per minute while the car is idling). Cabbies rarely allow more than four passengers in a cab (it's illegal, unless the fifth person is a child under seven), though it may be worth asking.

Not all drivers know their way around the city, so it helps if you know where you're going – and speak up. By law, taxis cannot refuse to take you anywhere inside the five boroughs or to New York airports, so don't be duped by a reluctant cabbie. They may still refuse; to avoid an argument, get out and try another cab. If you have a problem, take down the medallion and driver's numbers, posted on the partition. Always ask for a receipt – there's a meter number on it. To complain or to trace lost property, call the Taxi & Limousine Commission (1-212 227 0700, 8am-4pm Mon-Fri) or visit www.nyc.gov/taxi. Tip 15-20 per cent, as you would at a restaurant.

Late at night, cabs stick to fast-flowing routes. Try the avenues and key streets (Canal, Houston, 14th, 23rd, 34th, 42nd, 57th, 72nd and 86th). Bridge and tunnel exits are good for a steady flow of taxis returning from airports, and cabbies will usually head for nightclubs and big hotels. Otherwise, try the following:

Chinatown

Chatham Square, where Mott Street meets the Bowery, is an unofficial taxi stand. You can also try hailing a cab exiting the Manhattan Bridge at Bowery and Canal Street.

Lincoln Center

The crowd heads towards Columbus Circle for a cab; those in the know go west to Amsterdam Avenue.

Lower East Side

Katz's Deli (Houston Street, at Ludlow Street) is a cabbies' hangout; also try Delancey Street, where cabs come in over the Williamsburg Bridge.

Midtown

Penn Station, Grand Central Terminal and the Port Authority Bus Terminal attract cabs all night.

Soho

If you're on the west side, try Sixth Avenue; east side, the intersection of Houston Street and Broadway.

Times Square

This busy area has 30 taxi stands. Look for the yellow globes on poles.

Tribeca

Cabs head up Hudson Street. The Tribeca Grand (2 Sixth Avenue, between Walker & White Streets) is another good bet.

Directory

Car services

Car services are also regulated by the Taxi & Limousine Commission (*see p369*). Unlike cabs, they aren't yellow and drivers can make only pre-arranged pickups. If you see a black Lincoln Town Car, it most likely belongs to a car service. Don't try to hail one, and be wary of those that offer you a ride; they may not be licensed or insured, and you could get ripped off.

The following companies will pick you up anywhere in the city, at any time of day or night, for a set fare.

Carmel
1-212 666 6666.

Dial 7
1-212 777 7777.

Tri-State Limousine
1-212 777 7171.

Driving

Manhattan drivers (especially cabbies) are fearless; so taking to the streets is not for the faint of heart. It's best to try to restrict your driving to evening hours, when traffic is lighter and there's more street parking available. Even then, keep your eyes on the road and stay alert.

Car rental

Car rental is much cheaper in the city's outskirts and in New Jersey and Connecticut than in Manhattan; reserve ahead for weekends. Another way to save money is to rent from an independent agency, such as **Aamcar**. Log on to www.car rentalexpress.com for more independent companies.

Companies located outside New York State do not include LDW (loss/damage waiver) insurance in their rate, which means you will need to pay for any damage to the car unless you are covered under another policy or by your credit card.

Rental companies in New York State are required by law to insure their own cars, though the renter pays for the first $100 in damage to the rental vehicle. Personal liability insurance is advised wherever you rent (unless your travel insurance or home policy covers it). UK residents may find rental car insurance more cheaply on www.insurance 4carhire.com.

You will need a credit card (or a large cash deposit) to rent a car, and you usually have to be at least 25 years old. All car-rental companies listed below add sales tax (8.625 per cent). If you know you want to rent a car before you travel, ask your travel agent or airline to check for special deals and discounts, or look online.

Aamcar

315 W 96th Street, between West End Avenue & Riverside Drive (1-800 722 6923/1-212 222 8500/ www.aamcar.com). Subway: 1, 2, 3 to 96th Street. **Open** 7.30am-7.30pm Mon-Fri; 9am-3pm Sat; 9am-7pm Sun. **Credit** AmEx, DC, Disc, MC, V. Compact rates from $49.95 per day, unlimited mileage; $39.95 with 100 free miles.
Alamo *US: 1-800 462 5266/ www.alamo.com. UK: 0870 400 562/www.alamo.co.uk.*
Avis *US: 1-800 230 4898/ www.avis.com. UK: 0870 606 0100/www.avis.co.uk.*
Budget *US: 1-800 527 0700/ www.budget.com. UK: 0870 153 170/www.budget.co.uk.*
Dollar *US: 1-800 800 3665/ www.dollar.com. UK: 0800 085 578/www.dollar.co.uk.*
Enterprise *US: 1-800 261 7331/ www.enterprise.com. UK: 0870 350 3000/www.enterprise.com/uk.*
Hertz *US: 1-800 654 3131/ www.hertz.com. UK: 0870 844 8844/www.hertz.co.uk.*
National *US: 1-800 227 7368. UK: 0116 217 3884. Both: www.nationalcar.com.*
Thrifty *US: 1-800 847 4389/ www.thrifty.com. UK: 01494 51600/www.thrifty.co.uk.*

Street parking

Make sure you read parking and meter signs and never park within 15 feet of a fire hydrant (to avoid a $115 ticket and/or having your car towed). Parking is off-limits on most streets for at least a few hours every day. The Department of Transportation (dial 311) provides information on daily changes to parking regulations. If precautions fail, call 1-718 935 0096 for towing and impoundment information.

Emergency towing

Oz Towing

356 West Street at Clarkson Street (1-212-247-0445/www.towingnew yorkcity.com). **Open** 24hrs daily; repairs 9am-5pm daily. **Credit** AmEx, Disc, MC, V.
All types of repairs are carried out on domestic and foreign vehicles.

24-hour gas stations

Exxon

24 Second Avenue, at 1st Street (1-212 979 7000). **Credit** AmEx, MC, V. Repairs.

Hess

502 W 45th Street, at Tenth Avenue (1-212 245 6594). **Credit** AmEx, DC, Disc, MC, V. No repairs.

Cycling

Aside from the immensely pleasurable cycling in Central Park, and along the wide bike paths around the perimeter of Manhattan (now virtually circumnavigated by paths) biking in the city streets is no picnic and is not recommended for urban beginners. Still, zipping through bumper-to-bumper traffic holds a certain allure, especially for those with good cycling skills, a helmet and a motorists-be-damned attitude. For bike rentals and citywide bike paths, *see p336.*

Walking

One of the best ways to take in NYC is on foot. Most of the streets are laid out in a grid pattern and are relatively easy to navigate. Our full set of street maps (*pp402-412*) makes it even easier.

Resources A-Z

Age restrictions

In NYC, you must be 18 to buy tobacco products and 21 to buy or to be served alcohol. Some bars and clubs admit patrons between 18 and 21, but you'll be ejected if you're caught drinking alcohol. Always carry picture ID as even those well over 21 can be asked to show proof of age and identity.

Business

Consumer information

Better Business Bureau

1-212 533 6200/
www.newyork.bbb.org.
The BBB offers advice on consumer-related complaints (shopping, services, etc). Each phone enquiry costs $5 (plus New York City tax) and must be charged to a credit card; the online service is free.

New York City Department of Consumer Affairs

42 Broadway, between Beaver Street & Exchange Place (311 local, 1-212 639 9675 out of state/www.nyc.gov/ consumer). Subway: 4, 5 to Bowling Green. **Open** 9am-5pm Mon-Fri. File complaints on consumer-related matters here.

New York City 311 Call Center

311.
This non-emergency three-digit number was established in 2004 as a means for residents to get answers and register complaints about city issues ranging from parking regulations and small claims court to real-estate auctions and consumer tips.

International couriers

DHL Worldwide Express

Call to find the office nearest you or to arrange a pickup at your door (1-800 225 5345/www.dhl.com). **Credit** AmEx, DC, Disc, MC, V. DHL will send a courier to pick up packages at any NYC address, or you can deliver packages in person to one of its offices or drop-off points. Cash is not accepted.

FedEx

Call to find the office nearest you or to arrange a pickup at your door (1-800 247 4747/www.fedex.com). **Credit** AmEx, DC, Disc, MC, V. Packages headed overseas should be dropped off by 6pm for International Priority delivery (depending on destination), and by 9pm for packages to most destinations in the US (some locations have a later cut-off time; call to check).

UPS

Various locations throughout the city; free pickup at your door (1-800 742 5877/www.ups.com). **Open** Hours

vary by office; call for locations and times. **Credit** AmEx, MC, V. Like DHL and FedEx, UPS will send a courier to pick up parcels at any address in the five boroughs. The city's 30 retail locations (formerly Mail Boxes Etc) also offer mailbox rental, mail forwarding, packaging, phone-message service, copying and faxing. UPS provides domestic and international services.

Messenger services

A to Z Couriers

106 Ridge Street, between Rivington & Stanton Streets (1-212 253 6500/ www.atozcouriers.com). Subway: F to Delancey Street; J, M, Z to Delancey-Essex Streets. **Open** 8am-8pm Mon-Fri. **Credit** AmEx, MC, V. These cheerful couriers will deliver in the city (also national and international).

Breakaway

335 W 35th Street, between Eighth & Ninth Avenues (1-212 947 4455/ www.breakawaycourier.com). Subway: A, C, E to 34th Street-Penn Station. **Open** 7am-9pm Mon-Fri; 9am-5pm Sat; noon-5pm Sun. **Credit** AmEx, MC, V. Breakaway is a recommended local delivery service that promises to pick up and deliver within 90 minutes.

Jefron

55 Walker Street, between Church Street & West Broadway (1-212 431 6610/www.jefron.com). Subway: 1, 2, 3 to Chambers Street. **Open** 4am-8pm Mon-Fri. **No credit cards.** Jefron specialises in transporting import and export documents.

Photocopying & printing

The Copy Specialist

44 E 21st Street, at Park Avenue South (1-212 533 7560). Subway: N, R, W to 23rd Street. **Open** 8.30am-7pm Mon-Fri; 10am-4pm Sat. **Credit** AmEx, MC, V. Dependable provides offset, laser and colour printing; fax; large-format photocopies; binding and more. **Other locations:** 71 W 23rd Street, between Fifth & Sixth Avenues (1-646 336 6999).

Servco

1150 Sixth Avenue, between 44th & 45th Streets (1-212 575 0991). Subway: B, D, F, V to 47th-50th

---

Travel advice

For current information on travel to a specific country, including the latest news on health issues, safety and security, local laws and customs, contact your home country's government department of foreign affairs. Most have websites with useful advice for would-be travellers.

Australia
www.dfat.gov.au/travel

Ireland
www.irlgov.ie/iveagh

United Kingdom
www.fco.gov.uk/travel

Canada
www.voyage.gc.ca

New Zealand
www.mft.govt.nz/travel

USA
www.state.gov/travel

Directory

Streets-Rockefeller Center; 7 to Fifth Avenue. **Open** 8.30am-8pm Mon-Fri. **No credit cards.**
Photocopying, offset printing, blueprints and binding services are available.

Translation & language services

All Language Services
77 W 55th Street, between Fifth & Sixth Avenues (1-212 986 1688/ fax 1-212 265 1662). Subway: 42nd Street S, 4, 5, 6, 7 to 42nd Street-Grand Central. **Open** 24hrs daily. **Credit** AmEx, MC, V.
ALS will type or translate documents in any of 59 languages and provide interpreters.

Consulates

Check the phone book for a complete list of consulates and embassies. *See also p371* **Travel advice.**

Australia
1-212 351 6500.

Canada
1-212 596 1628.

Great Britain
1-212 745 0200.

Ireland
1-212 319 2555.

New Zealand
1-212 832 4038.

Customs

US Customs allows foreigners to bring in $100 worth of gifts (the limit is $800 for returning Americans) without paying duty. One carton of 200 cigarettes (or 50 cigars) and one litre of liquor (spirits) are allowed. Plants, meat and fresh produce of any kind cannot be brought into the country – not even a sandwich. You will have to fill out a form if you carry more than $10,000 in currency. You will be handed a white form on your inbound flight to fill in, confirming you have not exceeded any of these allowances.

If it is essential for you to bring prescription drugs into the US, make sure the container is clearly marked, and bring your doctor's statement or a prescription. Marijuana, cocaine and most opiate derivatives, along with a number of other drugs and chemicals, are not permitted: possession of them is punishable by a stiff fine and/or imprisonment. Check with the **US Customs Service** (www.customs.gov) before you arrive if you have any questions about what you can bring.

New York might be one of the world's great shopping destinations, but bear in mind that UK Customs still allows returning visitors to bring only £145 worth of 'gifts, souvenirs and other goods' into the country duty-free, along with the usual duty-free goods.

Disabled access

Under New York City law, all facilities constructed after 1987 must provide complete access for the disabled – restrooms, entrances and exits included. In 1990 the Americans with Disabilities Act made the same requirement federal law. In the wake of this legislation, many older buildings have added disabled-access features. There has been widespread (though imperfect) compliance with the law, but it's always a good idea to call ahead and check.

New York City can be challenging for disabled visitors. One useful resource is *Access for All*, a guide to New York's cultural institutions published by Hospital Audiences Inc (1-212 575 7660, www.hospaud.org). The online guide tells how accessible each location really is and includes information on the height of telephones and water fountains; hearing and visual aids; and passenger-loading

zones and alternative entrances. HAI's service for the visually impaired provides recordings of commentaries of theatre performances.

All Broadway theatres are equipped with devices for the hearing-impaired; call **Sound Associates** (1-212 582 7678, 1-888 772 7686) for more information. There are a number of other stage-related resources for the disabled. **Telecharge** (1-212 239 6200) reserves tickets for wheelchair seating in Broadway and Off Broadway venues while Theatre Development Fund's **Theater Access Project** (1-212 221 1103, www.tdf. org) arranges sign-language interpretation and captioning in American Sign Language for Broadway and Off Broadway shows. **Hands On** (1-212 740 3087, www. handson.org) does the same.

Lighthouse International
111 E 59th Street, between Park & Lexington Avenues (1-212 821 9200/www.lighthouse.org). Subway: N, R, W to Lexington Avenue-59th Street; 4, 5, 6 to 59th Street. **Open** 10am-6pm Mon-Fri; 10am-5pm Sat.
In addition to running a store that sells handy items for the vision-impaired, this organisation provides helpful information for blind residents of and visitors to New York City.

Mayor's Office for People with Disabilities
2nd Floor, 100 Gold Street, between Frankfort & Spruce Streets (1-212 788 2830). Subway: J, M, Z to Chambers Street; 4, 5, 6 to Brooklyn Bridge-City Hall. **Open** 9am-5pm Mon-Fri.
This city office provides a broad range of services for the disabled.

New York Society for the Deaf
315 Hudson Street, between Vandam & Spring Streets (1-212 366 0066/www.fegs.org). Subway: C, E to Spring Street; 1 to Houston Street. **Open** 9am-5pm Mon-Thur; 9am-4.30pm Fri.
The deaf and hearing-impaired come here for information and services.

Society for Accessible Travel & Hospitality

Suite 610, 347 Fifth Avenue, between 33rd & 34th Streets (1-212 447 7284/www.sath.org). Subway: B, D, F, N, Q, R, V, W to 34th Street-Herald Square.
This non-profit group was founded in 1976 to educate the public about travel facilities for people with disabilities and to promote travel for the disabled worldwide. Membership is $45 a year ($30 for seniors and students) and includes access to an information service and a quarterly travel magazine. No drop-ins; membership by mail only.

Electricity

The US uses 110-120V, 60-cycle alternating current rather than the 220-240V, 50-cycle AC used in Europe and elsewhere. The transformers that power or recharge many newer electronic devices such as laptop computers are designed to handle either current and may need nothing more than an adaptor for the wall outlet. However, most electrical appliances, including hairdryers, will require a power converter as well. Adaptors and converters of various sorts can be purchased at airport shops, at several pharmacies and department stores, and at Radio Shack branches around the city (consult the phone book for store locations), and they can sometimes be borrowed at better hotels.

Emergencies

Ambulance
In an emergency only, dial 911 for an ambulance or call the operator (dial 0). To complain about slow emergency service or poor treatment, call the Fire Department Complaint Hotline (1-718 999 2646).

Fire
In an emergency only, dial **911**.

Police
In an emergency only, dial **911**. For the location of the nearest police precinct or for general information about police services, call 1-646 610 5000.

Gay & lesbian

For gay/lesbian resources, *see pp300-310*.

Health & medical facilities

The public health-care system is virtually non-existent in the United States, and private health care is prohibitively expensive. If possible, make sure you have comprehensive medical insurance when you travel to New York.

Clinics

Walk-in clinics offer treatment for minor ailments. Most require immediate payment, though some will send their bill directly to your insurance company if you're a US resident. You will have to file a claim to recover the cost of prescription medication.

D•O•C•S
55 E 34th Street, between Madison & Park Avenues (1-212 252 6000). Subway: 6 to 33rd Street. **Open** *Walk-in* 8am-8pm Mon-Thur; 8am-7pm Fri; 9am-3pm Sat; 9am-2pm Sun. Extended hours by appointment. Base fee $80 and up. **Credit** AmEx, Disc, MC, V.
These excellent primary-care facilities, affiliated with Beth Israel Medical Center, offer by-appointment and walk-in services. If you need X-rays or lab tests, go as early as possible (no later than 6pm) Monday to Friday.
Other locations: 202 W 23rd Street, at Seventh Avenue (1-212 352 2600).

Dentists

NYU College of Dentistry
345 E 24th Street, between First & Second Avenues (1-212 998 9872/after-hours emergency care 1-212 998 9800). Subway: 6 to 23rd Street. **Open** 8.30am-7pm Mon-Thur; 8.30am-3pm Fri. Base fee $90. **Credit** Disc, MC, V.
If you need your teeth fixed on a budget, the final-year students here are slow but proficient, and an experienced dentist is always on hand to supervise. Go before 2pm to ensure a same-day visit.

Emergency rooms

You will be billed for emergency treatment. Call your travel insurance company's emergency number before seeking treatment to find out which hospitals accept your insurance. Emergency rooms are always open at:

Cabrini Medical Center
227 E 19th Street, between Second & Third Avenues (1-212 995 6000). Subway: L to Third Avenue; N, Q, R, W, 4, 5, 6 to 14th Street-Union Square.

Mount Sinai Hospital
Madison Avenue, at 100th Street (1-212 241 7171). Subway: 6 to 103rd Street.

New York – Presbyterian Hospital/Weill Cornell Medical Center
525 E 68th Street, at York Avenue (1-212 746 5454). Subway: 6 to 68th Street.

St Luke's – Roosevelt Hospital
1000 Tenth Avenue, at 59th Street (1-212 523 6800). Subway: A, B, C, D, 1 to 59th Street-Columbus Circle.

St Vincent's Hospital
153 W 11th Street, at Seventh Avenue (1-212 604 7998). Subway: F, V, 1, 2, 3 to 14th Street; L to Sixth Avenue.

Gay & lesbian health

See p374 Helplines.

House calls

NYHotel Urgent Medical Services
Suite 1D, 952 Fifth Avenue, between 76th & 77th Streets (1-212 737 1212/www.travelmd. com). Subway: 6 to 77th Street. **Open** 24hrs daily; appointments required. **Fees** Weekday hotel-visit fee $300; weekday office-visit fee $175 (higher for nights and weekends). **Credit** AmEx, MC, V.
Dr Ronald Primas and his partners provide specialist medical attention right in your Manhattan hotel room or private residence, from a simple prescription to urgent medical care.

Directory

Pharmacies

Be aware that pharmacies will not refill foreign prescriptions and may not sell the same over-the-counter products.

Duane Reade

224 W 57th Street, at Broadway (1-212 541 9708/www.duane reade.com). Subway: N, Q, R, W to 57th Street. **Open** 24hrs daily. **Credit** AmEx, MC, V.
This chain operates all over the city, and some stores are open 24 hours. Check the website for additional branches.
Other 24-hour locations: 24 E 14th Street, at University Place (1-212 989 3632); 155 E 34th Street, at Third Avenue (1-212 683 3042); 1279 Third Avenue, at 74th Street (1-212 744 2668); 2465 Broadway, at 91st Street (1-212 799 3172).

Rite Aid

303 W 50th Street, at Eighth Avenue (1-212 247 8736/www.riteaid.com). Subway: C, E to 50th Street. **Open** 24hrs daily. **Credit** AmEx, Disc, MC, V.
Selected Rite Aid stores have 24-hour pharmacies. Call 1-800 748 3243 or check the website for a listing of all branches.
Other 24-hour locations: 408 Grand Street, at Clinton Street (1-212 529 7115); 301 W 50th Street at Eighth Avenue (1-212 247 8384); 146 E 86th Street, between Lexington & Third Avenues (1-212 876 0600); 2833 Broadway at 110th Street (1-212 663 3135).

STDs, HIV & AIDS

Chelsea Clinic

303 Ninth Avenue, at 28th Street (1-212 239 1725). Subway: C, E to 23rd Street. **Open** 8.30am-4.30pm Mon-Fri; 9am-2pm Sat.
Hours of walk-in clinics may change, so call ahead before visiting. Arrive early, because testing is offered on a first-come, first-served basis. (Check the phone book or see www.nyc.gov for other free clinics.)

Women's health

Liberty Women's Health Care of Queens

37-01 Main Street, at 37th Avenue, Flushing, Queens (1-718 888 0018/ www.libertywomenshealth.com). Subway: 7 to Flushing-Main Street. **Open** By appointment only. **Credit** MC, V.

Size charts

Women's clothing

UK	Europe	US
4	32	2
6	34	4
8	36	6
10	38	8
12	40	10
14	42	12
16	44	14

Women's shoes

UK	Europe	US
33	36	5
4	37	6
5	38	7
6	39	8
7	40	9
8	41	10
9	42	11

Men's suits

UK	Europe	US
34	44	34
36	46	36
38	48	38
40	50	40
42	52	42
44	54	44
46	56	46

Men's shoes

UK	Europe	US
36	39	7
71/2	40	71/2
8	41	8
8	42	81/2
9	43	91/2
10	44	101/2
11	45	11

This facility provides surgical and non-surgical abortions until the 24th week of pregnancy. Unlike many other clinics, Liberty uses abdominal ultrasound before, during and after the abortion to ensure safety.

Parkmed Eastern Women's Center

7th Floor, 800 Second Avenue, between 42nd & 43rd Streets (1-212 686 6066/www.eastern womenscenter.com). Subway: 6 to 28th Street. **Open** By appointment only. **Credit** AmEx, Disc, MC, V.
Urine pregnancy tests are free. Counselling, contraception services and non-surgical abortions are also available.

Planned Parenthood of New York City

Margaret Sanger Center, 26 Bleecker Street, at Mott Street (1-212 965 7000/1-800 230 7526/www.pp nyc.org). Subway: B, D, F, V to Broadway-Lafayette Street; N, R, W to Prince Street; 6 to Bleecker Street. **Open** 8am-4.30pm Mon, Tue; 8am-6.30pm Wed-Fri; 7.30am-4.30pm Sat. **Credit** AmEx, MC, V.
This is the best-known, most reasonably priced network of family-planning clinics in the US. Counselling and treatment are available for a full range of needs, including abortion, contraception, HIV testing and treatment of STDs. Call for more information on other services or to make an appointment at any of the centres. Walk-in

clients are welcome for both emergency contraception and free pregnancy tests.
Other location: 44 Court Street, between Joralemon & Remsen Streets, Brooklyn Heights, Brooklyn (appointments 1-212 965 7000).

Helplines

Alcohol & drug abuse

Alcoholics Anonymous

1-212 647 1680.
Open 9am-10pm daily.

Cocaine Anonymous

24-hour recorded information 1-212 262 2463.

Drug Abuse Information Line

1-800 522 5353. **Open** 8am-10pm daily.
This hotline refers callers to recovery programmes around the state as well as to similar programmes in the rest of the US.

Pills Anonymous

24-hour recorded information 1-212 874 0700.
This helpline offers recorded information on drug-recovery programmes for users of marijuana, cocaine, alcohol and other addictive substances, as well as referrals to Narcotics Anonymous meetings. You can also leave a message so that a counsellor can call you back.

Child abuse

Childhelp USA's National Child Abuse Hotline

1-800 422 4453. **Open** 24hrs daily.
Counsellors provide general crisis consultation and can help in an emergency. Callers include abused children, runaways and parents having problems with children.

Gay & lesbian

See p374 Helplines.

Health

Visit the website of the Centers for Disease Control and Prevention (CDC) (www.cdc.gov) for up-to-date national health information, or call one of the toll-free hotlines below.

National STD & AIDS Hotline

1-800 342 2437.
Open 24hrs daily.

Travelers' Health

1-877 394 8747 or visit CDC website. **Open** 24hrs daily.
Provides alerts on disease outbreaks and other information via a recording.

Psychological services

Samaritans

1-212 673 3000. **Open** 24hrs daily.
People who may be thinking of committing suicide or suffering from depression, grief, sexual anxiety or alcoholism can call this volunteer organisation for advice and a listening ear.

Rape & sex crimes

Safe Horizon Crisis Hotline

*1-212 577 7777
/www.safehorizon.org.*
Open 24hrs daily.
Safe Horizon offers telephone and in-person counselling for any victim of domestic violence, rape or other crime, as well as providing practical help with court procedures, compensation claims and legal aid.

Special Victims Liaison Unit of the New York Police Department

Rape hotline 1-212 267 7273.
Open 24hrs daily.
Reports of sex crimes are fielded by a female detective from the Special Victims Liaison Unit. She will inform the appropriate precinct, send an ambulance if requested, and provide counselling and medical referrals. Other issues handled: violence against gays and lesbians, child victimisation, and referrals for the families and friends of crime victims.

St Luke's – Roosevelt Hospital Crime Victims Treatment Center

1-212 523 4728.
Open 9am-5pm Mon-Fri.
The Rape Crisis Center provides a trained volunteer who will accompany you through all aspects of reporting a rape and getting emergency treatment.

Holidays

See p383 Holidays.

Insurance

If you are not an American, it's advisable to take out comprehensive insurance before arriving here; insurance for foreigners is almost impossible to arrange in the US. Make sure you have adequate health coverage; medical costs are high. For a list of New York urgent-care facilities, *see p373* Emergency rooms.

Internet

Internet access

Cyber Café

250 W 49th Street, between Broadway & Eighth Avenue (1-212 333 4109). Subway: C, E, 1, 9 to 50th Street; N, R, W to 49th Street. **Open** 8am-11pm Mon-Fri; 11am-11pm Sat, Sun. **Cost** $6.40/30mins; 50¢/printed page. **Credit** AmEx, MC, V.
This is a standard internet access café that also happens to serve great coffee and snacks.

FedEx Kinko's

1-800 463 3339/www.kinkos.com.

Outposts of this ubiquitous and very efficient computer and copy centre can be found throughout the city.

New York Public Library

www.nypl.org.
The branch libraries throughout the five boroughs are great places to email and surf the web for free. However, the scarcity of computer stations may make for a long wait, and user time is limited. The Science, Industry and Business Library, 188 Madison Avenue, at 34th Street, has more than 40 workstations that you can use for up to an hour per day.

Wi-Fi

NYCWireless

www.nycwireless.net.
This group has established 113 nodes in the city for free wireless access. (For example, most parks below 59th Street are covered.) Visit the website for more information.

Starbucks

www.starbucks.com.
Credit AmEx, MC, V.
Many branches offer wireless access through T-Mobile (10¢/min).

Legal assistance

If you're arrested for a minor violation (disorderly conduct, harassment, loitering, rowdy partying, etc) and you are very polite to the officer during the arrest (and carry proper ID), then you'll probably get fingerprinted and photographed at the station and be given a desk-appearance ticket with a date to show up at criminal court. Then, you'll most likely get to go home.

Arguing with a police officer or engaging in more serious criminal activity (possession of a weapon, drunken driving, illegal gambling or prostitution, for example) might get you 'processed', which means a 24- to 30-hour journey through the system. If the courts are backed up (and they usually are), you'll be held temporarily at a precinct pen. You can make a phone call after you've been fingerprinted. When you get

Directory

through central booking, you'll arrive at 100 Centre Street for arraignment. A judge will decide whether you should be released on bail and will set a court date. If you can't post bail, then you'll be held at Rikers Island. The bottom line: try not to get arrested, and if you are, don't act foolishly.

Legal Aid Society
1-212 577 3300/www.legal-aid.org. **Open** 9am-5pm Mon-Fri.
Legal Aid gives general information and referrals on legal matters.

Sandback, Birnbaum & Michelen Criminal Law
1-800 640 2000. **Open** 24hrs daily.
You might want to carry these numbers with you, in case you find the cops reading you your rights in the middle of the night. If no one at this firm can help you, then you'll be directed to lawyers who can.

Libraries

See p375 New York Public Library.

Locksmiths

The emergency locksmiths listed below are open 24 hours. Both require ID and proof of car ownership or residency (driving licence, car registration, utility bill).

Champion Locksmiths
30 locations in Manhattan (1-212 362 7000). **Cost** $15 service charge; $39 minimum to replace the lock they have to break. **Credit** AmEx, Disc, MC, V.

Elite Locksmiths
152 E 33rd Street, between Third & Lexington Avenues (1-212 685 1472). Subway: 6 to 33rd Street. **Cost** $55 during the day; $85 at night. **No credit cards**.

Lost property

For property lost in the street, contact the police. For lost credit cards or travellers' cheques, *see p379*.

Buses & subways
New York City Metropolitan Transit Authority, 34th Street-Penn Station, near the A-train platform

(1-212 712 4500). **Open** 8am-noon Mon-Wed, Fri; 11am-6.30pm Thur. Call if you've left something on a subway train or a bus.

Grand Central Terminal
1-212 340 2555. **Open** 7am-6pm Mon-Fri; 8.45am-5pm Sat.
Call if you've left something on a Metro-North train.

JFK Airport
1-718 244 4444, or contact your airline.

La Guardia Airport
1-718 533 3400, or contact your airline.

Newark Liberty International Airport
1-973 961 6230, or contact your airline.

Penn Station
1-212 630 7389. **Open** 7.30am-4pm Mon-Fri.
Call for items left on Amtrak, New Jersey Transit or the Long Island Rail Road.

Taxis
1-212 692 8294/www.nyc.gov/taxi.
Call for items left in a cab.

Media

Daily newspapers

Daily News
The *News* has drifted politically from the Neanderthal right to a more moderate but tough-minded stance under the ownership of real-estate mogul Mort Zuckerman.

New York Post
Founded in 1801 by Alexander Hamilton, the *Post* is the nation's oldest continuously published daily newspaper. It has swerved sharply to the right under current owner Rupert Murdoch. The *Post* includes more gossip than any other local paper, and its headlines are often sassy and sensational.

The New York Times
As Olympian as ever after more than 150 years, the *Times* remains the city's, and the nation's, paper of record. It has the broadest and deepest coverage of world and national events and, as the masthead proclaims, it delivers 'All the News That's Fit to Print'. The mammoth *Sunday Times* can weigh a full 5lb and typically contains hundreds of pages, including a well-regarded magazine as well as book review, travel, real-estate and other sections.

Other dailies
The *Amsterdam News*, one of the nation's oldest black newspapers, offers a trenchant African-American viewpoint. New York also supports three Spanish-language dailies: *El Diario, Hoy* and *Noticias del Mundo*. Newsday is a Long Island-based daily with a tabloid format but a sober tone (it also has a city edition). *USA Today* keeps weary travellers abreast of national news. You may even find your own local paper at a Universal News shop (check the phone book for locations).

Weekly newspapers

Downtown journalism is a battlefield, pitting the *New York Press* against the *Village Voice*. The *Press* consists largely of opinion columns; it's full of youthful energy and irreverence as well as cynicism and self-absorption. The *Voice* is sometimes passionate and ironic but just as often strident and predictable. Both papers are free. In contrast, the *New York Observer* focuses on the doings of the upper echelons of business, finance, media and politics. *Our Town, Chelsea Clinton News*, the *West Sider* and *Manhattan Spirit* are on the sidelines; these free sister publications feature neighbourhood news and local political gossip, and they can be found in street-corner dispensers around town. In a class all its own is the hilarious, satirical national weekly the *Onion*.

Magazines

New York
This mag is part newsweekly, part lifestyle reporting and part listings.

The New Yorker
Since the 1920s the *New Yorker* has been known for its fine wit, elegant prose and sophisticated cartoons. Today, it's a forum for serious long-form journalism. It usually makes for a lively, intelligent read, in both paper form and on the well-made website.

Time Out New York
Of course, the best place to discover what's going on in town is *Time Out New York*. Based on the tried and trusted format of its London parent, TONY is an indispensable guide to the life of the city (if we do say so ourselves). Its Hot 100 restaurants are an essential read.

Other magazines
Since its launch in 1996, the bimonthly *Black Book Magazine* has covered New York high fashion

and culture with intelligent bravado. *Gotham*, a monthly from the publisher of the glossy gab-rags *Hamptons* and *Aspen Peak*, unveiled its larger-than-life celeb-filled pages in 2001. And for two decades now, *Paper* has reported monthly on the city's trend-conscious, offering plenty of insider buzz on bars, clubs, downtown boutiques – and the people you'll find in them.

Radio

Nearly 100 stations serve the New York area. On the AM dial, you can find talk radio and phone-in shows that attract everyone from priests to sports nuts. Flip to FM for free jazz, the latest Franz Ferdinand single or any other auditory craving. Radio highlights are printed weekly in *Time Out New York*, and daily in the *Daily News*.

College radio

College radio is innovative and free of commercials. However, smaller transmitters mean that reception is often compromised by Manhattan's high-rise topography. **WNYU-FM 89.1** and **WKCR-FM 89.9** are, respectively, the stations of New York University and Columbia; programming spans the musical spectrum. **WFUV-FM 90.7**, Fordham University's station, plays mostly folk and Irish music but also airs a variety of shows, including *Beale Street Caravan*, the most widely distributed blues programme in the world.

Dance & pop

American commercial radio is rigidly formatted, which makes most pop stations extremely tedious and repetitive during the day. Tune in on evenings and weekends for more interesting programming. **WQHT-FM 97.1**, 'Hot 97,' is a commercial hip hop station with all-day rap and R&B. **WKTU-FM 103.5** is the premier dance music station. **WWPR-FM 105.1**, 'Power 105,' plays top hip hop, and a few old-school hits. **WBLS-FM 107.5** showcases classic and new funk, soul and R&B.

Jazz

WBGO-FM 88.3 is strictly jazz. Dee Dee Bridgewater's weekly JazzSet programme features many legendary artists. **WKCR-FM 89.9**, the student-run radio station of Columbia University, is where you'll hear legendary jazz DJ Phil Schaap.

Rock

WSOU-FM 89.5, the station of Seton Hall University, a Catholic college, focuses primarily on hard rock and heavy metal. **WAXQ-FM 104.3** offers classic rock. **WXRK-FM 92.3**'s alternative music format attracts morning listeners with its 6-10am weekday sleaze-fest.

Other music

WQEW-AM 1560, 'Radio Disney', has kids' programming. **WNYC-FM 93.9** and **WQXR-FM 96.3** serve up a range of classical music; **WNYC** tends towards the progressive end of the classical spectrum. **WCAA-FM 105.9** and **WZAA-FM 92.7** spin Spanish and Latin.

News & talk

WABC-AM 770, **WCBS-AM 880**, **WINS-AM 1010** and **WBBR-AM 1130** (*see also below* Sports) offer news throughout the day, plus traffic and weather reports. **WABC** hosts a morning show featuring the street-accented demagoguery of Guardian Angels founder Curtis Sliwa along with civil-rights attorney Ron Kuby (weekdays 5-10am). Right-winger Rush Limbaugh also airs his views here (noon-3pm). **WNYC-AM 820/FM 93.9**, a commercial-free, public radio station, provides news and current-affairs commentary. **WBAI-FM 99.5** is a left-leaning community radio station. **WLIB-AM 1190** is the flagship station of Air America, a liberal answer to right-wing talk radio.

Sports

WFAN-AM 660 airs Giants, Nets, Mets and Devils games. Talk-radio fixture Don Imus offers his opinion on... everything (5.30-10am Mon-Fri). **WCBS-AM 880** covers the Yankees, New York's pride and joy. **WEPN-AM 1050** is devoted to news and sports talk and is the home of the Jets, Knicks and Rangers. **WBBR-AM 1130** broadcasts Islanders games. **WADO-AM 1280** provides Spanish-language coverage of many sports events.

Television

A visit to New York often includes some TV time, which can cause culture shock, particularly for British and European visitors.

Time Out New York offers a rundown of TV highlights. For full schedules, save the *Sunday New York Times* TV section or buy a daily paper.

Networks

Six major networks broadcast nationwide. All offer ratings-driven variations on a theme.

CBS (Channel 2 in NYC) has the top investigative show, *60 Minutes*, on Sundays at 7pm; overall, programming is geared to a middle-aged demographic, but CBS also screens reality shows like *Survivor*. NBC (4) is the home of Law & Order, the long-running sketch-comedy series *Saturday Night Live* (11.30pm, Sat), and popular primetime shows including *The Apprentice, Fear Factor, ER, Scrubs, The Office* and *My Name is Earl*. Fox-**WNYW** (5) is popular with younger audiences for shows like *The Simpsons* and *American Idol*. ABC (7) is the king of daytime soaps and family-friendly sitcoms. ABC continues to score with it's hits: *Desperate Housewives* and *Lost*.

WXTV and WNJU are Spanish-language channels that offer game shows and racy Mexican dramas. They're also your best non-cable bets for soccer.

Public TV

Public TV is on channels 13, 21 and 25. Documentaries, arts shows and science series alternate with *Masterpiece Theatre* and reruns of British shows like *Inspector Morse*. Channel 21 broadcasts BBC World News daily at 6am and at 7pm and 11pm.

Cable

For channel numbers for Time Warner Cable or for other cable systems, such as Cablevision or RCN, check a local newspaper's TV listings.

Nickelodeon presents shows suitable for kids and adults nostalgic for shows like *The Brady Bunch* and *Happy Days*. NY1 focuses on local news. The **History Channel**, **Sci Fi** and the **Weather Channel** are self-explanatory. **Discovery Channel** and the **Learning Channel** feature educational nature and science programmes.

VH1, MTV's mature sibling, features programmes that delve into the lives of artists such as Eminem, LL Cool J, Beyonce Knowles and Nick Lachey. You can also catch *Surreal Life* and *Best Week Ever*. **MTV** increasingly offers fewer music videos and more of its original programming (*Laguna Beach, My Super Sixteen* and *The Real World*). **FUSE**, a new music-video channel, aims for early MTV style. **FSN** (Fox Sports Network), **MSG** (Madison Square Garden), **ESPN** and **ESPN2** are all-sports stations. **Bravo** shows arts programming, such as *Inside the Actors Studio*, art-house films and *Queer Eye for the Straight Guy*.

Comedy Central is all comedy, airing *South Park* and *The Daily Show* with Jon Stewart.

Cinemax, the **Disney Channel**, **HBO**, the **Movie Channel** and **Showtime** are premium channels often available in hotels. They show uninterrupted feature films, exclusive specials and acclaimed series like *The Sopranos*, *Big Love* and *Deadwood*.

Money

Over the past few years, much of American currency has undergone a subtle facelift, partly to deter increasingly adept counterfeiters. However, 'old' money still remains in circulation. All denominations except for the $1 bill have recently been updated by the US Treasury. One dollar ($) equals 100 cents (¢). Coins include copper pennies (1¢) and silver-coloured nickels (5¢), dimes (10¢) and quarters (25¢). Half-dollar coins (50¢) and the gold-coloured dollar coins are less commonly seen, except as change from vending machines.

All paper money is the same size, so make sure you fork over the right bill. It comes in denominations of $1, $2, $5, $10, $20, $50 and $100 (and higher, but you'll never see those bills). The $2 bills are quite rare and make a smart souvenir. Small shops will seldom break a $50 or $100 bill, and cab drivers aren't required to change bills larger than $20, so it's best to carry smaller denominations.

ATMs

The city is full of automated teller machines (ATMs), located in bank branches, delis and many small shops. Most accept American Express, MasterCard, Visa and major bank cards, if they have been registered with a personal identification number (PIN). Commonly, there's a usage fee of $1.50 to $2, though the superior exchange rate often makes ATMs worth the extra charge. Holders of accounts at out-of-country banks can also use ATMs but the fees can be high. Though you don't always pay the local charge, some UK banks charge up to £4 per transaction plus a variable

---

Loo lowdown
Where to go when you got to go.

When nature calls in NYC, the real challenge lies in finding a legal public place to take care of your business. Although they don't exactly have an open-door policy, the numerous McDonald's restaurants, Starbucks coffee shops and Barnes & Noble bookstores contain (usually clean) restrooms. If the door to the loo is locked, you may have to ask a cashier for the key. Don't announce that you're not a paying customer and you should be all right. The same applies to most other fast-food chains (Au Bon Pain, Wendy's, etc), major stores (Barneys, Macy's, Toys 'R' Us) and hotels and bars that don't have a host stationed at the door. Here are a few other options that can offer sweet relief in the city (though you may have to hold your breath and forgo soap and towel).

Downtown

Battery Park

Castle Clinton. Subway: 1 to South Ferry; 4, 5 to Bowling Green.

Tompkins Square Park

Avenue A, at 9th Street. Subway: L to First Ave; 6 to Astor Pl.

Washington Square Park

Thompson Street, at Washington Square South. Subway: A, B, C, D, E, F, V to W 4th Street.

Midtown

Bryant Park

42nd Street, between Fifth and Sixth Avenues. Subway: B, D, F, V to 42nd St-Bryant Park; 7 to Fifth Avenue.

Grand Central Terminal

42nd Street, at Park Avenue, Lower Concourse. Subway: 42nd Street S, 4, 5, 6, 7 to 42nd Street-Grand Central.

Penn Station

Seventh Avenue, between 31st & 33rd Streets. Subway: A, C, E, 1, 2, 3 to 34th Street-Penn Station.

Uptown

Avery Fisher Hall

Broadway, at 65th Street. Subway: 1 to 66th Street-Lincoln Center.

Charles A Dana Discovery Center

Central Park, north side of Harlem Meer, 110th Street, at Malcolm X Blvd (Lenox Avenue). Subway: 2, 3 to 110th Street-Central Park North.

Delacorte Theater

Central Park, midpark, at 81st Street. Subway: B, C to 81st Street-Museum of Natural History.

payment to cover themselves against exchange rate fluctuations. Yes, it sounds as dodgy to us as it does to you.

US bank account holders who have lost their PIN or whose card is damaged can usually get cash from branches of their bank with proper ID.

Most ATM cards now double as charge cards, if they bear the Maestro or Cirrus logo. You can get cashback on this at supermarkets, British customers included (theoretically, and for a percentage charge), though in practice it seems only to work at certain outlets.

Banks & currency exchange

Banks are generally open from 9am to 3pm Monday to Friday, though some stay open longer and on Saturdays. You need a photo ID, such as a passport, to cash travellers' cheques. Many banks will not exchange foreign currency, and the bureaux de change, limited to tourist-trap areas, close between 6pm and 7pm. It's best to arrive in the city with a few dollars in cash and to pay mostly with credit cards or travellers' cheques (accepted in most restaurants and larger stores – but ask first, and be prepared to show ID). In emergencies, most large hotels will offer 24-hour exchange facilities; the catch is that they charge high commissions and don't give good rates.

Chase Bank
1-212 935 9935/www.chase.com.
Chase's website gives information on foreign currency exchange, banking locations and credit cards. For foreign currency delivered in a hurry, call the number listed above.

Commerce Bank
1-888 751 9000/
www.commerce online.com.
All of Commerce Bank's 17 Manhattan locations are open seven days a week.

People's Foreign Exchange
3rd Floor, 575 Fifth Avenue, at 47th Street (1-212 883 0550). Subway: E, V to Fifth Avenue-53rd Street; 7 to Fifth Avenue. **Open** 9am-6pm Mon-Fri; 10am-3pm Sat, Sun.
People's provides foreign exchange on bank notes and travellers' cheques of any denomination for a $2 fee.

Travelex
29 Broadway, at Morris Street (1-212 363 6206). Subway: 4, 5 to Bowling Green. **Open** 9am-5pm Mon-Fri.
A complete range of foreign-exchange services is offered.
Other location: 510 Madison Avenue, at 53rd Street (1-212 753 0117).

Credit cards

Bring plastic if you have it, or be prepared for a logistical nightmare. Credit cards are essential for renting cars and booking hotels, and handy for buying tickets over the phone and the internet. The five major cards accepted in the US are American Express, Diners Club, Discover, MasterCard and Visa. If cards are lost or stolen, contact:

American Express
1-800 528 2122.

Diners Club
1-800 234 6377.

Discover
1-800 347 2683.

MasterCard/Maestro
1-800 826 2181.

Visa/Cirrus
1-800 336 8472.

Travellers' cheques

Like credit cards, travellers' cheques are also routinely accepted at banks, stores and restaurants throughout the city. Bring your driver's licence or passport for identification. If cheques are lost or stolen, contact:

American Express
1-800 221 7282.

Thomas Cook
1-800 223 7373.

Visa
1-800 336 8472.

Wire services

If you run out of cash, don't expect the folks at your consulate to lend you money. In case of an emergency, you can have money wired to you from your home.

MoneyGram
1-800 666 3947/
www.moneygram.com.

Western Union
1-800 325 6000/
www.westernunion.com.

Postal services

Stamps are available at all US post offices and from drugstore vending machines and at most newsstands. It costs 39¢ to send a 1oz letter within the US. Each additional ounce costs 24¢. Postcards mailed within the US cost 24¢; for international postcards, it's 80¢. Airmailed letters to anywhere overseas cost 80¢ for the first ounce and 80¢ for each additional ounce.

For faster Express Mail, you must fill out a form, either at a post office or by arranging a pickup. Twenty-four-hour delivery to major US cities is guaranteed. International delivery takes two to three days, with no guarantee. Call 1-800 275 8777 for more information.

General Post Office
421 Eighth Avenue, between 31st & 33rd Streets (24hr information 1-800 275 8777/www.usps.com). Subway: A, C, E to 34th Street-Penn Station. **Open** 24hrs daily.
Credit MC, V.
This is the city's main post office; call for the branch nearest you. Queues are long, but stamps are available from vending machines. Branches are usually open 9am-5pm Mon-Fri; hours vary Sat.

General Delivery
390 Ninth Avenue, between 31st & 33rd Streets (1-212 330 3099).

Directory

Subway: A, C, E to 34th Street-Penn Station. **Open** 10am-1pm Mon-Sat. US residents without local addresses can receive their mail here; it should be addressed to the recipient, General Delivery, 390 Ninth Avenue, New York, NY 10001. You will need to show a passport or ID card when picking up letters.

Poste Restante

Window 29, 421 Eighth Avenue, between 31st & 33rd Streets (1-212 330 2912). Subway: A, C, E to 34th Street-Penn Station. **Open** 8am-6pm Mon-Sat.
Foreign visitors can receive mail here; mail should be addressed to the recipient, General Post Office, Poste Restante, 421 Eighth Avenue, attn: Window 29, New York, NY 10001. Be sure to bring ID.

Religion

Here are just a few of New York's many places of worship. Check the phone book for more listings.

Baptist

Abyssinian Baptist Church

For listing, see p150.

Buddhist

New York Buddhist Church

331-332 Riverside Drive, between 105th & 106th Streets (1-212 678 0305/www.newyork buddhistchurch.org). Subway: 1 to 103rd Street.

Catholic

St Patrick's Cathedral

For listing, see p131.

Episcopal

Cathedral Church of St John the Divine

For listing, see p148.

Jewish

UJA–Federation of New York Resource Line

1-212 753 2288/www.ujafedny.org. **Open** 9am-5pm Mon-Thur; 9am-4pm Fri.

This hotline provides referrals to other organisations, groups, temples, philanthropic activities and synagogues, as well as advice on kosher food in the city.

Methodist

Church of St Paul & St Andrew, United Methodist

263 W 86th Street, between Broadway & West End Avenue (1-212 362 3179/www.spsanyc.org). Subway: 1 to 86th Street.

Muslim

Islamic Cultural Center of New York

1711 Third Avenue, between 96th & 97th Streets (1-212 722 5234). Subway: 6 to 96th Street.

Presbyterian

Madison Avenue Presbyterian Church

921 Madison Avenue, at 73rd Street (1-212 288 8920/www.mapc.com). Subway: 6 to 72nd Street.

Restrooms

See p378 **Loo lowdown**.

Safety

New York's crime rate, particularly for violent crime, has waned during the past decade. Most crime occurs late at night in low-income neighbourhoods. Don't arrive thinking your safety is at risk wherever you go; it is unlikely that you will ever be bothered.

Still, a bit of common sense won't hurt. Don't flaunt your money and valuables, and try not to look obviously lost. Avoid deserted and poorly lit streets; walk facing oncoming traffic so no one can drive up alongside you undetected, and close to or on the street; muggers prefer to hang back in doorways and shadows. If you are threatened, hand over your valuables at once (your

attacker will likely be as anxious to get it over with as you), then dial 911 as soon as you can (it's a free call).

Be extra alert to pickpockets and street hustlers – especially in crowded tourist areas like Times Square – and be wary of diversionary jostles.

Smoking

New Yorkers live under some of the strictest anti-smoking laws on the planet. The 1995 NYC Smoke-Free Air Act makes it illegal to smoke in virtually all indoor public places, including the subway and cinemas. Recent legislation went even further, banning smoking in nearly all restaurants and bars; for a list of exceptions, *see p227* **Smoke signal**. Be sure to ask before you light up.

Students

Student life in NYC is unlike it is anywhere else in the world. An endless extracurricular education exists right outside the dorm room – the city is both teacher and playground. For further guidance, check the *Time Out New York Student Guide*, available in August for free on campuses, and $2.95 at Hudson News outlets (consult the phone book for locations).

Student identification

Foreign students should get hold of an **International Student Identity Card** (ISIC) as proof of student status and in order to secure discounts. These can be bought from your local student-travel agent (ask at your student union or *see p381* STA Travel). If you buy the card in New York, then you will also get basic accident insurance thrown in – a bargain.

Directory

Student travel

Most agents offer discount fares for those under 26. For specialists in student travel deals, visit:

STA Travel

205 E 42nd Street, between Second & Third Avenues (1-212 822 2700/ for other locations 1-800 777 0112/ www.statravel.com). Subway: 42nd Street S, 4, 5, 6, 7 to 42nd Street-Grand Central. **Open** 10am-6pm Mon-Sat.

Tax & tipping

In restaurants, it is customary to tip at least 15 per cent, and since NYC tax is 8.625 per cent, a quick method for calculating the tip is to double the tax. In many restaurants, when you are with a group of six or more, the tip will be included in the bill. For tipping on taxi fares, *see p369*.

Telephones

New York, like most of the world's busy cities, is overrun with telephones, cellular phones, pagers and faxes. (Check with your network operator that the service will be available here.) This increasing dependence on a dial tone accounts for the city's abundance of area codes. As a rule, you must dial 1 + the area code before a number, even if the place you are calling is in the same area code. The area codes for Manhattan are 212 and 646; Brooklyn, Queens, Staten Island and the Bronx are 718 and 347; 917 is reserved mostly for mobile phones and pagers. Long Island area codes are 516 and 631; codes for New Jersey are 201, 551, 848, 862, 609, 732, 856, 908 and 973. Numbers preceded by 800, 877 and 888 are free of charge when dialled from anywhere in the US.

General information

The Yellow Pages and the White Pages phone books

contain a wealth of useful information in the front, including theatre-seating diagrams and maps; the blue pages in the centre of the White Pages directory list all government numbers and addresses. Hotels will have copies; otherwise, try libraries or Verizon (the local phone company) payment centres.

Collect calls & credit card calls

Collect calls are also known as reverse-charge calls. Dial 0 followed by the number, or dial AT&T's 1-800 225 5288, MCI's 1-800 265 5328 or Sprint's 1-800 663 3463.

Directory assistance

Dial 411 or 1 + area code + 555 1212. Doing so may be free, depending on the payphone you are using; carrier fees may apply. Long-distance directory assistance may also incur long-distance charges. For a directory of toll-free numbers, dial 1-800 555 1212.

Emergency

Dial 911. All calls are free (including those from pay- and mobile phones).

International calls

Dial 011 + country code (Australia 61; New Zealand 64; UK 44), then the number.

Operator assistance

Dial 0.

Pagers & mobiles

Most US mobile phones will work in NY but since the US doesn't have a standard national network, visitors should check with their provider that their phone will work here, and whether they need to unlock a roaming option. Visitors from other countries will need a tri-band handset and a roaming agreement, and may find charges so high that rental, or, depending on the length of their stay, purchase of a US phone (or SIM card) will make better economic sense.

If you carry a mobile phone, make sure you turn it off on trains and buses and at restaurants, plays, movies,

concerts and museums. New Yorkers are quick to show their annoyance at an ill-timed ring. Some establishments even post signs designating 'cellular-free zones'.

InTouch USA

1-800 872 7626. **Open** 8am-5.30pm Mon-Fri. **Credit** AmEx, DC, Disc, MC, V.
InTouch is the city's largest mobile-phone rental company, leases equipment by the day, week or month.

Public payphones & phonecards

Public payphones are easy to find. Some of them even work (non-Verizon phones tend to be poorly maintained). Phones take any combination of silver coins: local calls usually cost 25¢ for three minutes; a few payphones require 50¢ but allow unlimited time on the call. If you're not used to US phones, then note that the ringing tone is long; the 'engaged' tone, or busy signal, is short and higher pitched.

To call long-distance or to make an international call from a payphone, you need to go through one of the long-distance companies. Most payphones in New York automatically use AT&T, but phones in and around transportation hubs usually contract other long-distance carriers, and charges can be outrageous. MCI and Sprint are respected brand names (*see above* Collect calls & credit-card calls). Make the call by either dialling 0 for an operator or dialling direct, which is cheaper. To find out how much a call will cost, dial the number, and a computerised voice will tell you how much money to deposit. You can pay for calls with your credit card.

The best way to make long-distance calls is with a phonecard, available from any post-office branch or from chain stores like Duane Reade or Rite Aid (*see p374* Pharmacies). Delis and newspaper kiosks sell phonecards, including the New York Exclusive, which has favourable international rates. Instructions are on the card.

Telephone answering service

Messages Plus Inc

1317 Third Avenue, between 75th & 76th Streets (1-212 879 4144). Subway: 6 to 77th Street. **Open** 24hrs daily. **Credit** AmEx, DC, Disc, MC, V.
Messages Plus provides an answering service with specialised (medical, bilingual, etc) receptionists, if required, and plenty of ways to deliver your messages. It also offers telemarketing, voicemail and interactive website services.

Tickets

It's always show time somewhere in New York. And depending on what you're after – music, sports, theatre – scoring tickets can be a real hassle. Smaller venues often have their own box offices. Large arenas like Madison Square Garden have ticket agencies – and many devoted spectators. You may have to try more than one tactic to get into a popular show.

Box-office tickets

Fandango

1-800 326 3264/www.fandango. com. 24hrs daily. **Surcharge** $1.50 per ticket. **Credit** AmEx, Disc, MC, V.
Fandango is one of the newer services to offer advance credit-card purchase of movie tickets online or over the phone. Tickets can be picked up at an automated kiosk in the theatre lobby (not available in all theatres).

Moviefone

1-212 777 FILM/www.moviefone. com. 24hrs daily. *Surcharge $1.50 ($1 if purchased online) per ticket.* **Credit** AmEx, Disc, MC, V.
Purchase advance film tickets by credit card over the phone or online;

Passport update

People of all ages (children included) who enter the US on the Visa Waiver Progam (VWP; *see p384*) are now required to carry their own machine-readable passport, or MRP. MRPs are recognisable by the double row of characters along the foot of the data page. All burgundy EU and EU-lookalike passports issued in the UK since 1991 (that is, all that are still valid) should be machine readable. Some of those issued outside the country may not be, however; in this case, holders should apply for a replacement even if the passport has not expired. Check at your local passport-issuing post office if in any doubt at all.

The US's requirement for passports to contain a 'biometric' chip applies only to those issued from 26 October 2006. By then, all new and replacement UK passports should be compliant, following a gradual phase-in. The biometric chip contains a facial scan and biographical data.

Though it is being considered for 2008 (when ID cards may be introduced), there is no current requirement for UK passports to contain fingerprint or iris data. The application process remains as it was, except for new guidelines that ensure that the photograph you submit can be used to generate the facial scan in the chip.

Further information for UK citizens is available from www.passport.gov.uk. Nationals of other countries should check well in advance of their journey whether their current passport meets the requirements for the time of their trip, at http://travel.state.gov/visa and with the issuing authorities of their home country.

pick them up at an automated kiosk in the theatre lobby. This service is not available for every theatre.

Telecharge

1-212 239 6200/www.telecharge. com. 24hrs daily. **Average surcharge** $6 per ticket. **Credit** AmEx, DC, Disc, MC, V. Broadway and Off Broadway shows are on offer here.

Ticket Central

416 W 42nd Street, between Ninth & Tenth Avenues (1-212 279 4200/ www.ticketcentral.com). Subway: N, Q, R, W, 42nd Street S, 1, 2, 3, 7 to 42nd Street-Times Square. **Box office & phone orders** noon-8pm daily. **Surcharge** varies with ticket price. **Credit** AmEx, MC, V.
Both Off and Off-Off Broadway tickets are available at the office or by phone.

Ticketmaster

1-212 307 4100/www.ticketmaster. com. **Surcharge** $3-$10 per ticket. **Credit** AmEx, DC, Disc, MC, V.

This reliable service sells tickets to rock concerts, Broadway shows, sports events and more. You can buy tickets by phone, online or at outlets throughout the city – Tower Records, J&R Music and Computer World, and Filene's Basement, to name a few.

TKTS

Duffy Square, 47th Street, at Broadway (1-212 221 0013/ www.tdf.org). Subway: N, Q, R, W, 42nd Street S, 1, 2, 3, 7 to 42nd Street-Times Square. **Open** 3-8pm Mon-Sat; 11am-7pm Sun. Matinée tickets 10am-2pm Wed, Sat; 11am-2pm Sun. **Surcharge** $3 per ticket. **No credit cards**.
TKTS has become a New York tradition. Broadway and Off Broadway tickets are sold at discounts of 25%, 35% and 50% for same-day performances; tickets to other highbrow events are also offered. The queue can be long, but it's often worth the wait.
Other locations: 199 Water Street; booth is at the corner of Front and John Streets.

Scalpers & standby tickets

When a show sells out, there's always the illegal scalper option, though the risk that you might end up with a forged ticket does exist. Before you part with any cash, make sure that the ticket has all of the correct details, and be warned: the police have been cracking down on such trade of late.

Some venues also offer standby tickets right before show time, while other places give reduced rates for tickets purchased on the same day as the performance for which they're for.

Ticket brokers

Ticket brokers function like scalpers but are legal because they operate from out of state. They can almost guarantee tickets, however costly, for sold-out events and tend to deal only in better seats. They also tend to be less seedy and more regularly patronised than their UK equivalents. For brokers, look under Ticket Sales in the Yellow Pages.

Apex Tours
1-800 248 9849/www.tixx.com.
Open 9am-5pm Mon-Fri.
Credit AmEx, Disc, MC, V.

Prestige Entertainment
1-800 243 8849/www.prestige entertainment.com. **Open** 8am-6pm Mon-Fri; 8am-5pm Sat; 11am-3pm Sun. **Credit** AmEx, MC, V.

TicketCity
1-800 765 3688/www.ticketcity.com.
Open 8.30am-8pm Mon-Fri; 10am-6pm Sat; 11am-4pm Sun. **Credit** AmEx, Disc, MC, V.

Time & date

New York is on Eastern Standard Time, which extends from the Atlantic coast to the eastern shore of Lake Michigan and south to the Gulf of Mexico. This is five hours behind Greenwich Mean Time. Clocks are set forward one hour in early March for Daylight Savings Time and back one hour at the beginning of November. Going from east to west, Eastern Time is one hour ahead of Central Time, two hours ahead of Mountain Time and three hours ahead of Pacific Time. In the United States, the date is written as month, day and year; so 2/8/05 is 8 February 2005. Forms that foreigners may need to fill in, however, are often the other way round, including immigration cards.

Toilets

See p378 **Loo lowdown**.

Tourist information

Hotels are usually full of maps, brochures and free tourist magazines that include paid listings (so the recommendations often cannot be relied on as being objective). Many local magazines, including *Time Out New York*, offer opinionated, reliable information and updates on events and exhibitions.

NYC & Company
810 Seventh Avenue, between 52nd & 53rd Streets (1-800 NYC VISIT/ www.nycvisit.com). Subway: B, D, E to Seventh Avenue. **Open** 8.30am-6pm Mon-Fri; 9am-5pm Sat, Sun.
The city's official (private, non-profit) visitors' and information centre doles out maps, leaflets, coupons and advice, and provides information on tour operators and travel agents.
Other locations: 33-34 Carnaby Street, London W1V 1CA, UK (020 7437 8300).

Times Square Visitors Center
1560 Broadway, between 46th & 47th Streets (1-212 869 1890).
Subway: N, Q, R, W, 42nd Street S, 1, 2, 3, 7 to 42nd Street-Times Square. **Open** 8am-8pm daily. This centre offers discount coupons for Broadway tickets, internet access, MetroCards, free maps and other useful goods and services, predominantly for Theatreland. Staff are multilingual. There are also ATMs, photo booths and free internet stations on site.

Holidays

The majority of banks and government offices are closed on the major US holidays, but you will usually find a smattering of restaurants and shops have stayed open, along with some museums. If you are in New York during or around a holiday, be sure to call the venues you'd like to visit to enquire about special hours.

New Year's Day
1 January

Martin Luther King Day
Third Monday in January

Presidents' Day
Third Monday in February

Memorial Day
Last Monday in May

Independence Day
4 July

Labor Day
First Monday in September

Columbus Day
Second Monday in October

Veterans Day
11 November

Thanksgiving Day
Fourth Thursday in November

Christmas Day
25 December

Directory

Visas & immigration

Visas

Some 27 countries participate in the **Visa Waiver Program** (VWP). Citizens of Andorra, Australia, Austria, Belgium, Brunei, Denmark, Finland, France, Germany, Iceland, Ireland, Italy, Japan, Liechtenstein, Luxembourg, Monaco, the Netherlands, New Zealand, Norway, Portugal, San Marino, Singapore, Slovenia, Spain, Sweden, Switzerland and the UK do not need a visa for stays in the US shorter than 90 days (business or pleasure) as long as they have a machine-readable passport valid for the full 90-day period and a return ticket. *See also p382* **Passport update**.

If you do not qualify for entry under the VWP, that is if you are not from one of the eligible countries or are visiting for any purpose other than pleasure or business, you will need a visa. Media workers and students note: this includes you. If you are in the slightest doubt, check ahead. You can obtain application forms from your nearest US embassy or consulate or its website. Enquire several months ahead of travel how long the application process is currently taking.

Canadians travelling to the US need visas only in special circumstances.

Whether or not you have a visa, it is not advisable to travel on a passport with six months or less to run.

If you lose your passport inside the US, contact your consulate (*see p372*).

Immigration

Your airline will give all visitors an immigration form to be presented to an official when you land. Fill it in clearly and be prepared to give an address at which you are staying (a hotel is fine).

Upon arrival, you may have to wait an hour or, if you're unlucky, considerably longer, in Immigration, where owing to tightened security you can expect slow-moving queues. You may be expected to explain your visit; be polite and prepared. Note that all visitors to the US are now photographed and fingerprinted on arrival on every trip. You will usually be granted an entry permit.

US Embassy Visa Information

In the US, 1-202 663 1225/in the UK, 09055 444546, 60p per minute/http://travel.state.gov/visa.

When to go

There is no bad time to visit New York, and visitor numbers are fairly steady year-round. The weather can be unpleasantly hot in summer and charmingly, then tediously, snowy in winter, but there are compensations at each season. *See below* **Climate**.

Working in NY

Non-nationals cannot work in the United States without the appropriate visa; these are hard to get and generally require you to prove that your job could not be done by a US citizen. Contact your local embassy for further details. Some student visas allow part-time work after the first academic year.

UK students who want to spend a summer vacation working in the States should contact the British Universities North America Club (BUNAC) for help in arranging a temporary job and the requisite visa (16 Bowling Green Lane, London, EC1R 0QH; 020 7251 3472, www.bunac.org/uk).

Climate

New York is fairly predictable: winters are windy and frigid (with a sun that sits low in the southern sky, so you might want to plan your walks northward, from Downtown to Uptown, to avoid the glare); summers are hot and often very humid, with occasional brief showers. Spring is typically blustery and changeable, and fall/autumn is generally dry, cool and gorgeous. Below is a snapshot of the city's weather averages.

	Temperature Hi °F/°C	Low °F/°C	Rain/snow days	Full sun days
Jan	38/3	25/-4	11	8
Feb	40/5	27/-3	10	8
Mar	50/10	35/2	11	9
Apr	61/16	44/7	11	8
May	72/22	54/12	11	8
June	80/27	63/17	10	8
July	85/30	68/20	11	8
Aug	84/29	67/20	10	9
Sept	76/25	60/16	8	11
Oct	65/18	50/10	8	12
Nov	54/12	41/5	9	9
Dec	43/6	31/-1	10	9

Source: National Weather Service

Directory

Further Reference

Books

See also p18.

Edward F Bergman *The Spiritual Traveler: New York City* A guide to sacred and peaceful spaces in the city.
Eleanor Berman *Away for the Weekend: New York* Trips within a 200-mile radius of New York City. *New York Neighborhoods* Foodie guide focusing on ethnic enclaves.
William Corbett *New York Literary Lights* A compendium of information about NYC's literary past.
Dave Frattini *The Underground Guide to New York City Subways*
Gerri Gallagher and Jill Fairchild *Where to Wear* A staple for shopaholics.
Suzanne Gerber *Vegetarian New York City.*
Alfred Gingold and Helen Rogan *Cool Parent's Guide to All of New York.*
Hagstrom *New York City 5 Borough Pocket Atlas* You won't get lost when you carry this thorough street map.
Colleen Kane (ed) *Sexy New York City* Discover erotica in the Naked City.
Chuck Katz *Manhattan on Film 2*
Lyn Skreczko and Virginia Bell *The Manhattan Health Pages*
Earl Steinbicker (ed.) *Daytrips New York*
Linda Tarrant-Reid *Discovering Black New York* Museums, landmarks, more.
Time Out *New York Eating & Drinking 2005* The annual comprehensive critics' guide to thousands of places to eat and drink in the five boroughs.

Architecture

Richard Berenholtz *New York, New York* Mini panoramic images of the city through the seasons.
Stanley Greenberg *Invisible New York* Photographic account of hidden architectural triumphs.
Landmarks Preservation Commission *New York City Landmarks Preservation Guide*
Karl Sabbagh *Skyscraper* How the tall ones are built.
Robert AM Stern et al *New York 1930* A massive coffee-table slab with stunning pictures.
Norval White & Elliot Willensky *AIA Guide to New York City* A comprehensive directory of important buildings.
Gerard R Wolfe *New York: A Guide to the Metropolis* Historical and architectural walking tours.

Culture & recollections

Irving Lewis Allen *The City in Slang* How NY has spawned new words and phrases.
Candace Bushnell *Sex & the City; Trading Up* Smart women, superficial New York.
George Chauncey *Gay New York* The evolution of gay culture from 1890 to 1940.
Martha Cooper and Henry Chalfant *Subway Art.*
Josh Alan Friedman *Tales of Times Square* Sleaze and decay in the old Times Square.
Nelson George *Hip Hop America* The history of hip hop, from Grandmaster Flash to Puff Daddy.
Robert Hendrickson *New Yawk Tawk* Dictionary of NYC slang.
Jane Jacobs *The Death and Life of Great American Cities.*
AJ Liebling *Back Where I Came From* Personal recollections from the *New Yorker* columnist.
Gillian McCain and Legs McNeil *Please Kill Me* Oral history of the '70s punk scene.

Frank O'Hara *The Collected Poems of Frank O'Hara* The great NYC poet found inspiration in his hometown.
Andrés Torres *Between Melting Pot and Mosaic* African-American and Puerto Rican life in the city.
Heather Holland Wheaton *Eight Million Stories in a New York Minute.*
EB White *Here Is New York* A clear-eyed love letter to Gotham.

Fiction

Kurt Andersen *Turn of the Century Millennial* Manhattan seen through the eyes of media players.
Paul Auster *The New York Trilogy: City of Glass, Ghosts, and the Locked Room* A search for the madness behind the method of Manhattan's grid.
Kevin Baker *Dreamland* A poetic novel about Coney Island's glory days.
James A Baldwin *Another Country* Racism under the bohemian veneer of the 1960s.
Michael Chabon *The Amazing Adventures of Kavalier and Clay* Pulitzer Prize-winning account of Jewish comic-book artists in the 1940s.
Bret Easton Ellis *Glamorama* A satirical view of dazzling New York City nightlife.
Jack Finney *Time and Again* An illustrator travels back to 19th-century NY.
Larry Kramer *Faggots* Devastating satire of gay NY.
Phillip Lopate (ed) *Writing New York* An excellent anthology of short stories, essays and poems.
Tim McLoughlin (ed) *Brooklyn Noir* An anthology of crime tales set in Brooklyn.
Time Out *Book of New York Short Stories* Naturally, we like

Directory

these original short stories by 23 US and British authors.

Toni Morrison *Jazz* 1920s Harlem.

David Schickler *Kissing in Manhattan* Explores the lives of quirky tenants in a Manhattan block.

Hubert Selby Jr *Last Exit to Brooklyn* Dockland degradation, circa 1950s.

Edith Wharton *Old New York* Four novellas of 19th-century New York.

Colson Whitehead *The Colossus of New York: A City in 13 Parts* A lyrical tribute to city life.

Tom Wolfe *The Bonfire of the Vanities* Rich/poor, black/white. An unmatched slice of 1980s New York.

History

See p24 **Further reading**.

Films

Annie Hall (1977) Woody Allen co-stars with Diane Keaton in this appealingly neurotic valentine to living and loving in Manhattan.

Breakfast at Tiffany's (1961) Blake Edwards gave Audrey Hepburn her signature role as the cash-poor socialite Holly Golightly.

Dog Day Afternoon (1975) Al Pacino makes for a great antihero as a Brooklyn bank robber in Sidney Lumet's uproarious classic.

Do the Right Thing (1989) The hottest day of the summer leads to racial strife in Bedford-Stuyvesant in Spike Lee's incisive drama.

The French Connection (1971) As detective Jimmy 'Popeye' Doyle, Gene Hackman ignores all traffic lights to chase down drug traffickers in William Friedkin's thriller.

The Godfather (1972) and **The Godfather: Part II** (1974) Francis Ford Coppola's brilliant commentary about capitalism in America is told

through the violent saga of Italian gangsters.

Mean Streets (1973) Robert De Niro and Harvey Keitel shine as small-time Little Italy hoods in Martin Scorsese's breakthrough film.

Midnight Cowboy (1969) Street creatures 'Ratso' Rizzo and Joe Buck face an unforgiving Times Square in John Schlesinger's dark classic.

Spider-Man (2002) The comic-book web-slinger from Forest Hills comes to life in Sam Raimi's pitch-perfect crowd pleaser.

Taxi Driver (1976) Robert De Niro is a crazed cabbie who sees all of New York as a den of iniquity in Martin Scorsese's bold drama.

Music

Beastie Boys 'No Sleep Till Brooklyn' These now middle-aged hip hoppers began showing their love for their fave borough two decades ago.

Leonard Cohen 'Chelsea Hotel #2' Of all the songs inspired by the Chelsea, this bleak vision of doomed love is on a level of its own.

Billy Joel 'New York State of Mind' This heartfelt ballad exemplifies the city's effect on the souls of its visitors and residents.

Charles Mingus 'Mingus Ah Um' Mingus brought the gospel to jazz and created a NY masterpiece.

Public Enemy 'It Takes a Nation of Millions to Hold Us Back' A ferociously political tour de force from the Long Island hip hop group whose own Chuck D once called rap 'the CNN for black America'.

Ramones 'Ramones' Four Queens roughnecks, a few buzzsaw chords, and clipped musings on turning tricks and sniffing glue – it transformed rock 'n' roll.

Frank Sinatra 'Theme song from New York, New York' Trite and true, Frank's

bombastic love letter melts those little-town blues.

Bruce Springsteen 'My City of Ruins' The Boss praises the city's resilience post-September 11 with this track from 'The Rising'.

The Strokes 'Is This It' The effortlessly hip debut of this hometown band garnered praise and worldwide attention.

The Velvet Underground 'The Velvet Underground & Nico' Lou Reed and company's first album is still the gold standard of downtown cool.

Websites

www.timeoutny.com The Time Out New York website covers all the city has to offer. When planning your trip, check out the New York City Guide section for a variety of itineraries that you can use in conjunction with this guide.

eatdrink.timeoutny.com Subscribe to the TONY Eating & Drinking online guide and instantly search thousands of reviews written by our critics.

www.nycvisit.com The site of NYC & Company, the local convention and visitors' bureau.

www.mta.info Subway and bus service changes are always posted here.

www.nyc.gov City Hall's official New York City website has lots of links.

www.nytimes.com 'All the News That's Fit to Print' from the *New York Times*.

www.clubplanet.com Follow the city's nocturnal scene and buy advance tickets to big events.

www.livebroadway.com 'The Official Website of Broadway' is the source for theatres, tickets and tours.

www.hipguide.com A short 'n' sweet site for those looking for what's considered hip.

www.forgotten-ny.com Remember old New York here.

www.manhattanusersguide. com An insiders' guide to what's going on around town.

Directory

Index

Where to stay

Advertisers' Index

Please refer to the relevant pages for contact details

Place of interest and/or entertainment	
Hospital or college	
Railway station	
Parks	
River	
Freeway	
Main road	
Main road tunnel	
Pedestrian road	
Airport	✈
Church	✚
Subway station	Ⓜ
Area name	SOHO
Hotels	❶
Restaurants	❶
Bars	❶

Maps

Street Index

Brooklyn

38th St - R13/S13/W6
39th St - R12/13/
    S13/W6
40th St - S13
41st St - R13/S13
42nd St - R13/W6
43rd St - R13/W6/7
44th St - R13/S13/W6
45th St - S13
46th St - S13/W6
47th St - S13/W7
48th Ave - p411 W6
48th St - S13/W7
49th Ave - p411 W6
49th St - R13
50th Ave - p411 W6
50th St - R13
51st Ave - p411 V6/W6
51st St - R13
52nd St - R 13
53rd St - R13
54th Ave - p411 W6
54th Dr - p411 W6
54th Rd - p411 W6
54th St - R13
55th Ave - p411 U6/W6
55th St - R13
56th St - R13
57th Ave - p411 W7
57th St - R13
58th Rd - p411 W7
58th St - R13

Adams St - p411 T9
Adelphi St - U10/T9
Ainslie St - p411 V8
Albany Ave - V11/12
Albee Sq - p411 T9
Albemarle Rd - T13/U13
Amity St - S10
Anthony St - p411 V7/W7
Apollo St - p411 V7
Argyle Rd - U13
Ashland Pl - T10
Atlantic Ave - S10/U10

Bainbridge St - W10
Baltic St - S10/T10
Banker St - p411 U7
Bartlett St - p411 V9
Bay St - R11/S11
Beadel St - p411 V7/W7
Beard St - R11
Beaver St - p411 V9/W9
Bedford Ave - U10/13/
    V10/U7/8/9
Bergen St - V11/W11
Berkeley Pl - T11
Berry St - p411 U7
Beverley Rd - U13/
    V13/W13
Boerum Pl - S10/V8
Bogart St - p411 W8
Bond St - T10
Borden Ave - p411 V6
Bowne St - R10/S10
Bradley Ave - p411 W6
Bridge St - p411 T9
Bridgewater St - p411 W7
Broadway - W10/U8/
    V9/W9
Brooklyn Ave - V11/12/13
Brooklyn Bridge - p411 S8
Brooklyn Queens Exwy -
    p411 U8/9/V7/W7
Buckingham Rd - U13
Buffalo Ave - W11
Bush St - S11
Bushwick Ave - p411 V8
Butler St - S10/T10/11

Cadman Plz E - p411 S9
Calyer St - p411 V6/7
Cambridge Pl - V10
Carlton Ave - T10/U10
Carroll St - S10/T11/V12
Caton Ave - U13
Central Ave - p411 W9
Centre St - S11
Chauncey St - W10
Cherry St - p411 W7
Chester Ave - T13
Church Ave - U13/W13
Clarendon Rd - V13/W13
Clark St - p411 S9
Clarkson Ave - W12
Classon Ave - U10/U9
Claver Pl - U10
Clay St - p411 U6/V6

Clermont Ave - p411 U9
Clifton Pl - U10
Clinton Ave - U10/U9
Clinton St - S10/11
Clymer St - p411 P411 U8
Coffey St - R11
Columbia St - R11/12/
    S10
Commerce St - R10/S11
Commercial St - p411 U6
Commercial Wharf - R10
Concord St - p411 T9
Congress St - S10
Conover St - R11
Conselyea St - p411 V8
Cook St - p411 W9
Cortelyou Rd - V13
Court St - S10
Cranberry St - p411 S9
Creamer St - S11
Crooke Ave - p410
Crown St - V12
Cumberland St - T10/T9

Dahill Rd - T13
Dean St - T10/U10/
    U11/V11/W11
Decatur St - W10
Degraw St - S10/T10/11
Dekalb Ave - T10/U10/
    V10/W9
Delavan St - R10/11
Devoe St - p411 V8/W8
Diamond St - p411 V7
Dikeman St - R11
Division Ave - p411 U8
Division Pl - p411 V7/W7
Dobbin St - p411 U7
Douglass St - T10/11
Downing St - U10
Driggs Ave - p411
    U7/8/V7
Duffield St - p411 T9
Dupont St - p411 U6/V6
Dwight St - R11

E 2nd St - T13
E 3rd St - T13
E 4th St - T13
E 5th St - T13
E 7th St - T13
E 8th St - U13
E 19th St - U13
E 21st St - U13
E 22nd St - U13
E 28th St - V13
E 29th St - V13
E 31st St - V13
E 32nd St - V13
E 34th St - V13
E 37th St - V13
E 38th St - V13
E 39th St - V13
E 40th St - V13
E 42nd St - V13/W13
E 43rd St - W13
E 45th St - W12/13
E 46th St - W12/13
E 48th St - W13
E 49th St - W12/13
E 51st St - W12/13
E 52nd St - W12/13
E 53rd St - W12/13
E 54th St - W12/13
E 55th St - W12/13
E 56th St - W12/13
E 57th St - W13
E 58th St - W12/13
E 59th St - W13
E 91st St - W12
E 93rd St - W12
E 95th St - W12
E 96th St - W12
E 98th St - W12
Eagle St - p411 U6/V6
East New York Ave -
    V12/W12
Eastern Pkwy - V11/W11
Eckford St - p411 V7
Ellery St - p411 V9
Empire Blvd - V12
Engert Ave - p411 V7
Erasmus St - V13
Evergreen Ave - p411 W9

Fairview Pl - V13
Fenimore St - V12
Ferris St - R11
Flatbush Ave - U12/13

Flushing Ave - p411 U9/
    V9/W8
Ford St - W12
Fort Greene Pl - T10
Fort Hamilton Pkwy - T13
Franklin Ave - U10/U9
Franklin St - p411 U6
Freeman St - p411 U6/V6
Frost St - p411 V7
Fulton St - T10/V10/11

Gardner Ave - p411
    W7/W8
Garfield Pl - T11
Gates Ave - V10
George St - p411 W9
Gerry St - p411 V9
Gold St - p411 T9
Graham Ave - p411 V8
Grand Ave - U10/U9
Grand St - p411 U8/W8
Grand St Ext - p411 V8
Grattan St - p411 W8
Green St - p411 U6/V6
Greene Ave - U10/W9
Greenpoint Ave - p411
    V6/W6
Greenwood Ave - T13
Guernsey St - p411 V7

Hall St - U10/U9
Halleck St - S11
Halsey St - W10
Hamilton Ave - S11
Hancock St - V10
Hanson Pl - T10
Harrison Ave - p411 V8/9
Harrison Pl - p411 W8
Hart St - p411 V9/W9
Hausman St - p411 V7
Havemeyer St - p411
    U8/V8
Hawthorne St - V12
Henry St - S10
Herkimer St - W11
Hewes St - p411
    U8/9/V8
Heyward St - p411 U9/V9
Hicks St - S10
Hooper St - p411
    U8/9/V8
Hopkins St - p411 V9
Howard Ave - W10
Hoyt St - S10/T10
Hudson Ave - T10
Humboldt St - p411 V7/8
Huntington St - S11
Huron St - p411 U6/V6

Imlay St - R10
India St - p411 U6/V6
Ingraham St - p411 W8
Irving Pl - U10
Irving St - S10

Jackson St - p411 V7/8
Java St - p411 U6/V6
Jay St - p411 T9
Jefferson Ave - W10
Jefferson St - p411 W8/9
Jewel St - p411 V7
John St - p411 T9
Johnson Ave - p411 W8
Johnson St - p411 S9/T9

Kane St - S10
Keap St - p411 V8
Kent Ave - p411 U8/9
Kent St - p411 U6/V6
King St - R11
Kingsland Ave - p411
    V6/7
Kingston Ave - V11/12
Knickerbocker Ave -
    p411 W9
Kosciusko St - V10/W9
Kossuth Pl - p411 W9

Lafayette Ave - U10/W9
Laurel Hill Blvd - p411 W6
Lawrence St - p411 T9
Lee Ave - p411 U8
Lefferts Ave - V12
Lefferts Pl - U10
Leonard St - p411 V8
Lewis Ave - W10/W9/W9
Lexington Ave - V10
Lincoln Pl - T11/V11/W11

Lincoln Rd - V12
Linden Blvd - V13
Livingston St - T10
Lombardy St - p411 W7
Lorimer St - p411 V8
Lorraine St - S11
Lott St - V13
Luquer St - S11
Lynch St - p411 U9/V9

Macdonough St - W10
Macon St - V10/W10
Madison St - W10
Malcolm X Blvd - W10
Manhattan Ave - p411
    U6/V6
Manhattan Bridge - p411
    S8
Maple St - V12
Marcy Ave - V10/U8/V8/9
Marginal St E - R12
Marion St - W10
Marlborough Rd - U13
Marshall St - p411 T9
Martense St - V13
Maspeth Ave - p411 W7
Maujer St - p411 V8
Mcguinness Blvd - p411
    V6/7
Mckeever Pl - U12
Mckibbin St - p411
    V8/W8
Meadow St - p411 W8
Melrose St - p411 W9
Meserole Ave - p411 U7/
    V7
Meserole St - p411 V8/
    W8
Metropolitan Ave - p411
    U7/8/W8
Middagh St - p411 S9
Middleton St - p411 U9/
    V9
Midwood St - V12/W12
Mill St - S11
Milton St - p411 U6
Minna St - T13
Monitor St - p411 V6/7
Monroe St - V10/W10
Montague St - p411 S9
Montgomery St - V12
Montrose Ave - p411 V8
Moore St - p411 V9/W9
Morgan Ave - p411 W8
Moultrie St - p411 V6/7
Myrtle Ave - p411 U9/W9

N 1st St - p411 U8
N 3rd St - p411 U7/8
N 4th St - p411 U7/8
N 5th St - p411 U8
N 6th St - p411 U7
N 7th St - p411 U7
N 8th St - p411 U7
N 9th St - p411 U7
N 10th St - p411 U7
N 11th St - p411 U7
N 12th St - p411 U7
N 13th St - p411 U7
N 14th St - p411 U7
N 15th St - p411 U7
N Oxford St - p411 T9
N Portland Ave - p411 T9
Nassau Ave - p411 V7
Nassau St - p411 T9
Navy St - p411 T9
Nelson St - S11
Nevins St - T10
New York Ave - V12
Newell St - p411 V7
Noble St - p411 U7
Noll St - p411 W9
Norman Ave - p411 V7
Nostrand Ave -
    V10/11/12/13/V9

Oak St - p411 U7
Ocean Pkwy - T13
Onderdonk Ave - p411 W8
Orange St - p411 S9
Orient Ave - p411 W8
Otsego St - R11

Pacific St - S10/T10/
    V11/W11
Paidge Ave - p411 V6
Parade Pl - U13
Park Ave - p411 V9
Park Pl - V11/W11

Parkside Ave - U12/13/
    V12
Patchen Ave - W10
Pearl St - p411 T9
Penn St - p411 U9
Pierrepont St - p411 S9
Pineapple St - p411 S9
Pioneer St - R10/11
Plymouth St - p411 T9
Poplar St - p411 S9
Porter Ave - p411 W7
Powers St - p411 V8
President St - S10/T11/
    U11/V11
Prince St - p411 T9
Prospect Exwy - S12/T12
Prospect Ave - T12
Prospect Park Southwest -
    T12/13
Prospect Park West -
    T11/12
Prospect Pl - U11/W11
Provost St - p411 V6
Pulaski Bridge - p411 V6
Pulaski St - p411 V9
Putnam Ave - U10/V10

Quincy St - V10

Raleigh Pl - V13
Ralph Ave - W10/11
Randolph St - p411 W8
Reed St - R11
Remsen Ave - W12
Remsen St - p411 S9
Review Ave - p411 V6
Rewe St - p411 W8
Richards St - R11
Richardson St - p411 V7
River St - p411 U7/8
Rochester Ave - W11/12
Rock St - p411 W9
Rockaway Pkwy - W12
Rockwell Pl - T10
Rodney St - p411 U8/V8
Roebling St - p411 U8/V7
Rogers Ave - V11/12/13
Ross St - p411 U8/9
Rugby Rd - U13
Russell St - p411 V6/7
Rutland Rd - U12/V12/
    W12
Rutledge St - p411 U8/9
Ryerson St - p411 U9

S 1st St - p411 U8/V8
S 2nd St - p411 U8/V8
S 3rd St - p411 U8
S 4th St - p411 U8
S 5th St - p411 U8/V8
S 6th St - p411 U8
S 8th St - p411 U8
S 9th St - U P411 U8
S 10th St - p411 U8
S 11th St - p411 U8
S Elliott Pl - T10
S Oxford St - T10
S Portland Ave - T10
Sackett St - S10/T10/11
Saint Edwards St -
    p411 T9
Saint Felix St - T10
Saint James Pl - U10
Saint Johns PL - T11/
    V11/W11
Saint Marks Ave -
    U11/W11
Saint Marks Pl - T10
Saint Pauls Pl - U13
Sandford St - p411 U9/V9
Sands St - p411 T9
Schenectady Ave -
    W11/12/13
Schermerhorn St - T10
Scholes St - p411 V8/W8
Scott Ave - p411 W7/8
Seabring St - R10/S10
Sedgwick St - S10
Seeley St - T13
Seigel St - p411 V8/9/W8
Sharon St - p411 V8/W8
Sherman St - T13
Skillman Ave - p411 V8
Skillman St - U10/U9
Smith St - S10/11
Snyder Ave - V13/W13
Spencer St - p411 U9
Stagg St - p411 V8/W8
Starr Ave - p411 V6,W6

400 Time Out New York

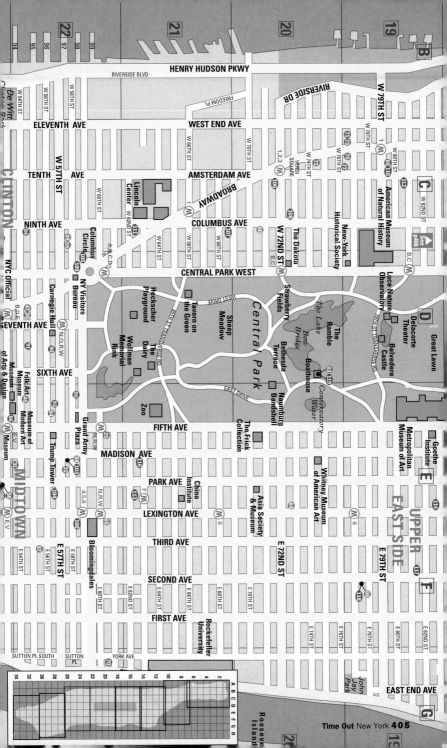

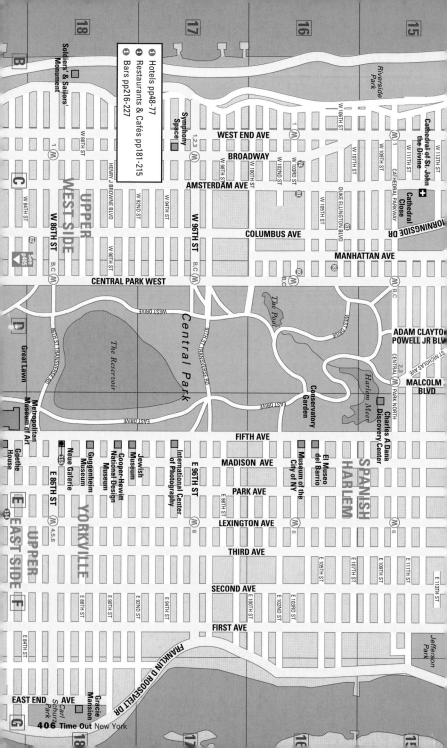

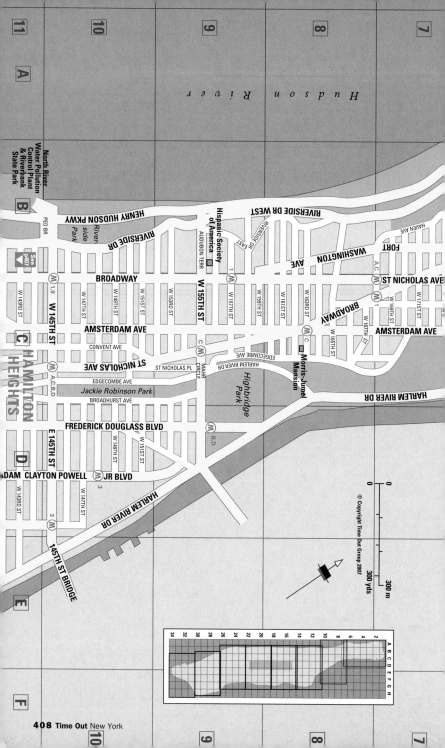

Hudson River

North River
Water Pollution
Control Plant
& Riverbank
State Park

PED BR

HENRY HUDSON PKWY

River-
side
Park

RIVERSIDE DR

RIVERSIDE DR WEST

RIVERSIDE DR

HAVEN AVE

Hispanic Society
of America

AUDUBON TERR

RIVERSIDE DR
EAST

WASHINGTON AVE

FORT

See
p407

BROADWAY

W 143RD ST

W 145TH ST

W 147TH ST

W 149TH ST

W 151ST ST

W 153RD ST

W 155TH ST

W 157TH ST

W 159TH ST

W 161ST ST

W 163RD ST

W 165TH ST

ST NICHOLAS AVE

BROADWAY

W 167TH ST

W 169TH ST

W 171ST ST

AMSTERDAM AVE

AMSTERDAM AVE

CONVENT AVE

ST NICHOLAS AVE

ST NICHOLAS PL

MADHR CIRCLE

HARLEM RIVER DR

EDGECOMBE AVE

Morris–Jumel
Mansion

Highbridge
Park

HAMILTON HEIGHTS

EDGECOMBE AVE

Jackie Robinson Park

BROADHURST AVE

FREDERICK DOUGLASS BLVD

W 145TH ST

W 151ST ST

HARLEM RIVER DR

E 145TH ST

DAM CLAYTON POWELL JR BLVD

W 143RD ST

W 147TH ST

HARLEM RIVER DR

145TH ST BRIDGE

© Copyright Time Out Group 2007

0

0

300 yds

300 m

34 32 30 28 26 24 22 20 18 16 14 12 10 8 6 4 2

A B C D E F G H

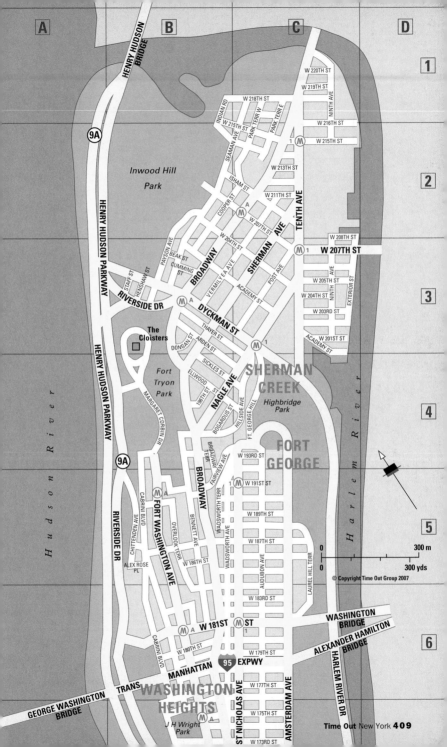

A

HENRY HUDSON BRIDGE

HENRY HUDSON PARKWAY

9A

Inwood Hill Park

RIVERSIDE DR

The Cloisters

Fort Tryon Park

HENRY HUDSON PARKWAY

9A

RIVERSIDE DR

Hudson River

B

STAFF ST

HENSHAW ST

PAYSON AVE

BEAK ST

CUMMING ST

MARGARET CORBIN DR

DONGAN ST

ARDEN ST

SICKLES ST

ELLWOOD ST

190TH ST

BOGARDUS ST

NAGLE AVE

BROADWAY

CABRINI BLVD

CHITTENDEN AVE

FORT WASHINGTON AVE

OVERLOOK TERR

BENNETT AVE

ALEX ROSE PL

CABRINI BLVD

MANHATTAN

TRANS

GEORGE WASHINGTON BRIDGE

WASHINGTON HEIGHTS

C

W 220TH ST

W 219TH ST

INDIAN RD

W 218TH ST

SEAMAN AVE

PARK TERR W

PARK TERR E

W 215TH ST

W 213TH ST

ISHAM ST

W 211TH ST

TENTH AVE

COOPER ST

A

W 207TH ST

W 204TH ST

BROADWAY

VERMILYEA AVE

SHERMAN AVE

ACADEMY ST

POST AVE

A

DYCKMAN ST

THAYER ST

1

SHERMAN CREEK

Highbridge Park

FT. GEORGE HILL

HILLSIDE AVE

BROADWAY TERR

FAIRVIEW AVE

W 193RD ST

FORT GEORGE

WADSWORTH TERR

1

W 191ST ST

WADSWORTH AVE

W 189TH ST

W 187TH ST

W 186TH ST

AUDUBON AVE

W 183RD ST

LAUREL HILL TERR

A

W 181ST ST

1

W 180TH ST

W 179TH ST

95 **EXPWY**

ST NICHOLAS AVE

W 177TH ST

AMSTERDAM AVE

W 175TH ST

A

J H Wright Park

W 173RD ST

D

W 220TH ST

W 219TH ST

NINTH AVE

W 216TH ST

W 215TH ST

TENTH AVE

W 208TH ST

1

W 207TH ST

W 205TH ST

NINTH AVE

EXTERIOR ST

W 204TH ST

W 203RD ST

ACADEMY ST

W 201ST ST

Harlem River

WASHINGTON BRIDGE

ALEXANDER HAMILTON BRIDGE

HARLEM RIVER DR

0   300 m

0   300 yds

© Copyright Time Out Group 2007

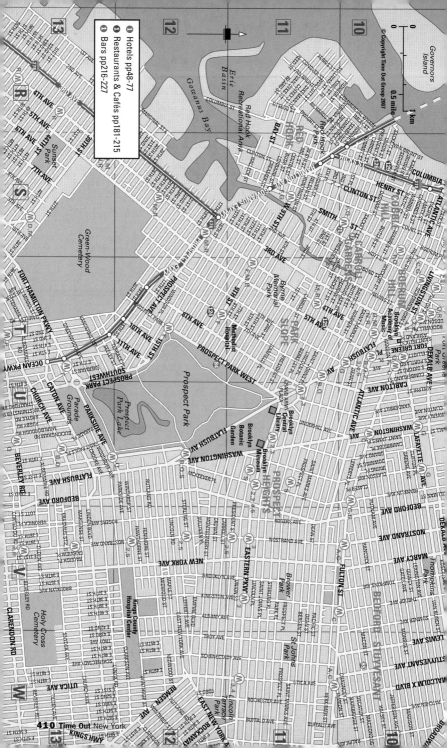

Hotels pp48–77
Restaurants & Cafés pp181–215
Bars pp216–227

Queens

Central Park

SPANISH HARLEM

Jefferson Park

TRIBOROUGH BRIDGE

East River

East River

Hell Gate

Bowery Bay

La Guardia Airport

0   1 km
0   0.5 mile
© Copyright Time Out Group 2007

❶ Hotels pp48-77
❶ Restaurants & Cafés pp181-215
❶ Bars pp216-227

YORKVILLE

E 86TH ST

UPPER EAST SIDE

E 79TH ST

E 72ND ST

Carl Schurz Park

John Jay Park

TRIBOROUGH BRIDGE

Astoria Park

MAIN AVE

ASTORIA BLVD

ASTORIA

St Michaels Cemetery

ASTORIA BLVD

DITMARS BLVD

Socrates Sculpture Park

VERNON BLVD

30TH AVE

Roosevelt Island

STEINWAY ST

31ST AVE

JACKSON HEIGHTS

31ST AVE

QUEENSBORO BRIDGE

Queens Bridge Park

LONG ISLAND CITY

American Museum of the Moving Image

NORTHERN BLVD

WOODSIDE

BROADWAY

ROOSEVELT AVE

BROADWAY

BAXTER

East River

See pp402-412

Sunnyside Yard

Greenland Park

SKILLMAN AVE

WOODSIDE AVE

45TH AVE

THOMSON AVE

QUEENS BLVD

43RD AVE

QUEENS BLVD

P.S.1

Dutch Kills

SUNNYSIDE

See pp410-11

New Calvary Cemetery

QUEENS-MIDTOWN TUNNEL

JACKSON

49TH AVE

BORDEN AVE

495

Newtown Creek

Calvary Cemetery

Mount Zion Cemetery

MIDDLE VILLAGE

GRAND AVE

GREENPOINT AVE

GREENPOINT

NORMAN AVE

MAURICE AVE

MASPETH

Mt Olivet Cemetery

ELIOT AVE

Juniper Valley Park

McCarren Park

LOMBARDY ST

MASPETH AVE

BEDFORD AVE

DRIGGS AVE

BERRY ST

KINGSLAND AVE

VANDERVOORT AVE

MANHATTAN AVE

HUMBOLDT ST

English Kills

GRAND ST

FLUSHING AVE

METROPOLITAN AVE

Linden Hill Cemetery

Lutheron Cemetery

Glen Ridge Park

CENTRAL AVE

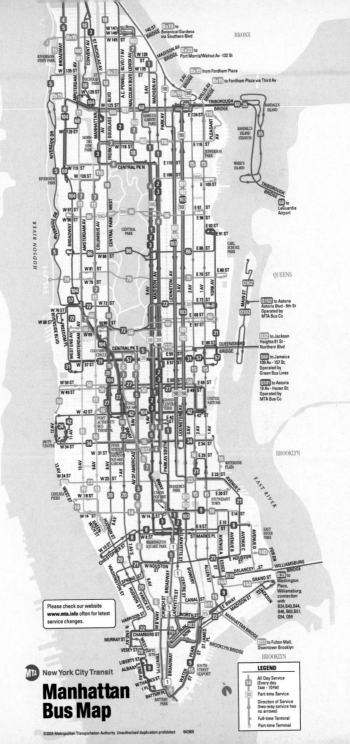

MTA New York City Transit

Manhattan Bus Map

Please check our website
www.mta.info often for latest
service changes.

LEGEND

14	All Day Service (Every day 7AM - 10PM)
30	Part-time Service
	Direction of Service (two-way service has no arrows)
	Full-time Terminal
	Part-time Terminal

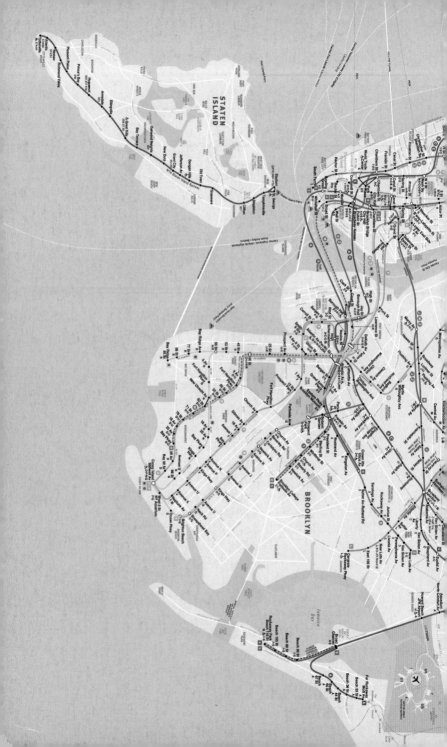